Postwar America

An Encyclopedia of Social, Political, Cultural, and Economic History

Volume Four

Edited by **James Ciment**

SHARPE REFERENCE

an imprint of M.E. Sharpe, Inc.

SHARPE REFERENCE

Sharpe Reference is an imprint of M.E. Sharpe, Inc.

M.E. Sharpe, Inc.
80 Business Park Drive
Armonk, NY 10504

© 2007 by M.E. Sharpe, Inc.

Library of Congress Cataloging-in-Publication Data

Postwar America: An encyclopedia of social, political, cultural, and economic history /
James Ciment, editor.
  p. cm.
Includes bibliographical references and indexes.
ISBN-13: 978-0-7656-8067-9 (alk. paper)
ISBN-10: 0-7656-8067-X (alk. paper)

1. United States—Civilization—1945—Encyclopedias. 2. United States—Social conditions—
1945—Encyclopedias. 3. United States—Economic conditions—1945—Encyclopedias.
4. United States—Politics and government—20th century—Encyclopedias. I. Ciment, James.

E169.12.P654 2005
973.92'03—dc22   2004013120

Cover images: Clockwise from top left corner, by Getty Images and the following:
Bill Pogue; Three Lions; Ralph Crane; Newsworld/New York Tribune; World Perspective;
Petrified Collection.

Printed and bound in the United States of America

The paper used in this publication meets the minimum requirements of
American National Standard for Information Sciences
Permanence of Paper for Printed Library Materials,
ANSI Z 39.48.1984.

MV (c) 10 9 8 7 6 5 4 3 2 1

Publisher: Myron E. Sharpe
Vice President and Editorial Director: Patricia Kolb
Vice President and Production Director: Carmen Chetti
Executive Editor and Manager of Reference: Todd Hallman
Senior Development Editor: Jeff Hacker
Project Editor: Laura Brengelman
Program Coordinator: Cathleen Prisco
Editorial Assistant: Alison Morretta
Text Design: Carmen Chetti and Jesse Sanchez
Cover Design: Jesse Sanchez

Contents

Sidebars

Topic Finder

Arts and Popular Culture

Advertising
Altamont Killings
Architecture
Arts, Fine
Arts Funding, Government
Automobile Culture
Baseball
Basketball
Beauty, Fashion, and Cosmetics
Bicentennial Celebrations
Boxing
Censorship
Classical Music
College Sports
Comic Books
Comic Strips
Consumer Culture
Counterculture
Country and Western Music
Dance
Dance, Popular
Diet and Food
Disco
Drug Culture
Extreme Sports
Fads
Film, Documentary
Film, Feature
Film, Independent
Folk Music
Football
Gambling
Gay and Lesbian Politics and Culture
Golf
Happenings
Hells Angels
Hobbies
Ice Hockey
Internet
Jazz
Jet Set
Literature, Fiction
Literature, Nonfiction
Love-Ins

Miller v. California (1973)
Music Videos
National Endowments for the Arts and
    Humanities
Newspapers and Magazines
Olympics
Payola Scandal
Photography
Poetry
Pornography
Radio
Rap and Hip Hop
Rat Pack
Rhythm and Blues
Rock and Roll
Sports, Participatory
Sports Broadcasting
Streaking
Surfing
Television
Tennis
Theater
Theme Parks
Woodstock Music Festival
World's Fairs

Civil Liberties and Civil Rights

Affirmative Action
Alexander v. Holmes County Board of Education
    (1969)
Bakke Decision (1978)
Birmingham Church Bombing
Black Panthers
Black Power Movement
Brawley (Tawana) Affair
Brown v. Board of Education (1954)
Busing
Censorship
Civil Liberties
Civil Rights Act of 1964
Civil Rights Legislation and Policy
Civil Rights Movement, Through 1965
Civil Rights Movement and Black Power,
    After 1965
Congress of Racial Equality

Science, Technology, and the Environment
Agriculture
AIDS/HIV Crisis
Air Pollution
Alaskan Pipeline
Anti-Nuclear Power Movement
Apollo Program
Atomic Weapons Testing
Atoms for Peace
Automobile Industry
Birth Control
Blackouts, Electrical
Club of Rome Report
Communications Technologies
Computers
Dalkon Shield Controversy
Defense Spending and Defense Industry
Donora (Pennsylvania) Smog Episode
Earth Day
Electronics Industry
Endangered Species Act
Energy
Energy, Department of
Environmental Protection Agency
Environmentalism
Exxon Valdez Disaster
Gemini, Project
Genetics
Global Warming
International Geophysical Year
Internet
Mass Transit
Medicine
Mercury, Project
Missile Gap
Moon Landing
Natural Disasters and Disaster
    Management
Nuclear Energy
Offshore Oil Drilling
Ozone Depletion
Planetary Exploration
Plastics
Reproductive Technologies
Robotics
Satellites

Science, Government Policy on
Silkwood Case
Skylab
Space Shuttle
Steel Industry
Television
Three Mile Island Disaster
Thresher Disaster
Tranquilizers
Tylenol Tampering Incident
Unabomber Affair
Unidentified Flying Objects
Water Pollution and Water Pollution Policy
Weapons, Nuclear
Weapons of Mass Destruction
Wildlife and Wilderness

Women's Issues
Abortion
Affirmative Action
Beauty, Fashion, and Cosmetics
Birth Control
Brawley (Tawana) Affair
Child Rearing
Citadel Affair
Consciousness Raising
Crime, Sexual
Dalkon Shield Controversy
Day Care
Emily's List
Family
Family Leave Act
Feminist Movement
Gay and Lesbian Politics and Culture
Griswold v. Connecticut (1965)
Kinsey Reports
Masters and Johnson Studies
National Organization for Women
National Women's Conference
Reproductive Technologies
Roe v. Wade (1973)
Test-Tube Babies
Toxic Shock Syndrome
Welfare and Public Assistance
Women and Work
Women's Studies

Postwar America

Volume Four

T

TAFT-HARTLEY ACT

The Taft-Hartley Act of 1947 was legislation passed by the conservative 80th U.S. Congress as a means of limiting the growing strength of labor unions. The bill, authored by two Republicans, Senator Robert Taft of Ohio and Congressman Fred Hartley of New Jersey, contained a number of important and controversial provisions.

Under Taft-Hartley, if a compelling national interest were deemed to be at stake, a strike could only begin after an eighty-day cooling-off period. The law prohibited the closed union shop, meaning that workers would no longer have to be members of the union as a condition of employment. Also forbidden were sympathy boycotts initiated by strikers against enterprises that had business dealings with the firm against which the original work stoppage was aimed. Another important clause stated that, in order to remain in the good graces of the government, union leaders had to sign affidavits professing their non-Communist credentials. Noncompliance would result in denial to rank and file members of access to the National Labor Relations Board (NLRB), the agency charged with certifying unions and the election of their representatives.

The year 1946 had been a watershed in the contentious relationship between workers and businesses in the United States. In that year alone, a total of 4,985 work stoppages by 4.6 million workers resulted in a loss of 116 million days of work. Especially crippling to the nation were strikes by the coal miners in March and the railway workers in May. The Truman Administration was implementing a policy of economic conversion that was designed to shift the U.S. economy from a war footing (one that produced tanks, planes, and other weaponry) to one that would generate a host of consumer goods for the civilian population. The prevalence of work stoppages served to undermine the president's plans and created a feeling of anxiety among the people. For most Americans, the economic malaise of the 1930s was hardly a distant memory, and the return of a peacetime economy ushered in a sense of disquiet.

The unions argued that strikes were an economic necessity. They claimed that real wages had not kept pace with inflation, despite the wartime gains made in employment and pay. Walter Reuther, chief of the United Auto Workers (UAW), believed that corporations were making substantial profits and could absorb worker salary increases without an increase in prices for goods and services. Repeated calls for companies to open their books went unheeded, however, and the costs of wage hikes were passed along to the consumer.

Sensing that the nation was descending into chaos, President Harry S Truman was spurred to action. In May 1946, when news of a possible railway strike reached Washington, D.C., the president called the respective heads of the Brotherhood of Railroad Trainmen and the Brotherhood of Locomotive Engineers to the White House for talks. When these unions vowed to walk off their jobs, Truman threatened to draft the strikers into the U.S. armed forces and have the government take over the railroads. Shortly after this exchange, the unions reached an agreement with their employers, averting any possible action by the president.

In November of that year, coal miners, led by union chief John L. Lewis, threatened a work stoppage. Fearing a winter with disrupted supplies of coal, President Truman went to court and received an order mandating a cessation of the strike. Defying the ruling, Lewis sent his unionists to the picket line. The court then fined Lewis and the coal miners union $10,000 and $3.5 million, respectively, for contempt. Seeking a truce, Lewis attempted to initiate talks with the White House, but he was openly rebuffed by the president, leaving the union leader distraught and with no choice but to call off the strike.

The president's bold stance against the labor movement denied him the support of the unions, one of the pillars of the New Deal coalition, in the congressional elections of 1946. Instead of openly campaigning for Democratic candidates, the unions offered only lukewarm support for the party of Franklin D. Roosevelt.

Meanwhile, the opposition Republican Party proposed a program that included an end to wartime restrictions on the economy, the need to weed out corruption in the government, and the desire to curtail the power of the union movement. The election of 1946 resulted in Republicans, for the first time since

1930, winning control of both the Senate (51–45) and the House of Representatives (246–188).

The Republicans went right to work and, in 1947, proposed what became known as the Taft-Hartley Act. When the details of the bill were made public, supporters of the union movement, such as Philip Murray and Lee Pressman of the Congress of Industrial Organizations (CIO), decried its "draconian provisions." President Truman vetoed the bill, but the Senate and House overrode his veto by mustering the support of two-thirds of both houses of Congress.

The veto enabled Truman to regain the support of organized labor in time for the presidential election of 1948. The unions backed the Democratic ticket, denouncing the Republican Party as pro-business and antiunion. This support of the president by a key interest group proved pivotal in Truman's surprise victory over Republican nominee Thomas Dewey.

At the time of its passage, union supporters believed that the Taft-Hartley Act would overturn the Wagner Act of 1935, which gave workers the opportunity to organize freely under union auspices through the NLRB. Such fears did not materialize, but Taft-Hartley did have a profound impact on intraunion politics.

With the rise of anticommunism throughout the nation, the trade unions came under scrutiny, both externally and internally, by those who believed the union movement had been infiltrated by individuals who were either pro-Soviet or members of the Communist Party. The unions, feeling revulsion toward those in their midst who supported the Soviet line and fearing domestic repercussions, took action to purge such individuals from their ranks. The CIO jettisoned twelve of its thirty-five member unions, including the International Longshoremen's Union, United Electrical Workers, National Maritime Union, and the Mine, Mill and Smelter Workers, because the leadership of their respective trades was dominated by Communist or pro-Soviet members. The results of this policy allowed the union movement to articulate a staunch anticommunist position that was maintained over the ensuing decades.

John Caulfield

See also: Election of 1946; Election of 1948; Landrum-Griffin Act; Strikes; Unions.

Bibliography

Donovan, Robert. *Conflict and Crisis: The Presidency of Harry Truman, 1945–1948.* New York: W.W. Norton, 1977.

Goulden, Joseph. *The Best Years, 1945–1950.* New York, Atheneum, 1976.

Hamby, Alonzo. *Beyond the New Deal: Harry S Truman and American Liberalism.* New York: Columbia University Press, 1973.

Patterson, James T. *Grand Expectations: The United States 1945–1974.* New York: Oxford University Press, 1996.

TAILHOOK SCANDAL

The Tailhook Association (TA) is a privately funded organization of active and retired naval aviators from both the U.S. Navy and the Marine Corps. The name of the association comes from the fact that all members are required to have made at least one landing on an aircraft carrier; such landings include hooking the plane's tail to slow it down. Although not officially part of the armed forces, the organization enjoys a close relationship with the Navy, and officials of the former often serve as high-level officers in the latter.

At the TA's thirty-fifth annual convention in September 1991, held at the Las Vegas Hilton hotel, members participated in sexual harassment of females—both organization members and passersby—that included verbal obscenities and unsolicited physical contact. After initial complaints to Navy leadership were ignored and Congress became involved, the episode came to be call the "Tailhook Scandal."

For years, the TA's annual convention had served as both a venue for networking among members and a time for drinking and carousing. Indeed, the meetings were notorious for the wild antics of attendees, and sexual harassment at these events was not new. But sexual politics in 1991 were highly charged following the Clarence Thomas hearings, in which the U.S. Supreme Court nominee was accused by former aide Anita Hill of sexual harassment.

The first stirrings of a problem surfaced at a convention panel meeting on the morning of September 7, 1991, when Lieutenant Monica Rivadeneira asked when the U.S. Navy would allow women to fly in combat. The audience response to her question consisted of sexist and obscene comments about women in general, and no one in attendance admonished the individuals who made them. Later that night, outside the hotel's "hospitality suites," numerous male attendees lined the halls to fondle and grope any women, both female military personnel and civilian women, who happened to walk past.

Unbeknownst to the assailants, one of the victims was Lieutenant Paula Coughlin, an accomplished helicopter pilot and an aide to a high-ranking Navy officer, Rear Admiral John W. Snyder. Coughlin's persistent requests that the men leave her alone and her pleas to bystanders for help went unheeded. When Coughlin reported the incident to Snyder, he brushed aside her complaints.

Within days, reports of the incident and several similar stories surfaced within the military community, and the Naval Investigative Service (NIS) launched an official inquiry in October 1991. On April 30, 1992, after months of examining the evidence, the NIS issued a report that found that twenty-six women, many of them military officers, had indeed been victimized at the 1991 convention. Of the estimated seventy men involved in the assaults, the report revealed the identities of only two; none of the accused faced criminal or disciplinary charges.

The lightness of the discipline outraged members of the public and Congress, which urged the Navy's inspector general to make his own investigation. As a result of that proceeding, the Navy ended its relationship with the Tailhook Association in 1992 but still failed to exact any punishment for the perpetrators.

A frustrated Coughlin went to the press on June 24, 1992, sharing her experiences with the print and television news media. Two days later, Secretary of the Navy Lawrence Garrett resigned his position, claiming full responsibility for the handling of the matter. Over the course of the next two years, the Navy began overhauling its official policies regarding women within its ranks, establishing a policy of "zero tolerance" for anyone accused of sexual harassment and the expansion of its investigative apparatus for such allegations, among other measures.

Kimberly Little

See also: Women and Work.

Bibliography

Ebbert, Jean, and Marie-Beth Hall. *Crossed Currents: Navy Women in a Century of Change.* 3rd ed., with a foreword by Captain Edward L. Beach. Washington, DC: Brassey's, 1999.

Stein, Laura W., ed. *Sexual Harassment in America: A Documentary History.* Westport, CT: Greenwood, 1999.

TEACH-INS

Teach-ins were a new form of demonstration that arose out of the anti-Vietnam War movement in the 1960s. Largely conducted on college campuses, teach-ins of professors, students, staff, and community members combined protest and pedagogy. Teach-ins swept through many college campuses in the spring of 1965 and quickly became a central feature of the growing anti-Vietnam War movement. Although their prominence diminished as students turned to more militant tactics, teach-ins remained an important vehicle for educating Americans about the Vietnam War and other issues of the 1960s and post-Vietnam era.

Concerned about the escalating war in Vietnam, a group of professors joined with students to organize the first teach-in at the University of Michigan on March 23–24, 1965. Despite at least two bomb scares and a scattering of hecklers, 3,000 students participated in the all-night program of lectures, debates, and discussion groups to raise awareness about U.S. foreign policy and the history and politics of Southeast Asia.

In the next days and weeks, the movement spread quickly. Held at such major institutions as Columbia University and the University of Wisconsin-Madison, as well as at many smaller colleges, teach-ins constituted a central expression of the burgeoning campus antiwar movement. Despite some attempts at coordinated action, however, teach-ins remained primarily local affairs and varied widely.

Initiated by students, professors, or sometimes student-faculty committees, teach-ins usually weighed heavily in favor of withdrawal or negotiation in Vietnam but tended to offer a variety of rationales and solutions. Some featured formal debates, while others favored discussion and informal workshops. Some, like Berkeley's May 1965 teach-in, turned into massive events. Organized by Berkeley's Vietnam Day Committee, 20,000 students participated in the thirty-six-hour event, and speakers included writer Norman Mailer, Senator Ernest Gruening (Democrat of Oregon), civil rights leader Bob Moses, and Socialist Norman Thomas.

The momentum of the early movement led to a national teach-in on May 15, 1965, in Washington, D.C. The Inter-University Committee for a Public Hearing on Vietnam, which had grown out of the initial Michigan teach-in, organized the fifteen-hour event. It featured a number of prominent scholars and policymakers debating the American position in Vietnam. Although the headline debate between National Security Advisor McGeorge Bundy and George Kahin, a Southeast Asia expert from Cornell, was cancelled when Bundy was sent to the Caribbean at the last minute, the gathering was successful in pushing the issue of Vietnam into the arena of public debate.

The teach-ins prompted a variety of reactions. The involvement of professors raised questions of academic freedom and the appropriate role of the professor. The Johnson Administration attempted to counter the influence of teach-ins by dispatching so-called "truth teams," or administration representatives, to several Midwest colleges beginning in May 1965.

Activists within the antiwar movement also clashed over the teach-ins. Some saw them as a vehicle for influencing administration policy by engaging it in public discussion and debate, while others, skeptical of working within mainstream political circles, saw the teach-ins more in the vein of protest. Frequent clashes between students and professors broke down the lines of communication and cooperation that had facilitated many of the early teach-ins. As the war dragged on, teach-ins did not fit as easily into the increasingly militant antiwar movement.

Although teach-ins were no longer as prominent after 1965, they continued to play an important role in the antiwar movement; they spread to other nations as well and started a trend that continues to today. Teach-ins were organized by antiapartheid activists in the 1980s and antiglobalization activists in the 1990s and early 2000s to educate students and others.

Matthew Levin

See also: Antiwar Movement, Vietnam Era; Education, Higher; Love-Ins.

Bibliography

DeBenedetti, Charles. *An American Ordeal: The Antiwar Movement of the Vietnam Era.* Syracuse, NY: Syracuse University Press, 1990.

Menashe, Louis, and Ronald Radosh, eds. *Teach-Ins, U.S.A.: Reports, Opinions, Documents.* New York: F.A. Praeger, 1967.

TEENAGERS

The word "teenager" was coined anonymously during World War II, which, sociologists and historians say, is entirely appropriate. Although teenagers have always existed in the technical sense—all human beings who survive to adulthood pass through the years thirteen to nineteen—it was during the postwar era that the concept of the teenage years as a uniquely formative stage in life came into its own.

In pre-industrial societies, and even in many industrial societies, humans passed directly from childhood into adulthood, from the protectiveness of the family and school directly into marriage and work. But with a growing urban population and middle class from the late nineteenth century onward, American parents increasingly came to realize that schooling and training must be extended into the teen years if their offspring were to succeed in life.

Such aspirations were confined to a minority of Americans until the postwar economic boom. By the 1950s, the vast majority of teenage Americans were in high school—though many worked on the side to make spending money—and no longer children. Yet, they were protected by their families and schools from the harsh realities of the marketplace, even as their bodies matured physically and their sexual drives emerged.

The rise of the teenager as a unique social cohort was not just a relative statistical fact of the postwar era—that is, a higher percentage of persons between the ages of thirteen and nineteen being able to extend their youth into years that previously were regarded as adulthood—but an absolute one as well. The surging U.S. birthrate after World War II—the so-called baby boom—meant there were far more Americans in their teenage years by the late 1950s and 1960s.

1950s: The Golden Age of the Teenager

The new and expanding teenage cohort had an immense impact on American society beginning in the 1950s. Teenagers became trendsetters—in music, fashion, food, media, and other lifestyle choices—in ways they never had before.

At the same time, teenagers were seen as a threat to the social order to an unprecedented degree. The 1950s witnessed growing concerns about everything from petty crime to gang activity to illegal car racing to out-of-wedlock births, all lumped together under the popular term of the day, "juvenile delinquency."

Like so much else in American society, World War II was a pivotal period in the transformation of the American teenager. With parents increasingly out of the home—fathers in the military and mothers in the workplace—teenagers gained autonomy and the freedom to run their own lives, and the booming wartime economy put money in their pockets. Freedom and money allowed teenagers to express themselves as consumers of products and culture. During the war, for example, the young singer Frank Sinatra drew mass crowds of screaming teenage girls to his concerts and appearances throughout the country.

Retailers were somewhat slow to recognize the teenage market, whereas the media were quicker to adapt. This was partly out of necessity. As television became more popular and parents were forced to stay home to take care of more children, the movie industry saw its profits begin to plummet during the early 1950s. Searching out new markets, the industry recognized that teenagers wanted to get out of the home and needed places to socialize.

Increasingly, moviemakers released horror and science fiction films, youth-oriented romances and dramas, and even employed gimmicks such as 3-D and drive-ins to get teenagers in front of the silver screen. The teen-oriented movie reached its apotheosis with the 1955 hit *Rebel Without a Cause*, which featured several young stars—Natalie Wood, Sal Mineo, and James Dean—in a high school drama about teen alienation.

Similarly, as television undercut radio drama, stations shifted to all-music formats that appealed to younger people who wanted to dance. And no music was more appealing—or danceable—than black rhythm and blues, played on late-night broadcasts across the South and increasingly in the urban North. Several music pioneers, including Cleveland radio deejay Alan Freed and Memphis-based record producer Sam Phillips, recognized the potential of marketing the highly infectious music to America's white teenagers. In 1954, Freed coined the term "rock and roll" for the new version of rhythm and blues that was gaining popularity among America's white teenagers, and he moved his program to the more influential New York media market. That same year, Phillips recorded a Mississippi-born teenager named Elvis Presley, whose music was heavily influenced by black rhythm and blues and gospel, as well as by white country and western music. Like Sinatra before him, Presley drew mobs of screaming teenagers to his concerts, further cementing adolescents as musical trendsetters in 1950s America.

By that decade, retailers also were beginning to recognize a potential teenage market. The first to do so was a marketing researcher named Eugene Gilbert, who conducted polls of teenage buyers and, by 1958, concluded that their purchasing power was an astounding $9.5 billion. Moreover, he advised his business clients that teenagers were influential in determining how their parents spent money on things such as vacations and clothing. More generally, he said, though parents had been shaped by the Depression—and therefore resisted impulse buying—teenagers had never known anything but prosperity, and so they were infusing their households with a buy-now attitude.

There also was a downside to the teenage phenomenon. Though the 1950s earned a somewhat-deserved reputation for social stability and calm—especially in contrast to the unrest of the 1960s—they were, say historians, a period of great anxiety, as fears of communism, organized crime, and the atomic bomb permeated the American consciousness. Some of this fear, clearly, focused on the new autonomous teenage culture. In 1953, for example, the federal Children's Bureau warned of a coming crime wave, as baby boom children matured into their teen years.

It was not long before studies of juvenile delinquency were becoming best-sellers and Hollywood, as is its wont, was marketing to this anxiety with films about teenage rebelliousness and crime, including *Rebel Without a Cause*, *The Wild One* (1953), and *The Blackboard Jungle* (1955). There also was talk that rock and roll music was infecting the nation's white youth with the heightened sexuality that racists associated with African Americans and their music. In some places, especially the Bible Belt states of the South and Midwest, rock and roll records were publicly destroyed.

Since the 1950s: Decline and Resurgence of Teen Culture

The 1950s might be described as the golden age of the teenager, but the more politically turbulent decade that followed saw the attention of the general public and media transferred to a slightly older contingent—the college student and dropout. Though teenagers could be found in college, in the political protest movement, and in the counterculture, these social institutions and phenomena were more associated with people in their early twenties. Indeed, no decade of the postwar era would see such a dominance of teenage culture as the 1950s. This is not to say that teenagers disappeared after 1960, but never again would they be the trendsetters they had been.

Still, many of the anxieties about teenagers persisted. With the rise of the crack culture in the 1980s, a new specter haunted the American imagination—the so-called superpredator. These were the supposed shock troops of the urban gangs, armed with high-power weapons, devoid of moral compasses—having been raised haphazardly in single-parent households—and intent on winning and holding lucrative territory in the drug wars that gripped American inner cities during the late 1980s and early 1990s.

Though many of these gangs were dominated by Latinos and African Americans, white suburban America was producing its own supposed predators in the form of alienated teenagers who took out their frustrations by opening fire on fellow students and teachers in the nation's high schools. A spate of such events included the 1999 massacre at Columbine High School in suburban Denver, Colorado, which left fourteen students, including the two perpetrators, and one teacher dead. The two teenage shooters were said to be part of an amorphous goth movement. Dressing in black and dabbling in occultism, goths were seen as antisocial types who disdained their parents, teachers, and all other figures of authority.

Just as the late 1980s and 1990s saw a resurgence of the perception of teenagers as a force for social instability, the period also witnessed a resurgence of media attention on teenage culture. With home theater systems and video rentals keeping older viewers at home, Hollywood began aiming at the teenage market with growing numbers of action-packed blockbusters.

Meanwhile, MTV and other music outlets were marketing new teenage megastars such as Britney Spears and Eminem to younger listeners. Some social observers have noted this may have been a matter of demographics, as the children of the baby boom generation—the so-called baby boomlet—entered their teen years.

James Ciment

See also: Child Rearing; Crime, Juvenile; Drug Culture; Education, Elementary and Secondary; Education, Higher; Extreme Sports; Family; Music Videos; Rap and Hip Hop; Rock and Roll; School Shootings.

Bibliography

Hine, Thomas. *The Rise and Fall of the American Teenager.* New York: Avon, 1999.

Palladino, Grace. *Teenagers: An American History.* New York: Basic Books, 1996.

Rollin, Lucy. *Twentieth-Century Teen Culture by the Decades: A Reference Guide.* Westport, CT: Greenwood, 1999.

TELEVISION

Arguably the most influential technology of the postwar era in America—its only real competitor, say historians, is the computer—television has shaped the American way of life in diverse and profound ways. The history of television is twofold—one of rapid technological change and one of the impact of that change on the broader culture.

With regard to technological change, television is really a series of evolving technologies—broadcast, cable, satellite, and broadband Internet—for capturing images and sounds, electronically and digitally. With regard to the cultural impact, television has evolved into such a powerful cultural influence, because it has produced programs that form a large and distinctive body of narratives and representations; they create audiences that share the social rituals of viewing and talking about the contents of these programs. As the primary means for socialization of the whole baby boom generation, television is not just a mirror held up to society but also a shaper of experiences and lifestyles.

Technological Developments

The first television patent was issued in 1923 to Russian-born physicist Vladimir Zworikyn, widely regarded as the "father of television," working for the Radio Corporation of America (RCA) in New Jersey; some historians argue that the self-educated inventor Philo Farnsworth developed the technology independently in California. Television was first broadcast in the United States to a small number of television set owners in 1939.

Television also was introduced that year to a larger public at the New York World's Fair exhibit, "The World of Tomorrow." There, RCA sponsored the Hall of Television, where a model in transparent Bakelite was on display. RCA's National Broadcasting Company (NBC) used its transmitter atop the Empire State Building in New York City to experiment with this new type of broadcasting. David Sarnoff, the so-called "televisionary" head of RCA, called it "radio with eyes."

RCA moved ahead fast because of European competition for standards: The first regular television program service had been started in Berlin, under the Nazis, in 1935; the British Broadcasting Company (BBC) broadcast the first public television programs in 1936. State-owned European television was defined as relevant to public service and used mostly for news and propaganda purposes. American television, following the model of radio, would be commercial and provide mostly entertainment.

Although nothing happened quickly, delays, caused both by regulatory requirements and by historical events, ultimately proved beneficial for mass production and consumption. First, the Federal Communications Commission (FCC), concerned about high fidelity and the quality of signal delivery, asked to delay commercialization of the new technology. Then, upon the entry of the United States into World War II, defense requirements turned all the cathode tube factories in the country into radar screen and military electronics providers.

This was followed by a "license freeze" from 1948 to 1952, allowing the newly established television networks to consolidate themselves and limiting the entry of independent stations and operators into the media market. When the FCC finally gave the industry the go-ahead, television benefited from the experience of Navy-trained radar operators, who in civilian life became set installers and repairmen.

By 1950, some 3 million U.S. homes were equipped with a television set. From there, growth in the number of sets and the amount of time spent in front of them was explosive. By 1955, there were 32 million sets, and by 1960, the average American family was watching six hours of television daily.

Color television technology was introduced in the United States in 1954. The National Television Systems Committee (NTSC) process became the standard, with 525 lines and 30 frames per second. In 1960, the United States launched the first communications satellite, *Echo 1A*, and the Japanese company Sony, developed the first television set assembled with solid-state transistors instead of electron tubes; the new technology allowed for miniaturization and, with it, portability.

The 1960s saw other profound technological changes. These included videotape, which allowed for the recycling of programs. Cable technology also developed in rural and suburban areas, making the medium pervasive.

Ties with the movie industry provided progressively more recorded programs. By 1955, the major motion picture studios in Hollywood and New York realized that they could not ignore the small screen and started producing hour-long films and series specifically for home consumption. The television industry relied on ratings to measure program popularity and to establish advertising prices. The ads paid for easy access to news and entertainment for a larger and larger audience.

An Adaptive Medium

As television evolved into a more complex system, the broadcasting industry asked for stronger regulation. Created by the Communications Act of 1934, the FCC's main role had been to distribute licenses to stations and administer their renewal. In the 1960s, responding to public dissatisfaction with poor quality content and the assessment of FCC Chairman Newton Minow that television programming was a "vast wasteland," the agency began enforcing the "fairness doctrine." Editorial content would henceforth be required to serve the public interest better. The Public Broadcasting System (PBS), partly funded by viewer donations and free of advertising, came into being to answer the criticisms of those who denounced profit-oriented programming and the management of airtime wholly for advertisers and sponsors.

In the early 1970s, to limit network control over both production and distribution, the FCC added two regulations: PTAR (1970) and "Fin-Syn" (1971). PTAR (the Prime Time Access Rule) limited the networks' share in programming to three hours of prime time per night to ensure airtime for local and independent first-run syndicated programs. Fin-Syn (Network *Fin*ancial and *Syn*dication Rules) encouraged independent producers by prohibiting networks from owning syndicated program rights.

This balanced partition of tasks was maintained for three decades. President Ronald Reagan undid the fairness doctrine in 1987, when he vetoed an attempt by Democrats in Congress to turn it into law. Deregulation pressure from an industry with far-reaching mergers and acquisitions strategies put an end to PTAR and Fin-Syn in the mid-1990s.

Such pressure culminated in the new Telecommunications Act of 1996. Together with the Cable Communications Act of 1984, this measure facilitated the vertical integration of station ownership, production, and distribution; it also lowered barriers for entry into local and regional media markets and reduced the number of players in the audiovisual sector.

Rise and Fall of the Big Three Networks

The three commercial broadcast networks—American Broadcasting Company (ABC), the Columbia Broadcasting System (CBS) and National Broadcasting Company (NBC)—had dominated television since its inception, but their "golden age" spanned from the 1960s to the 1980s. The quiz show scandals of 1957–1960, in which game shows were rigged to allow popular contestants to win, offered the networks an opportunity to claim total control of programming costs and content, when they changed their operating rules so as not to deceive the public.

The networks became full-blown brokers of programs and sellers of advertising time, rather than merely broadcasters of programs paid for by sponsors. The increased control led to their expansion into commercial advertising throughout the 1960s. It also led to the disappearance of live broadcasting and to the creation of catalogues of films and series, useful for reruns and foreign export. Having control of programs also allowed networks to tailor schedules for segmented audiences in regular time slots, such as daytime soaps for housewives and Saturday morning cartoons for children. Without real competition and with little pressure to take risks, network broadcasting became a formulaic closed system, leaving little space for other alternative or innovative content.

The three classic networks were not displaced until the 1990s, after technical innovations had matured and deregulation allowed challenges to what they had established in the 1950s. Fox Network appeared in 1986. Two minor, studio-owned, over-the-air networks merged in 1995: UPN (United Paramount) and WB (Warner Brothers), merging into the CW in 2006. In addition, several new technologies greatly widened viewers' choices: cable, Direct Broadcast Satellite (DBS), and VCR.

For three decades, the networks had held more than 90 percent of the American television audience. By the early 2000s, their share had fallen to under 40 percent, as other programming enticed audiences away. Yet their power as the producers of prototype shows for the whole industry endured.

Cable and Internet

Cable was originally developed in the late 1940s to deliver broadcast signals by wire in areas too remote to receive clear signals from over-the-air television stations. It remained in this ancillary status, until the FCC approved coupling with domestic communications satellites in 1973 and allowed extension to urban television markets.

In 1984, cable operators won the deregulation battle over terrestrial broadcasters with passage of the Cable Communications Act. The legislation allowed them to provide services (such as mail order, home video-shopping) and content that was not available on over-the-air networks. Subscription based and often commercial free, cable TV had great audience appeal. Providers also were able to avoid program content regulations imposed on the networks by the FCC, although they were required to increase local content by "must carry" rules (for public access channels). By 1990, about two-thirds of American households subscribed to cable service, with a choice of more than seventy channels. In 2002, cable surpassed over-the-air television in prime-time viewing.

Cable companies have modified the viewing experience of the American generations born since the 1980s as the supply side of the industry expanded. They benefit from a multichannel television system, whose use was enhanced by the remote control. Americans' viewing possibilities were also expanded by the VCR, which was enhanced by the rise of video rentals and sales stores. Home videotape technology offered a secondary market for television products.

This trend was followed by videotape's digital equivalent, the DVD, which can turn the computer screen into a television video display. In 2001, the sales of DVD films surpassed those of VHS, demonstrating the rapid adoption of DVD players and computer drives.

Cable found its audience by segmentation, identifying niche publics and desirable themes: HBO (1976, for feature films), Nickelodeon (1979, for children), CNN (1980, for live continuous news coverage), MTV (1981, for popular music), and others. The cable industry also underwent a process of concentration, with three major cable operators (Multiple System Operators) dominating the market by 2000: ATT-Comcast, Time-Warner, and Viacom. In response to their threat, the networks embarked on cable ventures of their own, such as NBC's offering of CNBC (news).

Quiz Show Scandals

Television quiz shows, in which contestants use their wits to compete for cash prizes and merchandise, were enormously popular in the medium's first decade, from the late 1940s to the late 1950s. Making the transition from radio, quiz shows were at first broadcast primarily in the daytime and aimed at the large audience of stay-at-home mothers. With their growing popularity, the networks decided to air them in prime time and to up the stakes of the prizes. The first of these programs was *The $64,000 Question*, which soon spawned a host of imitators, including NBC's *Twenty One*, which tested the contestants' knowledge of general facts.

The quiz show scandal of the 1950s was triggered by the revelations of one Herbert Stempel, a contestant on *Twenty-One*. In 1958, Stempel went to prosecutors in New York, where the show was aired, and claimed that he had been asked by the show's producers to lose to another contestant, Charles Van Doren, who was highly popular with audiences. Stempel's revelations were soon followed by others, which led to a grand jury empanelment from September 1958 to June 1959. The grand jury indicted only one person, Alfred Freedman, a producer of *Twenty-One*, for perjury.

The grand jury findings were not published, in order to avoid damaging the reputation of innocent contestants. Shocked by the findings, however, federal prosecutors took the case to Congress, which was holding hearings on the subject. The most dramatic moment of the investigation was Van Doren's soul-searching confession of accepting answers provided to him in advance by the show's producers.

While a number of contestants were eventually convicted of perjury for misleading investigators, none of the show's producers was ever convicted. To be found guilty of fraud, there had to be a victim; prosecutors could not prove that the public, who were really the only victims, had lost anything tangible.

Before the end of 1958, several quiz shows went off the air because the sponsors, mostly pharmaceutical and beauty product companies, did not want to be associated with the tainted programs. Consumer organizations and journalists used the incident to decry the deceptive practices and lack of ethics of the television industry and the failures of oversight on the part of the Federal Communications Commissions. Congress responded by passing a bill, the Communications Act Amendment of 1960, declaring illegal any contest or game show that used practices designed to deceive the public.

The networks responded with self-regulation, banning a number of quiz programs from the air, increasing internal monitoring, and creating departments dedicated to monitoring and enforcing standards and practices. By the early 1960s, TV quiz shows had made something of a comeback, although many were produced by local stations rather than networks.

Divina Frau-Meigs

The advent of commercial Internet at the end of the 1990s posed yet another challenge to television systems, as more than half of American households were equipped by the early 2000s with the new technology. Companies such as Microsoft, Cisco, and AOL started taking audience share from networks and cable as they provided games and music online. They offered "surfing" opportunities, such as home shopping, with the added value of interactivity. The response of the ever-changing television system was to create dedicated sites and to use virtual connections to deliver services and products alongside content. In an effort at "broadcastization" of the Internet, each TV network and each program developed its own official and unofficial websites and merchandizing offers.

As the Telecommunications Act of 1996 allowed media companies to acquire both Hollywood catalogues for content and telecommunications companies for hardware, vertically integrated megamedia mergers became possible and attractive. The FCC lifted ownership restrictions on broadcasters and broadcasting restrictions on content producers and cable and phone operators. The whole broadcasting industry was brought together through a process of swapping and cross-ownership agreements, in an effort to rationalize the fragmentation caused by the media explosion over the postwar decades.

By the end of the century, six media giants dominated the industry: Time Warner (Turner/CNN, AOL, HBO, TNT, WB); Disney (Capital Cities, ABC, Go.com); Viacom (Blockbuster, Paramount, UPN); General Electric (NBC, Microsoft, Dow Jones, MSNBC); Westinghouse (CBS and cable services); and the foreign News Corporation (Fox network, 20th Century Fox, BSkyB). Together, the six conglomerates claimed more than half the revenues generated by U.S. media consumption and more than 75 percent of the time Americans spent in front of their screens.

Television and Identity Politics

In the 1960s, television seemed to ignore the identity politics that rose in the wake of the civil rights movement. Its programs during the era largely continued to target middle-class suburban audiences, and they avoided any controversial material. Television entertainment generally eschewed representation of the counterculture. By the 1970s, however, the networks had come to participate more actively in American social transformations. The onscreen universe slowly started showing women at work, racial diversity, and a youth presence, in spite of the reticence on the part of advertisers and producers.

Happy Days (ABC, 1974–1984) and *Mork and Mindy* (ABC, 1978–1982) characterize the best of this trend to blend action and comedy around young people. For liberated women, programs such as *The Mary Tyler Moore Show* (CBS, 1970–1977) and *Charlie's Angels* (ABC, 1976–1981) toyed with both sexual exploitation and sex liberation. The debate over racial integration moved from comic radio transfers like *Amos 'n' Andy* shows to *The Cosby Show* (NBC, 1984–1992) for the black (and white) suburban middle class.

Genre cycles followed a similar pattern. The first television shows were copied from popular culture staples, including such early 1960s Westerns as *Rawhide* (CBS, 1959–1966), or such later 1970s comic book superheroes as *The Incredible Hulk* (CBS, 1977–1982). Innovation in genres revived or reinterpreted tested formulae with new themes or formats. Soap operas, with their mix of melodrama and romance, attest to

this process, with prime time hits such as *Dallas* (1978–1991) and *Dynasty* (1981–1989).

Genres limit risk while guaranteeing larger audiences with predictable content. The mix of suspense and confirmation of expectation creates pleasure and loyalty to the program and to the channel, hence television's drive for serialization. Successful shows such as *Bewitched* (ABC, 1964–1972) led to imitations such as *I Dream of Jeannie* (NBC 1965–1970) or to spin-offs such as *Lou Grant* (CBS, 1977–1982), lifted from the *Mary Tyler Moore Show*. When a genre was overexploited, reaching audience saturation, it was slowly dropped from the schedule and another genre cycle began.

Fragmentation of Identity Politics and the Rise of Morality Politics

The late 1980s and the 1990s saw television's second "golden age," with high-quality dramatic series, docudramas, and reality-based programming. Ensemble series replaced those with single heroes, as the shows adjusted to a more multicultural country. Series such as *L.A. Law* (NBC, 1986–1994), *thirtysomething* (ABC, 1987–1991), *Northern Exposure* (CBS, 1990–1995), *ER* (1994–), and *Friends* (NBC, 1994–2004), with snappy dialogue and realistic settings, expanded the scope of the audience.

Docudramas mixed theater and film. The early success of such productions as the miniseries *Roots* (1977), which was aimed at African Americans but captured a wide white audience as well, led to other controversial shows based on real-life situations; these included *The Ryan White Story* (ABC, 1989) on AIDS and *Roe v. Wade* (NBC, 1999) about abortion.

Reality-based programming, the most prominent television fare by the end of the 1990s, used the hybridization of several television genres (the cop serial, the soap, the amateur video) in programs such as *America's Most Wanted* (Fox, 1988–) and *COPS* (Fox, 1989–), while game shows came back with a mix of soap and romance in programs including *Survivor* (CBS, 2000–) and *Big Brother* (CBS, 2000–).

Talk shows, which boomed with the process of syndication, followed the trend of live audience participation. Driven by popular stars and personalities such as Oprah Winfrey, Jerry Springer, and Larry King, they allowed for the airing of controversial political and social concerns.

Television thus plunged into hyperfragmented identities, helped by the rise of new over-the-air networks and cable and satellite channels. Segmentation increased with gendered networks (Lifetime, 1984), broadcasting programs such as *Kate and Allie* (1984–1989) and *Cagney & Lacey* (1982–1988). Television moved away from the traditional middle-class family as pictured in *Father Knows Best* and *Leave it to Beaver* to cover changing perceptions of women, as in *Roseanne* (1988–1997) and *Married . . . with Children* (1987–1997). In these series, women balanced work and household duties, while dealing with such social issues as date rape, abortion, violence, and child care. Reality could intrude as well, as in the *Murphy Brown* (1988–1998) episodes about out-of-wedlock pregnancy that prompted Vice President Dan Quayle to lash out at feminism and extol traditional family values during the 1992 presidential campaign.

Shows about racial integration, including *The Fresh Prince of Bel Air* (NBC, 1990–1996) and *In Living Color* (Fox, 1990–1994), catered to urban viewers. At the same time, the 1990s also witnessed a new segregated divide, as some program featured leading casts that were all-white, such as *Friends*, or all black, such as *The Steve Harvey Show* (WB, 1996–) and *Moesha* (UPN, 1996–2001). This move was facilitated as minor or recently established networks such as WB, UPN, and BET appealed to black audiences with a black cast, allowing the big three networks to return to white audiences with a white cast.

Just as television in the 1960s and 1970s did not portray identity politics, so there has been a time lag in the TV appearance of the morality politics pressed by the New Right and its conservative agenda. Morality politics appeared in some mainstream series, as in *Highway to Heaven* (NBC, 1984–1989) and *Touched by an Angel* (CBS, 1994–2003), but it was mostly evident in talk shows and other participatory formats. The rise of regional cable networks such as the National Empowerment Television or the Goodlife TV network, together with evangelical channels such as the Christian Broadcasting Network (which became The Family Channel), allowed ministers Pat Robertson and Jerry Falwell (*The Old Time Gospel Hour*) and others to express their conservative views on race, ethnicity, and gender.

News Television

If fictional TV programming ignored the civil rights movement, there was news coverage from the Freedom Riders of the early 1960s to the 1968 assassination of Martin Luther King, Jr. In the early civil rights era, television gave Northern viewers contact with Southern black protesters' views, helping to form a liberal consensus around desegregation and black voting rights.

At the same time, the Vietnam War confronted politicians with the difficulty of controlling the public's perceptions as the war's violence regularly invaded people's living rooms. Walter Cronkite's news coverage of February 1968 during the Tet Offensive made the nation aware of the need for peace negotiations. With the civil rights movement, the Vietnam War, and the Watergate crisis, television provided a postwar vision of democracy reacting to public opinion.

Television news enhanced a feeling of national identity around mourning (the assassination of John Kennedy in 1963 or the *Challenger* space shuttle crash in 1986) and with joy (the walk on the Moon in 1969 or the fall of the Berlin Wall in 1989). Historical events were recorded on television and brought audiences closer to the political process through the broadcast of national conventions (first telecast in 1952) and presidential debates (beginning in 1960). While this brought political leaders closer to the public, a particularity of postwar politics, it also made them the object of political scrutiny, as in the Pentagon Papers or the Watergate scandals that led to the downfall of the Nixon Administration.

In the 1980s, the advent of continuous cable news reshuffled this relationship, as politicians became dependent on CNN for their decision making. Founded

CBS News—featuring such respected broadcasters as (left to right) Douglas Edwards, Walter Cronkite, and Edward R. Murrow—was the bellwether of early television journalism. It established standards to which the industry still aspires. *(CBS Photo Archive/Getty Images)*

Roots

From January 23 to January 30, 1977, more than 130 million Americans—or 70 percent of the national population—tuned their televisions to watch all or part of the six-part miniseries *Roots* on the ABC network. A dramatization of the 1976 book by Alex Haley, *Roots* traced the story of an African American family from the capture of Gambian ancestor Kunta Kinte by slavers in the 1700s to the post–Civil War era, when his descendents in America were granted freedom.

Besides setting records for viewership, the series sparked renewed interest in African American history. It helped change popular perceptions of race, and convinced entertainment producers that people of color were not only appropriate subjects of drama, but they also comprised a market for that drama.

The miniseries, a total of twelve hours in length, cost $6 million dollars to produce and featured such well-known actors as Leslie Uggams, Lou Gossett, and George Hamilton. Newcomers such as LeVar Burton, who played the young Kunta Kinte, became instant stars when they appeared on the show. Celebrities in other fields, such as the poet Maya Angelou and football star O.J. Simpson, took minor roles.

On average, each hour of the miniseries was filmed in twenty-one days, under the guidance of eight different directors. Critics fretted about distortions of history and sensationalism in the depiction of violence, but audiences found little to complain about; the final two-hour broadcast drew 80 million viewers. *Roots* remains the most watched dramatic show in television history.

The symbiotic relationship between the show and the book, which would win a Pulitzer Prize in 1977, was also unprecedented in publishing history. Series producer David Wolper claimed that publisher Doubleday initially planned a print run of only 50,000 books, and Wolper laughed at the figure, saying it would not come close to meeting demand. He was right. Doubleday printed 300,000 copies of *Roots* in September 1976; by March 1977, a few weeks after the show aired, 2 million hardcover books had been sold.

Coming on the heels of the American Bicentennial, *Roots* also sparked a nationwide interest in genealogy that crossed racial boundaries. More important, however, was its effect on race relations. Surveys found that one-third of those who watched *Roots* saw the entire miniseries and learned more about slavery and its brutality than they ever had in school. Viewers discussed the issues it raised, as well as slavery itself, at home and at work, often in interracial groups. *Roots* is even credited by some with making black studies programs and black history classes a popular option in colleges.

A subsequent production, *Roots: The Next Generations*, aired two years later, in February 1979. This time, 110 million people watched the series, making it a strong commercial success as well.

Vickey Kalambakal

in 1980, by cable pioneer Ted Turner, CNN was the first twenty-four-hour news network, with live coverage of major events around the planet. By 1990, it was viewed in more than ninety countries, with a global news service that made it a source, as well as a transmitter of media events. It had particular triumphs in the live coverage of the Tiananmen Square demonstrations in 1989 and the first Gulf War in 1991. The live coverage of CNN in competition with Fox News (1986) increased pressure on the three major networks to depart from their traditional desktop journalism, dominated by anchormen such as Tom Brokaw (*NBC Nightly News*), Peter Jennings (*ABC World News Tonight*), and Dan Rather (*CBS Evening News*).

As the FCC removed public service obligations and audience ratings were applied to news, the private life of politicians became the object of more intense public scrutiny. Sex politics occupied center-screen with the Clarence Thomas-Anita Hill hearings (1991) and the Clinton-Lewinsky affair (1998–1999). Identity politics turned race and ethnic news into a kind of informational entertainment

In the groundbreaking 1977 television miniseries *Roots*, Ben Vereen and Olivia Cole play slaves who set out for Tennessee after being freed. The multigeneration slave family saga was based on the best-selling book by Alex Haley. *(Evening Standard/Getty Images)*

(or "infotainment"), most notably with the murder trial of O.J. Simpson in 1994.

News programming also was affected by genre cycles and hybridization. Documentaries and public affairs programs such as the celebrated *60 Minutes* (CBS, 1968–) and *Frontline* (PBS, 1983–) declined as reality-based programming emerged. *A Current Affair* (Fox, 1986–1996) and similar programs contributed to turning news into a tabloid press format, which, according to critics, diminished the public trust in televised information and journalistic standards. Analysis and commentary were sacrificed to dramatic images and real-time live telecasts. The first Gulf War was said to look like a video game, when CNN showed laser-guided surgical strikes. The second Gulf War as presented on Fox and other channels featured reporting styles copied from reality shows with their seemingly unedited, continuous streams of images.

Audiences: From Mass to Niche

The concept of audience has undergone considerable change since the beginning of television. During the reign of the three networks, it was viewed as a mass audience, measured with ratings that were sold to advertisers. TV audiences were first conceived of as national communities: an unstructured, amorphous, homogeneous mass of people to whom the message could be sent directly and nationally. This concept prevailed until about the end of 1970s. Maintained by broadcast-

ers, advertisers, and politicians alike, it served them all as an integrative view of American society and built consensus.

This picture changed with the advent of cable, narrowcasting, and segmentation. The audience was then fractured into "niche publics," according to age, gender, ethnicity, race, and profession. Such demographic grouping has altered the way advertisers target their products for consumers, as their messages are distributed across a wider variety of channels. Not all audiences are equal, nor are all minority groups: conditions of income attract sponsors and broadcasters. The growing Latino community has become an increasingly desirable market as far as broadcasters are concerned, with several networks in Spanish to choose from— Telemundo (bought by NBC in 2002), Univision (associated with Latino entrepreneurs in the United States), and TV Azteca (broadcasting from Mexico).

Such changes in the postwar audience have pushed the industry toward a two-pronged strategy: multiple exposures to the same program and highly selective exposure to premium programs. New consumer trends allow the national public to receive the same product but with a different kind of exposure in an asynchronous manner (via VHS, cable reruns, DVDs, and TiVo digital video recording). The mass market is larger than before because of transnational trends that extend the audience beyond U.S. borders.

The networks also vie for niche publics likely to be attached to a product as a form of their cultural identity and expression. This is particularly the case for fan communities developing around series or for single-issue publics or communities, which are in demand of cultural expressions targeted to their needs— age (*Buffy, The Vampire Slayer*, WB/UPN, 1997–2003, for teenagers), sexual orientation (*Queer as Folk*, Showtime, 2000–), race (Black Entertainment Network), or ethnicity (Telemundo and Univision). These audiences, though narrow, are willing to pay premium prices for subscriptions. They also have to have disposable income to attract sponsors and advertisers.

Public Opinion: Citizens, Consumers, Participants

The reception of television content by the audience has followed a double trend, modeled on mass and niche perceptions of the audience. The first model holds that mass media has power over audiences and can, by incubation and cultivation, modify attitudes and values. The second model suggests uses and gratification, positing that individual appropriation of media by audiences deflects the power of the message.

In one case, the audience is passive and gullible; in the other, it is active and motivated by pleasure. In the first case, the concern is political and considers audiences as citizens; in the second case, the concern is economic and considers audiences as consumers. The two models, however, acknowledge the key role of television in the socialization of the public. Combined, the two models give a sense of the complex ways in which various publics are engaged by television.

The big postwar reception debates took place during the influence of effects theory and the conception of mass audience as reflecting citizens. There was audience mobilization on sensitive content issues, particularly violence, pornography, and children's advertising. The debate on television violence shaped the system, as it led to technological and legal changes and economic considerations of image and brand.

Legislation was passed and reached its climax with the 1993 Children's Protection From Violence Programming Act, completed in 1996 by an educational amendment. It imposed a three-hour per week minimal quota of educational and informational programs and a requirement that all new sets be equipped with a Violence chip (V-chip), which allows parents to control the sexual and violence content of programming available to their children.

But research findings, often complex and contradictory, have led the industry and its interest groups to invoke free-speech arguments and the First Amendment to help prevent public intrusion into its decision-making process. As a result, public discourse and criticism were primarily focused on fiction, not news, and on children's, not adult, programming. Although public authorities and policymakers led a series of federal inquiries (U.S. Senate 1969, 1974; the Surgeon General's Scientific Advisory Committee Report of 1972), little was gained in terms of legislation. There was a shift from solutions aimed at pushing responsibility onto producers (prime-time watershed or family hours in the 1960s) to solutions aimed at pushing responsibility onto parents (advisories and technological devices in the 1990s). The industry made sure there was no criticism of the commercial system, especially during the golden age of network domination. It successfully deflected debate from other important issues, such as market structure or media concentration.

Media reformers and critics found new hope in the arrival of commercial cable and the even newer satellite television, as a means of offering diversity of content and pluralism of ideas. The prospect for content quality was even further removed as deregulation policies prevailed and the Fairness Doctrine was demoted. The debate shifted to niche publics, especially as the uses and gratifications model gained currency.

Research from the 1980s focused largely on how race, ethnicity, and gender shape the reception of programs. The early sitcoms and soap operas were analyzed in relation to women in the suburbs. The debate over racial integration was stirred around the *Cosby Show* and race. Docudramas and their interpretation of history and memory (the Civil War, the Holocaust) also stirred controversial interpretations of meaning.

More recently, reception analysis has focused on fan communities, especially as they express themselves on the Internet around sites dedicated to such series as *Friends* and *The X-Files* (Fox, 1993–2002) or programs such as *Big Brother*. This trend follows the network strategy of developing home pages and official sites to complement their programming and encourage audience feedback. But there is also the perception that fans are producers of texts (making parodies, illustrations, and songs, for example) and participants (interacting with actors, writing sequels, and protesting the content of some episodes). As "textual poachers," they have derived several strategies of resistance to commercial media and transgress network copyrights by downloading programs illegally; as interactive players, they can mobilize against the cancellation of a program or campaign for a feature film to be made out of a series.

Such user attitudes, together with technological and social changes, will frame the future of television systems as they move to High Definition TV and other digital innovations. The potential for interactivity and self-expression they entail shift the dynamics of communication away from the transmission of values to a participatory model, fostering greater attention to self and to single, community-oriented issues.

This process leaves television at the hub of a content system that blurs off-line and online entities and supports the financing of the fragile virtual economy. With its built-in commercial power, television has retained its capacity for shaping popular culture well beyond the postwar era.

Divina Frau-Meigs

See also: Advertising; Fairness Doctrine; Film, Feature; Internet; Music Videos; National Endowments for the Arts and Humanities; Radio; Sports Broadcasting.

Bibliography

Anderson, Kent. *Television Fraud: The History and Implications of the Quiz Show Scandals.* Westport, CT: Greenwood, 1978.

Jenkins, Henry. *Textual Poachers: Television Fans and Participatory Culture.* New York: Routledge, 1992.

Lewis, Justin. *The Ideological Octopus: An Exploration of Television and Its Audience.* New York: Routledge, 1991.

Newcomb, Horace, ed. *Television: The Critical View.* 6th ed. New York: Oxford University Press, 2000.

Spigel, Lynn, and Michael Curtin, eds. *The Revolution Wasn't Televised: Sixties Television and Social Conflict.* New York: Routledge, 1997.

Tichi, Cecelia. *Electronic Hearth. Creating an American Television Culture.* New York: Oxford University Press, 1991.

Watson, Mary-Ann. *Defining Visions. Television and the American Experience Since 1945.* New York: Harcourt Brace, 1998.

TENNIS

Americans began playing tennis in the 1870s, when a Staten Island, New York, woman named Mary Ewing Outerbridge introduced the sport to the nation after seeing British soldiers playing the game in Bermuda. Outerbridge set up the first tennis court at the Staten Island Cricket and Baseball Club in 1874. The first U.S. national tennis championship, now known as the U.S. Open, was held in Newport, Rhode Island, in 1881.

Until the 1920s, tennis was largely played by members of upper-class country clubs, particularly in the Northeast. During the course of that decade, however, the game began to gain a middle-class audience and participants, as Bill Tilden, Helen Wills, and Suzanne Langlen, the top competitors, popularized the sport beyond the social elite. In 1938, American Don Budge became the first player to win the singles titles at the U.S., English, Australian, and French nationals, a group of tennis tournaments known collectively as the Grand Slam.

After the cancellation of major events because of World War II, competitive tennis resumed worldwide in 1946. The sport was to experience significant changes during the postwar era, especially in the professionalization of competition, televised promotion, desegregation, and expanded opportunities for women.

Until the late 1960s, tennis was largely an amateur sport, governed by the United States Lawn Tennis Association (USLTA), and the major tournaments were reserved for amateur players. This was part of an old tradition. During the late nineteenth and early twentieth centuries, amateurism, the idea that athletes competed for the love of the game, rather than monetary reward, prevailed for many sports. Determined to preserve that ideal, the USLTA would not permit players to profit directly from tournament play, teaching tennis, endorsing equipment, or writing about the sport. Nevertheless, the tennis establishment often paid the leading players liberal "expense" allowances for appearing in tournaments, and most of them could make a living from this income without becoming professionals who played for monetary prizes.

In the 1930s, Bill Tilden led a handful of top tennis players into a professional circuit; their turning pro robbed the major amateur tournaments of its best-known players. In the 1950s, Jack Kramer, who had won the U.S. Open in 1946 and 1947 and Wimbledon in 1947, launched a campaign to open tennis to both amateurs and professionals, offering prize money and renewing public interest in the sport.

Interest increased among USLTA officials in opening the game to professionals when Australian players won most of the U.S. Open championships from 1953 to 1968. Rod Laver, one of the leading Australians, turned pro in 1963 and played on the small but successful U.S. Professionals circuit established in 1964, which gained support from the Australian, British, and French tennis associations. In 1968, the British opened Wimbledon to professionals, and, in 1969, the USLTA opened the U.S. national championships to professionals. The USLTA changed its name to the U.S. Tennis Association (USTA) in 1975.

Influence of Television

In the 1970s, after the sport had opened up to professionals, American television began showing greater interest in tennis. TV ratings for tennis remained below those for team sports and golf, but the cost of televising tennis was much less than for the other sports, due to the small court size and maximum of four players. Moreover, many advertisers were eager to buy commercial time during tennis matches, because they believed the broadcasts reached a more affluent market than did other sports.

From 1970 to 1973, the major television networks—National Broadcasting Company (NBC), American Broadcasting System (ABC), and Columbia Broadcasting System (CBS)—tripled the amount of airtime devoted to tennis; NBC paid $100,000, then a record, for the rights to televise each of the eight World Championship Tennis Tournaments. Televised tennis peaked in 1975, when the networks telecast fifty matches and CBS paid $600,000 (more than was needed to telecast a National Football League game) to cover a match between Jimmy Connors and John Newcombe.

Despite its success, televised tennis did not fit neatly into any predetermined time slot, and television producers frequently responded by resorting to delayed videotapes, with parts of matches edited out. Producers also encouraged promoters to adopt the "sudden death" tiebreaker after each player in a match had won six games, to abandon the strict rules of all-white tennis attire, and to replace white tennis balls with the more visible yellow. None of these changes completely solved the problems of televised tennis. Fans objected to editing out any part of a match, and they complained that delayed telecasts destroyed the inherent drama of the contests, when they already knew who had won. Occasionally, fans were treated to the spectacle of the same player simultaneously playing different opponents on separate networks.

African Americans and Tennis

Before it accepted professionals and television popularized the sport, tennis opened up to African Americans. Althea Gibson, one of the leading amateurs from 1950 to 1958, is recognized as breaking the color barrier in what had been a largely white sport, becoming the first African American to compete in the U.S. Open in 1950 and the first to win a major championship, the French Open, six years later. Gibson also won at Wimbledon in 1957 and at both Wimbledon and the U.S. Open in 1958.

Arthur Ashe, who followed Gibson as the leading African American tennis player, won the National Collegiate Athletic Association (NCAA) singles title in 1965 and the U.S. national singles championship in 1968, the year before the tournament opened to professionals. In 1975, Ashe won the Wimbledon single's title, becoming the first black man to win that championship.

In the late 1990s, Venus and Serena Williams brought a powerful playing style, unlike most women before them, to the professional circuit. In 1999, Serena, the younger of the sisters, won the U.S. Open singles title, becoming the first African American woman since Gibson to do so. In addition to winning Wimbledon again in 2002 and 2003, she triumphed at the Australian Open in 2003 and 2005, the French Open in 2002, and the U.S. Open in 2002. After winning her first professional match in 1998, Venus won the women's single title in Wimbledon in 2000, 2001, and 2005, the U.S. Open in 2000 and 2001, and the Olympic gold medal in 2000.

The Williams sisters were among the most aggressive tennis players, male or female, in the history of the sport. Their style of play would have been completely unacceptable for women when they started playing tennis in the late nineteenth century. Originally, women tennis players were expected to demonstrate the same gentility, decorum, circumspection, and subordination on the tennis court as they did in

The young American stars John McEnroe (left) and Jimmy Connors (right), seen shaking hands after their Wimbledon semifinals match in 1977 (won by Connors), were dominant figures in men's international tennis from the mid-1970s to early 1980s. *(Roger Jackson/Central Press/Getty Images)*

Women's tennis icon Billie Jean King makes a grand entrance into the Houston Astrodome on September 20, 1973, for her highly publicized challenge match—the "Battle of the Sexes"—with the aging former men's champion Bobby Riggs. *(Sahm Doherty/Time Life Pictures/ Getty Images)*

other aspects of their life. Although players such as Helen Wills, Suzanne Lenglen, and Maureen Connolly challenged these expectations, they did not overthrow them in the way Billie Jean King would in the 1960s and 1970s.

A founding member of the women's professional tennis tour in 1973, King won thirty-eight Grand Slam tournaments from 1966 to 1980; in 1972, she won all four Grand Slam singles titles in a single year. Confident, articulate, and assertive, she led the crusade against sexism in tennis, erasing the stiff formality and pomposity from the sport. King is perhaps best known for her 1973 "Battle of the Sexes" exhibition match against Bobby Riggs, who had won the Wimbledon men's singles title in 1939. The largest audience in the history of the sport to date watched the twenty-nine-year-old King defeat the fifty-five-year-old Riggs, giving women's tennis an enormous boost.

While the interest drawn to the game by the King-Riggs match was a one-off event, the popularity of the game—both as a participatory and spectator sport—has continued to grow into the early twenty-first century. In 2005, many Grand Slam matches began to be broadcast over the Internet, promising an even greater audience for the sport.

Adam R. Hornbuckle

See also: Golf; Olympics; Sports Broadcasting; Sports, Participatory.

Bibliography

Baltzell, E. Digby. *Sporting Gentlemen: Men's Tennis from the Age of Heroes to the Cult of the Spectator.* New York: Free Press, 1995.

Collins, Bud, and Zander Hollander, eds. *Bud Collins' Modern Encyclopedia of Tennis.* Detroit: Gale Research, 1994.

Evans, Richard. *Open Tennis: The Players, the Politics, the Pressures, the Passions, and the Great Matches.* Lexington, MA: S. Greene, 1990.

King, Billie Jean. *We Have Come a Long Way: The Story of Women's Tennis.* New York: McGraw-Hill, 1988.

Rader, Benjamin G. *American Sports: From the Age of Folk Games to the Age of Televised Sports.* Upper Saddle River, NJ: Prentice Hall, 2004.

TERRORISM, DOMESTIC

Beginning in 1945, domestic terrorism in the United States became a growing concern for federal, state, and local authorities, as many Americans chose to express their discontent through political violence. Domestic terrorism can be defined as any act perpetrated on U.S. soil by American citizens against government institutions or against individuals belonging to any ethnic, religious, sexual, occupational, or other social minority. Such acts are usually designed to intimidate persons with opposing views or to disrupt public services and undermine public confidence in the organs of government.

Domestic terrorism is not monolithic. American terrorists may be individuals acting alone (such as abortion clinic bomber Eric Robert Rudolph or Unabomber Ted Kaczynski) or as part of an organization. Though predominately an expression of extreme-right political views, domestic terrorism in America also has sprung up as a left wing reaction to wars that are perceived as unjust, racial inequality, and environmental concerns. Whatever their political orientation, terrorist groups in the United States have remained outside the political mainstream and have built only limited constituencies.

Political violence in the United States has a long history. Examples include Ku Klux Klan violence against African Americans in the post–Civil War South, and, again, in the 1960s, against civil rights organizations, and bombings perpetrated by the extreme left wing Weather Underground during the 1960s. The best-known example of domestic terrorist violence is the 1995 bombing of the Alfred P. Murrah Federal Building in Oklahoma City by Timothy McVeigh, a right wing extremist. Other high-profile incidents have included the 1984 murder of Denver talk-show host Alan Berg by Colorado anti-Semites and a number of bombings of abortion clinics and shootings of abortion providers since the 1973 *Roe v. Wade* U.S. Supreme Court decision legalizing abortion.

Puerto Rican Nationalism

The period 1945–1960 saw relatively few instances of domestic terrorism in the United States. The most active source of political violence during the 1950s was a group of Puerto Rican separatists associated with a small, but volatile, Puerto Rican Nationalist Party headed by Harvard-educated Pedro Albizu Campos. His exposure to racism in the U.S. Army during World War I left Campos an embittered advocate of independence through violent revolution. Campos and his followers were further angered by discrimination against Puerto Rican immigrants living in the United States. Although they had failed miserably in the Puerto Rican elections of 1948 and attracted only a small following on the island, the nationalists believed that violent acts against government institutions would galvanize support for their movement.

On November 1, 1950, two of Campos's followers—Griselio Torresola and Oscar Collazo—attempted to assassinate President Harry S Truman in Washington, D.C., by shooting their way into Blair House, where the president and his family were living while the White House was being renovated. The attempt was foiled by the quick action of two White House security guards and a Secret Service agent; the shootout left one assailant and a Secret Service agent dead. The Puerto Rican Nationalist Party was also responsible for a March 1, 1954, incident, in which three individuals fired guns on the floor of the U.S. House of Representatives.

Campos and his followers had seriously misjudged the climate of opinion in the Puerto Rican community, both on the U.S. mainland and in Puerto Rico. Community leaders quickly disavowed the party, and the independence movement seemed to gain no support through violence. The Truman Administration defused pro-independence sentiment by granting Puerto Rico political autonomy as a self-governing commonwealth in 1952. Nevertheless, terrorist activity by Puerto Rican nationalists continued over the next twenty years, with considerable support from the radical American left.

Anti-Civil Rights Terrorism

The relative domestic quiescence of the 1950s did not last. Political divisions in the 1960s and early 1970 over civil rights, the Vietnam War, and the environment spawned considerable terrorist activity. Political violence by white supremacist groups sprang up in the southeastern United States in reaction to renewed civil rights activity.

Ku Klux Klan violence intensified in Mississippi during the 1964 "Freedom Summer" drive by the Student Non-Violent Coordinating Committee, which sought to register African Americans to vote. The violence manifested in a rash of burnings of black churches and the murder of three civil rights workers.

Far from slowing the civil rights movement, white supremacist political violence drew attention to racial injustice in the American South, increased support for the Civil Rights Act of 1964 and the Voting Rights Act of 1965, and brought increased law enforcement efforts against the Klan by federal authorities and the Federal Bureau of Investigation (FBI).

Left Wing Terrorism

Domestic terrorism on the left appeared in the late 1960s and intensified during the early 1970s. The initial catalyst was frustration on the part of many student leftists over the failure of nonviolent means to end the Vietnam War. In addition, many white student radicals and black militants were embittered by the slow progress toward ending racial inequality and achieving economic justice.

The largest of the leftist terrorist movements was the Weather Underground, a loose collection of small groups and individuals who engaged in bombings of installations identified with the military-industrial complex and in bank robberies. Most of its members had splintered from the Students for a Democratic Society, the largest of the New Left protest organizations that had emerged on college campuses.

Violent black militant groups looked to the Black Panther Party (which claimed that it was acting in self defense) as their inspiration. The best known of the black terrorist organizations was the Black Liberation Army (BLA).

Like the right wing violence in the South, left wing terrorism proved counterproductive. Mainstream antiwar and civil rights organizations disavowed the Weather Underground and the BLA. They lost much of their support and membership, as the United States gradually withdrew from Vietnam in the early 1970s and as it became clear that the revolution many members hoped for would not occur. Left wing terrorist activity continued into the 1980s and 1990s, nevertheless, sometimes making headlines. Best known among these incidents was the botched holdup by the BLA of a Brinks armored truck in Rockland County, New York, in October 1981, which resulted in the deaths of one BLA member, two police officers, and one security guard.

Since the early 1980s, terrorism on the left has carried over into the activities of new groups that have used violence in support of environmentalism (so-called eco-terrorists) and animal rights. Since the 1970s, hundreds of organizations in the United States have advocated stricter measures to preserve the natural environment (particularly wildlife habitats) and the reduction or abolition of the use of animals in scientific experiments.

Like extremists in the earlier civil rights and antiwar organizations, many on the fringes of the environmental and animal rights movements became frustrated by the slow pace of change in the legal and legislative process and created an underground movement to combat corporations and other organizations whose practices they considered immoral. Their acts have ranged from the sabotage of construction and logging machinery to the bombing of fast-food chain restaurants and car dealerships and the wrecking of fuel-inefficient sport utility vehicles; the total property damage has been estimated at more than $100 million. Most prominent among these organizations are PETA (People for the Ethical Treatment of Animals), the Animal Liberation Front, and the Earth Liberation Front.

Terrorism on the Right

Notwithstanding the activities of the Weather Underground, eco-terrorists, and animal rights groups, the largest source of domestic political violence since 1945 has been the extreme right wing. These groups range from older organizations, such as the Ku Klux Klan and the American Nazi Party, to newer groups, such as Holocaust deniers, neo-Nazi skinheads, and antigovernment white power groups such as Posse Comitatus; radical militias such as the Wisconsin and Michigan militias and the Militia of Montana; and racial separatists. Many of these groups, particularly

the Christian Identity Movement and the violent anti-abortion group Army of God, justify their actions in biblical terms.

Whatever organization they belong to, most right wing extremists share a hatred of government—particularly the U.S. federal government—as well as white-supremacist, anti-Semitic, sexist, and homophobic ideologies. They manifest in their extreme form the popular mistrust of big government, big corporations, and economic globalization.

The most violent groups—rural militias and Christian extremists—emerged during the late 1980s and early 1990s in the Farm Belt and Rust Belt areas of the Midwest and in the mountain and agricultural areas of the Far West. These areas were hit hard by the decline of the manufacturing sector and the loss of small family farms or, in the West, by environmental conflict and federal restrictions on land use. Many white men from small farms and industrial towns affected by factory closures and economic dislocation felt besieged, vulnerable, and angry, and they looked for someone to blame. For some, the scapegoat became federal or state government bureaucracy or large international corporations controlled, in their view, by liberals, blacks, Zionists, or all three. These "alien" elements, extremists believe, are out to destroy white, Anglo-Saxon Protestant Americans and traditional American institutions and replace them with world government.

The most immediate fear among many militia members is that such alien elements will assert their control by taking away their firearms. The FBI siege of a white supremacist militia compound at Ruby Ridge, Idaho, in 1992, which ended in a bloody shootout, and the tragic destruction of the Branch Davidian compound at Waco, Texas, in 1993 seemed to confirm their worst fears.

The literature of the militia movement reflects its members' fears. The best-known and most popular book is the blatantly racist *Turner Diaries* by William Pierce, the head of a neo-Nazi organization called the National Alliance. First published in 1978, the fictional *Turner Diaries* describe a 1990s race war triggered by the federal government's attempt to ban the possession of firearms by private citizens. The title character and other citizens fight back and eventually prevail, but only after the mass slaughter of racial minorities, "race traitors," and other undesirable elements. The book is an open call for terrorist violence against government workers, nonwhites, and non-Christians, and it directly advocates racial genocide. Pierce's message is that the only way to assert one's manhood is through the purifying test of racial violence. *The Turner Diaries*, said to have had a profound effect on convicted Oklahoma City bomber Timothy McVeigh, is an example of how the literature of the racist right encourages acts of violence.

The threat to public safety and homeland security posed by domestic terrorist organizations was brought home by the bombing in Oklahoma City on April 19, 1995. The explosion killed 168 people (including 19 children) and injured 850 others. Several days later, the FBI arrested McVeigh, an Operation Desert Storm veteran who had no criminal record. McVeigh was typical of many individuals who joined the militias. After leaving the army shortly after the Gulf War, he drifted from state to state and attended gun shows. Although he established a number of contacts with militia groups, he never formally joined any. Angered by the burning of the Branch Davidian compound in Waco two years earlier, McVeigh rationalized the Oklahoma City bombing as an act of retaliation.

Government Responses

The response of federal, state, and local authorities to domestic terrorism has been sporadic and inconsistent. The federal reaction to the acts of Puerto Rican separatists in the 1950s was to treat the instigators as criminals. The FBI and other investigative agencies were preoccupied with national security issues, such as Soviet espionage and the presence of Communists in government, and showed little concern for the threat of domestic terrorists. The pattern of federal response changed during the 1960s and 1970s, sometimes to the detriment of individual civil liberties.

With mandates from the Kennedy, Johnson, and Nixon administrations, the FBI conducted covert political operations against targeted organizations and individuals. Likewise, the Carter and Reagan administrations used instances of domestic political violence, such as the 1981 BLA Brinks robbery, to justify widening the scope of surveillance activities against all dissident organizations and to stiffen sanctions against dissenters.

Until the Oklahoma City bombing, law enforcement authorities at all levels had been reluctant to move against the political right. But the bombing, the loss of life, and the publicity surrounding the trials of McVeigh and accused co-conspirator Terry Nichols precipitated calls for the FBI to revise its guidelines for investigating terrorism and for Congress to enact new counterterrorism legislation. The main obstacle to federal legislation had been the reluctance of federal and state law enforcement agencies to define acts by domestic terrorists within a criminal justice framework. Moreover, the bureau previously had devoted relatively few resources to the monitoring of militias and other extremist organizations.

The FBI's rules of investigation, a product of the Watergate era, required an actual act of violence or proof of an imminent act of violence for an investigation to be launched. Groups violating weapons laws fell under the jurisdiction of the Bureau of Alcohol, Tobacco, and Firearms and state and local law enforcement. Following the Oklahoma City bombing, however, the FBI broadened the criteria to allow evidence showing that a group had the *potential* for violence.

The Clinton Administration proposed the Omnibus Counterterrorism Act in February 1995, giving the federal government the authority to increase covert surveillance against militia groups; to investigate groups that had not yet shown any signs of criminal activity; to allow law enforcement to tap phone lines and monitor Web sites and e-mail messages without obtaining court authorization; and to access hotel and library records, credit card accounts, and phone activities.

Partisan bickering—combined with the distrust of the federal government felt by some congressional conservatives and civil liberties concerns expressed by liberals—delayed passage of antiterrorist legislation for almost a year, when Congress passed the Antiterrorism and Effective Death Penalty Act of 1996. After September 11, 2001, Congress passed the USA Patriot Act, broadening the jurisdiction of both federal and state law enforcement to monitor and investigate groups with the potential for terrorist activity.

Congressional action has not been the only avenue of response for law enforcement. Groups such as the Southern Poverty Law Center and the Anti-Defamation League monitor and report on the activities of hate groups and the militias. The Southern Poverty Law Center drafted a model anti-militia law for states that do not have one, and the center has been active in helping state and local law enforcement set up guidelines for dealing with such private armies. It has supported lawsuits against groups such as the Aryan Nation, with the goal of tying up their funds and forcing them to shut down.

In addition, both state and federal law enforcement have made use of legislation already on the books to counteract the militias and other anti-government racist groups. Weapons laws, as well as anti–bank fraud laws, laws against abuse of the mail, tax laws, and RICO (Racketeer Influenced and Corrupt Organizations) laws have been used effectively against these groups. The Southern Poverty Law Center successfully used a Texas statute banning private military organizations to force the Ku Klux Klan to close militia-type training camps for members who were allegedly terrorizing Vietnamese fisherman along the Texas coast.

Perhaps the most innovative legislative measures taken against domestic terrorist groups are the growing number of hate crime laws passed by state legislatures and the U.S. Congress, a response to increasing acts of terror against racial minorities. The movement to enact such laws gained momentum during the mid-1980s after a rash of black church burnings. Pressure to include violence against gays and lesbians under hate crimes provisions increased after attacks based on the sexual orientation of the victims were publicized. The best-known example is the June 1998 murder of a gay Wyoming college student, Matthew Shepard.

As of 2000, forty-one states had enacted hate crimes laws, and federal and state law enforcement has prosecuted a number of cases under these statutes. The laws have raised civil liberties concerns, especially pertaining to the First Amendment to the U.S. constitution (guaranteeing freedom of speech and the right of free assembly). Attempts to link hate rhetoric to actual cases of violence and to prosecute individuals and groups who are not directly connected to specific crimes for incitement to violence have been particularly difficult to carry out successfully.

Domestic Terrorism Since September 11

The threat to homeland security posed by domestic militias and white supremacy groups has been obscured by the attacks of Islamic terrorists on the Pentagon and the World Trade Center on September 11, 2001. Since then, the focus of law enforcement at the federal, state, and local levels has been the threat posed by foreign-based Islamic fundamentalists, and the resources of the U.S. Department of Homeland

Security and federal law enforcement have concentrated on preventing foreign-based attacks. Concerns about terrorist cells in the United States focus predominately on Muslim groups with ties to al-Qaeda or other international organizations.

Although militias and other right wing extremist organizations have maintained a low profile and have been largely ignored by the mainstream media, these homegrown groups remain a real threat. Although they have little in common with Islamic fundamentalists and dislike ethnic Arabs, they share a common hatred of the U.S. government and the perceived Zionist influence. If domestic extremists should decide to make common cause with international terrorists, such an alliance would pose a grave threat to homeland security.

Walter F. Bell

See also: Birmingham Church Bombing; Greensboro Massacre; Homeland Security, Department of; Jewish Defense League; Oklahoma City Bombing; Puerto Rico and Puerto Ricans; Symbionese Liberation Army; Terrorism, Foreign; Unabomber Affair; Weathermen; White Supremacist Groups.

Bibliography
Barkun, Michael. "Religion, Militias, and Oklahoma City: The Mind of Conspiratorialists." *Terrorism and Political Violence* 8 (Spring 1996): 50–64.

Hamm, Mark S. *In Bad Company: America's Terrorist Underground.* Boston: Northeastern University Press, 2002.

Jacobs, Ron. *The Way the Wind Blew: A History of the Weather Underground.* New York: Verso, 1997.

Jenness, Valerie, and Ryken Grattet. *Making Hate a Crime: From Social Movement to Law Enforcement.* New York: Russell Sage, 2001.

Kimmel, Michael, and Abby Ferber. " 'White Men Are This Nation': Right-Wing Militias and the Restoration of Rural American Masculinity." *Rural Sociology* 65:4 (2000): 582–604.

Simon, Jeffrey D. *The Terrorist Trap: America's Experience with Terrorism.* Bloomington: Indiana University Press, 1994.

Snow, Robert L. *The Militia Threat: Terrorists Among Us.* New York: Plenum, 1999.

TERRORISM, FOREIGN

Since the end of World War II, foreign terrorism against U.S. citizens and facilities, both at home and abroad, has reflected changing political circumstances and has grown in frequency, sophistication, and danger.

The aircraft hijackings of the 1960s and 1970s have given way to the fundamentalist suicide bombers of the 1980s and 1990s. What began as the operations of small, self-contained revolutionary groups has become the domain of twenty-first century terrorist armies numbering in the tens of thousands. The political terrorism of the Red Army Faction and the Palestine Liberation Organization has become the religious terrorism of Hezbollah and al-Qaeda.

Cold War

During the Cold War period, the United States became involved in conflicts against groups that were thought to be displaying left wing or anti-Western tendencies. This placed America, Americans, and American interests worldwide firmly in the target zone. American involvement in anticommunist struggles led the United States to support unpopular right wing governments and various forms of dictatorship throughout the world. As the dominant Western power, the United States became the focus of attack. Since the early 1970s, the United States has been the target of more than 30 percent of all international terrorist attacks.

European terrorism in the 1970s and 1980s, for example, was aimed in part as a protest against U.S. involvement in Vietnam, in part as a protest against what left wing movements and groups (both those advocating peaceful demonstrations and those employing violence) saw as oppressive regimes, and in part as a protest at the ready acceptance of European states to acknowledge American dominance in NATO. An international anticapitalist, anti-imperialist terrorist group known as the Red Army Faction attacked U.S. Army headquarters in Frankfurt, Germany, on May 11, 1972, using a car bomb to kill one person and wound thirteen others. Later that month, the same group killed three American servicemen, when a car bomb exploded at U.S. Army headquarters in Heidelburg, Germany. On August 31, 1981, the Red Army Faction detonated a bomb in the car park at the U.S. Air Force base in Ramstein, Germany. And the group claimed responsibility for an unsuccessful assassination attempt on General Fred Kroesen, the U.S. Army commander in West Germany, on September 15, 1981.

On January 26, 1982, Italian special forces succeeded in rescuing U.S. Army Brigadier-General James Dozier, who had been kidnapped by the Italian Red Brigade—like the Red Army faction, an anti-imperialist, anticapitalist group—from his home in Verona, Italy, on December 17, 1981. On November 15, 1983, a U.S. Navy officer was shot dead while his car was stopped at a traffic light in Athens, Greece. Responsibility for this attack was claimed by yet another left wing terrorist group, the Greek November 17 group. In 1985, there was an attack on the Rhein-Main airbase in Germany; the Red Army Faction claimed responsibility for the deaths of three U.S. servicemen and the injuries of seventeen others.

Middle Eastern Terrorism

For the most part, European-based, left wing terrorist groups faded from the scene in the 1980s, victims of police crackdowns, internal quarrels, and a changing ideological environment. Far more lethal since then has been terrorism directed against the United States by Middle Eastern organizations, some nationalist and others religious.

On April 12, 1984, in a revenge attack for the U.S. Central Intelligence Agency (CIA) attempt on the life of Hezbollah leader Sheikh Mohammed Hussein Fadlallah, a bomb was detonated in a restaurant near the U.S. Air Force base at Torrejon, Spain. The blast killed eighteen U.S. servicemen and injured eighty-three others.

In an attack on a West Berlin nightclub on April 6, 1986, two U.S. servicemen were killed and seventy-nine injured by a bomb attributed to Libya. The United States retaliated ten days later with a bombing attack on Tripoli and Benghazi, Libya, that killed ninety-three Libyan civilians. The United States lost one aircraft, with two crewmen, in the attack. On April 14, 1988, the second anniversary of the U.S. raid on Libya, a car bomb set off by Japanese Red Army terrorists killed five people at a U.S. Navy club in Naples, Italy.

The *Achille Lauro*, an Italian cruise ship, en route from Genoa, Italy, to Ashdod, Israel, was captured on October 7, 1985, by four young Palestine Liberation Organization (PLO) members off the coast of Egypt. As had happened in previous hijackings, the terrorists targeted American and Israeli passengers and killed Leon Klinghoffer, a sixty-nine-year-old American Jew. In an agreement with the Egyptian government, the hijackers negotiated free passage in exchange for release of the hostages. The Egyptian plane flying the terrorists out of Egypt was intercepted by U.S. warplanes and forced to land at a NATO airbase in Sicily.

Rescue workers search for survivors or remains after a car bombing at the U.S. Marine barracks in Lebanon left 241 dead in October 1983. Lebanon was the site of kidnappings and terrorist bombings against Americans through much of the 1970s and 1980s. *(Philippe Bouchon/AFP/Getty Images)*

Beginning in the 1980s, the United States was faced with a new form of terrorist, the suicide bomber willing to become a martyr in the service of his or her faith. Islamic fundamentalist groups such as Hezbollah, Islamic Jihad, and the Muslim Brotherhood are primarily motivated by religion and are more interested in promoting the expansion of Islam than national or territorial gain. These groups consider themselves to be at war with the non-Islamic world. The United States has become the focus of much of their anger and is seen as the enemy of Islam, partly because of its own actions and partly because of its continuing political and military support for Israel. American personnel and aircraft in the Middle East have been targets for kidnapping and hijacking, because the United States is recognized as the main weapon supplier to Israel and the guarantor of Israeli security in the region. Indeed, as the relationship between Israel and America has strengthened, so, too, has the severity of the attacks on U.S. property and personnel.

Lebanon had become the site of a series of kidnappings and killings of Americans as early as the mid-1970s, amid civil war between Christian and Muslim groups. In June 1975, Colonel Ernest Morgan became the first of many Americans taken hostage by Hezbollah guerrillas, a radical Shiite group, in the environs of the Lebanese capital, Beirut. While Morgan was released unharmed just thirteen days later, a spate of other hostage-takings did not end so quickly or so bloodlessly.

On March 16, 1984, CIA Beirut station chief William Buckley was kidnapped in a revenge attack after the failed CIA attempt to assassinate the spiritual leader of Hezbollah. Buckley was tortured and then executed. Terry Anderson, a U.S. journalist, was kidnapped in Beirut on March 16, 1985, and held until his release in December 1991. Thomas Sutherland, a U.S. academic at the American University in Beirut, was taken on June 9, 1985, and held until November 1991. On September 12, 1986, another U.S. academic at the American University in Beirut, Joseph Cicippio, was taken and held until December 1991. Jesse Turner and Alan Steen were taken in Beirut on January 24, 1987, and held until late 1991. Marine Lieutenant-Colonel William Higgins was taken hostage in Beirut on February 17, 1988, and later killed by his Hezbollah captors. Hostage taking was a major component in Hezbollah terrorism, and the group was responsible for most, if not all, of the eighty Western hostages being held in Lebanon from the late 1970s through the early 1990s.

Further direct action took the form of suicide bombers willing to die for their religious beliefs. A suicide car bomb was used in an attack on the U.S. Embassy in Beirut in April 1983, resulting in forty-nine dead, including sixteen Americans, and 120 injured. A second suicide car bomb, on October 23 of the same year, was aimed at the U.S. Marine barracks in Beirut and resulted in the deaths of 241 U.S. servicemen.

In March 1985, eighty people were killed when a massive car bomb exploded outside the Beirut headquarters of Hezbollah. That organization's spiritual leader, Sheikh Mohammed Hussein Fadlallah, was the intended target, but he escaped injury. The most commonly voiced explanation for the bomb was that the CIA and Saudi Arabia had attempted to assassinate Fadlallah. In what was seen as an act of revenge against the CIA car bomb, Lebanese Shiite militants staged an international airplane hijacking. On June 14, 1985, TWA Flight 847, bound from Athens to Rome, was taken over by two hijackers connected to Hezbollah; the hijackers killed a U.S. serviceman aboard the plane before negotiating the release of the hostages and their own escape.

U.S. embassies have long been the target of terrorist attacks. On November 4, 1979, the U.S. Embassy in Tehran, Iran, was attacked and seized by a group of Iranian students who took sixty-six American citizens hostage. In August 1975, the U.S. consulate in Kuala Lumpur, Malaysia, was attacked and seized by Japanese Red Army terrorists as a means of securing the release of members held in custody. As noted above, sixty-three were killed and 120 were injured, when a suicide truck bomb, packed with 400 pounds of explosives, hit the U.S. embassy in Beirut in April 1983. Among the casualties was the CIA's Middle East director. This was only one of many attacks on the Beirut embassy. On December 12, 1983 there was a foiled suicide car bomb attempt to blow up the U.S. Embassy in Kuwait. Five people were killed when the device exploded outside the embassy. The U.S. Embassy in Beirut was once again the target for suicide bombers on September 20, 1984, when an attack killed twenty-three and wounded twenty-one, including the U.S. ambassador.

On August 7, 1998, the U.S. embassies in Nairobi, Kenya, and Dar es Salaam, Tanzania, were attacked simultaneously by car bombs attributed to al-Qaeda and its leader, Osama bin Laden. The explosion in Nairobi killed 214 people, including twelve U.S. nationals, and injured nearly 5,000, while the bomb in Dar es Salaam killed ten and injured seventy-two. This incident showed that the terrorists had the knowledge and skills to coordinate multiple and simultaneous attacks in different countries. On May 29, 2001, following a trial in a federal court in Manhattan, four men accused of the embassy attacks in Africa were convicted of conspiring to kill Americans; one of the defendants came from Jordan, one from Tanzania, one from Saudi Arabia, and one from Arlington, Texas.

On October 12, 2000, a suicide bomber in a small launch struck the USS *Cole* while the ship was refueling in harbor in Aden, Yemen. The *Cole,* an Arleigh Burke-class, or Aegis guided missile destroyer, suffered a forty-foot by sixty-foot hole in its side and the loss of seventeen U.S. personnel and thirty-seven wounded. Responsibility for the attack was attributed to al-Qaeda and bin Laden. On June 25, 1996, a truck bomb exploded outside the Khobar Towers U.S. military housing complex near Dharan, Saudi Arabia, killing nineteen Americans and injuring more than 500 Americans and Saudis. The building housed some 3,000 personnel directly involved in enforcing the no-fly zone in Iraq.

State-Supported Terrorism Against the United States

Sponsorship of terrorist groups is the most common form of state involvement, whether by means of financial assistance, military training of personnel, supply of arms and explosives, furnishing of documents, or provision of safe haven. States have used such groups to further their foreign policy aims by proxy. Most state sponsorship has taken place in the Middle East. Iran has exercised influence over Shiite groups such as Hezbollah, Syria has supported Palestinian organizations such as the Popular Front for the Liberation of Palestine, and Libya has sponsored the terrorist group led by Abu Nidal.

As in the seizure of the U.S. embassy in Teheran in 1979, government support for terrorism often follows popular sentiment. Although not initiating the attack, the hard-line, anti-American contingent in the regime of the Ayatollah Khomeini was quick to lend its support. At the same time, however, the hostage situation brought out into the open the power struggle between Khomeini and those hard-liners. At the request of Khomeini, the students released four women and six black hostages, while, at the same time, calling for the return of the shah from the United States to stand trial. Other demands by the Iranian regime included an admission of guilt by the United States for its past actions in Iran, the promise of no future interference in Iranian affairs, and the return of the shah's personal fortune to the Iranian people. But dialogue between Teheran and Washington was difficult, as the hard-liners refused to negotiate with the administration of President Jimmy Carter.

American oil imports from Iran were halted, and Iranian assets in the United State were frozen. Economic pressure and subsequent attempts at diplomatic solutions both failed. Under the code name Operation Eagle Claw, a rescue was attempted by the American Delta Force on April 25, 1980. The attempt failed, when rescue aircraft collided at Desert One, a forward refueling base some 200 miles south of Tehran. Eight American servicemen were killed and five injured in the accident, which ended all hope of rescue. The hostages were finally released after 444 days on January 20, 1981, when the situation was resolved politically by the new Reagan Administration, which released $8 billion in Iranian assets in the United States. It later was alleged in a 1986 magazine article that President Ronald Reagan had secretly exchanged arms for the release of the hostages.

On December 21, 1988, Pan Am Boeing flight 103 was destroyed after a suitcase containing a bomb detonated over the Scottish town of Lockerbie. The blast killed all 259 people on board the aircraft, 189 of whom were American, along with eleven on the ground. United Nations (UN) sanctions were imposed on Libya in 1992 and 1993, in an effort to bring those responsible for the attack to justice.

Abdel Baset Ali Mohmed al-Megrahi, a Libyan intelligence agent, was tried for the murder of 270 people at a specially convened court at a former U.S. airbase in the Netherlands. In negotiations among Great Britain, the United States, the UN, and Libya, it was agreed that the trial would be conducted under Scottish law, with one major exception: It would be conducted without a jury, relying solely on a panel of three judges. On January 31, 2001, Megrahi was found guilty and sentenced to life in prison, with a recommendation that he serve at least twenty years. As of 2006, he was serving out his sentence at Barlinnie

prison in Glasgow, Scotland. Co-defendant Al Amin Khalifa Fhimah was found not guilty of murder. In early 2003, as part of a continuing effort to have UN and U.S. sanctions lifted, Libya accepted responsibility for the 1988 bombing and provided substantial compensation to the families of the victims.

Hezbollah (Arabic for "Party of God") is a group of Muslim extremists united by anti-Western views. Created in 1982 by Shiite Muslims, sponsored initially by the regime of the Ayatollah Khomeini in Iran, and following a strongly anti-Western ideology, Hezbollah is viewed in the West as a relatively unstructured, informal, and loose-knit organization. Run by a group of twelve clerics known as the Consultative Council and led by a secretary-general, its system of committees deals with specific topics such as political, social, and military affairs. Formed in the aftermath of the successful Islamic revolution in Iran, Hezbollah is dedicated to the formation of an Islamic republic in Lebanon. By 1984, Hezbollah had joined forces with many smaller Shiite political groups, effectively absorbing the other Lebanese extremist Shiite factions and bringing them under central control. The party's goal was the creation of a Shiite Islamic state in Lebanon, and it saw both Israel and the United States as the main obstacles to that goal.

Within the Middle East, Israel is seen by fundamentalists as the primary source of evil and an extension of American influence and policy. Viewing Western influence as anathema to the true teachings of Islam, Hezbollah has directed much of its terrorist activity against Israel and the United States, which it depicts as the Great Satan. After the Israeli invasion of Lebanon in 1982 and the expansion of U.S. military presence in Beirut, Hezbollah began a twin-track policy of direct military action and hostage taking. Direct action was aimed at Israel and its Western allies in Lebanon, mainly the United States and France, the former colonial power in Lebanon. The U.S. military presence in Beirut was seen as a signal of support for the Israeli invasion, and the attacks on U.S. armed forces were a demonstration of the resolve within the Hezbollah movement. Attacks by Hezbollah have been directed at American interests in Lebanon or as revenge attacks for such U.S. actions as the 1985 CIA assassination attempt on the Hezbollah hierarchy.

Hezbollah has not taken the fight to the U.S. mainland or to U.S. interests worldwide, focusing instead on Islamic Lebanon. It is only through American intervention or interests in this area that any

Lockerbie Bombing

The incident that became known as the Lockerbie bombing was the downing of a Pan Am flight by a terrorist bomb over the small town of Lockerbie, Scotland, in December 1988, resulting in the death of more than 270 persons on the plane and the ground.

At 6:25 pm on the evening of December 21, 1988, a Pan Am Boeing 747 airliner took off from London's Heathrow Airport. Flight 103 had originated in Frankfurt, West Germany, bound for New York City and then Detroit. The airliner had climbed to its cruising altitude of 31,000 feet, when, approximately seven minutes after take-off, an explosion in the cargo hold ripped a hole in the thin aluminum skin of the airplane. The sudden loss of pressure caused the plane to break apart in midair. In all, 270 were killed in the crash—all 259 passengers and crew on board the jumbo jet, and eleven on the ground. Of the passengers, 189 were Americans, including thirty-five Syracuse University students heading home for the holidays.

After the explosion, airplane parts both large and small, luggage, thousands of gallons of burning aviation fuel, and human bodies fell toward the Scottish border town of Lockerbie, with parts crashing directly onto homes. One large piece of the aircraft, a sixty-foot section of fuselage with sixty bodies inside, crashed between two rows of houses, narrowly missing them. A large wing section, still filled with aviation fuels, fell directly on three houses and created a firestorm so hot that it obliterated the homes and the eleven people inside them.

Based on the nature of the crash and intelligence about terrorist activities, government officials declared the incident a bombing, as opposed to an accident, almost immediately. At that time, it was the worst single act of airline terrorism against the United States to date; only the terrorist events of September 11, 2001, would eventually surpass it. For eleven years it was the world's biggest unsolved case of mass murder.

Due to the nature of the crime, an investigative team was assembled from the United Kingdom and the United States to determine how the bomb was planted, how it caused the aircraft to crash, and who may have been responsible. The investigators faced formidable legal and forensic challenges; some 10,000 pieces of evidence had been scattered over 850 square miles of countryside.

At first, there was suspicion that Iran and Syrian terrorists agents had committed the act in retaliation for the 290 Iranian pilgrims killed while traveling to Mecca in July 1988, when the U.S. Navy cruiser *Vincennes* shot down their Iranian passenger jet over the Persian Gulf, believing it to be a military aircraft with hostile intentions. This was later rejected in favor of a Libyan connection, when the investigators found a small fragment of the timer that had caused the explosion in the cargo hold. The Federal Bureau of Investigation (FBI) traced it to Libya and then matched it to a timer seized from Libyan agents in West Africa. The case soon became entangled in a political standoff with Libyan leader Muammar Qaddafi, an opponent of U.S. foreign policy in the Middle East, who refused to allow extradition of the suspects.

Finally, in April 1999, an agreement was reached between the United States, Great Britain, the United Nations, and Libya to allow two Libyan men to face trial for the bombing. As part of the unusual agreement made to bring them to trial, they would stand before three Scottish judges in a neutral court in the Netherlands. Also as part of the deal, the United Nations agreed to suspend its sanctions against Libya. Without this agreement, the trial could not have proceeded.

Ultimately, justice would have to wait until March 14, 2002, fourteen years after the bombing, when, after a review of his trial and subsequent appeals, Libyan intelligence officer Abdel Baset Ali Mohmed al-Megrahi, was convicted and imprisoned for life for his part in the bombing. His co-defendant, Al-Amin Khalifa Fahima, another Libyan intelligence official, was found not guilty and released.

John C. Rock

clash occurs. Hezbollah operates mainly in southern Lebanon, southern Beirut, and the Bekaa Valley and is thought to have a membership of thousands.

Al-Qaeda

Al-Qaeda (Arabic for "The Network") was established in the late 1980s by Osama bin Laden. Like most other Middle East organizations, it is a loose coalition with the primary aims of overturning what it sees as corrupt regimes in the Muslim world and expelling Westerners and non-Muslims from Muslim countries, specifically the U.S. military from Saudi Arabia, home to Islam's holiest places. The original function of the group was to bring together those Arabs fighting the Soviet forces in Afghanistan.

Al-Qaeda is multinational in composition, and it acts primarily as an umbrella organization for other, smaller groups, funding Islamic militants worldwide. Members of al-Qaeda are usually also members of other terrorist organizations. The main role of al-Qaeda is to act in a central unifying role, directing the path of terrorist activity and providing necessary support.

In December 1992, bombs detonated in Aden, Yemen, and aimed at U.S. servicemen were attributed to al-Qaeda. The February 1993 bombing of the World Trade Center in New York, which killed six people and injured more than 1,000, was thought to be the work of al-Qaeda. In October 1995, a group of ten people, including the blind Egyptian cleric Umar Abd al-Rahman, were convicted of the bombing. They were also convicted of numerous other offenses, including conspiracy to bomb other New York landmarks, such as the Lincoln and Holland Tunnels and the United Nations building. Rahman was the spiritual leader of the al-Gamma al-Islamiyya (IG), an extremist Sunni Muslim group active in Egypt since the late 1970s and one of the groups aligned with al-Qaeda.

Prior to the U.S.-led invasion of Afghanistan in 2003, al-Qaeda maintained a number of terrorist training camps and a large presence in that country, including a so-called terrorist university. In 1995, five Americans were killed in the al-Qaeda bombing of a Saudi National Guard office in Riyadh used by U.S. military trainers.

On September 11, 2001, al-Qaeda was responsible for the hijacking of four commercial jets over U.S. airspace. Two of the aircraft were used to destroy the World Trade Center in New York City; a third was crashed into the Pentagon building near Washington, D.C., and the fourth jet was brought down in a field in Shanksville, Pennsylvania, when passengers rose up against the hijackers. Nearly 3,000 people died in the attacks.

In addition to all the above-mentioned attacks, al-Qaeda is believed responsible for conspiring to kill the pope during a 1994 visit to the Philippines, plotting to blow up a dozen U.S. airliners over the Pacific in 1995, and planning to bomb Los Angeles airport in 1999. Since the U.S.-led invasion of Afghanistan in 2002, in which al-Qaeda training camps and bases were destroyed, the group has dispersed worldwide and is still active.

While not necessarily planning all of the missions, bin Laden provides al-Qaeda cells with essential financial support, as well as arms, training, and intelligence. A son of a rich Saudi Arabian family and with a large personal fortune, bin Laden fought with, and helped to finance, the *mujahadin* resistance fighters during the Soviet occupation of Afghanistan in the 1980s and was seen as an ally of the United States, even to the extent of receiving military supplies such as Stinger ground-to-air missiles. After the defeat of the Soviet forces in the late 1980s, bin Laden returned to Saudi Arabia, but his calls for political reform and violent action against Saudi and U.S. interests got him expelled in 1991. He then went to Sudan, but he was expelled from that country under U.S. pressure in 1996, whereupon he found sanctuary with the fundamentalist Taliban regime in Afghanistan. In 1998, he called for a holy war (*jihad*) to force a U.S. withdrawal from Saudi Arabia.

In an effort to provide some degree of protection from terrorist attack, the George W. Bush Administration in early 2003 created the Department of Homeland Security, which, under Secretary Tom Ridge, brought together smaller, existing U.S. government agencies into a loose coalition. These agencies were organized into four main groups or directorates: Border and Transportation Security consists of the U.S. Customs Service, Immigration and Naturalization Service, Federal Protection Service, Transportation Security Administration (a new agency), Federal Law Enforcement Training Center, Animal and Plant Health Inspection Service, and Office for Domestic Preparedness. The Emergency Preparedness and Response directorate includes the Federal Emergency Management Agency, Domestic Emergency Support Teams, Strategic National Stockpile, Nuclear Incident Response Team, and National Domestic Preparedness Office. The third directorate is Science and Technology, comprising CBRN Countermeasures Programs, the Environmental Measurements Laboratory, the National BW Defense Analysis Center, and the Plum Island Animal Disease Center. The fourth, the Information Analysis and Infrastructure Protection directorate, is comprised of the Critical Infrastructure Assurance Office, Federal Computer Incident Response Center, National Infrastructure Protection Center, National Communications System, and Energy Security and Assurance Program.

The United States has emerged as the main target for international terrorism primarily because of its involvement on the world scene and its sometimes dubious choice of allies. U.S. interests have been the target of extremist groups in countries throughout the world that consider the United States, which has supported many authoritarian regimes, as the main obstacle to radical political and religious change. The U.S. presence, whether military, diplomatic, or cultural, has continuously attracted controversy and, in its wake, terrorism.

U.S. military personnel and civilians in Saudi Arabia also have become targets of terrorist attacks in response to the U.S.-led invasion of Iraq in 2003. Indeed, many Middle East experts argue that, as long as the United States continues to maintain a military presence in the Arab world, its personnel and interests will continue to be the target of attacks from those who see the United States as a superpower attempting to control the region's resources and imposing an alien Western culture.

Derek Young

See also: Hijackings; Homeland Security, Department of; Iran Hostage Crisis; Islam; Middle East, Relations with (Except Israel); September 11 Attacks; Terrorism, Domestic.

Bibliography

Crockatt, R. *America Embattled: 9/11, Anti-Americanism and the Global Order.* London: Routledge, 2002.

Dekmejian, R. Hrair. *Islam in Revolution: Fundamentalism in the Arab World.* Syracuse, NY: Syracuse University Press, 1995.

George, Alexander, ed. *Western State Terrorism.* New York: Routledge, Chapman, and Hall, 1991.

Gerson, Allan, and Jerry Adler. *The Price of Terror: One Bomb, One Plane, 270 Lives: The History-Making Struggle for Justice after Pan Am 103.* New York: HarperCollins, 2001.

Jacquard, Roland. *In the Name of Osama bin Laden: Global Terrorism and the bin Laden Brotherhood.* Durham, NC: Duke University Press, 2002.

Kegley, Charles W. *The New Global Terrorism: Characteristics, Causes, Controls.* Upper Saddle River, NJ: Prentice Hall, 2003.

Laqueur, Walter. *A History of Terrorism.* New Brunswick, NJ: Transaction, 2002.

Lesser, Ian O., et al. *Countering the New Terrorism.* Santa Monica, CA: Rand, 1999.

Long, David E. *The Anatomy of Terrorism.* New York: Free Press, 1990.

Matar, Khalil I., and Robert W. Thabit. *Lockerbie and Libya: A Study in International Relations.* Jefferson, NC: McFarland, 2004.

Menashri, David. *Iran: A Decade of War and Fear.* New York: Holmes and Meier, 1990.

———, ed. *The Iranian Evolution and the Muslim World.* Boulder, CO: Westview, 1990.

Mickolus, Edward. "September 11 Attacks." In *Encyclopedia of World Terrorism,* edited by Frank Shanty and Raymond Picquet. Armonk, NY: M.E. Sharpe, 2003.

Ranstorp, Magnus. *Hizballah in Lebanon.* New York: St. Martin's, 1996.

Rezun, Miron. ed. *Iran at the Crossroads: Global Relations in a Turbulent Decade.* Boulder, CO: Westview, 1990.

Smith, G. Davison. *Combating Terrorism.* London: Routledge, 1990.

Wilkinson, Paul. *Technology and Terrorism.* London: Frank Cass, 1993.

TEST-TUBE BABIES

Louise Joy Brown, the world's first successful "test-tube baby," was born to a family in Great Britain on July 25, 1978. The parents, John and Lesley Brown, had been infertile and underwent an experimental procedure known as in vitro fertilization (IVF). Louise was the first live human birth fertilized outside the mother's body.

For more than a decade, Drs. Patrick Steptoe and Robert Edwards had been seeking a successful alternative to traditional conception that would help infertile couples. Steptoe and Edwards had developed a method to fertilize an ovum outside of a woman's body, but none of these pregnancies had lasted more than a few weeks.

The IVF process begins by removing an egg from a woman's ovaries and mixing it with a man's sperm. After the ovum is fertilized, it is placed in a solution designed to nurture the egg as it begins to replicate. The fertilized egg is then placed in the uterus in the hope that it will attach to the uterine wall. Doctors usually position multiple eggs in the uterus, hoping that at least one will implant.

With the Brown pregnancy, Steptoe and Edwards decided to reimplant the ovum earlier than with the other pregnancies. This was probably the difference that allowed Lesley and John Brown to become the first parents whose IVF pregnancy continued past the first trimester. While all parties involved tried to maintain secrecy, the press caught wind of the revolutionary procedure, and soon the world nervously awaited Louise's birth.

Many reproduction specialists and infertile parents were hoping for an effective treatment that would result in a healthy child. But critics across the world denounced the process as an immoral and potentially disastrous incursion of science into human reproduction. A heated public debate emerged, with those opposed to IVF calling up images of deformed babies, monstrous animal-human hybrids, and the resumption of eugenics programs. Supporters of IVF emphasized that the procedure would allow countless infertile parents to have their own children. The debate raged until the moment Louise was born. The world's first test-tube baby turned out to be a perfectly healthy five-pound, twelve-ounce baby girl.

The first American test-tube baby was delivered on December 28, 1981. Named Elizabeth Jordan Carr, she was born in Norfolk, Virginia, at the first IVF center in the United States, a clinic run by Drs. Howard Jones and Georgeanna Jones.

Since that time, this once-controversial procedure has become more and more commonplace, and reproduction clinics that specialize in IVF have emerged all over the world. In the United States alone, there have been an estimated 45,000 test-tube babies born since 1981.

IVF has emerged as a viable option for adults who have not been able to have children for a variety of reasons. However, the steep price tag for the procedure has made it an unaffordable option for many working- and middle-class people, although some health insurance plans are beginning to cover at least a portion of the costs for this procedure.

Despite the success of the IVF procedure, Louise Brown's birth set the stage for later debates on science, morality, and humanity. These questions con- tinue to surround other scientific advances such as cloning and the human genome project.

Richard Santos

See also: Reproductive Technologies.

Bibliography

Henig, Robin Marantz. *Pandora's Baby: How the First Test Tube Babies Sparked the Reproductive Revolution.* New York: Houghton Mifflin, 2004.

TET OFFENSIVE

A surprise attack by forces of the National Liberation Front (NLF) and North Vietnamese Army (NVA) forces during Vietnamese New Year celebrations in January 1968, the Tet Offensive proved to be a critical turning point in the Vietnam conflict. Devastating television coverage of urban warfare challenged assurances from the administration that the war was being won and ultimately led to President Lyndon B. Johnson's announcement that he would not seek reelection that November.

General Vo Nguyen Giap started planning the Tet Offensive in 1967 as a way to regain the initiative the North Vietnamese had lost in the fighting over the previous two years. Crafting a coordinated political, diplomatic, and military strategy known as "General Offensive, General Uprising," Vo Nguyen Giap attempted to spur defections from the South Vietnamese armed forces, create diplomatic tension between Washington and Saigon, and spark a popular uprising in the South. In preparation for the Tet campaign, Vo Nguyen Giap initiated a conventional offensive against U.S. forces to draw them away from the most populated areas in the South in late 1967. The strategy succeeded; by January, more than half of U.S. combat battalions had been moved to counter the siege at Khe Sanh.

The offensive caught the American and South Vietnamese troops off guard. The commander of the U.S. Military Assistance Command, General William Westmoreland, did not anticipate the attack, failing to consider the possibility of such an unorthodox strategy. On January 30 and 31, NLF and NVA troops began coordinated attacks throughout the South, including more than half of the provincial capitals. South Vietnamese government installations, military bases, and communications centers were the primary

Vietcong soldiers climb onto a U.S. tank abandoned during the Tet Offensive of January 1968. The widespread North Vietnamese attacks, beginning on the Tet lunar holiday, came as a shock to U.S. military and political leaders—as well as the public. *(AFP/Getty Images)*

targets, and the South Vietnamese population was bombarded with leaflets urging them to revolt.

The American response was quick and decisive. Fighting continued for only a few days in some cities, but in Saigon, protracted combat lasted for more than a week as the NLF attacked the presidential palace, police headquarters, and a government radio station and commandos took control of the U.S. embassy for several hours. But the most vicious fighting took place in the old imperial capital of Hue, where fighting continued house to house through March.

For the NLF and NVA forces, the Tet Offensive was an unmitigated military disaster. Their attacks failed, and they suffered enormous losses; some estimates put the casualty rate at over 50 percent of the 84,000 troops committed to the offensive, with the NLF bearing the brunt of the casualties. From a political perspective, the offensive did not spark the uprising expected by Hanoi, and the diplomatic breach between the United States and South Vietnam never materialized.

Despite these obvious failures, however, the Tet Offensive was a public relations success for the North. The televised pictures of the fighting—especially occupation of the embassy—were instrumental in changing U.S. domestic opinion on the war and accelerating public discontent with the administration and the seemingly endless fighting. The shift in perception of the war was crystallized by Walter Cronkite, the avuncular CBS anchor, who exclaimed as he watched footage of the fighting, "What the hell is going on? I thought we were winning this damned war!"

Although a decisive military victory for the United States and South Vietnam and a major political miscalculation by the NLF and Hanoi, the Tet Offensive dealt a devastating psychological blow to the United States and hastened the decline of public support for the American commitment to South Vietnam.

Andrew L. Johns

See also: Antiwar Movement, Vietnam Era; Election of 1968; Vietnam War.

Bibliography

Gilbert, Marc Jason, and William Head, eds. *The Tet Offensive.* Westport, CT: Praeger, 1996.

Oberdorfer, Don. *Tet!: The Turning Point in the Vietnam War.* Garden City, NY: Doubleday, 1971.

Spector, Ronald H. *After Tet: The Bloodiest Year in Vietnam.* New York: Free Press, 1993.

THALIDOMIDE

In 1954, Chemie Grünenthal, a small West German pharmaceutical company, synthesized a drug called thalidomide under the brand name Contergan in West Germany and Kevadon in Canada. Thalidomide was subsequently licensed worldwide and manufactured by several pharmaceutical companies with slightly different formulas.

At first, the drug was marketed as an anticonvulsive for gastritis; later, the manufacturers claimed the drug was suitable for treating anxiety disorders and insomnia. Additionally, the drug was considered safe for pregnant women, who used it as a preventative for nausea and morning sickness. It was touted as a wonder drug and became the best-selling sedative in Europe. It was sold over the counter.

But the positive press accounts often failed to take account of poorly designed clinical tests on animals and a lack of systematic follow-up tests on human beings, as well as efforts by the manufacturers to quash adverse reports. Because the drug proved nonfatal when given in large doses to various mammals, the developers of the drug concluded that it was safe for human use. Before conducting proper tests on humans and establishing a proper monitoring regimen,

Chemie Grünenthal offered free samples to doctors in West Germany and Switzerland in 1955.

The first clinical indication for the use of thalidomide was as an anticonvulsant, although studies had not demonstrated this effect. Patients reported a soporific, or sleep-inducing, effect when they ingested the drug and a few other minor side effects. Before the sale of thalidomide could be approved, however, the West German government required more data from animal studies to support the manufacturer's claims that the drug could be marketed as a soporific. To demonstrate the drug's sedating powers, Grünenthal scientists designed an unorthodox animal study. Using a jiggle cage that measured slight movements of the mice who were given thalidomide, the researchers persuaded the German licensing agency that the mice showed much less movement while under the influence of thalidomide.

In October 1957, Contergan (thalidomide) became widely available for sale in Germany, and then in other parts of Europe, as an over-the-counter drug. Ten months previously, however, a child had been born without ears to a mother who had taken the drug during her pregnancy. Ironically, the father of the child was employed by Chemie Grünenthal and had given free samples of the drug to his wife. The case was ignored by West German regulatory officials.

Without any further independent testing, thalidomide became the drug choice for pregnant women worldwide who suffered from nausea and morning sickness. In 1960, the U.S. Food and Drug Administration (FDA) received a marketing application for thalidomide from Richardson-Merrell Company. Frances Kelsey, the physician assigned to the review, rejected the application, because it failed to disclose patient reports of nerve damage.

Reports from Australia and Germany linked thalidomide to a dramatic increase in infants born with extremely deformed arms and legs. Their mothers had taken thalidomide during a critical point in embryonic development, from twenty to thirty-six days after conception. Immediately, Chemie Grünenthal withdrew the drug, and it was never sold in the United States.

In the countries where it was available, the various trade names for thalidomide confused both the public and doctors, however, so it was still several months before the drug was no longer available throughout the world. It has been estimated that 8,000–12,000 thalidomide babies were born with birth defects, virtually none of them in the United States, as the drug was not approved by the Food and Drug Administration. The true number will never be known, however, because of lapses in record keeping by physicians and pharmaceutical companies.

Since 1968, thalidomide has been prescribed to nonpregnant women in the United Kingdom and elsewhere as treatment for skin conditions related to leprosy. In 1998, the FDA approved the use of thalidomide in the treatment of that disease. Ongoing research suggests that the drug also may be beneficial in treating multiple sclerosis, Kaposi's Sarcoma, and a number of other disorders.

Suzanne M. Carter

See also: Medicine.

Bibliography

Botting, J. "The History of Thalidomide." *Drug News Perspective* 15:9 (2002): 604–11.

Bren, L. "Frances Oldham Kelsey: FDA Medical Reviewer Leaves Her Mark on History." *FDA Consumer* 35:2 (2001): 24–9.

Critchley, E. M. "Was the Thalidomide Tragedy Preventable?" *Lancet* 351:9115 (1998): 1591.

Shah, R. R. "Thalidomide, Drug Safety and Early Drug Regulation in the UK." *Adverse Drug Reaction and Toxicology Review* 20:4 (2001): 199–255.

THEATER

American theater came into its ascendancy after World War II. Even as it lost some of its audience to television and urban flight, it gained artistic, political, and psychological substance.

The great prewar playwrights who had revolutionized the quality of American stage writing in the 1920s and 1930s, notably Eugene O'Neill and Thornton Wilder, wrote some of their best work in the 1940s. They were joined by a new generation of writers: Tennessee Williams, Arthur Miller, and Edward Albee, among others.

This cohort of playwrights established the American drama as a literary form that could bear comparison both to its European counterparts and to American novels and poetry. Successive writers such as Sam Shepard, David Mamet, August Wilson, and John Guare, to name a few, have met this high standard.

Early Postwar Masters

The decades after the war saw a transformation in acting, direction, and production. Method acting, politically or psychologically charged staging, and experimental theaters and troupes moved American theater into realms of greater verisimilitude and intensity. The emergence of African American, Asian American, and women playwrights and actors broadened the scope of who was represented on the American stage. At the same time, American theater underwent a process of decentralization and diffusion, as theaters located off Broadway and outside of New York City increasingly became the incubators for new works of drama. Broadway became the destination of great plays rather than their birthplace. With its increasing verisimilitude, relevancy, and diversity, American theater came to reflect the anxieties and preoccupations of the American people, and its history is therefore closely bound to the country's social and political history.

Tennessee Williams emerged as one of America's great playwrights with his second play, *The Glass Menagerie* (1945). The play's protagonist, Tom Wingfield, recalls the night he brought home a suitor for his awkward sister, Laura. The suitor's revelation that he is already engaged and his breaking of one of Laura's glass animals upsets the delicate balance that exists among Tom, Laura, and their mother, Amanda. The play is notable for its lyrical grace, the intensity of its dialogue, and its use of memory as a framing device.

Two years later, Williams's *A Streetcar Named Desire* (1947) was produced at the Ethel Barrymore Theater on Broadway. Its characters have become American cultural archetypes: the volcanic Stanley Kowalski, his wife Stella, and Stella's sister, the faded ingenue Blanche Dubois. The play was directed by Elia Kazan, perhaps the most important director of the postwar decade, who would later direct Williams's *Cat on a Hot Tin Roof* (1955). *Streetcar* starred Jessica Tandy, Kim Hunter, and a mesmerizing Marlon Brando.

A student of the distinguished actress Stella Adler, Brando achieved his famously brooding, primal portrayal of Stanley through so-called Method acting. Drawing on the work of the Russian director Konstantin Stanislavsky, Lee Strasberg's "Method School" encouraged actors to rely on their own emotions and experiences rather than on the mandates of the play's text. When Brando reprised the role in the subsequent film version of the play (1951), he helped establish the Method as an alternative to traditional modes of acting.

A second great playwright to emerge in the 1940s was Arthur Miller, who established himself with *All My Sons* (1947). A response to the war, the play tells the story of Joe Keller, a manufacturer whose shoddy airplane parts cause the death of a number of fighter pilots. One of Joe's sons, a pilot himself, learns of his father's actions and, in response, flies a suicide mission. Realizing he is responsible for his son's death, Keller takes his own life.

Miller followed this play with his masterpiece, *Death of a Salesman* (1949). Like Williams's Stanley Kowalski, Miller's Willy Loman became an American everyman. Loman, whose name itself implies his low social status, is a traveling salesman who looks back on his life's failures, particularly his failures as a father to Happy and Biff. Upon losing his job, Loman kills himself so that his family will receive a $20,000 insurance policy. The play was staged nonnaturalistically, with different sets juxtaposed to reflect the processes of Loman's memory. Writing of his play that same year, Miller declared, "I believe that the common man is as apt a subject for tragedy in its highest sense as kings were." This is perhaps the defining element of the postwar drama: the discovery of tragedy in everyday life.

Miller's *The Crucible* (1953) was both a period piece and a contemporary social commentary. Set in Puritan America, the play challenged the hypocrisy of the anticommunist hearings of Senator Joseph McCarthy (Republican of Wisconsin) by tacitly comparing them to a witch hunt. A great allegory, the play has endured in part, because it functions so effectively even when not read as an indictment of McCarthy.

Eugene O'Neill, widely considered the most important playwright in America, had not staged a play in the ten years after he received the Nobel Prize in Literature in 1936. He had written one, however: *Long Day's Journey into Night*, the autobiographical masterpiece that he gave to his wife Carlota in 1941 with the request that it not be produced until twenty-five years after his death. O'Neill broke his silence not with this play, but with his *The Iceman Cometh* (1946), a work that combines the gritty realism of the neighborhood bar in which it is set with the mythic and existential weight of a Greek tragedy. The play was revived in 1956, in the wake of which Carlota O'Neill released *Long Day's Journey*

Willy Loman (played by Lee J. Cobb) is restrained by sons Biff (left, Arthur Kennedy) and Happy (right, Cameron Mitchell) in the original 1949 Broadway production of Arthur Miller's jolting tragedy, *Death of a Salesman. (W. Eugene Smith/Time Life Pictures/Getty Images)*

into Night (a decade earlier than O'Neill had wished). The story of the broken, addiction-ridden Tyrone family, *Long Day's Journey* is a searing, frank portrayal of the tragedies of a normal family. It culminates with the haunting image of the drug-addled matriarch Mary Tyrone coming onstage in her wedding dress.

Yet the postwar stage was not populated entirely by tragedies. The musical continued to flourish, and shows like Cole Porter's *Kiss Me, Kate* (1948) were wildly popular. Richard Rodgers and Oscar Hammerstein produced a string of landmark musicals during the 1940s and 1950s: *Oklahoma!* (1943), *Carousel* (1945), *South Pacific* (1948), *The King and I* (1951), and *The Sound of Music* (1959).

Picking up the torch around the time of Hammerstein's death in 1960 was a new generation of composers and librettists. Librettist Alan Jay Lerner and composer Frederick Loewe produced *My Fair Lady* (1956), based on Shaw's *Pygmalion*, and *Camelot* (1960), which was later adapted to characterize the Kennedy era.

Leonard Bernstein and Stephen Sondheim collaborated on *West Side Story* (1957). Subsequently, Sondheim composed the score and lyrics for a series of musical comedies, notably *A Funny Thing Happened on the Way to the Forum* (1962), *Company* (1970), and *Sweeney Todd* (1979), the grotesque musical comedy about a cannibalistic barber.

Meanwhile, in London, the American poet T.S. Eliot was writing plays in verse. *The Cocktail Party* (1950) and *The Confidential Clerk* (1954) challenged the notion that twentieth-century drama had to be written in vernacular prose.

The 1950s also witnessed the increasing presence of African American playwrights and actors on the Broadway Stage. *A Raisin in the Sun* (1959), written by Lorraine Hansberry and starring Sidney Poitier, was one of the first plays to represent the life of an African American family as a subject worthy of serious treatment. The Younger family, due to receive a $10,000 check from the life insurance policy of the family patriarch, clashes over whose dreams the check will help to realize and whose dreams will be deferred.

Comedies, like musicals, proved enduringly popular Broadway vehicles. Neil Simon's tremendous success began with *Barefoot in the Park* (1963) and continued with such modern classics as *The Odd Couple* (1965) and *Last of the Red Hot Lovers* (1969). Later shows included the autobiographical *Brighton Beach Memoirs* (1983), *Biloxi Blues* (1985), and *Lost in Yonkers* (1991). Simon's popularity was bolstered by many of his plays being made into movies.

Edward Albee roared onto the American stage with *The Zoo Story* (1960), a play that foreshadowed the social turmoil of the coming decade. Set on a pair of benches in New York City's Central Park, the play presents a chance encounter between Jerry, a conventional family man, and Peter, a disturbed but prescient resident of a rooming house. Through storytelling and incisive questioning, Peter draws Jerry into an increasingly menacing relationship that culminates in a shocking act of violence.

Two years later, Albee's *Who's Afraid of Virginia Woolf?* depicted a similarly destructive relationship in the marriage of George and Martha, who, over the course of an evening, savage both each other and the younger couple they have invited over for cocktails. A much longer play than *The Zoo Story*, Albee's masterpiece is a harrowing work that draws on both psychological realism and the European theater of the absurd.

Rise of Off-Broadway and Regional Theater

The Zoo Story heralded the new decade not only in the darkness of its subject matter, but also in its premiering off Broadway at the pioneering Provincetown Playhouse on Cape Cod in Massachusetts. By the 1960s, some of the best plays, actors, and directors could be found in off-Broadway venues, such as Circle in the Square and the Negro Ensemble Company.

Economic, political, and demographic changes all help to account for this migration away from Broadway.

Hair   Premiering in 1967, the rock musical *Hair* enjoyed unprecedented success even as it stirred up controversy for celebrating the lifestyle of the counterculture: Its characters were hippies who protested the Vietnam War, practiced free love, and took drugs. Originally an off-Broadway production, *Hair* ran on Broadway for five years, spawned fourteen touring companies in the United States alone, earned millions of dollars for its promoters, and became an enduring symbol of the 1960s.

Hair was conceived and written by two actors, Gerome Ragni and James Rado. Both had worked in legitimate and experimental theater, and they saw theatrical potential in the hippie movement. The plot revolved around one man's decision whether to join the U.S. Army or evade the draft.

Galt MacDermot, a jazz musician and composer, scored the play, using musical styles he had been exposed to during his college years in South Africa. Unlike most contemporary musicals, *Hair* focused not on characters or storyline, but on the social conflicts and anti-establishment attitudes of the time. The emphasis was not on dialogue, but on music, imagery, and theme.

Hair ran for eight weeks, beginning on December 2, 1967, at the Public and Cheetah theaters in New York. The original producer, Joseph Papp, had not intended to take the show to Broadway, but positive response to the play attracted new backers—liberal politician Michael Butler and producer Bertrand Castelli. The show was revamped, with new songs and a larger band and, under award-winning director Tom O'Horgan, it opened at the Biltmore Theater on Broadway on April 29, 1968.

Among *Hair*'s innovations was an integrated cast, one-third of which was African American.

The Broadway production also included profanity, as well as male and female nudity, to express both the rebellious flouting of authority and the spirit of liberation that were major themes of the play.

No musical had ever featured rock music or had showcased "concept" over story line. During the performances, improvisation in dance and words was encouraged, and actors frequently ran into the aisles or sat on audience members' laps. To some critics, *Hair* seemed plotless. In effect, the play was as rebellious as its youthful characters. Written and produced by outsiders to Broadway, it broke with all traditions.

Many critics and important showmen, such as Jack O'Brien and David Merrick, hated *Hair*. Others enjoyed it. A former theater critic of *The New York Times*, Brooks Atkinson, found it "fresh and spontaneous." Controversy brought more publicity, and a younger audience came to the theater. In April 1970, *Hair* celebrated its two-year anniversary with a free concert in Central Park attended by 10,000 people.

Road productions of *Hair* shocked some communities. Legal motions to bar the show from opening in Boston and Chattanooga were finally argued before the U.S. Supreme Court, which affirmed the "right of free expression" in two rulings. International touring companies also encountered occasional problems because of the nudity and antigovernment attitude. In Acapulco, Mexico, the cast and crew were jailed after only one performance.

By the mid-1970s, interest in *Hair* waned, and most shows had closed. The musical was revived on Broadway in 1977, without acclaim. It was made into a movie in 1979, directed by Milos Forman.

Vickey Kalambakal

New York City itself was, by the 1960s, feeling the drain of citizens and capital to the newly constructed suburban housing developments that now ringed the city, and this demographic shift, coupled with the ubiquity of television, was siphoning off some of the Broadway audience. Broadway theaters, always concerned with the bottom line, were increasingly driven to bring in big audiences with sure-fire hits. The established venues therefore proved both an increasingly difficult market for new playwrights to break into and an inhospitable one for the political radicalism and artistic experimentation that fired the imagination of many writers, actors, and directors.

Actors and directors created off-Broadway theaters, particularly nonprofit ones, out of a desire to engage in experimental works that would not necessarily receive the popular response required by Broadway. Such experimental, nonprofit theater groups include The Living Theater (based in New York City), the San Francisco Mime Troupe (in California), the Bread and Puppet Theatre (of Vermont), and the Open Theater (also founded in New York).

Yet Joseph Papp, for one, proved that shows produced off Broadway could be as or more popular than those produced on Broadway. His New York Shakespeare Festival, founded in 1954, settled into Central Park's outdoor Delacorte Theater in 1962, where it became a beloved icon of New York City culture. Papp opened the Public Theater, located in New York's East Village, in 1967. The first show to be produced in the new theater was *Hair*, the antiwar musical famous for its psychedelic score and infamous for the nude scene with which concludes Act 1. More graphic and outraged representations of the Vietnam War followed with productions such as David Rabe's *The Basic Training of Pavlo Hummel* (1971) and *Sticks and Bones* (1972).

Broadway faced competition outside of New York City as well, as cities across America developed theatrical centers over the course of the 1950s and 1960s. In 1958, for example, President Dwight D. Eisenhower authorized construction to begin on a national theater center located in Washington D.C. Five years later, after the assassination of President John F. Kennedy, the institute opened as the Kennedy Center for the Performing Arts.

Not only such state-sponsored theater centers, but nonprofit theaters, too, blossomed in and outside New York, including the Dallas Theater Center (Texas, 1959), the Cincinnati Playhouse in the Park (Ohio, 1964), the Long Wharf Theatre (Connecticut, 1965),

The 1967 Broadway musical *Hair*, produced by Joseph Papp, both epitomized and celebrated the hippie counterculture with its themes of peace and love, songs about sex and drugs, rambling storyline, and on-stage nudity. *(Ralph Morse/Time Life Pictures/Getty Images)*

Yale Repertory Theatre (Connecticut, 1966), and the Wooster Group (New York, 1967).

Many of the great playwrights of the 1960s and 1970s would emerge not from Broadway, but from the new off-Broadway, regional, and experimental theater scenes. Sam Shepard began writing for off-Broadway theaters in 1964, producing a series of dark meditations on the American gothic, pop culture, and myth. *Buried Child* (1978), which won a Pulitzer Prize, is a story of incest and family violence, which fuses realism with the regenerative myth of a child killed to propitiate the gods of the harvest. Other well-known Shepard plays include *True West* (1980) and *Fool for Love* (1983). Like so many contemporary playwrights, Shepard also has had a career in film, in his case as an actor as well as a screenwriter.

David Mamet began writing in the late 1960s for a theater group he founded in his native Chicago. His first off-Broadway production was *Sexual Perversity in Chicago* (1976), followed by *American Buffalo* (1977) and *Glengarry Glen Ross* (1984); the latter, a story of cutthroat businessmen struggling to outdo each other, won Mamet the Pulitzer Prize. Other Mamet plays include *The Spanish Prisoner* (1985), *Speed the Plow* (1988), *Oleanna* (1991), and *Romance* (2004). Mamet's great strength is his facility with language; his profanity-laced, rapid-fire dialogue, at once colloquial and mannered, has become a new American stage and screen vernacular.

African American Theater

August Wilson, perhaps the most important voice in contemporary African American drama, got his start in small theaters in Pittsburgh and later in Minneapolis-St. Paul. He began to receive critical acclaim with *Ma Rainey's Black Bottom* (1984), which he followed with *Fences* (1986), *Joe Turner's Come and Gone* (1986), *The Piano Lesson* (1987), *Two Trains Running* (1990), *Seven Guitars* (1995), *King Hedley II* (1999), and *The Gem of the Ocean* (2003). Wilson's scope was ambitious: He created a cycle of plays dealing with the African American experience, each covering a different decade of the twentieth century. One of the striking contrasts in his works is that of the lyric, elegiac tone of his stage directions and the powerful Black English of his spoken dialogue.

Although Wilson was the most significant name in post–World War II African American theater, other black playwrights were active. Among the most notable of these were Ntozake Shange, best known for his 1975 *for colored girls who have considered suicide/when the rainbow is enuf;* the prolific Amiri Baraka (LeRoi Jones); and Lorraine Hansberry, whose 1959 *Raisin in the Sun* earned her the first New York Drama Critics' Circle's Best Play award presented to a female African American playwright.

Gay and Lesbian Theater

Much as Wilson gave voice to African American history, so other playwrights gave voice in the 1970s and 1980s to gay and lesbian issues. Harvey Fierstein's *Safe Sex* (1991) and John Guare's *Six Degrees of Separation* (1990) are two plays that broach issues of sexual orientation.

Similarly, much as the theater had reflected the cultural upheavals of the civil rights movement and the Vietnam War during the 1960s and 1970s, so it reflected the ravages of the AIDS epidemic during the 1980s and 1990s. Among the many plays to ad-

dress the AIDS crisis directly were Wendy Wasserstein's *The Heidi Chronicles* (1988), Tony Kushner's two-part *Angels in America: Millennium Approaches* (1990) and *Perestroika* (1991), and Terrence McNally's *Lips Together, Teeth Apart* (1991).

Legacy and Future

The 1990s and the beginning of the new century found several generations of playwrights sharing the stage. Arthur Miller, for example, premiered four plays: *The Ride Down Mt. Morgan* (1991), *The Last Yankee* (1993), *Broken Glass* (1994), and *Finishing the Picture* (2004). Edward Albee was also active, premiering *Three Tall Women* (1990), *The Play about the Baby* (2001), and *The Goat* (2000).

The fact that two figures who helped set the bar for American drama in the years following World War II were still staging plays in the new millennium speaks to the relatively short time in which the American theater has achieved its greatness.

Matthew Bolton

See also: Arts Funding, Government; Dance; Film, Feature; National Endowments for the Arts and Humanities.

Bibliography

Bigsby, C.W.E. *Modern American Drama, 1945–1990.* Cambridge, UK: Cambridge University Press, 1991.

Bordman, Gerald. *The Oxford Companion to American Theater.* New York: Oxford University Press, 1993.

Frenz, Horst, ed. *American Playwrights on Drama.* New York: Hill and Wang, 1965.

Kolin, Philip C., ed. *American Playwrights Since 1945: A Guide to Scholarship, Criticism, and Performance.* Westport, CT: Greenwood, 1989.

Parker, Dorothy, ed. *Essays on Modern American Drama: Williams, Miller, Albee, and Shepard.* Toronto: University of Toronto Press, 1987.

Roudane, Matthew C. *American Drama Since 1960: A Critical History (Twayne's Critical History of American Drama Series).* New York: Simon and Schuster, 1996.

THEME PARKS

Although amusement parks in America—featuring Ferris wheels and carousels, arcade games, sideshow attractions, and food booths—date back to the late nineteenth century, the theme park was an invention of the post–World War II era. Theme parks differ from amusement parks in several important ways.

As their name implies, theme parks are either organized around a motif—such as Southern California's Knott's Berry Farm, which in 1968 became a theme park based on an Old West motif—or, more typically, divided into distinct spaces, each with its own theme. For example, the original Disneyland, which opened in 1955, featured five theme areas: Main Street, U.S.A. (turn-of-the-century America), Adventureland (exotic and faraway places), Frontierland, (Old West), Fantasyland (rides based on fantasy literature), and Tomorrowland (utopian or futuristic rides).

Theme parks also differ from the older amusement parks in that they are generally located in the suburbs, rather than in urban areas. They were created especially to appeal to families, eschewing the dance halls, saloons, and other adult-oriented entertainments typical of prewar amusement parks such as Coney Island in New York.

From the beginning, theme parks were a bit less tawdry than old-style amusement parks and carnivals. They did away not only with drinking and dancing, but also with the gambling element that was so much a part of the old-style Midway, with its games of chance. To do away with the image of the scruffy drifter who ran the rides and games at carnivals and prewar amusement parks, theme parks tended to hire younger, well-groomed employees who were rigorously trained in the art of hospitality. In short, modern theme parks are very much a product of the postwar baby boom culture, with its focus on family, suburban life, and wholesome entertainment.

Traditional amusement parks had their heyday in the first half of the twentieth century, but two decades of the Great Depression and war caused many of them to become run-down by the early postwar period. Most were located in urban areas, and the flight of families to the car-oriented suburbs was draining them of clientele; most had no or inadequate parking facilities, having relied on urban rail transport for their customers. With falling revenues, little money was invested to renovate and update the parks, and many of the attractions—built out of wood—were vulnerable to fire. Indeed, the reputation for fires kept many suburban families away from the old amusements parks and hungering for something they could enjoy together.

Disneyland

Walt Disney, the pioneer of the modern theme park, realized this hunger. Born in Chicago in 1901 and raised in Kansas City, Missouri, Disney traveled first to New York and then to Hollywood, where he made a fortune in the 1920s through the 1940s producing animated films featuring cartoon characters of his own invention—including Mickey Mouse and Donald Duck—or retelling traditional fairy tales such as Snow White and Cinderella.

According to Disney himself, he was inspired to create a new kind of amusement park out of the same frustration that other postwar generation parents faced: He felt he had no place to take his daughters. Amusement parks seemed too dangerous, too adult oriented, and too run-down for suburban parents (now accustomed to the clean and safe environments of their suburban neighborhoods) to take their children to. Originally, Disney envisioned a small park for his employees, built on a backlot of his Burbank, California, studios. As he began to develop his ideas, however, the park expanded beyond the scope of an employee-only, backlot facility.

Recognizing his potential customer base and how they would get to the park, Disney bought land in Anaheim, California, an emerging suburb in the Orange County section of metropolitan Los Angeles, located along a newly expanded freeway connecting Los Angeles to Orange County and San Diego. Opened in July 1955, Disneyland, as the park was called, with its theme areas and employees dressed up as cartoon characters, was an immediate success. By the end of that summer, it had welcomed more than a million customers. Within a decade, no less than fifty million people had passed through its gates.

It is not surprising that the park inspired imitators. In 1959, the Busch Entertainment Corporation, a division of the Anheuser-Busch brewing company, opened Busch Gardens in Florida, a park with an African safari theme. Two years later, Angus Wynne, Jr., the son of an oil tycoon, launched Six Flags Over Texas, outside Dallas. Like Disneyland, Six Flags was divided into themed areas, including a Native American village, a wilderness cruise, and a pirate adventure ride.

Most of the early amusement parks were located in the Sun Belt, usually in popular tourist destinations where the climate allowed the parks to remain open year-round. Recognizing that there was a need for such parks near the urban centers of the Northeast and Midwest, the Marriott Corporation opened two Great America theme parks during the 1970s in Illinois and California. Though Disneyland and other theme parks featured a few thrill rides, the Great America parks made them their centerpiece, gradually engaging in a competition to build the fastest, most daring roller coasters and thrill rides.

Marine and Movie-Based Theme Parks

Two other types of theme parks were opening their doors during the early postwar period. One type focused on animals, specifically marine animals. In 1954, Marineland of the Pacific opened its gates on the Palos Verdes peninsula, an upscale suburban area of Los Angeles. This was followed ten years later by Sea World in San Diego. Unlike zoos, which sometimes featured marine creatures, the sea-oriented theme parks emphasized trained animal acts that featured large marine mammals such as dolphins, seals, and killer whales performing in shows for audiences.

A second kind of theme park emerged out of the old movie lot. Whereas Disney had decided to separate his theme park from his studio, the executives of Universal Studios in Los Angeles sought to capitalize on the public's fascination with motion pictures and how they were made. In 1962, the studio opened its backlot to walking tour groups; soon this was followed by bus tours. By the late 1960s, the studio was staging Old West gunfights for the tourists, and by the 1970s, it was offering special-effects shows, including one that featured the mechanical shark from the studio's hit movie *Jaws* (1975).

The final evolution in the development of the postwar theme park was orchestrated by the man who had pioneered the institution itself, Walt Disney. Even as Disneyland attracted millions of customers, Disney was disappointed with what was going on around the park, specifically the spread of strip malls, fast-food restaurants, low-priced motels, and other forms of entertainment such as miniature golf courses and pinball arcades. To Disney, it was all rather chaotic and unsightly. And so he began to envision a theme park embedded in a planned community, where every element would be subject to his company's control.

Beginning in the early 1960s, Disney secretly began to buy up large parcels of land around the central

Florida town of Orlando. There, he planned the Experimental Prototype Community of Tomorrow (EPCOT), which would include the latest technological advances to improve the lives of its residents and visitors. Upon Disney's death in 1966, however, the theme park component of his plan, Disney World, was given priority, opening up as a larger version of Disneyland in 1971. Epcot, too, eventually opened in 1982, but it was very different from Disney's original vision. It was more like a permanent version of a traditional world's fair, hosting exhibits that featured the latest in technology.

Like so many other businesses since the 1970s, the theme park industry has seen its share of corporate consolidation. By 2005, Six Flags was running forty parks, including Marine World, a branch in the Bay Area of California; the various Sea World Parks; Great Adventure, originally an independent theme park founded in New Jersey in 1974; and Magic Mountain, a theme park north of Los Angeles, launched in 1971. Meanwhile, the parent corporation of Disneyland and Disney World, the Walt Disney Company, acquired the media company Capital Cities/ABC in 1996. And Universal Studios' parent company, Universal Pictures, after being purchased by several other firms in the 1990s and early 2000s, became part of the General Electric group of companies in 2004.

James Ciment

See also: Automobile Culture; World's Fairs.

Bibliography

Adams, Judith A. *The American Amusement Park Industry: A History of Technology and Thrills.* Boston: Twayne, 1991.

Bryman, Alan. *Disney and His Worlds.* New York: Routledge, 1995.

THIRD PARTIES

In U.S. politics, "third party" refers to any political party outside the two main ones—that is, the Democratic and Republican parties. A two-party system has dominated U.S. politics since the 1790s. For the last 150 years, the Democratic and Republican parties have held sway; all others are known as third, alternative, or minor parties.

Third parties represent views and aims different from those of the main parties in some way; their focus is often (not always) narrowed to one ideological issue. By their nature, third parties represent fewer voters and thus have less clout in the electoral system. Nevertheless, most third parties do not wish to compromise or be subsumed into the larger parties.

Third parties have put forth candidates for most presidential elections and many local and state offices. In spite of this, they are often ignored. The media does pay some attention to third parties, but often solely in the context of their role as spoilers—taking votes away from the major parties—while ignoring the issues the third parties are trying to raise.

To complicate matters, different states qualify political parties for ballot inclusion and other matters differently. Before the party can be recognized, some states require that parties have a certain percentage or number of registered voters, or that a specific number of people vote for the party's candidate in certain elections. Recognition affects funding, participation in debates, and even the printing of a candidate's name and party on the ballot. For many third parties, establishing and boosting membership in all states is an important part of being included in the political process.

While some third parties have coalesced around charismatic leaders, many others serve as protest movements and highlight issues ignored by the major parties. As such, they not only give voice to a fringe or extremist group, but may, if they attract enough attention and adherents, influence the platforms and policies of other parties. Minor parties that become very popular often draw attention to dissatisfaction among voters and alert the major parties to their own failures.

While third parties have seen candidates elected to state office, no third party candidate has ever come close to the presidency since Abraham Lincoln, the first candidate of the fledgling Republican Party in 1860. Candidates are often promoted by third parties to get attention for a cause that the major parties have ignored or as a protest against the policies of the major parties. As such, they can be an effective method of generating publicity and attention for new ideas and reform movements. Ironically, once the attention of the Democrats or Republicans is focused on the new issue (usually because of votes won by the third party), and it is incorporated into the major party platform, the third party often fades into obscurity.

Types of Third Parties

Some political parties focus on a single issue. The Republican Party in the 1850s was perceived as an anti-slavery party. It was only after the Civil War that the Republicans expanded their platform and appeal, which allowed them to stay in power. Currently, the Right-to-Life Party, the Hawaii Independence Party, and many groups supporting legalization of marijuana are examples of one-issue parties.

The Prohibition Party, established in 1869 to fight for the criminalization of alcoholic beverages, is an example of a party that has survived into the twenty-first century by expanding its appeal. The Prohibition Party's platform today is based on a particular Christian moral code. Besides opposing American participation in international institutions and treaties and federal interference in the state and local matters, the party advocates legislation banning homosexuality, gambling, and pornography, as well as alcohol.

By broadening its agenda, the Prohibition Party became an example of another type of third party—one based on a particular ideology or doctrine. Other examples of this type are the many Socialist parties that have formed over the decades. By their nature, these parties keep themselves on the periphery of American politics. Their adherence to a philosophy that the mainstream parties deem unacceptable limits their effectiveness and the support they receive.

By design, some political parties exist only in one state. The Hawaii Independence Party falls into this category. The Green Party of Virginia, the Wisconsin Green Party, and those of many other states are all part of a national confederation, but they are also state parties working independently of each other.

The Peace and Freedom Party of California (PFP) developed out of the social upheaval of the 1960s; it was founded in 1967 to embrace a modified socialist creed, which included environmentalism, tolerance, and, by 1974, feminism. The PFP remains an active community organization today, establishing food co-ops and health clinics, as well as organizing protest marches. Although it puts presidential candidates on the ballot, the PFP does most of its work in California.

A more right-leaning group, the Conservative Party of New York, established in 1962, now claims 117,000 members. The Conservatives link themselves strongly with the major parties in New York State, supporting conservative candidates, judges, and ballot measures.

Some third parties have coalesced around strong personalities. In 1948, the States' Rights Democratic Party formed around presidential candidate Strom Thurmond, then governor of South Carolina. Party members, mostly disillusioned Democrats who called themselves Dixiecrats, were incensed by the civil rights initiative of President Harry S Truman, a Democrat. In that sense, the party also focused on a single issue: preserving the racial hierarchy of the Southern states. Together with the Progressives, who also put forward a presidential candidate in 1948, former Vice-President Henry Wallace, the third parties garnered more than 1 million votes.

Twenty years later, the American Independent Party (AIP) was established to promote the presidential aspirations of Alabama Governor George Wallace. Supporters, who endorsed his views on segregation and the Vietnam War, felt alienated by the major political parties. Nationwide, nearly 10 million votes were cast for the AIP in 1968. By 1972, 80 percent of AIP members voted for the Republican candidate, Richard M. Nixon, and the party was largely forgotten.

Third parties that depend on one person are usually short-lived, but they often influence the major parties. Thurmond's Dixiecrats and Wallace's Independents were disenchanted Democrats, and the Democratic Party suffered when they left. Although the Democrats did not change their platform to accommodate these third parties, on some occasions, minor parties have caused major parties to reevaluate their goals and policies. The Republican Party in 1968, for example, took up the AIP's platform of dealing more harshly with crime and attracted many new voters.

Major Minor Parties

Imported to America with European immigrants, socialist ideas influenced labor unions and spawned several political third parties, including the Socialist and Communist parties. These groups have splintered and reformed over the years; some have had close ties with international communism, especially with the Soviet Union, while others distanced themselves from the USSR. Labor unions never really joined these groups in large numbers, although the parties have traditionally claimed to represent the interests of workers.

During the early 1950s, the McCarthy Senate hearings damaged socialist parties in America, and few citizens wished to be affiliated with them. The Socialist and Social Democratic Parties united in 1956, but the new organization was rocked by as many schisms as mergers throughout the next decade. Rather than nominate their own candidates, socialist parties often supported Democrats. In 1973, the Socialist Party USA reformed itself out of several other groups, but again this unification caused many new divisions.

The socialists began to run their own candidates for president in 1980, starting with David McReynolds, and they focused much of their energies on local elections. Many candidates endorsed by the Socialist Party are supported by coalitions of socialist, progressive, and other left-leaning groups. In 2000, several Socialist Party presidential candidates split about 16,000 votes.

A completely new party, the Libertarians, started in 1971 by eight antigovernment conservatives, steadily increased its membership to become, by 1978, the third-largest political party in America. Believing that government should not interfere in the private or public lives, businesses, or education of its citizens, the Libertarians have been called both ultraconservative and radical. In the 2000 elections, 1,436 candidates of the Libertarian Party were listed on ballots throughout the United States, including 280 vying for congressional seats on the federal level. The party's presidential candidate, Harry Browne, received almost 383,000 votes. In 2003, more than 500 Libertarians held elective office, most of them on the local level. The party has more than a quarter million registered members.

The Green Party, a confederation of several state Green parties, claimed over 280,000 registered members as of August 2003. Of the 285 Green candidates who ran in 2000, 49 won their elections. Green presidential candidate Ralph Nader got 2.7 million votes, or 3 percent of all ballots cast. Officially founded nationally in 1996, the fast-rising Green parties have been active in some states since 1985. Their platform emphasizes environmentalism and social justice. Like the earlier socialist parties, Greens are unusual in American politics in that the party's roots are in Europe, where several parties concerned about ecological issues formed in the 1970s and 1980s and joined to create the European Coordination of Green Parties in 1984.

In 1992, independent presidential candidate H. Ross Perot organized what many considered a third political party, called United We Stand America. Perot received 20 million votes in his bid to become president, but he ran as an Independent, not as a candidate of United We Stand America. Perot founded the Reform Party in 1996, and United We Stand America was dissolved the next year. In 1998, the Reform Party saw its candidate, Jesse Ventura, win the gubernatorial

Libertarians

Libertarians in the United States represent a continuation of the European classical liberal tradition of Edmund Burke, which emphasizes the freedoms of the individual from government coercion and interference, as opposed to the rights of people to expect services from their government. As a result, libertarians do not fit well within the typical left-right political dichotomy; they tend to agree with Republicans that government should stay out of private industry's way and agree with Democrats that the government should not meddle in the personal affairs of consenting adults. Libertarians often argue that their philosophy is closest to those of the Founding Fathers, and they avoid use of the term "liberal" because of its association with government activism and large-scale social welfare programs.

One of the formative libertarian thinkers in the United States was Friedrich von Hayek, a Nobel laureate economist (1974), originally associated with the Austrian School of economics centered around the University of Vienna and Ludwig van Mises. Unwilling to live under Nazi rule, Hayek became a British subject in the 1930s and moved to the United States in the 1950s. At the University of Chicago, he trained a number of well-known free-market economists, including James M. Buchanan, who won the Nobel Prize in Economic Sciences in 1986 for demonstrating that the relationship between politicians and their constituents follows the rules of the marketplace.

One of the best-known libertarians and popularizers of the libertarian philosophy of individual liberty, responsibility, and property against collectivism was the science fiction writer Robert A. Heinlein. In his novels, particularly *The Moon Is a Harsh Mistress* (1966), Heinlein wove libertarian philosophy into the fabric of his created worlds, immersing readers in those concepts with such expressions as TANSTAAFL, a common Lunarian acronym standing for "There ain't no such thing as a free lunch," a pithy warning that all government gifts have strings attached.

As a result of Heinlein's persuasive championship of libertarian philosophy, the science fiction community has been a strong bastion of libertarian thought. Jim Baen, head of the science fiction publishing company Baen Books, includes in his guidelines for writers a warning against submitting novels that glorify the "nanny state."

Spelled with a lower-case "l," libertarian is a general term for any person holding to the libertarian philosophy. Capitalized, the term "Libertarian" generally is restricted to mean a member of the Libertarian Party. The Libertarian Party in the United States was founded in 1971 by David Nolan and others in response to price controls and other so-called socialist policies being imposed by Republican President Richard M. Nixon and a Democratic-controlled Congress. The party has run a presidential candidate in every election since that time, generally obtaining ballot access in most or all states. It claims to be the largest third party in the United States, although the Greens and others dispute this claim.

In 2004, the Libertarians ran retired business executive Michael Badnarik as their presidential candidate. Badnarik received nearly 400,000 votes, or 0.33 percent of the total vote, running fourth behind Republican candidate George W. Bush, Democratic candidate John Kerry, and independent candidate Ralph Nader.

Leigh Kimmel

election in Minnesota. Because of its popularity, the Reform Party's views on balancing the national budget, campaign reform, and protecting American jobs had an impact on both the rhetoric and platforms of the major parties and their candidates throughout the 1990s.

The Reform Party also has, in its short history, been rocked by factionalism. In the 2000 elections, unable to agree on a presidential candidate, the party wound up putting forth two: Pat Buchanan and John Hagelin. The latter was also the candidate of the

Attracting followers with a plainspoken, down-home style, billionaire Texas businessman H. Ross Perot ran for president as an independent in 1992 and as the candidate of the Reform Party, which he founded, in 1996. The Reform Party exerted national political influence through the end of the decade. *(Bill Pugliano/Getty Images News)*

Natural Law Party. The two Reform Party candidates received almost half a million votes.

The Natural Law Party was also founded in 1992. The philosophy of this party centered more on process than crisis management. The Natural Law Party emphasized "prevention-oriented" government and scientific solutions to the nation's problems. As an example, the party would use intensive educational programs to reduce the number of abortions in the United States, rather than legislation that restricts abortion. The Natural Law Party also supported a flat tax and balanced budget. Its approach and platform garnered it more than 83,000 votes in the 2000 elections, even though the party was not listed on all state ballots.

The Constitutional Party was formed in 1996 out of the U.S. Taxpayers Party, a coalition of state parties dating from 1992. Constitutionalists supported conservative interpretations of the Constitution and the Declaration of Independence that shift power to local and state governments and eliminate many federal taxes. Like the Natural Law Party, the Constitutional Party was not listed on all ballots, but it received almost 98,000 votes in 2000.

The Prohibition Party received just over 200 votes in 2000. Other third parties that got roughly 10,000 votes, but were confined to one or more state, are the Conservative Party in New York and Virginia and the American Independent Party in California.

Although third-party officials and candidates hate to admit it, the major impact of their organizations on presidential elections in recent years has been that of spoilers. Republicans claim that Ross Perot's 19 percent of the popular vote in 1992 denied George H.W. Bush a second term in the White House, although post-election surveys have found that Perot voters would probably not have changed the outcome, as enough of them would likely have voted for Clinton to give the Democratic candidate a majority in the electoral college.

Democrats claim that Ralph Nader's Green Party effectively threw the election to Republican George W. Bush in 2000. Indeed, in several states where Bush won the popular vote by a razor-thin margin—most notably, Florida—there were more than enough Nader votes to make a difference. As Nader was on the left end of the political spectrum, the assumption is that most of his votes were "taken" from the Democratic candidate, Al Gore.

Vickey Kalambakal

See also: American Independent Party; American Nazi Party; Dixiecrats; Election of 1948; Election of 1968; Election of 1980; Election of 1992; Election of 1996; Election of 2000; Peace and Freedom Party; Progressive Party, 1948.

Bibliography

Gillespie, J. David. *Politics at the Periphery: Third Parties in Two-Party America.* Columbia: University of South Carolina Press, 1993.

Hazlett, Joseph M. *The Libertarian Party and Other Minor Political Parties in the United States.* Jefferson, NC: McFarland, 1992.

Ness, Immanuel, and James Ciment, eds. *Encyclopedia of Third Parties in America.* Armonk, NY: M.E. Sharpe, 2000.

THOMAS (CLARENCE) HEARINGS

Broadcast live on television, the Senate confirmation hearings of Clarence Thomas for a seat on the U.S. Supreme Court in 1991 turned into a highly charged national drama after lawyer Anita Hill, a former co-worker of his, accused the nominee of sexual harassment.

In June 1991, Republican President George H.W. Bush was given the unenviable task of replacing Supreme Court Justice Thurgood Marshall, the revered pioneer of civil rights and a strong voice for the liberal bloc on the Supreme Court. Unfortunately for Bush, his choice would become the most notorious and controversial Supreme Court nominee of the twentieth century.

Given the importance of an African American voice on the Court, it was highly unlikely that Bush would replace the first African American on the Court with anyone other than another African American. Because of Bush's conservatism, however, it was expected that he would not nominate a liberal replacement. As a result of the controversy that Ronald Reagan had created by nominating Robert Bork, whose opinions on crucial issues were well documented, it seemed likely to many Washington observers that Bush would choose a nominee without a national reputation or a body of documented opinions.

Nomination

The nomination of Clarence Thomas, a Georgia native who had been a U.S. Appeals Court judge for the Washington, D.C. Circuit since March 1990, was appealing to most Republicans. He was against liberal activism on the court, sympathized with the anti-abortion movement, and was generally supportive of states' rights.

Thomas was a conservative African American who had worked throughout the 1980s in the Department of Education and the Equal Opportunity Commission (EEOC). With only two years as a federal court judge, Thomas had almost no judicial experience and had written relatively few opinions. The fact that he was Southern was a bonus, since there were no Southerners on the Supreme Court.

The investigation of Clarence Thomas by members of the Senate Judiciary Committee, journal-

ists, and special interest groups was even more exacting than is usual in such cases. The impetus came from many sources, but the controversy was essentially twofold. First, Thurgood Marshall had represented the political ideology of most African Americans, and Clarence Thomas did not. Second, the Court's positions on liberal social issues, such as a woman's right to choose and affirmative action, were apparently in jeopardy, and liberals were up in arms.

In the course of discovering as much background information as possible, two journalists uncovered information that led them to Anita Hill, a law professor at the University of Oklahoma who had alleged that Thomas sexually harassed her when she worked with him at the Department of Education and again at EEOC. Hill, who had never filed formal charges against Thomas, agreed to cooperate with the Senate Judiciary Committee.

In 1991, most women were well aware of the prevalence of sexual harassment in the business world and academia, but it was not a topic that had received a lot of coverage by the mainstream media. When the Thomas hearings turned to possible sexual harassment on October 11, the world was both stunned and intrigued by the drama that unfolded on their television screens. While Thomas narrowly won the seat on the Supreme Court by a vote of 52 to 48, Hill's testimony forever changed perceptions of sexual harassment and male-dominated politics.

U.S. Supreme Court nominee Clarence Thomas responds to a question at his Senate confirmation hearings in September 1991. The televised proceedings became highly contentious when a former employee, attorney Anita Hill, testified that Thomas had sexually harassed her. *(J. David Ake/AFP/Getty Images)*

Much criticism was directed at Democrat Joseph Biden of Delaware, the chairman of the Senate Judiciary Committee, for his handling of the hearings. A number of critics believed that the hearings should never have been televised. Since they were made accessible to the American viewing public, however, it was argued that the hearings should have been involved with uncovering the truth. Women's rights advocates contended that expert testimony on sexual harassment should have been introduced and that Hill should never have been required to stand alone in her charges.

Without providing a precise definition of sexual harassment and by not allowing testimony concerning Thomas's documented interest in pornography, the Senate Judiciary Committee allowed the entire scenario to develop into "he said, she said" and left many unanswered questions. Thomas claimed he was the victim of a "high-tech lynching" by the committee, "categorically denied" all charges, and accused the American media of feeding the frenzy.

Anita Hill's Testimony

Hill, in contrast to Thomas's angry public stance, appeared calm and professional throughout eight hours of testimony, as she charged Thomas with physically and verbally sexually harassing her. Hill was forced to depend on the Democrats on the committee for fair play. Republicans on the committee were successful at introducing witnesses who painted Hill as a neurotic female who imagined sexual attentions and who sought revenge when male attention was not reciprocated. As for the Democrats, Hill's supporters claimed they failed to defend her, fearing that they would be seen as obstructive to the nomination process.

No final proof or consensus on the facts of the sexual harassment allegations has arisen in the years following the Thomas nomination. Public opinion polls have tended to support Hill as being more believable. A *USA Today*/CNN poll revealed that the number of respondents who believed Thomas declined from 54 percent in 1991 to 39 percent in 1992.

Hill's testimony before the all-white, all-male Senate Judiciary Committee, which included senators from both parties, had a significant impact on the 1992 election and the future makeup of the Senate Judiciary Committee. While Thomas remains on the Supreme Court, with a reputation as one of its

more conservative members, Hill left her position at the University of Oklahoma in 1996, citing harassment by Thomas supporters. She went on to write her memoirs, *Speaking Truth to Power* (1997) and became a law professor at Brandeis University in 1997.

Elizabeth Purdy

See also: Bork Nomination; Conservatism; Courts.

Bibliography

Hill, Anita. *Speaking Truth to Power.* New York: Doubleday, 1997.

Mayer, Jane, and Jill Abramson. *Strange Justice: The Selling of Clarence Thomas.* Boston: Houghton Mifflin, 1994.

Ragan, Sandra L., et al. *The Lynching of Language: Gender, Politics, and Power in the Hill-Thomas Hearings.* Urbana: University of Illinois Press, 1996.

Siegel, Paul. *Outsiders Looking In: A Communication Perspective on the Hill-Thomas Hearings.* Cresskill, NJ: Hampton, 1996

THREE MILE ISLAND DISASTER

Since the first U.S. nuclear energy plant was built in the 1950s, the government has insisted that a nuclear meltdown is virtually impossible because of the complex system designed to ensure safety. The incident at the Unit 2 nuclear plant at Three Mile Island (TMI), ten miles from Harrisburg, Pennsylvania, on March 28, 1979, proved that accidents can happen, because human error and vulnerability may override emergency measures. A tragic chain of circumstances, involving both technical and human failure, led to the disaster.

The accident at TMI remains the most serious accident ever to occur at a nuclear power plant in the United States. Approximately 140,000 residents of nearby Harrisburg, Pennsylvania, evacuated either out of fear or in response to the government's suggestion that small children and pregnant women should leave at once. Once the incident was made public, citizens all along the Eastern seaboard were afraid that radiation would become airborne and spread contaminants for hundreds of miles. Americans nationwide demanded to know what had caused the accident, whether the situation could have been avoided, and what conclusions could be drawn about potential nuclear accidents at other plants.

Reactor Design

In the early morning hours of March 28, 1979, the cooling system in the Unit 2 reactor—which maintains a flow of water around the reactor core—failed. Like all U.S. nuclear plants, TMI had an emergency back-up cooling system, but it had been turned off during routine maintenance. The two workers in charge of monitoring the system that morning were both tired, having worked long shifts, and they failed to note that the back-up cooling system was turned off.

The reactor vessel began to super-heat what cooling water was still in the system, forcing open a relief valve. Cooling water then began pouring onto the reactor flow at the rate of 220 gallons a minute. Responding to the leak, the operators shut off other cooling water pumps. Without the emergency coolants, the reactor began to tear itself apart as the trapped, heated water turned into steam.

Sophisticated computer analysis of the system at TMI had predicted that no more than 1 percent of the metal inside the reactor would be likely to produce hydrogen by mixing with water in case of such an emergency. In reality, in the nuclear accident at TMI, 25–30 percent of the metal inside the reactor reacted with water to produce hydrogen. The hydrogen that was produced had the potential to cause a major explosion inside the containment building.

The Number Two power station (twin cooling towers at the left) at Three Mile Island in Pennsylvania was the site of the worst commercial nuclear accident in U.S. history. Malfunctioning pumps and valves caused a partial meltdown in March 1979. *(Bill Pierce/Time Life Pictures/Getty Images)*

What actually happened was that, as the reactor core began to break apart, large amounts of radioactive material were released into the surrounding containment vessel.

Initial investigation by officials at TMI identified five separate equipment breakdowns involving valves, pumps, and fuel rods. The investigation also revealed that a reactor valve had malfunctioned during a test in 1978, but this information was not acted upon to prevent future malfunctions. The TMI investigation also identified serious problems with data analysis that should have been able to pinpoint problems and identify them before the initial blockage set off a chain of events that created major problems.

People around the country blamed the National Regulatory Commission (NRC) for inadequate safety procedures; members of Congress accused the NRC of inefficiency and placing too much emphasis on public relations and not enough on safety. It was reported that the NRC had ignored vital information issued by reactor inspectors before the accident occurred. One inspector stated that he had been given a bad personnel performance evaluation after reporting that instructions for dealing with conflicting pressure readings were inadequate.

In the six months devoted to investigating the incident at TMI, the Kemeny Commission, a twelve-member investigating team appointed by President Jimmy Carter and chaired by mathematician and Dartmouth College President John G. Kemeny, discovered a plethora of problems with the TMI reactor, as well as potential problems at other U.S. nuclear power plants. In effect, the investigating team concluded that the situation at TMI was an accident waiting to happen. Much of the blame was assigned to the National Regulatory Commission, which, according to the Kemeny Commission, could not ensure an acceptable level of safety at the nation's nuclear power plants.

Problems

Specifically, the problems at TMI were summed up by the Kemeny Commission as follows:

1. *Design errors.* Two months after the incident at TMI, it was reported that plant operators had been unable to halt the chain of events that took place on March 28 because of confusing or erroneous data generated by reactor computers.

2. *Inadequate training of operators.* Subsequent investigation of the TMI incident uncovered an appalling lack of basic and emergency training required of plant operators. When the accident happened, not a single qualified nuclear engineer was present at the plant. None of the personnel present had ever received detailed training on what to do if an emergency occurred, although all had participated in the basic one-year course required by the NRC. Even the supervisors of the plant had no formal training in emergency procedures.

3. *Safety violations.* On August 3, 1979, NRC Director of Investigation Victor Stello announced that the commission was considering filing thirty-five separate charges against officials at Three Mile Island for, among other things, failing to maintain safety and emergency equipment. Charges were also being considered against Metropolitan Edison, which had violated a number of federal rules before the accident and was being blamed for exposing TMI workers to high levels of radiation after the accident.

4. *Human fatigue.* Investigation revealed that TMI maintenance workers had worked forty consecutive days without a day off since March 1, and shifts on all but three days of that month had involved ten-hour workdays.

5. *Insufficient manufacturer warnings.* Even after Babcock and Wilson, the reactor manufacturer, had been warned of the reactor's unreliability in January and February by NRC investigators, it failed to warn the plant operators that monitors might not adequately indicate the effective operation of the cooling system. It was also revealed on July 19 that internal memos from two Babcock and Wilson engineers warning of potential accidents at nuclear power plants had been ignored.

Within weeks of the TMI incident, lawsuits had been filed by virtually every business within twenty-five miles of the plant. More than 2,000 cases were also filed by individuals in the area who claimed they had contracted acute lymphocytic leukemia, chronic myelogenous leukemia, thyroid cancer, cell carcinoma, thyroid adenoma, osteogenic sarcoma, breast cancer, adenocarcinoma of the ovaries, bladder cancer, and acoustic neuroma from radiation emanating from TMI. In 1996, a federal district judge dismissed all cases, claiming that no connection had been proved between the diseases and the incident at TMI. In 2000, the U.S. Supreme Court refused to hear the case.

Elizabeth Purdy

See also: Energy, Department of; Environmentalism; Nuclear Energy.

Bibliography

Curtis, Richard, and Elizabeth Hogan. *Nuclear Lessons: An Examination of Nuclear Power's Safety, Economic, and Political Record.* Harrisburg, PA: Stackpole, 1980.

Ford, Daniel R. *Three Mile Island: Thirty Minutes to Meltdown.* New York: Viking, 1981.

Martin, Daniel. *Three Mile Island: Prologue or Epilogue?* Cambridge, MA: Ballinger, 1980.

Panati, Charles, and Michael Hudson. *The Silent Intruder: Surviving the Radiation Age.* Boston: Houghton Mifflin, 1981.

THRESHER DISASTER

The nuclear attack submarine USS *Thresher* sank east of the Massachusetts coast on April 10, 1963. All 129 men on board were killed in the worst submarine accident on record.

The *Thresher* was originally designed as a Skipjack-class submarine, but extensive upgrades of its sonar and its ability to run silently and in deeper waters later prompted the U.S. Navy to designate it as the lead ship of an entirely different class called the Thresher Class. The *Thresher* was built at the Portsmouth (New Hampshire) Naval Shipyard and launched on July 9, 1960. After successful sea trials, it was formally commissioned on August 3, 1961, whereupon it patrolled the Atlantic for a year before heading back to Portsmouth for a nine-month overhaul.

The USS *Thresher* returned to sea on the morning of April 9, 1963, under the command of Lieutenant Commander John M. Harvey. After conducting a shallow-water test dive, the submarine headed eastward, having arranged to rendezvous with the surface vessel USS *Skylark* the following day for deep-water dive tests.

The two ships met early on April 10 some 200 miles east of Cape Cod, Massachusetts, and began the tests. The exercise proceeded without incident until approximately 9:12 A.M., when the *Thresher* reported a minor difficulty, but failed to indicate exactly what it was. Sailors aboard the *Skylark* then heard sounds consistent with a submarine trying to blow water out of its ballast tanks in order to surface. Subsequent attempts to contact the *Thresher* failed until 9:17, when it issued a brief, garbled message, followed by the sounds of a ship breaking up.

The Navy quickly organized a search for the *Thresher*, but few naval officials entertained hopes of finding survivors in waters approaching depths of 8,400 feet. Although the remains of the submarine would not be discovered until August 1963, U.S. Navy Chief of Naval Operations Admiral George W. Anderson declared the *Thresher* lost on April 11.

To discern the cause of the *Thresher* disaster, the Navy named a court of inquiry that heard testimony from numerous sources, including Vice Admiral Hyman G. Rickover, naval engineers, shipyard personnel, *Skylark* crew members, and former *Thresher* crew members. The court's findings, made public on June 20, 1963, concluded that a failure in the engine room piping system had most likely flooded the submarine and damaged its electrical circuits. The resulting loss of power and propulsion, in the court's estimation, caused the *Thresher* to slow, sink, and implode.

In the wake of the accident, the U.S. Navy reviewed its submarine operation and safety procedures and revamped submarine construction techniques. It also temporarily restricted the operating depths of Thresher-class and Polaris-class submarines, pending the findings of a review of the deep-water capabilities. This review, completed in March 1964, made several recommendations for improving safety on all submarines. Although the precautions undoubtedly improved safety, the Navy suffered another tragedy five years later with the loss of the submarine USS *Scorpion*.

H. Matthew Loayza

See also: Nautilus; Nuclear Energy.

Bibliography

Polmar, Norman. *The Death of the USS Thresher.* Guilford, CT: Lyons, 1964, 2001.

Polmar, Norman, and Thomas B. Allen. *Rickover.* New York: Simon and Schuster, 1982.

TILL (EMMETT) LYNCHING

In the summer of 1955, a Chicago youth named Emmett Till boarded a train to visit relatives in the Mississippi River Delta. The small town of Money, Mississippi, was characterized by strict racial segregation and hatred that was brutally manifested when the mutilated corpse of the fourteen-year-old boy floated to the surface of the Tallahatchie River. With this act, the vigilantism dating back to the post-Reconstruction era was resurrected, and the outrage it generated would fuel the burgeoning civil rights movement.

It was an August afternoon when the African American Till and several friends ventured to the white-owned Bryant grocery store in Money. The sequence of events remains unclear, as accounts vary, but it seems that Till was boasting about interacting with white girls in the North, and he was challenged by one of the boys to flirt with Carolyn Bryant, a former beauty queen, who was operating the cash register. After purchasing some candy, Till made a gesture, perhaps a whistle, that Mrs. Bryant deemed inappropriate.

A few days later, Bryant's husband Roy and a man named J.W. Milam kidnapped Till from the home of his great uncle, Moses Wright, in the early hours of the morning. Till was not seen again until the river washed up a virtually unrecognizable body that Wright identified by a ring on its finger. Roy Bryant and Milam were arrested for murder, and a media frenzy descended upon the court proceedings. Some seventy periodicals sent reporters to cover the trial, including African American newspapers such as the *Pittsburgh Courier* and the *Chicago Defender,* as well as pro-segregation Southern newspapers such as the *Jackson Daily News.*

A little over an hour of deliberation produced two acquittals from the all-white jury, which found that the evidence did not establish the murder victim to be Till. The verdict told African Americans that they could expect little justice in the courts of the South. Journalist James L. Hicks, writing for the *Baltimore Afro-American,* postulated in a series of articles that there was a conspiracy among Mississippi authorities to prevent incriminating evidence and missing witnesses from appearing during the trial. Moreover, no effort was made to determine how long the victim had survived before being cast into the river or who else may have been involved in the murder.

The boy's mother, Mamie Till, insisted that her son's body be shipped north for an open casket funeral. She spoke out against the act of violence that left her childless and the crime of allowing those

The lynching of African American teenager Emmett Till in rural Mississippi during the summer of 1955 added fuel to the burgeoning civil rights movement. The two men accused of the abduction were acquitted because the body was not identifiable; an exhumation in 2005 confirmed that it was Till. *(Library of Congress, LC-USZ62–111241)*

responsible to go unpunished. For days, mourners filed past the crushed skull, its partially decomposed flesh, and the bullet wound that ended Emmett Till's life.

Jet magazine ran the story of the funeral with photographs that brought the gruesome reality of lynching to the eyes of thousands. This vivid testimony of injustice was a turning point that helped spawn the boycotts, sit-ins, and marches for civil rights in the late 1950s and 1960s.

Lindsey Swindall

See also: Civil Rights Movement, Through 1965; Crime, Violent.

Bibliography

Hudson-Weems, Clenora. *Emmett Till: The Sacrificial Lamb of the Civil Rights Movement.* Troy, MI: Bedford, 1994.
Whitfield, Stephen J. *A Death in the Delta: The Story of Emmett Till.* Baltimore: Johns Hopkins University Press, 1991.

TOBACCO AND TOBACCO INDUSTRY

No industry in postwar America has seen its fortunes—if not in revenue, then in prestige and acceptance—fall faster and farther than the tobacco industry. Whereas cigarette smoking—and, to a lesser extent, the use of cigars, pipe tobacco, and smokeless tobacco—was once seen as a relatively harmless habit, over the course of just a few decades, the practice came to be recognized as the single most preventable cause of disease and death in modern society. Once permitted almost anywhere at any time, smoking has been banned from most public indoor spaces.

As for the tobacco companies themselves, which were once seen as no better or worse than any other corporate interest providing a product for consumers, they are now mistrusted and even reviled as deceitful purveyors of sickness and death. With their revenues declining in the United States, the tobacco companies have been forced to seek new markets overseas and diversify into other businesses.

1940s–1960s: A Growing Industry

The tobacco plant, as every school child has learned, was originally domesticated and cultivated by Native Americans, and smoking its leaf was incorporated into their rituals and everyday life. Early European explorers brought tobacco back to their home countries, and English colonists in the Chesapeake Bay region soon became wealthy by growing it for export.

Whereas tobacco was primarily smoked in cigars and pipes (or snorted or chewed) for much of its history, cigarettes became the primary tobacco product in the late nineteenth century, especially after the invention of machine rollers, which made mass production possible. Like many industries, tobacco became more consolidated during the late nineteenth and early twentieth centuries, even despite a successful antitrust suit against the American Tobacco Company in 1911. By 1945, a handful of companies—Philip Morris, R.J. Reynolds, Brown and Williamson, Liggett, and Lorillard—controlled the vast majority of sales in the United States.

The government aided tobacco in a number of ways. When falling demand threatened the nation's tobacco farmers during the Great Depression, the federal government offered them subsidies to keep them in business. During World War II, the administration of President Franklin D. Roosevelt declared tobacco an essential wartime crop, and army manuals encouraged soldiers to smoke as a way to reduce battlefield tensions. In fact, cigarettes were included in the rations given to soldiers in both World War I and World War II. World War II also saw the spread of domestic consumption of cigarettes: Whereas Americans smoked an average of 2,236 cigarettes in 1941, the figure had jumped 50 percent, to 3,449, by 1945.

Smoking also was promoted by Hollywood studios during the war and in the immediate postwar era. Cigarettes and cigarette smoke became symbols of sophistication when smoked by men, signals of seduction when smoked by women, and rebelliousness when smoked by youths. Cigarettes were ubiquitous in the late 1940s and 1950s, with smoking permitted everywhere from airplanes to hospitals. Major movie stars such as John Wayne endorsed them in advertisements.

Even some doctors got into the act, touting one brand or another as smoother on the throat. Indeed, the widespread introduction of filtered cigarettes during the early postwar period was promoted as a health measure. In 1952, Lorillard introduced Kent filtered cigarettes as "the greatest health protection in cigarette history," and Liggett announced that its L & M filter brand was "just what the doctor ordered." Still, filtered cigarettes got off to a rocky start; as late as 1954, they accounted for just 10 percent of total U.S. sales.

Then came the Marlboro Man. With sales slumping in favor of rival R. J. Reynolds's new Winston filter brand, Philip Morris introduced the Marlboro brand in 1954, a filtered cigarette aimed at the growing women's market. It proved a disaster, and the company went back to its marketing division to retool the brand's image. After extensive market research, advertising pioneer Leo Burnett suggested a different approach, aimed at men and featuring one of the great icons of advertising history, the rugged cowboy image of the Marlboro Man. The new Marlboro became an instant best-seller, and it was the top-selling brand in America by the late 1960s. It also established the popularity of filtered cigarettes and the importance of advertising.

Initially focused on print, advertisers soon recognized the power of television in advertising cigarettes, and, by the late 1960s, they were devoting 80 percent of their advertising dollars to that medium. The money was well spent: By the early 1960s, roughly half of all American men and a third of women were regular cigarette smokers. In 1963, the year before the U.S. Surgeon General's office published its landmark report on the dangers of smoking, the average American smoker consumed 4,345 cigarettes per year, up more than 25 percent from 1945.

Health Warnings

Warnings about the dangers of tobacco and complaints about smoking were nearly as old as the industry itself. As early as 1604, King James I of England issued his famous essay "Counterblast to Tobacco," in which he denounced the new practice of "tobacco taking" as a "vile custome" that was more fit for the barbarian natives of the New World than civilized Englishmen. But he was in the minority. By the 1700s, tobacco—smoked, snorted, chewed, or even delivered as an emetic—was being used as a treatment for everything from dysentery to hernias.

It was not until the twentieth century that scientists began to recognize the dangers of tobacco. In 1929, German scientists published the first study showing a statistical link between tobacco smoking and lung cancer. In 1950, an article in the *Journal of the American Medical Association* reported that 96.5 percent of the lung cancer patients interviewed were moderate to heavy smokers. Indeed, whereas the lung cancer rate among white men in the United States was 4.9 per 100,000 in 1930, it had grown to 27.1 per 100,000 by 1950; during the same period, per capita consumption of cigarettes rose from 1,500 to 3,600. In 1955, CBS aired the first documentary on the dangers of smoking.

Yet the message failed to sink in, and cigarette smoking continued to rise during the late 1950s and early 1960s. The 1964 *Surgeon General's Report on Tobacco* began to change that pattern. A meta-analysis of findings from more than 7,000 studies conducted during the 1950s and early 1960s, the report drew several alarming conclusions: Tobacco smoking was a major cause of lung cancer in women and of lung and throat cancer in men (the latter disease because more men tended to smoke cigars and pipes, where the smoke sits in the throat rather than entering the lungs). Smoking, the report declared, was also the leading cause of chronic bronchitis and other diseases of the lung, and it was closely linked to heart disease.

Bearing the government's imprimatur, the surgeon general's report had a dramatic effect on cigarette smoking, causing a 20 percent drop in consumption in the first three months after its release. The decline was only temporary, however, as consumption returned to pre-report levels soon thereafter.

Anti-Smoking Laws and Lawsuits

In any event, the government had now gone into the business of discouraging people from smoking, even as it continued to provide subsidies to tobacco farmers. In 1965, Congress passed the Cigarette Labeling and Advertising Act, followed four years later by the Public Health Cigarette Smoking Act; both acts restricted advertising, called for increasingly strong health warnings on tobacco packaging and advertising, and mandated an annual government report on tobacco use and health. In 1970, tobacco advertising on television was banned, effective the following year. The tobacco companies did win a reprieve, as the federal government prohibited states from passing additional advertising bans, as long as tobacco companies adhered to the federal regulations.

For their part, the tobacco companies refused to admit, at least publicly, that tobacco presented health risks; they also denied the addictiveness of nicotine. Both claims not only flew in the face of the consensus developing within the health professions, but they also went against the findings of the tobacco companies' own researchers. One internal 1963 memo at Brown and Williamson, for example, read, "Nicotine is addictive. We are, then, in the business of selling nicotine, an addictive drug effective in the release of stress mechanisms."

What the tobacco companies could not deny, however, was the fact that tobacco smoke was annoying and unpleasant for nonsmokers. Beginning in the 1970s, nonsmokers began to make their weight felt; as consumers of services, they began to demand freedom from cigarette smoke. The first to defer to this growing constituency were the airlines, where passengers were forced to sit for long periods within airtight vessels. In 1969, Pan Am became the first airline to offer a nonsmoking section, and, by 1990, smoking had been banned from virtually all U.S. flights.

Nonsmokers also began to put pressure on politicians. In 1973, Arizona passed the first statewide law requiring that smoking be restricted to designated indoor public places. Such bans and the adverse health news were having an effect. Between 1965 and 1980, the percentage of adults who regularly smoked tobacco fell from 42.4 percent to 33.2 percent, a drop of more than 20 percent.

The 1980s and 1990s saw more blows to tobacco consumption and the tobacco industry. In 1986, the annual *Surgeon General's Report on Smoking and Health* linked secondhand smoke to health problems for the first time, giving municipalities and states a medical reason for imposing ever harsher bans on indoor smoking. The report also stated that even smokeless tobacco is both cancer-causing and addictive.

Adding to the tobacco industry's woes were lawsuits pressed by tobacco users and their families. From 1954, when the first suit was filed, to the early 1990s, big tobacco faced more than 1,000 lawsuits demanding restitution for lost health and lost lives. But tobacco lawyers proved adept at deflecting the suits. First, they claimed that partaking of tobacco products was a choice made by the smoker; then, once the 1964 surgeon general's report came out, they effectively argued that smokers were aware of the dangers and still chose to smoke. Tobacco companies fought every case, fearing that settling a single one would lead to a cascade of new suits. The strategy was simple: The companies would use their deep pockets to bleed plaintiffs dry. As an attorney for R. J. Reynolds explained, "The way we won these cases was not by spending all of Reynolds' money, but by making that other son of a bitch spend all his."

Still, tobacco companies were hurting, as fewer and fewer Americans chose to smoke. Though the decline slowed, it remained inexorable; the percentage of smokers in America had fallen to just 28 percent by 2000, pushed downward by higher taxes on cigarettes and the introduction of new products to help people quit smoking, such as nicotine patches and chewing gum that eases the quitter's cravings.

Surgeon General's Report on Tobacco (1964)

On the morning of January 11, 1964, the surgeon general of the United States, Dr. Luther L. Terry, released a document that would have a profound and enduring effect on the health, habits, and lifestyle of the American people—the *Surgeon General's Report on Tobacco*. The report, which established a direct link between smoking and cancer, irrevocably altered the way that tobacco was seen and used in the United States.

Cigarette consumption had increased steadily during the early postwar period. Soldiers who had been given free cigarettes during the war became loyal customers when they returned home. Although German scientists had linked smoking to cancer as early as the 1930s, in the United States, smoking was generally seen as a harmless vice.

The first American study to link smoking to cancer was conducted in 1953 by researcher Ernst L. Wynders, who found that applying cigarette tar on the backs of mice caused tumors. Throughout the 1950s and early 1960s, American tobacco companies flatly denied the danger of cigarettes, but they did begin to promote "safer" filtered and reduced-tar cigarettes.

By the mid-1960s, more than half of all adult American men smoked, and more than 46 percent of all Americans smoked. Tobacco was a multibillion-dollar industry, and smoking was acceptable in most public areas, including offices, airplanes, and hospitals. But scientists and health officials in the federal government were troubled by the mounting evidence of smoking's dangers, and the administration of President John F. Kennedy commissioned the first surgeon general's report to learn the truth about tobacco. The report confirmed what scientists had been saying for years: Smoking causes cancer.

Government scientists knew the report would be controversial; others worried about its effects on Wall Street. To limit the damage to tobacco stocks, the press conference announcing the report was held on a Saturday morning in a highly guarded auditorium at the U.S. Department of State. At 7:30 A.M., the first copies of the 387-page document were delivered to the White House. Ninety minutes later, 200 accredited members of the press were "locked in" without telephones and given an hour and a half to review the report. After a two-hour question-and-answer period with Surgeon General Terry and his advisory committee, the press release was issued. By dinnertime, news of the report was sending shock waves across the country.

Based on more than 7,000 previously published articles, the *Surgeon General's Report on Tobacco* flatly stated that smoking was a major cause of lung cancer and laryngeal cancer in men and of lung cancer in women. It also noted that cigarette smoking was directly related to heart disease and was the leading contributory cause of death from chronic bronchitis and other lung disorders. "Cigarette smoking is a health hazard of sufficient importance in the United States to warrant appropriate remedial action," it affirmed.

Remedial actions were not explicitly stated, but the U.S. Congress responded to the report by passing two pieces of legislation—the Federal Cigarette Labeling and Advertising Act of 1965 and the Public Health Cigarette Smoking Act of 1969. These laws called for health warnings on cigarette packages, limited advertising in the broadcast media, and mandated an annual report on the health consequences of smoking. Additionally, the Public Health Service founded the National Clearinghouse for Smoking and Health (now the Office on Smoking and Health) in 1964.

Within three months of the report's release, cigarette consumption in America had dropped 20 percent. Although the number returned to pre-report levels in a matter of months, the number of Americans who smoke today has decreased from 46 percent in 1964 to approximately 20 percent.

Dawn Alexandrea Berry

Tobacco companies have been nothing if not resourceful in maintaining their profits. In an effort to blunt the image of smoking as unhealthful, R. J. Reynolds introduced the first low-tar nicotine cigarette, Vantage, in 1970, and several companies launched secret programs to develop "safe" cigarettes. In 1988, the company introduced Premier, a cigarette that merely heated rather than burned its tobacco, producing less carcinogenic smoke; it proved unpopular and was terminated.

The big tobacco companies also diversified. In 1988, Philip Morris bought Kraft Foods, and R. J. Reynolds merged with Nabisco. Recognizing that their product tended to kill the very people who bought it—and that greater numbers of people were quitting—some tobacco companies launched advertising campaigns to lure young people to smoke. The most notorious of these was R. J. Reynolds's Joe Camel campaign. Although the name had been used as early as 1975, the company decided to make Joe Camel a cartoon character in 1988. The move was highly effective: Within just three years, Camel's share of the U.S. market jumped from 3 percent to 13 percent. Critics said the campaign—with its point of purchase advertising near store candy counters and its sponsorship of sporting events popular with children—was a callous attempt to lure minors into smoking. Facing Federal Trade Commission complaints that the campaign violated federal law on children's advertising, the company reluctantly retired Joe Camel in 1997.

The U.S. tobacco industry's most successful effort to revive its fortunes came overseas. Recognizing that domestic demand was essentially flat or declining, American tobacco companies began to eye the more lucrative Asian market during the 1980s. Many governments there were resistant to U.S. tobacco penetration into their markets, either because they understood the health dangers of tobacco or, more typically, because they wanted to protect their own domestic manufacturers. Through heavy lobbying, however, the big American tobacco companies persuaded the Reagan Administration to put pressure on the Asian countries, threatening trade sanctions if the nations such as Japan and South Korea did not drop their restrictions on tobacco imports. Fearful of losing their biggest trade market, Asian governments conceded. By the early 1990s, sales of American cigarettes in Japan, as an example, were up 600 percent over the previous decade,

and heavy advertising pushed up average consumption there by nearly 10 percent.

At home, tobacco companies faced their biggest challenge yet. In 1994, Mississippi attorney general Michael Moore filed suit against the tobacco industry to make it pay the Medicaid costs the state had incurred for the 200,000 elderly Mississippians suffering from smoking-related illnesses. When the state government abandoned Moore and refused to pay for the lawsuit, he convinced some local plaintiff attorneys to fund the action, in return for a portion of the proceeds—which promised to be very large if Moore won the case.

In Congress, that same year, tobacco company executives were forced to testify under oath about their products. Their collective denial raised the ire of both Congress and the public. One member of the public, a former legal assistant at Brown and Williamson named Terrell Williams, was in a position to do something about it. In a celebrated example of corporate whistle-blowing, he turned over to the Mississippi lawyers thousands of internal documents showing that the tobacco companies had known their products were both hazardous to health and addictive.

Liggett Tobacco was the first to cave. In 1994, the company settled with Moore and twenty-one other state attorneys general who had joined the Mississippi suit. "We at Liggett," an official statement from the company read, "know and acknowledge that, as the Surgeon General and respected medical researchers have found, cigarette smoking causes health problems, including lung cancer, heart and vascular disease and emphysema. Liggett acknowledges that the tobacco industry markets to 'youth,' which means those under 18 years of age, and not just those 18–24 years of age."

Three years later, in 1997, the major tobacco companies offered a path-breaking settlement that included Food and Drug Administration regulation, bans on outdoor advertising and vending machines, and money for anti-smoking campaigns. The U.S. Senate banned the deal because, it concluded, the agreement protected the companies from further legal action.

Later that year, however, the tobacco industry reached a settlement with Mississippi, Florida, Minnesota, and Texas, offering $40 billion to reimburse the four states for their smoking-related Medicaid costs. In 1998, a settlement was reached with the remaining forty-six states and territories. Along with paying Medicaid costs—to the tune of nearly $250 billion over twenty-five years—the tobacco industry agreed to pledge hundreds of millions of dollars for anti-smoking campaigns.

Despite these huge settlements, the tobacco industry was not out of the legal woods yet. It still faced hundreds of private lawsuits. Though several tobacco companies had lost individual suits during the 1990s, juries had been persuaded to accept their argument that the plaintiffs were primarily responsible for their health problems and had rewarded them no damages. In 2000, however, a California jury ordered Philip Morris to pay $51.5 million to a woman suffering from inoperable lung cancer. Later that year, an Oregon jury ordered the company to pay $81 million to the family of a man who had died after smoking Marlboro cigarettes for forty years.

Meanwhile, in 1999, the Clinton Administration opened a case to get the tobacco industry to pay for the federal government's smoking-related health costs. By the early 2000s, the administration of George W. Bush was demanding a settlement of $130 billion from the industry for a twenty-five-year anti-smoking program.

Suddenly, in 2005, the U.S. Department of Justice announced it would accept a $10 billion settlement, claiming that its case was weak. Many legal experts, as well as Democrats in Congress, were shocked and dismayed by the settlement, claiming that the case was strong and that the Bush Administration, as well as pro-administration Republicans in Congress, had caved in to big tobacco—which had spent an estimated $129 million lobbying on Capitol Hill since 1999 and donated roughly $13 million to federal candidates (most of it to Republicans) between 2000 and 2004.

James Ciment

See also: Agriculture; Diet and Food; Health Care; Medicine; Science, Government Policy on.

Bibliography

Hilts, Philip J. *Smokescreen: The Truth Behind the Tobacco Industry Cover-Up.* Reading, MA: Addison-Wesley, 1996.

Kluger, Richard. *Ashes to Ashes: America's Hundred-Year Cigarette War, the Public Health, and the Unabashed Triumph of Philip Morris.* New York: Vintage Books, 1997.

Parker-Pope, Tara. *Cigarettes: Anatomy of an Industry from Seed to Smoke.* New York: New Press, 2001.

TONKIN GULF RESOLUTION

SEE Gulf of Tonkin Resolution

TORT LAW

Until the 1940s and, in particular, immediately after the end of the World War II, doctrines of American tort law remained relatively stable, reflecting trends that harkened back to the nineteenth century. Particularly notorious among the nineteenth century holdovers were limits to recovery that heavily favored industry, such as assumption of risk, absence of recovery for the loss of a loved one, and the "fellow-servant" rule, which barred damages caused by an injured employees' co-workers.

1950s and 1960s

Especially during the 1950s and 1960s, however, tort law began to erode timeworn defenses and expanded theories of liability. One example appeared in the defense of contributory negligence, which barred plaintiffs from recovering any damages whatsoever if they had played even the smallest role in the incident leading to their injuries. The defense reflected the extreme reluctance of late-nineteenth- through early-twentieth-century legislators and judges to allow large tort damages because of their fear that such awards could discourage technological innovation and modernization, ironically, because of the great amount of harm that they caused. For example, according to one legal historian, in a single, one-year period, between 1888 and 1889, 1,972 railway employees lost their lives and 20,028 were injured.

Gradually, during the pre–World War II period, another tort defense, comparative negligence, proportionately allocating damages between defendant and plaintiff, came into being, thus making it possible for victims to recover part of their damages even if they were partially at fault. In the first decade following the end of the war, comparative negligence gained recognition among a handful of states; by the 1970s, it coexisted with or displaced the contributory negligence defense.

During the 1960s, another postwar change, strict liability for manufacturers of defective products, emerged. Previously, plaintiffs had to rely on contract

The Ford Pinto and Product Liability

In 1972, thirteen-year-old Richard Grimshaw sustained life-changing injuries in a car accident while riding in a Ford Pinto. The car's driver was killed, one of dozens of deaths in the 1970s attributed to a design flaw in the vehicle. Grimshaw sued the Ford Motor Company and was awarded millions of dollars on the grounds that the company knew about the flaw but did not fix it. The verdict laid the foundation for other product liability cases of the 1980s and 1990s.

At the start of the 1970s, the Ford Motor Company and other American automobile makers found themselves fighting off competition from overseas companies that offered fuel-efficient compact cars as opposed to the larger American models. Scrambling to keep up, Ford introduced the Pinto in 1971. Advertised as weighing under 2,000 pounds and costing under $2,000, the car was an immediate hit, with 250,000 sold in the first year.

One was purchased by Lilly Gray, who drove to Barstow, California, with Grimshaw as a passenger in April 1972. The vehicle stalled on the freeway and was rear-ended by the car behind it, causing the Pinto to burst into flames. Gray was killed. Grimshaw suffered disfiguring burns over 90 percent of his body and lost four fingers, his nose, and an ear. Grimshaw sued, arguing that the location of the Pinto's gas tank made the car unsafe.

Evidence revealed that Ford had known about the vulnerability but had not fixed it, fearing that it would cost money and add weight, putting the car over the $2,000 and 2,000-pound thresholds. The jury sided with Grimshaw, awarding him $2.5 million in compensatory damages for his injuries and a shocking $125 million in punitive damages against Ford.

Until this time, awards of punitive damages in product liability cases were rare. Most American courts subscribed to the theory of strict tort liability and did not allow such awards at all. Companies were responsible for their products, it was thought, not their conduct. But what if a company's conduct was so unethical that it needed to be deterred from similar conduct in the future? In that case, juries began favoring large punitive damage awards, as in *Grimshaw v. Ford Motor Company*.

In *Grimshaw*, however, the judge found $125 million to be excessive; he cut the punitive damage award to $3.5 million, which Ford appealed. In 1981, a California appeals court sustained the $3.5 million award, noting that it amounted to only .005 percent of Ford's net worth.

The *Grimshaw* case was only the beginning of bad Pinto publicity. The September/October 1977 issue of *Mother Jones* magazine featured an investigatory article called "Pinto Madness"; it cited internal company reports and other documents on problems with the vehicle. After a petition from the Center for Auto Safety, the National Highway Transportation Safety Administration launched a defect investigation and found thirty-eight cases of fuel system damage, gas leakages, and fire. Lawsuits piled up, and Pinto sales dropped. By 1978, twenty-seven people had died in Pinto crashes. In June of that year, Ford recalled 1.5 million Pintos to improve the filler pipe and install a polyethylene shield that would protect the gas tank.

After the *Grimshaw* verdict, a lawyer called the jury's decision "the loudest noise that a jury has made in any civil suit in American jurisprudence." Thereafter, juries assigned liability to companies with increasing frequency, especially if plaintiffs could prove foreknowledge of problems that a company failed to correct.

In the Ford Pinto case, early tests had shown that the car's fuel tank design was dangerous, but a cost-benefit analysis had balanced "human lives and limbs against corporate profits." It would have cost about $10 per car to fix the flawed automobile.

Melissa Stallings

theories in order to hold a manufacturer liable for defective products. Such theories assumed a contractual relationship between the manufacturer and the purchaser through warranties, which could make manufacturers liable for defects. However, the greatest hurdle for plaintiffs under contract theories was that there was often no direct relationship between the manufacturer and buyer; this was particularly true if there were a chain of events between manufacture and sale. The proliferation of large manufacturing concerns distributing products across the country further debilitated the connection between manufacturer and buyer, making it difficult for plaintiffs to prove that the manufacturer was the cause of injuries.

Under strict liability, however, manufacturers were liable for whatever injuries their products caused, regardless of any intervening events. The change occurred for various reasons. Legislatures and courts in the postwar era recognized that the rise of large manufacturing and distribution networks—arising, in part, as an offshoot of the huge war industry—had made anachronisms of prewar notions about direct contractual relationships between manufacturers and consumers. Another reason was that the tens of thousands of automobile accident victims each year necessitated a revision of earlier doctrines, especially if manufacturing defects were involved. A third reason was that legal scholars, judges, and legislators realized that the United States was one of the few countries retaining the contributory negligence defense, something that the majority of other developed nations had replaced with comparative negligence.

During the postwar period, change occurred also in the safeguarding of privacy. Prior to the mid-1940s, the main remedy for intrusion into one's private life had been a lawsuit based on infliction of emotional distress. This, however, required that the plaintiff prove that the distress was severe to an imaginary, hypothetical average person; if such a hypothetical plaintiff would not have suffered from severe distress, there was no recovery. Torts based on invasion of privacy, however, changed that. It became possible to sue because of embarrassment to the actual victim, not to a hypothetical average person.

During the 1960s, privacy gained even more protection. In the 1965 case of *Griswold v. Connecticut*, the U.S. Supreme Court held that a Connecticut law prohibiting the dissemination of advice to married couples about contraceptive use violated federal constitutional protections of privacy. The Court decided the case in an historical era of growing consciousness about civil liberties as manifested in protests against the draft, of Southern states' continuing segregationist policies, and of gender discrimination across the country.

1970s and 1980s

Nor were changes in negligence defenses, product liability, and privacy the only changes in the first few decades of the postwar period. Between the 1940s and early 1970s, there was also a notable expansion of tort liability in areas such as occupational safety, landowner and tenant relationships, professional malpractice, and environmental and consumer protection. The election of John F. Kennedy, Lyndon Johnson's Great Society and the War on Poverty, and the civil rights, women's, environmental, and antiwar movements further encouraged reconsideration of public policies.

At the other end of the spectrum, there was a gradual movement away from expanding liability. This appeared in the guise of "tort reform" movements, which gained momentum after the 1970s and which, in spite of the progressive-sounding phrase, have often masked the interests of major corporations and the health care industry. Between the mid-1970s and mid-1980s, such limited liability movements enjoyed only minimal success.

The presidential administrations of Gerald Ford and Jimmy Carter witnessed an effort to encourage uniformity in tort liability through the promulgation of a model tort law, but few states adopted it, and those that did copied only parts of it. From 1981 to 1993, the presidential administrations of Ronald Reagan and George H.W. Bush made relatively unsuccessful attempts to limit liability by shifting some types of lawsuits from state to federal courts.

The lack of success that big business and the health care lobby experienced during the 1970s and the 1980s led them to shift their focus to eroding liability under consumer protection laws and changing regulations for specific industries. By the mid-1990s, the new strategy began to bear fruit when President Bill Clinton, although generally favoring consumers over big business, signed into law legislation limiting liability in aviation.

1990s and 2000s

However limited the successes of the tort reform lobby had been until the mid-1990s, one of the pivotal events leading to future limitations on corporate, health care, and professional liability had occurred in 1986, when a broad range of powerful business interests, including Johnson & Johnson, the Sporting Arms & Ammunition Manufacturers Association, Ruger and other gun manufacturers, Philip Morris and tobacco companies, and various health-care organizations formed the American Tort Reform Association.

Persistent corporate lobbying eventually led to rewards, such as Congress's 1995 overriding of President Clinton's veto of legislation limiting liability in securities fraud. The administration of George W. Bush then announced that the president would do at the federal level what he did in his home state of Texas, which, until the mid-1990s, had been one of the most consumer-friendly states, but, by the time Bush entered the White House, had become one of the most pro-business.

Beginning in the mid-1990s, limitations on tort liability gained momentum across the country. By 2001, at least forty-five states had enacted tort reform legislation, much of it aimed at limiting punitive damages to two or three times the amount of actual harm. In the first eight months of 2005, forty-eight states introduced a total of at least 400 bills addressing tort liability, with about two-thirds enacting approximately fifty new laws, many of which limited liability for medical professionals.

At the same time, corporate interests stepped up their efforts to cut down liability to consumers by contributing as much as $12 million to a single state judicial election campaign, thus also raising questions about impairing the democratic process. And yet, even as the tort lobby made significant inroads, its efforts did not always go without check, as state courts in about a half dozen states have declared some caps on damages to be unconstitutional.

Other trends have also become apparent in recent decades. One has been a general retreat from massive jury awards, as judges, legislators, and the American public noticed that juries were awarding huge damages for seemingly trivial lawsuits. Another trend has been a critique of the decades-old concept of the "reasonable person" standard for gauging the boundaries of legally acceptable conduct.

Feminist scholars began to argue in favor of a gender-specific standard, asserting that the "reasonable person" in negligence cases implicitly assumes the perspective of a male and should not apply to females. In some instances, racial minorities began

making analogous claims, asserting that it is not the perspective of a hypothetical, supposedly race-neutral "reasonable person," but that of a "reasonable person" of a particular race that should be the standard in cases such as those based on emotional distress from race-based victimization.

Tort law evolved significantly between the pre–World War II era and the postwar period. Although postwar doctrines remain largely rooted in prewar frameworks, there have been variations on the earlier theories. In general, there has been an expansion of tort liability favoring victims over their prewar tortfeasor (person committing the tort) counterparts. As the period between the mid-nineteenth century and the present seems to indicate, however, the evolution of tort law seems to be cyclical, sometimes limiting and sometimes expanding liability.

Michael Serizawa Brown

See also: Automobile Industry; Crime, Property; Dalkon Shield Controversy; Insider Trading Scandals; Toxic Shock Syndrome; Tylenol Tampering Incident.

Bibliography

Bogus, Carl T., *Why Lawsuits Are Good for America: Disciplined Democracy, Big Business, and the Common Law.* Critical America series, edited by Richard Delgado and Jean Stefancie. New York: New York University Press, 2001.

Davies, Julia A., Lawrence C. Levine, and Edward J. Kionka, eds. *A Torts Anthology.* 2nd ed. Cincinnati, OH: Anderson, 1999.

Friedman, Lawrence M. *A History of American Law.* 2nd ed. New York: Simon and Schuster, 1985.

Huber, Peter W. *Liability: The Legal Revolution and Its Consequences.* New York: Basic Books, 1988.

Rabin, Robert L. *Perspectives on Tort Law.* 4th ed. New York: Little, Brown, 1995.

White, G. Edward. *Tort Law in America: An Intellectual History.* New York: Oxford University Press, 2003.

TOXIC SHOCK SYNDROME

Toxic shock syndrome (TSS) is marked by a sudden onset of fever, rash, vomiting, hypotension, and low blood pressure. It is caused by *Staphylococcus aureus* infection. This bacterium is found on the skin and mucous membranes of most people. While its presence does not necessarily lead to disease, *Staphylococcus aureus* can result in the development of skin infections (boils and abscesses), wound infections, blood infections, and some forms of food poisoning.

The most susceptible groups are menstruating women, women using barrier contraceptive devices, and persons who have undergone nasal surgery. In the United States, the annual incidence of TSS is 1–2 per 100,000 women aged fifteen to forty-four. About 5 percent of cases are fatal.

TSS was first described in 1978, when seven children aged eight to seventeen became infected in Wisconsin. It was not until April 1983, however, when a Kansas mother of two, Betty O'Gilvie, died of TSS, that it became associated with menstruation and tampon use.

Procter & Gamble had released a line of superabsorbent tampon products called Playtex Rely made of compressed beads of polyester and carboxymethyl cellulose. This material, which could hold nearly twenty times its weight in fluids, caused a drying out of the normally mucus-coated vaginal vault. Women had complained that if they wore one of these tampons too long, residue remained, and tears appeared on the vaginal walls when the device was removed. Some women even had to seek medical treatment to get the tampons removed. Food and Drug Administration (FDA) regulations at the time did not cover tampons.

O'Gilvie's family sued the manufacturer on the grounds that the product's warning label was inadequate. Although Proctor & Gamble had followed FDA labeling standards, a federal jury awarded compensatory damages and $10 million in punitive damages to the deceased woman's family in 1987. Although Proctor & Gamble had met the minimum criteria, the jury believed that stronger product warnings were warranted under these circumstances. Following the verdict, Rely tampons were withdrawn from the market, Playtex strengthened its warnings on other products about the association between tampons and TSS, and the company initiated a public education program to warn about the dangers of TSS.

Since its association with tampons was identified, the incidence of TSS has declined significantly. Key factors attributed to the decline include changes in the composition and absorbency of tampons. Withdrawal of the Rely brand, which consisted of a unique composition, forced other manufacturers to lower the absorbency of all tampons. The FDA now regulates tampons as a medical device and sets the absorbency standards. Tampons identified as ultra-absorbent are 15-to-18-gram tampons that may help women manage heavier menstrual flows.

Compared with the 813 menstrual TSS cases in 1980, only three cases were confirmed in 1998 and six in 1997. Consequently, TSS induced by tampon use became virtually nonexistent.

Suzanne M. Carter

See also: Dalkon Shield Controversy; Health Care; Tort Law.

Bibliography

Hanrahan, S.N. "Historical Review of Menstrual Toxic Shock Syndrome." *Women Health* 21:2–3 (1994): 141–45.

Higgins, S.P., and J.R. Horsley. "The Toxic Shock Syndrome." *BMJ* 300:6738 (1990): 1523.

Meadow, Michelle. "Tampon Safety: TSS Now Rare, but Women Still Should Take Care." *FDA Consumer* 34:2 (2000).

Reingold, A.L. "Toxic Shock Syndrome: An Update." *American Journal of Obstetrics and Gynecology* 165:4, Pt. 2 (1991): 1236–39.

Riley, Tom. *The Price of a Life: One Woman's Death from Toxic Shock.* Bethesda, MD: Adler and Adler, 1986.

TRANQUILIZERS

At their peak use in 1975, sedative-hypnotics—better known as minor tranquilizers—were by far the most widely prescribed class of drugs in the history of the United States. The best known of these drugs, diazepam, sold as Valium, became a household name. Sedative-hypnotic drugs relieve anxiety and insomnia by depressing the central nervous system. Since the 1960s, controversy over the addictiveness and efficacy of tranquilizers has been widespread among doctors, medical researchers, the media, and the public at large.

Valium, and nearly all of the other widely used tranquilizers that became popular in the 1960s, belongs to a class of drugs called the benzodiazepines. Before the synthesis of the first benzodiazepine in 1957, barbiturates were the sedative drug of choice—phenobarbital, in particular, was popular. Although doctors had been using barbiturates since 1903, concern was growing that they were too addictive, and researchers began exploring newer, less potent agents. In 1955, the first nonbarbiturate sedative, meprobamate (brand name Miltown), hit the market, and it became, for a time, the most well known of the minor tranquilizers.

In 1957, researchers at the pharmaceutical giant Hoffmann-La Roche synthesized the first benzodiazepine, called chlordiazepoxide (Librium). The drug was approved for marketing in February 1960, and it soon surpassed Miltown in popularity. Its own popularity was eclipsed three years later with the introduction of one of its analogues, diazepam (Valium), another Hoffmann-La Roche product.

The proliferation of new drugs was spurred by the enormous profits to be had in a nation that, by 1960, was spending $280 million a year on tranquilizers. At the same time, the marketing of such drugs was facilitated by relatively lax FDA requirements then in effect. The pharmaceutical advances of the 1950s were well publicized, and the development of Miltown, and later Valium, sparked plenty of controversy—from glowing endorsements to impassioned criticism. Especially in the earlier days, the media tended to embrace the new "happy pills" (or, as one headline dubbed them, "aspirin for the soul"), deeming them effective, modern, and safe.

By the end of the decade, though, people were expressing concern that America's use of tranquilizers was getting out of hand. One of the main currents of the growing and varied objections to tranquilizers was the so-called "Pharmacological Calvinism" response: the idea that "escaping" from the problems of daily life with a pill was an indication of moral weakness or character deficiency. Another criticism was that widespread anxiety was indicative of a larger societal problem and should be addressed through fundamental social changes rather than individual medication. Other objections targeted the drugs' potential for addiction and abuse. Senator Estes Kefauver (Democrat of Tennessee) led a Congressional investigation of the drug industry in 1957 and attacked the advertising and corporate policies of the big pharmaceutical companies that produced tranquilizers.

Despite the controversy, tranquilizer use continued to rise through the 1960s. Jacqueline Susann's *Valley of the Dolls,* a best-selling 1966 novel, chronicled the terrible impact of tranquilizers and other drugs on the lives of young single women in New York City.

By 1970, tens of millions of Americans were taking sedative-hypnotic medications: 20 percent of women and 8 percent of men. Tranquilizer use peaked in 1975, with more than 100 million prescriptions written that year, although use began to decline after mid-decade. In 1977, after two decades of uncertainty over diagnostic and prescription procedures among doctors, the FDA published its official "Guidelines for the Clinical Evaluation of Anti-Anxiety Drugs."

An FDA report in the early 1980s still identified Valium as the number-one prescription drug in the country, but criticism of the tranquilizers continued. Ralph Nader's consumer-rights group Public Citizen exposed the medical dangers in *Stopping Valium* (1982). The book charged that the drug was addictive and especially dangerous for pregnant women, the elderly, and drivers.

Prescriptions for tranquilizers declined steadily through the 1980s. Alprazolam (Xanax), another benzodiazepine, became the most widely prescribed of the minor tranquilizers in 1986. Tranquilizer prescriptions had leveled off at around 61 million per year by 1990.

All benzodiazepines—in fact all of the sedative-hypnotics—are habit forming, even at therapeutic doses. The evidence is quite clear that tolerance and dependency can develop in both the long-acting type (used to treat anxiety) and the short-acting type (used to treat insomnia) of benzodiazepine. Even after only a few months of medication, getting off tranquilizers can be difficult. Upon stopping the medication or moving to a lower dose, patients frequently experience "rebound insomnia" and/or "rebound anxiety," becoming overly alert as their brains continue to compensate for the CNS-depressant effects of the (now absent) drug. The "rebound" symptoms feel very much like the original anxiety, and patients are likely to get back on medication to relieve them.

Abuse of tranquilizers is not common. When it does happen, it is almost always in conjunction with the abuse of other drugs, most frequently opiates like heroin. It is more prevalent in people with a history of addiction. Some tranquilizers are abused more often than others.

Flunitrazepam (Rohypnol), introduced by Hoffmann-La Roche in 1975, became infamous in the early 1990s for its use as a club drug and so-called "date rape" drug. Although no longer legally available in the United States, it is often prescribed in Western Europe and elsewhere. Similarly, the highly addictive methaqualone (Quaaludes), used to treat insomnia, was widely abused in the 1960s and 1970s. The Drug Enforcement Agency (DEA) decreed it a "Schedule I" drug in 1984, putting it in the category of substances deemed to be highly addictive and with no medical use.

The DEA began to regulate tranquilizers in general in 1975, classifying the benzodiazepines and meprobamate (Miltown) as "Schedule IV" drugs, or drugs with low abuse potential that the federal government leaves up to states and localities to regulate. Still, the classification meant stricter prescription-refill controls and record-keeping requirements, as well as an official acknowledgment that the drugs have "abuse potential."

Although their use has declined, tranquilizers are still a popular prescription drug in the United States, disproportionately so among women. Some of the more common benzodiapines are alprazolam (Xanax), clonazepam (Klonopin), clorazepate (Tranxene), diazepam (Valium), flurazepam (Dalmane), lorazepam (Ativan), oxazepam (Serax), temazepam (Restoril), and triazolam (Halcion). Benzodiazepines are also prescribed for reasons other than inducing sleep and lowering anxiety, including prevention of convulsive disorders, pre-surgical sedation, and alcohol detoxification.

The terminology can be confusing, because antipsychotic drugs—used to treat schizophrenia and the manic phase of bipolar disorder—are sometimes also called the "major tranquilizers." They are not merely stronger versions of the minor tranquilizers but a different class of drugs entirely (called the neuroleptics). These, too, were developed in the 1950s.

Suzanne Julian

See also: Drug Culture; Drug and Alcohol Rehabilitation Programs; Medicine; Mental Health; Psychiatry.

Bibliography

Gibe, Jonathan, ed. *Understanding Tranquilliser Use: The Role of the Social Sciences.* London: Tavistock, 1991.

Gorman, Jack M., M.D. *Essential Guide to Psychiatric Drugs.* New York: St. Martin's, 1998.

Smith, Mickey C. *Small Comfort: A History of the Minor Tranquilizers.* New York: Praeger, 1985.

TRANSCENDENTAL MEDITATION

Pioneered in the 1950s by Maharishi Mahesh Yogi, a Hindu monk from India, transcendental meditation (TM) is a relaxation technique designed to reduce stress and enhance a person's physical and mental potential. The word "transcendental" was intended to

The Indian Hindu monk Maharishi Mahesh Yogi (center) introduced transcendental meditation—a form of yogic relaxation—to the West during the 1960s. Adherents such as the Beatles George Harrison (left) and John Lennon (right) helped spread the movement. *(Keystone/ Getty Images)*

signify that the practitioner transcends ordinary reality and achieves a higher state of consciousness. Adopted by celebrities, most notably the Beatles, the practice gradually caught on with the public during the late 1960s. By the middle of the 1970s, it was estimated that more than 350,000 Americans were practicing TM. Maharishi also began referring to the practice as the "Science of Creative Intelligence" in 1971, but the name TM stuck with the public.

Ideally, the practice involves several sessions of meditation per day. The practitioner chooses a word or phrase, known as a mantra, drawn from the Vedas (Hindu holy scripture) that has special spiritual significance to the practitioner. By repeating the mantra, focusing on breathing, and attempting to prevent wandering thoughts from entering the mind, the practitioner loses ordinary consciousness and enters a meditative state. At the end of the meditation, usually lasting between ten and thirty minutes, the practitioner is said to experience enhanced calmness and energy.

During the late 1960s and 1970s, the practice became increasingly institutionalized with teachers and centers helping people learn the practice. Maharishi developed a course that included seven steps: an introductory lecture, a preparatory lecture, an interview with a TM teacher, personal instruction, assessment, understanding of TM mechanics, and understanding of the meaning of higher states of consciousness. Most practitioners of TM insist, however, that these steps are merely part of a technique and not rituals in a religion. TM, they argue, is thus a practice and not a faith.

Maharishi first introduced the technique to others in 1957 and began training teachers in the early 1970s. Prior to that, those who wanted to learn TM had to learn from him directly, either in India or during his frequent travels to Europe and the United States. In 1974, he established Maharishi International University (renamed Maharishi University of Management in 1995) in Fairfield, Iowa. The university offers instruction in how to apply the techniques of TM to business, medicine, and other professions.

Western science has verified the benefits of TM in several hundred studies since the 1960s. While the findings vary, the general consensus is that TM can reduce stress and anxiety, while helping to alleviate the physical ailments associated with those mental states. In addition, research sponsored by the National Institute of Mental Health concluded that TM can help people reduce or eliminate their addictions to drugs, alcohol, and tobacco. Both the U.S. Army and U.S. Bureau of Prisons have officially recognized TM as an addiction recovery program.

Today, it is estimated that some 5 million people around the world practice TM, with about 2 million of them in the United States. Explaining the popularity of the practice in the United States, Maharishi maintained that "creative intelligence can only be appreciated in a country that is more evolved . . . [The] United States is the most creative country in the world."

Part of the lasting success of this practice in the United States in the 1990s and 2000s is attributed to the writings and lectures of best-selling author and medical doctor Deepak Chopra, an advocate of transcendental meditation.

Matthew N. Drumheller

See also: Counterculture; Encounter Groups; New Age and Eastern Religions; Self-Awareness Movements.

Bibliography

Forem, Jack. *Transcendental Meditation: Maharishi Mahesh Yogi and the Science of Creative Intelligence.* New York: Dutton, 1973.

Maharishi Mahesh Yogi. *Science of Being and Art of Living: Transcendental Meditation.* New York: Dutton, 1963.

Mason, Paul. *The Maharishi: The Biography of the Man Who Gave Transcendental Meditation to the World.* Rockport, MA: Element, 1994.

TRANSPORTATION

At the beginning of the postwar era, trains remained the dominant form of land transportation in the United States. This was true for both passengers and freight, as well as for urban and intercity transportation. There was, of course, competition. Highway construction and mass-produced automobiles had come to have a significant impact on railroad passenger traffic and intercity freight traffic by the 1920s. Air travel, however, remained a luxury of the rich into the early postwar era, and air freight was confined to high-value, low-weight items such as mail.

With the establishment of the interstate highway system and the development of urban expressways and freeways in the 1950s, buses and automobiles became the primary form of urban and intercity transportation, while trucks became increasingly competitive with railroads for the hauling of freight. Similarly, the advent of the jet age in the 1950s and falling airfares by the 1970s made airline transport the dominant form of long- and medium-distance passenger transportation in the United States.

Railroads

Railroads provided the backbone for America's industrial economy from the Civil War through World War II, facing little competition in transporting raw materials, manufactured products, business travelers, and tourists. The late 1800s and early 1900s have been remembered as the "golden age" of railroading, but trains carried the vast majority of intercity passengers as late as 1945. By the 1960s, competition from trucks, airplanes, buses, and other modes of transportation had forced railroads to specialize in hauling long-distance bulk freight.

The economics and technologies of railroading encouraged its shift to a more specialized role. The high fixed costs of building and maintaining railroad infrastructures—rails, cars, switches, and terminals—have historically been offset by relatively low unit costs for fuel and labor. Overall operating costs were thus lowest, and freight rates were most competitive, on long-distance shipments of bulk goods requiring little specialized service. As competition from trucks increased in the 1940s, railroads began modernizing equipment to improve operating efficiency and to lower unit costs still further. Diesel engines, with vastly better fuel economy and lower maintenance costs than steam locomotives, were first deployed in 1941 and were used in 92 percent of rail services by 1957. Service was also improved during the 1950s by heavy welded rails, longer and faster trains, new custom cars, such as automobile racks and "Big John" grain hoppers, and improved traffic control for speedier, more reliable service.

Despite these efforts, railroads faced continual difficulties in competing with other transportation modes, partly because of rate floors set by the Interstate Commerce Commission (ICC). The early 1970s brought a series of bankruptcies, halted only in 1976, when Congress salvaged the remains of six major freight lines by creating Conrail, a corporation established to receive federal funds for infrastructure modernization. Railroad profits improved over the next two decades, particularly following the expansion of containerized shipping—the use of standardized cargo boxes that could be moved seamlessly between ships, trains, and trucks to maximize the advantages of each mode of transport.

In 1984, the double-stack container was successfully engineered, giving a single train the capacity of 200 trucks. Between 1980 and 1997, intermodal traffic grew from 3 million containers to 8.7 million, accounting for 17 percent of all rail revenues. Railroads intensified their efforts to capture profitable cargoes; by 1997, rails carried 70 percent of the nation's automobiles from factories to dealerships, as well as 65 percent of coal shipments. Measured in ton-miles (the movement of one ton of freight one mile), railroads in 1997 led all other forms of transportation, hauling 40 percent of intercity shipments compared to 28 percent for trucks, 14 percent for boats and barges, and 18 percent for pipelines.

With the expansion of the interstate highway system in the 1940s and 1950s, however, long-haul trucking became the nation's primary mode of freight transportation. Railroads continued to haul more ton-miles of freight, but trucks captured the most valuable hauls by the 1970s, especially manufactured products, machinery, food, livestock and perishable agricultural products, household goods, and chemicals. Shippers increasingly chose trucks for their flexibility—their ability to travel anywhere there were roads, to pick up

and deliver loads on short notice, and to provide customized hauling capabilities such as reliable mechanical refrigeration, livestock trailers, and hazardous chemical tankers. The trucking industry became a major political, economic, and cultural force in the 1960s and 1970s, the latter signaled by a string of hit country and western songs such as "Six Days on the Road" (1963) and popular movies like *Convoy* (1978).

In 1964, the International Brotherhood of Teamsters achieved unprecedented power with the signing of the Master Freight Agreement, which established wage scales for some 400,000 truck drivers across the nation. Plagued by scandals involving organized crime and racketeering charges, Teamster membership dwindled to 300,000 by 1980, with the union representing less than 25 percent of all truck drivers by 2000. The American Trucking Associations, meanwhile, maintained a strong lobbying force representing the interests of large commercial trucking firms in Washington on issues of taxation, regulation, and highway funding.

Barges and pipelines also became major competitors to the railroads in postwar America, particularly in the shipment of heavy basic commodities such as coal, grain, petroleum, and natural gas. The Army Corps of Engineers had revived the nation's rivers as major transportation arteries by the 1940s, as the 12,000 miles of inland water routes formerly traversed by steamboats were overhauled with deep dredging, jetties and levees for flood control, and intricate lock-and-dam systems to assure smooth and reliable barge movement.

The cost efficiency of moving dry bulk cargo by water—more than twice as energy-efficient as rail freight and eight times more efficient than trucking—proved especially important on the Mississippi River system during the postwar period. More than one-third of all barge traffic, or 700 million tons of cargo, traveled on the Mississippi and Ohio rivers and their tributaries by the mid-1990s.

Pipelines, like waterways, had been in use since the nineteenth century, but the network expanded dramatically in the postwar period in response to rising demand for petroleum products. Pipe diameters grew from 24 inches to the "Big Inch" standard of 56 inches after 1945, while total interstate pipeline mileage rose from 137,500 in 1945 to 313,000 in 1975. The era of giant pipeline building culminated with the construction of the $9 billion Trans-Alaska Pipeline between 1973 and 1981, after which concerns about environmental damage from oil spills,

Interstate Highway System

Despite its name, the National System of Interstate and Defense Highways emerged not out of military necessity but from a widespread public commitment to high-speed, intercity and interstate automobile travel. Considered the largest public works project in world history, the 41,000-mile, $27-billion system created by the Federal Aid Highway Act of 1956 resulted from a decades-long drive for a coordinated network of limited-access freeways.

Before 1956, highway users could agree on little more than the desire for more roads. Automobile clubs wanted fast intercity highways, funded by either gasoline taxes or tolls, which truckers refused to pay. Farmers wanted farm-to-market roads funded by general tax revenues, while urban planners saw expressways as tools for slum clearance. In the Federal Aid Highway Act of 1944, Congress responded to these demands by appropriating $1.5 billion for roads, but without designating funds to build the planned 40,000 miles of interstate expressways. Construction was left to state engineers who were committed to moving traffic efficiently over existing roads rather than building a new system.

By 1950, the number of registered passenger cars in the United States had doubled from the 1940 figure of 27 million, while trucking freight had increased by one-third since 1949. State-funded highway construction fell behind, leading to congestion and deterioration of outdated roads.

The National Highway Users Conference (established in 1932 by General Motors chairman Alfred Sloan) initiated Project Adequate Roads in 1951 to demand strict highway rating standards to force federal financing of intercity expressways. Although backed by powerful lobbyists—including the American Trucking Association, American Automobile Association, petroleum firms, road contractors, and auto manufacturers—the project resulted in little more than publicity, after truckers refused to accept higher gasoline taxes to finance the plan.

Serious federal commitment to interstates did not come until 1954, when President Dwight D. Eisenhower, influenced by his Council of Economic Advisers, sought dramatically

---

fires, and lost wildlife habitat discouraged new projects. Nonetheless, by 1990, pipelines carried approximately 50 percent of the nation's refined petroleum at lower cost than other modes of transportation.

Airline and Bus Competition

Airlines dominated commercial intercity passenger travel beginning in the 1950s. Commercial airlines before World War II served the U.S. Postal Service almost exclusively, since travelers considered airlines expensive, unreliable, and unsafe. The availability of sturdy but inexpensive surplus military planes like the DC-3 gave a boost to the postwar industry, leading to a fiftyfold increase in the number of miles traveled by passengers on airlines between 1940 and 1963.

Airlines developed special services to entice customers who would otherwise travel by rail or bus, including discounted "coach" tickets and special vacation packages to faraway places like Alaska and Europe. Government funding of airport construction, automated scheduling services and air traffic control, and the creation in 1958 of the Federal Aviation Agency (later Administration) helped improve the reliability, comfort, and safety of air travel. In the late 1950s, the implementation of jet engines, adapted from military aeronautics, significantly reduced fuel costs, while boosting travel speeds. By the 1970s, airlines carried three of every five commercial intercity passengers, becoming especially dominant in long-distance travel.

Buses competed successfully for medium-distance passenger traffic from the 1940s to the 1960s. Offering cheaper rates than trains and faster service than airplanes on short trips, commercial bus lines such as Greyhound (founded in 1926) saw their peak ridership of 27 billion passenger miles in 1945 remain steady for the next twenty years.

increased highway construction to create jobs and economic growth. In July 1954, the president established the Advisory Committee on a National Highway Program to work with the groups represented in Project Adequate Roads, along with state governors and congressional representatives, to hammer out a compromise that would allow such an increase in federal highway funding.

The solution came in June 1956 with the invention of the Highway Trust Fund, which tied highway financing directly to federal taxes on fuel and tires. The more cars and trucks Americans bought and drove, the more highways they would get. At the same time, the fund's revenues were not allowed to support public transportation or pollution abatement. With federal funding guaranteed at 90 percent of construction cost through the target completion date of 1969, interstates rapidly expanded.

The interstate system changed the face of America. Interchange exits sprouted chain restaurants, motels, and gas stations willing to pay inflated land prices for these locations in order to take advantage of the guaranteed trucker and tourist traffic. Suburbs expanded as freeway commuters halved their travel time to downtown jobs.

Three-quarters of the system's mileage was in place or under construction by 1969, but the results of untrammeled expansion led to criticism. Environmental groups such as the Sierra Club condemned the increase in air pollution and the covering of rural landscapes in concrete. Residents in Boston, New Orleans, Washington, D.C., and other U.S. cities blamed expressways for intensifying racial segregation by dividing white and black neighborhoods and destroying the downtown neighborhoods they plowed through.

By the mid-1970s, state and local politicians canceled planned portions of the system. The number of new highway miles constructed in 1979 dropped to 66,000 from a high of 172,000 in 1970. Rising social and economic costs forced governments to focus on repairing and maintaining a system that was no longer universally desired.

Shane Hamilton

Rapid growth of automobile ownership eventually diminished the role of buses in intercity travel, with Greyhound losing 30 million passengers, or about half of its ridership, between the mid-1960s and the mid-1980s. Motorcoach firms responded to tough times by eliminating service to small towns and rural areas—places where there were already few mass transportation services available.

The development of mass automobility in postwar America transformed medium-distance passenger travel from a commercial enterprise into a personal convenience. With funding provided by the Federal Aid Highway Acts of 1944, 1954, and 1956, metropolitan developers constructed expressways connecting downtown business districts with expanding suburbs and interstate highways. Mass-produced automobiles became necessities for suburban families, not only for commuting between homes, workplaces, and shopping centers, but also for visiting increasingly popular tourist destinations such as the Grand Canyon and Disneyland. New car sales quadrupled between 1946 and 1955, with three-quarters of American households owning at least one car by the end of the 1950s.

Compared to other forms of travel, automobiles brought high rates of traffic fatalities and very high per-mile operation costs, along with the hassles of traffic jams and air pollution. The apparent convenience of personal transportation proved irresistible in the postwar era, however, especially for the growing number of suburban Americans whose neighborhoods were designed with the assumption of universal car ownership.

In the 1950s, railroads made a short-lived attempt to lure commuters and tourists off the highways by updating their passenger services. Streamlined diesel-electric locomotives provided quiet, smooth, and stylish rides on lines such as the *California Zephyr,* a high-speed stainless-steel passenger train connecting

A public works project of unprecedented scope, the 41,000-mile interstate highway system was authorized by federal legislation in 1956. The network of multiple-lane expressways was also designed for military and civil defense purposes. *(Harold M. Lambert/Getty Images)*

Chicago and San Francisco beginning in 1949. New glass-domed observation cars afforded unobstructed views of passing scenery on selected Western routes, while "slumbercoaches" provided private bedrooms for little more than the cost of a coach ticket.

Such efforts proved temporary, however, as railroads suffered estimated losses of $400 million per year on passenger service through the 1960s. Railroads increasingly focused their investments on improving freight service, so that, by 1967, passenger rail routes had declined to 68,000 miles, down from 160,000 miles in 1947.

Most railroad firms officially ended passenger service in 1971, when Congress created the National Rail Passenger System, commonly known as Amtrak. Despite being a quasi-public corporation subsidized by the federal government, Amtrak had, by 2004, never shown a profit, even after introducing high-speed service for commuters in the densely populated Northeast Corridor between Boston, New York, and Washington.

Effects of Deregulation

New political and economic concerns attended the increasingly competitive postwar transportation system. All of the major modes of transportation took part in the deregulation wave of the late 1970s and early 1980s, with trucking and airlines experiencing the greatest impacts.

The Motor Carrier Act of 1980 effectively ended forty-five years of ICC oversight, which had limited market entry and regulated routes and freight rates to minimize predatory competition in the trucking industry. More than 19,000 new trucking firms were established between 1980 and 1982 alone, increasing competition and driving down freight rates as desired by proponents of deregulation, but also forcing several large companies such as Consolidated Freightways, along with thousands of smaller firms, into bankruptcy. The number of trucking business failures jumped from 400 in 1980 to more than 1,500 in 1986. The companies that survived often did so by relying on low-wage, nonunionized drivers who were encouraged to haul heavier loads and drive longer hours.

The Airline Deregulation Act of 1978 led to comparable restructuring in the airline industry. Following a wave of mergers and bankruptcies in the 1980s, major airlines were forced to slash ticket prices to attract enough customers to offset rising fuel costs. Nearly 90 percent of all passengers traveled on discounted fares during the 1980s. Airlines also instituted the hub-and-spoke system, sending passengers via feeder flights to central hubs before rerouting them to their final destinations in order to minimize fuel costs. Business, nonetheless, remained unstable, as only one major airline posted a profit in 1992, and a series of bankruptcies in the early 1990s brought requests for federal bailouts.

The signing of the North American Free Trade Agreement (NAFTA) in 1993 led to increased cross-border traffic between Canada, Mexico, and the United States. Traffic between Canada and the United States was already strong following a 1989 agreement to promote cross-border commerce, but within seven years of NAFTA's signing, the annual value of merchandise trucked between the two countries increased by $100 billion.

Integrating U.S. and Mexican highway transportation proved more difficult, with the two countries maintaining very different standards for wages, safety, equipment maintenance, and highway construction.

Lady Bird Bill (Highway Beautification Act)

The Highway Beautification Act of 1965 was enacted as part of President Lyndon B. Johnson's Great Society. His wife Lady Bird Johnson was the legislation's strongest advocate. By publicly supporting the bill, sitting in on legislative sessions, and lobbying for its passage, she broke ground for the role of the first lady, while helping to enact important environmental legislation that limited the spread of outdoor billboards.

The first lady's lifelong love of the outdoors and the many wildflower species of her native state of Texas led her to seek a strong role in the White House on behalf of "beautification," though this was a term she never cared for. After President Johnson's election in 1964, his ad hoc Task Force on Natural Beauty recommended that his administration focus on the nation's natural beauty, the preservation of open space, highway beautification, and the regulation of billboards. Lady Bird Johnson saw this effort as a chance, she later wrote, "to repay something of the debt I owed nature for the enrichment provided from my childhood onward."

She initially focused her efforts on Washington, D.C., through the private Committee for a More Beautiful Capital. But the interstate highway system built across the United States in the 1950s was in need of beautification as well. The Bonus Act of 1958 regulated the billboards that sprang up along the highways, but by the early 1960s, it had proven largely ineffective. In his 1965 State of the Union address, President Johnson called for "a new and substantial effort to landscape highways to provide places of relaxation and recreation wherever roads run." He asked his special assistant, Bill Moyers, to draft a bill on highway beautification, which he called "Lady Bird's bill."

Moyers had little knowledge of the complicated billboard industry, which, along with the Bureau of Public Roads, helped draft the legislation. In April 1965, a four-bill highway beautification package was introduced in Congress. It called for eradication of eyesores along highways, including billboards and junkyards, using money from the Highway Trust Fund. Critics later charged that the influence of the powerful billboard industry helped create a program that left many billboards standing. Talks went on for months between legislators and the billboard lobby, and it seemed that the entire package would stall indefinitely. Estimates of the program's cost ranged from $780 million to $1.2 billion.

The Highway Beautification Act was finally signed into law on October 22, 1965. It gave states the power to regulate billboards and junkyards along federal highways, and it called for the Department of Commerce to withhold 20 percent of highway funds for states that did not implement stronger standards.

Lady Bird Johnson's involvement in the passage of the bill was both applauded and criticized. Throughout, she took part in strategy conferences and lobbied openly on behalf of the bill. Some White House staff and members of Congress resented her involvement and thought the bill was not worth the political trouble. In Montana, a billboard appeared that read, "Impeach Lady Bird." After the bill's passage, the first lady retreated from the controversy and focused her efforts on public appeals for landscaping and better highway design.

Even if the final Highway Beautification Act lacked the teeth the Johnsons had hoped for, it still called attention to the enormous network of roads snaking across the country and their cost to natural beauty. "Though the word beautification makes the concept sound merely cosmetic," Lady Bird Johnson later wrote, "it involves much more: clean water, clean air, clean roadsides, safe waste-disposal, and preservation of valued old landmarks as well as great parks and wilderness areas. To me, in sum, beautification means our total concern for the physical and human quality we pass on to our children and the future."

Melissa Stallings

By 2000, the total value of merchandise transported via truck between the two countries amounted to only 65 percent of the Canadian trade. The future integration and coordination of America's transportation systems, either within or across U.S. borders, remained uncertain.

Shane Hamilton

See also: Automobile Culture; Automobile Industry; Energy; Hijackings; Mass Transit; September 11 Attacks.

Bibliography

Bilstein, Roger E. *Flight in America: From the Wrights to the Astronauts.* Baltimore: Johns Hopkins University Press, 2001.

Goddard, Stephen. *Getting There: The Epic Struggle between Road and Rail in the American Century.* Chicago: University of Chicago Press, 1994.

Gould, Lewis L. *Lady Bird Johnson and the Environment.* Lawrence: University Press of Kansas, 1988.

Johnson, Lady Bird, and Carlton B. Lees. *Wildflowers Across America.* New York: Abbeville, 1988.

Rose, Mark H. *Interstate: Express Highway Politics, 1939–1989,* 2nd ed. Knoxville: University of Tennessee Press, 1990.

Russell, Jan Jarboe. *Lady Bird: A Biography of Mrs. Johnson.* New York: Charles Scribner's Sons, 1999.

Stover, John F. *The Life and Decline of the American Railroad.* New York: Oxford University Press, 1970.

Thomas, James Harold. *The Long Haul: Truckers, Truck Stops, and Trucking.* Memphis, TN: Memphis State University Press, 1979.

TRAVELGATE

"Travelgate" was the name given to one of the early scandals in the administration of President Bill Clinton. In May 1993, the White House announced that it had fired all seven employees of the White House Travel Office because of financial mismanagement. Allegations of false statements, improper use of law enforcement, obstruction of justice, and patronage were leveled at President Clinton and First Lady Hillary Clinton; they denied any wrongdoing.

Travelgate primarily dealt with issues surrounding the office's services in providing air and ground transportation, lodging, and office space on the road for the media that covers the president. Payment is typically made for these services to travel providers by the travel office, which is then reimbursed by the news organizations. Seven employees, all of whom had served during several administrations, worked in the travel office in 1993, with Billy Ray Dale serving as director.

On May 19, 1993, the White House announced that all seven employees had been fired after an internal investigation by the auditing firm of KPMG Peat Marwick found financial mismanagement and questionable accounting practices. The White House said it consulted the Justice Department, which agreed that action should be taken. The firings took place, the White House said, in order to initiate reform in the travel office. Critics immediately claimed the White House was covering up an attempt by the Clintons to hire a firm from Arkansas, their home state, to handle the arrangements.

Media coverage of the Travel Office firings was so great that by the end of May, the White House had eased off its initial allegations. Five members of the travel office staff were placed on leave with pay and later reinstated. White House Chief of Staff Thomas McLarty began an internal review of the events leading up to the firings and released his report, the "White House Travel Office Management Review," in July. The report found no evidence of patronage, held that the firings of the office's director and deputy director were justified, and made suggestions for reform within the office. Media attention died down after Dale was indicted for embezzlement in December 1994.

Dale's acquittal in November 1995 renewed interest in Travelgate, however, as critics charged that the White House had used the Federal Bureau of Investigation (FBI) to drum up false allegations against him. In 1996, the House of Representatives began an inquiry, and Attorney General Janet Reno asked Independent Council Kenneth Starr to look into the firings. Reno's request came after a memo was found that implied Hillary Clinton had ordered the firings to benefit a travel firm tied to a close friend, Harry Thomason. In March 1996, the first lady denied any involvement and said that she learned of trouble within the Travel Office from Thomason and White House Counsel Vincent Foster, who had committed suicide in 1993.

In 2000, Independent Counsel Robert Ray finished the Travelgate investigation and exonerated Hillary Clinton of perjury, obstruction of justice, and knowingly making false statements, while acknowledging that she probably had some role in firing the travel office officials. This scandal was one of several that dogged the early Clinton Administration, and it revived interest in the Whitewater scandal. That, in turn, started the investigation that ultimately led to Bill Clinton's impeachment.

Melissa Stallings

See also: Impeachment of President Clinton; Whitewater Scandal.

Bibliography

Roberts, Robert N., and Marion T. Doss, Jr. *From Watergate to Whitewater: The Public Integrity War.* Westport, CT: Praeger, 1997.

Walden, Gregory S. *On Best Behavior: The Clinton Administration and Ethics in Government.* Indianapolis, IN: Hudson Institute, 1996.

TRUMAN DOCTRINE

First articulated in a speech by President Harry S Truman to a joint session of Congress on March 12, 1947, the Truman Doctrine, as it came to be known, openly declared a U.S. commitment to contain Communist expansion for the first time. Specifically, Truman requested $400 million in economic and military aid to bolster anticommunist regimes in Greece and Turkey. More generally, and of far greater consequence, Truman's speech implied a global commitment to aid any country threatened by Communist insurgency. This implication fundamentally altered American foreign relations in the postwar era and contributed to the burgeoning Cold War with the Soviet Union.

The Truman Doctrine capped almost two years of deepening tension and suspicion in relations with America's World War II ally, the Soviet Union. The source of the friction was rooted principally in divergent visions of the postwar world. U.S. officials, mindful of American disengagement and failure to follow through on President Woodrow Wilson's post–World War I vision for an international order based on democracy, free markets, and the rule of law, advocated a postwar structure built upon free trade, capitalist development, representative government, and collective security. Institutions such as the International Monetary Fund, the World Bank, and the United Nations epitomized this worldview.

The Soviet Union, on the other hand, stressed territorial spheres of influence that reflected the major powers' own interests. From the Soviet perspective, this meant friendly, Communist neighbors. The "Big Three," U.S. President Franklin D. Roosevelt,

British Prime Minister Winston Churchill, and Soviet Premier Joseph Stalin, attempted to resolve their respective differences at wartime conferences at Tehran (December 1943) and Yalta (February 1945).

In April 1945, a month before V-E day, Roosevelt died, and Truman assumed the presidency. Truman believed the Yalta accords affirmed America's Wilsonian outlook, particularly its dedication to self-determination and free elections. Citing perceived Soviet violations of the Yalta agreements in Poland and Eastern Europe, Truman initiated a "get tough" policy that included blunt language and suspension of lend-lease shipments to the Soviet Union. This hard-line approach became firmer in 1946 following Soviet reluctance to withdraw troops from Iran, pressure on Turkey to allow Soviet bases in that country, and a speech by Stalin that implied the inevitability of future world conflict with capitalist powers.

Meanwhile, Truman received warnings about Soviet intentions from both inside and outside his administration. First, a little-known State Department official in Moscow, George Kennan, responded to Washington requests for an analysis of the Soviet regime with an 8,000-word indictment known as the "Long Telegram." Kennan provided the intellectual framework for the policy that would become known as "containment," arguing that the Soviets were committed fanatically to the belief that there could be no permanent, practical compromise with the United States. Shortly after Kennan's analysis, Churchill visited the United States and gave a speech at Fulton, Missouri, that alluded to an "iron curtain" falling across Eastern Europe. Both the Long Telegram and the Iron Curtain speech crystallized assumptions in ascendance among U.S. policymakers. Indeed, a comprehensive White House study of U.S.-Soviet relations, completed in September 1946, found a firm consensus within the government regarding a perceived Soviet threat.

This was the context on February 21, 1947, when Britain notified the United States that its dire financial situation prevented further material and military support for the royalist Greek government under siege by Communist rebels. On February 24, President Truman met with Secretary of State George C. Marshall and Undersecretary of State Dean Acheson, both of whom urged prompt and vigorous action in assisting Greece. At stake, they argued, was not only Greece, but the strategically vital Middle East, as well. The advisers did not fear a Soviet invasion, but rather political and diplomatic pressure from

Moscow that would send weakened nations into the Soviet orbit and undermine the creation of a liberal internationalist order. The harsh European winter of 1946–1947 broadened those worries to all of Western Europe; American officials feared that desperate Western Europeans would see communism as an answer to their economic woes.

Congressional Approval

On February 27, Truman, Marshall, and Acheson met with Congressional leaders to apprise them of the situation and solicit support for concerted action. Marshall repeated his warnings about Europe and the Middle East succumbing to Soviet domination. Acheson, concerned that Marshall's presentation failed to hit the alarmist mark, conjured up images of a rotten apple (Greece) infecting an entire barrel (Middle East and beyond), an analogy later invoked as the domino theory. Impressed by Acheson's apocalyptic scenario, the congressmen, led by former isolationist Senator Arthur Vandenburg (Republican of Michigan), promised to support Truman on condition that he explain the situation to the American people in the same vivid language. All agreed that it was time to take a firm stand against the Soviets.

Acheson immediately assembled a State Department committee to draft a message. Truman's closest advisers revised and completed the final draft, and, on March 12, the president felt confident enough to address Congress and the American public. Truman spoke for eighteen minutes. He asserted that Communists threatened the Greek government, which had sent an urgent appeal for American assistance. The United States, he said, must supply this assistance. He added that Turkey also needed U.S. support.

Then came the key statement: "At the present moment in world history nearly every nation must choose between alternative ways of life. The choice is too often not a free one. . . . I believe it must be the policy of the United States to support free peoples who are resisting attempted subjugation by armed minorities or by outside pressures."

The declaration marked a watershed moment in U.S. foreign affairs. Without naming the Soviet Union, Truman drew a line in the geopolitical sand and declared U.S. commitment to containing communism throughout the world. Containment remained the fundamental strategy of U.S. foreign policy through-

out the Cold War. The Korean and Vietnam wars were fought in its name. Military and foreign aid budgets were dramatically increased to sustain it.

Some scholars have argued the Truman Doctrine was couched in inflammatory rhetoric that unnecessarily fueled the Cold War. Others, however, claim it simply put into words what had been unspoken realities and that the policy's wisdom bore fruit forty years later, when the Soviet empire collapsed.

John Gripentrog

See also: Alliances, Foreign; Anticommunism; Berlin Airlift; Containment; Foreign Aid; Middle East, Relations with (Except Israel); Soviet Union/Russia, Relations with; Western Europe, Relations with.

Bibliography

Cohen, Warren. *The Cambridge History of American Foreign Relations.* Vol. IV, *America in the Age of Soviet Power, 1945–1991.* Cambridge, UK: Press Syndicate of the University of Cambridge, 1993.

LaFeber, Walter. *America, Russia, and the Cold War, 1945–2000.* 9th ed. New York: McGraw-Hill, 2002.

Truman Doctrine, excerpted from *Congressional Record,* March 12, 1947.

TRUTH-IN-LENDING ACT

A massive expansion of credit fueled postwar prosperity by allowing ordinary Americans to purchase consumer goods that previously had been out of reach. By the 1960s, however, the increasing number and complexity of credit transactions led to a great deal of confusion and expense for consumers. A 1964 study revealed that families far underestimated the true cost of consumer credit, believing their average annual interest rate to be 8 percent rather than the actual 24 percent.

To prevent such misunderstanding, Congress in 1968 passed the Truth-in-Lending Act (TILA), which introduced uniform disclosure requirements for all consumer loans. The law represented a major advance for the burgeoning consumer protection movement and a step toward the greater regulation of the financial industry.

The idea behind TILA was conceived by former economics professor Paul Douglas, when he served on the Consumers Division of the National Recovery Administration in 1934. Douglas's suggestion that the calculation of interest rates be standardized in a fair and easily understood manner was poorly received by industry-friendly regulators. In 1960, Douglas, now a Democratic senator from Illinois, raised the issue again before the Senate Banking Committee. The proposal immediately triggered controversy and strong opposition from senators who sided with numerous business trade groups. Critics argued that annual interest rates were difficult to calculate, that disclosure would hurt small retailers already burdened by complex federal regulations, and that consumers would spend less if they perceived that they were paying more in interest.

Over the next seven years, Douglas and his allies held frequent public hearings to raise awareness of the issue. As the consumer movement gained strength, support for the bill grew. A local version of it was passed in Massachusetts in 1966 without the dire consequences that its critics had predicted. Organized labor, credit unions, and mutual savings banks all joined the campaign for a federal bill.

Although Douglas failed to win reelection in 1966—partly because business groups threw their support behind his opponent—momentum for uniform credit disclosure continued to grow. In 1968, Wisconsin Senator William Proxmire and Missouri Representative Leonor Sullivan, both Democrats, won passage of the Consumer Credit Protection Act. That bill, which extended well beyond disclosure of requirements for consumer loans, incorporated TILA as its principal component.

The TILA provision required the disclosure of consumer loan finance charges (the fees charged by the creditor for issuing the loans) and the annual percentage rate (a complex calculation of interest based on annual repayment and regulated by the Federal Reserve Board). The law allowed consumers to sue creditors for illegal or excessive finance charges, and the creditors would be forced to pay major penalties and face criminal liability for noncompliance.

The effectiveness of TILA has been a source of continual debate. Advocates have used the law to win relief for low-income consumers who are often targeted by deceptive advertising. Studies have shown, however, that many consumers were slow to gain a better understanding of the cost of credit. Moreover, high-cost lenders have used existing disclosure requirements to counter calls for more aggressive and substantive regulations to protect vulnerable debtors.

Eduardo Canedo

See also: Banking and Credit; Consumer Movement; Redlining; Regulation and Deregulation.

Bibliography

Douglas, Paul H. *In Our Time.* New York: Harcourt, Brace and World, 1968.

Peterson, Christopher L. "Truth, Understanding, and High-Cost Consumer Credit: The Historical Context of the Truth in Lending Act." *Florida Law Review* 55 (July 2003): 807–903.

TYLENOL TAMPERING INCIDENT

On September 29, 1982, when twelve-year-old Mary Ann Kellerman woke up at her Chicago home with a sore throat, her parents gave her an Extra-Strength Tylenol (acetaminophen) capsule. Within three hours, she was dead, having accidentally taken a capsule laced with cyanide. By October 1, 1982, six more people in the Chicago area died after taking contaminated Tylenol capsules, including an eighteen-year-old theater worker and a thirty-five-year-old flight attendant.

These incidents sparked a nationwide panic, an outbreak of copy-cat crimes, and the recall of 31 million bottles of Tylenol products with a retail value of more than $100 million. They also brought the issue of tamper-resistant food and drug packaging to the forefront of national affairs.

As the mystery unfolded, Chicago Mayor Jane M. Byrne ordered stores in the city to remove all Tylenol products while the city sponsored collection sites for concerned citizens to turn in Tylenol capsules for testing. Area paramedics received training on how to counter cyanide poisoning, and Illinois State Lottery officials halted the sale of tickets for the number 2880 in the daily pick-4 game, the reported lot number for the batch of tainted capsules.

State and federal investigators searched for suspects in the Chicago area and at manufacturing centers in Texas and Pennsylvania. They received thousands of leads, but no one has ever been formally charged. Although the crime was never solved, investigators theorized that the capsules had been tainted by a person in the local area. One scenario centered on an individual who shoplifted bottles of Tylenol capsules, filled the capsules with cyanide, and then returned the bottles to the shelves of area drug stores.

James Lewis, an unemployed accountant and previously convicted con artist, became a prime suspect after he sent a letter to Johnson & Johnson, the Tylenol parent company, demanding $1 million to "stop the killing." He was convicted on federal extortion charges for sending the letter, but he was never tried for contaminating the Tylenol capsules. Even ten years after the incident, Lewis maintained his innocence. Another primary suspect, Roger Arnold, was imprisoned for slaying a co-worker at Jewel Food and Drug Stores who identified Arnold as a potential suspect.

Johnson & Johnson suffered significant financial losses from the 1982 recall. In addition, families of the victims sued Johnson & Johnson for not packaging its products in tamper-resistant bottles, which had been readily available since the 1960s. In 1991, Johnson & Johnson paid between $35 million and $39 million to survivors of the seven victims in Chicago.

The company had to rebuild its reputation by designing packages with warnings and safety features.

Tylenol stopped being manufactured in capsules altogether in 1986, after a separate cyanide-poisoning incident killed one woman in Bronxville, New York. Johnson & Johnson then opted to produce pills that could not easily be manipulated.

The incident changed how the pharmaceuticals and food industries packaged their products. On the federal level, new laws were enacted that strengthened criminal penalties for product tampering and required seals on all nonprescription drugs.

Jenny Barker

See also: Medicine; Tort Law.

Bibliography

Flynn, James, Paul Slovic, and Howard Kunreuther, eds. *Risk, Media, and Stigma: Understanding Public Challenges to Modern Science and Technology.* Sterling, VA: Earthscan, 2001.

Food and Drug Letter, Washington Drug Letter, and Product Safety Letter. *Product Survival: Lessons of the Tylenol Terrorism.* Washington, DC: Washington Business Information, 1982.

U

U-2 INCIDENT

From the moment the Soviet Union set off its first atomic device in August 1949, America's intelligence agencies sought as much knowledge as possible about Soviet nuclear capabilities. Attempts to penetrate the Soviet Union with weather balloons failed in the face of Soviet air defenses. To counter those defenses, the United States developed the U-2, a spy plane that flew at an altitude of 70,000 feet with a range of 4,000 miles and whose cameras took excellent pictures of objects on the ground fourteen miles below. These pictures allowed President Dwight D. Eisenhower to decide crucial foreign policy issues.

In 1959, Eisenhower grew uneasy about the U-2 flights. Attempting to improve relations with Soviet Premier Nikita Khrushchev, Eisenhower knew that disclosure of the U-2's activities would damage the chances for a nuclear test ban treaty. The U-2 pilots were nervous themselves, as Soviet surface-to-air-missiles came closer to each flight, while the planes grew heavier and slower as more equipment was added to them.

In April 1960, Eisenhower ordered the Central Intelligence Agency (CIA) to halt the flights, but CIA Director Allen Dulles convinced him to allow

Wreckage of the American U-2 surveillance plane shot down over the Soviet Union in May 1960 was put on display in a Moscow museum. The captured pilot, Francis Gary Powers, was returned in a spy exchange in 1962. *(Carl Mydans/Time Life Pictures/Getty Images)*

one more flight over the Soviet missile installation at Tyuratam in the Soviet Republic of Kazakhstan. For the first time, a U-2 would fly the entire 3,800 miles across the Soviet Union. The CIA chose Francis Gary Powers, the senior U-2 pilot, to fly the mission.

On May 1, 1960, Powers's flight left Pakistan and headed northwest across the Soviet Union. Near Sverdlovsk, in Russia's Ural Mountains, Powers felt a dull thump hit the plane and saw a flash of brilliant orange flame flicker across the cockpit. As the plane began to plummet, Powers managed to eject and land safely. Spotted by Russian farmers, Powers was arrested by KGB agents and taken to Moscow, where he admitted to spying for the United States.

When informed that a U-2 was lost, the CIA assured Eisenhower that there was no way the pilot could have survived. On May 3, a cover story claimed that an air weather service mission had crashed in Turkey. A furious Khrushchev felt personally betrayed and embarrassed by his repeated promises to the Soviet Politburo that Eisenhower was a man who could be trusted. On May 7, Khrushchev announced that the Soviet Union had shot down a spy plane and had captured both the pilot and incriminating film.

A week later at a summit meeting of leaders from France, Great Britain, the Soviet Union, and the United States, Khrushchev demanded that the flights be suspended and that those responsible be punished. Eisenhower suspended the flights and took responsibility for them, but he refused to apologize. In response, Khrushchev withdrew his invitation to Eisenhower to visit the Soviet Union. Eisenhower's hopes of peaceful relations, arms limitations, and a nuclear test ban treaty were dashed. Khrushchev's power eroded as critics within the Politburo withdrew their political support.

A Soviet court sentenced Powers to three years in prison and seven years of hard labor. He served a little less than two years before being exchanged for a Soviet spy on February 10, 1962.

Jason Dikes

See also: Cuban Missile Crisis; Election of 1960; Soviet Union/ Russia, Relations with; Spies and Spying; Strategic Arms Treaties.

Bibliography

Beschloss, Michael. *Mayday: Eisenhower, Khrushchev, and the U-2 Affair.* New York: Harper and Row, 1986.

Taubman, William. *Khrushchev: The Man and His Era.* New York: W.W. Norton, 2003.

Wise, David, and Thomas B. Ross. *The U-2 Affair.* New York: Random House, 1962.

UNABOMBER AFFAIR

"Unabomber" was the name given by the Federal Bureau of Investigation (FBI) to Theodore Kaczynski, who, over a period of seventeen years, mailed a number of bombs to scientists, academics, and others that killed three people and injured many more. The name was a combination of "university," where many of the explosive devices were sent, and "bomber." Kaczynski was finally arrested in 1996 after a tip-off from his own brother.

Raised in a middle-class suburban Chicago home, Kaczynski showed signs of being extremely gifted academically. He skipped two years of school and, by the age of fifteen, was accepted at Harvard; Kaczynski studied there from 1959 to 1962. By 1967, he had earned a doctorate in mathematics from the University of Michigan. He then joined the Department of Mathematics at the University of California at Berkeley, as an instructor.

In 1971, Kaczynski moved to Great Falls, Montana. It was also in this year that he wrote an essay containing many of the ideas that would later surface in his manifesto, "Industrial Society and Its Future," published in 1995 in *The Washington Post* and *The New York Times.*

On May 26, 1978, the first bomb mailed by Kaczynski slightly injured Northwestern University public safety officer Terry Marker. Between 1978 and 1987, a number of individually targeted bombs were attributed to the Unabomber. On December 11, 1985, a bomb sent by Kaczynski killed Hugh Scrutton, the owner of a computer store in Sacramento. After the placement of a bomb in Salt Lake City, Utah, on February 20, 1987, a witness was able to provide a description of the man who placed it. No more attacks attributed to the Unabomber occurred until 1993.

In September 1995, the *Washington Post* and *The New York Times* agreed to publish the unedited, anti-technology manifesto of the so-called Unabomber, in the hope of ending his seventeen-year letter bombing campaign. He was apprehended the following April. *(Evan Agostini/Getty Images News)*

The assistant managing editor of *The New York Times,* Warren Hoge, received a letter from Kaczynski on June 23, 1993. Hoge was given a nine-digit number, which, Kaczynski said, Hoge could use to identify any correspondence at a later date as genuine. In San Francisco that July, the federal UNABOMB Task Force, composed of agents from the treasury department, postal service, and FBI, was formed.

Thomas Mosser became Kaczynski's second fatality, when he opened a package on December 10, 1994. Gilbert Murray, president of the California Forestry Association, the third and final fatality, lost his life on April 24, 1995. The intended target had been William Dennison, whom Murray had replaced in the position of president.

On the same day as Murray's death, Hoge received another letter from Kaczynski, this one outlining the reasons for targeting those who had received his parcels. In late June 1995, Hoge and Michael Getler of *The Washington Post* received a copy of Kaczynski's "Industrial Society and Its Future," in which he argued that the Industrial Revolution had been a disaster for mankind. The text was published in *The Washington Post* on September 19, 1995, with the two newspapers splitting the cost of publication.

Kaczynski's younger brother, David, recognized the phrasing in the manifesto, and, in February 1996, he initiated contact with the FBI. Theodore Kaczynski was arrested in his cabin in Montana on April 3, 1996.

Psychiatric testing was requested prior to the trial, but Kaczynski would not submit to it. The trial began on November 12, 1997, and, on January 8, 1998, Kaczynski asked to be allowed to represent himself. He was found competent to do so, but U.S. District Judge Garland Burrell refused the request. Kaczynski then made a deal for a plea bargain, and, on January 22, 1998, pled guilty to thirteen counts of bombing and murder. He was given four consecutive life sentences, to be served at a maximum security prison in Colorado.

Shannon Schedlich-Day

See also: Crime, Violent; Terrorism, Domestic.

Bibliography

Chase, Alston. *Harvard and the Unabomber: The Education of an American Terrorist.* New York: W.W. Norton, 2003.

Douglas, John, and Mark Olshaker. *Unabomber: On the Trail of America's Most-Wanted Serial Killer.* New York: Pocket Books, 1996.

UNEMPLOYMENT

The history of employment and unemployment in postwar America has followed a predictable and timeworn pattern. When the economy has undergone growth, unemployment has tended to fall; when the economy has fallen into recession—officially defined by the U.S. government as two consecutive quarters of declining gross domestic product (GDP)—unemployment has tended to rise. At the same time, however, another trend has defied most historical precedents. With each recovery period immediately following a recession, unemployment has been ever slower to decline.

As in previous periods in American history, unemployment in the postwar era has tended to be more acute among more economically marginal groups, such as ethnic minorities and the young. Through the 1980s, unemployment in the United States also tended to be more acute among blue-collar workers—especially those in the shrinking manufacturing sector—than among professionals and white-collar workers. But this, too, has changed in the decades since, as increasing numbers of clerical and managerial employees find themselves in the unemployment lines.

Measuring and Defining Unemployment

Unemployment is measured by the Bureau of Labor Statistics (BLS), which draws a sample of 65,000 households each month and completes interviews with the vast majority of them. Each interviewed household answers questions concerning the work activity of members sixteen years of age or older during the calendar week containing the twelfth day of the month. If a household member sixteen years of age or older worked one hour or more as a paid employee, either for someone else or in his or her own business or firm, he or she is classified as employed. A household member is also considered employed if he or she worked fifteen hours or more without pay in a family enterprise. Finally, household members are counted as employed if they held a job from which they were temporarily absent due to illness, bad weather, vacation, labor-management disputes, or personal reasons, whether they were paid or not.

Those who are not employed fall into one of two categories: 1) unemployed or 2) not in the labor force.

To be considered unemployed, a person must be available for work and have made specific efforts to find work during the previous four weeks. A person not looking for work, either because he or she does not want a job or has given up looking, is classified as not in the labor force. People not in the labor force include full-time students, retirees, individuals in institutions, and those staying home to take care of children, elderly parents, or other family members.

The total labor force is defined as the number of people employed plus the number of unemployed. The total population sixteen years of age or older is equal to the number of people in the labor force plus the number not in the labor force. With these figures, several ratios can be calculated. The unemployment rate is the ratio of number of people unemployed to the total number of people in the labor force.

Keynesian Economics and Unemployment

Prior to the industrial and commercial revolutions of the nineteenth century, unemployment was not a well-known phenomenon, as most people worked on the land and their labor followed the natural seasons of the calendar. Indeed, the term "unemployment" did not come into widespread use until the turn of the twentieth century.

As more and more Americans found themselves working for others in nonrural settings, unemployment became an inevitable by-product of recessionary times. The peak unemployment rate in U.S. history came at the depths of the Great Depression in 1933, when it exceeded 25 percent. Unemployment remained high throughout the 1930s, until World War II defense contracting and military recruitment sent it to historical lows of under 2 percent.

With the end of the war, many economists and policymakers feared a return of high unemployment rates and advocated a so-called Keynesian approach to government economic policy. The English economist John Maynard Keynes had argued that governments could lessen the impact of economic recession by increasing spending on public works and other projects. This, it was said, would have a multiplier effect. That is, one dollar earned by a worker on a government project would be spent on goods and services that would create employment for others.

This view contradicted traditional laissez-faire economics and conservative ideology. First, pre-Keynesian economists said that for a government to spend in recessionary times, it would have to borrow, thereby drying up funds for private sector economic activity and exacerbating unemployment. Laissez-faire ideologues also argued that government help weakened individualistic enterprise. But the lessons of the Great Depression and World War II had convinced both Democrats and moderate Republicans that Keynesian economics was necessary to avoid mass unemployment. As once conservative Republican Richard M. Nixon was reputed to have said during his tenure in the White House, "We are all Keynesians."

The Keynesian solution seemed to work, at least through the 1970s. While there were recessions between the late 1940s and early 1970s, they were short and not very deep. In only one year—the recession year of 1958—did the unemployment rate stay above 7 percent for more than a single month in a row. Generally, unemployment rates during this period were in the 4 to 5 percent range, what some economists call "natural unemployment"—that is, joblessness caused by people willingly quitting jobs or refusing to take jobs they deem beneath their skill level or expected income level.

Stagflation

Two key factors brought these halcyon employment days to an end. One was international competition. Coming out of World War II, the United States was the economic powerhouse of the world; the nation's GDP in 1945 was estimated to equal that of the rest of the world. In addition, America's major competitors, such as Japan and Western Europe, had seen their economic infrastructures destroyed by war. By the early 1970s, however, they had recovered and were taking markets away from U.S. exporters, as well as selling directly to U.S. consumers.

The second key factor was rising energy prices. By the early 1970s, the United States was ever more dependent on imported oil. When the price of that oil rose dramatically—as it did in 1973 and 1979—the results were harsh recessions and a disturbing new phenomenon called "stagflation," a portmanteau word combining stagnation and inflation.

Typically, economies experienced one or the other phenomenon. When the economy was expanding too fast, demand for workers and products rose, resulting in wage and price inflation but low unemployment.

Reagan Recession

In February 1981, just weeks after Ronald Reagan was inaugurated president of the United States, Congress received his new economic plan. The Economic Tax Recovery Act was legislation he proposed to lower taxes, balance the budget, and reduce government spending. The underlying premise was a theory, fashionable in some academic circles, known as "supply-side economics," which held that lowering taxes would encourage economic growth, bring more revenues into government coffers, and thereby avoid a budget deficit.

Reagan and his Republican administration believed that lower personal and corporate taxes would result in greater consumer spending. The budget would be balanced by reduced spending in every government department and with the elimination of many government-run programs. Medicare and Social Security would not be touched, however, and military spending actually would be increased in the face of Cold War tensions. Overall, the government was to play a lesser role in the economy, and many industries underwent deregulation.

After initial skepticism from many congressmen and an assassination attempt on Reagan in March 1981, the charismatic president began to see a marked increase in support. By July, nearly two-thirds of Americans were in favor of the measures, and support was growing from the Democrats in Congress. In August 1981, the Economic Tax Recovery Act was passed by the legislators and signed by Reagan into law.

Projections indicated that there would still be a budget deficit of $80 billion, and Reagan promised additional cutbacks. As the largest deficit in American history loomed, and with inflation rising to 14 percent per year, the Federal Reserve Board raised interest rates. An economic recession was now inevitable. By November, unemployment had reached 9 million and 17,000 businesses had failed. Many blue-collar workers were jobless, farmers had to relinquish land, and the homeless rate rose. The poverty and unemployment numbers had not been this high since the Great Depression.

As 1982 began, inflation declined to 8.9 percent, but the decrease could not mask the reality for many Americans. The economy remained stalled in a recession and, with the deficit rising, many politicians called for changes. Reagan decided to raise taxes on businesses, but he would not raise the income tax or cut defense spending. By January 1983, his approval rating had fallen to 35 percent, down from 60 percent during the summer of 1981.

In his 1983 State of the Union address, Reagan admitted, "the recession was much deeper than those inside and out of the government had predicted." He continued to state his belief in economic recovery, however, and, as the year continued, inflation slowly dropped, federal defense spending resulted in a rise in production in the technology and aerospace industries, and commercial construction prospered. The unemployment lines shortened dramatically.

One year later, memories of the harshness of the recession seemed to evaporate for many Americans, and Reagan was reelected for a second term in a landslide. The severe economic measures implemented three years earlier, which had resulted in the recession, appeared to be successful in the end, although federal deficits continued to balloon into the 1990s. After a brief period of surpluses in the late 1990s, a new round of tax cuts in the early 2000s led to record deficits once again.

Gavin J. Wilk

When recessionary times hit, demand fell, and so did prices, even as unemployment rose. But in the 1970s—due to declines in manufacturing and rapid hikes in the crucial energy sector—came both inflation and unemployment. From 1975 to 1986, U.S. unemployment rates hovered in the 6 to 7 percent range at the same time that inflation stayed consistently above 10 percent. These two statistics were combined into what economists called the "misery index," which stayed in the upper teens in the late 1970s, damaging the presidency of Jimmy Carter.

His replacement, conservative Republican Ronald Reagan, brought in an economic team with a tough monetarist philosophy. Inspired by the teachings of University of Chicago scholar Milton Friedman, Reagan's economic policymakers believed that inflation was the key economic problem, because it created uncertainties for businesses concerning costs, revenues, and profits. To solve the problem, Reagan's team took a monetarist approach, shrinking the nation's money supply (actually, slowing its growth, which, in a growing population, meant a smaller money supply per capita) to wring inflation out of the system. With less money to chase goods and services, the thinking went, prices would fall.

The strategy worked; inflation was brought under control. But there was a cost: the worst recession in postwar American history. The manufacturing sector was shrinking in response to increased international competition and automation. Such industries as steel and automobiles saw mass layoffs in the 1970s and 1980s.

Thus, at the peak of the so-called "Reagan recession," in November and December of 1982, unemployment reached a postwar high of 10.8 percent and did not fall back to the 5 percent range until 1988. Another recession in the early 1990s, this one shorter but sharper, brought the unemployment rate back up to the 7 percent range until 1994.

Clinton Boom and September 11

As with the recession of the late 1970s, that of the early 1990s led to a change in administrations, with Democrat Bill Clinton defeating incumbent Republican George H.W. Bush in 1992. The irony was that the economy was just beginning to come out of recession. The problem for Bush was that, with each such recovery period, employment levels lag behind economic growth; voter anxiety over joblessness contributed mightily to Bush's defeat. Indeed, Clinton campaign strategist James Carville emphasized the importance of unemployment as a campaign theme by posting a sign at Clinton's campaign headquarters that read: "It's the economy, stupid."

While economists say some of Clinton's policies were effective in promoting economic growth—particularly by bringing down the national deficits

through selective tax hikes on the wealthy, which brought down interest rates and led to increased business investment—the new president also got lucky. Clinton presided over one of the great bursts in productivity in postwar history, a by-product of the computer revolution, which made for greater efficiencies in business (enabling the average worker to produce more per hour so that the economy can grow without creating inflation). This allowed the Federal Reserve Board to keep the money supply expanding without fear of inflation. The results were historically low unemployment rates. In April 2000, the U.S. jobless rate fell to its lowest level since the early 1950s—3.8 percent.

Several factors led to increases in unemployment during the early 2000s. One was the collapse of the "dot.com bubble," which erased hundreds of billions of dollars in stock wealth. A second was the September 11, 2001, terrorist attacks, which hit the travel and airline sectors particularly hard but created a sense of uncertainty throughout the economy.

Liberal economists also pointed to the huge tax cuts of the first George W. Bush Administration, which created vast budget deficits, driving up short-term interest rates and reducing business investment. Whatever the reason, Bush became the first president since Herbert Hoover, at the onset of the Depression, to preside over a net job loss during his first term in office.

James Ciment and S.S. Rath

See also: Blue-Collar Workers; Corporate Consolidation; Downsizing, Corporate; Economic Policy; Employment Act of 1946; Enterprise Zones; Globalization; Job Corps; Keynesian Economics; North American Free Trade Agreement; Poverty; Reaganomics; Rust Belt; Service-Sector Workers; Stagflation; Unions; White-Collar Workers; Women and Work.

Bibliography

Aronowitz, Stanley. *Just Around the Corner: The Paradox of the Jobless Recovery.* Philadelphia: Temple University Press, 2005.

Schaller, Michael. "The Republican Party 1981–1992: Renewal and Illusion." In *History of U.S. Political Parties*, Vol. V, edited by Arthur Schlesinger, Jr. Philadelphia: Chelsea House, 2002.

Vedder, Richard K., and Lowell E. Gallaway. *Out of Work: Unemployment and Government in Twentieth-Century America.* New York: New York University Press, 1997.

UNIDENTIFIED FLYING OBJECTS

An Unidentified Flying Object (UFO) is an object in the sky that cannot be readily identified. U.S. government investigations into UFOs have dismissed the vast majority of sightings as either some type of aircraft or unusual weather phenomena. The investigations also have implied that the rest of the sightings remain unidentifiable due to a lack of evidence. Although the skeptical dismiss UFO sightings as figments of overactive imaginations and the reports of crackpots, in the popular imagination, UFOs are often assumed to be alien spacecraft, evidence of which the government keeps secret for national security reasons.

The modern UFO phenomenon began on June 24, 1947, when pilot Kenneth Arnold reported seeing a line of disc-shaped aircraft flying through the Cascade Mountains of Washington State. Arnold reported that the silvery objects looked like saucers that had been skipped across water. Thus was born the image of the flying saucer. The media and the public soon became locked into a UFO frenzy, and sightings were reported all over the country and around the world.

In 1951, the U.S. Air Force established "Project Blue Book," an in-depth scientific study to discover the truth behind the UFOs. Between 1951 and 1969, Project Blue Book analyzed thousands of flying saucer sightings and failed to find even one verifiable case of an alien spacecraft. Most reported sightings turned out to be atmospheric phenomena or commercial or military aircraft. Of the almost 13,000 cases examined, however, almost 600 were classified as truly unidentifiable.

The fact that there are so many unexplained reports and that so many people see UFOs every year has convinced millions of Americans that some UFO sightings are proof of visiting aliens. The more extreme UFO enthusiasts claim there is a decades-old government conspiracy to hide the existence of aliens from the public. These conspiracy theorists point to events such as the Roswell (New Mexico) incident to prove their case.

On July 8, 1947, the *Roswell Daily Record,* the local newspaper, reported that the U.S. Air Force had recovered the wreckage of a crashed flying saucer at a nearby ranch. The news quickly spread and was taken to be the proof of alien visitors. But the next day, the story was retracted by the Air Force, which claimed that the wreckage was, in fact, a weather balloon. Recent declassified government documents have revealed that the unusual balloon was part of Project Mogul, a

The town of Roswell, New Mexico, has been the focus of attention among UFO enthusiasts, who believe that an alien spaceship landed there in 1947. Protestors in Washington, D.C., demand the release of documents that they claim will prove their case. *(Joshua Roberts/ AFP/Getty Images)*

top-secret operation designed to test the atmosphere for evidence of Soviet nuclear weapons testing.

Despite the lack of conclusive evidence, continued reports of sightings, popular science fiction films, and pervasive conspiracy theories of a government cover-up have fueled public interest in UFOs ever since. Hollywood was quick to capitalize on the interest, and, in the 1950s, it began releasing the first in a long line of alien invasion movies. Many of these films, such as *The Thing from Another World* (1951) and *The Day the Earth Stood Still* (1951), used alien invasions as allegories for Communist infiltration and nuclear proliferation.

There also have been countless books, magazines, television shows, toys, and a wide assortment of alien paraphernalia consumed by the public. Television shows such as *The X-Files* (1993–2002) and movies such as *Men in Black* (1997) and the remake of the classic *War of the Worlds* (2005) promise to carry the American obsession with UFOs well into the twenty-first century.

Richard Santos

See also: Conspiracy Theories.

Bibliography

Peebles, Curtis. *Watch the Skies! A Chronicle of the Flying Saucer Myth.* Washington, DC: Smithsonian Institution, 1994.

Steiger, Brad, ed. *Project Blue Book: The Top Secret UFO Findings Revealed.* New York: Ballantine, 1976.

UNIONS

As the nation emerged from World War II, American labor unions found themselves at the height of their power. The Great Depression had brought an explosion in union membership, from fewer than 3 million in 1932 to more than 9 million by 1939, and to nearly 14.5 million (35 percent of the work force) by 1945.

The Congress of Industrial Organizations (CIO) was responsible for a large part of the massive gain in union membership. Founded by John L. Lewis, president of the United Mine Workers, as an offshoot of the American Federation of Labor (AFL) in 1935, it was originally named the Committee for Industrial Organizations; it was renamed in 1938.

The CIO had an agenda of organizing workers in America's mass-production industries, such as steel, auto, and rubber—industries that the AFL's strategy and history of organizing along craft and skill lines rather than across a whole industry had all but ignored. Throughout the 1930s, the CIO was a dynamic force in the American labor movement, working with any and all allies, from President Franklin D. Roosevelt and the Democratic Party to the Communist Party to achieve dramatic union victories—for example, with General Motors (GM) in Flint, Michigan—and the recognition of the Steel Workers Organizing Committee by the nation's largest steel manufacturer, U.S. Steel, in 1937.

With such victories under their belt, the CIO and its affiliated unions, such as the United Auto Workers (UAW) and the United Steel Workers of America (USWA), entered World War II as a major force in American politics and business. Following the attack on Pearl Harbor in December 1941, the CIO and its competitor, the AFL, entered into a No-Strike Pledge. For the good of wartime production and national unity, unions would forgo work stoppages for the duration of the conflict.

The effects of the No-Strike Pledge on organized labor in America were twofold. On one hand, labor leaders such as the UAW's Walter Reuther, the AFL's William Green, and the International Ladies Garment Workers Union's (ILGWU) Sidney Hillman were able to gain entrance to the highest circles of the American state in the form of the National War Labor Board, which was made up of equal parts labor, corporate, and government officials. In so doing, labor leaders were given a major voice in state policy for the first time in U.S. history. On the other hand, the pledge had the effect of stifling rank-and-file militancy and

accepting a government with which, outside of the National War Labor Board, labor had little pull in comparison to the corporate interests that the Roosevelt Administration turned to for wartime support.

Peak Years: 1940s and Early 1950s

At the end of the war, union leadership faced a major dilemma. Organized labor's support for the war and wartime administration had gained unions influence in government previously unheard of in American history. World War II also resulted in major gains for union membership and a bevy of new contracts. Yet rank-and-file workers were growing increasingly frustrated by the rise of what the left wing sociologist C. Wright Mills called "the new men of power"—that is, a labor movement led by unresponsive leaders who were entrenched in the state apparatus and removed from the everyday concerns of the membership they supposedly represented.

Without the potent weapon of the strike at the unions' disposal, manufacturers often violated their commitment to pay raises and took away some of the hard-fought, shop-floor control that militant workers had won during the 1930s. The result, during the war, was a series of wildcat (unauthorized) strikes.

When the war ended, these strikes multiplied into the largest strike wave in American history. Virtually every major U.S. industry experienced work stoppages in the period from the fall of 1945 through 1946. The latter year witnessed more than 5,000 strikes, involving some 4.6 million workers, by far the largest strike wave in American history. Navigating the divide between an increasingly corporatist involvement in the American state through the National Labor Relations Board's role as labor mediator and the militancy of labor's rank and file would prove to be a key issue for unions, as the nation moved from wartime production to peacetime economic boom.

One way that organized labor sought to increase its power, along with its membership, was a massive attempt to organize America's central area of anti-union sentiment—the South. In 1946, the CIO embarked on the most ambitious organizing drive in American history, dubbed Operation Dixie. Though unions had witnessed huge gains in the Northeast, Midwest, and West Coast during the Great Depression and World War II, the South had remained largely outside their grasp.

The Jim Crow system of racial segregation kept African American and white workers from identifying and working with each other. This provided antiunion business leaders and politicians with a potent wedge to further divide and thus conquer previous spurts of Southern working-class militancy, such as the populist revolt of the late-nineteenth century.

Furthermore, as compared to the rest of the nation, the South largely (though decreasingly) still had an agricultural-based economy. Where manufacturing had taken root in the South—in places such as the Piedmont textile centers of Virginia, the Carolinas, and Georgia—unionism had been foiled time and again through local leaders' willingness to use the most violent of means to keep organized labor out.

For the CIO, despite the huge odds against it, the potential benefits of an organized South were too tempting to pass up. These benefits included a union voting bloc capable of dislodging antiunion Southern Democrats, a work force less tempting to the so-called runaway shops in industries, such as automobiles and electrical, that were already closing plants in search of cheaper labor in Southern states, and a huge gain in Southern living standards, which were by far the worst in the country.

Despite the CIO's massive investment of organizers and money in the South, by 1948, it had largely been defeated in this area, though it did succeed in organizing hundreds of thousands of textile and communication workers. Business and political leaders across the South portrayed CIO leaders as anti-American Communists, played on the racism of Southern white workers, threatened violence against organizers, and painted pictures of de-industrialized ghost towns that would result from textile mills leaving for cheaper work forces if Operation Dixie succeeded. The CIO forced many of these problems on itself, as it refused to turn Operation Dixie into a wider struggle against the Jim Crow system of employment by largely ignoring African American workers (by far the CIO's most sympathetic Southern audience) in favor of the mostly white Piedmont textile workers and by pulling organizers and money out of towns and whole states at the first sign of defeat.

The failure of the CIO in the South was also aided by the increasingly anticommunist sentiment that pervaded America and the labor movement during the 1940s. Throughout the CIO's early history, a large portion of its most energetic, experienced, and effective organizers had been in one way or another associated with communism during the Popular Front period of the Great Depression.

Following the war, however, the CIO experienced a growing split between left-led unions such as the United Electrical Workers and the Walter Reuther–led UAW. The left-led unions were critical of the "labor liberalism" and growing ensconcement with state and business leaders that characterized groups such as the UAW. They saw the stifling of rank-and-file militancy during the war and its aftermath as a function of an increasingly conservative and unrepresentative CIO leadership.

The split turned into outright division with the passage—by the Republican Congress, over President Harry S. Truman's veto—of the Taft-Hartley Act in 1947. Among the many provisions of this legislation was a requirement that all trade-union officials sign a pledge declaring they were not Communists, the effect of which was to purge many of the most energetic and experienced CIO organizers, as well as those who were most vehemently working for integration and against Jim Crow unionism, which limited membership to white workers only, in the South. The CIO leadership, unsympathetic and hostile to the left-led unions and organizers who had been Communist Party members or fellow travelers during the 1930s, took the opportunity to push out some of its most dynamic colleagues and officials well before the hysteria of McCarthyism reached full force.

The purge of Communists finalized by Taft-Hartley was only the most immediate and dramatic effect that the law had on American labor. More important for the long-term future of the labor movement were two other provisions. Section 14b of the act gave states the right to outlaw the union shop and pass "right-to-work" laws that gave workers in a unionized shop the freedom to not join a union. The effect was that even after a union recognition election had been won, a company could destroy shop-floor solidarity and, eventually, defeat the union by selectively hiring antiunion employees. Right-to-work laws, not surprisingly, were mostly passed across the nation's most antiunion region, the South.

Perhaps even more important in the long run, Taft-Hartley outlawed the sympathy strike. This weapon had been used successfully in some of organized labor's most dramatic moments of the 1930s, such as the general strikes in Toledo, Minneapolis, and San Francisco, California, in 1934. The effect of outlawing such strikes was to deprive labor of the ability to mobilize an entire community in response to the intransigence of employers and industry. No longer were workers able to enlist their friends and family as active participants against an individual employer or industry by taking their struggle beyond the confines of their individual job into a broader critique of local or even national economic conditions and systems.

Although both the AFL and CIO worked against passage of the Taft-Hartley Act, upon its enactment, there was little they could do to protest. Refusal to abide by its provisions would have meant the loss of access to government mediation of labor disputes through the National Labor Relations Board, a prospect that was unfathomable to America's increasingly bureaucratized unions.

Taft-Hartley represented the beginning of the dominant trend of postwar American unionism: corporate liberalism. Though the effect of Taft-Hartley was to deprive unions of their militancy, its stated purpose was industrial peace and a decline in labor

Hoffa and the Teamsters

Ever combative and constantly in the limelight, Jimmy Hoffa ruled the militant International Brotherhood of Teamsters union from the late 1950s through the mid-1970s with a mix of patronage and coercion that made him one of the most powerful figures in the history of American labor. But nothing about Hoffa was as memorable as his exit from the national stage in 1975.

James Riddle Hoffa was born on February 14, 1913, in Brazil, Indiana. His father, a coal miner, died when he was seven, and James moved with his mother to Detroit, Michigan. From the age of seventeen, he worked in a grocery warehouse, and, by the age of twenty, he had become a well-known local Teamsters union organizer.

Hoffa was elected vice president of the Teamsters in 1952 and president in 1957, after the conviction and imprisonment of then-president Dave Beck for misappropriation of union funds. A Senate investigation of the Teamsters accused union officials of misdealings, and the American Federation of Labor-Congress of Industrial Organizations (AFL-CIO) released the union from the federation as a result of the pressure. Despite a variety of charges and indictments against him—most notably connections with organized crime—the charismatic Hoffa was reelected in 1961 by an overwhelming number.

Investigations into the Teamsters' activities were conducted by the U.S. Department of Justice beginning in 1957 under Attorney General Robert F. Kennedy. Hoffa was charged with bribery and attempting to influence the Senate McClellan Commission, but he was found not guilty of the former charges in 1964. Finally, in 1967, he was convicted of jury tampering and the misuse of union pension funds and sentenced to thirteen years in prison. In December 1971, after Hoffa had served only four years of his term, President Richard M. Nixon commuted his sentence on the condition that he remove himself from union activity.

Despite the Nixon agreement, Hoffa continued to work behind the scenes in the union. On July 30, 1975, he was parked at a restaurant lot in Bloomfield Hills, Michigan, purportedly meeting to negotiate his reentry into the union. It was the last time anyone saw him alive, and his body was never found.

Hoffa's disappearance continues to be the subject of popular speculation and urban legend. Fingers have been pointed at other union leaders, organized crime, and even the Federal Bureau of Investigation. Hoffa was declared legally dead in 1983. New evidence in the case was found in 2001 and again in 2003, but charges were never filed. One investigation had police excavating building sites and portions of a football field in New Jersey. Police still consider the disappearance an open case.

Hoffa's son, James Philip Hoffa, a trained labor lawyer, was elected president of the Teamsters in 1998 and again in 2001.

Pamela Lee Gray

disputes and strikes. Corporate liberalism was the idea, increasingly at the forefront of many business leaders' thinking in the 1950s and beyond, that consistent and strong profits required peaceful labor relations, which, in turn, required workers to be paid relatively high wages and given benefits in exchange for renouncing their right to strike and ceding control over production and the shop floor.

Corporate liberalism, and its attendant economic philosophy of Fordism, was epitomized by the historic 1950 contract agreement between General Motors and the UAW. Dubbed the "Treaty of Detroit" by *Fortune* magazine's Daniel Bell, the five-year contract guaranteed benefits such as health care, a union shop, and cost-of-living wage adjustments. In exchange, the UAW and its members not only gave up the right to strike and control the shop floor, but essentially they

As longtime head of the Teamsters union, Jimmy Hoffa was one of the most powerful and controversial figures in the postwar labor movement. In July 1975, having served prison time for jury tampering and misusing union pension funds, he disappeared. *(Lynn Pelham/Time Life Pictures/Getty Images)*

ceded their right to contest who controlled and owned production in America.

Such an accord became the prototypical agreement for postwar labor relations: It represented the unquestioned acceptance of industrial capitalism by unions, while simultaneously expressing the goal of such capitalism. It envisioned a partnership between organized labor and industry to move industrial workers, at least in terms of wages and benefits, into America's growing middle class.

Between the rise of collective bargaining agreements epitomized by the GM–UAW accord of 1950, the complete expulsion of Communists from the CIO, and the passage and codification of Taft-Hartley, the differences that once separated the AFL from its breakaway rival, the CIO—craft unionism versus industrial unionism, pragmatism versus militancy—became less stark. It seemed only natural in 1955 when the two federations merged to become the AFL-CIO. Because it was still decidedly bigger than the CIO, the AFL, with its cautious, antiradical approach to unionism, took the lead in the merged organization and produced its first president, George Meany.

Meany had been secretary-treasurer of the old AFL, and, despite his strong background and adherence to craft-union principles, he was more sympathetic than many of his AFL brethren to the upsurge in industrial unionism during the 1930s and 1940s. Yet Meany was far from a radical—he was virulently anticommunist and accused of taking little or no action to end the rampant discrimination against African Americans in union membership and hiring within the member unions of the AFL-CIO.

Stasis: Late 1950s and 1960s

From the late 1950s through the end of the 1960s, unions and the American labor movement were in a period of stasis. Though some unions, such as the UAW, enthusiastically supported the civil rights movement, the AFL-CIO mostly found itself no longer on the cutting edge of social change. During much of this period, unions seemed to lose their dynamism, as organizing became less of a priority in relation to the AFL-CIO's new emphasis on political action within and for the Democratic Party.

The one exception to this lag in organizing growth was public-sector unionism. Organizations such as the American Federation of State, County and Municipal Employees and the American Federation of Teachers organized unprecedented numbers of workers at all levels of government. Indeed, public employee union membership rose from fewer than 500,000 in the middle of the 1950s to more than 4 million by the early 1970s.

The closeness of the American labor movement to the Democratic Party had been growing exponentially since the Great Depression and the presidency of Franklin D. Roosevelt. Before World War II, the CIO had firmly aligned itself with Roosevelt and the Democratic Party, helping to deliver working-class votes not only to Roosevelt, but also to sympathetic labor candidates across the nation, such as Michigan governor Frank Murphy. In 1943, the CIO's political involvement became official with the formation of the Congress of Industrial Organizations Political Action Committee (CIO-PAC), which sought to mobilize the masses of urban industrial workers to support pro-labor candidates who usually hailed from the Democratic Party.

In 1947, the AFL followed suit and created Labor's League for Political Education (LLPE), a radical departure for the federation that had been shaped by Samuel Gompers and his vision of a complete separation between unionism and politics. The strength of the LLPE lay in the tight-knittedness of its member unions, such as the United Brotherhood of Carpenters and Joiners, whereas the CIO-PAC was colored by the idealism and organizing fervor that had been such a part of the breakaway federation during its massive organizing campaigns of the 1930s and 1940s.

Upon the 1955 merger of the AFL and CIO, a new political arm, the Committee for Political Education (COPE), was formed. By the 1960s, the success of COPE in mobilizing working-class and union voters for candidates and in support of pro-labor legislation had given the AFL-CIO a major voice in the Democratic Party. Though bureaucratized and often unresponsive to the desires of rank-and-file union members, COPE and its predecessors in the CIO-PAC and LLPE had given organized labor its most influential relationship with a major political party in U.S. history.

Crisis Years: 1970s–2000s

The 1960s was a time of growing political influence, gains in social welfare provisions as part of President Lyndon B. Johnson's Great Society programs, and a relatively static though still strong labor movement, but the 1970s pushed American unions into crisis. To many historians, the postwar Fordist system of stable production, high wages, and a growing middle class based on unionized industrial jobs came to an abrupt end in 1973 with the oil crisis and the end of the Bretton Woods trade agreement. The period that followed, often dubbed "post-Fordism," saw the frequency of recessions rise, while the country went through a period of "stagflation" (stagnant growth coupled with inflation). The 1970s would also see the first great national wave of de-industrialization and capital flight.

De-industrialization had been a fixture of industrial capitalism for centuries, as new technologies and the search for cheaper labor led companies to close production in certain areas in favor of others. Areas such as the textile centers of New England had seen many of their jobs migrate to Southern states such as North and South Carolina during the first half of the twentieth century. Still, little could have prepared America and its unions for the factory closings that hit virtually every region of the country; the toll was particularly brutal on the industrial Midwest and Northeast.

As a result of layoffs and closings in such centers of steel production as Youngstown, Ohio, and Gary, Indiana, the once extremely powerful United Steel Workers of America saw its membership cut in half during the 1970s and early 1980s, from approximately 1 million to less than a half million. The USWA was the rule rather than the exception throughout the 1970s and 1980s, as the United Auto Workers, International Brotherhood of Teamsters, and International Ladies Garment Workers Union all lost hundreds of thousands of union members. Union membership declined from 29 percent of the population in 1973 to 16 percent by 1989.

With the drop-off came a new round of union busting. Although vehemently antiunion practices on the part of employers have never been entirely absent from American business, the postwar period and its corporate liberalism initially made such outright hostility more episodic than continual across America's main industries. Despite the limitations of the Wagner Act and Taft-Hartley, the postwar federal government did not engage in explicitly antiunion practices, as it had during the Gilded Age and the post–World War I period.

In 1981, however, newly elected President Ronald Reagan changed this by dramatically crushing the Professional Air Traffic Controllers Organization (PATCO, one of the few unions that had endorsed him in 1980), whose 13,000 members walked off the job for better working conditions. Not only did Reagan end the strike by firing all 13,000 workers and delegitmizing the union, but he sent a loud-and-clear message to unions around the country by announcing that the government would refuse to rehire any air traffic controller who had walked off the job.

What was most disturbing about the PATCO affair to union leaders was the fact that although Reagan was proving himself to be the most antiunion president since the 1920s, he continued to garner millions of votes from white, blue-collar union members to whom he appealed with his emphasis on patriotism and old-fashioned values. In so doing, he helped to throw organized labor into further crisis, as its members could not be counted on as much to deliver their votes to the Democratic Party. Thus, as the 1970s turned into the 1980s, the prospects for organized labor, already critically wounded by plant closures and macro-structural changes in the U.S. and global economy, began to look even worse.

The period from the 1980s to the present has seen union membership continue to erode across virtually every American industry. Whereas union members represented more than 20 percent of the labor force in 1983, they accounted for less than 16 percent by 1993 and less than 13 percent in 2003. But not all unions declined after the 1970s.

The United Farm Workers (UFW), led by Cesar Chavez, successfully organized against the California grape industry by sending the migrant grape workers out on numerous strikes and leading a national boycott of grapes. By the mid-1970s, Chavez and the UFW had won union contracts for 65 percent of California's grape workers.

The Service Employees International Union (SEIU), led by John Sweeney (who would later head the AFL-CIO) and Andy Stern, succeeded in organizing hundreds of thousands of workers in the nation's rapidly growing service economy throughout the 1980s and 1990s. The SEIU concentrated much of its energy on health care, building service, and public-sector workers and became one of the few bright spots of the labor movement. By 2005, the SEIU had become the nation's largest union with more than 1.8 million members.

The growth of the SEIU and its place in the emergent service economy highlighted growing divisions in the labor movement. A debate erupted between many of the old-guard unions, such as the UAW and USWA, and the SEIU and the newly merged Union of Needletrades, Industrial and Textile Workers and Hotel Employees and Restaurant Employees International Union (which became known as UNITE-HERE). The old-guard unions argued that in order for labor to regain its power, it should concentrate on politics and changing institutions such as the National Labor Relations Board, which had become increasingly more hostile to labor since 1970. Groups such as the SEIU saw this strategy as ineffective, arguing that labor could only regain its influence in politics by vastly increasing its membership, especially in low-wage service jobs. The debate turned into open division in 2005, when the SEIU, joined by the Teamsters, the United Food and Commercial Workers, and UNITE-HERE, left the AFL-CIO to form the Change to Win Coalition.

The split caused many to recall the last time labor had experienced such turmoil—seven decades earlier, when John L. Lewis founded the CIO. Though some of the issues seem similar, such as the Change to Win Coalition's emphasis on organizing in new areas (a goal that bears much resemblance to the CIO's focus on previously unorganized industrial workers), the historical contexts of 1935 and 2005 look exceedingly different.

The seventy years between the founding of the CIO and the Change to Win Coalition saw the American labor movement rise to its peak of social and political influence during and immediately after World War II, then begin a slow weakening. The decline picked up steam with waves of deindustrialization, the end of Fordism and corporate liberalism, a rebirth of union busting by corporations and the federal government, and the election of presidents such as Ronald Reagan who gained support from union members while launching all-out attacks on unions themselves. Although on an institutional level, the American labor movement has seemingly come full circle, the challenges it faces in the next seventy years and beyond look less clear and more difficult.

Thomas Jessen Adams

See also: Agricultural Workers; Air Traffic Controllers' Strike; Automobile Industry; Blue-Collar Workers; Globalization; Landrum-Griffin Act; North American Free Trade Agreement; Pensions, Private; Rust Belt; Service-Sector Workers; Strikes; Taft-Hartley Act; Unemployment; Women and Work.

Bibliography

Cohen, Lizabeth. *Making a New Deal: Industrial Workers in Chicago, 1919–1939.* New York: Cambridge University Press, 1990.

Davis, Mike. *Prisoners of the American Dream: Politics and Economy in the History of the U.S. Working Class.* New York: Verso, 1986.

Lichtenstein, Nelson. *Labor's War at Home: The CIO in World War II.* Ithaca, NY: Cornell University Press, 1982.

———. *State of the Union: A Century of American Labor.* Princeton, NJ: Princeton University Press, 2002.

Mills, C. Wright. *The New Men of Power, America's Labor Leaders.* New York: Harcourt, Brace, 1948.

Stein, Judith. *Running Steel, Running America: Race, Economic Policy and the Decline of Liberalism.* Chapel Hill: University of North Carolina Press, 1998.

Tomlins, Christopher. *The State and the Unions: Labor Relations, Law, and the Organized Labor Movement in America, 1880–1960.* New York: Cambridge University Press, 1985.

Zieger, Robert. *American Workers, American Unions.* Baltimore: Johns Hopkins University Press, 1986.

UNITED NATIONS, RELATIONS WITH

The United States, a key player in the creation of the United Nations (UN) during and immediately after World War II, has had a rocky relationship with the world body in the decades since. Although the United States is the organization's largest source of funds and holds one of five permanent, veto-wielding seats on the critical Security Council, America has often found itself the odd nation out on many controversial votes taken by the UN.

In addition, the UN has come under fire from U.S. politicians and the American public at large. In particular, conservatives in the United States have criticized the organization as corrupt and leaning too far to the political left. From time to time, Washington has chafed at the influence of the large bloc of developing countries in the General Assembly and the decisions they have made, especially those criticizing America's key ally in the Middle East, Israel.

In return, many UN members have used the forum to express their dissatisfaction with American hegemony in the world; some have complained that Washington holds too much power within the organization. American frustration with the UN—as well as UN member nations' suspicion of the United States—reached a high point during the early 2000s, when the George W. Bush Administration dismissed the effectiveness of UN-led weapons of mass destruction (WMD) inspections in Iraq and bypassed the Security Council to launch a preemptive, largely unilateral war against that country in early 2003.

Origins

For the first century or so of its history, the United States—protected by vast oceans and focused on settling its Western territories—largely avoided involvement in affairs outside its borders. With its rising industrial might and the closure of the Western frontier in the late nineteenth, America—or at least some of its key policymakers—began to assert the country's military, political, and especially economic power overseas, first in Latin America, then in East Asia, and finally, in Europe during World War I.

But U.S. involvement in World War I proved a painful lesson for most Americans. Frustrated that the costly war had not brought democracy and freedom to the world, as President Woodrow Wilson had promised, many in Congress and the public longed for a return to the country's isolationist traditions. This thinking led to a decisive 1919 Senate vote against America joining the League of Nations, an international peacekeeping organization championed by Wilson. Although Washington participated in international military, political, and economic forums during the 1920s and 1930s, it did so on an ad hoc basis, remaining aloof from full participation in the League. Indeed, many historians have argued that the League's inability to prevent aggression by the Fascist powers of Germany, Japan, and Italy during the 1930s was a result, in part, of America's absence from the organization.

But the United States could not avoid involvement in world affairs altogether. By late 1941, the country had largely dropped its position of neutrality in the great conflict between the Fascist powers on one hand and the antifascist forces of Great Britain, the Soviet Union, and China on the other, providing materiel and armaments to the latter group. With Japan's December 7, 1941, attack on Pearl Harbor, Washington found itself a full participant in World War II.

Even before U.S. entry into the war, however, President Franklin D. Roosevelt had begun to consider America's role in the world after the war was over. In August 1941, he met with British Prime Minister Winston Churchill aboard a British battleship off the

Newfoundland coast. The result of the meeting was the Atlantic Charter, a document outlining the two countries' war aims. These included national self-determination, disarmament, and a collective security mechanism for ensuring peace and preventing aggression. As World War II ground on through the early 1940s, and as its cost in money and human life mounted, policymakers in Washington became increasingly determined to prevent a replay of what had happened after World War I, when the country withdrew from the world and aggression went unpunished.

At a 1943 conference in Tehran, Roosevelt proposed to his allies (Churchill and Soviet premier Joseph Stalin) an institution that he called the Four Policemen, consisting of the four great powers (the United States, Great Britain, the Soviet Union, and China), which would act as international law enforcers to prevent aggression and ensure the peaceful settlement of conflicts between nations. A year later, representatives of the four countries met at Dumbarton Oaks, a mansion in Washington, where they approved a preliminary charter for a UN organization. The body would include a General Assembly of all member nations, as the League of Nations had, but it bowed to *Realpolitik* by centralizing power in a Security Council consisting of the five great powers (Britain insisted on including France), each of which would have a veto over key security decisions made by the organization.

In April 1945, representatives from fifty countries met in San Francisco to write a permanent charter for the new organization, based largely on the plan outlined at Dumbarton Oaks, but providing more room for other nations to participate and decide organizational policy. With the fate of the League of Nations in mind, one of the decisions reached at the time was to headquarter the body in New York, to ensure U.S. participation.

Cold War Tensions

The United Nations began with great hopes, but it soon fell victim to Cold War hostilities between two of its founders and Security Council members, the United States and the Soviet Union. In 1946, President Harry S Truman presented a plan for the international control of the new atomic weapons developed by the United States during World War II and used against Japan. At the time, the United States alone possessed the bomb, and it was determined to maintain that monopoly. Under the plan, the United States would keep its small stockpile of atomic weapons, forgo building more, and give the UN power to punish countries that tried to develop them. Such UN action, under the U.S. plan, would be exempt from Security Council veto. But because the Soviet Union was determined to develop atomic weapons of its own—to counter those possessed by the United States—the plan was doomed to failure.

Four years later, U.S. efforts to involve the UN in halting aggression by Communist nations was more successful. Following Communist North Korea's invasion of South Korea in June 1950, the United States went to the UN asking for Security Council approval to send troops to South Korea.

Normally the pro–North Korean Soviet Union would have vetoed such a move, but Moscow was boycotting the organization after the General Assembly's refusal to seat the Communist Chinese delegation. Communists under Mao Zedong had taken power in mainland China the year before, forcing the ruling nationalists to flee to the island of Taiwan. The UN General Assembly, dominated by the United States and its allies in Europe and Latin America, chose to recognize Taiwan over Beijing. Although U.S. forces were joined in Korea by troops from dozens of other nations—all technically part of a UN "police action"—in fact, the Korean War was largely a fight between the United States and South Korea on one side and North Korea—and later Communist China—on the other.

As the Korean War illustrated, the United States wielded enormous influence over the world body during the late 1940s and 1950s, even after the Soviet Union returned to the UN in late 1950. Indeed, to overcome Soviet Security Council vetoes, the United States pushed its "United for Peace" resolution through the General Assembly. Under this resolution, the General Assembly could initiate military action over the objection of a single Security Council nation. Although many UN experts doubted the legality of the resolution, it gave the United States cover to maintain a military presence in Korea despite numerous Soviet vetoes of resolutions to maintain a UN police presence on the Korean peninsula.

Dominated by the United States and its image burnished by a number of high-profile peacekeeping efforts in Cyprus and the Sinai, the UN enjoyed the solid support of the Dwight D. Eisenhower Administration and the American public during the 1950s and early 1960s. Still, there were elements on the far right of the American political spectrum, including Senator Joseph McCarthy (Republican of Wisconsin) and the John Birch Society, who saw the organization as a front for a worldwide Communist conspiracy. One group, the Minutemen, even claimed that the UN had plans for the occupation of American cities.

Relations between the United States and the UN, however, grew more contentious during the 1960s. One reason was the worldwide decolonization movement. Between the late 1940s and the early 1960s, vast areas of Asia and Africa (outside the southern regions of the latter) were granted or won their independence from European colonizers. These new developing world nations became UN members, increasing the General Assembly ranks from 51 in 1945 to 113 by 1965. A large number of these new nations had leftist, or at least anti-Western, governments. Following the lead of the first nonaligned nations conference at Banung, Indonesia, in 1955, many opted for a neutral stance in the Cold War, which often meant voting against U.S. interests at the UN. In addition, a global opposition to perceived U.S. imperialism, and especially to the United States's war in Vietnam, often evinced itself in harsh anti-American rhetoric at the UN.

America's strong support for Israel after the 1967 and 1973 Arab-Israeli Wars added fuel to the fire. In the former conflict, Israel seized the Golan Heights, the West Bank, East Jerusalem, the Sinai Peninsula, and the Gaza Strip from its Arab neighbors, becoming an occupying force in regions with large Palestinian populations. As formerly occupied countries themselves, the vast majority of developing world states sympathized with the Palestinians, or at least wanted to cultivate friendly relations with the oil- and cash-rich Arab countries. Numerous General Assembly resolutions were passed from the 1960s on calling for Israel to pull out of the occupied territories and condemning the Jewish state for its seizure of Palestinian land, its policy of settling Jews on Palestinian territory, and its efforts to crush the Palestinian insurgency. In the mid-1970s, the UN General Assembly voted to grant the Palestine Liberation Organization—which Jerusalem and Washington considered a terrorist organization—observer status, invited its chairman, Yasir Arafat, to address the body, and declared that "Zionism is a form of racism." The United States voted against all of these resolutions and measures, but, in doing so, it found itself increasingly isolated from the world body's vast majority of states.

American Conservative Hostility

With Ronald Reagan's victory in the 1980 U.S. presidential election and the preeminence of conservative ideology in American politics, old right wing shibboleths about UN leftism and anti-Americanism came to the fore. In 1984, the Reagan Administration pulled the United States out of the UN Educational, Scientific, and Cultural Organization (UNESCO). But it was not only the perceived left wing bias of the UN and its organizations that upset conservatives in Washington.

The Christian right, a major component of the Republican base, strongly objected to the policies of the UN Population Fund (UNPF). Founded in 1969, the UNPF became a strong supporter of birth control and, where it was accepted by member states, abortion as well. Republican lawmakers, in control of America's purse strings after taking a majority in Congress in the 1994 midterm elections, began cutting America's contribution to the UNPF unless it stopped funding organizations that advocated or provided abortions.

There were also complaints about wastefulness and corruption in the UN. Led by Senator Jesse Helms of North Carolina, Republican members of Congress voted to withhold hundreds of millions of dollars in America's UN dues until reforms were made to streamline the organization and end the supposed anti-American bias of some of its component organizations. Some political observers said that Republican hostility had less to do with corruption and waste than it did with a general hostility toward the UN's mission.

That is to say, many of the UN's toughest critics were part of an ideological faction known as the neoconservatives, or "neocons." A central tenet of neocon foreign policy is that the United States should be able to pursue its military, political, and economic interests unilaterally, without having to seek the approval of other countries or international bodies such as the UN. Other observers of U.S.-UN relations say that the neocons' hostility seems misplaced. Since the demise of the Soviet Union, they point out, the UN has once again become an organization dominated by the United States and its Western allies.

September 11 and the Iraq War

Nevertheless, with the inauguration of President George W. Bush in 2001, the neocons were in control of American foreign policy. Following the September 11 terrorist attacks, they felt more embold-ened to act on their unilateral instincts. In October, the administration launched a full-fledged invasion of Afghanistan, whose Taliban regime, it was said, was harboring the September 11 mastermind, Osama bin Laden, and his al-Qaeda terrorist organization. Though it did not seek Security Council approval for the invasion, the Bush Administration nevertheless enjoyed broad international support for its effort to overthrow the Taliban.

The Bush Administration's decision to attack Iraq in 2003 was a different story. Ironically, the dispute over Iraq grew out of one of the greatest moments in the history of U.S.-UN amity. In 1990, after the Iraqi dictator Saddam Hussein had invaded neighboring Kuwait without provocation, U.S. President George H. W. Bush—with UN backing—organized a broad international coalition to force Hussein out of Kuwait. The UN also voted to impose economic sanctions on Iraq and sent inspectors to uncover and destroy Iraq's Weapons of Mass Destructiion (WMD) and missile-building facilities. Frustrated by the continuing sanctions and inspections, Hussein made it increasingly difficult for the inspectors to do their job. In 1998, citing the obstacles put in front of them by the Iraqi government, the inspectors pulled out.

In the aftermath of the September 11 terrorist attacks, the George W. Bush Administration became increasingly insistent that Iraq had somehow been connected to the attacks and that the regime possessed—or would soon possess—WMDs, including nuclear weapons. Most of the international community was suspicious of the Bush Administration's claims or else felt the best way to handle the situation was to send the inspectors back with an ultimatum for Hussein: Cooperate or face possible invasion. In late 2002, the Security Council voted to send inspectors back into Iraq. For several months, they conducted investigations, reporting that they had found some evidence of WMDs but no serious violations of earlier UN resolutions.

The Bush Administration—along with its ally, Great Britain—was not satisfied. In February 2003, it dispatched Secretary of State Colin Powell to make a case to the Security Council that Hussein was developing WMDs and that inspections were not enough to stop him. When the Security Council proved unwilling to authorize immediate military force against Iraq, the Bush Administration opted not to seek that authorization, claiming that earlier Security Council resolutions were sufficient. In March, it launched a massive invasion of Iraq that led to the rapid collapse of the Hussein regime and the occupation of Baghdad.

In the years since, the Bush Administration has failed to find WMDs or provide compelling evidence linking Iraq to the September 11 attacks. Meanwhile, UN General Secretary Kofi Annan repeatedly condemned the preemptive invasion as a violation of the UN Charter. Nevertheless, the UN committed itself to helping end the occupation by readying Iraq for elections and sovereignty and by establishing a presence in the country.

As the anti-American insurgency grew, however, the UN found itself under attack as well. In August 2003, its headquarters in Baghdad were attacked by a suicide bomber who killed the organization's top envoy in the country, Sergio Vieira de Mello, along with twenty-three others. The UN substantially reduced its activities in Iraq, though it did help to organize democratic elections in the country.

An Easing of Tensions?

As of the mid-2000s, U.S.-UN relations were at an ebb, aggravated not just by the Iraq War but also by the Bush Administration's decision to appoint the UN-bashing John Bolton as its ambassador to the body. Bolton has repeatedly been at the forefront of those criticizing the organization for its anti-Americanism, corruption, and waste.

Meanwhile, the United States insisted on a thorough investigation of corruption in the UN's oil-for-food program, which had been established in the late 1990s to allow Iraq to sell its oil in exchange for needed food and medicine. The Bush Administration and members of Congress demanded that an outside investigator, former Federal Reserve chairman Paul Volcker, investigate. Although Volcker's team did find some evidence of UN corruption, many UN members found the outrage of the U.S. administration hypocritical, given the billions of missing dollars in U.S. reconstruction money destined for Iraq.

For all the acrimony, there were some signs that U.S.-UN relations were on the mend, if slowly. Though the Bush Administration continued to insist on American unilateralism, it came to realize the need for international cooperation in the War on Terrorism and the rebuilding of Iraq. For its part, the UN has become increasingly receptive to the U.S. criticism that it needs to cut some of its more wasteful practices and become a more efficient organization.

James Ciment

See also: China and Taiwan, Relations with; Cuban Missile Crisis; Haiti Incursion; International Institutions; Iraq War; Israel, Relations with; Korean War; Somalia Intervention; Terrorism, Foreign.

Bibliography

Franck, Thomas M. *Nation Against Nation: What Happened to the U.N. Dream and What the U.S. Can Do About It.* New York: Oxford University Press, 1985.

Gregg, Robert W. *About Face? The United States and the United Nations.* Boulder, CO: Lynne Rienner, 1993.

Meisler, Stanley. *United Nations: The First Fifty Years.* New York: Atlantic Monthly Press, 1995.

Stoessinger, John G. *The United Nations and the Superpowers: China, Russia, and America.* New York: Random House, 1977.

Weiss, Thomas G., David P. Forsythe, and Roger A. Coate, eds. *United Nations and Changing World Politics.* Boulder, CO: Westview, 2004.

URBAN RENEWAL

Urban renewal was the term applied to postwar efforts to raze impoverished inner-city neighborhoods and replace them with a variety of civic improvement projects, such as new government centers, office buildings, and retail complexes; improved public and private housing; and an infrastructure for automobiles that included limited-access highways and parking garages. Begun during the late 1940s, urban renewal reached its zenith in the 1960s, before it tapered off, a victim of its own failures—the destruction of once-vibrant if poor neighborhoods and the creation of what critics called soulless urban spaces—and rising political conservatism that looked on government-financed social improvement projects with disdain.

By the 1950s and 1960s, it was obvious to politicians, planners, and urban residents that many downtown areas were in serious decline. The suburbs were draining the middle class from the cities. Though the suburban lifestyle—private homes, open space, and better public facilities such as schools—was the major lure, government programs contributed to the exodus. The Federal Housing Administration, established in 1934, favored government-guaranteed, low-cost mortgages for new rather than existing housing, and the Federal-Aid Highway Act of 1956 provided vast subsidies for an interstate system that would make it easier to live in the suburbs and commute to the cities.

Moreover, fewer people were moving into urban areas after World War II. Restrictive immigration laws had cut off the flow of foreigners into cities, and black migration from the South had subsided by the 1960s. Race played another role as well. Although black migration was down from its peak during World War II, the prewar and war years had seen the development of large African American populations in the inner cities, which caused increasing numbers of middle-class whites to flee to the suburbs, especially after the urban rioting of the mid-1960s.

To reverse the decline, many city governments began to lobby Washington for money to redevelop their inner-city cores. The redevelopment consisted of two stages. One was slum clearance: the destruction of overcrowded and substandard tenements and other types of prewar housing that were viewed as eyesores, depressed property values, and discouraged suburbanites and tourists from visiting and spending money in the central city. Most cities made promises to residents that comparably priced housing units would replace those that had been cleared out, but this was often left out of the final plans for urban renewal.

Some black activists came to call urban renewal "Negro removal." Rather than rebuild neighborhoods, the cities erected high-rise public housing projects on the peripheries of downtown. As crowded as the tenements they replaced but with few of the previous commercial amenities and little sense of neighborhood, these public housing projects became little more than vertical slums, beset by crime and the very physical decay they had been intended to eradicate.

With cutbacks in public housing funding initiated during the recessionary 1970s and accelerated under the conservative anti–public housing administration of President Ronald Reagan in the 1980s, there was little maintenance, as the infrastructure deteriorated. So poorly thought-out and badly run were some of the projects that a number of them, beginning with St. Louis's Pruitt-Igoe Project in 1973, had been torn down by the end of the twentieth century.

Rather than replacing the neighborhoods, then, urban renewal led to the building of new civic centers, office buildings, and indoor shopping malls. The reason, say urban experts, was politics. Inner-city residents, many of them poor and uneducated, had little say in the running of city government. Instead, business interests predominated. Politicians, though sometimes sympathetic to the needs of their poor, inner-city constituents, nevertheless accepted the business community's argument that revitalization depended on creating a healthier tax base. To do that, it was necessary to attract businesses and commerce by putting up office buildings and shopping malls. To make the inner city more attractive, modern civic centers—some with theaters and concert halls—were also seen as vital.

The constituency for these new commercial and government projects would be suburbanites. To lure them back into the city, new highways and multi-level parking structures were built. But the highways cut through poor urban neighborhoods, and the parking structures created an urban no-man's land that led to further deterioration of inner-city neighborhoods. Once again, much of this building was financed by the federal government, which allowed interstate highway funds to be used for urban beltways and spurs.

Even as the push for such projects was reaching its apex in the 1960s, so were the forces of resistance. A number of architects and urban planners began to criticize the form these projects were taking. The monumental plazas, the office buildings without ground-floor stores, the blank facades of parking garages, and the lack of housing all combined to discourage human interaction and community. Moreover, with their emphasis on drawing in suburbanites, the projects often became empty and, thus, dangerous places at night.

More compelling for politicians was the reaction of urban residents. The rioting that broke out in cities from Los Angeles, California, to Newark, New Jersey, during the mid-1960s led politicians at both the local and federal level to rethink the planning process behind urban renewal. Under new federal regulations of the period, resident participation and one-for-one replacement of razed housing became mandatory.

In 1966, the administration of Lyndon B. Johnson, responding to the first wave of rioting, inaugurated the ambitious Model Cities Program, which would combine urban renewal with housing, education, and job programs. Initially aimed at only a few urban centers, the program was soon expanded to encompass about 150 of them. Budgetary constraints resulting from the Vietnam War ensured that little funding was made available, however, and the program limped along until 1974, when it was killed by Congress. The era of urban renewal effectively came to a close.

In 1978, President Jimmy Carter launched the Urban Development Action Grant program, which created low-tax or tax-free enterprise zones in inner cities. But this was largely a jobs program rather than an urban renewal one. By 1986, it, too, had been shut down as part of the Reagan Administration's cuts in urban funding.

James Ciment

See also: Automobile Culture; Housing; Inner Cities; Model Cities Program.

Bibliography

Isenberg, Alison. *Downtown America: A History of the Place and the People Who Made It.* Chicago: University of Chicago Press, 2004.

Keating, W. Dennis, and Norman Krumholz, eds. *Rebuilding Urban Neighborhoods: Achievements, Opportunities, and Limits.* Thousand Oaks, CA: Sage, 1999.

Teaford, John C. *The Rough Road to Renaissance: Urban Revitalization in America, 1940–1985.* Baltimore: Johns Hopkins University Press, 1990.

V

VESCO (ROBERT) AFFAIR

The Vesco affair was a financial and political scandal of the 1970s involving financier Robert Vesco. Under investigation by the Securities and Exchange Commission (SEC) for embezzling money from a mutual funds investment company he owned, Vesco contributed money to the 1972 reelection campaign of President Richard M. Nixon. Investigators alleged that the donation was part of a quid pro quo, whereby the Nixon Administration would quash the SEC investigation. Vesco fled the country before he could be arrested, and administration officials were eventually cleared of wrongdoing by a federal grand jury. Still, the affair added to the general sense of corruption surrounding Nixon during his second term in office.

Born the son of Detroit autoworkers in 1935, Vesco became a chemical engineer. He was also a self-taught financier who learned to use fights, mergers, and other tools of corporate aggression to take over a host of small companies. In three years, from 1964 to 1967, he bought a number of small companies with collective annual sales of $1.3 million and turned them into a financial empire with sales of more than $100 million per year. The national press touted him as the "boy wonder" of the merger mania gripping Wall Street in the mid- to late 1960s.

In 1971, Vesco gained a controlling interest in a mutual fund firm called Investors Overseas Services (IOS). Soon thereafter, the SEC began to look into allegations that Vesco had embezzled some $224 million from IOS. In March 1972, Vesco met with Maurice Stans, head of the Nixon Committee to Re-Elect the President (popularly referred to by its acronym, CREEP), offering him a $250,000 contribution, allegedly in exchange for the Nixon Administration stopping the SEC investigation. Adding to the suspicion of investigators, it was learned that Stans had told Vesco the contribution would have to be made before April 7, when a new law would go into effect requiring the campaign to release the names of all contributors and the amounts given.

In fact, IOS officials did not turn over the money—in $100 bills—until April 10. Vesco gave only $200,000 at that time, with the rest scheduled to come later. Stans claimed that the donation had been made earlier and therefore did not have to be declared. That same day, a meeting was arranged, allegedly by Attorney General John Mitchell, for Vesco lawyer Harry Sears to meet with SEC Chairman William Casey. Other meetings were also set up, and Vesco contributed another $250,000. The SEC prosecution continued, however.

In 1973, Vesco was indicted for making illegal contributions to the Nixon campaign. Three years later, he was also indicted by a federal grand jury on embezzlement charges. Stans, Sears, and Mitchell were eventually found innocent of conspiracy charges related to the case.

Vesco himself had fled the country in 1972, first for Costa Rica and then the Bahamas, Nicaragua, and Antigua. Living in luxury with his allegedly purloined wealth, he was said to use bribery with local officials to avoid extradition to the United States or Switzerland, where the IOS was headquartered. In 1984, Vesco moved to Cuba, where he and his Cuban wife were indicted by the government in 1995 for fraud. The two were sentenced to prison, Vesco for thirteen years and his wife for nine. Even as he remained in a Cuban jail, the U.S. government continued to demand his extradition.

John Barnhill

See also: Crime, Property; Wall Street.

Bibliography

Herzog, Arthur, Jr. *Vesco.* New York: Doubleday, 1987.
Hutchinson, Robert A. *Vesco.* New York: Praeger, 1975.

VIETNAM WAR

The Vietnam War, although never formally declared by Congress, was the longest foreign conflict in American history and the most politically divisive since the Civil War. U.S. involvement began with support for French colonizers in the late 1940s and 1950s, expanded to the provision of military advisers in the early 1960s, and culminated in full-scale combat involving U.S. ground troops from 1965 to 1973.

In support of an anticommunist regime in the southern half of the country, the United States committed more than 500,000 troops by 1968 and ultimately suffered nearly 60,000 dead by the end of the fighting. The war was also costly in political and economic terms, dividing the nation between those who supported the U.S. effort and those who both opposed the war and questioned the honesty of America's political leaders. Without concomitant tax increases, wartime spending also set off an inflationary cycle that helped push the nation into prolonged economic recession during the 1970s and early 1980s. For Vietnam, the costs were far greater, including a devastated countryside and several million dead combatants and civilians.

Ultimately, North Vietnam, along with its southern-based revolutionary allies—the National Liberation Front, better known as the Viet Cong—defeated the U.S.-backed regime of South Vietnam in 1975. Widely regarded as the only major military defeat in U.S. history, the Vietnam War instilled an enduring reluctance on the part of the American people to engage in foreign conflict—a feeling that lingered even after the terrorist attacks of September 11, 2001.

Background

French colonial rule was established in Indochina—the area now comprising Vietnam, Laos, and Cambodia—in the mid-nineteenth century. Over the next hundred years, France extended its control over the region's economy, establishing rubber plantations and exploiting the tin reserves of the region. Along with this imperial control, the French introduced Christianity and replaced traditional Buddhist officials with Catholics. By the mid-twentieth century, Catholics, who represented a mere 20 percent of the population, had become the political elite, serving in low- and mid-level posts within the colonial administration. The French preference for Catholics created antagonisms within Vietnamese society that would linger through the late twentieth century.

World War I represented the first setback for French control over Indochina and other parts of France's far-flung colonial empire. Not only did the war devastate the French economy and military, but it spawned new ideas about self-determination for subject peoples throughout what is now called the developing world. U.S. President Woodrow Wilson actively promoted independence for colonies, an idea much resisted by imperialists in Paris, London, and other European capitals.

At the Versailles Peace Conference of 1919, where the postwar world order was negotiated, decolonization was placed on the agenda, when Vietnamese representatives argued their case for independence. The great powers at the conference, however, turned a deaf ear to the Vietnamese pleas and confirmed continuing French control over Indochina for the foreseeable future. Frustrated, some of the representatives—including a former chef named Nguyen Ai Quoc (later known by his *nom de guerre,* Ho Chi Minh)—returned to Vietnam and, in 1930, established a national resistance organization heavily infused with communist ideas. For the next decade, the resistance made little headway.

Then, in 1941, Japan invaded Indochina, seizing control of the region from France. That same year, Ho Chi Minh formed a new resistance organization, the Viet Minh, to fight the Japanese invaders. Although communist in its politics, the Viet Minh received aid from the United States, which was also at war with the Japanese. In late 1945, with Japan's unconditional surrender to the United States and its allies, the Viet Minh seized control of the administration in the capital at Hanoi. But the United States and Great Britain, now concerned about Communist expansion around the world, refused to recognize Ho Chi Minh's government.

To reassert control over its former colony, France reinvaded Vietnam in 1946, unleashing a massive shelling of the port of Haiphong, a major redoubt of Viet Minh forces near Hanoi. The attack left more than 6,000 civilians dead and outraged millions of Vietnamese, who now turned to the Viet Minh as a means of getting rid of the hated French. A bitter guerrilla struggle ensued.

In 1949, Bao Dai, the scion of an old ruling family of Vietnam, returned to the country to take over as figurehead emperor of a Vietnam that was independent in name only. Most Vietnamese neither accepted this quasi-independent state nor Bao Dai, who had long been out of the country and had a reputation as a dissolute playboy, as their leader. Still, Bao Dai was recognized in 1950 as the leader of Vietnam by the United States, Great Britain, and much of the West.

Meanwhile, both the Soviet Union and the new Chinese Communist government extended recognition to Ho Chi Minh and the Viet Minh as the legitimate rulers of Vietnam. By the early 1950s, the Viet Minh and the French were locked in an ever-expanding war, with the United States paying much of the latter's costs in the conflict, some $1 billion in all.

The stalemate was finally broken in the spring of 1954, when French forces were decisively defeated at the battle of Dien Bien Phu in the northern part of Vietnam by General Vo Nguyen Giap and his Vietnamese Liberation Army, the military wing of the Viet Minh. France asked for U.S. air support, including the possible use of nuclear weapons, but President Dwight D. Eisenhower, a former general, recognized the untenable military position the French had found themselves in and refused the request. The French were forced to sue for peace, thereby ending what is known to historians as the first Vietnamese War (The so-called second Vietnamese War was against the Americans from 1964 to 1975; the Vietnamese refer to the wars by their enemies—the first Vietnamese War is called the French War, and the second is called the American War).

Peace talks to determine the future of Vietnam began in Geneva in the summer of 1954, culminating in the signing of a peace treaty, called the Geneva Accords, on July 21 by France and the new countries of Indo-China. While not signatories to the agreement, the Soviet Union, Communist China, and the United States agreed to abide by the accords. Under the agreement, Laos, Cambodia, and Vietnam were granted independence. Vietnam, however, was divided into two halves at roughly the 17th parallel. North of that line, the government was led by Ho Chi Minh and the Viet Minh; south of the line, the government was headed by Emperor Bao Dai, with the administrative center at Saigon.

Ho Chi Minh was not happy with the arrangement and was pressured into it by his patrons in Beijing and Moscow who did not want continued conflict in the region, having just seen the Korean War come to an end the year before. He was reconciled to the arrangement, however, by a stipulation in the accords calling for national elections in 1956 that would lead to the uniting of the country under a single administration. As the widely recognized leader of the independence struggle, Ho Chi Minh was certain he would win a fair election.

America Steps In

With the French leaving Vietnam, the United States moved in. In June 1954, the Central Intelligence Agency (CIA) established a station in Saigon and began cultivating Ngo Dinh Diem, an anticommunist former exile as a new leader for Vietnam. Soon, the American press was referring to Ngo Dinh Diem as the "George Washington of Vietnam." While little known in Vietnam, he had long opposed French colonial rule and so, unlike many educated Vietnamese, was untainted by collaboration. In addition, Ngo Dinh Diem was a Catholic, a fact that appealed to U.S. Secretary of State John Foster Dulles, himself a devout Christian.

In subsequent years, historians have cited the backing of Ngo Dinh Diem as America's first major error in Vietnam. Possessing little knowledge of the country's history, U.S. policymakers had little understanding of the long-standing antagonisms between Vietnam's minority Catholic elite and its majority Buddhist population. Nevertheless, within days of Ngo Dinh Diem's assuming power, the Eisenhower Administration began sending military and economic aid to his government.

Although the Eisenhower Administration may have been unaware of Vietnam's religious issues, it was fully conscious of Ho Chi Minh's overwhelming popularity in the country. The administration knew, as did Ho Chi Minh himself, that should the unification elections proceed in 1956, as called for in the Geneva Accords, the country would have a government dominated by the Communist Viet Minh.

As early as 1954, during the battle of Dien Bien Phu, Eisenhower had talked of the "domino theory," whereby if Vietnam fell to the Communists, so, too, would neighboring Asian countries. With the Cold War struggle between the democratic West and the Communist East at its height, Eisenhower felt that a Communist Vietnam would be a major strategic setback to the United States. To prevent that from happening, Washington, in 1955, encouraged Ngo Dinh Diem to hold his own elections in the southern half of the country, which he then declared the independent Republic of Vietnam, better known as South Vietnam. Holding this election effectively repudiated the Geneva Accords.

By the late 1950s, U.S. support for Ngo Dinh Diem's regime was largely coordinated by the CIA, which established a quasi-independent company called Air America to fly in supplies. It also supplied information about political opponents to Ngo Dinh Diem. In 1959, a law was passed giving the government in Saigon sweeping powers to arrest and hold political opponents without charge. Ngo Dinh Diem's

Assassination of Ngo Dinh Diem

In the late 1950s and early 1960s, Ngo Dinh Diem was America's man in Vietnam. Having ousted the Emperor Bao Dai in 1955, Ngo Dinh Diem had proclaimed himself president of the newly created Republic of South Vietnam. A strict Catholic in a largely Buddhist nation, he had never collaborated with the hated French colonialists, who had pulled out of Vietnam the year before; however, his repression of Buddhists, harsh measures to crush a Communist insurgency, and autocratic rule antagonized many of his countrymen. By the early 1960s, the United States found itself backing a hated figure.

The French colonial masters had been driven out in 1954 by a Communist-nationalist insurgency led by Ho Chi Minh. Under the 1954 Geneva Accords, Vietnam was temporarily divided into two halves—the Communist North and the non-Communist South. After Ngo Dinh Diem cancelled nationwide elections in 1956, Communist insurgents renewed their struggle against what they perceived as a U.S.-dominated regime in Saigon. Indeed, the administration of President Dwight D. Eisenhower, fearing a Communist takeover of Southeast Asia, had begun providing military and economic aid to the Diem regime.

Ngo Dinh Diem used the aid to help settle Catholic refugees from the North, but he also embarked on a hated relocation program of South Vietnamese peasants, moving them into armed camps to keep them from supporting Communist insurgents. Suspecting that Buddhists might be supporters of the rebels, he and his brother, Ngo Dinh Nhu, head of the national police, engaged in a nationwide crackdown against Buddhist monks, priests, and temples. In October 1963, several monks set fire to themselves in protest, and the shocking images were spread by the news media around the world. In response, Ngo Dinh Diem's high-profile wife dismissed the protests as a "monk barbecue show."

By this time, the administration of President John F. Kennedy was further committing the United States to defending South Vietnam. By late 1963, some 17,000 U.S. military advisors were training the South Vietnamese military and helping direct its counterinsurgency efforts in the field.

Kennedy feared he would be politically tarnished if he let South Vietnam fall to the Communists, but Ngo Dinh Diem's regime was becoming an embarrassment. Secretly, feelers were sent out to a number of South Vietnamese generals by U.S. officials, including Ambassador Henry Cabot Lodge, that Washington would not be displeased if Ngo Dinh Diem were to be overthrown.

On November 1, the generals acted, not only capturing Ngo Dinh Diem but assassinating him as well. Most historians believe that while the United States was definitely behind the coup, it was not necessarily implicated in Ngo Dinh Diem's murder.

The government of South Vietnam underwent a series of army coups through 1965, and it was eventually stabilized under President Nguyen Van Thieu after 1967. By that time, the United States was fully engaged in the Vietnam War, with more than 400,000 troops in the country.

John Barnhill and James Ciment

government used this new power to jail thousands of Buddhists, intellectuals, students, and any other persons suspected of being sympathetic to the Viet Minh. The crackdown forced his opponents to go underground, and, in December 1960, they formed the National Liberation Front (NLF).

Determining that political opposition to Ngo Dinh Diem was futile, the NLF organized a military wing, known in the West as the Viet Cong, to engage in guerrilla warfare against the Saigon government. (In fact, Viet Cong, a derogative Vietnamese slang word, was the name given the guerrillas by their enemies.)

While the NLF insisted that it was an autonomous organization with non-Communists in its leadership ranks, both Washington and Saigon assumed from the beginning that it was organized and aided by the regime in the Democratic Republic of Vietnam, or North Vietnam.

With guerrilla attacks by the NLF increasing against the Saigon regime, the new administration of President John F. Kennedy began sending U.S. military advisers in February 1961 to aid the Army of the Republic of Vietnam (ARVN). While not supposed to engage in combat themselves, the advisers were under orders to fire back in self-defense if attacked.

Later that year, Kennedy sent Vice President Lyndon B. Johnson and a team of experts to investigate military and economic conditions in Vietnam and to suggest where future aid might best be served. The team's report, the "December 1961 White Paper," said that stabilizing the regime and defeating the NLF would require increases in economic, technical, and military aid, as well as a major increase in the number of American advisers.

While Kennedy was still determined to avoid sending U.S. combat troops to South Vietnam, he did agree in 1962 to create the Military Assistance Command Vietnam (MACV) and to increase the number of advisers. By the time of his assassination in November 1963, Kennedy had placed some 17,000 U.S. military advisers in South Vietnam.

Meanwhile, the NLF had increasing success in the countryside, leading the United States and South Vietnam to implement the Strategic Hamlet Program, which forced villagers into barbed wire-surrounded hamlets built and operated by ARVN. The idea was to cut off villager support for the NLF and to turn large areas of the countryside into free-fire zones. That is, if the villagers were concentrated in the hamlets, the military could assume anyone outside the hamlets was with the NLF. Rather than cutting off aid to the NLF, however, the program antagonized millions of Vietnamese peasants and turned them against the regime of Ngo Dinh Diem. The NLF benefited from an upsurge in recruits as a result.

By the summer of 1963, it was clear to most American observers that the NLF was winning in the countryside. As for the cities, the Ngo Dinh Diem regime was creating problems for itself there as well. Suspecting that Buddhist temples and monasteries were secretly aiding opponents, national police head

Ngo Dinh Nhu, Ngo Dinh Diem's brother, launched systematic raids, setting off massive street protests. In addition, several monks had themselves set on fire to protest Ngo Dinh Diem's crackdown; photographs reprinted in newspapers in the United States and around the world helped undermine support for Ngo Dinh Diem in Washington. The country appeared to be in chaos, and Ngo Dinh Diem's regime looked increasingly isolated and vulnerable.

On November 1, several South Vietnamese generals captured Ngo Dinh Diem and Ngo Dinh Nhu and assassinated them. While it was widely believed that the Kennedy Administration and the CIA had encouraged the generals in their coup plot, most historians have concluded that Kennedy himself did not expect or want Ngo Dinh Diem to be killed.

Nevertheless, just three weeks after Ngo Dinh Diem's murder, Kennedy himself was assassinated; his successor, Lyndon B. Johnson, decided that a new approach was needed. He appointed U.S. Military Academy at West Point superintendent William Westmoreland to lead MACV and imposed a trade embargo against North Vietnam. These actions had little effect, as NLF attacks against the South Vietnamese government, now undergoing a series of coups, escalated.

America Commits Itself to War

While the guerrilla struggle continued in South Vietnam, the Johnson Administration decided to take the war to the North, helping South Vietnamese forces launch sea-based guerrilla attacks on North Vietnamese military and economic targets. In retaliation, North Vietnamese gunboats launched two attacks in early August 1964 on the USS *Maddox,* an American destroyer cruising in international waters in the Gulf of Tonkin off the North Vietnamese coast. Controversy has surrounded the events ever since. North Vietnam claimed from the beginning that it never attacked the *Maddox,* and secret White House tapes, released to the public in the late 1990s, record even Johnson himself questioning whether both attacks had really occurred.

Regardless of what happened, Johnson used the alleged incident to win broad powers from a highly supportive Congress to conduct military action against North Vietnam and the NLF. (The House voted unanimously, and only two senators demurred: Democrats

Wayne Morse of Oregon and Ernest Gruening of Alaska.) Still, Johnson was initially reluctant to commit U.S. forces to the struggle.

Facing reelection in November, Johnson wanted to run as a peace candidate, especially as his opponent was the hawkish Barry Goldwater, an ultraconservative Republican Senator from Arizona. At the same time, Johnson did not want to look weak in the face of supposed Communist aggression. The president decided to take the middle road, keeping out U.S. ground forces but launching limited air attacks against North Vietnamese military targets. He won the 1964 election in a landslide.

The compromise Johnson struck in August soon gave way to a more aggressive U.S. posture. In February 1965, Johnson launched "Rolling Thunder," a military operation involving continuous bombing of North Vietnam rather than retaliatory strikes for specific attacks by the North Vietnamese-supported NLF against the regime in Saigon. By this time, Hanoi had established a network of dirt roads and paths along the border with Laos and Cambodia to funnel arms and men to the South, the so-called Ho Chi Minh Trail.

From 1965 to 1968, when Johnson called it off, Operation Rolling Thunder resulted in the dropping of more than 1 million tons of bombs on North Vietnam—more than had been dropped in all other wars of the twentieth century to that time. Johnson and his military advisers hoped that by steadily increasing the pain on North Vietnam, Hanoi would cut off aid to the NLF and sue for peace.

In fact, the bombing had little, if any, effect on either North Vietnam's capacity or willingness to support the NLF and, ultimately, Vietnamese unification under the Hanoi regime. Partly, this was because the North Vietnamese were being heavily supplied by the Soviet Union and China. Meanwhile, the supplies and men North Vietnam was sending south allowed the NLF to conduct attacks against U.S. airbases in South Vietnam.

In March, Johnson took the fateful step of sending the first U.S. combat troops to Vietnam; the first U.S. Marines waded ashore near the South Vietnamese city of Da Nang on March 8. Initially, their mission was confined to protecting the bases, but Westmoreland and MACV soon realized that the only way to do this effectively was to take the war to the NLF. By April, U.S. troops were patrolling the countryside and con-

ducting so-called search and destroy missions against NLF fighters.

In November, the first major battle between U.S. forces and the North Vietnamese Army (NVA) took place in the Ia Drang Valley in the northern part of South Vietnam. Some 450 men of the Air Cavalry, backed by other U.S. forces, fought 2,000 NVA troops, resulting in 305 American troops killed and 240 wounded, along with hundreds of NVA dead. The battle saw the first extensive use of helicopter-borne troops, which would become MACV's standard tactic against an elusive guerilla force enemy.

While the U.S. military leadership proclaimed victory at Ia Drang, it recognized that the enemy was more formidable than first thought. MACV called for more troops, and Washington obliged. By the end of 1965, the United States had roughly 150,000 troops in South Vietnam, many of them draftees. Of the roughly 1,000 combat deaths that year, 16 percent were draftees. By 1967, that percentage would rise to more than one-third.

Aside from straightforward combat, U.S. forces also engaged in other forms of counterinsurgency warfare. In 1965, Johnson directed the CIA to launch its Phoenix program, which used U.S. military units as cover as it pursued suspected Vietnamese collaborators. Interrogations were arbitrary and outside judicial control, as CIA recruits were often Green Berets and SEALS, the special force units of the U.S. Army and U.S. Navy, respectively. Between 1965 and 1970, U.S. and South Vietnamese intelligence services assassinated suspected members of the Viet Cong, at one point, setting a goal of 1,800 killings per month. Total deaths by assassination were at least 21,000 in the five years of the program. While it resulted in the assassinations of many innocent people, Phoenix also had a certain brutal success. In some Southern areas, the program compromised or killed 95 percent of the Communist force.

All of this effort was on behalf of a regime in Saigon that seemed to be in turmoil, with military coup after coup. Finally, in late 1965, Air Marshall Nguyen Cao Ky, one of the anti-Diem coup leaders from 1963, seized power along with ARVN commander Nguyen Van Thieu. Washington soon backed away from supporting Nguyen Cao Ky, who was seen as too unpredictable, and supported Nguyen Van Thieu.

In 1967, with roughly 400,000 troops in Vietnam, Johnson wanted elections to validate his choice

President Lyndon B. Johnson (center), Secretary of Defense Robert McNamara (right), and Secretary of State Dean Rusk ponder strategy at a cabinet meeting in 1967. The Vietnam War was already consuming much of their time, energy, and political capital. *(Hulton Archive/Getty Images)*

of leaders. The subsequent election proved a disaster, however, as Nguyen Van Thieu won only 30 percent of the vote. Worse, the runner-up campaigned with a plan for an immediate cease-fire. Nguyen Van Thieu had him tossed him in jail, causing demonstrations in Saigon that nearly led to nationwide rioting.

Both the NLF and NVA, like the United States, also had to readjust their strategies. In the early 1960s, they expected a quick victory against a corrupt regime in Saigon and an ineffective and demoralized ARVN. But the arrival of large numbers of U.S. troops changed the equation. After the battle at Ia Drang, the Communist forces eschewed major military engagements against the far better equipped U.S. military and instead focused their efforts on small-scale guerilla attacks. The strategy now was not to defeat the U.S. military—an impossible task given the sheer might of the U.S. military machine—but to wear down the resolve of the government and people.

The war ground on through 1966 and 1967, with U.S. troops launching countless search-and-destroy missions and dumping millions of bombs. By the beginning of 1968, there were some 400,000 U.S. troops in "Nam," as the "grunts," or regular U.S. troops, referred to the war zone. And the fighting was difficult. Not only was the thickly jungled terrain unforgiving and the enemy elusive, but the troops could never even be sure who the enemy was. NLF forces, in particular, blended effectively into the civilian population. At the same time, civilians often provided food and hiding places for NLF forces. Frustrated, many U.S. troops came to see all Vietnamese—even the very young and very elderly—as the enemy. Attacks against civilians turned ever-larger sections of the population against the Americans. U.S. troops and Vietnamese peasants became caught in a deepening cycle of suspicion and hostility.

Meanwhile, the strategy of the NLF and NVA to wear down American resolve was beginning to have an effect on the U.S. home front. As early as 1965, when the first combat troops were sent to Vietnam, the Students for a Democratic Society (SDS), founded in the early 1960s as a radical pro-civil-rights, antipoverty group, was organizing its first major antiwar rally. Within two years, the antiwar movement, while still largely confined to college-age Americans who feared being drafted once they left college, had expanded dramatically. In early 1967, an SDS organizer named David Dellinger organized the National Mobilization Committee to End the War in Vietnam, popularly known as the Mobe. In April, the Mobe organized a march against the war that brought 100,000 people into the streets of New York City. An October protest at the Pentagon in Washington brought fewer numbers, but resulted in greater publicity as numerous protesters engaged in civil disobedience by trying to shut down the defense headquarters.

Still, as 1968 dawned, the majority of Americans still supported the war and President Johnson's conduct of it. All that soon changed. In late January 1968, the NVA and the NLF launched the Tet Offensive, named after the Vietnamese New Year holiday. It was a coordinated attack against more than 100 locations across South Vietnam. Many areas considered relatively safe, particularly in cities, were suddenly plunged into conflict. Even the U.S. Embassy in Saigon was briefly occupied by guerrillas.

The Tet Offensive was considered a failure by military experts; the Communist forces suffered 37,000 dead, while the United States lost 2,500 and eventually recaptured all its lost territory. The political outcome, however, was another matter. Launched by the Communists to bring the Johnson Administration to the negotiating table, the offensive worked. In March, Johnson agreed to a partial bombing halt, extended to a full cessation in October. Moreover, although they soon became bogged down in endless procedural details, preliminary negotiations to bring an end to the war opened in Paris. In reality, Johnson's new willingness to negotiate had less to do with events in Vietnam than they did with developments at home.

Vietnam was called the "first television war," because regular news footage of the fighting was conveyed to the American people in their living rooms on nightly news broadcasts. By early 1968, Americans had become used to seeing endless footage of the fighting, followed by rosy Pentagon assessments of progress. The Tet Offensive exposed the contradiction. Two months before Tet, Westmoreland confi-

dently told journalists that he saw "light at the end of the tunnel"—that is, that the United States would soon win the war. That prediction rang hollow with voters following Tet, especially after CBS News anchor Walter Cronkite, seen as the most trusted man in America in public opinion polls, turned against the war.

In the New Hampshire Democratic presidential primary that February, peace candidate Senator Eugene McCarthy of Minnesota won an unexpectedly large margin of the vote against the incumbent. On March 31, following his announcement of the partial bombing halt, Johnson dropped a bombshell of his own on the American people: He would not be running for reelection.

The race became wide open in both parties. Ultimately, the Democrats nominated Vice President Hubert H. Humphrey, who largely supported the war, at a strife-filled convention in Chicago. Republicans turned to former Vice President Richard M. Nixon, who promised voters he had a "secret plan" to end the war. Nixon won a narrow victory in November, by which time the number of U.S. troops in Vietnam had peaked at 543,000.

Nixon and "Vietnamization"

Nixon did have a secret plan to end the war, but if the people who voted for him thought that meant a quick exit from Vietnam, they were mistaken. Nixon's plan for ending the war—"peace with honor," he said—had two components.

One was gradually to develop ARVN as an effective fighting force, allowing it to take increasing responsibility for the fighting and enabling America to gradually withdraw its troops. Nixon called this the "Vietnamization" of the war. And, indeed, he did bring the troops home, albeit slowly. While he announced a token withdrawal shortly after taking office in January 1969, there were still 334,000 troops in Vietnam at the end of 1970.

Nixon's hopes to cool the antiwar movement at home failed in the face of the other component of his Vietnam strategy: to expand the war geographically to neighboring Laos and Cambodia. The NVA and NLF troops had long retreated to these supposedly neutral countries, when things got too hot in South Vietnam, using them to regroup and as places to move and stash weapons and materiel.

At first, Nixon tried to keep this second component secret, engaging in elaborate ruses to prevent the American people from learning that he had ordered bombing runs on Laos and Cambodia. In April 1970, however, Nixon revealed his "secret" war by launching a massive invasion of Cambodia to find and destroy the alleged NVA/NLF headquarters there. The invasion produced little in tangible military gains.

In April 1969, Americans had been horrified to learn of a massacre perpetrated by U.S. troops at a South Vietnamese village called My Lai. The killing of hundreds of unarmed civilians had further undermined the people's faith that the war was justified. By the time of the Cambodian invasion, polls revealed that a majority of Americans were against the war. The Cambodia invasion only added to the unrest in the United States; it resulted in a renewed wave of antiwar protests, including a protest at Kent State University in Ohio at which National Guardsmen shot and killed four unarmed students.

Vietnamization proceeded, as the number of American troops in the country dropped to about 140,000 by 1971 and just 43,000 (largely aircrews and their support teams) by the end of 1972, despite another major NVA/NLF offensive that spring. The gradual pull-out helped dampen some antiwar protesting and gave Nixon a landslide victory over the Democratic peace candidate, Senator George McGovern of South Dakota, in the 1972 presidential election.

In Paris, the peace talks proceeded as well. Finally, in the fall of 1972, North Vietnamese negotiators Le Duc Tho and Xuan Thuy and U.S. National Security Advisor Henry Kissinger agreed on a draft peace plan. Under it, the last U.S. ground troops would withdraw from Vietnam and a ceasefire would take effect in advance of national elections to unify the country. In addition, North Vietnam would release all of the nearly 600 American prisoners of war (POWs) it held.

President Nguyen Van Thieu of South Vietnam, however, refused to accept the agreement, since it left NVA troops in the south. While Nguyen Van Thieu's signature was not necessary to put the agreement into effect—indeed, he had long resented being left out of the Paris talks—his loud protestations about being abandoned by the American government were an embarrassment. The peace talks were temporarily off. In December, the United States launched the most massive bombing yet of North Vietnam, killing thousands of civilians in Hanoi and Haiphong and outraging public opinion in much of the United States and around the world.

Most historians agree that the bombing was conducted to show both Nguyen Van Thieu and the North Vietnamese government that Washington was

Remaining U.S. Marines in Vietnam help in the evacuation of American and South Vietnamese civilians during the fall of Saigon in April 1975. *(Dirck Halstead/Getty Images News)*

committed to protecting the Saigon regime. While the North Vietnamese government protested the bombings vigorously, they also made overtures to the Americans about returning to Paris.

Finally, on January 23, 1973, both sides initialed the final draft of the agreement, and North Vietnam began releasing American POWs. The war, at long last, was over, at least for the United States.

Agent Orange

Agent Orange was an herbicide developed in the early 1960s by the U.S. military for use in Vietnam. A 50–50 mix of two chemical sprays, first manufactured in the 1940s as weed killers, Agent Orange was used chiefly as a defoliant on Vietnam's dense tropical plant and tree life, which provided cover for enemy movement. Deriving its name from orange stripes on its 55-gallon drum storage containers, the herbicide was mixed with kerosene or diesel fuel and dispersed principally by air.

Between 1962 and 1971, the U.S. Air Force sprayed approximately 20 million gallons of fifteen different defoliating chemicals over 6 million acres of South Vietnamese territory. These included other color-coded herbicides such as Agents Blue, Purple, Pink, White, Green, and Orange II (also called "super orange"). Agent Orange, however, used from 1965 to 1970, comprised 80 percent of all defoliants released.

In the 1970s, some of the 2.5 million American veterans of the Vietnam conflict began to suspect exposure to Agent Orange as the cause of delayed, and diverse, health problems. The herbicide contained small amounts of dioxin, an unavoidable by-product of the chemical's manufacturing process and a potent toxin.

In a 1965 internal report, one manufacturer of Agent Orange, Dow Chemical, had declared dioxin "exceptionally toxic" to humans. Four years later, a U.S. study found a link between the chemical agent and birth defects in laboratory animals. In 1970, the U.S. Surgeon General reported that herbicides containing dioxin were a human health hazard.

In 1991, Congress passed legislation providing for limited medical benefits for Vietnam veterans exposed to Agent Orange. Not until March 2000 did the U.S. Air Force, having been criticized by the General Accounting Office for releasing flawed studies, concede the existence of credible evidence regarding, specifically, the onset of diabetes in Vietnam veterans who had handled Agent Orange.

Throughout the 1990s, the Department of Veterans Affairs (DVA) acknowledged a growing number of diseases and medical conditions associated with exposure to Agent Orange. In 1996, the National Academy of Sciences found a "suggestive" connection between exposure and the development of prostate cancer and peripheral neuropathy. President Bill Clinton ordered the DVA to provide medical benefits to Vietnam veterans in these cases. The list of diseases covered by disability benefits soon included, among others, Type II diabetes, Hodgkin's disease, non-Hodgkin's lymphoma, soft tissue sarcoma, multiple myeloma, and cancers of the lung, larynx, and trachea. The DVA also began covering treatment of birth defects in the children of female Vietnam veterans.

Legal proceedings against Agent Orange's private manufacturers began in 1979 with a class action suit (informally known as *In re Agent Orange Product Liability Litigation*) filed by veterans. The chemical-company defendants—Dow, Monsanto, Diamond Shamrock, Hercules, Uniroyal, T-H Agricultural and Nutrition, and Thompson Chemicals—settled out of court in 1984 for $180 million. The settlement decreed that no other lawsuits could be filed against the manufacturers. In 1994, the U.S. Supreme Court refused to hear a second, class action suit, *Ivy v. Diamond Shamrock Chemical Company et al* (1989), declaring "the matter is settled."

Phillip M. Carpenter

Endgame

For Vietnam, the war ground on through the spring of 1975, when a massive North Vietnamese and NLF offensive toppled the government of Thieu and led to the fall of Saigon on April 30, 1975. Utterly disgusted with the war, a majority in Congress refused to give President Gerald Ford the hundreds of millions in funds for military support for the South that he requested. Amid utter chaos, the United States abandoned its presence in South Vietnam after some two decades of support.

Hundreds of thousands of Vietnamese allies escaped the country in fear of their lives, most eventually finding sanctuary in the United States. In Cambodia, the genocidal Khmer Rouge took power in April; their policy of forcibly eliminating all traces of Western and urban culture led to the deaths of an estimated 2 million Cambodians, or one-third of the population, until their regime was toppled by Vietnamese invaders in 1979.

With American troops safely out of Vietnam, the postwar adjustment for the United States began. Among the most emotional episodes was the arrival of POWs under Operation Homecoming, from February through April 1973. The demands for a full accounting of all U.S. prisoners of war and missing in action (MIAs) would continue for decades afterward. Post-traumatic stress disorder, a psychological malady caused by the brutal fighting conditions in Vietnam, became a recognized illness in 1980. Two years later, Vietnam agreed to begin talks about American MIAs, and the Vietnam Veterans Memorial was dedicated in Washington, D.C.

In 1988, Vietnam and the United States finally began actually working together to account for the MIAs. By 1991, the United States was ready to normalize relations with Vietnam, which it did incrementally, as Vietnam became more cooperative on the MIA issue.

Full normalization came under President Bill Clinton in 1995. A U.S. ambassador was posted to Hanoi in 1997. Clinton visited Vietnam in 2000, the first president to travel there since Nixon in 1969. Final trade normalization came in 2001.

Costs and Effects

The war in Vietnam cost the United States roughly $176 billion and some 58,000 lives lost, 153,000 wounded, and untold thousands psychologically damaged. It also cost roughly 2 million Vietnamese lives and a massive displacement of the rural population. In the years 1964–1969 alone, U.S. planes dropped more than nine times the tonnage of high explosives that it did in World War II's Pacific Theater. The Vietnamese countryside remained littered with the toxic and dangerous remnants of the war. The legacy of Operation Ranchhand was equally damaging. Ranchhand was the defoliation effort, designed first to clear vegetation from along highways and then expanded to clear whole forests in order to deny the enemy sanctuary or a secure position from which to ambush U.S. troops. The chemical of choice, Agent Orange, was a dioxin-based herbicide. From 1962 to 1971, U.S. forces sprayed almost 19 million gallons of herbicide, 11 million of which were Agent Orange, in Vietnam and Laos. Six million acres of jungle and cropland were sprayed during the ten-year effort. After decades of denial that Agent Orange caused medical problems for G.I.s, the Veterans Administration began treating veterans for dioxin-induced conditions, just as it had earlier treated the mental and emotional problems the war provoked.

The war also produced in the United States a political aftereffect, known as the "Vietnam syndrome." Americans became increasingly wary of overseas military entanglements following the fall of Saigon. While the United States became involved in several small-scale invasions and occupations during the 1980s, it was not until the Persian Gulf War of 1991 that it committed any large number of troops to a foreign war.

While President George H.W. Bush claimed that America "kicked the Viet Nam Syndrome once and for all" in 1991, many historians maintain that that may not have been the case. One of the complaints about Vietnam was that America got into the war incrementally, with no "exit strategy" and no clear objective. In fighting the Persian Gulf War, Bush made it clear that he would fight to win—and then get out—so as not to repeat Vietnam. As for the Iraq War, the prolonged occupation stirred renewed talk in some circles of "another Vietnam." The only foreign war America has ever lost continued to haunt the nation into the new century.

John Barnhill and James Ciment

See also: Anticommunism; Antiwar Movement, Vietnam Era; China and Taiwan, Relations with; Domino Theory;

Draft, Military; Green Berets; Gulf of Tonkin Resolution; My Lai Massacre; Nixon Doctrine; Southeast Asia, Relations with; Southeast Asia Treaty Organization; Soviet Union/Russia, Relations with; Tet Offensive; War Powers Act.

Bibliography

"Agent Orange: Information for Veterans Who Served in Vietnam." Department of Veterans Affairs, Washington DC, April 2001.

Baritz, Loren. *Backfire: A History of How American Culture Led Us into Vietnam and Made Us Fight the Way We Did.* New York: William Morrow, 1985.

Buzzanco, Robert. *Vietnam and the Transformation of American Life.* Malden, MA: Blackwell, 1999.

Catton, Philip E. *Diem's Final Failure; Prelude to America's War in Vietnam.* Lawrence: University Press of Kansas, 2003.

Davidson, Phillip B. *Vietnam at War.* Novato, CA: Presidio, 1988.

DeBenedetti, Charles, and Charles Chatfield. *An American Ordeal: The Antiwar Movement of the Vietnam War.* Syracuse, NY: Syracuse University Press, 1990.

FitzGerald, Frances. *Fire in the Lake: The Vietnamese and the Americans in Vietnam,* Boston: Little, Brown, 1972.

Garrow, David. *Protest at Selma: Martin Luther King, Jr., and the Voting Rights Act of 1965.* New Haven: Yale University Press, 1978.

Karnow, Stanley *Vietnam: A History.* New York: Arrow, 1983.

Kousser, J. Morgan. *Colorblind Injustice: Minority Voting Rights and the Undoing of the Second Reconstruction.* Chapel Hill: University of North Carolina Press, 1999.

Sheehan, Neil. *A Bright Shining Lie: John Paul Vann and America in Vietnam.* New York: Random House, 1990.

Spector, Ronald H. *United States Army in Vietnam: Advice and Support: The Early Years, 1941–1960.* Washington, DC: Center of Military History, 1983.

Tucker, Spencer C., et al., eds. *Encyclopedia of the Vietnam War.* 3 vols. Santa Barbara, CA: ABC-CLIO, 1998.

VanDerMark, Brian. *Into the Quagmire: Lyndon Johnson and the Escalation of the Vietnam War.* New York: Oxford University Press, 1991.

Wilcox, Fred. *Waiting for an Army to Die: The Tragedy of Agent Orange.* Cabin Lock, MD: Seven Locks, 1989.

Young, A.L., and G.M. Reggiani, eds. *Agent Orange and Its Associated Dioxin: An Assessment of a Controversy.* New York: Elsevier Science Publishing, 1988.

VINCENNES INCIDENT

On July 3, 1988, the U.S. Navy cruiser USS *Vincennes* shot down Iran Air Flight 655 over the Strait of Hormuz in the Persian Gulf, killing all 290 passengers on board. The *Vincennes* crew mistook the plane for a hostile Iranian aircraft. Nevertheless, the Muslim world was outraged and vowed revenge for what it saw as an American crime. The administration of President Ronald Reagan expressed remorse and paid compensation to the families of those killed, but it stood by the right of the United States to shoot when threatened.

Iran and Iraq had been at war since 1980. The U.S. presence in the Persian Gulf was ordered by Reagan to protect Kuwaiti oil tankers flying the U.S. flag from attacks by Iran. While in the Persian Gulf, U.S. naval vessels routinely encountered mine fields, missile attacks, and speedboat raids. In 1987, an Iraqi missile killed thirty-seven Americans aboard the USS *Stark*. After that, U.S. naval policy did not require warning shots to be fired in order to elicit a response.

After Iranian naval speedboats fired on a U.S. reconnaissance helicopter, the *Vincennes* and the speedboats began firing at one another around 10 A.M. on the morning of July 3. The *Vincennes* was equipped with the state-of-the-art Aegis radar system, the most sophisticated in use by the U.S. Navy. During the battle, the Aegis radar screen suddenly showed a high-altitude aircraft approaching at high speed.

Vincennes commander Captain William C. Rogers gave the unidentified craft several chances to identify itself but received no response. Believing that the *Vincennes* was about to be attacked, Rogers ordered his men to shoot down the unidentified aircraft. Two surface-to-air missiles were fired, one of which hit the plane six miles away. No one on the *Vincennes* ever saw the Iranian passenger plane.

Reagan issued a statement that afternoon saying that it was a terrible tragedy and sending sympathy and condolences to the families of the passengers and crew. Chairman of the Joint Chiefs of Staff Admiral William J. Crowe, Jr. told the press that Rogers was given wide latitude to protect his men from Iranian aggression. For weeks after the *Vincennes* incident, the Pentagon and White House stood by this explanation: Thinking the *Vincennes* was under attack by an F-14 fighter jet, Rogers had no choice but to order the plane shot down.

In August, the Pentagon released its official report on the *Vincennes* incident. It placed the blame on human error and the fog of war. In the confusion of battle with the speedboats, psychological stress affected decision making aboard the *Vincennes*. Defense Secretary Frank Carlucci said that no one would be punished because "these mistakes were not due to negligence or culpability." In 1989, Rogers and Lieutenant Commander Scott Lustig were commended for their conduct during the speedboat skirmish on July 3. No mention was made of Iran Air Flight 655.

Protests in Iran after the incident called for "Death to America" and "Death to Reagan." Iran asked the United Nations (UN) for international condemnation of the United States but was refused. Before the UN Security Council, Vice President George H.W. Bush placed responsibility on Iran for allowing a passenger airliner to fly over a war zone and for continuing the war with Iraq. The United States, nonetheless, paid compensation to the families of the 290 people killed.

Still, Iranians called for revenge. When Pan Am Flight 103 crashed over Lockerbie, Scotland, in December 1988, many Americans felt that revenge had come. In 1991, intelligence revealed the bombing to be the work of Libyans, not Iranians.

Some questions about the *Vincennes* incident will never be answered, such as how the multimillion-dollar Aegis radar system failed to distinguish a fighter jet from a passenger airliner and why the airliner did not respond to requests for identification. Certainly, the 290 passengers en route from Bandar Abbas, Iran, to Dubai, United Arab Emirates, did not expect to fly over a battle zone.

Melissa Stallings

See also: Middle East, Relations with (Except Israel); *Stark* Incident.

Bibliography

Kemp, Geoffrey. *Forever Enemies? American Policy and the Islamic Republic of Iran.* Washington, DC: Carnegie Endowment for International Peace, 1994.

U.S. House of Representatives. *The July 3, 1988 Attack by the* Vincennes *on an Iranian Aircraft.* Washington, DC: U.S. Government Printing Office, 1993.

U.S. Senate. *Investigation Into the Downing of an Iranian Airliner by the U.S.S. "Vincennes."* Washington, DC: U.S. Government Printing Office, 1989.

VIOLENCE, POLITICAL

Political violence in American history has not, of course, been confined to the postwar era. Of the four American presidents assassinated, only one—John F. Kennedy—has been murdered since the end of World War II.

Indeed, the late nineteenth and early twentieth centuries were marked by a wave of assassinations around the world, usually perpetrated by anarchists hoping to trigger civil unrest or revolution by targeting political leaders. This was partially the motivation of Leon Czolgosz, the self-declared anarchist and Polish immigrant who assassinated President William McKinley in 1901. As in many of the postwar assassinations, historians concluded that Czolgosz's motivation was political but that the man was also mentally unbalanced. Like previous political assassinations, and several of the postwar era, the McKinley murder has since been surrounded by conspiracy theories spun by people who believe that larger forces were at work in both the assassination and the subsequent cover-up.

Puerto Rican Nationalists

The first major acts of political violence during the postwar period were a departure from the American tradition of lone gunmen, politically motivated but mentally disturbed, stalking and then attempting to kill their high-profile political targets. On November 1, 1950, Oscar Collazo and Griselio Torresola, two members of the Puerto Rican independence movement—the Armed Forces of the National Liberation (FALN is its Spanish acronym)—opened fire on Blair House in Washington, D.C. (the temporary home of the president while the White House was being renovated) in an attempt to kill President Harry S Truman. The president had recently signed Public Act 600, establishing the Commonwealth of Puerto Rico, a move that nationalists saw as a means to thwart Puerto Rican independence. More immediately, the assassination attempt followed a botched coup by the FALN in San Juan in late October that had included a failed assassination attempt on Puerto Rican governor Luis Muñoz Marín, a supporter of commonwealth status for the island.

One of the Blair House assassins (Torresola) and an agent of the Secret Service—the Treasury Department police force assigned to protect the president, among its other duties—were killed in the attempt, though Truman himself was unhurt. Collazo was sentenced to life in prison after refusing to follow his lawyer's advice to plead insanity. Instead, Collazo defended his actions by delivering a rambling but impassioned courtroom indictment of U.S. exploitation of Puerto Rico. In 1979, the sixty-five-year-old

Collazo was granted clemency by President Jimmy Carter and allowed to return to Puerto Rico.

On March 1, 1954, Puerto Rican nationalists struck again, firing machine guns from the floor of the U.S. House of Representatives, wounding five congressmen, one seriously. The four would-be assassins—Lolita Lebron, Rafael Cancel Miranda, Andres Figueroa Cordero, and Irvin Flores—were sentenced to life in prison and, like Collazo, granted clemency by Carter in 1979. (Puerto Rican nationalists were involved in other crimes following this 1954 assault on Capitol Hill, including a series of bombings in New York and Chicago during the 1970s and 1980s that left six people dead.)

Assassination Attempts on Presidents and Candidates

Aside from these few events during the 1950s, political violence in America is most closely associated in the public mind with the 1960s. Indeed, that single tumultuous decade saw the murder of a president (John F. Kennedy in 1963), a senator and leading presidential candidate (Robert F. Kennedy in 1968), and the nation's two most recognized African American leaders (Malcolm X in 1965 and Martin Luther King, Jr., in 1968).

Undoubtedly, the most politically significant of the assassinations was that of President Kennedy. On November 22, 1963, during a political fence-mending trip to Dallas, Texas, the forty-six-year-old president was shot and killed, while he was riding through the city in a motorcade. Texas governor John Connally, also in the car, was hit by a bullet but survived. Ex-marine Lee Harvey Oswald was apprehended hours later, but, before he could be put on trial, he was himself killed by Dallas nightclub owner Jack Ruby.

Kennedy's successor, Lyndon B. Johnson, put together a high-profile commission headed by Chief Justice Earl Warren of the U.S. Supreme Court to investigate the assassination. The Warren Commission concluded that Oswald, a mentally unbalanced individual, had acted alone, a verdict that most of the American public believed to be flawed. A variety of conspiracy theories have been advanced in the years since, tying the assassination to everybody from Johnson to Cuban leader Fidel Castro and to organizations and groups as diverse as the Central Intelligence Agency, the mafia, and anti-Castro Cuban exiles.

On June 6, 1968, Kennedy's younger brother, Senator Robert F. Kennedy of New York, was assassi-nated while campaigning for the Democratic presidential nomination in California. Having just won the all-important Golden State primary, Kennedy appeared poised to win the party's nomination. Following a victory speech at the Los Angeles Ambassador Hotel, Kennedy was gunned down by Sirhan Bishara Sirhan, a Palestinian nationalist who had immigrated to the United States in the 1950s. Unlike Oswald, who shot President Kennedy from the upper floors of the Texas School Book Repository and whose direct involvement in the crime was not witnessed by anyone, Sirhan fired at Senator Kennedy at close range in a crowded hotel kitchen, with dozens of witnesses.

Sirhan survived to go on trial and was sentenced to death—a fate that was commuted to life in prison after the U.S. Supreme Court ruled the death penalty unconstitutional in 1972. Sirhan never denied shooting Kennedy, although he said that he had been too intoxicated to remember firing the gun and that his motivation was the senator's strong support for Israel. Because of the many eyewitnesses present and the fact that Sirhan survived to go on trial, far fewer conspiracy theories have surrounded this political crime. Still, some have speculated whether Sirhan was hypnotized or manipulated in some way to commit the crime by forces that did not want to see Senator Kennedy become president. In the aftermath of Senator Kennedy's assassination, Congress passed legislation making the Secret Service responsible for protecting the lives of major presidential candidates. Sirhan, who remains in prison, has since asserted that he was framed, but there is no credible evidence to prove the allegation.

Sirhan's murder of Kennedy was the last successful assassination of a national political figure in postwar America, but several attempts were made to kill presidents and presidential candidates during the 1970s and 1980s. On May 15, 1972, Alabama governor George Wallace was shot four times by a janitor named Arthur Bremer; three others, including a Secret Service agent, were also wounded in the attack. Although Wallace survived, he was permanently paralyzed and confined to a wheelchair. As in the Robert Kennedy assassination, Bremer fired at close range, was witnessed doing so by many people, was immediately apprehended, and survived to go on trial.

Because Wallace himself was a controversial figure—a popular Democratic pro-segregationist who threatened to run as an independent in 1972—many believed the assassination had been politically motivated. As details of Bremer's life and personality came out at trial, however, it became clear that the assassin was a mentally unbalanced loner who had had psychological motivations for committing the crime. Bremer, too, remains in prison.

Three years later, in 1975, President Gerald R. Ford was the target of two unsuccessful assassination attempts less than three weeks apart. On September 5, Lynette Alice "Squeaky" Fromme, a follower of the murderous cult leader Charles Manson, pointed a pistol at the president in Sacramento, California, but failed to fire. Fromme claimed the act was a fulfillment of Manson's teachings, but no evidence was uncovered at trial to link Manson directly to the crime. Less than three weeks later, on September 22, another would-be assassin, former left wing radical Sara Jane Moore, fired a single shot at Ford outside a San Francisco hotel.

Moore had been recruited by the Federal Bureau of Investigation (FBI) as an informant with connections to the Symbionese Liberation Army, the radical group that had kidnapped newspaper heiress Patty Hearst the year before. At trial, Moore claimed that she had wanted to abandon her FBI role and return to her radical roots. By shooting the president, she said, she had hoped to win back the trust of her former radical friends. Although both Fromme and Moore were declared fit to stand trial and sentenced to life in prison under a 1965 federal law against threatening the president, many psychologists believe them to be mentally unbalanced. Fromme and Moore, both of whom briefly escaped prison in the 1980s, remain incarcerated to the present day.

As for the perpetrator of the latest serious assassination attempt of the postwar period, John Hinckley, Jr., there is little doubt that he was delusional. On March 30, 1981, Hinckley fired six shots at President Ronald Reagan outside a Washington, D.C., hotel. Reagan, White House press secretary James Brady, a policeman, and a Secret Service agent all were hit by bullets. Brady suffered lasting brain damage, but Reagan was luckier: A bullet, lodged in his lung, was quickly removed, and the president suffered no long-term effects from his wounds.

Hinckley had no political ax to grind with the conservative Republican president; indeed, he had been stalking Reagan's predecessor Jimmy Carter and liberal Massachusetts Democratic senator Ted Kennedy the year before. Instead, Hinckley was motivated by the movie *Taxi Driver* (1976), in which the lead character goes on an anticriminal shooting spree and is hailed as a hero. The lead actress in the film, a young Jodie Foster, was the object of Hinckley's obsession; by shooting the president, Hinckley had hoped to win her affection. Represented by high-powered defense attorneys hired by his wealthy father, Hinckley was acquitted on grounds of insanity—the only presidential assassin or would-assassin in American history to win such a verdict to date—and has been institutionalized ever since, although he was granted limited leaves to visit his parents in 2005.

Assassination of African American Leaders

Two major African American leaders were also the targets of assassination attempts during the postwar era. The first, Malcolm X, died in a hail of gunfire at the Audubon Ballroom in New York City on February 21, 1965. A former street criminal who had discovered the teachings of Elijah Muhammad, the head of the Black Muslim movement, while in prison, Malcolm X became one the movement's top organizers and spokespersons upon his release. In 1964, however, Malcolm X resigned over differences with Nation of Islam leaders and announced that he would set up an alternative Muslim organization. There were several reasons for his decision. First, he resented Muhammad's decision to silence him after he had declared President John F. Kennedy's assassination a case of "chickens coming home to roost" (he believed the president had condoned violence against African Americans in the South). Malcolm X was also deeply disappointed to learn that his leader, Muhammad, had carried on affairs and impregnated several young female followers. Finally, Malcolm X believed that Muhammad had issued orders for his assassination.

Malcolm X's followers appealed to him to keep a low profile, especially after his home was firebombed, but the black nationalist leader refused. Although the murder took place in front of a large audience Malcolm X was addressing, the perpetrators were never identified. Most historians believe that Malcolm X was assassinated by followers of Muhammad who, they say, feared and resented the disciple's growing influence in the black community. Many white Americans, who saw Malcolm X as a perpetrator of anti-white hate and an advocate of violence—charges disputed by his followers—were not surprised by his violent fate.

No such thinking accompanied the murder of the Reverend Martin Luther King, Jr., three years later. A leader of the civil rights movement since the mid-1950s, King advocated a nonviolent approach to ending racial segregation and discrimination in America. That approach won him the disdain of radical black leaders such as Malcolm X but a wide following among mainstream African Americans and liberal whites. By the mid-1960s, however, though he did not abandon his nonviolent approach to social change, King was becoming more outspoken and politically radical, questioning America's involvement in the Vietnam War and criticizing its economic system, which had left so many poor people behind. In April 1968, while in Memphis, Tennessee, to support a strike by the city's predominantly African American garbage collectors, King was killed on the balcony of the Lorraine Motel by a single shot fired from a high-powered rifle several hundred yards away. No one actually saw the perpetrator, but a petty criminal with a history of racial animus named James Earl Ray was arrested for the crime.

Ray never pleaded guilty, but he agreed to a plea bargain that sent him to prison for the rest of his life. Ray, who had led police on a chase through several states and Canada before being arrested in Montreal, claimed that he had been coerced into accepting the plea bargain and maintained his innocence until his death in prison in 1998. A year later, a jury in a civil suit brought by the King family against several private citizens and government agencies for King's death resolved that he had indeed been murdered by a conspiracy involving the mafia, several private individuals, and local, state, and federal agencies.

James Ciment

See also: Birmingham Church Bombing; Black Panthers; Conspiracy Theories; Crime, Violent; Greensboro Massacre; Kennedy (John F.) Assassination; Manson Murders; Oklahoma City Bombing; Puerto Rico and Puerto Ricans; Riots, Race; Symbionese Liberation Army; Terrorism, Domestic; Unabomber Affair; Warren Commission; White Supremacist Groups; Wounded Knee.

Bibliography

Clarke, James W. *American Assassins: The Darker Side of Politics.* Princeton, NJ: Princeton University Press, 1982.

Crotty, William J., ed. *Assassinations and the Political Order.* New York: Harper and Row, 1972.

McKinley, James. *Assassination in America.* New York: Harper and Row, 1977.

VISTA   *SEE* Volunteers in Service to America

VOICE OF AMERICA

The Voice of America (VOA) was the U.S. government's first international shortwave radio broadcasting network. As part of the Office of War Information (OWI), the VOA—established in February 1942, shortly after the U.S. entry into World War II—played an important role in Europe, Asia, and Latin America in countering Axis propaganda and building indigenous support for the Allied cause. Following the war, the VOA remained on the air and became an integral part of American foreign policy during the Cold War, as the United States sought to discredit the Soviet Union and stop the spread of communism. After the Cold War ended in the early 1990s, the VOA continued to broadcast news and information about the United States and the American way of life to overseas listeners.

The VOA's first broadcast was transmitted from New York City on February 25, 1942. Early programs were produced in four languages (English, French, German, and Italian) and transmitted abroad in fifteen-minute segments over the British Broadcasting Corporation's (BBC's) shortwave relays, while the VOA sought to obtain its own frequencies. The first VOA-broadcast programs carried a blend of war news, commentaries about Allied war policies and aims, and information about the U.S. government and the American people.

An executive order signed by President Franklin D. Roosevelt in June 1942 created the OWI to explain U.S. war policies, domestically and internationally, to the general public and news media. The Overseas Branch of the OWI administered the VOA, which, along with the United States Information Service (USIS), served as an overseas propaganda agency for the U.S. government. The VOA's reach and scope continued to expand throughout the war, finally broadcasting around the world twenty-four hours a day in more than fifty languages. By the close of the war in September 1945, the VOA had become an important part of the United States' wartime foreign policy.

Intense, domestic, political postwar pressure drastically reduced the size and output of the VOA. Congressional critics, many of whom were conservative Republicans and Southern Democrats, were anxious to demobilize after the war and put pressure on the government to dismantle its propaganda machine. Despite the success of wartime broadcasts, both the VOA and OWI had been subjects of controversy during the war, as opponents questioned the loyalty of broadcast personnel. Critics also charged that VOA broadcasts had been biased in their support of the Democratic Party and the New Deal, and they argued that any postwar broadcasts should be conducted by private media outlets. While President Harry S Truman favored the continuation of overseas broadcasts, he abolished the OWI on August 31, 1945, and transferred a much smaller VOA to an interim information agency within the State Department.

Over the next year and a half, the VOA underwent a transformation as its size and range were drastically reduced to meet peacetime standards. The VOA engaged in a series of struggles with Congress to retain its budget in 1946 and 1947, when opponents attempted to take it off the air permanently. Ironically, the emergence of Cold War hostilities between the United States and the Soviet Union in 1947 saved the VOA from extinction. As tensions between the two powers increased, lawmakers began to see the VOA as a vital tool for building support abroad for American initiatives like the Marshall Plan and the Truman Doctrine, while also countering the anti-American propaganda of the Soviet Union.

The Voice of America was established in 1942 to disseminate news and information about World War II. In the postwar years, the radio network focused its broadcasts on promoting U.S. policies and opposing anti-American propaganda. *(Three Lions/Getty Images)*

As a result, Congress in January 1948 passed the Information and Education Exchange Act, also known as the Smith-Mundt Act, which gave the State Department the legislative authority to operate the VOA and the rest of the international information program. The legislation, which sought to "promote a better understanding of the United States among the peoples of the world," nearly doubled funding for the VOA and enabled it to expand its reach globally. While it is difficult to measure the number of listeners, given the secrecy of the societies to which the VOA broadcast, VOA officials claimed they were reaching hundreds of millions in the Soviet bloc, mainland China, and elsewhere.

The deepening of the Cold War and the anticommunist hysteria that engulfed the United States in the late 1940s and early 1950s dramatically affected the VOA. Conservatives in Congress, such as Representative John Taber (Republican of New York), Senator Joseph P. McCarthy (Republican of Wisconsin), and Representative Richard M. Nixon (Republican of California), routinely questioned the competence and loyalty of VOA personnel. In the spring of 1948, a scandal developed, when congressional critics read a script from the VOA series "Know North America" that, in conservative eyes, disparaged the American people and their way of life. Similar content battles were waged between conservatives in Congress and the executive branch throughout the 1940s and 1950s, as the VOA attempted to take a fair and unbiased approach to programming, while critics repeatedly attacked it for focusing on the problems of American society, such as racial unrest and labor dissension, instead of refuting the continual stream of anti-American propaganda emanating from the Soviet Union.

Despite conservatives' accusations of inaccuracy and disloyalty, the VOA continued to be an important tool of American cultural diplomacy throughout the Cold War. In 1953, the VOA was incorporated into the newly created United States Information Agency (USIA). The USIA removed the VOA and the rest of the government's international information program from the State Department and placed them in an independent agency, whose director reported directly to the president. This action sought to immunize the VOA from congressional attacks, while emphasizing the importance of the information program to the achievement of U.S. Cold War objectives.

Throughout the 1950s, 1960s, and 1970s, the VOA, along with Radio Liberty and Radio Free

Europe, continued to be an important instrument of American foreign policy, particularly in Eastern Europe and the Soviet Union. There, listeners ignored prohibitions from their own governments, tuned in clandestinely, and heard a variety of news, informational, and entertainment programming.

After the end of the Cold War in the early 1990s, the VOA continued to broadcast abroad, providing a new generation of listeners with vital news and information about the United States, along with glimpses into the American way of life. In 2005, the VOA broadcast over 1,000 hours of weekly programming, via satellite television and the Internet, as well as radio, in more than forty languages, and estimated its worldwide audience at more than 100 million.

Terry R. Hamblin

See also: Propaganda, U.S.; Radio.

Bibliography

Krugler, David F, *The Voice of America and the Domestic Propaganda Battles, 1945–1953.* Columbia: University of Missouri Press, 2000.

Pirsein, Robert William, *The Voice of America: A History of the International Broadcasting Activities of the United States Government, 1940–1962.* Chicago: Arno, 1979.

Shulman, Holly Cowan. *The Voice of America: Propaganda and Democracy. 1941–1945*, Madison: University of Wisconsin Press, 1990.

VOLUNTEERS IN SERVICE TO AMERICA

Volunteers in Service to America (VISTA) is a domestic volunteer program established in 1964. Senator Hubert Humphrey, Democrat of Minnesota, first envisioned a national service corps during the 1950s, and President John F. Kennedy pursued the idea after the success of the Peace Corps. In changing the name from National Service Corps to VISTA, Congress hoped for a "great new vista, free of poverty" for all Americans.

In his 1963 State of the Union address, President Kennedy praised the success of overseas volunteers in the Peace Corps, which had been founded in 1961 to help people in underdeveloped countries. That success, he said, "suggests the merit of a similar corps serving our own community needs: in mental hospitals, on Indian reservations, in centers for the aged or for young delinquents, in schools for the illiterate or

the handicapped. As the idealism of our youth has served world peace, so can it serve the domestic tranquility." Kennedy was assassinated before he could launch the domestic corps of volunteers.

The concept finally came to fruition in 1964, when President Lyndon B. Johnson signed the Economic Opportunity Act as a key component of his War on Poverty. The law created the Office of Economic Opportunity (OEO), which administered hundreds of programs aimed at fighting poverty, including Head Start and VISTA. Up to 5,000 VISTA volunteers would be recruited and trained to work within the OEO and other antipoverty programs.

Volunteers had to be over the age of eighteen and without dependents. They would enlist for one year and attend six weeks of training. Draft deferments (not exemptions) of up to two years were available for VISTA volunteers. They would receive a small rent and food allowance, plus an additional amount set aside for them to collect after their service was concluded, in return for their work with the poor. They were required to live where they worked, under the assumption that only then could they truly become a part of the community.

"Your pay will be low; the conditions of your labor will often be difficult. But you will have the satisfaction of leading a great national effort, and you will have the ultimate reward which comes to those who serve their fellow man," Johnson told the first group of VISTA volunteers in December 1964.

The volunteers were mostly white, middle class, under the age of twenty-four, and had attended college. The OEO attempted to recruit minorities and the retired as the program progressed. VISTA was heavily advertised in print, film, television, and radio. In 1965, the OEO received 11,000 applications, which rose to 17,000 in 1967 and 23,000 in 1969.

The notion of living and working among the poor appealed to young people in the 1960s, when more than 32 million Americans were below the poverty line. By the end of 1965, some 2,000 VISTA volunteers were serving in the Appalachians, migrant worker camps, and poor neighborhoods. They did whatever work was needed in the communities—building, teaching, farming, mentoring, and more. Some volunteers decided to stay. Jay Rockefeller came to West Virginia as a VISTA volunteer in 1964 and was later elected governor and one of the state's senators.

VISTA merged with the Peace Corps in the 1970s and began recruiting professionals like doctors, lawyers, and architects to serve in poor communities. In the 1980s, it changed its focus to teaching local individuals and setting up local institutions to help the communities, rather than having VISTA volunteers do the work themselves. The VISTA Literacy Corps was created in 1986 to teach adults and children across the nation how to read.

In 1993, VISTA merged with AmeriCorps, a similar program established by the Clinton Administration, to form AmeriCorps*VISTA. Volunteers rededicated themselves to many of VISTA's original programs and ideals, helping the poor with low-income housing, finances, and transition from welfare to work. In 2006, there were 6,000 VISTA volunteers across the United States.

Melissa Stallings

See also: AmeriCorps; Peace Corps.

Bibliography

AmeriCorps. http://www.americorps.org.

Crook, William H. *Warriors for the Poor: The Story of VISTA, Volunteers in Service to America.* New York: William Morrow, 1969.

Reeves, T. Zane. *The Politics of the Peace Corps & VISTA.* Tuscaloosa: University of Alabama Press, 1988.

Whittlesey, Susan. *VISTA: Challenge to Poverty.* New York: Coward-McCann, 1970.

VOTING ISSUES

Two great ironies permeate the history of voting in the United States since the end of World War II. First, while securing the right to vote for African Americans in the South represented one of the great civil rights struggles of the past half-century, Americans still have one of the lowest voter-turnout rates of any major industrialized democracy in the world. At first glance, the drop from the 63.1 percent turnout of registered voters in 1960 to 55.3 percent in 2004 may not seem great; the 2004 turnout was the largest in almost forty years. In fact, while presidential elections in the 1960s saw increased voting rates, turnout since 1972 has fallen from the mid-50 percent range to the low-50 percent range, hitting bottom in 1996 with 49.1 percent. For midterm elections, the numbers are even lower—high 40s in the 1960s to mid- and high-30s in the 1990s and 2000s.

Second, while the United States champions free and fair elections around the world, its own system of voting, according to an increasing number of experts, has become deeply flawed. Partisan politicians not only run the mechanics of voting—how ballots appear, how votes get counted, and other critical aspects of the process—but they also determine who votes where. That is, in an age of sophisticated computer software, partisan state legislatures have drawn district lines—for both their own elections and those for Congress—which ensure that incumbents are rarely successfully challenged in their bids for reelection. (It is also true that incumbents have advantages in fund-raising and generally outspend their opponents.) From 1996 through 2004, more than 98 percent of incumbents won races to keep their seats in the House of Representatives. In 1968, the figure was 73 percent.

Securing the Southern Black Vote

The fact that fewer and fewer voters bother to show up at the polls—and that incumbents have an ever greater lock on their seats—should not be construed to mean that the great civil rights campaign to secure the franchise for African American voters in the South was unimportant. It represented one of the greatest campaigns for democracy in American history.

Through the 1960s, Southern governments used a variety of means to restrict African American voting. Some methods were legal, within the context of the times. For example, many Southern states had whites-only primaries. Since these elections were technically intraparty affairs, they were deemed constitutional by the courts. But the reality was that the South was essentially a one-party region through the 1960s, dominated by the Democrats. Excluding blacks from party voting was to exclude them from the political process altogether.

Other legal methods of voter restriction used in the South included poll taxes and literacy tests, both of which had a greater impact on blacks than on whites. As late as 1959, the U.S. Supreme Court ruled in *Lassiter v. Northampton County Board of Elections* that literacy tests for voting in North Carolina did not violate the Fourteenth and Fifteenth Amendments.

There were also extralegal means to deny blacks the vote. Registrars kept odd hours, and the locations of their offices were not publicized in the black community. Literacy tests were applied capriciously;

Baker v. Carr (1962)

Baker v. Carr was a landmark U.S. Supreme Court decision that gave federal courts the jurisdiction to scrutinize legislative apportionments, or the designation of voting districts, even for state elections.

In 1962, citizen Charles Baker won a suit brought against the state of Tennessee, claiming that the state was violating the Fourteenth Amendment of the Constitution by not reapportioning its voting districts according to population. The second clause of the amendment clearly states that representation shall be based on the total number of citizens.

The numbers spoke in Baker's favor. In 1961, the skewed apportionment of voting districts meant that just 37 percent of the voters elected fully 60 percent of Tennessee state senators and that just 40 percent chose nearly two-thirds of the state house members. As of 1962, the Tennessee state legislature had failed to reapportion its voting districts for sixty years in spite of interim population growth and redistribution.

Baker faced a setback when a federal district court ruled that it had no jurisdiction in the matter, because the case involved apportionment for state elections. He then appealed to the Supreme Court, which ruled in his favor.

The *Baker v. Carr* decision has been important to voters in urban areas because it gave greater weight to their votes. As urban areas grow faster than rural ones, the need for fair reapportionment is more critical to them. Before *Baker v. Carr,* urban areas were underrepresented because of geographical districting policies, which gave rural votes greater weight. In New Jersey, for example, each county elected one member to the State Senate. This meant that if one county had a larger population than another, votes in the county with a smaller population would be stronger than those in a county with a larger one. *Baker v. Carr* abolished this inequality, underlining the principle of "one person, one vote."

Although the U.S. Constitution holds that population must be the determining factor in electing representatives, state legislatures are not bound by federal constitutional restrictions. Prior to *Baker v. Carr,* states had often practiced gerrymandering—drawing new districts and dividing the political body so as to favor the party in power or special interests. The Supreme Court decision opened the door for suits to be brought against states that still participated in such "legislative appointment." Within nine months, suits were brought along similar lines to *Baker v. Carr* in at least thirty-four other states.

Arthur Holst

whites were given questions with easy answers, blacks with obscure and esoteric ones. But mostly it was sheer intimidation that kept the vast majority of blacks out of the Southern political process through the 1960s. Any black person who tried to register and vote knew that he or she faced potential retaliation by whites. This could be economic—losing a job—or, in extreme cases, physical violence (or threats) against the potential voter and his or her family.

The statistics bear out how well these methods worked. In 1960, just 5 percent of eligible black voters were registered in Mississippi. In fact, in only one state of the Old Confederacy, Tennessee, was the rate above 50 percent.

The civil rights movement, said to have begun in Montgomery, Alabama, in 1955, with the struggle to desegregate the city's bus system, soon became engaged in winning back the franchise granted to black (males) after the Civil War and then lost over the course of the late nineteenth and early twentieth centuries. In particular, younger members of the movement—led by the Student Nonviolent Coordinating Committee—struggled to overcome violence and racism to register black voters in the Mississippi Freedom Summer project of 1964.

At the same time, national civil rights organizations and leaders were struggling to win congressional passage of laws that would require the federal government to more actively guarantee black voting rights. The result of this campaign was the Twenty-Fifth Amendment to the U.S. Constitution (ratified in 1964), which banned the poll tax, and the Voting Rights Act of 1965, which empowered the U.S. attorney general to take over the election process in jurisdictions where less than 50 percent of potential minority voters were registered.

The result of these campaigns was nothing short of astonishing. In Mississippi, the registration rate among blacks jumped to nearly 60 percent by 1968. Indeed, no Southern state had a black registration rate beneath 50 percent that year.

Guaranteeing the Franchise to Other Groups

The Voting Rights Act also provided protections for non-English-speaking citizens. The law provided that states must guarantee that bilingual ballots are available in counties where 5 percent or more of the population speaks a language other than English. The legislation was extended three times after 1965. The first extension was in 1970, when Congress renewed the temporary provisions of the Act for another five years; the law was extended again in 1975 and in 1982. While there was some progress in registration and voting under the 1970 legislation, Congress found that many states, especially in the South, ignored the provisions in Section 5, which allowed for the legal changes in voting procedures and election laws.

The 1970 legislation also allowed eighteen-year-olds to vote in federal elections. Some states disputed the law's constitutionality, but the Supreme Court ruled in *Oregon v. Mitchell* (1970) that Congress had the authority to lower the voting age in federal but not state elections. Several states challenged the law in court by arguing that the Constitution does not grant the government power to control other aspects of state voting law. But with the Vietnam War raging—and young people contending that being drafted for the military meant that they should have the right to vote—the Twenty-Sixth Amendment was ratified in July 1971, lowering the voting age to eighteen in all elections.

Before 1972, in order to vote, a citizen eighteen years or older had to reside in a state for a specified period of time. The residency requirements varied from state to state and depended on the type of election. Most jurisdictions excluded people from voting who did not fulfill a lengthy state residency requirement. Others, such as Maine, Minnesota, Oregon, and Wisconsin, allowed prospective voters to register and cast their ballots on the same day as they established residency.

In 1972, in *Dunn v. Blumstein,* the U.S. Supreme Court confirmed that lengthy residency requirements for voting in state and local elections were unconstitutional; it suggested that a person who lives in a state for at least thirty days should be eligible to vote. Since that time, no state has imposed a residency requirement of more than thirty days; registering and voting on the same day was authorized in 1976.

In most states, people who have been found guilty of a felony or who are confined in a prison or mental institution cannot register to vote. In most jurisdictions, registering to vote requires that a person must place his or her name on the list of eligible citizens at a local government office or by mail with a designated authority.

The 1975 Voting Rights Act banned all literacy tests and established federal policies designed to increase voter turnout among Native Americans and Spanish-speaking Americans. In 1982, Congress extended the Voting Rights Act for twenty-five years. This latest version permits private parties to sue in federal court and to overturn any election law or procedure that produces de facto discriminatory results. However, regions can escape oversight by the federal examiners if they maintain a clean voting rights record for at least ten years.

A law passed in 1984 required that all polling places and voter registration sites must be accessible to people with physical disabilities. Localities without such facilities are required to make alternate arrangements to accommodate disabled voters.

Making Registration Easier

Despite all of these provisions, voter registration and turnout in the United States have remained relatively low. To increase participation in the electoral process, Congress passed the National Voter Registration Act, also known as the "motor voter" law, in 1993. The legislation has three provisions. First, it requires states to allow people to register to vote whenever they apply for a renewal or change of address on their drivers' license. Second, it requires states to allow people to register to vote at public assistance offices, armed forces recruiting centers, public libraries, schools, or any other state and local government offices. And third, it requires all states to provide for voter registration through the mail.

The motor voter law took effect in 1995, and within just two months, a total of 630,000 new voters signed up in twenty-seven states. Despite the increase in registration, however, voter turnout in the presidential election of 1996 was one of the lowest in U.S. history. Just 49.1 percent of eligible voters cast a ballot.

The 2000 Election and Its Legacy

No improvement in registration or turnout matters, of course, unless the votes are fairly and accurately counted. This process was tested and, to many, found wanting in the 2000 presidential election between Democratic Vice President Al Gore and Republican Texas Governor George W. Bush.

That election was one of the closest in the nation's history. In Florida, because the vote was so close, a recount automatically went into effect under state law. (Florida was critical to the outcome of the election because its twenty-five electoral votes would provide the margin of victory for either Bush or Gore.) After numerous legal challenges and recounts, the U.S. Supreme Court, in the case of *Bush v. Gore* on December 12, voted 7–2 to end the recounts on the grounds that they constituted an equal protection violation, because different standards were applied in different counties. For example, some counties required full hand recounts of all precincts, while others, like Miami-Dade, required them only for selected precincts. The Court also voted, 5–4, that no new recount with uniform standards could be conducted in time to meet the December 12 deadline for declaring a final vote count as stipulated by state law. Thus, Republican candidate George W. Bush was declared the winner in Florida, giving him enough electoral votes to win the race for president.

After the discrepancy over Florida's vote count, a number of suggestions were made to renovate America's voting system. In 2002, Congress passed the Help America Vote Act, requiring that each state have in place a system for counting disputed ballots. In addition, the legislation provided federal funds for improving voting equipment and for the training of election officials. No steps were taken, however, to create a uniform national voting system. In the 2004 election, electronic machines were used in some areas but not in others. Many experts question the precision of electronic voting and the security of machines; others question the reliability of nonelectronic voting.

Florida's recount catastrophe of 2000 was of great concern to many Americans, especially minority groups who felt their votes had been unfairly discarded. The fears of electoral gridlock in 2004 proved unfounded, even though the balloting was close (though not razor-thin, as in 2000). This time, the decisive state was Ohio, whose electoral votes—and the final outcome—Democratic candidate Senator John Kerry conceded without dispute or overt controversy. Still, issues raised by the Florida recount dispute and various concerns over the use of electronic voting machines have made the American people, public officials, and the media all the more vigilant about the fairness and credibility of the election process.

Sherrow Pinder

See also: Constitutional Amendments; Election of 2000; Election of 2004; Voting Rights Act.

Bibliography

Converse, Phillip, E. "Change in the American Electorate." In *The Human Meaning of Social Change,* ed. Angus Campbell and Phillip E. Converse. New York: Russell Sage Foundation, 1972.

Graham, Gene S. *One Man, One Vote:* Baker v. Carr *and the American Levellers.* Boston: Little, Brown, 1972.

Hasen, Richard L. *The Supreme Court and Election Law: Judging Equality from Baker v. Carr to Bush v. Gore.* New York: New York University Press, 2003.

Keller, Morton. *Affairs of State: Public Life in Late Nineteenth-Century America.* Cambridge, MA: Harvard University Press, 1977.

Keyssar, Alexander. *The Right to Vote: The Contested History of Democracy in the United States.* New York: Basic Books, 2002.

Kousser, Morgan J. *Colorblind Injustice: Minority Voting Rights and the Undoing of the Second Reconstruction.* Chapel Hill: University of North Carolina Press, 1999.

VOTING RIGHTS ACT

The Voting Rights Act of 1965 is generally regarded as one of the most effective civil rights laws in American history. The legislation changed the landscape of electoral politics in Southern states where African Americans had been effectively disfranchised since the 1890s.

After the Civil War and Emancipation, Reconstruction had granted formerly enslaved African Americans freedom, citizenship, and the right to vote under the Thirteenth, Fourteenth, and Fifteenth Amendments to the U.S. Constitution. Yet these amendments did not assure a fair and equal vote, because the federal courts acquiesced in determined efforts by Southern whites to prevent black suffrage. During Reconstruction, and for years after, whites used large-scale violence, intimidation, and fraud to minimize the electoral participation of African Americans. Beginning in the 1890s, Southern state legislatures and constitutional conventions adopted disfranchising measures such as the grandfather clause, the poll tax, literacy tests, and the white primary to restrict the ballot box.

By the early twentieth century, these methods had effectively disfranchised most Southern African Americans, and, even after the U.S. Supreme Court struck down white primary laws as unconstitutional, registration barriers continued to handicap black political participation. In 1958, the U.S. Civil Rights Commission reported that there were forty-four counties in the Deep South where there was not a single black voter registered. Many of these counties had large African American populations; some had an African American majority. Every time the federal courts struck down one registration barrier, Southern white officials came up with some new measure to limit black registration and voting. Thus, in 1965, Congress passed the Voting Rights Act to establish an enforcement mechanism with the power to guarantee all citizens the right to a free and effective ballot.

The Voting Rights Act suspended literacy tests and provided for the appointment of federal examiners with the power to register qualified citizens. In addition, Section 5 of the legislation required certain jurisdictions—those states with the most egregious history of racial discrimination in voting—to obtain "preclearance" for any change in their electoral procedures. An immediate effect of more minority voters was the sharp decrease, almost elimination, of blatant bigotry in electioneering. A longer-term effect has been the election of minority citizens at almost every level of government.

South Carolina, joined by other Southern states, challenged the constitutionality of the Voting Rights Act, claiming that it violated the state's right to control and implement elections. In 1966, the Supreme Court upheld the Act in *South Carolina v. Katzenbach,* and federal courts have continued to sustain it against repeated challenge. In 1970, despite the opposition of the Nixon Administration, Congress extended the law for another five years. In 1975, testimony from Asian, Hispanic, and Native American voters persuaded Congress, with bipartisan support, to add special protections for language-minority citizens and to extend the preclearance requirements of Section 5 to new states and localities for another seven years.

As African Americans began to vote in larger numbers after 1965, many Southern jurisdictions, from state legislatures to county and city councils and school boards, changed their method of elections from wards to at-large voting in order to dilute minority voting strength. In the former, heavily African American wards were likely to elect African American representatives; in the latter, African Americans, often a minority in the larger jurisdiction, would be unable to elect African American representatives to office. Under the Voting Rights Act, the Department of Justice frequently blocked such changes in jurisdictions covered by the preclearance requirement; where at-large elections were in place before 1965, separate litigation was necessary. African American citizens brought a class action lawsuit against the city of Mobile, Alabama, arguing that its at-large election system diluted the strength of the African American vote. The Supreme Court ruled in *Mobile v. Bolden* (1980) that minority plaintiffs had to prove that voting procedures such as at-large elections were adopted or maintained with a racially discriminatory purpose in order to be overturned. No longer was an outcome of racial discrimination sufficient; the plaintiffs had to show intent.

In 1982, Congress extended the preclearance provisions of Section 5 and the provisions protecting minority language voters for another twenty-five years. Congress also created a new results test by revising Section 2 of the Act so that vote dilution could be challenged without requiring proof of discriminatory intent. Not just in the South, but throughout the country, hundreds of at-large systems and other election practices with a racially discriminatory effect have been successfully challenged under the new Section 2 results test.

The Voting Rights Act has resulted in a substantial increase in minority elected officials, especially African Americans in the South, Native Americans in the West, and Hispanics in California and Texas. A pivotal piece of legislation in modern American history, the Voting Rights Act continues to have a tremendous influence on the nation's political life.

Orville Vernon Burton

See also: Civil Rights Act of 1964; Civil Rights Legislation and Policy; Civil Rights Movement, Through 1965; Selma March; Voting Issues.

Bibliography

Davidson, Chandler, and Bernard Grofman, eds. *Quiet Revolution in the South: The Impact of the Voting Rights Act, 1965–1990.* Princeton, NJ: Princeton University Press, 1994.

Garrow, David. *Protest at Selma: Martin Luther King, Jr., and the Voting Rights Act of 1965.* New Haven, CT: Yale University Press, 1978.

Kousser, J. Morgan. *Colorblind Injustice: Minority Voting Rights and the Undoing of the Second Reconstruction.* Chapel Hill: University of North Carolina Press, 1999.

WACO INCIDENT

Located in north central Texas, the city of Waco was the site of the deadliest federal law-enforcement action in U.S. history. On April 19, 1993, after a fifty-one-day standoff with federal agents, seventy-five members of the Branch-Davidians religious cult, including twenty-one children, died in a fire that consumed their Mount Carmel compound.

At the time of the tragedy, the members of the compound and their leader, David Koresh, were under investigation by the Bureau of Alcohol, Tobacco, and Firearms (ATF) for allegedly stockpiling illegal weapons in preparation for the Apocalypse. The Federal Bureau of Investigation (FBI) took over hostage negotiations during the standoff and ultimately made the decision to carry out the final assault on the compound.

While it is still unclear how the fire started, flames simultaneously erupted in several locations a few minutes after FBI tanks breached the compound's walls. The buildings, which spanned an area the size of a city block and were made mostly of wood, took less than forty-five minutes to be consumed by the fire. Except for nine members who managed to escape, everyone inside the compound, including David Koresh, died in the flames.

The origins of the Branch-Davidians can be traced back to a splinter sect of the Seventh Day Adventist Church. The original sect, called Davidians, was founded in 1942 by Victor Houteff, who believed that Christ would return once a specific number of Christians had been purified and the Seven Seals in the Book of Revelations had been opened by an anointed messenger. Following Houteff's death in 1955, there was a split within the sect that led to the founding of the Branch-Davidians.

Like Houteff's group, the Branch-Davidians believed in the imminent return of Christ and the importance of the Seven Seals, but they did not believe that Houteff or his successor were the prophesied agents of God. The Branch-Davidians would not find the man destined to lead them toward the Apocalypse until 1981, when twenty-four-year-old David Koresh joined their ranks.

Koresh was born Vernon Howell in Texas in 1959. He grew up in Dallas as a member of the Seventh Day Adventist Church but became disillusioned with the church in his late teens. Shortly thereafter, Koresh moved to Waco, where he joined the Branch-Davidians as a handyman and quickly rose to a position of importance. A ninth-grade dropout with a formidable knowledge of Scripture, Koresh provided numerous biblical explanations for his ascension within the group. By 1987, he had assumed full control of the Branch-Davidians and proclaimed himself to be the seventh and final angel, destined to be the agent of God and to bring about the end of the world.

The Branch-Davidian faith allows for apocalyptic prophets who have been anointed by God. Koresh was not the only prophet within the Mount Carmel group, but he was definitely the most charismatic. In 1990, he legally changed his name to David Koresh ("David" referring to the king of the Israelites, and "Koresh" being another name for Cyrus, the king of Persia who was commanded by God to "subdue nations before him"). He then began prophesizing that the great battle to cleanse the earth in preparation for the New Jerusalem would take place in Texas at the hands of the U.S. government. Koresh also ordered members of the Branch-Davidians to begin collecting firearms in preparation for the end of the world. By 1993, enough weapons had been amassed within the Mount Carmel compound to capture the attention of investigators within the ATF.

The ATF monitored Koresh and his followers for ten months before deciding to raid the compound and arrest him on firearms violations. While Koresh could have easily been arrested outside Mount Carmel, ATF agents wanted to arrest him in close proximity to the weapons at the compound.

On February 28, 1993, ATF authorities carried out the raid, despite warnings from an undercover agent that Koresh knew of the impending assault. A shot was fired during the confusion of the raid, which led both sides to respond with additional gunfire. The firefight that ensued ended with six Branch-Davidians and four ATF agents dead and an additional twenty-five wounded. The ATF withdrew later

The Branch Davidian compound in Waco, Texas, is engulfed by flames during the April 1993 confrontation with federal authorities. Cult members, under siege for stockpiling weapons, apparently committed mass suicide in the final FBI assault. *(Bob Daemmrich/AFP/Getty Images)*

that day, leaving the FBI to take over what they then determined to be a hostage situation.

The FBI surrounded the seventy-seven-acre compound with 400 federal agents. David Koresh and about a hundred of his followers locked themselves in Mount Carmel with enough food and water to last a year and allegedly enough firepower to fend off the Apocalypse itself. Koresh told his lawyers and FBI negotiators that he had a number of illegal firearms in his possession but was unspecific as to how many. Without a clear idea of what was inside the compound, FBI officials had no choice but to wait for Koresh and his followers to surrender.

Koresh initially agreed to surrender to authorities three days into the standoff. According to telephone conversations, he offered to turn himself in peacefully if the FBI agreed to broadcast his fifty-eight-minute sermon over local radio airwaves. The FBI complied with his request, and the first of two dozen Branch-Davidians were allowed to leave Mount Carmel. But Koresh later recanted his offer to surrender, claiming that God had told him to wait for a sign. The FBI continued to surround Mount Carmel for nearly two months, while Koresh waited for his message from God.

In addition to the weapons charges, Attorney General Janet Reno had received several reports of child abuse within the compound during the course of the standoff. Although Koresh had never been arrested for molestation, it was well known that he had performed marriage ceremonies for girls as young as four-

teen. Reno, who was in charge of federal operations at Waco, finally decided that the FBI could not risk waiting any longer and authorized the use of force to end the standoff.

Assault by Government Forces

On the morning of April 19, the FBI warned everyone in the compound to surrender or face an assault. The Branch-Davidians ignored the warning and prepared for the attack. In an effort to drive Koresh and his followers out of the compound, the FBI punched holes in the walls of Mount Carmel and pumped CS gas (tear gas) inside. Flames broke out shortly after the tanks breached the compound.

Critics of Reno and the FBI claim that the CS gas mixed with other burning compounds to contribute to the fire. Federal officials contended that the Branch-Davidians started the fire themselves in an effort at martyrdom. The factual evidence surrounding the fire is confusing at best. Satellite images showed several small fires breaking out simultaneously throughout the compound, while eyewitnesses reported that they saw the tanks knock over kerosene lamps. An independent consulting firm, hired by the National Rifle Association (NRA) to investigate the fires in 1995, found that the small series of fires seen in satellite images were most likely set by the Branch-Davidians themselves.

The debate over how the fire began eventually led to a Congressional investigation in 2000, which cleared FBI agents of any wrongdoing and placed responsibility for the deaths with Koresh. Attorney General Janet Reno took public responsibility for her decision to use force, but she also placed the blame for the fire on Koresh. "The fate of the Branch-Davidians was in David Koresh's hands, and he chose death for the men and women who had entrusted their lives to him," Reno said. "And he, David Koresh, chose death for the innocent children of Waco."

Catherine Griffis

See also: Crime, Violent; Cults; Evangelical Christianity; Oklahoma City Bombing; Ruby Ridge Shooting.

Bibliography

Reavis, Dick. *The Ashes of Waco: An Investigation.* New York: Simon and Schuster, 1995.
Wright, Stuart. *Armageddon in Waco: Critical Perspectives on the Branch Davidian Conflict.* Chicago: University of Chicago Press, 1995.

WALL STREET

Wall Street, the popular term for the American stock market or U.S. securities industry, was named after a street in lower Manhattan that was the first permanent home of the stock exchange in New York. At the heart of the American financial market, it is largely composed of publicly traded companies on the New York Stock Exchange (NYSE), the American Stock Exchange (AMEX), and other lesser exchanges, including the National Association of Securities Dealers Automated Quotation (NASDAQ), founded in 1971, which deals largely in technological stocks.

Like the American economy itself, Wall Street has gone through several major phases during the postwar era: a period of transition following World War II; a boom period, or bull market, stretching from the mid-1950s through the early 1970s; a time of retrenchment, or bear market, from the early 1970s through the early 1980s; a time of accelerated gains through the end of the 1990s; and a period of stagnation in the early 2000s.

Prior to the Great Depression and the New Deal, the U.S. securities industry was largely unregulated and subject to manipulation by traders with significant financial resources and information that was unavailable to the public. During the nineteenth century, several attempts were made to corner the market on securities, thereby manipulating the price. This could set off panics in the larger economy, as was the case in the 1870s.

Until the 1920s, most trading was done by and for major financial players in New York and the Northeast. During that decade, the electronic ticker tape, which flashed prices electronically across the country, allowed ordinary citizens to invest in the stock market more easily. This brought in more financial resources and fed the great boom market of the late 1920s. The inflated stock prices of the period generally did not represent real values; instead, they reflected speculation by insiders. Thus, when the stock market crashed in October 1929, millions of Americans lost their investments.

In response to these manipulations and to ensure that the markets were more transparently honest—a critical factor in their success, as few investors would put their money into an institution that was rigged by insiders—the administration of Franklin D. Roosevelt established the Securities and Exchange Commission (SEC) in 1934, as part of its New Deal package of reform programs. The SEC continued to act as a government watchdog on Wall Street throughout the postwar era, regulating brokers and exchanges, as well as setting financial disclosure rules for publicly traded companies, all in a generally successful effort to prevent insider manipulation.

War and Transition

World War II was a relatively quiet time on Wall Street. To a much greater extent than in previous wars, with the possible exception of the Civil War, the government borrowed enormous sums of money to pay for the struggle, soaking up much of the funds available for private investment. In addition, through the Federal Reserve Board (commonly known as the Fed), the Roosevelt Administration kept bond rates stable, and, through other acts and regulations, prices and wages were regulated or capped. Thus, new stock offerings fell to their lowest level since the depths of the Great Depression. Most of the trading during the war was in U.S. Treasury bonds.

The volume of government-issued bonds dropped dramatically after the war, but the decline was not matched by a heady increase in securities investment, as had occurred after World War I. The main reason was action taken by the Fed. Fearing a surge in inflation, the government established measures to prevent margin buying—that is, purchasing stocks by borrowing money—and to force investors to use cash to buy securities. This kept speculation down, but it also limited investment on Wall Street.

At the same time, the U.S. Department of Justice began antitrust cases against major trading firms, including Morgan Stanley, which had an adverse effect on investment, until the case was dropped in 1953. The Korean War also had an impact on stock market investment, as, once again, government borrowing and efforts to keep inflation in check had a dampening effect on stocks and other securities.

Boom Years: Mid-1950s to Early 1970s

The general postwar economic boom began during the late 1940s, but it was not until the immediate post–Korean War period that the prosperity began to be reflected on Wall Street. Indeed, it was not until late 1954 that the Dow Jones Industrial Average (commonly known as the Dow)—a composite index of thirty key industrial, transportation, and utility stocks established in 1896 and altered over the years to reflect the changing American economy—climbed above 381.17, its peak before the 1929 crash.

Unlike the speculative stock market boom of the 1920s, say economic historians, the upsurge of the 1950s and 1960s was based on what financial analysts call "fundamentals." The American economy was experiencing dramatic growth in productivity and output. Individual incomes and corporate profits were rising, as two decades of depression and war gave way to a postwar boom in consumer spending and business investment. Before it was over in late 1972, the great postwar boom period had sent the Dow to well over 1,000.

There were parallels between the two eras as well. The crash of 1929 soured middle-class Americans on investing in securities through the 1930s and 1940s, especially after evidence of market manipulation emerged in the investigations of the early 1930s. By the mid-1950s, however, ordinary Americans, buoyed by prosperity, increasingly optimistic about the economy, and attracted by stock prices that were finally climbing again, returned to securities as an investment. This was encouraged by commission brokerage houses such as Merrill Lynch, which set up offices in cities across the United States, and by the development of mutual funds, whereby small investors could pool their resources and allow financial experts to invest in carefully defined "baskets" of stocks or bonds for them. Finally, the government eased up on margin requirements, allowing investors to use borrowed money to buy stocks.

Once again, stock market news transcended the financial pages and became the talk in offices and homes around the country. As stocks continued to gain in price, more Americans invested in the market, sending stock prices to further heights. By the 1960s, more than 10 million shares were being traded on an average day, up from a few hundred thousand during the 1930s and early 1940s.

Rising share prices not only put profits in the pockets of ordinary investors, but they also bolstered the accounts of the companies being traded, as many corporations kept some of their shares in house. Rising prices provided publicly traded companies with assets beyond what they needed for investment in new production facilities. The result was a wave of corporate mergers during the 1960s, fueled not only by excess capital but also by the belief that the more diversified a company was, the better it would be able to survive downturns in specific industries.

No corporation reflected this trend more than International Telephone and Telegraph (IT&T). A manufacturer of telephone equipment and owner of telephone systems in several countries, IT&T began to diversify after 1959 under the leadership of its chief executive officer, Harold Geneen. By the early 1970s, IT&T owned subsidiary companies in fields as diverse as rental cars (Avis) and hotels (Sheraton).

Recession and Retrenchment: Early 1970s to Early 1980s

The great postwar boom came to an end in the early 1970s, a victim of economic problems at home and abroad. The country had experienced recessions—defined as two consecutive quarters of zero or negative growth in gross national product (GNP)—from time to time between the late 1940s and early 1970s, but these were usually brief episodes followed by renewed upsurges in growth. By the 1970s and 1980s, the recessions were becoming longer and deeper.

Part of the problem was inflation. Easy credit and government borrowing to pay for the Vietnam War started sending prices dramatically higher in the 1970s, undermining economic stability. Adding to this was the problem of lagging productivity. From the late 1940s to the mid-1960s, productivity had averaged more than 3 percent annually; by the 1970s, it had fallen to just 1.5 percent and to near zero in the second half of the decade. Increased competition from the newly resurgent economies of Western Europe and Japan, which had finally recovered from World War II, also was having an impact on American exports.

But nothing marked the transition from the postwar boom to the 1970s slump more dramatically than the rise in energy prices. Once an exporter of oil, the United States had become the world's largest importer by the early 1970s, a significant downside to the boom of the 1950s and 1960s. Much of the oil was being imported from the politically volatile Middle East. When Arab countries decided to penalize the United States for aiding Israel in the 1973 Arab-Israeli War by cutting off oil supplies, the price of oil shot up by nearly 40 percent in a matter of months. Because oil affected virtually every industry in America, this sent the prices of all kinds of commodities and services radically higher, resulting in a combination of unemployment and inflation that experts referred to as "stagflation."

The steep recession of 1973–1975 undercut corporate profitability and stock prices. From late 1972 to early 1975, the Dow plummeted from about 1,050 to nearly 550, a decline of almost 50 percent. Though it made a comeback in 1976, rising above the 1,000 mark again, further shocks—including a second energy crisis near the decade's end—sent stocks tumbling. In early 1980, the Dow had fallen again to just under 700. Falling stock prices hurt both individuals, who lost much of their savings, and industry, which was forced to retrench through layoffs and a reduced investment in productive capacity. With the recession affecting virtually every sector of the economy, even companies that had diversified found themselves with reduced profits or even losses.

The recessionary 1970s also had an impact on politics, giving rise to a new conservative movement that argued government regulation was to blame for the economic hard times. In 1980, voters threw out Democratic president Jimmy Carter and elected conservative Republican Ronald Reagan, who came into office on a platform that investment needed to be encouraged through a reduction in taxes on corporations and the wealthiest Americans.

At the same time, the Fed was undergoing a change in focus. Whereas it had promoted easy credit in the 1960s as a way to keep the economy growing, it now became more concerned with inflation. After taking over as chairman of the Fed in 1979, Paul Volcker moved to cut the supply of credit by increasing the interest rates that banks paid for loans. This tightened the money supply and sent the country into its worst recession since the 1930s. Unemployment soared to above 10 percent in the early 1980s, and the stock market stagnated. Between the time Reagan came into office in early 1981 and the end of the recession in late 1982, the Dow remained under 1,000 and usually below 800.

Second Boom: Early 1980s Through 2000

The Reagan Administration's efforts to wring inflation from the economy were successful, as were its efforts to bolster investment through tax cuts. The so-called "supply-side economics," which emphasized increased productivity over consumption, revived Wall Street, even if it widened the gap between rich and poor in the overall economy. Beginning in late 1982 and lasting through the crash of October 1987, the Dow climbed dramatically, from roughly 700 to more than 2,700, a gain of nearly 400 percent.

The era not only witnessed unprecedented corporate profitability, but it also spurred a new wave of mergers. Unlike the conglomerations of the 1960s, the new mergers were not aimed at creating recession-proof diversification. Instead, the consolidation was spurred by a perception that many companies were poorly managed and that greater profits could be wrung out of them if redundant capacity and personnel were eliminated. Whereas once mass layoffs signaled that a company was in serious trouble, triggering a decline in its stock price, corporations that reduced their payrolls now were being rewarded by Wall Street investors and saw their stock prices rise.

Still other acquisitions were instigated for even more ruthless motives, such as raiding companies for their assets, both financial and productive. Once the acquired company had been stripped of these assets, it was sold. The result was a wave of corporate bankruptcies and more mass layoffs.

Some of the acquisitions were funded with junk bonds. Corporate bonds are the opposite of stock shares. Whereas an investor who purchases a share is buying a piece of a company's assets, a bond is a kind of investor loan to the company. Bonds are rated by firms such as Standard & Poor's on the basis of their yields, how much interest they will pay, and their investment quality (the degree of risk that they will be paid back in full). Normally, yields stand in inverse proportion to investment quality. That is, bonds with low investment quality attract purchasers only by offering high yields. Beginning in the late 1970s and accelerating in the 1980s, a number of brokerage houses on Wall Street, most notably Drexel Burnham Lambert, began to specialize in the issuance of high-yield, low-quality bonds, which soon gained the popular name "junk bonds." The vast sums of money raised by the issuance of junk bonds were used to acquire other companies, which were stripped of their assets to pay off the bonds. Once the bonds were paid off, those who had purchased the companies reaped huge profits; the brokerage houses, meanwhile, pocketed large fees.

This kind of financial legerdemain was rife with fraud, as many companies doctored their books to appear more profitable so that they could issue more junk bonds. A number of major players in the junk bond field were convicted of insider trading, profiting on knowledge that was unavailable to regular investors. A slew of SEC investigations and convictions resulted in the late 1980s, as high-flying arbitrageurs—the name for those who engaged in these risky mergers and acquisitions—such as Ivan Boesky and Michael Milliken were prosecuted and sent to jail.

On October 19, 1987, Wall Street experienced another blow, the single largest one-day drop to that time—508 points, or nearly 25 percent of the Dow. Many explanations have been offered for the crash; some believe it was a reaction to the scandals of Wall Street. But the reason that most economists agree on is that a normal adjustment got out of hand because of automation and institutionalization. That is to say, two critical factors fundamentally altered who invested in Wall Street and how they invested during the 1970s and 1980s.

Increasingly large institutional investors—especially pension funds—were becoming key players on the market, investing vast sums of money in stocks and fund shares. At the same time, the market was becoming computerized, allowing investors to institute automatic sell orders, outside the control of human brokers, when a stock price fell below a certain value. When stock prices started to fall, the electronic triggers kicked in. When the huge share holdings of institutional investors began to be sold automatically, there were few buyers to purchase them, sending the prices tumbling and triggering more sales. As a result of "Black Monday," as the day came to be called, the NYSE and other exchanges instituted safety measures to prevent such electronic cascading.

Despite the crash, the scandals, and a sharp recession in the 1990s, Wall Street continued to thrive. Between October 20, 1987, and the end of 1994, the Dow climbed, albeit more slowly, from around 1,700 to nearly 4,000.

But it was the late 1990s that saw the greatest surge in stock prices in history, as the Dow climbed to nearly 12,000 by the first months of the new millennium. Much of the surge was fueled by technology stocks. By the 1990s, the computer revolution had begun to pay off, as businesses began to utilize the technology's immense power to crunch numbers and process information. Computers fueled new gains in productivity that matched the boom years of the 1950s and 1960s. In other words, the fundamentals behind the stock surge were good, but some of the gains were based on pure speculation.

What investors were speculating on was the Internet: With its potential to revolutionize virtually every aspect of the way business is conducted, the Internet offered the potential for a quantum leap in productivity and growth. Numerous start-up companies raised vast sums of venture capital and then went public, drawing in large numbers of inexperienced and undiscerning investors. Many of the companies listed themselves not on the NYSE but on the upstart NASDAQ, which witnessed gains that made the growth in the Dow look positively weak by comparison. Whereas the latter index tripled during the late 1990s, NASDAQ soared by more than 500 percent—from under 1,000 at the end of 1994 to over 5,000 by early 2000.

But many of the new companies were poorly organized and had weak business plans, their profitability sustained by little more than speculation, a potential for future growth, and a widespread belief that the new economy was not subject to the old laws of supply and demand. Indeed, even some of the most successful Internet companies—such as Amazon.com, which originally specialized in online book and music sales—consistently lost money, remaining in business only by drawing in new investors.

Ultimately, the old economic laws so disdained by Internet entrepreneurs began to make themselves felt, as investors grew wary of companies that showed no sign of realizing their potential and earning profits. The result was a winnowing out of the weaker companies, a stagnating Dow, and the utter collapse of the NASDAQ, which fell as precipitously in the early 2000s as it had risen in the late 1990s. By early 2003, the NASDAQ had bottomed out at just over 1,200.

Adding to Wall Street's woes was a series of corporate scandals involving such high-flying companies as Enron, Worldcom, and Adelphia. Executives of these companies were either under investigation or had been indicted for manipulating the books to bolster share prices.

The September 11 terrorist attacks did not help Wall Street either. Not only did much of the securities industry feel a direct impact—Wall Street was literally hundreds of yards from the World Trade Center, and many employees were killed in the collapse of the towers—but the attack further weakened an economy that was already heading into recession. After shutting down for several days after September 11, the market plunged—the Dow lost 1,370 points, or 14.3 percent of its value—in just one week. Average share prices gradually rebounded, but a general stagnation set in, with the Dow hovering just above 10,000 throughout 2005.

Early Twenty-First Century: Time of Uncertainty

The prospects for Wall Street remained eminently uncertain at the beginning of the twenty-first century, and the uncertainties went far beyond the mere ups and downs of the American economy. No doubt as the economy revives, so would Wall Street. But other factors are not so easy to predict.

One unknown factor is the effect further automation will have on Wall Street. The NYSE is almost unique among the world's great stock exchanges in that much of its trading continues to be performed by people. In August 2004, the NYSE announced plans to conduct more electronic trading; many companies and investors still preferred the old system, trusting in the human traders with whom they had established close, long-term relationships. In 2005, the NYSE announced that it would become a publicly traded company itself, hoping to raise investor capital to modernize and expand.

These changes reflect a fear among exchange leaders that the NYSE must adapt to the new age of globalization or risk becoming an irrelevant anachronism. With global communications becoming ever more seamless, it is increasingly possible for investors to move their money around the world, trading on exchanges as far away as Johannesburg and Hong Kong. To retain its share of the global trading market, the NYSE and other U.S. stock exchanges must attract investors—and companies to list—from all over the world.

Even with globalization, Wall Street clearly remained the center of world finance in the early years of the twenty-first century, with the NYSE at its hub. Nothing illustrated this better than the fact that business leaders from the newest major player in the world economy—mainland China—were rushing to have their companies listed on a stock exchange that had begun with twenty-four brokers and merchants meeting under a buttonwood tree on a narrow street in lower Manhattan in 1792.

James Ciment

See also: Banking and Credit; Corporate Consolidation; Crime, Property; Downsizing, Corporate; Economic Policy; Enron Bankruptcy; Insider Trading Scandals; Junk Bonds; New York City Financial Bailout; Regulation and Deregulation; Stock Market Crash of 1987; White-Collar Workers.

Bibliography

Benn, Alec. *The Unseen Wall Street of 1969–1975, And Its Significance for Today.* Westport, CT: Quorum, 2000.

Brooks, John. *Go-Go Years: The Drama and Crashing Finale of Wall Street's Bullish 1960s.* New York: Allworth, 1998.

Geisst, Charles R. *Wall Street: A History.* New York: Oxford University Press, 1997.

Gordon, John Steele. *The Great Game: The Emergence of Wall Street as a World Power, 1653–2000.* New York: Charles Scribner's Sons, 1999.

Mahar, Maggie. *Bull! A History of the Boom, 1982–1999.* New York: HarperBusiness, 2003.

WAR ON POVERTY

Immediately identifiable with the idealism of the 1960s and the cornerstone of the Great Society domestic program, President Lyndon B. Johnson's War on Poverty was intended to eliminate economic want in the United States. Johnson's program created a multitude of social service programs designed to improve conditions for millions of impoverished Americans.

In its broad scope, the program sought to bring aid to inner cities and suburbs, as well as to rural areas. Federal programs targeted young and old, whites, blacks, Native Americans, and immigrants. As the 1960s progressed, however, the harsh fiscal realities of the Vietnam War undermined the Great Society. Funds were soon being cut from domestic programs and redirected to military operations in Southeast Asia.

By 1968, say historians, the War on Poverty had become a casualty of the war in Vietnam. That year, the election of Richard M. Nixon ushered in a new, more conservative era and a growing public hostility to social engineering programs. Over the next thirty years, both Republican and, to a lesser extent, Democratic administrations worked to undo many of the War on Poverty programs. The final defeat, say some historians, was the Personal Responsibility and Work Opportunity Reconciliation Act, better known as the Welfare Reform Bill, signed into law by Democratic President Bill Clinton in 1996.

Johnson first proposed the War on Poverty as a tribute to his assassinated predecessor, John F. Kennedy, in his first State of the Union message to

Congress in January 1964. As the centerpiece of his speech, Johnson declared "unconditional War on Poverty in America" and called for a variety of programs to support the new campaign. Youth employment, an expanded food stamp program, increased unemployment insurance, upgraded educational programs, hospital insurance for seniors and the poor (Medicare and Medicaid, respectively), housing assistance, and federally funded public transportation were among the litany of programs Johnson demanded from Congress.

Two months later, the president submitted the Economic Opportunity Act of 1964 for consideration by the Congress, targeting five specific aspects of the poverty problem. To help eliminate future poverty, the Job Corps and several work-study programs for younger workers would be created. Through "Community Action" programs, individual towns and cities would be empowered to develop solutions for their individual antipoverty needs. Patterned after the Kennedy Administration's highly successful Peace Corps, a volunteer "army" would be recruited under the VISTA Program to fight the War on Poverty throughout America. Additional programs were developed to help poor farmers and the unemployed. Finally, to coordinate the entire effort, the Office of Economic Opportunity would be created. Once Congress had passed the legislation, Johnson appointed Sargent Shriver, former Peace Corps head, as the first director of the new agency.

As the momentum of the Great Society continued to build throughout 1964 and 1965, most notably in the landslide victory of Johnson and the Democrats in the 1964 election, other federal programs were added to the War on Poverty's arsenal with an intensity not seen since the heyday of the New Deal in the mid-1930s. The free and reduced cost lunch program and federal aid to poor schools were instituted to boost public education. The Department of Housing and Urban Development was created to administer the dozens of new programs to support urban renewal, public housing, housing assistance, and community development. The high-water mark of the Great Society and War on Poverty was passage of the Medicare and Medicaid acts in July 1965, which Johnson described as the fulfillment of the Social Security system developed under Franklin D. Roosevelt.

The summer of 1965 also marked a turning point in the War on Poverty. Within the span of only a few weeks, two events occurred that were the beginning of the end of the Great Society. On the international side, Johnson announced the first significant commitment of ground forces to the Vietnam theater, beginning the escalation of the war that would eventually rob the financial resources needed to address domestic issues. In domestic affairs, serious internal conflicts in American society also began to erupt. Rioting in the Watts section of Los Angeles marked the beginning of several years of racial violence and undermined white liberal support for Johnson's legislative efforts to improve the status of African Americans.

By the time Johnson was forced to abandon his reelection bid in 1968, in the face of the growing quagmire in Vietnam, the nation's attention had been diverted from defeating poverty to the military crisis in Southeast Asia and the escalating level of violence in America's cities. The assassinations and riots of 1968 seemed to crush the idealistic spirit of the Great Society era and ushered in a new era of hostility to "big government" programs.

Nixon, who succeeded Johnson in January 1969, spent much of his first term in efforts to achieve "peace with honor" in Vietnam and left many of the War on Poverty programs intact. After his reelection in 1972, however, his administration began to dismantle the Great Society programs. The original Office of Economic Opportunity was shuttered in 1974. The continuing economic problems of the 1970s left federal, state, and local officials with few resources to support social welfare programs.

By the time the national economy rebounded in the 1980s, social conservatives in the administration of Ronald Reagan were demanding an end to the last vestiges of the War on Poverty. In the 1990s, President Bill Clinton was faced with a national consensus that federal efforts to eliminate poverty had been unsuccessful, a demand for greater local control of social programs, and huge budget deficits. He endorsed welfare reform legislation that turned many social programs over to state governments for administration and effectively ended much of the federal government's efforts to, as Johnson had put it at the outset, "pursue victory over the most ancient of mankind's enemies."

William E. Doody

See also: Democratic Party; Department of Housing and Urban Development; Economic Policy; Inner Cities; Liberalism; New Frontier; Office of Economic Opportunity; Poverty; Rural America.

Bibliography

Gillette, Michael L. *Launching the War on Poverty: An Oral History*. New York: Twayne, 1996.

Katz, Michael B. *The Undeserving Poor: From the War on Poverty to the War on Welfare*. New York: Pantheon, 1989.

Zafresky, David. *President Johnson's War on Poverty: Rhetoric and History*. Tuscaloosa: University of Alabama Press, 1986.

WAR POWERS ACT

The War Powers Act of 1973 was passed by the Democrat-dominated 93rd Congress as a means to reassert the authority of the Senate and the House of Representatives in American foreign policymaking and the placement of U.S. military personnel in areas of conflict. The bill contained two important provisions: The president of the United States must inform the Congress within forty-eight hours after the deployment of American forces abroad, and troops must return home within sixty days unless Congress gives an extension to the deployment.

The genesis of the legislation was Congress's wish to find a legal means to overcome the foreign policy powers of the president, which had grown substantially during the course of the Cold War. Historically, the president had routinely sent American troops into harm's way without consulting or seeking the approval of the House and the Senate. The resolution signaled the end of bipartisanship in the conduct of U.S. foreign policy.

Since the end of World War II, both parties had reached a tacit agreement to support the president, when U.S. troops were committed to battle, regardless of the president's political affiliation. Throughout the Cold War, American policy was characterized by an active anticommunism, in which U.S. pressure was applied or forces deployed as a means to contain the global spread of Marxism.

The conflict in Southeast Asia, however, illustrated the impotency of Congress in the war-making process. In 1964, both Houses passed legislation (by votes of 416–0 in the House of Representatives and 88–2 in the Senate), known as the Gulf of Tonkin Resolution, giving the president sweeping powers to deal with North Vietnamese aggression. The ambiguity of the bill's wording served as a pretext enabling President Lyndon Johnson to dispatch U.S. combat troops to South Vietnam and deepen the nation's involvement in that conflict.

While the Vietnam quandary would serve as a rallying point for the reassertion of congressional authority, there was a long history of presidential power in the use of the U.S. military abroad. From 1798 to 1972, the president had sent forces to foreign lands nearly 200 times without seeking legislative approval, while asking for a congressional declaration of war only five times.

In the mid-to-late twentieth century, there were numerous examples of troop deployments that occurred both before and during the Cold War. Prior to American involvement in World War II, President Franklin D. Roosevelt sent U.S. naval forces into situations that would potentially bring the American military face to face with a hostile Germany. During this period, U.S. forces convoyed with British supply ships in the Atlantic Ocean, even though Nazi submarines were patrolling in their midst. Roosevelt did not seek congressional approval for this policy, nor did he consult with Congress about the efficacy of the action.

Roosevelt's successor, President Harry S Truman, ordered U.S. forces into battle during the opening days of the "police action" in Korea in 1950. The president briefed congressional leaders regarding the unfolding drama on the Korean peninsula, but he did not actively seek their advice.

Over the next several years, U.S. military forces were also sent to Lebanon (1958) and the Dominican Republic (1965). In neither case did the Congress pass a bill authorizing or approving the deployments. The belief in actively containing communism as a paramount objective of U.S. foreign policy held firm.

It was the conflict in Vietnam that ultimately led Congress to reassert its authority in foreign policymaking. The war was long, lasting from 1965 to 1973, and grew increasingly unpopular with the public and many members of Congress. Fueling that unpopularity was a growing awareness that the administrations of both Democrat Lyndon B. Johnson and Republican Richard M. Nixon had lied to the public and Congress about the causes, conduct, and progress of the conflict in Southeast Asia.

Two months after American participation in the war ceased in January 1973, Congress opened hearings regarding its role in American foreign policymaking and the deployment of troops in foreign lands. Liberals in Congress proposed the War Powers Resolution as a remedy for a perceived institutional imbalance. Opponents of the bill, such as Arizona Republican Senator Barry Goldwater, argued that the founding fathers had given the executive branch the power of war making, because the president was designated as commander in chief. Goldwater maintained that if the War Powers Resolution passed, the United States would be relegated to the status of a second-rate power, because it could not respond forcefully to situations vital to national security. Senator Jacob Javits, a New York Republican, disputed Goldwater's argument, asserting that modern presidents justified *every* military action on the basis of national security.

Both the Senate and the House passed the War Powers Resolution in the fall of 1973, but President Nixon vetoed the bill on the grounds that it would negate nearly 200 years of precedent. Opponents of the bill abandoned their opposition for fear of being too closely associated with a president battling for his political life over the Watergate scandal. On November 7, 1973, the Senate (by a vote of 75–18) and the House (by a vote of 284–135) overrode the presidential veto, and the bill became law.

John Caulfield

See also: Congress; Gulf War; Iran-Contra Affair; Iraq War; Presidency; Vietnam War.

Bibliography

Friedman, Leon, and William Levantrosser, eds. *Cold War Patriot and Statesman: Richard M. Nixon.* Westport, CT: Greenwood, 1993.

Garthoff, Raymond. *Detente and Confrontation.* Washington, DC: The Brookings Institute, 1994.

Patterson, James T. *Grand Expectations: The United States, 1945–1974.* New York: Oxford University Press, 1996.

WARREN COMMISSION

The Warren Commission was an investigative body set up in 1963 to look into the assassination of President John F. Kennedy. The commission was named after its chairman, Supreme Court Chief Justice Earl Warren. President Lyndon B. Johnson issued Executive Order Number 11130 establishing the Warren Commission, on November 29, 1963, exactly seven days after the assassination. The seven men appointed to the Warren Commission were given the imposing task of investigating the circumstances surrounding Kennedy's murder and the subsequent shooting of his alleged assassin, Lee Harvey Oswald.

Kennedy's death on November 22 had stunned the nation, but Oswald's death on November 24 stimulated wild speculation surrounding the chain of events, including rumors that Communist Russia or Cuba was behind the assassination. Johnson felt a growing need to cut off the public's "explosive and dangerous" speculations before the United States found itself in a potentially explosive international situation.

Because the U.S. judicial system does not allow for a defendant to be tried posthumously, Oswald's assassination meant that normal judicial procedures could not be used to uncover the truth behind Kennedy's death. While President Johnson wanted to conduct an investigation into his predecessor's assassination, he also wanted to avoid jurisdictional competition among various federal and state agencies. Thus, he created the President's Commission on the Assassination of John F. Kennedy, commonly known as the Warren Commission to concentrate all investigatory efforts in a single body with the broadest national mandate. Presidential commissions are created on the president's own authority and for his own purposes. Unlike a congressional investigation, which has limited jurisdiction and deals with internal misconduct, a presidential commission is better suited for dealing with matters outside the government. The Warren Commission was directed to act as a forensic fact-finding body and to report its findings to the public.

The commission was composed of members of both the Republican and Democratic parties and represented each branch of the federal government. Richard Russell, a Democrat from Georgia, and John Sherman Cooper, a Republican from Kentucky, represented the Senate; Louisiana Democrat Hale Boggs and Michigan Republican Gerald Ford were from the House of Representatives. Members from the executive branch included former Central Intelligence Agency (CIA) Director Allen W. Dulles and former Secretary of War John J. McCloy. Johnson then named Warren as the head of the commission.

Warren was initially hesitant to take part, because he believed that his service on a presidential commission would undermine the independence of the judiciary. Johnson, arguing that failure to fully investigate the assassination might lead to misplaced public outcries for retaliation, won Warren over.

By November 29, details of the assassination had disseminated throughout the world and had led to a growing number of conflicting reports. Following Oswald's arrest and denial of guilt, global attention focused on the possibility of a domestic or foreign

Chief Justice Earl Warren, joined by other members of the Commission on the Assassination of President John F. Kennedy, delivers the commission's final report to President Lyndon B. Johnson in September 1964. The commission concluded that Lee Harvey Oswald had acted alone in killing JFK. *(Francis Miller/Time Life Pictures/Getty Images)*

conspiracy; Johnson feared that the nation was quickly approaching a state of emergency. As such, the Warren Commission was intended to provide the public with the answers they were looking for and to assure the rest of the world of the government's stability. Before the Commission's proceedings, only 29 percent of Americans believed that Oswald acted alone; after the Commission's findings were released, 87 percent believed he was guilty.

Unrestricted Powers

The commission was given unrestricted investigative powers in order to present a complete report to the public. In December 1963, Congress passed Senate Joint Act 137 granting the commission power to subpoena witnesses and evidence relating to any matter under its jurisdiction. The resolution also gave it the right to compel testimony from witnesses and grant immunity. Although members of the commission weighed the testimony of 552 witnesses, they never once granted any of them immunity. As a concession to privacy, however, proceedings were closed to the public unless the witness specifically requested an open hearing. The commission encouraged witnesses to testify to any rumors that might prove to be evidence of a conspiracy. This, in addition to the fact that the trial of Oswald's assassin, Jack Ruby, was ongoing at the time

of the commission's investigation, caused many witnesses to shy away from testifying in open court.

The commission met for a period of ten months. During that time, it reviewed evidence from ten different federal and state agencies, including the Federal Bureau of Investigation (FBI), Secret Service, and CIA. It reassessed all reports and investigated all assertions and rumors relating to the possibility of a conspiracy or accomplices that were brought to their attention.

On September 24, 1964, the Warren Commission released its unanimous findings to President Johnson and the American public. Officially titled *Report of the President's Commission on the Assassination of President Kennedy,* it included a number of conclusions, the most important of which was that Oswald fired all three shots that killed President Kennedy and injured Texas Governor John Connally.

The Warren Commission also determined that there was no evidence of a conspiracy of any kind and that Oswald had acted alone. The commission could not clearly identify Oswald's motive without his testimony and chose not to ascribe to any single theory. Instead, it offered a myriad of factors in his background and earlier antisocial behavior that might help explain his behavior.

Prior to the Warren Commission, there had never been a federal mandate for the investigation of a president's death. A variety of investigations had followed previous presidential assassinations, but the Warren Commission was unique in that it was created under presidential authority. Following Kennedy's assassination, it became apparent that there was a need to establish a law making presidential assassinations a federal crime, subject only to federal investigation. Such a law was passed in 1964.

Despite the distinguished membership of the Warren Commission and the extensive report it put out, conspiracy theories about the Kennedy assassination have lingered ever since. While widely criticized, director Oliver Stone's 1991 film *JFK,* which posed a variety of theories about who may have been responsible for the killing, was a box-office hit. On the fortieth anniversary of the assassination in 2003, a poll conducted by ABC News found that 70 percent of Americans still felt that the crime was the "result of a plot, not the act of a lone killer."

Catherine Griffis

See also: Conspiracy Theories; Kennedy (John F.) Assassination.

Bibliography

Lane, Mark. *Rush to Judgment: A Critique of the Warren Commission's Inquiry into the Murders of President John F. Kennedy, Officer J.D. Tippit, and Lee Harvey Oswald.* New York: Holt, Rinehart and Winston, 1966.

Mosk, Richard M. "The Warren Commission and the Legal Process." *Case and Comment* 72:3 (May–June 1967): 13–20.

Warren Commission. *Report of the Warren Commission on the Assassination of John F. Kennedy.* New York: McGraw-Hill, 1964.

WATER POLLUTION AND WATER POLLUTION POLICY

Since the end of World War II, water pollution has become one of the most persistent and pervasive issues in American politics and public policy. Concerns about clean water are linked to the increasing possibility of water shortages, as economic and population growth strains supplies. Water pollution also has become a major public health issue, as toxic substances have found their way into the water supply in many metropolitan areas. Environmental and public health concerns frequently collide with fears of job loss; companies often claim that they must cut back on their payrolls, if not close down completely, because of the cost of complying with stringent clean water standards.

The ecological impact of water pollution is the greatest source of concern among environmental activists. Major environmental disasters in coastal and inland waters—such the oil spill off the coast of Santa Barbara, California (1969), the Cuyahoga River fire in Ohio (1969), and the disastrous *Exxon Valdez* oil spill in Alaska's Prince William Sound (1989)—have attracted the greatest media and public attention. All of these incidents caused massive damage to fish and other wildlife, as well as to local economies and the tourism industry.

Government water pollution policy is a product of conflict between special interest groups and the divided structure of governance in the United States, as well as of changes in the political climate and technology. Federal policy has evolved to focus on setting goals through national legislation and giving state and local governments responsibility for implementing national law. At the same time, Washington has taken a more activist stance on public health issues at both the national and local levels.

Policy Before the 1970s

Historically, the U.S. federal government maintained a low profile on water-related issues. Washington was content to leave the establishment of policies and priorities to local, state, and regional authorities. Indeed, until the end of World War II, water quality was not a primary concern of government at any level.

Public policy pertaining to water focused primarily on irrigation for commercial agriculture, electric power for industry and a growing urban population, and the improvement of inland waterways for recreational and commercial boat traffic. Policies pertaining to water quality were based on use—that is, bodies of water were classified according to the highest desired use, and water-quality standards were set accordingly. Implicitly, waste disposal and transport were accepted as legitimate uses of the nation's water resources.

Public concern about clean drinking water first surfaced early in the twentieth century. Early efforts to improve water quality rested on local initiatives. Jersey City (New Jersey), Oberlin (Ohio), and Chicago (Illinois) were among the first municipalities to experiment with chlorination and to build chemical plants to treat drinking water.

Until the early 1970s, federal efforts to address the growing problem of water pollution were feeble at best. The Water Pollution Control Act of 1948 provided construction loans and technical assistance to municipalities building water treatment facilities, but Congress failed to appropriate any money to support the legislation's provisions. Likewise, although the act established Public Health Service hazard abatement procedures for interstate waterways, it barred enforcement without state consent.

Water quality remained mostly a state and local concern, and the federal government's role was limited to providing grants to municipalities for wastewater treatment (Congress finally began appropriating money for these grants in 1956) and information and planning assistance to the states. By the early 1970s, however, there was a growing consensus that the restricted federal role and traditional use-based policies of state and local governments had not prevented a steady nationwide decline in water quality—a decline that posed increasing public health and environmental threats. The well-publicized disasters in Santa Barbara and on the Cuyahoga River dramatized the growing problem.

Clean Water Act

Pressure from environmental groups and public demands for action finally brought legislative action. In 1972, President Richard M. Nixon signed the Clean Water Act and amendments to the Water Pollution Control Act. These measures, along with the Safe Drinking Water Act of 1974, gave the federal government greater powers and a more direct role in the control of water pollution and set a national goal of nothing less than the elimination of pollutant discharges into the nation's waters by 1985. This meant that waste disposal and assimilation were no longer acceptable as uses of water resources.

The Clean Water Act set two interim goals: First, the waters of the United States were to be fit for fishing and swimming by 1983. Second, toxic pollutants in amounts harmful to human activities or aquatic ecosystems were to be eliminated. The act provided two tools to achieve these goals. The first was the Construction Grants Program, which gave massive federal support to wastewater treatment plants owned and operated by municipalities and local sewer districts. With $18 billion in funding to begin with, these grants would pay 75 percent of the construction costs for new treatment facilities or for the expansion of existing plants. The program operated from 1973 to 1988, paying out more than $60 billion in grants over that period. In 1989, the George H.W. Bush Administration replaced the program with a revolving loan fund.

The second tool was a system of technology-based regulations governing the discharge of water pollutants from point sources. These included both publicly owned treatment facilities and two classes of industrial facilities: direct dischargers, which release effluent directly into receiving waters, and indirect dischargers, which discharge pollutants into a sewer, where they are carried to a treatment plant.

Taken together, these provisions brought the U.S. Environmental Protection Agency (EPA), created in 1970, and other federal agencies into unprecedented involvement in state and local pollution control operations. They also signified a new concern for ecological issues beyond human water uses. The Clean Water Act was amended in 1977 and again in 1987 to extend the deadlines for promulgation and compliance with the standards. In addition, in 1987, the EPA was ordered to establish effluent guidelines for additional point-source categories.

The Clean Water Act was at the vanguard of a major shift in the federal government's monitoring of economic activity. From the New Deal of the 1930s until the late 1960s, federal regulation focused on economic concerns—namely, the prices of goods and services produced by industries that were thought to be natural monopolies and whose activities crossed state lines. The 1970s began an era of social regulation concerned with workplace safety and health, environmental quality, exposure to hazardous chemicals, and unsafe consumer products. Social regulation and the accompanying federal involvement in all levels of industrial and commercial activity grew, until a conservative turn in the political climate led to demands for a loosening of regulations in the late 1970s and into the 1980s.

Rollback of Federal Influence

The legislation of the early 1970s, with its emphasis on the ecology of waterways rather than their human and economic uses and its unyielding adherence to technology-based standards, left little room for discussion between the EPA and industrial interests with a long-standing stake in water policy or with traditional water agencies at the federal, state, and local government levels. The EPA was essentially on its own, having responsibility for the largest of the federal programs but the smallest expert manpower pool to administer them.

Toxic chemicals known as PCBs were found to have seeped into the Hudson River from this General Electric plant in upstate New York some time before 1977. The company and Environmental Protection Agency finally agreed in 2005 on a massive dredging project to clean up the site. *(William Waldron/Getty Images News)*

Driven by technology-based standards—best practicable technology by 1977 and best available technology by 1983—the cleanup effort proved more complex than originally envisioned. The EPA's administrative capacity was severely overtaxed. The issuance of rules, regulations, permits, and guidelines was too great a task for the agency's personnel resources. Shortfalls in appropriations for the grant program and slow progress in allocating the available funds led to delays in achieving the Clean Water Act's targets.

Confronted by bureaucratic conflict between the EPA and other federal and state agencies, as well as by claims from industry and state interests that stringent enforcement of the standards threatened economic growth and jobs, the National Commission on Water Quality (mandated by the Clean Water Act) set about formulating midcourse corrections to the act. Sensitive to political and economic realities but equally aware of the powerful environmental lobby that opposed any relaxation of standards, the commission recommended that the 1977 and 1983 shortfalls be addressed by issuing deadline waivers and extensions on a case-by-case basis, rather than by announcing a general extension of the deadlines. For the 1985 deadline, however, the commission advocated a blanket extension of five to ten years, along with the establishment of a review process to measure progress and recommend further revisions. Commission members also suggested alleviating the strain on the EPA's personnel resources by giving the states a greater role in devising regulations and standards on water pollutants.

The administration of President Jimmy Carter moved toward implementing the commission's recommendations. Federal officials sought full funding for the Construction Grants Program, while increasing the role of the states in developing regulations and procedures for the control of pollutants. In general, the 1977 amendments to the Clean Water Act led to a dramatic increase in the number of regulations and growing concern over the economic burden these new regulations entailed. A 1979 EPA report prepared at the direction of Congress estimated that American manufacturers would spend $3.8 billion per year in capital costs and $15.9 billion a year in operating costs to meet the standards set by federal and state regulators.

This maze of regulations and the costs involved in compliance triggered a political backlash. The administrations of Republican presidents Ronald Reagan and George H.W. Bush put renewed emphasis on water use for societal purposes and, correspondingly, less concern with water pollution control to preserve ecological systems. This change occurred in the wider context of a dramatic shift in overall federal water policy. The influence of the EPA was reduced, and control of federal policy went to a new agency—the Office of Water Policy—in the U.S. Department of the Interior. This was largely a response to ranching and mining interests in the western United States, which had become increasingly resentful of the federal restrictions on land and water use that had formed the prevailing policies of the outgoing Carter Administration.

In general, by the early 1980s, there was a growing feeling that the country had committed itself to unrealistic goals. The change in political climate found expression in efforts by the pro-business Reagan Administration to modify the rules and regulations regarding water content and to cut back on federal support for the construction of new treatment facilities.

The new priorities were incorporated in the omnibus Water Resources Development Act, which Congress, with the administration's support, passed in November 1986. The legislation was, in many ways, a milestone in the history of U.S. water policy in general and water pollution control in particular. It authorized $16.5 billion in new funds for water projects, some of which would be supported at a level as high as 100 percent. Full funding, however, was hardly the rule. The act reduced the general percentage of federal financial support for new water pollution control projects from 75 percent to 50 percent, and it required the states to match the federal contribution before the money would become available.

In addition, President Reagan vetoed the 1986 amendments to the Clean Water Act, because he regarded the $18 billion cost as excessive. In the next term, the 100th Congress reintroduced and re-passed the amendments, this time overriding another presidential veto. Unlike the money appropriated in the Water Resources Development Act, the availability of these funds did not depend on corresponding state and local financing.

Almost in spite of itself, the Reagan Administration oversaw some significant advances in the control of water pollution. In 1986, Congress passed amendments to the Safe Drinking Water Act that emphasized standards for more than eighty newly designated contaminants and for the filtration of most surface pollutants.

These developments aside, however, the Reagan Administration's central goal remained getting the federal government out of direct participation in water pollution control. President Reagan's successors continued in this direction. The administrations of George H.W. Bush and Bill Clinton both sought to extricate Washington from the Construction Grants Program. By the early 1990s, it was clear that the time had come to pass most water-quality-related activities back to the states.

Despite setting goals that many critics regarded as unrealistic, the Clean Water Act, the Safe Drinking Water Act, and their amendments brought about dramatic improvements in water quality in the United States. The evidence suggests that the states have, by and large, succeeded in protecting the nation's water supply.

Determining the extent of the improvement and the possible dangers has been difficult, however, because of limited information. Since the 1970s, only one-third of all water bodies (including surface water and underground aquifers) have been assessed by the EPA to determine pollution levels. Of the water bodies assessed by states, however, 65 percent of rivers and streams, 55 percent of lake acres, and 56 percent of estuary square miles met clean water standards.

Progress toward controlling water pollution notwithstanding, the degree of regulation and the controversy over whether ecological preservation or economic growth should have priority in making water-quality policy continues to agitate activists on both sides of the issue. The Clinton Administration, while seeking to streamline the federal bureaucracy and reduce spending on treatment plants and other facilities, still supported strict regulations and pressed states to accelerate their efforts to limit sources of water pollution.

When George W. Bush took office in January 2001, it soon became clear that his administration had a different set of priorities. In line with his pro-business outlook, President Bush began a general review of federal regulations and suspended all regulatory actions that had not been made final during the closing days of the Clinton presidency. Many regulations pertaining to water pollution were affected. Before the end of March 2001, the Bush Administration had rejected higher standards for arsenic in drinking water, reversed course on pressuring states to

speed up their efforts to limit non-point water pollutant emissions, and relaxed standards on farm runoff. These steps enraged environmental activists and led them to accuse the Bush Administration of sacrificing water quality and public health for the sake of higher corporate profits.

Walter F. Bell

See also: Environmental Protection Agency; Environmentalism; *Exxon Valdez* Disaster; Offshore Oil Drilling; Science, Government Policy on; Wildlife and Wilderness.

Bibliography
Bacot, A. Hunter. "Environmental Pollution Control, State Government Regulation of." In *Encyclopedia of Public Administration and Public Policy*, edited by Jack Rabin. New York: Marcel Dekker, 2003.

Davis, Devra. *When Smoke Ran Like Water: Tales of Environmental Deception and the Battle Against Pollution.* New York: Basic Books, 2002.

Jordon, Jason. "A Paler Shade of Green." *Planning* 70:8 (August/September 2004): 10–15.

Ringquist, Evan J. "Political Control and Policy Impact in the EPA's Office of Water Quality." *American Journal of Political Science* 39:2 (May 1995): 336–63.

Rogers, Peter. *America's Water: Federal Roles and Responsibilities.* Cambridge, MA: MIT Press, 1993.

WATERGATE

Watergate is the catch-all term given to a series of political scandals surrounding the presidency of Richard M. Nixon during the early 1970s. Named after the Washington, D.C., hotel complex where the scandal first became public in June 1972, Watergate ultimately resulted in the indictment and conviction of several Nixon Administration officials and the August 1974 resignation of the president himself.

On the night of June 17, 1972, five men were arrested for breaking into the headquarters of the Democratic National Committee (DNC) at the Watergate Hotel in Washington, D.C. One of the men in police custody was in possession of the phone number of a member of Nixon's staff.

Soon, the entire nation was embroiled in a public spectacle that went all the way to the White House and seriously damaged the reputation of the American presidency. A simple intrusion for the purpose of political espionage would, within two years, ruin the lives of everyone connected with it and pose a direct challenge to the constitutional system of the United States.

1972 Election

The Watergate saga began with the reelection campaign of President Nixon during the summer of 1970. Nixon wanted to win, and he was willing to do anything to ensure an easy victory. At the president's insistence, White House staffers created a special division of the Internal Revenue Service (IRS) to investigate so-called "dissident" political organizations. This group, known as the Special Services Staff, looked into the financial records of such liberal organizations as the Ford Foundation and the Brookings Institution, and it even investigated DNC chairman Larry O'Brien. By the end of 1970, it had compiled financial information on 4,000 left-leaning individuals and close to 2,000 organizations.

Still reeling over the "Pentagon Papers" scandal, the White House entered a tense period of lockdown during the 1972 campaign. Obsessed with the idea of secrecy, President Nixon authorized the creation of a group called the "Plumbers." Working under

Nixon domestic policy adviser John Ehrlichman, the Plumbers consisted of men recruited from both the Federal Bureau of Investigation (FBI) and the Central Intelligence Agency (CIA). Their mission was to determine the cause and potential results of the Pentagon Papers leak and to keep the president informed as to any further leaks.

Though Nixon did not want to identify with the covert investigations of his political opponents, he did want to be informed of any discoveries. The president took a behind-the-scenes approach when it came to the methods through which the Plumbers were to obtain their information, but he was certainly aware that the methods might be considered extralegal.

Nixon adopted a similar philosophy when it came to his 1972 reelection campaign, vesting total control in the Committee to Re-Elect the President (CRP). Attorney General John Mitchell was placed in charge of this organization as the campaign's director, and its White House contact was Nixon adviser Robert Haldeman, who kept the president informed as to the campaign's activities. With Mitchell in charge of the campaign and Haldemen as a conduit to the White

Chairman Sam Ervin (right) and co-chairman Howard Baker (left) headed the U.S. Senate committee whose investigation into the Watergate scandal held the nation enthralled in 1973 and led to the resignation of President Richard M. Nixon the following August. *(Gjon Mili/Time Life Pictures/Getty Images)*

House, President Nixon was able to keep his distance, while at the same time remaining in control.

CRP, more commonly referred to as CREEP, began to work with the Plumbers, specifically a former FBI operative named G. Gordon Liddy. Liddy's mission was to gather information about the Democratic Party and its leadership.

At this point in the campaign season, the Democratic headquarters was located at the Watergate Hotel, in Washington, D.C. From a command center at the Howard Johnson hotel located directly across from the Watergate, the Plumbers began bugging the phones of key Democratic leaders in an effort to gain information about their activities. The observation post looked down on the Democratic offices, giving the Plumbers a clear view of their target. Finding nothing of any political value through phone taps, the Plumbers moved to the next phase of their espionage.

The concept of a covert intrusion into the Democratic headquarters originated in two schemes by Liddy and fellow CREEP member John Caulfield. The latter proposed that CREEP set up a business front to conduct the campaign's investigations into the DNC. This was called Project Sandwedge. Liddy felt that surveillance and wiretappings were the most effective way to keep up with the president's opponents. His plan was called Project Gemstone. Both ideas were proposed to campaign director John Mitchell and rebuffed. The attorney general was extremely loyal to the president, but he did not think such intelligence gathering methods were necessary. Liddy was not dissuaded.

Former CIA agent E. Howard Hunt finally combined the two plans and conceived the clandestine operation along with Charles Colson, another Nixon aide. Initially, the plan was a success. The team managed to infiltrate the Watergate and install the necessary equipment to bug the DNC headquarters. It was only after a second team returned to the building to recover their taping equipment that the scheme was uncovered and five team members were arrested.

Although Liddy and Hunt were no longer working directly with the Plumbers, they retained their White House credentials and worked from the Plumbers' suite across the street from the Watergate. Hunt used his former colleagues in the CIA to recruit a new team of covert operatives for the Watergate job. His main contact in this effort was Bernard Barker, a Cuban-born former CIA operative who was now living in Miami. Early in 1972, Hunt had approved of Barker's short list of possible accomplices and began to recruit individuals who would be essential for the action. While the president was beginning his reelection campaign, Liddy and Hunt were traveling around the country on government vouchers in search of the perfect team. Once more, Liddy had broached the topic with campaign director John Mitchell, and once more Mitchell did not approve. Hunt and Liddy went ahead with their scheme anyway.

Haldeman was made aware of the plan through his intermediary at CREEP, Jeb Magruder, who sent a memo to Haldeman's White House office in April 1972 outlining the plan. While the memo, along with most of the CREEP documents, was shredded to guard against political espionage, Magruder and his aide, Gordon Strachan, later testified that Haldeman was aware that Liddy and Hunt were going ahead with the operation.

The irony of the break-in was that it was unnecessary. With the opening of diplomatic relations with China, aptly staged in the months before the election, and the efforts of the Nixon Administration to reduce the number of American forces in Vietnam, Nixon's reelection to the presidency was assured.

Though Hunt and Liddy were co-conspirators, each played a distinct part in the mission. Hunt was the main organizer, gathering loyal individuals who were willing to participate in the scheme. Liddy was the operations officer, in charge of the timing and execution of the break-in.

Shortly after 1 A.M. on July 17, 1972, Watergate security guard Frank Willis became a part of the biggest political scandal in American history, simply by removing a piece of tape covering a door lock. The tape had been placed by one of the burglars over the lock of a garage-level door that provided access to the interior of the Watergate. When Willis discovered that other doors had been taped in the same manner, he became suspicious and phoned the police.

Meanwhile, Liddy was observing his team as it began to remove recording devices from the DNC headquarters. At 1:52, an unmarked police car, carrying three officers from the Washington, D.C., plain clothes unit arrived at the scene. Alfred Baldwin, the Watergate lookout, saw the car arrive, but he was unaware of its objective and paid no attention. While the CREEP team searched O'Brien's office, they were unaware that they were about to be discovered.

Officer John Barrett of the D.C. police depart-

Recording tape proved to be the downfall of the Nixon White House, as secretly recorded conversations—and eighteen minutes of them that were inexplicably erased—suggested a cover-up in the Oval Office. *(Library of Congress, LC-USZ62–84034)*

ment was the first to catch the strange men in blue rubber gloves in the midst of their search of the DNC offices. The men were arrested without incident, as Liddy listened in on his radio. As the arrests were taking place, Hunt and Liddy bolted from the scene. After Liddy went home to establish an alibi for himself, Hunt returned to the Plumbers' surveillance room at the Howard Johnson hotel and instructed the remaining members of his team to get rid of the evidence.

By 5 A.M., Hunt was concerned enough to retain a lawyer, in case he and Liddy were indicted for their activities. Liddy approved Douglas Caddy as a potential defense counsel. The move was prophetic, as within a matter of hours, the FBI was brought into the case by the police. While Liddy was shredding the essential documents at CREEP headquarters, the five men who were caught during the break-in were being identified as Bernard Barker, James McCord, Eugenio Martinez, Frank Sturgis, and Virgilio Gonzales. Liddy, who still had his White House credentials, placed a secure phone call from the tactical situation room to Magruder and informed him that the plan had gone awry. When the *Washington Post* reported the story of the break-in, little was known about the intention of the men; all the *Post* knew was that the DNC headquarters had been breached.

Nixon was made aware of the break-in upon his return from a trip to Key Biscayne, Florida. On June 20, 1972, he met with advisers to discuss the potential outcome of the incident. It was after this meeting that Haldeman was reminded that several documents from Liddy concerning the break-in bore his approval. Haldeman told his staff to make sure all files concerning the break-in were disposed of. The last

thing the presidential adviser wanted was to link the incident to the White House. As Haldeman would soon discover, however, that ship had sailed. By this time, reports within the media were beginning to link CREEP with the mysterious burglars.

Cover-Up and Investigation

One of the men arrested at the Watergate, former CIA operative James McCord, was also the security chief for CREEP. McCord was identified by the FBI, which was ordered to pursue the matter further when his government connection was discovered. In the meantime, the White House made efforts to stall the media's inquiries into the break-in. Spokesman Ron Ziegler reiterated the president's feeling that the break-in was nothing more than a "third-rate" burglary.

At this point, the media grew even more interested in the story. Speculation as to the involvement of several individuals, including Hunt and Colson, began to grow within the first week after the initial arrests. In response, DNC chairman O'Brien announced that the Democrats were seeking recompense from CREEP in excess of $1 million. On June 25, 1972, O'Brien demanded that the president appoint a special prosecutor to look into any further involvement of the White House.

The issue of the break-in became an increasing concern for the president, as it was revealed that more White House staffers were involved. When Magruder was questioned about his knowledge of the planning and execution of the break-in, the president and White House counsel John Dean discussed the idea of immunity. Furthermore, Nixon ordered Ehrlichman and Haldeman to deny any involvement in the break-in, when they were questioned by the press. The objective was to refuse comment and avoid any reporter who asked questions about the incident. On September 15, 1972, Nixon ordered the FBI to drop the matter and cease its investigation. This did not stall what had already been set in motion, and a two-year odyssey was about to begin.

According to tapes recorded in the Oval Office, the subject of payoffs to the conspirators was brought up during the week following the break-in. A June 30, 1972, tape has Nixon promising to pay the five men to keep silent about their White House connections—the money was to come out of the CREEP political fund. L. Patrick Gray, acting director of the FBI, began to review all documentation concerning the break-in and the burglars and passed this information on to Dean. Thus, the White House knew where the FBI investigation was going and which witnesses were about to be interviewed.

In the spring of 1973, U.S. district court judge John Sirica sentenced the Watergate burglars to exceptionally long jail terms, prompting McCord to tell his story in the hopes of clemency. In March 1973, he told of the payoffs from the White House, and the U.S. Senate convened a special committee to investigate the matter further. This was the beginning of the end for the Nixon Administration.

Within weeks, Dean sought a deal with the Senate committee to protect himself from prosecution for his role in the cover-up; Nixon fired him as White House counsel in April 1973. One by one, the dominos began to fall for the men surrounding the president. Soon, Nixon aides Haldeman and Ehrlichman were implicated for their connection to CREEP and to the burglars, and the president was forced to ask for their resignations.

When it was revealed that Nixon possessed a recording system for the Oval Office, Watergate special prosecutor Archibald Cox demanded that he turn over the tapes to Judge Sirica. Claiming executive privilege, Nixon refused to comply, saying that the tapes might contain information vital to national security. When Cox again requested that the president turn over the tapes, Nixon had him fired.

In June 1974, the U.S. Supreme Court ruled that executive privilege could not be claimed and that the president was required to turn over the tapes. Meanwhile, the House Judiciary Committee agreed that enough information was available to link the president to a cover-up. In July, the committee voted on three articles of impeachment against Nixon—obstruction of justice, abuse of power, and contempt of Congress.

There was no place for the president to turn; he had exhausted all of his delaying tactics. On the night of August 8, 1974, Nixon announced to the nation that he would resign the presidency the following day. Vice President Gerald R. Ford grimly took the oath in the Oval Office at noon on August 9 and announced that the "long national nightmare" was over. Though the break-in at the Watergate Hotel had been the work of overzealous aides, it was the president's efforts to stall the investigation that tainted the White House.

Jeffrey R. Gudzune

See also: Campaign Finance; Enemies List; Federal Election Campaign Act; Freedom of Information Act; ITT Affair; Presidency; Republican Party.

Bibliography

Emery, Fred. *Watergate: The Corruption of American Politics and the Fall of Richard Nixon.* New York: Simon and Schuster, 1994.

Kutler, Stanley I. *The Wars of Watergate: The Last Crisis of Richard Nixon.* New York: Alfred A. Knopf, 1990.

Olson, Keith W. *Watergate: The Presidential Scandal That Shook America.* Lawrence: University Press of Kansas, 2003.

Oudes, Bruce, ed. *From the President: Richard Nixon's Secret Files.* New York: Harper and Row, 1989.

Woodward, Bob, and Carl Bernstein. *All the President's Men.* 2nd ed. New York: Simon and Schuster, 1994.

WEAPONS, NUCLEAR

Since the dropping of the U.S. atomic bombs over Hiroshima and Nagasaki, Japan, in August 1945, ending World War II, nuclear weapons have never been used in combat. Nevertheless, their presence has overshadowed postwar America and the world with the possibility of a civilization-destroying nuclear war between superpowers.

With the collapse of the Soviet Union in 1991 and end of the Cold War, many Americans hoped the threat of nuclear weapons had receded. Since the September 11, 2001, attacks, however, a new fear has arisen—that nuclear weapons might find their way into the hands of terrorists.

Origins

Nuclear weapons originated in discoveries in physics dating to the turn of the twentieth century. In 1905, Albert Einstein published his theory that a form of energy exists in mass-binding, positively charged particles (protons) in an atom's nucleus. If the protons could somehow be separated, splitting the nucleus, vast quantities of energy would be released in a process known as fission.

A number of experiments conducted in the late 1930s proved that a human-made fission reaction was theoretically possible. At the same time, the scientists conducting these experiments in the United States, many of them exiles from Nazi Europe, feared that the Hitler regime was developing such nuclear weapons. Einstein and others urged President Franklin D. Roosevelt to do the same.

On September 17, 1942, Roosevelt appointed Army Corps of Engineers Brigadier General Leslie Groves as head of a classified atomic weapons program known as the "Manhattan Engineer District," later known familiarly as the Manhattan Project. This $2 billion endeavor, the largest and most expensive yet undertaken by the federal government, developed installations throughout the United States. At one of those facilities, in Los Alamos, New Mexico, physicist Robert Oppenheimer was put in charge of building the atomic bomb itself.

The first atomic explosion at Alamogordo, New Mexico, on July 16, 1945, was produced by a plutonium device and created a fireball with a temperature of about 100 million degrees. The benchmark for the energy yield of fission weapons came to be measured in increments of thousands of tons of conventional explosive, known as kilotons. This bomb registered a 15-kiloton explosion.

By the first week of May 1945, Germany had surrendered to Allied forces, and the chief rationale for atomic weapons had disappeared. Japan, however, continued to fight. Concerned about the human cost of an assault on Japan's home islands, Roosevelt was anxious to secure Soviet support. A deal had been reached at the Yalta Conference in February 1945, by which the Soviets would attack the Japanese army in Manchuria within two or three months of victory in Europe.

Roosevelt died on April 12, 1945, however, and his successor, Harry S Truman, had a more cynical view of the Soviet Union than his predecessor, seeing it more as a competitor than an ally. The Potsdam Conference in July and August featured the first instance of "atomic diplomacy": bolstered by the Alamogordo test (unknown to the Soviets until after the conference), Truman took an uncompromising line in renegotiating Yalta's terms for Soviet concessions in Manchuria.

On August 6, nine days before the Soviets were scheduled to attack Japanese forces, a U.S. bomber dropped a U-235 device on Hiroshima with a force of 12.5 kilotons, killing about 100,000 people; an equal number succumbed to radiation sickness by 1950. Nagasaki was attacked three days later with a 22-kiloton plutonium bomb, causing another 40,000–75,000 deaths.

After the war, administration officials were divided on whether to internationalize control of atomic weapons and research or to preserve America's "atomic monopoly." In early 1946, Secretary of State James Byrnes successfully promoted a United Nations resolution creating the UN Atomic Energy Commission (UNAEC) to facilitate scientific exchange, peaceful use of atomic energy, and disarmament. Undersecretary of State Dean Acheson and Tennessee Valley Authority chief David Lilienthal developed a plan, largely Oppenheimer's brainchild, to establish an Atomic Development Authority (ADA), providing for U.S.-Soviet collaboration in controlling atomic materials and facilities. But with Truman's appointment of financier Bernard Baruch to lead the UNAEC negotiations, the bilateral protocols of the proposed ADA were abandoned, and the Soviets were required to make transparent their atomic program, cease research, and submit to inspections before talks could proceed. Soviet officials, predictably, declined to participate.

The Truman Administration thus sought to retain the U.S. atomic monopoly, despite warnings that it was impossible to keep the theoretical principles of such weapons secret. The U.S. atomic program was also compromised by espionage. In early 1950, Klaus Fuchs, a German-born physicist and naturalized British citizen who had worked at Los Alamos between 1944 and 1946, was arrested and convicted of spying for the Soviets. The following year, Julius and Ethel Rosenberg were convicted of passing top-secret information about the atomic bomb to Soviet agents in 1944 and 1946.

In 1946, the U.S. Atomic Energy Commission (AEC) was established, inheriting all wartime atomic weapons facilities; it eventually expanded into a national research and industrial complex. Though responsible for civilian and military atomic research, the AEC's priority after 1947 was bomb making.

The Soviet Bomb

In August 1949, the Soviets exploded their first fission device. While this event surprised some military officials, including Groves, who believed it would take twenty years for the Soviets to develop the atomic bomb, scientists such as Vannevar Bush and Hans Bethe had, following the war, estimated the Communists could achieve the feat in five years. Ten months later, the Cold War escalated, when North Korean forces crossed the 38th parallel into South Korea.

These events contributed to the Truman Administration's decision to develop the hydrogen bomb, a quantum leap in nuclear explosive power based on the fusion principle. The maximum yield of such "thermonuclear" devices is measured in millions of tons of conventional explosive, or megatons.

The leading advocate of the hydrogen bomb was Edward Teller, a Hungarian émigré physicist. Oppenheimer, however, opposed the new weapon, maintaining that it would begin an arms race with the Soviets. In 1950, defense policy analysts produced the NSC-68 paper, which claimed that the Soviet Union was the most dangerous threat to the United States and called for the rapid expansion of the conventional and atomic arsenal to "contain" communism.

A major author of Cold War policy was the mathematician John von Neumann, who developed the influential "game theory" of international relations: Although two opponents might take an action beneficial to both, the only way one party can be absolutely sure it will not be betrayed is to take swift action in self-interest. Where U.S. foreign policy was concerned, this meant building as many advanced nuclear weapons as quickly as possible. The first hydrogen bomb was tested at the South Pacific atoll of Eniwetok on November 1, 1952.

With the Korean War a costly stalemate, the Eisenhower Administration introduced the "New Look" defense program in the fall of 1953, predicated on the assumption that nuclear weapons would be a cheap and effective way of containing Soviet expansionism. In 1954, von Neumann participated in a scientific panel that recommended the Air Force develop

The characteristic mushroom cloud—icon and nightmare of the Nuclear Age—takes shape after the first explosion of the hydrogen bomb, by the United States, at Eniwetok atoll in the Pacific Ocean in November 1952. *(Three Lions/Getty Images)*

missiles armed with hydrogen bombs. In that same year, Oppenheimer, declared a security threat in 1953, was stripped of his security clearance to the nuclear weapons program.

As Oppenheimer had predicted, neither the hydrogen bomb nor the new long-range bombers and missiles had deterred the Soviets; indeed, they provoked an arms race that would last four decades. Between 1945 and the late 1960s, the United States maintained a large advantage in both delivery systems (aircraft and missiles) and warheads, despite claims from hawkish politicians that there was first a bomber and then a missile "gap" favoring the Soviets.

The U-2 reconnaissance aircraft confirmed in 1956 that the Soviets possessed only several dozen strategic bombers at a time when the U.S. had several hundred. The U-2 could find no evidence that the Soviets had more long-range missiles than the United States. In November 1960, a spy satellite project, code-named "Corona," located only four Soviet intercontinental ballistic missiles (ICBMs). Photo analysis, moreover, suggested that the missile type, the unwieldy SS-6, was a technical failure and that the Soviets had discontinued its production. In 1960, the United States possessed nearly 1,000 strategic warheads and bombs, while the Soviets had about 200.

Kennedy and Nuclear Weapons

The U.S. advantage in nuclear weapons produced what President John F. Kennedy's defense secretary Robert S. McNamara later acknowledged as the "Action-reAction" phenomenon: the United States innovated new nuclear weapons technologies, and the Soviets succeeded in emulating them several years later. This undermined the "New Look" assumption that nuclear superiority would yield political advantages.

Although superiority in nuclear weapons conferred no real diplomatic or military benefit, it became politically unacceptable for the United States to lose ground to the Soviets in the arms race. This logic underpinned the development of new nuclear weapons technologies and "strategic use" doctrines in an effort to outpace the effects of the Action-reAction phenomenon.

The use doctrine of the 1950s, "massive retaliation," was based on the premise that Soviet or Chinese expansionism could be contained by the threat of utter destruction using every nuclear weapon in the

New Look Defense Policy

The "New Look" defense policy was drafted by the administration of President Dwight D. Eisenhower during the post–Korean War era as a means to contain Communist expansionism through reliance on nuclear weapons.

U.S. policymakers believed that the war had demonstrated the ineffectiveness of traditional large infantry, armor, and artillery formations against opponents, such as the Chinese and the Soviets, with larger conventional forces than the United States. The costly stalemate in Korea convinced Budget Director Joseph Dodge, Treasury Secretary George Humphrey, and, ultimately, Eisenhower himself, that national security and the preservation of the civilian economy were tied together. As such, the security of the United States would be jeopardized not only by Communist aggression, but also by a budget-busting overreaction to the threat. These officials believed that the rapid inflation of the defense budget and the suspension of civil liberties, as called for by more militant anticommunist politicians, would destroy the democratic fiber of American society, producing a "garrison state" almost as undesirable as Communist domination.

It was on these assumptions that nuclear weaponry was promoted as a cheap and effective means to deter aggression, as well as to retain military superiority over the Soviet Union. These considerations were enshrined in National Security Policy Paper 162/2, adopted on October 30, 1953. The plan called for downsizing the Army and Navy and placing increased reliance on a large nuclear arsenal controlled mainly by the Air Force. This "New Look" was the impetus for the development of long-range bombers, medium-range missiles, and, later, long-range missiles.

An overall strategy for how the weapons would be used to fulfill these objectives did not exist beyond the threat of an all-out attack on the Soviet Union and China by every branch of the U.S. armed forces in a policy that came to be known as "massive retaliation." Most importantly, no quantitative study confirming the assumption that nuclear weapons could, in fact, be used to contain Soviet or Chinese expansionism in a cost-effective way had yet been conducted. The Soviet launch of the *Sputnik I* satellite in fall 1957 fostered a public perception that the United States trailed the USSR in missile technology; this resulted in demands from politicians and pundits that America embark on a crash program to expand its strategic arsenal.

Eisenhower, under pressure to take action, augmented and accelerated existing nuclear weapons projects, authorizing the concurrent development of three kinds each of intermediate and long-range ballistic missiles in the late 1950s. Preparedness at any cost, not cost-efficient performance, had become the prime operating principle of U.S. nuclear weapons strategy, undermining the original premise of New Look.

As a result, the national defense budget expanded from about $3.2 billion in 1950 to $52.2 billion by 1960. This caused the Kennedy Administration, led by Defense Secretary Robert S. McNamara, to employ "scientific management" in reforming strategic weapons policy, in order to deliver the cost-effectiveness that the New Look had promised but failed to deliver.

Matthew Eisler

U.S. arsenal. By the late 1950s, with the Soviets possessing a limited number of nuclear weapons themselves, the prospect of a war triggered by Soviet interventions in Eastern Europe had become unacceptable to American planners, who feared that such a war might now lead to thermonuclear destruction.

The high cost of the proliferation of nuclear weapons and the inability of massive retaliation to influence Soviet behavior convinced McNamara to rethink American strategy. In 1962, he introduced the concept of "counterforce/no cities." Because the United States possessed more accurate delivery systems, it could knock out Soviet weapons. Lacking such accurate delivery capabilities of their own, the Soviets would have to attack larger targets, such as cities. But McNamara reasoned that they would not do so, fearing American retaliation against Soviet metropolitan areas. According to this new doctrine, U.S. nuclear weapons could be used to contain Soviet conventional military aggression without risking total nuclear devastation. However, this doctrine also justified an unending arms race, because targets proliferated as the Soviet arsenal expanded.

In late 1963, faced with demands from the U.S. Air Force for large numbers of new missiles and the prospect of a spiraling defense budget, McNamara introduced a new policy as an economy measure to balance counterforce/no cities. Nuclear firepower would be limited to 1,200 megatons in total, and the nuclear missile force would be fixed at 1,054 land-based and 656 sea-based weapons in a parallel doctrine called "assured destruction"—that the United States would have adequate firepower to destroy the USSR even after suffering a hypothetical Soviet first strike. Until the end of the decade, the declared U.S. strategic policy combined assured destruction and counterforce.

The latter, however, was ultimately destabilizing and counterproductive, because it impelled the Soviets to react similarly. Believing that McNamara's policy laid out "ground rules" for a winnable nuclear war, the Soviets worked to develop counterforce weapons and strategies of their own. Further, McNamara's formula was predicated on the large U.S. advantage in strategic nuclear weaponry in the early 1960s. Yet, as the decade wore on, this advantage diminished as the Soviets gradually produced more nuclear weapons.

The Soviet attempt to overcome the USSR's technical and numerical inferiority led to a close brush with nuclear war in October 1962. With the Americans possessing a five-to-one advantage in long-range missiles (370 to 75) and seven-to-one superiority in bombers (1,350 to 190), and with additional short-range missiles based in Europe capable of striking the USSR, Premier Nikita Khrushchev was under pressure from Soviet hard-liners to redress the balance of power. And so, the Soviets placed short-range nuclear missiles in Cuba that were capable of reaching American cities. In what history has come to call the Cuban Missile Crisis, President Kennedy imposed a quarantine on offensive weapons shipments to Cuba and, after a brief showdown, the Soviets were compelled to remove their missiles in exchange for a U.S. pledge not to invade the Communist island.

The arms race then resumed, with the Action-reAction phenomenon continuing to dictate the technology and strategy of both sides. Soviet defense planners worked to achieve parity in nuclear weaponry, while the United States sought to maintain its qualitative and quantitative advantages within McNamara's cost-efficiency guidelines.

With no additional missile fuselages then being built, McNamara approved the development of the multiple independently targeted reentry vehicle (MIRV) as a way to meet the requirements of efficiency and superiority. Part of the existing single-warhead Minuteman I missile fleet underwent conversion in 1970 to accept three smaller and more accurate warheads, in effect transforming one missile into several, resulting in the Minuteman III. The number of missiles remained static, but the total number of warheads increased.

New Delivery Technologies

Because the Soviets trailed the United States in miniaturization and guidance technologies, which eventually led to U.S. and Soviet MIRVs in the late 1960s and early to mid-1970s, respectively, they built larger warheads, and thus larger missiles, to compensate. By the late 1960s, the Soviets had developed the SS-9 ICBM, which was primitive and inaccurate compared to the advanced Minuteman III, but, with its huge, multimegaton warhead, it was still capable of destroying American missiles in underground reinforced silos. Although the United States enjoyed a two-to-one advantage in total strategic nuclear warheads and bombs in 1970 (about 4,000 to 2,000), the Soviets then had enough SS-9s for American planners to realize that fighting a limited nuclear war was impossible. Thus, the U.S. superiority in nuclear weapons was only nominal—meaningless when both sides possessed enough firepower to destroy civilization many times over. Consequently, U.S. planners dropped counterforce in the early 1970s as part of the declaratory policy, and assured destruction became "mutually assured destruction" (MAD), the acknowledgement that both superpowers were too heavily armed for either one to risk a pre-emptive attack on the other.

With the U.S. defense budget swollen from the Vietnam War, President Richard M. Nixon and National Security Advisor Henry Kissinger hastened to formalize the status quo in the Strategic Arms Limitation Talks (SALT) of 1972. Rather than signaling an end to the arms race, however, the SALT agreement had flaws that led to renewed strategic arms development and deployment in the 1980s. SALT had two parts, the Anti-Ballistic Missile (ABM) Treaty and the Interim Agreement, the latter placing a five-year moratorium on the development of MIRVs and other offensive weapons.

The only strategic arms specifically banned were antiballistic missiles, the construction of which, both parties agreed, simply spurred the other side to build more nuclear warheads. But U.S. negotiators did not attempt to restrict or ban MIRVs, as they hoped to preserve the American advantage in such weapons. Critics warned that this was a mistake, since it was only a matter of time before the Soviets developed such technology. When they did, they might have an advantage, since the larger Soviet missiles would be able to carry more MIRVs than American missiles.

The Interim Agreement simply set ceilings for the number of total launchers and did not reduce weapons inventories. The protocol's great flaw was that it accounted for launch vehicles only, not total warheads. Because of the asymmetrical technological progress of the superpowers, the agreement did not reflect the true scope of their respective strategic nuclear weapons forces, producing misunderstandings.

Hawkish critics of SALT were scandalized that it allowed the Soviets 1,618 land-based nuclear missiles and 950 sea-based ones, compared to U.S. limits of 1,054 and 710 respectively. The Soviets, possessing 740 submarine-launched ballistic missiles in 1972 and entitled to 210 more under SALT terms, continued construction, an act interpreted by conservatives in the United States as a treaty violation and an attempt to seek superiority. But because its arsenal was configured differently, the United States continued to maintain a two-to-one advantage in total warheads in the 1970s as MIRV construction proceeded. Furthermore, the U.S. Joint Chiefs of Staff approved SALT on condition that the latest generation of highly accurate counterforce nuclear weapons be developed, including the MX, Trident, Cruise, and Pershing II missiles, as well as the B-1 and B-2 bombers. Thus, although superpower officials publicly made reference to MAD and the acceptance of the status quo, both countries continued to develop weapons and strategies suitable for a first strike.

By 1983, the United States possessed 9,719 strategic warheads (13,113 including weapons carried by short-range aircraft capable of reaching the USSR from nearby bases and aircraft carriers), compared to 8,040 analogous Soviet warheads. Plans to deploy Cruise and Pershing II missiles in Europe, coupled with public statements from Reagan Administration officials regarding the increased likelihood of nuclear war, helped foster massive demonstrations against the arms race throughout North America and Europe. Popular concern over the threat of global nuclear war was reflected in a series of graphic television films including *The Day After* (1983), *Testament* (1983), and *Threads* (1985).

Nuclear Freeze Movement

Arising out of popular fears of nuclear war came the Nuclear Freeze Movement (NFM) of the 1980s, which demanded a halt to all new nuclear weapons production and deployment by the United States and the Soviet Union, as well as other nuclear powers such as Great Britain, France, and China, and a halt to all nuclear weapons testing. (In 1963, the United States, the Soviet Union, and Great Britain, had signed the Nuclear Test Ban Treaty, outlawing aboveground testing, but underground tests continued.) The movement was enormously popular. In 1982, an estimated 1 million people demonstrated in New York's Central Park, the largest protest rally in American history before or since.

NFM members and leaders were most concerned about the bellicose language and arms buildup of the Reagan Administration. Specifically, the opposition focused on the development of the MX missile, an enormously expensive project to develop mobile missiles that would evade Soviet attack, and the deployment of U.S. medium-range nuclear missiles to Western Europe. Ultimately, the first project was killed, but the second went ahead.

More worrisome to advocates of a nuclear freeze was President Ronald Reagan's decision to develop the Strategic Defense Initiative (SDI) in 1983. Referred to as "Star Wars" for its concept of space-based laser weapons, SDI was intended to shoot down incoming missiles before they could hit their targets in the United States.

Critics argued that SDI was extremely costly and destabilizing, since it would lead the Soviets either to develop a system of their own or expand their arsenal to overwhelm an American missile defense system. Most of the scientific community also expressed its disapproval, arguing that SDI was simply beyond the capabilities of twentieth-century technology. Proponents in the administration and elsewhere, however, claimed that SDI was feasible and offered the first opportunity of the nuclear era for the development of effective defensive, as opposed to offensive, weapons.

End of the Cold War

In 1985, a new leader came to power in the Soviet Union. Recognizing his country's failing economy and inability to keep up with U.S. nuclear weapons production, including SDI, the reform-minded Mikhail Gorbachev proposed eliminating both arsenals at a U.S.-Soviet summit in Iceland in 1986. But Reagan, although intrigued by the offer, ultimately declined. Eventually, Gorbachev would set in motion reforms in the Soviet Union that would lead to the collapse of his country's hold over Communist Eastern Europe in 1989 and the breakup of the Soviet Union itself in 1991. With these developments, the nearly half-century-long Cold War came to an end.

This development led to much talk in the United States of a "peace dividend" in the early 1990s. Indeed, the Strategic Arms Reduction Treaties (START) of the early 1990s resulted in a vast reduction in U.S. and Soviet arsenals, from a combined total of more than 15,000 active strategic nuclear warheads in 1975 to roughly 5,000 in 2004. Still, both sides maintained arsenals on high alert that were capable of destroying the other side several times over.

The breakup of the Soviet Union also presented new problems. First, there was the matter of nuclear weapons based in former republics of the Soviet Union that were now independent countries, including Belarus, Kazakhstan, and Ukraine. By 1994, the last of these, Ukraine, agreed to destroy its nuclear weapons, under international aegis, or transfer them back to Russia.

Second was nuclear material scattered about the former Soviet Union. Some of it was unaccounted for, and security measures protecting much of it were deemed inadequate by U.S. inspectors. In addition, many Soviet scientists with the expertise to build nuclear weapons remained unemployed and impoverished in the wake of their country's economic collapse in the 1990s. The fear was that these scientists would be hired by developing countries seeking to develop their own nuclear weapons. In fact, nuclear proliferation became a pressing issue after the testing in 1998 of nuclear devices by Pakistan and India, two countries, then and later, locked in a tense confrontation over Kashmir.

Another fear connected with nuclear proliferation and the collapse of the Soviet Union was terrorism, specifically the fear that nuclear weapons or, more likely, nuclear material, might fall into the hands of terrorists. As the September 11, 2001, attacks on the United States demonstrated, the al-Qaeda terrorist network sought to inflict massive damage on the West. And nothing is more capable of doing that than nuclear weapons.

Still, experts said that obtaining nuclear weapons, even in the wake of the Soviet collapse, would not be easy. More likely would be the use of a "dirty bomb," a device in which radioactive material is wrapped around a conventional explosive. While not nearly as destructive as a nuclear weapon, a "dirty bomb" set off in a major metropolitan area would cause extraordinary panic and economic losses, although, experts say, probably not an immediate loss of many lives, since the radioactive doses would be small. Long-term illness, however, probably would be a major problem.

Conclusion

The history of nuclear weapons in the postwar era is full of ironies. First, the weapon that the United States used to end World War II turned into a specter that has haunted the country and the world ever since. Second, a weapon that was supposed to be an economically efficient way to deter attack—nuclear bombs are far cheaper to build and maintain than conventionally equipped armies—has cost the United States treasury dearly and came to bankrupt the Soviet Union.

Finally, while conservatives argue that the Reagan nuclear weapons buildup ultimately broke the back of the Soviet Union, the collapse of the Communist superpower may have exposed the United States to the far more insidious dangers of nuclear proliferation in the developing world and the use of nuclear materials and weapons by international terrorists.

Matthew Eisler

See also: Arms Race; Atomic Weapons Testing; Atoms for Peace; Ban the Bomb Movement; Baruch Plan; Cuban Missile Crisis; Hotline, U.S.-Soviet; Military-Industrial Complex; Missile Gap; Mutual Assured Destruction; MX Missiles; Neutron Bomb; Nuclear Test Ban Treaty; Soviet Union/ Russia, Relations with; Strategic Air Command; Strategic Arms Treaties; Strategic Defense Initiative; Weapons of Mass Destruction.

Bibliography

Barash, David P. *The Arms Race and Nuclear War.* Belmont, CA: Wadsworth, 1987.

Eisler, Matthew. "The Strategic Defense Initiative and the Evolution of Cold War Military-Technological Policy." Master's thesis, University of Alberta, Canada, 2002.

Hughes, Thomas P. *American Genesis: A History of the American Genius for Invention.* New York: Penguin, 1989.

Kaplan, Fred. *The Wizards of Armageddon.* Stanford, CA: Stanford University Press, 1991.

MacKenzie, Donald. *Inventing Accuracy: A Historical Sociology of Nuclear Missile Guidance.* Cambridge, MA: MIT Press, 1990.

Offner, Arnold A. *Another Such Victory: President Truman and the Cold War, 1945–1953.* Stanford, CA: Stanford University Press, 2002.

Paterson, Thomas G., and Dennis Merrill, eds. *Major Problems in American Foreign Relations.* Vol. II: *Since 1914.* 4th ed. Lexington, MA: D.C. Heath, 1995.

Stoll, Richard J. *U.S. National Security Policy and the Soviet Union: Persistent Regularities and Extreme Contingencies.* Columbia: University of South Carolina Press, 1990.

York, Herbert. *The Advisors: Oppenheimer, Teller, and the Superbomb.* San Francisco: W.H. Freeman, 1976.

WEAPONS OF MASS DESTRUCTION

Weapons of mass destruction (WMDs) are, as their name implies, weapons that are capable of producing great loss of life or property, usually with little discrimination between military forces and civilian populations.

They are generally divided into four categories: biological, chemical, radiological (weapons that spread radioactivity but do not involve a nuclear chain reaction), and nuclear. All of these WMDs, with the exception of radiological weapons, have been used—whether by nation-states, individuals, or groups—since 1945. Of the four, the most widespread and most destructive are nuclear weapons.

Nuclear Arms Race

On July 16, 1945, the U.S. military detonated an atomic device in the desert of New Mexico; the test was the culmination of a top-secret, three-year, multibillion-dollar effort known as the Manhattan Project. Less than a month later, on August 6 and 9, the United States dropped two atomic bombs on the Japanese cities of Hiroshima and Nagasaki, precipi-

tating the end of World War II. Since that time, no other nuclear weapon has been used in combat. These events marked the beginning of the nuclear age.

There are essentially two types of nuclear weapons. Atomic weapons utilize a process known as fission, whereby the nuclei of atoms are bombarded with neutrons and split, releasing enormous amounts of energy. Fusion weapons—also known as hydrogen bombs—exploit the process by which the sun generates energy by fusing hydrogen atoms to form heavier atoms.

The energy released by hydrogen weapons is of exponentially greater magnitude than that of atomic weapons. Whereas the atomic bomb dropped on Hiroshima released explosive energy equal to about 12 kilotons (1 kiloton = 1,000 tons) of dynamite, the hydrogen bombs can release 1 million tons or more. (In this article, the term "atomic" is used to refer to fission weapons and "nuclear" is used to refer to both types.)

As the scientists of the Manhattan Project understood—and explained to their military overseers—there was no way to maintain an American monopoly on nuclear weapons. Any country with an advanced technology and science sector—and access to uranium or plutonium, the raw material of atomic weapons—could build such weapons. The first country expected to do so was the Soviet Union, which had been America's ally in World War II but, within a few years of the war's end, was emerging as its major international adversary.

At first there was talk in U.S. policymaking circles of internationalizing atomic weapons, placing them in the hands of the United Nations (UN). But the so-called Baruch Plan—named after its main sponsor, financier and policy adviser Bernard Baruch—put a moratorium on atomic weapons development by other countries while allowing the United States to keep the weapons, about a dozen in number, that it had already produced. Not surprisingly, the Soviets rejected the plan. In 1949, several years ahead of American expectations, Moscow tested its first atomic bomb, and the arms race was on.

The next major advancement in nuclear weapons technology came with the development of the hydrogen bomb. In 1952, the United States exploded the first such device, followed a year later by the Soviets. Over the course of the 1950s, both nations produced H-bombs at an ever more feverish pace, joined by Great Britain, which successfully tested its first hydrogen bomb in 1953.

Still, the United States maintained a huge lead in nuclear weapons. By 1960, the United States had more than 20,000 of them—including tactical battlefield weapons and strategic weapons designed to destroy military bases and even cities—whereas the Soviet Union possessed just over 1,600. To counter the Soviet Union's vast superiority in conventional weapons and personnel on the critical European front of the Cold War, the North Atlantic Treaty Organization (NATO)—the anti-Soviet, Western European–North American alliance—accepted some 7,000 tactical nuclear weapons for its European arsenal.

Despite America's nuclear superiority, a number of politicians—including 1960 Democratic presidential candidate John F. Kennedy—argued that the Republican administration of President Dwight D. Eisenhower had left the United States vulnerable to Soviet attack. Kennedy spoke of a "missile gap," citing a Soviet lead in rocket technology that allowed it to be the first to test a suborbital intercontinental ballistic missile (ICBM), which was capable of reaching the United States in less than an hour, in 1957. Previously, nuclear weapons had to be delivered by aircraft, which could take up to half a day to reach their U.S. targets.

In fact, the United States was very close on the heels of the Soviet Union, developing the liquid-fueled Atlas rocket within a year of the Soviet missile test and the more reliable solid-fuel Minuteman missile by 1962. At roughly the same time, the Soviet Union developed solid-fuel rockets of its own. Both nations now began to develop what was called the "triad" defense, consisting of three delivery systems—airplane-delivered bombs, as well as land-based and submarine-based nuclear-equipped missiles—designed to withstand any first-strike nuclear assault by the other. By the early 1960s, experts agreed that the two countries possessed enough nuclear weapons to kill all of humanity.

As early as the mid-1950s, peace groups in the United States and Western Europe began to protest the nuclear arms race and the policy of mutually assured destruction, whereby peace between the superpowers was maintained by the idea that whichever nation launched a nuclear war would be destroyed by it, along with its adversary. But it was the Cuban Missile Crisis of 1962, in which the United States and the Soviet Union nearly went to war over the latter's deployment of nuclear weapons on the Caribbean island, that forced the superpowers to take the first steps toward arms limitation. Not only did the Soviets agree to take their weapons off the island—winning a secret assurance that America would do the same with its

missiles in Turkey—but a hotline was set up between Moscow and Washington for quick communication in a crisis, and both sides signed a ban on atmospheric testing. (An international treaty to ban all testing was not ratified until 1996.) Scientists were beginning to suspect that the radioactive fallout from such tests was endangering the health of the world's people.

Still, the arms race continued throughout the 1960s. America's nuclear stockpile grew to a peak of 31,700 in 1966, then began to decline, falling to just over 26,000 by 1970. The reduction was a function of improved missile navigation and the development of the multiple, independently targeted reentry vehicle (MIRV), a missile capable of delivering nuclear devices to several targets. For their part, the Soviets, lagging in navigation and MIRV technologies, kept expanding their stockpile to match America's. By the 1970s, the Soviets possessed nearly 12,000 nuclear devices.

Meanwhile, other nations were getting in on the act. In 1964, China and France exploded nuclear devices of their own, bringing the so-called nuclear club to five. Still, none of these nations possessed arsenals anywhere close to that of the superpowers; Britain's stockpile, estimated at about 350 in the mid-1970s, was the largest.

Policymakers in both Washington and Moscow began to fear that more nations, including potentially unstable ones, might join the nuclear club. Indeed, a number of countries, some in their own regional arms races, began to pursue nuclear weapons. India, locked in a decades-long confrontation with Pakistan, tested its first nuclear weapon in 1974. Israel, surrounded by hostile Arab states in the Middle East, was believed to have secretly developed nuclear weapons as early as the late 1960s. To control the spread of weapons, the United States, Soviet Union, Great Britain, and fifty other nations signed the UN-sponsored Nuclear Non-Proliferation Treaty in 1968, although the countries most actively involved in starting nuclear arsenals of their own refused to sign.

With the beginnings of détente—warmer relations between the Soviet Union and the United States—and the development of better surveillance systems, such as spy satellites, for monitoring the other side's weapons systems, the United States and Soviet Union signed two arms-control treaties in 1972. Both were the result of an ongoing series of negotiations known as the Strategic Arms Limitation Talks, or SALT. In the Antiballistic Missile Treaty, the two sides agreed to limit the number of strategic offensive weapons and strategic defensive systems;

a separate accord froze production of long-range ballistic missile launchers (delivery systems).

With the collapse of détente in the late 1970s, however, the United States and Soviet Union went back to improving and, in the case of the latter, expanding their nuclear arsenals. The Soviets increased their stockpile from about 30,000 warheads in 1980 to a peak of more than 40,000 in 1986, before cutting back to about 34,000 in 1990. With its superiority in technology, the United States was able to reduce its stockpile to just over 22,000 by the end of the decade without any drop-off in lethality. During the late 1970s, there was talk in Washington of a neutron bomb, a nuclear device that could produce a small explosion but spread large quantities of radiation, leaving buildings standing but populations dead. Widespread protest in official circles and among the public at large killed development of the weapon.

Protests against new deployments of major nuclear warheads were less successful. In the early 1980s, the United States and several European powers agreed to deploy a new generation of medium-range ballistic missiles in Western Europe. That deployment, as well as talk by the administration of Ronald Reagan of creating an antiballistic missile system in space—the so-called strategic defense initiative (SDI), or "Star Wars" defense—provoked a wave of massive protests in Western Europe and the United States.

End of the Arms Race

Though such protests were unlikely in the tightly controlled police state atmosphere of the Soviet Union, changes were nevertheless occurring in Moscow. As the accelerating arms race began to bankrupt the Soviet economy, reformers led by Mikhail Gorbachev took control of the Kremlin. Within a short time of taking power in 1985, Gorbachev made it clear that he did not want to continue the arms race. Over the next several years, the United States and the Soviet Union signed a series of treaties that eliminated medium-range ballistic missiles and further reduced long-range missiles.

Even as the last of these treaties was being signed, both the Soviet Union and the Communist bloc it controlled in Eastern Europe were collapsing. In December 1991, the Soviet Union officially dissolved, and its fifteen component republics became independent nations. Although this put an end to the Cold War and long-standing tensions in East–West relations, it did

not mean that the dangers posed by the arms race were over. Both sides continued to point thousands of nuclear-equipped missiles at each other, and, as the new Russian economy collapsed, there was less funding to maintain the monitoring and control devices to prevent an accidental missile launch. Perhaps even more dangerous was the threat that weapons components or nuclear material—poorly guarded and sometimes unaccounted for in the increasingly anarchic Commonwealth of Independent States (CIS, or association of former Soviet republics)—might fall into the wrong hands, whether those of states hostile to the United States or terrorist organizations.

Several measures were taken to prevent this eventuality. Part of the agreement between Moscow and the new nations of the CIS was that all nuclear weapons would be returned to Russia. Indeed, the three states that possessed them—Belarus, Kazakhstan, and Ukraine—quickly did so. Meanwhile, in December 1991, U.S. president George H. W. Bush signed the Soviet Nuclear Threat Reduction Act—also known as the Nunn-Lugar act—which provided billions of dollars in aid to the countries of the CIS to store, dismantle, and destroy nuclear weapons and materials, as well as other weapons of mass destruction, still on their territory. At the same time, new talks and treaties between Russia and the United States allowed both sides to reduce their arsenals even further. By the early 2000s, both nations' arsenals were under 10,000 weapons each.

Fears that nuclear material from the former Soviet Union might fall into the wrong hands persisted, however, as reports that material had gone missing came to light during the 1990s and early 2000s. Though few experts believed terrorists or even "rogue states" were capable of building nuclear weapons, they might use the nuclear material—widely available in medical and research institutions—to build radiological weapons. Such devices, popularly known as "dirty bombs," consist of nuclear material wrapped around conventional explosives. When ignited, the explosives spew radioactivity over a wide range. Although they result in few immediate deaths, they can cause costly, long-term health and contamination problems.

Finally, there remained the problem of non-Soviet-related nuclear proliferation. In 1998, both India and Pakistan, locked in a bitter conflict over the long-disputed territory of Kashmir, conducted a series of nuclear tests. Though Libya renounced its nuclear ambitions in 2004, Iran continued to insist that it had a right to pursue peaceful nuclear power development, even though many experts in the United States and Western Europe suspected that the oil-rich country was, in fact, using that story as a cover for developing nuclear weapons. Meanwhile, fears in the administration of George W. Bush about Iraqi nuclear weapons programs in the 1990s and early 2000s, though they led to a U.S. invasion in 2003, proved to be false.

The threat from North Korea was more concrete: There, a secretive and repressive regime was believed to have begun its nuclear weapons program as far back as the late 1980s or early 1990s. The country withdrew from the Nuclear Non-Proliferation Treaty in 1993 and began medium-range missile tests five years later. By the early 2000s—despite on-again, off-again talks with the United States, Russia, China, Japan, and South Korea—it was widely believed that the Pyongyang regime was in possession of up to a dozen nuclear weapons.

Biological and Chemical Weapons

Biological weapons—agents capable of causing disease in humans, crops, or domestic animals—have existed for centuries. During the Middle Ages, for example, armies hurled disease-ridden bodies into besieged cities to spread the plague. Chemical weapons have a shorter history; they were first widely used in the trench warfare of World War I.

Since the Geneva Protocol of 1925, nations have agreed to prohibit the use of biological and chemical weapons. Of the two, biological weapons, which are capable of spreading such scourges as anthrax, Ebola, pneumonic plague, cholera, and smallpox, are the most dangerous and the most restricted. In 1972, the United States, the Soviet Union, and a number of other countries signed the Biological and Toxin Weapons Convention, an international treaty making it illegal for any group or country to produce, store, or transport biological weapons. After the hundredth nation signed on in 1975, the treaty became binding. Still, it is believed that the Soviet Union and perhaps the United States have engaged in some testing and storage of biological weapons.

The use of biological weapons by individuals and groups, including terrorist organizations, has been more clearly documented. In 1972, and again in 1993, members of white supremacist groups were arrested for plotting to release biological agents into the water supplies of major American cities. In 2001, a still-unknown person or persons sent anthrax bacteria through the mail to media outlets and politicians, resulting in five deaths. Coming in the immediate aftermath of the September 11 terrorist attacks, the incidents created widespread alarm and forced the government to consider more seriously ways to fight and respond to biological weapons threats from terrorists.

Because chemical weapons are easier to control—biological weapons can also infect those who deploy them—they have been more commonly used. Mustard and other gases that effect the lungs, skin, and eyes were deployed heavily in World War I, and large stockpiles of more lethal nerve gases were maintained by a number of countries, including the United States and Soviet Union, throughout the Cold War decades. In 1961, President Kennedy increased federal funding for chemical weapons and deployed them on jets during the Cuban Missile Crisis the following year.

Still, neither superpower has ever used chemical weapons, and, as tensions between the two sides declined during the late 1980s, both pledged to stop stockpiling them. Washington and Moscow shared the hope that ceasing production would prompt other countries to do the same, and many did. One major exception was Iraq, which used chemical weapons against both Iran and its own Kurdish population, many of whom were allied with Iran, during and shortly after the Iran-Iraq War from 1980 to 1988. Indeed, Iraq's pursuit of chemical weapons—as well as its alleged pursuit of biological and nuclear weapons—prompted UN weapons inspections after the Gulf War of 1991 and a U.S. air attack on facilities allegedly containing WMD in 1993.

Although most experts believed that Iraq had been forced to stop producing and stockpiling chemical weapons during the 1990s, the George W. Bush Administration continued to suspect that it was secretly doing so. These allegations were a major reason behind the administration's decision to invade Iraq in 2003. Subsequent inspections conducted by U.S. experts following the invasion affirmed that the UN inspectors had done their job—that is, there were no chemical weapons or facilities to produce them in Iraq.

The chemical weapons threat posed by Iraq, at least during the 1980s and early 1990s, prompted the United States and other nations to sign the Chemical

Weapons Convention, which prohibited the development, production, stockpiling, and use of such weapons, in 1993. Four years later, with fifty nations having signed, the treaty went into effect. Like the international treaty against biological weapons, the chemical weapons accord includes provisions for on-site inspection of potential chemical weapons facilities and the destruction of existing stocks.

The Paradox of WMDs

The great paradox in the postwar history of weapons of mass destruction is that the most horrible of them—nuclear weapons—also have been the most widely stockpiled, deployed, and accepted, at least in the policymaking circles and general public of the nations that possess them. Although international treaties have prohibited the production of chemical and biological weapons, they have allowed members of the nuclear club to continue to possess such weapons.

But there is a method to the madness: Because of their sheer destructive power, nuclear weapons are far less likely to be used than chemical and biological weapons. For the same reason, tactical nuclear weapons, such as the neutron bomb, have produced the same negative reaction among the public as chemical and biological weapons.

As postwar history has demonstrated, these fears have proved well founded: Chemical and biological weapons have been used by nation-states and terrorists, whereas nuclear weapons have not. Still, few experts believe that the most nihilistic of these terrorists, notably al-Qaeda, would hesitate to use or threaten to use nuclear weapons if they came into their possession.

James Ciment

See also: Arms Race; Iraq War; Terrorism, Foreign; Weapons, Nuclear.

Bibliography

Cirincione, Joseph. *Deadly Arsenals: Tracking Weapons of Mass Destruction.* Washington, DC: Carnegie Endowment for International Peace, 2002.

Gaddis, John Lewis. *The United States and the End of the Cold War: Implications, Reconsiderations, Provocations.* New York: Oxford University Press, 1992.

Lavay, Peter, Scott D. Sagan, and James J. Wirtz, eds. *Planning the Unthinkable: How New Powers Will Use Nuclear, Chemical, and Biological Weapons.* Ithaca, NY: Cornell University Press, 2000.

Newhouse, John. *War and Peace in the Nuclear Age.* New York: Vintage Books, 1990.

WEATHERMEN

Radical activists known as the Weathermen, later the Weather Underground, emerged from a robust counterculture movement that helped define the political climate of America's colleges and universities during the 1960s. The group began as a faction of the Students for a Democratic Society (SDS), a broad-based national organization founded in 1960 and dedicated to promoting participatory democracy.

The SDS was united by opposition to the Vietnam War, but, by 1969, many in the organization were frustrated that its nonviolent methods had failed to end or even deescalate the war. As the group's membership clashed over future direction, the organization splintered. In the context of these debates, eleven SDS members issued a June 1969 statement that drew its title from the lyrics the 1965 song "Subterranean Homesick Blues" by Bob Dylan: "You don't need a weatherman to know which way the wind blows." The authors and proponents of this document became known collectively as the Weathermen. The group advocated violence in the struggle against the federal government and its Vietnam policies.

In June 1969, at the SDS National Convention in Chicago, the Weathermen insisted that the larger organization work in solidarity with oppressed peoples worldwide; in service of that cause, the Weathermen called for armed struggle to expose and contest systems responsible for oppression, particularly the U.S. military-industrial complex. They also proclaimed that anyone who declined the core views they had espoused would no longer be considered a member of the SDS. In this way, a small but devoted faction seized control of SDS organizational resources and the group's national office.

The Weathermen sought to turn back the forces of racism, sexism, and imperialism. As revolutionaries, they responded to state militarism with their own form of guerrilla warfare. They envisioned a high-profile event that would both publicize and advance this agenda, an SDS National Action, scheduled for October 1969 in Chicago. When dramatically fewer activists appeared than predicted, the situation culminated in a violent street confrontation with city police. By the end of the incident, referred to as the "Days of

Rage," hundreds of participants were arrested and several of the protest's leaders were indicted on rioting charges.

The Weathermen were already targets of government suspicion and surveillance, but the event in Chicago only intensified the attention of the Federal Bureau of Investigation (FBI) on the group. Regardless of the small turnout and violent outcome in Chicago, the Weathermen persisted in their efforts; members assembled for a December 1969 "War Council" in Flint, Michigan. At what would prove to be the last full meeting of the Weathermen, attendees decided to go "underground"; that is, they would conceal themselves by assuming false identities and living in safe houses with small Weather clusters, or affinity groups. In this way, they could conduct the work of the Weathermen undetected.

Thereafter calling themselves the Weather Underground Organization (WUO), members undertook a bombing campaign that would last from 1969 to 1975, bringing the group public notoriety. During that span, WUO claimed responsibility for more than twenty explosions, each targeting symbolic sites. In solidarity with people of color and their treatment in the criminal justice system, the Weather Underground set bombs at the California Department of Corrections, the Office of California Prisons, and the 103rd Precinct of the New York City Police Department. To protest military research and recruitment conducted at institutions of higher education, they bombed selective service offices as well as Reserve Officers Training Corps (ROTC) buildings on college campuses. Expressing their opposition to imperialism, they placed bombs in buildings said to epitomize the problems posed by multinational capitalism, such as the offices of Chase Manhattan Bank, General Motors, and Mobil Oil. To hasten an end to the Vietnam War, Weather bombers also struck at locations they regarded as most implicated in the nation's war machine, including the U.S. Capitol Building in March 1971 and the Pentagon in May 1972.

The bombings were intended as symbolic acts of property destruction, so detonations were typically preceded by telephone calls warning building occupants to evacuate. The group also issued public statements to communicate the rationale for bombings at chosen locations. (One explosion was not intentional. On May 6, 1970, a bomb exploded at the Greenwich Village, New York, townhouse of one of the Weathermen's parents, who were out of the country. Police believed the detonation was accidental; none of the Weathermen at the house was injured or arrested.)

By 1976, a few Weather fugitives had been captured and still more had resumed life aboveground. While some fugitives faced criminal prosecution, many of the charges against Weather members were dropped because of the illegal methods of surveillance, search, and investigation conducted by the FBI.

Although former "Weatherpeople" reentered the world they had criticized, they did not capitulate to its values and practices. Today, many—such as Bill Ayers, a professor at the University of Wisconsin, and Bernardine Dohrn, a Northwestern University law professor and human rights advocate—pursue careers that reflect their political commitments and convictions about social justice, as educators, health-care advocates, human rights champions, civil rights lawyers, social workers, and activists.

Linda S. Watts

See also: Antiwar Movement, Vietnam Era; Black Panthers; New Left; Students for a Democratic Society; Terrorism, Domestic; Yippies.

Bibliography

Gilbert, David. *SDS/WUO: Students For a Democratic Society and the Weather Underground Organization.* Montreal, Canada: Guillen, 2002.

Jacobs, Harold. *Weatherman.* Berkeley, CA: Ramparts, 1970.

Jacobs, Ron. *The Way the Wind Blew: A History of the Weather Underground.* New York: Verso, 1997.

Prairie Fire: The Politics of Revolutionary Anti-Imperialism. San Francisco: Communications Company, 1974.

WELFARE AND PUBLIC ASSISTANCE

With its tradition of rugged individualism going back to frontier days, the United States has been among the most parsimonious of major industrialized countries when it comes to providing welfare and other forms of public assistance. Even as the countries of Western Europe were developing generous social welfare states in the early post–World War II years, the United States remained the odd country out, offering only limited payments of cash and other assistance to single mothers raising children.

Although the U.S. federal government offered Social Security payments—and after 1965, Medicare payments—to the elderly, orphaned, and disabled, and states offered various forms of unemployment insurance, these were not welfare programs per se. They were not means-tested programs—requiring recipients to prove need—and they were funded, at least theoretically, by the recipients themselves. That is to say, mandatory paycheck deductions of current workers were used to fund pensions and other payments

National Welfare Rights Organization

From 1968 to 1975, the National Welfare Rights Organization (NWRO) organized thousands of American welfare recipients into a powerful national movement for welfare reform. At its peak, the organization had as many as 100,000 members, most of them African American women. Supporters credited the NWRO with helping to restore dignity and higher payments to many welfare recipients before internal conflicts ended its work in 1975.

The NWRO was created during a fertile time for activism and poverty programs. The civil rights movement was in full swing, and President Lyndon B. Johnson's Great Society programs were attempting to address the problems of the poor. Seized with a desire to join the action, George Wiley, an African American chemistry professor at Syracuse University, abandoned his academic career in 1966 to form the Poverty Rights Action Center. Such organizations were springing up all over the country, and in August 1967, more than sixty of them met in Washington, D.C. Together they formed the NWRO, a coalition of welfare organizations that would work to reform the federal welfare system and establish need-based payments.

Wiley became the organization's director and quickly got it involved in protests and lobbying. It received little public attention at first—the needs of minority women were not considered a priority. But the NWRO continued to raise its profile, sitting in on Senate Finance Committee hearings in 1967 while lobbying against work-incentive provisions proposed as amendments to the Social Security Act.

In 1968, the NWRO became part of Martin Luther King, Jr.'s, Poor People's Campaign, and it was given a meeting with the secretary of health, education and welfare. The same year, the NWRO received a government contract to help monitor the federal Work Incentive Program.

Money from the contract also helped the organization expand its staff and efforts in cities across the country. At a convention in Detroit in August 1969, the NWRO estimated that it had somewhere between 30,000 and 100,000 members, with 22,000 dues-paying families. Most members were from New York City, followed by Boston, Detroit, Los Angeles, and Chicago.

The NWRO developed a welfare "bill of rights" that called for prompt decisions on applications, hearings on denial of aid, and the right to spend welfare money without interference from welfare departments. Improvements to the U.S. welfare system were made through the NWRO's efforts, most notably an increase in benefit outlays—from $1.2 million in New York City in 1963 to $40 million in 1968. Welfare offices also responded to the NWRO's requests to treat welfare recipients with respect and made manuals and application documents more accessible to their clients.

Perhaps the NWRO's most lasting legacy was its empowerment of African American women, who had never before been organized into a national movement. Johnnie Tillmon succeeded Wiley as the NWRO's director and argued in a famous essay in *Ms.* magazine, "Welfare Is a Woman's Issue," that all women have a right to an adequate income, even if that income comes from welfare.

The NWRO membership was 90 percent African American and female, but its leadership was not. The organization was run by activist-minded white males and depended on wealthy whites and corporations for support. This dichotomy caused internal friction that the NWRO could not survive. Most of the staff resigned by 1972, and the national office closed in 1975.

Melissa Stallings

made to those who were retired, disabled, or unemployed. Moreover, reforms passed during the 1990s made welfare in America even more limited, difficult to get, and limited in duration.

New Deal Origins

Until the New Deal of the 1930s, no federal programs provided welfare to poor and disabled persons. For the most part, those left behind were forced to fend for themselves, rely on family support, or seek out aid from private or church-run charities.

Even during times of extreme economic distress, the government generally turned a deaf ear to the pleading of poor people and their advocates. When thousands of veterans who had lost their jobs because of the Great Depression came to Washington in 1932 to demand an early payment of the bonus they had been promised for their service in World War I, Congress refused to meet their demand and President Herbert Hoover had them rousted from their encampments around the city.

The states were a bit more generous, especially to single mothers and their children. Beginning with Illinois in 1911, a number of states began instituting what were called "mothers' pension programs." By 1933, forty-six of the forty-eight states had such programs in place, but many were forced to drop them in the face of the fiscal crisis of the Depression.

Soon after his inauguration in March 1933—when unemployment peaked at 25 percent—President Franklin D. Roosevelt established the Federal Emergency Relief Administration, offering federal relief grants to individuals for the first time in American history. Still, Roosevelt feared that direct relief payments would sap people's initiative and make them dependent on the government; he preferred to put poor, unemployed people to work, and so his administration initiated a host of public works programs.

Concerned about the large number of elderly poor, Roosevelt inaugurated Social Security in 1935. One of the provisions of the Social Security Act offered funds on a matching basis for states to reinstitute public assistance programs. In 1936, the Roosevelt Administration established the nation's first permanent federal welfare program, called Aid to Dependent Children (ADC). The program provided small grants to families with dependent children, although technically the money was not to be used to support parents or guardians—only those children living with parents or guardians were eligible. Compared to other New Deal programs, however, ADC was relatively small and its funding limited; the initial act appropriated just $25 million for the program.

Expansion of Welfare

Several key legislative changes expanded the ADC program during the 1950s and 1960s. In 1950, the federal government began reimbursing states for the maintenance of caretaking relatives and, more importantly, in 1961, aid was provided directly to both children and their unemployed parent. A year later, the rules were changed so that two parents could receive aid, as long as one of them was incapacitated, and the program's name was changed to Aid to Families with Dependent Children (AFDC).

The real legislative expansion of the AFDC program came in the mid-1960s, with President Lyndon B. Johnson's "War on Poverty." Among the many programs initiated under this heading were the Food Stamp Program, which provided AFDC recipients with vouchers that could be exchanged for groceries, and Medicaid, a health care program for destitute and disabled persons. In 1972, Congress established the Supplemental Security Income program, which provided additional funding for needy elderly and blind and other disabled persons.

As important as the legislative alterations was social change. By the 1960s, the number of single parents in America had grown dramatically. Whereas just 500,000 children and parents received ADC aid in the late 1930s, the number had climbed to more than 7 million by 1969. By the 1990s, fully 15 percent of all U.S. children were supported by AFDC. Contributing to the expansion was the so-called "poor people's movement" of the 1960s, which organized a series of marches and demonstrations by welfare recipients to ease bureaucratic restrictions on receiving aid and increase the amount paid out to recipients.

Backlash and Change

The growing costs and number of recipients concerned many Americans, both inside government and outside, for several reasons. First, there were fiscal concerns—chiefly, that welfare was driving up government spending and taxes. In reality, even at the program's height in the early 1990s, less than 1 percent of the federal budget was devoted to AFDC. In addition, there were charges of abuse, as some recipients of the program had been accused of fraud.

Welfare Reform Bill (1996)

On August 22, 1996, President Bill Clinton signed a landmark welfare reform bill into law. Over the previous two years, Congress had sent Clinton two measures, which he vetoed, because they "failed to protect our children and did too little to move people from welfare to work." The Personal Responsibility and Work Opportunity Reconciliation Act of 1996, however, was the culmination of a bipartisan effort to reform America's welfare system. Welfare, under the new system, was to be used as a transition to work rather than an open-ended means of financial support. Critics argued that it was a cynical way for Clinton, facing reelection in 1996, to show that he was not a "pro-welfare liberal" and win backing from swing voters.

The new law obligated welfare recipients on government assistance for two years to work. During the first year after the law was passed, single welfare parents were to work at least twenty hours per week, and, by 2000, the hours were to increase to thirty. By July 1997, two-parent welfare families were to work thirty-five hours per week.

State work requirements included participation in unsubsidized or subsidized employment, on-the-job training, community service, work experience, or twelve-month vocational training. Some $14 billion in child-care funding was allotted for the next six years to encourage and aid single mothers in moving into jobs. Government health coverage was continued for all welfare families, and a five-year cumulative limit on welfare assistance was established.

The 1996 legislation also included child-support enforcement measures. States had the power to implement tougher penalties on persons who failed to provide support, such as seizing assets, requiring community service in certain cases, and even revoking drivers' licenses.

Teen parents also were subject to the new rules. Unmarried minor parents were required to live with a responsible adult or in a supervised setting. In order to receive welfare assistance, young parents were to participate in certain educational and training activities, and, in 1998, $50 million was added to the Maternal and Child Health Block Grant for abstinence education.

All in all, the number of families receiving welfare dropped nearly 60 percent during the five years after the bill was passed, falling to 2.1 million by December 2001. Three million children were affected positively by the new measures, resulting in the lowest African American child poverty rate ever. Critics of the bill argued that the gains were likely to have come without the bill, given the prosperity of the times. They also pointed out the fact that many people who dropped from the welfare rolls were not finding work but ending up homeless or living with relatives.

In the spring of 2002, the House of Representatives passed measures that would strengthen the work requirements of the 1996 law, requiring welfare recipients to participate in work activities for forty hours per week. The new bill was still waiting a vote in the Senate in mid-2006.

Gavin J. Wilk

In 1980, Republican presidential candidate Ronald Reagan scored political points by denouncing "welfare queens" who showed up at government offices to pick up welfare checks in their Cadillacs. Liberal defenders of the programs argued this was not true, pointing out that bureaucracy, red tape, and hostile welfare caseworkers made the poor more likely to shun the program than to try to game it. They also claimed that talk of Cadillac-driving welfare queens was racism in disguise that played on white middle-class perceptions that most welfare recipients were black. In fact, although African Americans were disproportionately represented in the program, they remained a minority of recipients.

Finally, there were growing concerns, expressed by both Republicans and conservative Democrats, that AFDC was creating a "culture of dependency" in which the children of welfare recipients modeled their own behavior after their parents, perpetuating a cycle of dependency on government handouts. In addition, according to Christian conservatives, the program discouraged stable family life, because it made it difficult for mothers to collect welfare if there was an employed man living in the home. Caseworkers conducted spot inspections to make sure that AFDC recipients did not have a breadwinner in the house.

Despite the Reagan Administration's hostility to the program, AFDC not only survived but, as the numbers indicate, continued to expand. With Democrats in control of Congress, conservatives in the White House were forced to abandon their plans to limit or eliminate welfare programs for all but the most extremely disabled. For their part, Democrats were not happy with the program but were reluctant to reform it for fear of alienating key constituencies, such as urban and black voters.

By the mid-1990s, however, the political will to radically reform welfare was gathering. In 1992, centrist Democratic presidential candidate Bill Clinton vowed to "end welfare as we know it." Two years later, conservative Republicans took control of both houses of Congress, reflecting a new conservatism in the electorate at large. Fearing that a failure to fulfill his 1992 campaign promise would jeopardize his reelection chances, Clinton decided to steal the issue from the Republicans by initiating his own welfare reform.

Clinton's changes began in 1996 with a sharp increase in the Earned Income Tax Credit (EITC), a section of the tax code, dating back to 1975, that gave low-income parents a rebate for each dependent child. The more fundamental change in welfare came with the Personal Responsibility and Work Opportunity Reconciliation Act (PRWORA) of 1996. The legislation scrapped the sixty-year-old AFDC and replaced it with the new Temporary Assistance for Needy Families (TANF) program.

More than just a name change, TANF represented a whole new approach to welfare. Rather than perpetuating the old matching-fund system, TANF provided block grants to the states and allowed them wider discretion in determining eligibility and conditions for receiving welfare. More controversially, it set time limits on welfare payments: Adult recipients had to find work within two years or their payments would be cut off. In addition, the law established a lifetime limit of five years of welfare payments. States that failed to reduce their caseloads by 25 percent within one year and by 50 percent by 2002 would see

their block grants cut (although 20 percent of their caseloads could be exempted from this rule).

Despite their anger that the Democratic president had received most of the credit for the changes, conservative Republicans were generally pleased with the new law. Not so with liberals and advocates of the poor. Senator Ted Kennedy (Democrat of Massachusetts) called the law "legislative child abuse," and the Urban Institute, a liberal think tank, declared that the PRWORA threatened to send more than a million children into poverty. Even President Clinton said the bill was flawed, arguing that he and the Democrats should be reelected that year to fix it with more funding for jobs training and child care. Opponents of the bill argued that without such reforms, the law was a punitive measure that would put families onto the streets. Although Clinton won reelection in November 1996, the Republicans maintained their control over Congress, and little extra money was allocated for training and child care.

Supporters of TANF say the program has worked as planned, putting more and more welfare recipients to work. Whereas in 1996, about 4.4 million families were receiving aid under the old AFDC program, by the early 2000s, the number had fallen to just over 2 million. Critics contend that most of the drop came during the economic boom of the 1990s and that the figures have remained roughly the same since the 2001 recession.

More importantly, critics argue, the TANF figures disguise the fact that people pushed off the welfare roles by time limits have not found jobs or lifted themselves out of poverty but have moved in with relatives or been forced into homelessness. They point out that the official poverty rate in America climbed steadily during the early 2000s, up from 11.3 percent (31.6 million) in 2000 to 12.7 percent (37 million) in 2004. Poverty rates going up and welfare cases going down, they argue, is a sure sign that people are falling through the holes in the nation's social safety net.

James Ciment

See also: Family Assistance Plan; Family Support Act; Medicare and Medicaid; Poverty; Social Security; Unemployment; Women and Work.

Bibliography

Bailis, Lawrence. *Bread or Justice.* Lexington, MA: Lexington, 1974.

Coll, Blanche D. *Safety Net: Welfare and Social Security, 1929–1979.* New Brunswick, NJ: Rutgers University Press, 1995.

Finegold, Kenneth, and Alan Weil. *Welfare Reform: The Next Act.* Washington, DC: Urban Institute Press, 2002.

Gabe, Thomas. *Trends in Welfare, Work, and the Economic Well-Being of Female-Headed Families With Children.* New York: Novinka, 2003.

Katz, Michael B. *In the Shadow of the Poorhouse: A Social History of Welfare in the United States.* New York: Basic Books, 1996.

Kotz, Nick, and Mary Lynn Kotz. *A Passion for Equality: George Wiley and the Movement.* New York: W.W. Norton, 1977.

West, Guida. *The National Welfare Rights Movement: The Social Protest of Poor Women.* New York: Praeger, 1981.

WESTERN EUROPE, RELATIONS WITH

The post–World War II relationship between the United States and Western Europe has largely been a close and friendly one, with America helping to rebuild Europe after the war and defend it against Soviet aggression during the Cold War. Since the collapse of communism in the late 1980s and early 1990s, the relationship has become somewhat more strained, as an emerging European Union has attempted to chart a foreign policy independent of that of the United States. The 2003 U.S. invasion of Iraq, in particular, created tension, as much of Western Europe—with the major exception of Britain and, to a lesser extent, Spain and Italy—opposed the war.

For much of its history, the United States tried to stay out of European affairs. That tradition ended with World War I and President Woodrow Wilson's efforts to create an international order based on democracy and self-determination for the peoples ruled by European empires. Europe's twisting of Wilson's idealism caused many Americans to reject the international role the president envisioned.

Republican administrations in the 1920s concentrated on developing prosperity at home while limiting involvement abroad. This left the defense of liberal democratic capitalist ideals in the hands of pacific Britain and shell-shocked France. As events in the 1930s and 1940s proved, Britain and France alone did not possess the power, the will, or, in light of their continued colonial policies, the moral authority to lead the democratic world.

Aftermath of World War II

The United States after World War II faced twin challenges. Most leaders understood that the conflict might have been prevented by increased U.S. involvement, yet many of the people were more worried about a return of the Great Depression or simply putting their lives back in order.

Across the ocean, the nations of Europe faced disastrous circumstances. Allied and Axis air forces both had targeted urban areas and infrastructure, destroying not only industry and residences, but also the means by which food and supplies reached the people. Stalin's forces occupied the eastern half of the continent. His success, combined with the misery of peoples in the democratic regions, encouraged Western Communists to expect great changes. The changes came, but not in the manner the Communists hoped.

The first two years after the official end of fighting in Europe saw the Western democracies in dire straits. France and Britain had difficulty meeting any of their formidable commitments—satisfying their obligations in Germany, maintaining their imperial possessions abroad, and, most importantly, providing for their own people. Remnants of the Nazi paramilitary SS continued to launch terrorist attacks and assassinations against the Allied occupation and its German helpers.

Thus, the suffering and economic distress of Western Europe continued to grow, while the United States found prosperity as one of the sole producers of many manufactured goods. Costly transitions to more socialized systems of economics and government in Europe did not relieve the malaise. Meanwhile, the nations of Eastern Europe found their initial forays into democracy crushed by the heavy hand of Soviet interference.

By 1947, fear had developed in U.S. policymaking circles of the possibility of European democracy being undermined from without by the opportunistic Stalin and from within by populations desperate for help. Making matters worse, Greece's fragile anticommunist government was in danger of falling and could expect no more assistance from Britain.

Two years earlier, the American presidency had been inherited by the dogged Midwesterner, Harry S. Truman, upon the death of Franklin Roosevelt. Since the Potsdam Conference in the summer of 1945, at which the Allies discussed peace treaties and the occupation of Germany, Truman and his administration grew increasingly wary of Soviet ambitions in the rest of Europe. George Kennan, a U.S. dimplomat in Moscow, warned of a combination of old czarist expansionism combined with Communist revolutionary ideology. Advisers Clark Clifford and George Elsey wrote a major report that cited Soviet antagonism to Anglo-American efforts to maintain world peace through agreements and its willingness to support Communist expansion in the West. These alarm bells sounded in the halls of the State Department bureaucracy and the White House, even as pundits condemned Winston Churchill's "Iron Curtain" speech in March 1946 as overly belligerent.

Aiming his sights on a world where "we and other nations will be able to work out a way of life free of coercion," Truman introduced his groundbreaking (and eponymous) doctrine to Congress in March 1947. The president's speech described a world in which some nations could choose their government, while the fates of others were "based upon the will of a minority forcibly imposed upon the majority." Truman's specific request was for aid to Greece and Turkey to resist Communist subversion, but most in Congress understood that help would be available to any nation threatened in such a way.

The same year saw Truman wrest from a Republican Congress a massive aid package to reconstruct Europe. Although most of the work and ideas were Truman's, the package bore the name of Secretary of State George Marshall because of his influence among congressional Republicans. The United States made loan packages available to all nations that suffered damage during World War II, including the Soviet Union and its Eastern European satellites.

Western Europe eagerly signed up for the no-strings money even though this demonstrated a new era of dependence on the United States. In the short term, Western Europe relied on U.S. economic assistance and, in the long term, on U.S. military protection from the Soviet Union. Dependence meant ceding continental decision making—regarding the fate of Germany, for example—as well as initiative on defense and even foreign policy matters.

Some nations, such as Britain, accepted the role of deputy to the United States' sheriff, but France declined such a position. French politicians who subscribed to the ideas of Charles de Gaulle, leader of Free French forces in World War II, preferred to have France serve as the loyal opposition within America's benevolent empire. Still, the German people had served as the keystone of European affairs for centuries, and debate

over their future dominated the early Cold War and U.S.-Western European relations.

West Germany

Germany presented the Western democracies with their first major test. Divided after the war among the Soviet Union, Britain, France, and the United States, it, in turn, divided those that fought to defeat it. The Soviets, whose infrastructure had been ravaged by Germany's World War II invasion, demanded reparations in the form of factories and other physical assets—not just from their sphere of control but also from the American, British, and French zones. Additionally, Moscow desired a unified and neutralized Germany, one that might more easily choose socialism on its own.

Western Europe realized that its economy could not function with a Germany stripped of its industrial base and so worked to help restore that country's economy in the Western zones. Even worse from the Soviet perspective, the postwar agreement divided Berlin into occupation zones. Naturally, the Western democracies governed their zones with a measure of freedom, while all of Eastern Germany began to lose its individual freedoms and the ability to acquire material wealth.

Berlin became a symbol for the United States, Soviet Union, and Western Europe of the American commitment in Europe. Although the United States had never shown a deep attachment to the international community, its determination in West Berlin grew into a test of its determination to hold the line against the Soviets in Europe. The Soviets over and over again tried to force the United States to abandon Berlin, while America persevered in its occupation. The initial move toward getting the United States out of Berlin came in 1948, when the Soviets blocked land access to force the Western allies into either a shooting war or a humiliating retreat. Truman maneuvered out of the predicament by using American airpower to deliver needed supplies—the Berlin Airlift, from June 1948 to September 1949—while daring the Soviets to begin a shooting war.

Germany itself faded as an issue, even as Berlin flared repeatedly as an issue between the superpowers. After the late 1940s decision to create the separate liberal democratic Federal Republic of Germany in the Western zones, division was accepted as an accomplished fact, at least by the West. Thus, Germany grew more oriented to the Western powers and played a key role in the initial stages of the European Union.

That the Federal Republic of Germany (or West Germany) could play such a role among its former enemies was because of its economic recovery. Despite the best efforts of the Allied air forces, West Germany retained the most complete infrastructure on the Continent. Large banks, an extensive chemical industry, and a potent steel-making capacity helped to rejuvenate the country's economy by the 1950s. This recovery caused alarm, especially in France. But instead of keeping Germany an outcast state, as they had in the early 1920s, neighbors on the Continent looked for ways to reintegrate it into the family of nations.

While West Germany was achieving official status as a legitimate democratic state, the United States and Europe busily solidified their front against potential Soviet aggression. In 1947, the United States passed the National Defense Act, which expanded and reorganized the military, created the Central Intelligence Agency (CIA), and transformed the American defense establishment in numerous other ways. The European nations still feared the Soviets, however, and a movement emerged to create a more solid defensive pact. In 1949, the North Atlantic Treaty Organization (NATO) united Western Europe with the United States and Canada in a collective security arrangement that bound all to respond if one state fell under attack. Despite this show of unity, cracks started to appear in the Western world before the ink from the treaty signatures even dried.

France

The first sign that the United States would have trouble maintaining a unified front emerged with resistance from France over U.S.-European defense policy. De Gaulle, who, though not in power, nevertheless dominated French politics during much of the 1950s, occupied an interesting position with regard to the United States in that decade. While trying to stake out an independent position in the Western democratic world with regard to Europe, France increasingly relied on American aid under the Truman Doctrine to shore up its colonial empire in Southeast Asia.

De Gaulle navigated a troubled ship, seeking ways to replace its constitution, deal with colonial unrest, and maintain, at least, France's perception of its own power and position in the world. Certainly,

by giving France a share in the German occupation and a permanent seat on the UN Security Council, the United States saw France as one of the victors of World War II instead of one of the collaborators. France also benefited from a postwar boom in manufacturing that saw the nation producing large numbers of automobiles and aircraft by the 1970s.

Great Britain

Great Britain was at a crossroads, an imperial power trying to find a role in an increasingly postcolonial world. It had commitments to its commonwealth of former colonies, but also to its new European allies. The United States had emerged in the previous decades as a nation with which Britain had a special relationship, but this also strained its commitment to a new Europe. What made matters worse was that Britain entered a period of economic malaise as the United States and the Continent experienced growth. Because the British needed less help rebuilding after the war, its industrial machine remained slow and inefficient in comparison to the French and Germans. Sitting astride the Atlantic threads of power had helped maintain Britain as a preeminent nation for more than two centuries, but as it declined, its position betrayed more weakness than strength.

Both France and Britain's postwar weakness and lack of independence became evident in the Suez Canal Crisis of 1956. Egypt under Gamal Abdel Nasser had wrested itself free of British control and sought to lead an Arab revival. European ownership of the Suez Canal remained a symbol of colonial rule, and Nasser seized it. Britain, France, and Israel provoked a conflict with Egypt to allow the Europeans to sweep in and regain possession of the canal. But the world had changed. London and Paris no longer held the same weight as Washington and Moscow, both of which, for different reasons, opposed the old colonial methods of operation.

President Dwight D. Eisenhower saw the conflict as an especially untimely headache, taking place just as the Soviets crushed a Hungarian revolt against its oppressive Communist regime. Pressure from Eisenhower forced Britain and France to disengage and climb down in a humiliating manner. Cold War realities meant that Western Europe depended heavily on the United States in every meaningful way, but they had to seek a way to reestablish some manner of independent action.

The use and availability of weapons systems defined independence for Western European nations, principally France and Great Britain. The United States preferred that nuclear technology remain in a single set of hands. But the leaders of these nations, who saw their imperial basis for world power crumbling, saw another prospect for world power status in nuclear weapons. France and Britain developed nuclear technology fairly quickly, France going so far as to remove its weapons from NATO control. Britain also yearned for a method by which to deploy and launch strategic nuclear weapons and invested heavily in an American-made system in the early 1960s that was soon found to possess fatal flaws. West Germany fumed at the restrictions in the postwar peace treaty that barred it from creating such weapons and demanded, at least, control over the tactical nuclear arsenal stored in Germany by the United States. Washington saw this as potentially alarming the USSR unnecessarily and declined to permit the transfer of control. Control and policy regarding nuclear weapons in Western Europe remained a difficult issue throughout the century.

The Vietnam War and its aftermath created some strain on the alliance. Economic problems, as well as student disorder, appeared toward the end of the 1960s, and President Lyndon B. Johnson's laser-beam focus on Vietnam to the exclusion of other world affairs troubled Europe. Western Europe's student protesters opposed the war in Vietnam as much as their U.S. counterparts, and anti-Americanism grew.

The leaders of Western European nations questioned America's ability to deploy power in all parts of the world and continue to protect Europe effectively. President Richard M. Nixon's widening of the foreign policy focus helped ease these anxieties. His accession to the presidency also coincided with the emergence of the leftist Willy Brandt in West Germany. Surprisingly, the two shared a goal of somewhat normalizing relations with the Soviet Union.

Détente worked for a time, but it was a policy of necessity caused by the growing relative weakness of the United States and its perceived inability to meet every Cold War commitment. As social and economic problems continued to consume America in the 1970s, Europe grew steadily more alarmed. The Carter Administration often confused other nations who tried to figure out whether the dovish Secretary of State Cyrus Vance or the hawkish National Security Advisor

U.S. President Dwight D. Eisenhower (right) confers with British Prime Minister Harold MacMillan (center) and French President Charles de Gaulle (left) after their 1960 summit in Paris with Soviet leader Nikita Khrushchev. Cold War dynamics dictated U.S.-European relations. *(Keystone/Getty Images)*

Zbigniew Brzezinski actually owned the president's ear. This decade saw Europe become somewhat fearful of the growing tensions between the United States and the Soviet Union, but it also witnessed the Continent working on establishing its own system of unity and potential power.

Although it started as a small league of coal- and steel-producing nations in Western Europe, the European Economic Community developed quickly into a vehicle through which Europe might deliver a unified voice capable of registering with the same force as that of its American partner. That voice would not take shape until after the end of the Cold War, however.

The immediate post-Vietnam era, with its energy supply problems and serious economic difficulties, produced a "crisis of confidence" not only in America but among its allies as well. For a short time, the United States seemed to falter in its will to support its worldwide responsibilities. Then came a remarkable partnership between a rejuvenated America and two determined European leaders.

Fall of Communism

The election of Pope John Paul II and selection of hawkish and conservative Margaret Thatcher as British prime minister in the late 1970s formed two sides of a staunch anticommunist coalition that would find completion in 1981 with the inauguration of President Ronald Reagan. Each in his or her own way saw communism as a moral, as well as a political, threat and endeavored to increase the pressure upon the Soviet Union's Eastern European empire.

In the United States, Reagan not only increased the rhetoric, he also proposed the development of additional conventional and nuclear weapons systems. His speeches indicated a belief that an arms race would overload the increasingly fragile and corrupt Soviet economy. Reagan additionally advocated the creation of a space-based defense system against nuclear arms, an escalation that might have pushed the Soviets beyond their ability to compete. Although antiwar and anti-nuclear groups marched and demonstrated against Reagan in Europe, consistent election returns favoring parties with pro-American positions indicated that public opinion in many nations supported the acceleration of the Cold War.

From the Vatican came a different kind of pressure. Poland formed, in many ways, the lynchpin and the Achilles heel of the Soviet empire. Its geographical position and its inability to bring under control national and religious expressions of the people made it a prime target of subversion from the democratic West. The Polish pope took the lead in applying increasing pressure on his native country, with material assistance from British and American intelligence. The partnership between the Holy See and Washington grew closer than at any prior time in the history of the United States, with Reagan establishing full diplomatic relations with the Vatican.

This partnership achieved one of its major goals in 1985, although no one in the Western world knew it at the time. Soviet Premier Mikhail Gorbachev, who came to office that year, faced with a crumbling economy and unrelenting pressure from the outside world, considered the future of the empire he ruled and issued an order that countermanded Soviet policy since 1945. Soviet military support for its satellite regimes in Eastern Europe had ended. They were now on their own. By 1989, the nations of the Soviet bloc started breaking away from their former masters, and by 1992, the USSR itself was in the dustbin of history.

Throughout the 1990s, planners moved ahead with the goal of transforming Europe from an economic community into a union. This decade saw Europeans and Americans at pains to redefine their relationship in a post-Soviet world. NATO expanded to include still-wary members of the former Eastern Bloc, and the European Union later followed suit. Priorities and policies coming out of Washington started to lose the weight they had carried before. As Europe tried to unify its currency and its government, Britain strained to continue its special relationship with the United States and to remain connected with a Europe trying to redefine itself as an independent power in the world.

Europe and the United States started the 1990s with few points of disagreement. It was a decade of prosperity for America, if not so much for Europe, which found the weight of its prized socialized government programs and worker protections draining many of the Continent's nations' economies of their former vitality. Europe's relationship with the United States faced a new century of challenges, as a new threat emerged on both sides of the Atlantic.

Divisions Over the Iraq War

President George W. Bush represented a different kind of leader than many in Europe preferred. The defining events of his presidency also defined America's relationship with Europe—not just between governments, but also on a personal level. The terror attacks of September 11, 2001, reminded many Americans that the United States retreats from world power only at its own peril. Bush signaled to the world that America intended to be resurgent and even more active.

France, joined generally by Russia and Germany, served as the chorus of concern designed to urge restraint upon the United States. This circumstance once again strained Britain's position, as it sought to be both a good American ally and a contributor in Europe.

The buildup to the war in Iraq and the 2003 invasion by coalition forces headed by the United States and Britain opened up rifts between the United States and the Continent that appeared serious. France, led by President Jacques Chirac, attracted the ire of many in the United States. Not only did high-ranking government officials on both sides disparage each other's conduct, but the feelings of the general population were involved. For a short time, some Americans boycotted

French products and even dropped "French" from the names of foods. The French people could not understand America's eagerness to overturn the dictator Saddam Hussein's regime, and people in the United States fumed at French ingratitude. The squabble over the war overshadowed many areas of enduring Franco-American cooperation, especially in the War on Terror.

Fallout from the war in Iraq threatened some European governments with scandal. American journalists eagerly pursued links connecting Iraq, the United Nations, and French government officials. Other revelations suggested that French, German, and Russian industrialists maintained secret dealings with Saddam Hussein. France, in particular, underwent political turmoil as a result of these scandals. This was followed by a "no" vote on ratification of a new constitution for the European Union that would have solidified its sovereignty over individual states.

Despite the problems and differences of opinion, the likelihood of the United States and Western Europe drawing apart entirely remains remote. Economic dependency ties the two sides of the Atlantic together, even though the European Union from time to time flexes its muscles in regard to such issues as genetically altered food or the dominance of Microsoft. Even more significant, European public opinion is unlikely to approve the massive increases in defense spending that would be necessary to secure true independence from the U.S. defense umbrella.

As far as America is concerned, even sharp irritation does not signal a real intention to cut off nations such as France. Protecting Europe has grown into a traditional responsibility that, although sometimes wearying to public opinion, will not be rejected by the American mindset soon. As has been the case since at least the nineteenth century, Europe and the United States continue to need each other, no matter how hard they try to convince themselves otherwise.

Stephen Smoot

See also: Alliances, Foreign; Berlin Airlift; Berlin Wall; Containment; Eastern Europe, Relations with; Immigration; MX Missiles; North Atlantic Treaty Organization.

Bibliography

Barnet, Richard J. *The Alliance—America, Europe, Japan: Makers of the Postwar World.* New York: Simon and Schuster, 1983.

Gaddis, John Lewis, *We Now Know: Rethinking Cold War History.* Oxford, UK: Clarendon, 1997.

Giauque, Jeffrey Glen. *Grand Designs and Visions of Unity: The Atlantic Powers and the Reorganization of Western Europe, 1955–1963.* Chapel Hill: University of North Carolina Press, 2002.

Levy, Daniel, Max Pensky, and John Torpey. *Old Europe, New Europe, Core Europe: Transatlantic Relations after the Iraq War.* New York: Verso, 2005.

Moore, R. Laurence, and Maurizio Vaudagna. *The American Century in Europe.* Ithaca, NY: Cornell University Press, 2003.

Ninkovich, Frank, *The Wilsonian Century: U.S. Foreign Policy Since 1900,* Chicago: University of Chicago Press, 1999.

Ullman, Richard. *Securing Europe,* Princeton, NJ: Princeton University Press, 1991.

WHITE CITIZENS' COUNCILS

White Citizens' Councils were organizations founded in a number of towns, largely in the South, during the 1950s and 1960s to counter the civil rights movement and preserve traditional social and legal segregation between the races.

The first Citizens' Council was founded by a local farmer, Robert "Tut" Patterson, in Greenwood, Mississippi, in July 1954. The organization sought to preserve segregation in public schools in the wake of the May 1954 U.S. Supreme Court ruling in *Brown v. Board of Education.*

Unlike the Ku Klux Klan (KKK), a more violent group dominated by working-class whites, Citizens' Councils were generally made up of community leaders, who used legal and political means to preserve traditional race relations. Beginning with the first council in Greenwood, these organizations established a process of screening local candidates to verify that they opposed black voting rights and integration. The councils also coordinated economic boycotts of businesses that integrated their facilities.

By August 1955, the councils claimed an aggregate membership of 60,000, not only in the South; there were a total of 253 councils nationwide by mid-decade. In August 1956, the councils of thirty states joined together to establish the Citizens Councils of America (CCA), located first in Greenwood, Mississippi, and then in Jackson. The CCA's stated purpose was to maintain the "natural rights" of racial separation and the right of states, under the Constitution, to regulate public morals, education, health, marriage (such as barring interracial marriage), and public order (such as stopping civil rights demonstrations).

At its height, say political historians, the CCA was able to influence a few statewide elections, for instance, when it helped elect segregationist Ross Barnett to the governorship of Mississippi in 1960. Barnett would go on to fight James Meredith's efforts to integrate the University of Mississippi in 1962.

To counter their image as ignorant Southern racists, CCA members sought to demonstrate that the organization was mainstream and modern. Compared to the KKK, it was less coarse in its rhetoric and recruited more educated people as leaders and spokespersons. To its opponents, however, the CCA was known as the "uptown KKK," and its members—state representatives, bankers, attorneys, and other local elites—were unapologetic and clear in their expressions of white supremacy.

While separating itself from the KKK and deemphasizing violence, the councils persisted in intimidating and harassing African Americans and sympathetic whites through inflammatory speeches and pamphlets. Frequent accusations—standard among the anti-integrationist groups of the time—were that the National Association for the Advancement of Colored People (NAACP) and other mainstream civil rights organizations were Communist fronts and that most African Americans were essentially satisfied with the traditional racial order of the South.

Ultimately, the councils proved unable to deter the civil rights movement and, as African Americans gained influence in the 1960s and 1970s, elected officials shifted with the times or found themselves voted out of office. By the early 1960s, Citizens' Councils were losing membership to other anti-integration and anticommunist groups such as the John Birch Society. By the late 1970s, the CCA had almost disappeared from the political scene. Inactivity was not the same as a change of heart for former CCA leaders, however, and the movement underwent a resurgence in the mid-1980s, albeit under a new name.

In Atlanta, in 1985, Patterson and about two dozen supporters, including several former CCA organizers, used the earlier organization's mailing lists to establish the Council of Conservative Citizens (CCC). Patterson, now in his sixties, served as editor of the CCC's publication, *The Citizen Informer.* While reluctantly accepting the fact that integration was a permanent fixture in American society, the CCC embraced a number of conservative issues, including op-

position to immigration, gun control, and affirmative action. By the early 2000s, the CCC claimed about 15,000 members in twenty states; most were in the Deep South, especially Alabama, Georgia, and Mississippi. The new organization had far less clout than its predecessor, and all but far-right politicians shunned its endorsements.

John Barnhill

See also: *Brown v. Board of Education* (1954); Civil Rights Movement, Through 1965; National Association for the Advancement of Colored People; White Supremacist Groups.

Bibliography

McMillen, Neil R. *The Citizens' Council: Organized Resistance to the Second Reconstruction, 1954–1964.* Urbana: University of Illinois Press, 1971.

WHITE ETHNICS

White ethnics—a generic designation for Italians, Germans, Poles, Irish, and, to some extent, Jews in America—have played a vital, if controversial, role in the nation's postwar history. These communities have played an often-decisive part in the political trends of the era, particularly as the United States began its move to the right in the late 1960s.

At the same time, white ethnics have helped redefine such concepts as race, ethnicity, and rights in the postwar period, and their demands on the American state undoubtedly shaped the concept of governance in the period from 1945 through the early twenty-first century. Their presence has helped to reveal the limitations of assimilation in the United States while, at the same time, illustrating the inclusive tendencies of American culture.

Legacy of the New Deal

World War II marked a significant turning point for many white ethnics in the United States. On the home front, they discovered their political muscle, helping President Franklin D. Roosevelt win an unprecedented third term in 1940. Ethnic communities in such cities as Chicago, New York, Philadelphia, Detroit, and Boston became key constituents of the Democratic Party, as their place in Roosevelt's New Deal coalition became unquestioned. (In Irish South

Boston, for example, Roosevelt consistently received close to 80 percent of the ethnic vote).

As for the war effort itself, the presence of large numbers of white ethnics in the armed services helped solidify their status as true Americans. If, as many scholars conclude, the first half of the twentieth century featured an uncertainty surrounding the "whiteness" and civic fitness of white ethnics, the events of the 1940s put to rest the Anglo-American fear that such individuals lacked true commitment to the United States. In return for such acceptance, many white ethnics sought to "Americanize" themselves and their communities, believing that too much evidence of their ethnic heritage would only hinder their effort to assimilate further into the cultural mainstream.

Yet such developments had another series of effects on many white ethnics. A large part of Roosevelt's appeal to such individuals, particularly those in the middle and working classes, was his insistence on an active federal government that worked hard to protect the "legitimate rights" of all citizens. At the same time, white ethnics felt that their patriotic service in the armed forces further strengthened their claim on the benefits bestowed by the federal government. The programs associated with New Deal liberalism came to be seen as rightful entitlements by many white ethnics who believed that the federal government—as well as its local representatives—owed them for the support they gave the Democratic Party.

Thus, entering the postwar era, two aspects of white ethnic identity became clear: A claim to "legitimate rights" and a sense of entitlement toward the federal government. As white ethnics began to participate more in national politics, many grew to feel that such protection was something they deserved. As one white working-class ethnic from Chicago expressed it, "I gave the best part of my life to the American country, and I spent every cent I made here. They owe it to me to take care of me."

Racial Backlash

Such an insistence could often take a darker turn, as evidenced by the words of one white ethnic resident of Detroit in 1945: "Our boys are fighting in Europe, Asia, and Africa to keep those people off our soil. If [and] when these boys return they should become refugees who have to give up their homes because their own neighborhood with the help of city fathers had been invade[d] and occupied by the Africans, it would be a shame which our city fathers could not outlive."

This attitude, say many historians, reflected a continued belief among white ethnics that they had a right to live among their own and that the government should protect this right. The large-scale migration of African Americans to Northern ethnic communities during World War II and its immediate aftermath played a major role in the evolution of white ethnic identity. In Detroit, for example, the black population skyrocketed from 120,066 to 482,229 between 1930 and 1960, growing from 7.7 percent of the city's population to 28.9 percent. Other cities known for their preponderance of white ethnics underwent similar population shifts.

The large-scale infusion of African Americans into their communities led many white ethnics to begin to define themselves fully as "white," rather than as members of a particular ethnic group. Faced with dramatic changes in the racial composition of their neighborhoods, such white ethnics came to stress what historian Thomas J. Sugrue termed their "common bond of whiteness."

Ethnicity had long been a divisive factor in many Northern communities because ethnic groups often struggled over turf and political influence. By the mid-1950s, however, such ethnic hostility had dissipated (though it never entirely disappeared), when many aspects of ethnic life came to be understood in racial terms. The African American "invasion" provided a common enemy for white ethnics, and Italians joined Poles and Germans in homeowners' associations and other community groups that sprang up in numerous Northern cities to help combat the process of integration.

Yet even as these ethnic groups met under the banner of whiteness, they did not entirely give up their ownership of ethnicity. Instead, the concept of ethnicity became a means of their addressing both federal and local governments as a specific group not afforded all of the rights and privileges of other white Americans. To many white ethnics, housing projects and economic assistance programs designed particularly for the growing African American population overlooked the fact that their own hold on financial stability was tenuous at best. (From 1951 to 1953, for example, 4,185 workers lost their jobs to automation in Detroit-area Ford plants; there were similar tales of job insecurity in other cities.) African Americans,

Hardhats and the Vietnam War

"Hardhats," a colloquial term used to refer to construction workers, is derived from the protective headgear they wear on the job. In the late 1960s and early 1970s, however, the phrase became shorthand for white, working-class males who were angry at the protest movements of the era. In May 1970, hundreds of hardhats in New York City showed their support for President Richard M. Nixon and the war in Vietnam by attacking an antiwar protest.

The incident was a manifestation of the anger and resentment felt by lower- and middle-class Americans, mostly white and male, toward the preferential treatment they felt was being given to protesting college students, minorities, and the poor. Their actions also revealed the extent to which the war in Vietnam had divided Americans, especially along class lines. Solidarity among this group, historians have noted, was also the product of skillful political manipulation by the Nixon Administration.

Protests against the war in Vietnam, racial discrimination, and the plight of the poor had been part of the American landscape throughout the 1960s, peaking in May 1970, when Nixon announced that U.S. forces had invaded Cambodia, a neighbor of South Vietnam that had tried to remain neutral in the war. At one protest on the campus of Kent State University in Ohio, four youths were shot dead by National Guardsmen, fueling more student protests. It was in the midst of these protests that the hardhats emerged on the political landscape.

While the majority of national media attention was fixed on the drama being played out on college campuses and in inner cities, little attention was paid to what was going on elsewhere. Years of government spending on the war and on programs to help the poor and minorities had left many white working-class and middle-class suburbanites wondering what was being done for them. By the late 1960s, earning power had declined in the face of growing inflation, and a faltering economy was putting many out of work.

In addition, the behavior of college students, who seemed to occupy a position of privilege in the view of their working-class counterparts, seemed especially galling. A *Newsweek* magazine poll taken in 1969 showed that 84 percent of the respondents believed campus protestors were being treated too leniently by the police. The Nixon Administration took advantage of this mood to mobilize political support among white working-class and middle-class suburbanites, while simultaneously bolstering support for its policies.

Shortly after the Kent State shootings, the White House claimed that the incident was the fault of the demonstrators and not the National Guardsmen who had opened fire. New York City Mayor John Lindsay denounced the White House statement, pointing to the killings as proof that "the country is virtually on the edge of spiritual, and perhaps even a physical, breakdown."

Nixon Administration officials responded by urging New York construction workers to demonstrate in support of the president and against Lindsay and the antiwar protestors. On May 8, 1970, construction workers attacked antiwar demonstrators outside New York's City Hall, while police stood by. Several antiwar protesters were injured.

Two weeks later, thousands of union workers staged a parade through Manhattan, carrying American flags, singing patriotic songs, and denouncing the antiwar movement. The demonstration prompted unions in cities across the United States to stage marches of their own in support of the war.

Later, President Nixon met with union leaders, who presented him with his own hardhat. Symbolism aside, Nixon had tapped into the anti-antiwar protest sentiment typified by the hardhats and would use that sentiment in an effort to realign American politics to his advantage.

John Morello

argued many white ethnics, were not the only group that deserved to have their rights protected.

Such a reality led, in the 1960s, to what can best be described as a "crisis of assimilation" among white ethnics. Many in the industrial North began to believe that the Democratic Party they had supported so devoutly was beginning to forget them and that it seemed uninterested in their concerns.

To many white ethnics, African Americans were benefiting unjustly from Democratic housing programs, busing strategies, and economic assistance programs. The state was not living up to its end of the bargain, they said. White ethnics had "played by the rules" and had attempted to assimilate into American culture, but now their rights no longer seemed to matter.

In response to this circumstance, real or perceived, many white ethnics borrowed a page from black protesters and began to press for their rights as a distinct interest group. In this time of burgeoning political pluralism, the concept of ethnicity continued its comeback, this time, as a means for white ethnics to make the political process speak to their specific concerns.

At the same time, the renewed interest in ethnicity also was used to draw a critical distinction between these two groups—i.e., to differentiate between white ethnics and the putatively undeserving African Americans. Describing this turn of events, historian Thomas C. Holt characterized the view as "Race is something blacks have; ethnicity belongs to whites."

White Ethnic Politics

Politicians such as Republican George Wallace, the segregationist governor of Alabama, took notice of the emergence of this "white backlash" and crafted political campaigns that spoke to the anger of white ethnics. Wallace himself garnered substantial votes in his presidential campaigns of 1964, 1968, and 1972 in the ethnic neighborhoods of New York, Pennsylvania, Wisconsin, Michigan, and Ohio.

In a 1972 speech to Serbs and Poles at Serbian Hall in Milwaukee, Wallace explained how Democrats were not only forgetting white ethnics, but they were actively conspiring against them. To a thunderous round of approval, Wallace told his ethnic audience that the Civil Rights Act of 1964 would eliminate job security, control over neighborhood school systems, and the right of homeowners to sell their homes to whomever they choose. Wallace knew

his audience well, since all of these issues were near and dear to the hearts of white ethnics.

Other politicians, particularly Republicans, quickly followed Wallace's example. President Richard M. Nixon undoubtedly learned much from Wallace, as his references to "Middle America" and the "Silent Majority" seemed directed at white ethnics. One also sees this in Nixon's opposition to "forced" integration, a stance that endeared him to many white ethnics, particularly those Irish in Boston who were struggling against a 1974 court-ordered busing plan.

Liberal Democrats such as Senator Edward Kennedy and Congressman Thomas ("Tip") P. O'Neill, Jr., both of Massachusetts, supported the busing plan, which led some Irish to continue to move away from the party. By 1976, it was clear that, at least in Irish South Boston, the age of Democratic Party dominance was over. In that year's presidential election, the majority of the two Irish Catholic wards of Boston (6 and 7) voted Republican, with percentages of 55.4 and 50.9, respectively.

Similar concerns over busing in the Canarsie neighborhood of New York City also led to a turn away from the Democrats among white ethnics. In New York in 1968, all of Nixon's top eighteen New York assembly districts were largely Catholic in makeup. Whereas in 1960, New York City's German, Irish, and Italian Catholics had favored John F. Kennedy by an approximately 5–4 ratio, in 1968, they appeared to have preferred Nixon to Humphrey by a ratio of at least 5–3.

Nixon clearly understood the importance of white ethnics in his victories, and his support for the Ethnic Heritage Act of 1973 endeared him to even more ethnic communities. Through this act, the state, at least symbolically, finally recognized the "rights" of white ethnics; it even gave them grants for the sponsorship of ethnic festivals, ethnic history projects, and ethnic associations.

The "New Ethnicity"

Such recognition contributed greatly to the ethnic revival—or "new ethnicity"—of the 1970s. Once again, this revival had its roots in the 1960s. Many whites, in response to the "Black is Beautiful" rhetoric of the Black Power movement, began to see the beauty and worth in their own heritage, particularly in comparison to the perceived inauthentic values of mainstream Anglo-Saxon culture.

Scholar Michael Novak, a leading voice of this new ethnicity, saw such values as repressed, hyperrational, and soulless, and he blamed the "WASP elite" for both the domestic and international traumas of the previous decade. Speaking of this power elite (which increasingly became synonymous with those of the left of the political spectrum), Novak wrote: "What price is exacted by America when into its maw it sucks other cultures of the world and processes them? What do people have to lose before they can qualify as true Americans?" In the face of such questions, many white ethnics began to rediscover the traditions and histories of their ancestors.

This newfound renaissance of ethnicity had few immediate political or class implications. The effects instead were predominantly cultural. The popularity of Novak's *The Rise of the Unmeltable Ethnics* (1973), the *Godfather* movies, and ethnic cuisine, as well as the concept of the ethnic shopper in corporate marketing strategies, all spoke to the growing cultural influence of white ethnics in the United States.

In many ways, the ethnic revival of the 1970s can be read not as a rejection of mainstream American culture but as a celebration of the fact that such a culture now seemed to recognize the importance of such white ethnics. The previously impenetrable Anglo-Saxon mainstream culture now provided a space for the expression of ethnic identity and went so far as to see such an identity as undeniably "American."

Nothing illustrates this better than the fact that Ronald Reagan began his second presidential campaign not in the United States, but in a small Irish village called Ballyporeen. Throughout the 1984 campaign, Reagan stressed his ethnic roots and made frequent public appearances with such ethnic luminaries as Frank Sinatra. Yet Reagan offered no specific programs for white ethnics (many of whom were losing their jobs in the face of massive deindustrialization). He addressed all of these diverse groups simply as "Americans," and white ethics seemingly welcomed this spirit of inclusion.

On November 6, 1984, Democratic presidential candidate and former Vice President Walter Mondale, lost to Republican candidate Ronald Reagan by the margin of 59.2 percent to 40.8 percent. Ethnic whites in traditionally Democratic areas, such as southwest Chicago, northeast Philadelphia, and Cleveland all voted for Reagan over Mondale by a 2–1 margin. Across the country, Reagan carried every major European immigrant group, except for the Jewish community, by commanding majorities.

Just as it appeared that the white ethnic had reached the peak of its influence, immigration trends dramatically altered the American landscape. As recently as 1960, Europeans accounted for more than two-thirds of all new arrivals. By 1985, Europe's share had shrunk to just one-ninth. The top ten countries for new immigrants were all in Latin America and Asia. The liberalizing effects of the Immigration and Naturalization Act of 1965, originally intended to help Europeans reunite with their families in America, had created the environment for a new age of immigration.

Attention previously paid to white ethnics now focused on the potential influence of these new immigrant groups on American culture. By the 1990s, white ethnics found themselves struggling to find a voice in the growing chorus of "multiculturalism." This theory, in its rejection of "melting pot" metaphors and policies of assimilation in favor of celebrating the diverse cultures of all racial and ethnic groups, undoubtedly (and a bit ironically) drew from the rhetoric surrounding the ethnic revival of the 1970s.

Michael Carriere

See also: Blue-Collar Workers; Democratic Party; Immigration; Republican Party.

Bibliography

Chafe, William H. *The Unfinished Journey: America Since World War II.* New York: Oxford University Press, 1999.

Fraser, Steve, and Gary Gerstle, eds. *The Rise and Fall of the New Deal Order: 1930–1980.* Princeton, NJ: Princeton University Press, 1989.

Jacobson, Matthew Frye. *Whiteness of a Different Color: European Immigrants and the Alchemy of Race.* Cambridge, MA: Harvard University Press, 1998.

Moss, George Donelson. *Vietnam: An American Ordeal.* 4th ed. Upper Saddle River, NJ: Prentice Hall, 2002.

Novak, Michael. *The Rise of the Unmeltable Ethnics.* New York: Macmillan, 1971.

Steinberg, Stephen. *The Ethnic Myth: Race, Ethnicity, and Class in America.* Boston: Beacon, 1989.

WHITE SUPREMACIST GROUPS

In 1944, thirty leading American right wing extremists were put on trial by the federal government for sedition. In the same year, the national Ku Klux Klan (KKK) organization disbanded because of conflict with the Internal Revenue Service. Despite these difficulties, white supremacism made a surprisingly successful return in the postwar period. "White power" groups, buoyed by desegregation, social disaffection, and technological developments, have continued to spread their message of racial animosity. While a return to the mass appeal experienced by the KKK in the 1920s seems unlikely, groups of white nationalists (the name preferred by most in the movement) appear to be a permanent fixture on the fringe of American politics.

The first successful white nationalist group in the postwar period was James Madole's National Renaissance Party (NRP), established in 1949 in the New York City area. Madole's group, which probably never numbered more than 100 members, promoted National Socialism (including prominent usage of swastikas) and advocated complete racial segregation. The NRP continued to operate until Madole's death in 1978, but the party had been marginalized since the 1950s due to allegations that many members were government informants, Jewish "spies," or homosexuals. Several leading white supremacists began their careers in the NRP, including Eustace Mullins, a prolific author of white supremacy books, and Matt Koehl, the head of the National Socialist White People's Party, or the American Nazi party, in the 1970s.

In 1955, segregationist lawyer J. B. Stoner and Edward Fields, an anti-Semitic chiropractor, created the Georgia-based National States Rights Party (NSRP). The NSRP advocated total geographical separation of the races and anti-Semitism, but it differed from many groups on the far right by defending federal social welfare programs that benefit working-class Americans. Although Fields was the NSRP's chief writer and theoretician, Stoner was the party's public face (running for a variety of state offices during the 1960s and 1970s). The NSRP was the largest white nationalist group of the postwar period, with a peak membership of 2,000–3,000 and more than 10,000 subscribers to its magazine, *The Thunderbolt*. The group disbanded in 1984 after Stoner's conviction as a conspirator in a 1958 Birmingham church bombing.

Ku Klux Klan

The rise of the civil rights movement and early desegregation attempts helped propel the creation of several new KKK organizations in the mid-1950s. Unlike the "second" Klan of the 1920s, the Klan of the 1950s was actually a multitude of rival organiza-

tions that steadfastly refused either to recognize each other or refrain from internal bickering. The largest of the national Klan groups were the U.S. Klans, the National Knights of the Ku Klux Klan, the United Klans of America, and Robert Shelton's Alabama Knights of the Ku Klux Klan. Despite the welter of competing organizations, all of these groups exhibited the traditional KKK hatred of blacks, Jews, and Catholics.

The violent attacks on civil rights workers by Klan units during the late 1950s and early 1960s encouraged a growth in support among segregationist-minded Southerners, but a series of investigations by the House Committee on Un-American Activities in 1965–1966, concerted anti-Klan activity by the Federal Bureau of Investigation's (FBI's) Counterintelligence Program (COINTELPRO), and the futility of the antidesegregation campaign spelled disaster for the Klans.

Membership dropped precipitously in the early 1970s, and many Klan groups folded. Numerous small groups survived, but often only as personal organizations based around charismatic leaders such as Louis Beam, the author of anti-Semitic books denying the Holocaust, and David Duke, a former Louisiana legislator.

American Nazi Party

The other significant white supremacist group to emerge during the 1950s was George Lincoln Rockwell's American Nazi Party (ANP). With a hardcore following of no more than 100, Rockwell utilized marketing techniques and publicity stunts to achieve national fame for himself and the ANP, and it served as a model for countless later neo-Nazi organizations. During the early 1960s, Rockwell engaged in widely publicized speaking tours of American university campuses, traveled throughout the South in the "Hate Bus," and, thanks to the ANP's base in Arlington, Virginia, led almost weekly picketing of the White House.

In 1966, Rockwell changed the organization's name to the National Socialist White People's Party (NSWPP). In August 1967, Rockwell was assassinated by former ANP member John Patler, and former NRP and NSRP member Matt Koehl took over the organization. Koehl's leadership was frequently challenged in bitter internecine squabbles. NSWPP leaders left the group to found, among other organizations, the White Party of America, the new

American Nazi Party, and the National White People's Party. Rocked by continued defections and government scrutiny, Koehl changed the group's name to the New Order in 1982 and, two years later, relocated his dwindling band of followers to New Berlin, Wisconsin.

The most significant of the NSWPP splinter groups was the National Socialist Party of America (NSPA), established by Frank Collin in 1970. The NSPA gained national attention with its 1977 attempt to hold a rally in the predominantly Jewish town of Skokie, Illinois, and a 1979 shootout in Greensboro, South Carolina, between Communist Workers Party demonstrators and a combined group of KKK and NSPA members that left five of the Communists dead. The group fell apart after it was discovered that Collin's father was Jewish and that his successor was an FBI informant.

Nontraditional and Christian Identity Groups

The 1980s witnessed the growth of a variety of nontraditional neo-Nazi organizations. These groups diverged from the Rockwell-style aping of Nazi Germany and propounded anti-Semitic white nationalism under the guise of Christian Identity religions or decentralized localism, spreading their ideas through rock music and the Internet. These new-style groups also exhibited a higher level of conspiracy theory and paranoia in their rhetoric, which often revolved around the machinations of the Zionist Occupational Government (ZOG). While struggle for control of the movement continued, these newer groups often reached out to form bonds with the like-minded.

Christian Identity groups extol a belief system that posits that whites are the true children of Israel, that Jesus was a white man descended from the same line that produced the Germanic and Scandinavian peoples, and that Jews are products of a pre-Adamic, Satanic "seed line."

The leading Christian Identity group is Richard Girnt Butler's Aryan Nations, based in Hayden Lake, Idaho. The group has about 200 active members and hosts the annual World Aryan Conference at its compound. Frequent guests at the Aryan Nations headquarters include members of the National Alliance (a West Virginia group founded by William Pierce, author of *The Turner Diaries*, 1978), violence-prone skinheads (often followers of Tom Metzger's White

Aryan Resistance), and members of the Posse Comitatus (a militia-style organization that recognizes no legal entity above the county sheriff).

Conclusion

White nationalist groups have continued to survive and attract new followers by embracing developing technologies. Home computers enable them to print vast quantities of literature quickly and inexpensively, and compact-disk-burning systems allow for the easy distribution of "hate rock" (typified by the products of Detroit's Resistance Records).

They also quickly latched upon the Internet as a method of spreading their messages. Despite the small number of avowed white nationalists, cyberspace is littered with Web sites such as Stormfront, the Nizkor Project, and the Aryan News Agency. With the deaths of leaders such as Pierce and Butler in 2002 and 2003, respectively, the World Wide Web may prove to be the instrument that keeps this isolated fringe of American society alive.

Scott M. Beekman

See also: Birmingham Church Bombing; Civil Rights Movement, Through 1965; Greensboro Massacre; Little Rock School Desegregation Crisis; Terrorism, Domestic; Till (Emmett) Lynching; White Citizens' Councils.

Bibliography

Barkun, Michael, *Religion and the Racist Right: The Origins of the Christian Identity Movement.* Chapel Hill: University of North Carolina Press, 1994.

George, John, and Laird Wilcox. *American Extremists: Militias, Supremacists, Klansmen, Communists, and Others.* Amherst, NY: Prometheus, 1996.

Simonelli, Frederick J. *American Fuehrer: George Lincoln Rockwell and the American Nazi Party.* Champaign: University of Illinois Press, 1999.

WHITE-COLLAR WORKERS

The fortunes of white-collar workers in post–World War II America have undergone dramatic changes as the larger corporate economy, for which the vast majority of them work, has experienced major structural changes of its own.

Many sociologists and economists speak of a "golden age" of the white-collar worker—from the end of the war to the late 1970s—when a booming corporate sector offered expanding employment opportunities, job security, an array of benefits, and rising salaries. Since then, however, recession, corporate consolidation, and global competition have combined to squeeze the white-collar worker, limiting opportunities, job security, and benefits while forcing employees to put in longer hours for less inflation-adjusted pay.

Late 1940s to Early 1970s: Golden Age

White-collar workers—the term is derived from the button-down shirts traditionally worn by professionals and managers—constitute a wide range of professions. They include professionals such as doctors, lawyers, and teachers, as well as administrative and clerical employees; some economists also include management in the ranks of white-collar workers. There are great variations in pay in the ranks of white-collar professionals: Doctors are likely to earn more than teachers, for example, and managers can earn salaries exponentially higher than those of secretaries. What differentiates white-collar from blue-collar workers is that the former do not perform manual labor and are more likely to be salaried employees, as opposed to hourly wage workers.

The 1944 G.I. Bill was a critical catalyst for the growth of the white-collar sector in the postwar American work force. By providing massive grants and loans to veterans, the program helped create a vast pool of college graduates who could fill the ranks of corporate America, as it expanded to meet the postwar economic boom. The federal government committed itself in other ways to aiding corporate America grow, usually as an adjunct to Cold War military spending. Spending on research and development, for example, spurred the growth of a high-tech industry that became a leading employer of white-collar employees.

In the first few years after World War II, corporate America offered job security to a generation of employees, who had been scarred by the Depression and war. "In the immediate postwar years," wrote journalist William H. Whyte, author of the most influential book on American white-collar workers of the time, *The Organization Man* (1956), "college seniors seemed almost psychotic on the subject of a depression, and when they explained a preference for the big corporation, they did so largely on the grounds of security."

Indeed, it was not just a booming economy that promised white-collar workers job security; long-term employment was also part of the emerging corporate ethos of the 1950s and 1960s. As one General Electric executive noted in *Management Record*, a major business publication of the period, "Guarantees of employment cannot be made by businesses whose markets are as unpredictable as General Electric's. Nevertheless, we recognize the desire of employees for job continuity, and we have long striven to provide the greatest measure practicable. . . . Maximizing employment security is a prime company goal."

Many of corporate America's managers of the 1950s and 1960s held to this notion—that offering job security led to greater employee loyalty and thus higher productivity, all benefiting the bottom line. But security from layoffs was only half of the equation: Security also meant freedom from worry, especially with regard to health emergencies and money for retirement.

Part of the early postwar boom in fringe benefits such as health care and pensions was a direct function of the war. During the early 1940s, with employment on the home front tight and wage freezes in effect, companies were forced to offer these fringe benefits in order to recruit new employees. Once offered, the programs were hard to cancel once the war was over, especially as general economic prosperity was filling corporate coffers.

By 1970, most corporations in America were offering their employees sick leave, vacation time, and health care benefits; indeed, benefits rose an average of 6 percent annually through the 1960s and early 1970s. Of the health care plans offered by corporate America in 1970, more than 60 percent required no monetary contribution whatsoever from the employee.

As for retirement, the number of corporations offering pension plans rose from 7,000 in 1945 to more than 11,000 by 1950. In the latter year, Ford Motor Company extended its pension plan for unionized blue-collar workers to cover nonunionized white-collar workers. By 1970, roughly 25 million Americans were covered by $115 billion in pension funds.

Pay went up, too. In inflation-adjusted terms, salaried employees saw their annual compensation more than triple between 1945 and 1970, from roughly $2,000 to about $7,600. And it was relatively equally distributed. During the 1950s, the ratio of chief executive officer compensation to average worker compensation was about 50:1; by the early, 1970s, the ratio had fallen to about 35:1, a postwar low. Meanwhile, work hours shrank, and the five-day, forty-hour workweek became the norm.

Late 1970s to Early 2000s: Decline and Retrenchment

The 1970s were a difficult time for the American economy. During the 1960s, the federal government had tried to expand social welfare programs, even as it paid for an expensive war in Vietnam. Rather than raise taxes, the government borrowed; by pumping more money into the economy and driving up interest rates through its borrowing, it contributed to an inflationary cycle that would last through the deep recession of the early 1980s.

Adding to the inflationary cycle were energy costs. As America became more dependent on foreign oil, it made itself more vulnerable to price hikes by foreign suppliers and disturbances in the oil-rich Middle East. Twice during the 1970s, forces combined to raise oil prices. As a crucial component of the cost of virtually every service and product, rising energy prices set off general inflation throughout the economy.

This situation was exacerbated by increased foreign competition—as Europe and Japan finally caught up with American manufacturing prowess—and the stagnating productivity of American workers. Profit margins in corporate America leveled off, declined and, in some cases, disappeared altogether.

Still, many big businesses were forced to maintain generous wage and benefit packages to attract trained labor. Strong unions for blue-collar workers had established a floor beneath which white-collar workers could not fall as well. In addition, most corporations remained in the hands of the same executives who had managed them during the 1950s and 1960s, and so they were committed to keeping salaries and benefits generous. But falling profit margins could not be ignored, and for the first time in postwar American history, the corporate economy began to shed large numbers of workers to cut costs. Most of the burden fell on the blue-collar work force, because the vast ranks of clerical and middle-management employees were deemed necessary to run companies in an age of relatively uncomputerized operations.

The great shift in fortune for white-collar employees began in the 1980s, a by-product of a wave of corporate mergers, computerization, and a weakening union movement. Ironically, it was the growth of large corporate pension funds that helped trigger the corporate mergers that led to so many layoffs.

By the early 1980s, a number of corporate executives, as well as Wall Street arbitrageurs (those who arrange corporate buyouts and mergers), recognized that many large businesses were performing poorly but still rich in assets, mostly in the form of pension funds. As the decade proceeded, these executives and arbitrageurs put together deals—often based on the issuance of high-risk, high-yield bonds (so-called junk bonds)—to buy out bigger and bigger companies. Having made these buyouts, the acquiring companies found themselves deeply in debt, which they paid off by raiding corporate pension funds and lowering costs by laying off employees.

Until that time, mass layoffs in American business had largely been confined to the blue-collar ranks. Now, they reached up into middle management. From 1988 to 1991, more than 1 million middle managers were downsized annually. Using computer technology to automate ordinary clerical and mid-level management work allowed heavily indebted corporations to shed large numbers of white-collar workers.

Defenders of the practice said that U.S. corporations were spending too much on the salaries of white-collar workers, especially as compared to foreign competitors. Whereas white-collar salaries represented 26.6 percent of manufacturing costs in the United States during the late 1980s, the corresponding figure was 21.6 percent in Germany and just 17.9 in Japan.

Job security was not the only aspect of white-collar employment to be affected by the recession and mergers of the 1970s, 1980s, and early 1990s. A weakening union movement was another consequence of these economic trends, as well as a contributing factor to the problems faced by white-collar workers. After peaking at 37 percent of the U.S. work force in 1960, private sector union membership had fallen to less than 10 percent by the early 2000s. Although few white-collar employees were part of the labor movement, union-negotiated contracts provided a kind of protection: Pay and benefit packages won by unions set a floor beneath which white-collar workers' compensation rarely fell.

The result of these forces was that the average salary for white-collar workers stagnated and even declined slightly between the early 1970s and 2000. In 1973, the last year before the major economic shocks of the 1970s, a college graduate could expect to earn $16,000 in the first year of employment (in 2000 inflation-adjusted dollars); by 2000, the figure had declined to $15,000.

Benefits were cut as well. Whereas companies paid roughly two-thirds of pension costs during the late 1970s—usually in the form of defined benefits (a guaranteed amount paid upon retirement)—the figure had fallen to under 40 percent by the early 2000s—now usually in the form of defined-contribution benefits (a specified amount paid in each salary period). Health care benefits were also declining. As late as 1986, 60 percent of major U.S. corporations were still offering full medical coverage, with no employee contributions; ten years later, the figure had fallen to just 10 percent, even as health care costs nationwide doubled from roughly $700 billion in 1985 to about $1 trillion by 1995 (in 1995 inflation-adjusted dollars).

Other than a temporary growth spurt in white-collar hiring and pay during the tech-fueled boom economy of the late 1990s, the fortunes of white-collar workers have continued to decline in both relative and absolute terms. With each recession, more white-collar workers have been laid off, and with each recovery period, fewer employees have been rehired. In the recession months of September 2001 through January 2002, for example, corporations laid off nearly 1 million employees, many of them white collar; during the recovery year of 2003, the country shed 1.5 million jobs, many of them in white-collar fields.

Increasingly, many of the downsized white-collar jobs are going overseas. Before the rise of the Internet and the dramatic drop in telecommunications costs during the 1990s, most outsourcing of jobs occurred in the blue-collar sector—assembly work that could be done cheaper in countries such as Mexico and, increasingly, China. But in the early 2000s, skilled white-collar American labor was being outsourced as well—many of the jobs going to developing-world countries, where large numbers of citizens speak English and are relatively well educated. Computer software and consumer service jobs were being outsourced to India—where a software programmer makes about $10,000 annually, versus the $66,000 average in the United States—while jobs filling out paperwork and forms were sent to English-speaking Caribbean nations. And the trend shows no sign of stopping: The U.S. Department of Labor estimates that nearly 1.7 million white-collar jobs will be outsourced in the next fifteen years, including nearly half a million in the computer industry alone.

Meanwhile, work hours have continued to increase. By the early 2000s, an estimated 20 million white-collar workers were putting in more than fifty hours a week. Technology was contributing to the stress, with cell phones and e-mail making it possible—and, increasingly, necessary—for white-collar workers to take their jobs home or on vacation. A 2005 survey found that more than 8 million American white-collar workers checked in with their companies during off hours.

Moreover, in relative terms, white-collar compensation was declining in relation to executive pay. In the early 2000s, economists estimated that the average chief executive officer's total compensation was roughly 300 times that of the average clerical employee and 100 times that of the average mid-level manager.

James Ciment

See also: Advertising; Banking and Credit; Blue-Collar Workers; Computers; Crime, Property; Pensions, Private; Service-Sector Workers; Unemployment; Wall Street; Women and Work.

Bibliography

Ehrenreich, Barbara. *Bait and Switch: The (Futile) Pursuit of the American Dream.* New York: Metropolitan, 2005.

Fraser, Jill Andresky. *White-Collar Sweatshop: The Deterioration of Work and Its Rewards in Corporate America.* New York: W.W. Norton, 2001.

McColloch, Mark. *White-Collar Workers in Transition: The Boom Years, 1940–1970.* Westport, CT: Greenwood, 1983.

Whyte, William H. *The Organization Man.* New York: Simon and Schuster, 1956.

WHITEWATER SCANDAL

Whitewater, the name of a real estate development in Arkansas, became the popular name for a scandal implicating President Bill Clinton and his wife, Hillary. A complicated series of allegedly illegal loans taken out by the Clintons and their business partners in the 1970s and 1980s were at the heart of the case.

Whitewater gained national notoriety after Clinton's Attorney General Janet Reno authorized a special prosecutor, Kenneth Starr, to investigate any financial wrongdoing by the Clintons. The investigation came to be regarded by many as a witch-hunt, especially after Starr expanded the investigation to look into charges that the president had lied under oath about an affair he had with a White House intern named Monica Lewinsky. Ultimately, Clinton was impeached by the House of Representatives on charges stemming from the investigation, but he was acquitted by the Senate.

Clinton had been elected governor of Arkansas for the first time in 1978. In that same year, the Clintons borrowed approximately $200,000 from the local Citizen's Bank to purchase a scenic parcel of land in Flippin, Arkansas. Without notifying Citizen's Bank, the Clintons and their longtime friends, James and Susan McDougal, borrowed an additional $20,000 from another bank to make a down payment. In 1979, the Clintons and the McDougals formed the Whitewater Development Company for real estate development, specifically to build vacation homes on the property. In 1981, Jim McDougal loaned $30,000 to Hillary Clinton to build a model house on a Whitewater lot.

The following year, McDougal, who would also serve as an economic adviser to Governor Clinton, purchased the local Madison Bank and Trust Company. The majority of the plots in the Whitewater development had still not been sold, leaving the McDougals and the Clintons with financial losses. Miscellaneous loans were taken from the bank to pay off interest on the loan, and funds were shifted between accounts, as the McDougals struggled to keep the mortgages from defaulting.

In 1984, federal regulators initiated proceedings to investigate the questionable business practices of Madison Bank. The regulators criticized Madison's speculative land deals, insider lending, and hefty commissions paid to the McDougals and others. The pressure increased as the questionable practices came to the attention of the national media and the Madison Bank was failing miserably. The next year, McDougal held a fundraising event at Madison Guaranty to collect donations for a $50,000 Clinton campaign debt. Investigators later determined that some of the money was improperly withdrawn from depositor funds.

Under pressure from government investigators, McDougal decided to hire the Rose Law Firm, where Hillary Clinton worked as a lawyer, to handle its problems. While dealing with the crisis, Mrs. Clinton and another Rose lawyer sought state regulatory approval for a recapitalization plan for Madison. Over the next few years, the Madison Bank collapsed financially because of too many bad outstanding loans. In 1986, federal regulators removed McDougal as bank president, citing improper practices, but he retained

ownership. Two years later, Mrs. Clinton reacted to the impending crisis by asking McDougal for power of attorney to sell off any remaining Whitewater lots and clear up bank obligations.

Madison Bank and Trust Company collapsed the following year after a series of bad loans and a change in government accounting procedures. The federal government shut it down and spent $60 million to bail it out. James McDougal was indicted on federal fraud charges related to his mismanagement of a Madison real estate subsidiary.

The scandal went national when, in 1992, Governor Clinton announced his candidacy for president. As a way to head off potential bad publicity, the Clinton campaign commissioned an investigation into the candidate's involvement in the Whitewater episode. The report claimed that the Clintons had lost a substantial amount of money, approximately $68,000 from the Whitewater episode. However, the federal Resolution Trust Corporation (RTC), investigating the causes of Madison Bank's failure, sent a referral to the Justice Department that named the Clintons as potential beneficiaries of illegal activities at Madison.

In November 1992, Clinton defeated President George H.W. Bush in the national election. In June 1993, Deputy White House Counsel Vincent Foster filed three years of delinquent tax returns related to the Clintons' Whitewater investment. The next month, Foster was found dead in a Washington, D.C., park, apparently having committed suicide. Federal investigators were not allowed access to Foster's law office immediately after the discovery of his body, though White House aides were, increasing speculation that aides had removed files from his office on the order of the Clintons. In September 1993, Treasury Department officials tipped off Clinton aides about the progress of the RTC investigation.

Meanwhile, the Clinton Administration had become increasingly concerned over Republican political attacks based on the Whitewater episode. In December 1993, the pressure for an investigation had reached such an intense level that the White House agreed to turn over Whitewater documents to the Justice Department, which had been preparing to subpoena them. Attorney General Janet Reno named New York lawyer and former U.S. attorney Robert B. Fiske, Jr., as a special counsel to investigate the Clintons' involvement in Whitewater. Immediately, Fiske announced his intention to delve into the possible associations between Foster's suicide and his intimate knowledge of the developing Whitewater scandal.

Wanting a full accounting of the Whitewater issue, the House of Representatives and the Senate called for the creation of an investigatory committee in the summer of 1994. The committee subpoenaed many of Clinton's closest friends and advisers. In total, twenty-nine officials in the Clinton Administration testified in front of the committee; all of the subpoenaed officials were cleared of any possible wrongdoing.

Meanwhile, Attorney General Reno appointed Starr, a former federal appeals court judge and U.S. solicitor who had worked in the Reagan and first Bush administrations, as the independent counsel to look into the Madison-Whitewater scandal. Starr immediately reissued subpoenas for documents, such as the Rose Law Firm billing records of Hillary Clinton.

Independent counsel Kenneth Starr, appointed to investigate charges against President Bill Clinton in the Whitewater affair, is sworn in before the House Judiciary Committee before testifying in November 1998. His report to Congress, widely criticized as overzealous, culminated in impeachment proceedings. *(Pool/Getty Images News)*

After a lengthy initial investigation, the Democratic majority on the Senate Banking Committee declared that no laws had been broken in the Whitewater matter.

Meanwhile, prosecutors were unable to link the Clintons to the malfeasance of Madison Bank and Whitewater. In April 1998, a new series of tax evasion and fraud charges was brought against long-time Clinton associate Webster Hubbell for trying to cover up Mrs. Clinton's work for Madison while working at the Rose Law Firm. By May 1998, Susan McDougal was indicted on charges of criminal contempt and obstruction. By November 1998, Starr had stated that he would not be pursuing impeachment against President Clinton for the Whitewater scandal, but his investigation continued.

In 1998, it came to light that Clinton had been having an affair with White House intern Lewinsky. At first, Clinton tried to cover up the affair and lied under oath to investigators. Starr, who had few limits placed on him by Attorney General Reno's original special prosecutor order, turned his attention to the affair. Eventually, the House impeached Clinton on charges relating to the Lewinsky affair, though he was acquitted by the Senate.

Whitewater, most experts agree, was a highly politicized scandal. For many Republicans, it was evidence of the supposedly sleazy ethics of Bill and Hillary Clinton. Some opponents of the Clintons even charged that the couple had ordered the murder of Vincent Foster to prevent him from exposing their illegal activities.

To the Clintons and their defenders, however, Whitewater was a minor scandal, if that, and politically exploited. Compared to the hundreds of billions lost in the national savings and loan scandal of the 1980s, the several hundred thousands lost by Madison was inconsequential. Besides, defenders pointed out, the Clintons had lost money on the deal, so where was the financial wrongdoing?

Supporters claimed Clinton was being targeted by Republicans and the political right in an effort to destroy his reputation, and the whole Whitewater investigation was part of what Hillary Clinton called "a vast right-wing conspiracy." Ultimately, the Clintons were never indicted for anything, and Clinton left office in 2001 with extremely high approval ratings.

Jaime Ramón Olivares

See also: Impeachment of President Clinton; Travelgate.

Bibliography

Gross, Martin. *The Great Whitewater Fiasco: An American Tale of Money, Power, and Politics.* New York: Ballantine, 1994.

McDougal, Jim. *Arkansas Mischief: The Birth of a National Scandal.* New York: Henry Holt, 1998.

Stewart, James B. *Blood Sport: The President and His Adversaries.* New York: Simon and Schuster, 1996.

WILDLIFE AND WILDERNESS

The destruction of wilderness areas and the decline of wildlife populations have concerned Americans for more than a century, but since the end of World War II, these concerns have grown to become one of the nation's hottest political issues. From the use of pesticides to the destruction of old-growth forests in the Pacific Northwest and the threat of oil development in the Arctic National Wildlife Refuge, environmental concerns have driven a great deal of U.S. public policy, particularly since the 1960s.

Americans since Henry David Thoreau in the 1840s have expressed environmental concerns, but it was not until the beginning of the twentieth century that the environment became an important public issue. Progressives such as Theodore Roosevelt and Gifford Pinchot, along with precursors to modern environmentalists like John Muir, turned to the government to protect the nation's natural resources around 1900. Laws controlling the hunting of game, the creation and expansion of the National Park Service protecting areas such as Yellowstone, Yosemite, and the Grand Canyon, and the creation of the national forest system under Pinchot's management were among the major achievements of the early conservation movement.

After 1920, however, environmental concerns took a back seat to other problems in American life. The New Deal administrators of the 1930s revived some conservation programs, but they had little interest in the issues of wilderness and wildlife. It was not until after World War II that wilderness and wildlife again became a major issue in American life.

Birth of the Modern Environmental Movement

Historians have usually viewed the immediate years after World War II as the nadir of the postwar environmental movement. The widespread use of harmful pesticides, testing of nuclear weapons in the American West, and aggressive programs to dam many of America's rivers superceded most environmental concerns during the early years of the Cold War. By the 1950s and early 1960s, however, new developments put the environmental movement back into the mainstream.

The first was the Echo Park controversy in the early 1950s. As part of the push to build dams on every river in the United States in order to increase electrical capacity and prevent flooding, the U.S. Bureau of Reclamation planned to construct a dam on the Green River in Dinosaur National Monument in a remote region on the Colorado-Utah border. The Bureau of Reclamation and its rival in dam building, the U.S. Army Corps of Engineers, had rarely faced any opposition to their projects in the past and were shocked when the Wilderness Society and other conservation organizations led a highly organized fight to save the unique wilderness area from being flooded by the proposed Echo Park Dam. Beginning in 1950, using tactics such as lobbying and direct mail, both of which would become staple strategies of the environmental movement, opponents of the project made the dam a public issue that would determine the future of the National Park System. By 1954, mail to Congress ran 80 to 1 against the dam. Congress was unable to pass a bill covering the project, and, by 1956, environmentalists and the Bureau of Reclamation had reached a compromise that killed Echo Park in exchange for allowing other dams.

The second major event was the publication of *Silent Spring* by Rachel Carson in 1962. Carson wrote of the disastrous impact of pesticides, particularly DDT (dichloro diphenyl trichloroethane), upon wildlife. The book became an instant best-seller and woke up large sections of the American public to the everyday dangers they and their environment faced from pesticides. The book led to the banning of DDT in the United States in 1972 and, perhaps more importantly, brought knowledge of environmental problems into the cities and suburbs. Millions of people became interested in taking on these issues.

The final major event that galvanized the environmental community during the early decades of the Cold War was passage of the Wilderness Act of 1964. The legislation set aside more than 7 million acres of federal land as permanent wilderness. Along with the Echo Park campaign, the Wilderness Act marked a major transition in the environmental movement from conservation to preservation. Little of the land protected by the Wilderness Act had important resources that needed to be conserved for later use. Rather, environmentalists argued that land deserved protection simply for its intrinsic beauty. Echo Park, the high reaches of the Rocky Mountains, and the deserts of the Southwest, they contended, all deserved permanent protection so that Americans could enjoy their natural features.

By the late 1960s, two streams of environmental concern fused to create the modern environmental movement. One, represented by the Wilderness Act and the Echo Dam controversy, focused on preserving open spaces. The other, marked by the publication of *Silent Spring* and increasing pollution in developed areas, centered on cleaning up and preventing further man-made messes. Together, the two concerns created a powerful new movement in American society.

The first large-scale, public manifestation of this new movement occurred on April 22, 1970, the initial Earth Day. Earth Day became an annual observance, dedicated to environmental issues from recycling and pollution control to opposing nuclear energy and protection of endangered species. Earth Day was designed to allow Americans to express their concerns about the environment in nonconfrontational ways, reflecting the heavily middle-class character of the movement. Environmentalism became a community whose mainstream appealed strongly to middle-class optimism to change problems from within the existing political and economic system. All Americans could make a difference through recycling and picking up litter, and virtually everyone could agree that preserving animals such as elk, bear, and moose in places such as Yellowstone National Park was desirable.

The widespread support for environmental legislation manifested itself in the early 1970s with the creation of the Environmental Protection Agency (EPA) in 1970 and the passage of the Endangered Species Conservation Act of 1973, both signed into law by President Richard M. Nixon. The EPA created the first federal agency dedicated to protecting the environment. The agency became particularly effective in protecting water supplies, regulating pollution, and advising the public of environmental hazards. In particular, the EPA took a proactive approach to the Love Canal crisis in the late 1970s, advising residents of this heavily polluted neighborhood in Niagara Falls, New York, to evacuate, even before the city officially recognized the problem.

Endangered Species

The Endangered Species Act of 1973 protected individual species by limiting or banning economic activity or development in the habitat necessary for those species to survive. Tremendously popular at its passage, it soon came under attack from Americans concerned that such laws served to undermine the nation's economic power at a time when the economic growth that fueled the postwar boom came screeching to a stop.

Environmentalists and their opponents soon battled over the Endangered Species Act, when University of Tennessee zoology professor David Etnier discovered a tiny fish called the snail darter in the Little Tennessee River near the planned Tellico Dam project in 1973. Environmentalists took the government to court, charging it with violating the Endangered Species Act, because the Tellico project would destroy the habitat of the snail darter. Proponents of the dam, including powerful government agencies such as the Tennessee Valley Authority, eventually won the battle in court in 1978. The snail darter's Little Tennessee River habitat became a large lake, but other specimens were later found in smaller streams in the southeast.

When the Endangered Species Act came up for renewal in 1978, Congress weakened it and added economic provisions to it making it more difficult to list a species as endangered. This would not end the controversy over the Endangered Species Act, however, as seen in the 1980s and 1990s with the so-called spotted owl controversy in the Pacific Northwest.

Although President Jimmy Carter signed the bill allowing for the construction of the Tellico Dam, he did support environmental causes and worked to pass environmental legislation when he could. Wide-ranging environmental legislation tailed off after the economic crisis of 1973, but support remained strong for bills that did not seem to threaten economic interests. Thus, near the end of his term, Carter signed the Alaska National Interest Lands Conservation Act of 1980, which protected approximately 32 million acres of Alaska wilderness.

The protection of the Alaska lands may be the height of aesthetic environmentalism. The vast majority of this land was so remote as to be inaccessible for almost all Americans. Yet, outside of Alaska, the bill had strong support from people who felt that the nation had a duty to protect its wild places, even if they would never enjoy them personally.

Spotted Owl Controversy

The spotted owl controversy raged throughout the Pacific Northwest in the late 1980s and early 1990s. The controversy arose from the declining numbers of northern spotted owls, as a result of the loss of old-growth forests in the region, which this species needs to survive.

Responding to consumer demands for cheap housing and Cold War ideals of using America's resources to defeat communism, the U.S. Forest Service (USFS) became an agency increasingly devoted to timber production over other uses of the nation's forests, such as recreation and wildlife management. After World War II, the enormous stands of ancient timber in the Pacific Northwest began to decline due to a massive increase in harvesting by lumber companies under agreements with the USFS.

By the 1970s, scientists and the burgeoning environmental community began to express concern over the state of the region's forests. Scientists began to research the northern spotted owl, and they became increasingly concerned over its diminishing habitat. Also during the 1970s and 1980s, the Northwest became a hotbed for environmental activism. Many environmentalists viewed the declining number of spotted owls as a sign that the lumber industry was destroying the region's forests.

Environmental groups in Oregon and Washington began to take the USFS to court to halt lumber sales, until the agency developed a proper plan to save the owl under the auspices of the 1973 Endangered Species Act. The success of several lawsuits polarized the Northwest, with environmental groups on one side, and timber companies and loggers on the other. Environmental groups claimed that the lumber industry did not care about the future of the region or about the health of the environment, while the lumber industry, its workers, and local governments accused the environmentalists of trying to destroy the region's economy. Finally, after much resistance, the U.S. Fish and Wildlife Service listed the northern spotted owl on the endangered species list in 1991.

By early 1993, tensions between environmentalists and the lumber industry reached a fever pitch. Lawsuits had almost entirely halted old-growth logging throughout the region. The USFS withdrew its workers from the field for fear of physical attack. Loggers went to the forests to kill spotted owls.

In order to attempt a solution, recently inaugurated President Bill Clinton and Vice President Al Gore came to Portland for a forest conference. The discussions did little to please either side, but they did lead to a plan to protect the spotted owl and continue to allow for some timber harvesting.

Since the forest conference, the controversy has subsided somewhat, but old-growth logging remains heavily restricted. Perhaps most importantly for the forests of the Pacific Northwest, the spotted owl controversy—combined with a slowdown in the lumber industry and a shift of many timber operations to the American South and the developing world—ended the industry's dominance over the regional economy. It also demonstrated the power of the environmental movement in the region.

Erik Loomis

1980s and 1990s

The 1980s saw a rise in conflict between environmentalists and developers. Much of this was spurred when President Ronald Reagan named James Watt as secretary of the interior. Watt, a vocal pro-development advocate, fired up the environmental movement, inadvertently helping it out of a decade-long stagnation in membership growth. Groups such as the Wilderness Society and Sierra Club saw their membership skyrocket, as Watt and Reagan looked to turn back many of the environmental policies passed in the

1970s, including the Endangered Species Act, by loosening the regulations around economic development in wilderness areas. While the increased membership of the major environmental groups helped them to foil many of Watt and Reagan's policies, it also helped lead to the most important environmental conflict of the 1980s—the spotted owl controversy.

By the 1980s, it had become increasingly clear to environmentalists that production levels of timber in the Pacific Northwest were well out of line with any kind of sustainable harvest and that the destruction of old-growth timber had led to population declines for many of the region's plant and animal species. The environmental community pushed to list the spotted owl under the Endangered Species Act, which the government did in 1991. Environmentalists capitalized on this victory to challenge many lumber sales in court; in many cases, their victories put the lumber industry, which had long supported the economy of the Pacific Northwest, in jeopardy. Tensions remained high through the early 1990s, as old-growth logging ceased almost entirely and some lumber workers took to shooting spotted owls. In 1993, President Bill Clinton convened a Portland, Oregon, summit among environmentalists, lumber companies, lumber worker representatives, and government officials. At the summit, a plan was developed that pleased neither side but did allow for some timber harvesting, while protecting most of the old-growth forest for owl habitat.

The spotted owl controversy led to many calls to revoke the Endangered Species Act, especially when the economy of a whole region was threatened. The law remains in place, but environmental groups claim that the United States Fish and Wildlife Service has proceeded very slowly in listing new species in order to avoid future controversy.

Although the environmental community was not particularly pleased with Clinton's compromise in the spotted owl controversy, he remained committed to environmental causes throughout his presidency. Critics argued that he ignored solving any real problems such as global warming or developing alternative energy vehicles, but Clinton did use his presidential power to create new national monuments throughout the American West, including Grand Staircase-Escalante (the largest U.S. national monument) in Utah, the Sonoran Desert in Arizona, and the Hanford Reach in Washington. These monuments infuriated conservatives who believed that the land should remain open for development.

As the twenty-first century opened, the major battle over wilderness and wildlife occurred in Alaska's Arctic National Wildlife Refuge (ANWR), which was established in 1960 to protect 8.9 million acres of northeast Alaska. Like the regions in the state placed under protection by President Jimmy Carter, this wilderness area was known to few Americans and visited by even fewer. However, President George W. Bush's 2001 campaign to open ANWR for oil development invigorated the environmental community more than anything since the policies of Ronald Reagan and James Watt. Bush argued that the nation needed the oil from the area as a hedge against unstable Middle Eastern supplies; for their part, environmentalists contended that drilling would destroy precious ecosystems, critical to species such as the caribou, in exchange for oil that would supply the needs of the country for less than a year. Environmentalists remained confident that wilderness protection in the United States had gained popular support strong enough to defeat the project.

Yet the Bush Administration moved to open other areas of wilderness to industry, including large areas of the West for natural gas and oil development. In 2003, the Bureau of Land Management issued new rules defining roads in wilderness areas. Listing paths and even streambeds as right-of-ways, the Bureau effectively opened up the tracts to further development. Also in 2003, Secretary of the Interior Gale Norton announced that more than 1 million acres of wilderness in Utah would be taken off the list of lands to be considered for designation as federally protected wilderness. In 2006, the Bush Administration announced its intention to sell off 200,000 acres of national forest land.

Erik Loomis

See also: Alaskan Pipeline; Earth Day; Endangered Species Act; Environmental Protection Agency; Environmentalism; Global Warming; Science, Government Policy on; Water Pollution and Water Pollution Policy.

Bibliography

Clark, Tim, Richard P. Reaching, and Alice L. Clarke, eds. *Endangered Species Recovery: Finding the Lessons, Improving the Process.* Washington, DC: Island, 1994.

Hays, Samuel P. *Beauty, Health, and Permanence: Environmental Politics in the United States, 1955–1985.* Cambridge, UK, and New York: Cambridge University Press, 1987.

Rothman, Hal. *Saving the Planet: The American Response to the Environment in the Twentieth Century.* Chicago: Ivan R. Dee, 2000.

Yaffee, Stephen Lewis. *The Wisdom of the Spotted Owl: Policy Lessons for a New Century.* Washington, DC: Island, 1994.

WOMEN AND WORK

When the Japanese attacked Pearl Harbor on Sunday morning, December 7, 1941, plunging the United States into World War II, the place of American women in the nation's workforce was changed forever. Even though many women returned to hearth and home when the war ended in 1945, ideas on what women were capable of had changed, and American women no longer saw themselves as restricted to occupations that had been considered suitable to women in the past. During World War II, women had shown that they could build weapons, fly airplanes, serve as executives, and fill important government posts. To many women, opportunities for the future seemed infinite.

Impact of World War II

During World War II, more than 300,000 women were employed in the U.S. aircraft industry, building planes and assembling bombs. Other women joined the ranks of factory workers, becoming draftsmen and machinists. Still others built tanks and warships and manufactured ammunitions. For the first time in American history, women made up more than half of the workforce. The image of Rosie the Riveter appeared on posters around the country, urging American women to serve their country by joining the war effort.

A number of studies were conducted during World War II that documented the high productivity levels of female workers. For instance, a 1943 survey of 146 executives conducted by the National Industrial Conference Board revealed that the productivity levels of women workers was equal to or greater than those of males engaged in similar work. In California, a survey of several war plants by the Bureau of Employment Security found that productivity of both male and female workers improved and that costs per hour were lowered when females were present in the plants.

Even before Pearl Harbor, European allies that had already suffered through two years of war turned to the United States to supply their war needs. American men, who had worried about feeding themselves and their families during the Great Depression, suddenly found themselves working long hours and enjoying newfound prosperity. Once the United States became a participant in the war, however, the government put out a call for men to join the military and to fill crucial government jobs. The positions left vacant by men were soon filled by women. As the war progressed, so did the need for new employees, and the government launched a campaign to lure women into the workforce, invoking patriotism and promising unprecedented salaries in return.

Large numbers of women also answered the call for service by joining the military. They were able to choose among the Women's Army Corps (WAC), the Navy Women's Reserve (WAVES), the Marine Corps Women's Reserve, and the Coast Guard Women's Reserve (SPARS), in which women served both stateside and abroad. While many women were employed in the same kinds of service jobs for which they were eligible in the civilian workforce, others branched out into jobs that had been closed to them before the war. The Women's Air Force Service Pilots (WASPS), for instance, was created to leave male pilots free for combat service and performed admirably in flying supply planes to hazardous areas.

While minority women lagged behind white women both in wartime salaries and in the jobs available to them, they also made enormous gains during the war years. African American women, for example, who had been chiefly employed in domestic jobs before the war, advanced to various kinds of factory and service jobs. During the war, the number of black women employed in factories doubled.

The number of other minority women in the workplace also increased during and after World War II. In 1920, only 11.5 percent of Native American women had been in the workforce; by 1960, the number had increased to 55.1 percent. Similarly, the number of Chinese American women in the work force rose from 12.4 percent in 1920 to 59.2 percent in 1960.

Because of the increased opportunities for employment, discrimination against black workers was rampant. Some white workers actively campaigned against the employment of African Americans in jobs that had previously been designated as whites-only positions, and violence sometimes resulted. In 1941, President Franklin D. Roosevelt signed Executive Order 8802, which banned discrimination in national government and defense industries, and established the Fair Employment Practices Committee. When those actions failed to stop workplace discrimination, a group of African American women picketed Ford automotive plants, demanding jobs.

In addition to women who entered the workforce, large numbers of women volunteered their time and energies to the war effort. For instance, more than 3 million women gave their time to the American Red Cross during World War II. Other women were involved in driving ambulances, volunteering for Civil Defense positions, collecting food and other materials for the war effort, and selling war bonds.

The call for more female workers was answered by large numbers of older married women who had no young children at home, as well as by mothers of young children. For the latter, day care became an issue of major importance. The government's efforts to deal with the needs of working mothers never came close to solving the problem. Throughout the war, the government allotted only $400,000 for subsidized child care, and on-site child care at defense plants proved to be seriously inadequate. Most mothers were forced to depend on relatives, neighbors, and friends for child care. Some employers did try to assist working mothers. The shipbuilding firm of Kaiser Industries, for example, provided meals that working mothers could carry home to their children.

Once World War II ended, from the standpoint of the federal government and most employers, American women had served their purpose in filling in for male workers. At least one-fourth of all married female workers were unemployed at war's end. Many who remained in the workforce were demoted to minor, low-paying jobs. Some women, particularly those with small children, were happy to return home, but many others were infuriated at the wide-scale dismissal of their abilities and contributions to the war. Some states went so far as to pass laws restricting the employment of married women, so as to open up more jobs for returning veterans.

The courts also contributed to keeping women in their place during the post–World War II period. In *Goesaert v. Cleary* (1948), for example, the U.S. Supreme Court upheld a Michigan law that banned the employment of women in bars unless the female employee were the wife or daughter of the proprietor. The Court's rationale was that women in bars provided a constant temptation for male patrons.

Still, the number of women in the workplace continued to rise in the decades following World War II. In 1940, roughly one-quarter of American women worked outside the home. Approximately 15 percent of those were married women. By 1950, the number of women in the workforce had risen to 29 percent. By 1970, 34.5 percent of women held jobs outside the home, and, by 1980, the number had increased to 40 percent. At the beginning of the twenty-first century, the Census Bureau reported that 61 percent of American women over the age of 16 were in the workforce.

Women's Movement

In 1963, Betty Friedan published *The Feminine Mystique,* in which she identified the "problem that had no name" as "the feminine mystique." According to Friedan, this was the idea, accepted by men and women alike, that even educated women could find intellectual fulfillment by being the best mothers and wives they could be. Friedan also argued, that after World War II, women had been maneuvered back to the domestic scene by Madison Avenue executives who convinced them that their chief goals in life should be to have the cleanest house, the neatest clothes, and the most well-cared-for children and husbands.

Friedan's findings echoed those of anthropologist Margaret Mead, who had earlier recognized the role of the American media in generating anxieties among women in order to force them back to hearth and home at the end of World War II. At that time, studies had been published "proving" that working women were unhappier, while a number of other studies suggesting that working women made happier and better-adjusted mothers were ignored.

In her efforts to understand the actions that had created the feminine mystique, Friedan examined women's magazines after World War I and after World War II, discovering that post–World War I women had been encouraged to expand their horizons by choosing careers that were not dominated by women or by opting to stay single for longer periods. After World War II, however, Friedan contended, magazines depicted women who were unhappy in careers, because they realized true happiness lay only in being good wives and mothers.

Between the mid-1940s and the mid-1960s, women were encouraged to seek education not as a means of establishing career goals but as opportunities for obtaining what became known as an "MRS degree." During that period, the number of women attending college fell sharply, and only one-third of those women who did attend ever received a degree.

Friedan insisted that, as a result of the postwar campaign to return women to their homes, millions of American women had been "buried alive." She concluded that many had lost their personal identities in the quest for perfect domesticity and had lost their voices by accepting the advice of the popular media to eschew education and politics. The *Feminine Mystique* launched the modern women's movement, also known as the Second Wave.

In 1966, Friedan cofounded the National Organization for Women (NOW), which became the largest women's organization in the history of the United States. By the twenty-first century, NOW had 500,000 contributing members and chapters in all fifty states. Since its inception, NOW has worked to promote justice and equality for women throughout society, to protect reproductive rights, and to end violence against women. When the group rejected the liberal views of Friedan and her cohorts for the more radical leadership of Gloria Steinem and congresswoman Bella Abzug, a New York Democrat, NOW also pledged to end homophobia in American society. NOW's Legal Defense Fund has been instrumental in challenging laws that discriminate against women in the workplace and in society at large.

With the growth of the Second Wave of American feminism, women raised their political voices for the first time since 1920, when passage of the Nineteenth Amendment had quieted the First Wave feminists. The result was that women entered politics at all levels in unprecedented numbers, introducing legislation that was more responsive to the new perceptions of women's roles and to the needs of working women. Feminists put pressure on male politicians as well, and their persistence led to the inclusion of women as a protected class under Title VII of the landmark Civil Rights Act of 1964, which banned discrimination in employment on the basis of race, color, religion, sex, or national origin. Subsequently, women filed charges against discriminatory employers, forcing them to recognize the legitimacy of women in the workplace.

In 1971, Friedan co-founded the National Women's Political Caucus (NWPC), which raised funds to elect female candidates for office. Other groups, such as EMILY's List (Early Money Is Like Yeast) and WISH (Women in the Senate and House), soon followed. Feminists argued that having women in policymaking positions would be instrumental in ending all forms of discrimination against women.

Pay equity continued to be a priority issue among women, who were often paid less for doing the same jobs as their male colleagues because of the societal belief that only men deserved to be paid "family wages." At the end of World War II, a poll conducted by *Fortune* magazine revealed that 57 percent of women and 63 percent of men believed that married women whose husbands earned a living wage should be banned from the workplace.

In 1955, the prejudice against working women meant that, on the average, women made sixty-four cents for every dollar that a male worker made for equivalently skilled work. Six years later, that number had dropped to sixty-one cents on the dollar. Congress passed the Equal Pay Act in 1963, which banned the practice of paying women less than men for the same jobs. The law allowed a number of exceptions, and employers sometimes rewrote job descriptions of male workers to justify paying them more. Since the early 1990s, women have tended to make around seventy cents for every dollar made by male workers.

Feminists responded to continued inequities in pay with increased calls for legislation on "comparable worth," which would have devised a pay scale of jobs that were relatively equal according to education, skills, responsibility, and effort. For instance, comparable worth might equate the educational level required of a teacher with the physical demands placed on a truck driver and determine that pay for the two jobs should be approximately equal. In reality, truck drivers (mostly male) draw appreciably higher salaries than elementary and secondary school teachers, who are predominantly female.

Revised attitudes about women's place in society also influenced the views of the American courts in the 1970s. The turning point came in *Reed v. Reed* in 1971, when the U.S. Supreme Court was asked to determine whether or not an Idaho state court had erred in giving the divorced father of a deceased adopted child the right to manage the child's estate, even though the lower court acknowledged that both parents were equally capable of doing so. In its landmark decision, the Supreme Court determined that giving mandatory preference in order to streamline the judicial process was "the very kind of arbitrary legislative choice forbidden by the Equal Protection Clause of the Fourteenth Amendment." As a result, arbitrary classification that relegated women to second-class citi-

Title VII

Title VII of the Civil Rights Act of 1964 prohibits employment discrimination on the basis of race, gender, religion, or national origin. A long fought-for provision, it was finally enacted under President Lyndon B. Johnson, though it would be many years before it was enforced with any regularity or applied to all of the categories of discrimination it addressed.

One of the most pressing goals of the civil rights movement always had been fair hiring practices. Unlike welfare, aid for dependent children, or Social Security, such initiatives were seen as helping people achieve a better standard of living on their own, rather than by receiving a direct government subsidy. For a variety of reasons, however, employers had been slow to adopt fair hiring practices.

World War II did bring an increase in the number of women and minorities employed in industrial jobs, but the advance proved largely temporary. At the end of the war, most of the women who worked in industry were pushed out to make way for male veterans, and African American employees who hoped to use seniority to advance through the ranks found themselves limited to maintenance and janitorial positions.

Fair hiring legislation had been enacted, in one form or another, several times throughout the interwar and postwar periods. President Franklin D. Roosevelt created the Fair Employment Practices Commission in 1941 to eliminate racial bias in wartime industry, and, in 1961, President John F. Kennedy established the President's Committee on Equal Employment Opportunity. But both bodies were created by executive order only, and they had little enforcement authority and no official legislative support.

Title VII of the Civil Rights Act of 1964 contained strictures against racism in public places, as well as support for African American voting rights. Unlike the previous executive orders, Title VII provided for enforcement by creating the Equal Employment Opportunity Commission (EEOC). This body would be made up of five presidential appointees, confirmed by the Senate, and it would evaluate complaints against employers accused of discrimination.

While regulating racial discrimination was always a major goal of the Kennedy and Johnson administrations, the inclusion of gender discrimination as part of Title VII was a more radical departure. Historians disagree as to the origins of the gender clause. Some suggest that it was incorporated in the bill by opponents to kill the measure, as there were far fewer members of Congress willing to support antidiscrimination legislation against women than there were members who supported antidiscrimination legislation against African Americans. Still other historians suggest that women in Congress, backed by Deputy Secretary of Labor Esther Peterson, recognized the need for a strong piece of gender-equality legislation, particularly after they were ridiculed by male legislators during the battle over the Equal Pay Act of 1963. Whatever the explanation, gender was included, somewhat unexpectedly, in the final bill, which was voted into law on June 15, 1964.

It would be many years before Title VII was comprehensively enforced. Initially, the new commission was swamped with complaints and focused almost exclusively on racial concerns.

Gender issues were largely ignored in the early years, but, in the late 1960s, the EEOC began to take cases to court challenging exclusionary and protective legislation aimed at keeping women out of the workplace. Fighting for maternity leave and equal pay, and against sexual harassment and racism in the workplace, the EEOC has helped women and minorities in the workplace make significant progress against discrimination.

Anthony Todd

zenship were henceforth prohibited, making it more difficult to legally discriminate against women in all realms of society.

Changes in the Workplace and Benefits

Awareness of the distinct needs of working mothers created a demand for rethinking the structure of the workplace. Many employers began to experiment with innovations such as "flex-time," part-time, and share-time. Women who opt for flex-time choose to work nontraditional hours that leave them more time with their families, while mothers who work part-time generally choose to work only a few hours a day or a few days a week. Share-time allows two workers to divide a job so that, together, the traditional eight hours and all work responsibilities are covered. The prevalence of computers in the workplace has provided women with even more flexibility, allowing large numbers to telecommute. With this method, women can e-mail or fax material to their offices without ever leaving their homes.

In the postwar period, day care continued to be an issue of concern for employers as well as for working mothers and fathers. Many large companies and educational institutions provided on-site day care centers, while other employers offered to help pay for day care at other locations. Giving in to the ongoing pressure by feminists and other advocates of women's rights, the U.S. government also provided supplemental day care for lower-income women in the private sector.

In 1971, Congress passed the Comprehensive Child Development Act, which appropriated $750 million to provide child care for American mothers on welfare. Child Care and Development Block Grants were established in the late 1980s to assist states in providing aid to poor working mothers and their children. The national government also established the Earned Income Tax Credit for low-income working parents and provided a child-care income tax exemption for *all* working parents.

Special considerations for women in the workplace have sometimes proved detrimental to the financial health of women. Such was the case with the introduction of the so-called "Mommy Track," which gave women the option of choosing either family or work as a top priority. Women who chose the Mommy Track option soon found that their salaries lagged behind those of their male and other female colleagues. Mommy-Track workers were also frequently passed over for promotions. On the other hand, women who chose work as a priority discovered what came to be identified as the "glass ceiling," beyond which few women were able to progress. In all professions, even those dominated by females, males continued to make up the upper echelons of the pay scale and organizational chart.

Various forms of discrimination against women in the workplace continued throughout the decades following World War II. For instance, pregnant women were sometimes forced to give up their jobs once their pregnancies became evident. Additionally, medical insurers often refused to pay pregnancy-related costs for female employees at the same time that they paid for pregnancy-related coverage for the wives of male employees.

In 1976, in *General Electric Company v. Gilbert,* the U.S. Supreme Court upheld the practice of pregnancy discrimination. In 1978, however, with the support of President Jimmy Carter, Congress passed the Pregnancy Discrimination Act, which used Title VII of the Civil Rights Act of 1964 as the basis for banning pregnancy discrimination. The measure required employers and insurers to treat pregnancy, childbirth, and related medical conditions in the same way as other medical conditions, extending medical coverage and allowing time off from work for pregnancy and childbirth. Because of the ongoing controversy over abortion, employers were not expected to treat abortions in the same way as other conditions of pregnancy.

As divorce rates and the incidence of babies born to unmarried mothers increased, poor women began to experience what feminists and social scientists called "the feminization of poverty." This meant that the poorest segment of the population tended to be children under age six and their single-parent mothers. Because women's wages continued to lag behind those of males, poor mothers were often unable to hold down jobs while paying for child care. For many, welfare proved to be the only means of survival. An overhaul of the welfare system in 1996 provided states with incentives to assist poor women in entering the work force, allowing them to retain Medicaid benefits for a limited period in order to continue medical coverage during the transition period.

The Congressional Caucus for Women's Issues, made up of female members of the U.S. Senate and

House of Representatives, sponsored a family leave bill to take some of the burden off working mothers and to provide a means for fathers to share family responsibilities. The Family and Medical Leave Act, signed into law by President Bill Clinton in 1993, requires employers to grant unpaid leave to care for newborn, adopted, or foster children, to tend ailing members of the immediate family, and to deal with cases of personal illness. The unpaid leave may encompass as much as twelve weeks in a calendar year. A number of companies have been amenable to allowing pregnant women to build up personal leave and vacation time so that employees can receive a salary throughout their pregnancy leaves.

Title VII of the Civil Rights Act of 1964 had also been the basis of President Lyndon B. Johnson's program of affirmative action, which mandated the hiring and promotion of women and other minorities in the workplace. Before the 1980s, legal challenges to affirmative action were usually unsuccessful. For instance, in *Steelworkers v. Weber* (1979), the Supreme Court upheld a Kaiser Aluminum affirmative action plan, ruling that Title VII "does not condemn all private, voluntary, race-conscious affirmative action plans." Likewise, in *Fullilove v. Klutznick* (1980), the Court upheld the Public Works Employment Act of 1977, which set aside a certain proportion of federal contracts for women and other minorities.

During the Reagan-Bush years, however, the conservative Supreme Court withdrew support for affirmative action in several related cases, even though it did not back down on its stand against discrimination as defined by Title VII. In 1991, in *Automobile Workers v. Johnson Controls,* the Court determined that the company's policy of barring all women of childbearing age from certain jobs because of possible damage to unborn fetuses unfairly discriminated against women.

Sexual Harassment

The increased number of women in the workplace has sometimes provided a fertile environment for male employers who use their power to treat women as sexual objects rather than as fellow workers. This practice, which has come to be known as "sexual harassment," ranges from pressure for dates to being forced to listen to tales of sexual prowess to unwelcome physical contact. The practice has been particularly common in male-dominated workplaces, where men have been known to use sex as a way of making female workers feel uncomfortable. For instance, a small group of women who worked at the Forbes Fairlane mining plant in Virginia, Minnesota, won a $3.5 million class-action lawsuit against the plant owner, Evalth Mines, because employers had turned a blind eye over a period of years to a concentrated campaign of harassment by male employees, which included derisive remarks, inappropriate physical contact, and sexually explicit graffiti and jokes.

Despite the prevalence of sexual harassment in the workplace, it was not until 1986 that the Supreme Court held in *Meritor Savings Bank v. Vinson* that sexual harassment constitutes a form of sex discrimination that is unacceptable under Title VII of the Civil Rights Act of 1964. The *Meritor* case began when a female employee accused her immediate supervisor of forcing her to have sex with him over a period of years by threatening her with the loss of her job or the denial of promotions. The Court's new "hostile environment test" meant that employers must thereafter be responsible for the conduct of their employees. Many companies subsequently developed sexual harassment policies and conducted training sessions aimed at ensuring nonhostile working environments.

It was not until October 1991, however, that the general public was forced to deal with the issue of sexual harassment. At the time, President George H. W. Bush had chosen Clarence Thomas, a black Republican judge from Georgia, to replace retiring Thurgood Marshall, the first African American member of the Supreme Court. During the course of the investigation into Thomas's background, reports surfaced that Thomas has sexually harassed Anita Hill, a University of Oklahoma law professor who had worked for him years earlier. Although Thomas eventually won confirmation to the Court by a narrow margin, sexual harassment became part of the American psyche, and workplace conditions began to improve for many American women.

In 1993, the Supreme Court again addressed the issue of sexual harassment in *Harris v. Forklift Systems.* Expanding on *Meritor*'s hostile environment test, the Court held that victims of sexual harassment did not have to prove damage to their physical well-being or that they had suffered specific injuries in order to show that they had been sexually harassed. In June 2004, a federal judge ruled that roughly 1.6 million past and present female employees of Wal-Mart could join a class action suit claiming that the world's largest retailer had routinely underpaid women in the same work positions as men and had systematically overlooked females for promotion.

Conclusion

There is no doubt that women have made great strides in the workplace since the end of World War II. Not only have they effectively asserted their right and their ability to take on jobs normally associated with men, but they have brought to light previously ignored workplace problems such as sexual harassment. Still, significant issues remain.

Women continue to be paid substantially less than men for equivalent work, and they continue to be overlooked for promotion at many companies, large and small. Finally, the United States still lacks an adequate and affordable child-care system, a problem of increasing proportions as more and more mothers enter the workforce.

Elizabeth Purdy

See also: Day Care; Family Leave Act; Feminist Movement; Service Industries; Service-Sector Workers; White-Collar Workers.

Bibliography

Amott, Teresa, and Julie Matthaei. *Race, Gender, and Work: A Multi-Cultural History of Women in the United States.* Boston: South End, 1996.

Evans, Sara M. *Born for Liberty: A History of Women in America.* New York: Free Press, 1989.

Friedan, Betty. *The Feminine Mystique.* New York: Dell, 1963.

Kerber, Linda K., and Jane Sharron DeHart. *Women's America: Refocusing the Past.* New York: Oxford University Press, 1991.

Kessler-Harris, Alice. *In Pursuit of Equity: Women, Men and the Quest for Economic Citizenship in 20th Century America.* New York: Oxford University Press, 2001.

Lindgren, J. Ralph, and Nadine Taub. *The Law of Sex Discrimination.* Minneapolis, MN: West, 1993.

May, Elaine Tyler. *Pushing the Limits: American Women, 1940–1961.* New York: Oxford University Press, 1994.

Mills, Kay. *From Pocahontas to Power Suits: Everything You Need to Know About Women's History in America.* New York: Penguin, 1995.

Papachristou, Judith. *Women Together.* New York: Alfred A. Knopf, 1976.

Rix, Sara E., ed. *The American Woman, 1990–91.* New York: W.W. Norton, 1988.

Sapiro, Virginia. *Women in American Society: An Introduction to Women's Studies.* Mountain View, CA: Mayfield, 1994.

Smuts, Robert W. *Women and Work.* New York: Columbia University Press, 1959.

Sugrue, Thomas. *The Origins of the Urban Crisis: Race and Inequality in Postwar Detroit.* Princeton, NJ: Princeton University Press, 1998.

Women's Action Coalition. *WAC Stats: The Facts About Women.* New York: New Press, 1993.

WOMEN'S STUDIES

With the onset of the civil rights movement during the 1960s, some members of the academic community began to reconsider the traditional approach to research and knowledge. As ethnic minorities and women voiced demands for equality, those in the humanities and social sciences questioned the influence of race, class, and gender on the human experience. Women's studies emerged on college campuses as part of this trend in the late 1960s. Those involved in the women's liberation movement challenged the traditional curriculum, which often excluded women or presented only token figures and exceptional cases.

Also at this time, as more women became faculty members and female enrollment increased, several universities commissioned studies to examine the status of women on campuses. Finding that female students were at an academic and social disadvantage in a male-dominated atmosphere, faculty and students designed new courses to recognize the contributions of women and to refute stereotypes and sexist assumptions. Women's studies courses drew ideas and concepts from history, literature, psychology, sociology, economics, law, and other disciplines in order to explain women's inferior status in society, while searching for solutions to the problem.

During the 1969–1970 academic year, when the first women's studies programs appeared at San Diego State University in California and at Cornell University in New York, there were only about seventeen courses related to women's issues taught in the entire United States. The concept spread rapidly, however, and, by 1971, there were 610 courses, fifteen undergraduate programs, and one master's degree program.

Despite such growth and popularity, administrators often put up resistance to women's studies programs by offering courses but prohibiting the establishment of a degree program and limiting funding for faculty and supplies. In 1973, for example, the year-old program at the University of New Mexico received only $50 for supplies, while a part-time work-study student assistant was paid through a $100 donation. To counter these shortcomings, graduate students and faculty often taught on a volunteer basis.

Initially, instructors and students emphasized change in the existing curriculum and promoted general introductory courses. The purpose of the introductory course was to raise student awareness by combining academics with personal experiences. They were often modeled on consciousness-raising groups utilized by feminists.

Programs often maintained ties with activist groups and encouraged students to work for women's issues outside the classroom. At Cornell, for example, a 1970 course titled "The Evolution of Female Personality" took an interdisciplinary approach and addressed six major topics: status of women in law, marriage, and society; women's history; images of women in popular culture; family roles; social ecology; and prospects for change.

While scholars worked to define women's studies as a distinct field, many colleges and universities introduced women's studies through established disciplines, such as history and literature. Gerda Lerner, a historian at Sarah Lawrence College, designed a history course called "The Many Worlds of Women," as what she called "an experiment." She presented broad concepts in women's history, in order to give her students a frame of reference in which to understand the present day. In 1972, Lerner wrote, "We have to create a history in which man is no longer the measure, but *men* and *women* are the measure."

1980s and 1990s

By the early 1980s, nearly 100 universities offered women's studies majors and close to 400 had operating programs. Such programs became institutionalized, receiving greater financial support for instructors and staff. Yet a number of scholars started to question the validity of a general "female experience," and others sought a greater integration of women's issues into more disciplines.

Women's studies programs and research received criticism from ethnic minorities and lesbians that the mostly white, heterosexual women in academia had overlooked them. Because women's studies traditionally utilized an interdisciplinary approach, the field began to incorporate materials from African American, Hispanic, Native American, and Asian sources, as well as sources that considered the limitations of economic class.

At the same time, universities sought gender balance in mainstream courses and scientific fields. In 1983, Montana State University mandated that course materials be reviewed for sex bias and revised to include content on women. This proved a difficult challenge for the sciences, such as chemistry and biology, but as Harvard psychologist Carol Gilligan explained, women and men approach their work with different moral principles. Therefore, scientists had to consider how gender might play a role in ethics and decision making.

In the next decade, the primary challenge for women's studies was to accept racial, ethnic, sexual, and economic differences among women, while concurrently promoting the belief in a common female experience shared by all women. This became increasingly difficult in the 1990s, a decade defined by a multicultural movement in which women's studies struggled to retain a unique approach and avoid duplication with other interdisciplinary programs. Ultimately, efforts to include race, class, and sexuality, along with attempts to integrate women's studies into the mainstream, raised questions about whether women's studies could be an independent discipline. In some cases, women's studies programs gave way to gender studies, in which scholars considered interactions between men and women and the ways in which society shaped the male experience as well. Despite these debates and new directions, women's studies programs continued to grow, so that by 1995, 130 universities offered graduate degrees.

In order to broaden their scope, women's studies scholars in the 1990s focused increasingly on globalization and international issues. Most often associated with sustainable development, education, and politics in Third World countries, this departure from a Eurocentric worldview brought about the creation of numerous international organizations and conferences and was introduced as a subject in more and more introductory women's studies courses.

Women's studies was originally intended as a distinct discipline, but since the 1970s, the methods, theories, and methodologies developed by feminist scholars have had a far-reaching impact on higher education in the United States. By promoting cooperative learning, making curriculum more inclusive, and encouraging students to examine personal experiences, women's studies offered students and instructors in all disciplines an alternative to the traditional educational approach. Although women's studies programs have come under fire since their inception for imposing liberal ideologies on college campuses, they have enabled scholars to forge links between disciplines and to reconsider long-held assumptions.

Jenny Barker

See also: Consciousness Raising; Education, Higher; Ethnic Studies Programs.

Bibliography

Bystydzienski, Jill M. "Women's Studies Programs." *Ready Reference: Women's Issues.* Vol. 3, edited by Margaret McFadden. Pasadena, CA: Salem, 1999.

Howe, Florence. *Seven Years Later: Women's Studies Programs in 1976.* A Report of the National Advisory Council on Women's Educational Programs, June 1977.

Howe, Florence, and Carol Ahlum. "Women's Studies and Social Change." In *Academic Women on the Move,* edited by Alice S. Rossi and Ann Calderwood. New York: Russell Sage Foundation, 1973.

Lerner, Gerda. "On the Teaching and Organization of Feminist Studies." *Female Studies* V (1972): 34–37.

Williams, Dennis A., Marsha Zabarsky, and Dianne H. McDonald. "Out of the Academic Ghetto." *Education* (October 31, 1983).

Winkler, Barbara Scott, and Carolyn DiPalma, ed. *Teaching Introduction to Women's Studies: Expectations and Strategies.* Westport, CT: Bergin and Garvey, 1999.

WOODSTOCK MUSIC FESTIVAL

In August 1969, an estimated 500,000 people gathered at Max Yasgur's dairy farm outside Bethel, New York, to participate in an event that came to be regarded as the defining moment of the 1960s counterculture movement. The Woodstock Music and Arts Festival brought together people from all over the country for what was billed as "Three Days of Peace and Music."

Festival organizers Michael Lang and Artie Kornfeld originally planned the concert as a promotional event to support the construction of a state-of-the-art recording studio in the nearby artist's colony of Woodstock, New York. Because most bands had already set their summer touring schedules, Lang and Kornfeld were finding it difficult to secure big-name groups. This changed when Joel Rosenman and John Roberts, the financial backers, started offering appearance fees two to three times the going rate. Bands started to roll in, and the roster was soon filled with some of the top stars of the day.

Anticipation grew throughout the country as word spread that Jimi Hendrix, Janis Joplin, the Grateful Dead, and a host of other bands were going to perform at Woodstock. The concert originally was to be held in the town of Walkill, but with only thirty-one days left until the festival began, the city caught wind of the true magnitude of the event. Fearing a mass influx of hippies, the town altered the zoning and sound laws, forcing the festival organizers to find a new location. Yasgur offered his farm as a replacement site, and the organizers quickly set about preparing the festival grounds.

The stage was the first priority, with the result that there were barely any ticket booths, bathrooms, or fences to keep out people with no tickets. The crowd began showing up on Wednesday, August 13, and by Sunday at least half a million people had descended on the site. The rudimentary security was quickly overrun by thousands of gatecrashers. Just as the festival was beginning, the organizers were forced to declare Woodstock a free event.

Concert attendees effectively formed a makeshift hippie commune on Yasgur's farm, complete with free food tents and free school tents for children. There was also a hospital tent, where patients were separated by the three most common ailments: There was the "freak-out tent," where workers and nurses tried to talk down and comfort people on a "bad trip" from hallucinogenic drugs. There was an area set aside for the dozens of people whose feet had been cut by rocks or broken glass. Another area addressed the third most prevalent injury, burned eyes caused by lying on one's back and staring at the sun, evidently a common pastime for audience members who were "tripping" on drugs.

The narrow country roads and lack of adequate parking led to traffic jams of up to twenty miles long. Toilet facilities were woefully inadequate, heavy rain caused muddy conditions and other problems, and organizers were forced to fly in thousands of pounds of food and water. There was also rampant drug and alcohol use. Despite all this, Woodstock stands as the pinnacle of the hippie experience. To most attendees and fans, it remains an enduring testament to the spirit of peace and love.

The quality of the music was debated, with both the Dead and Jefferson Airplane claiming that Woodstock was one of the worst sets they ever played. But despite some lackluster performances and lack of basic comforts, Woodstock remains a cultural flashpoint.

Organizers tried to re-spark the spirit of Woodstock with anniversary festivals in 1994 and 1999. Woodstock '94, dubbed "Three More Days of Peace and Music," took place on one of the alternative sites for the original festival. With performances by contemporary bands such as the Red Hot Chili Peppers, Aerosmith, and Nine Inch Nails, Woodstock '94 was intended to unite Generation X the way the original festival had united the 1960s generation. This second event also suffered from inadequate sanitary facilities and mud caused by rain. And many attendees complained that ticket prices were too high and that food and water were too expensive to afford for three days.

These issues were even more pronounced in Woodstock '99, also held in upstate New York. Performances by such popular groups as Korn, Limp Bizkit, and Ice Cube did not keep the audience from ending the festival early by looting the food, alcohol, and merchandise tents. High temperatures, high prices, and too much alcohol led to riots in which dozens of fires were set and at least four women reportedly were raped. The spirit of the summer of 1969 was long gone.

Richard Santos

See also: Altamont Killings; Counterculture; Dance, Popular; Drug Culture; Love-Ins; Rhythm and Blues; Rock and Roll.

Bibliography

Eliscu, Jenny. "Rape Charges Latest Blow to Woodstock '99." *Rolling Stone* (July 30, 1999).

Makower, Joel. *Woodstock: The Oral History.* New York: Doubleday, 1989.

WORLD'S FAIRS

Since the nineteenth century, Americans have used world's fairs to showcase inventions, culture, and artwork, to celebrate historic events, to amuse themselves, and to redefine their country and way of life. Since World War II, a secondary motivation for host cities has been the economic and civic revitalization that can accompany such an international event. Literally millions of visitors, citizens of the United States and other

The Woodstock Music and Arts Festival in upstate New York brought together dozens of top musical performers, half a million attendees, and all the accoutrements of the counterculture from August 15 to 17, 1969. *(Library of Congress, LC-USZC4–1911)*

To its detractors, Woodstock remains the ultimate example of the counterculture's naiveté and vapidity—nothing more than thousands of kids drugged out of their minds, wandering through fields and harassing strangers. There were dozens of arrests for selling or possessing drugs, and the food, medicine, and police resources of Bethel were quickly stretched thin.

The music began on Friday, August 15, with a performance by folk singer and guitarist Richie Havens. Over the next three days, more than thirty-five bands and individuals performed for the crowd, including Ravi Shankar, Joan Baez, Santana, Credence Clearwater Revival, the Grateful Dead, Janis Joplin, Sly and the Family Stone, the Who, and Jefferson Airplane. The festival ended with a performance by Jimi Hendrix, in which he played his now-famous electric-guitar version of "The Star Spangled Banner."

countries across the globe, have visited the world's fairs held in the United States during the postwar era.

Due to the popularity and proliferation of fairs, the Bureau International des Expositions (BIE) was established in Paris in the 1920s under the aegis of the League of Nations. After the League's demise, the BIE continued to regulate the timing of world's fairs by giving or withholding its sanction. The United States did not join the BIE until 1968.

Seattle, Washington, nevertheless hosted the Century 21 Exposition in 1962, with forty-nine nations participating. Americans were still smarting from the 1957 launch of the satellite Sputnik by the Soviet Union, and the fair rebuilt confidence in U.S. technology and other achievements. Science was showcased at this fair, which officially opened when President John F. Kennedy pushed a telegraph key on the East Coast, 3,000 miles away.

The U.S. Science Pavilion, designed by Seattle native Minora Yamasaki (whose later work included the World Trade Center in New York), featured films shown on the huge "Spacearium" screen. Fair visitors could travel on a monorail or in a spherical elevator dubbed the "bubbleator," or tour a home of the future, with disposable dishes and climate control. Corporate exhibitors presented their views of future commerce and transportation with displays predicting satellite communications, cordless phones, and underwater farms. The fair's legacy can be seen today in Seattle's skyline, which includes the 600-foot-tall Space Needle and its monorail system. A financial success, the 1962 fair drew more than 10 million visitors.

New York City celebrated the 300th anniversary of its becoming a British colony with the World's Fair of 1964–1965. "Peace Through Understanding" was the fair's theme, carried through zones designated Industry, Transportation, Government, and Amusement. The symbol of the fair was the Unisphere, a stainless steel globe twelve stories high with the continents fixed to a grid of longitude and latitude bars. African and Asian nations had a more visible presence than at previous fairs, but many European countries declined to host exhibits because the fair lacked BIE sanction. Commercial presentations dominated the fair, which lasted for two summers and closed in 1965.

The New York World's Fair left a mixed legacy: More than 50 million visitors viewed its diverse wares, from Michelangelo's Pietà at the Vatican City's pavilion, to General Motors' visions of future life on spaceships or beneath the sea. Civil rights protests on opening day, however, cast a pall over the optimistic theme and exhibits. The city's tourism and hotel industries saw small profits, but the fair itself yielded a $20 million deficit for the city.

Alaska '67, celebrating the centennial of the purchase of Alaska from Russia, is often forgotten in the list of world's fairs. This international exhibition in Fairbanks was closed after only a few weeks because of a disastrous flood that killed five people and caused millions of dollars in damage to the fairgrounds.

HemisFair '68 opened in San Antonio, Texas, with an emphasis on Latin American culture and trade, combined with local urban renewal programs. Although more than 6 million visitors enjoyed exhibits celebrating the Hispanic influence on the Americas, the fair operated at a financial loss and probably lost visitors to the previous year's Expo '67 in Montreal, Canada. HemisFair Park is still a major civic attraction, however, and the fair's theme structure, the 622-

The Unisphere, a 140-foot-high stainless steel globe, was the centerpiece of the 1964 New York World's Fair. From the opening day parade on April 22, 1964, to the closing ceremonies on October 17, 1965, the fair attracted more than 50 million visitors. *(Marvin Lichtner/ Time Life Pictures/Getty Images)*

foot-tall Tower of the Americas, was renovated and reopened in 1990.

Spokane, Washington, marked its civic centennial by hosting Expo '74. The theme, "Celebrating Tomorrow's Fresh, New Environment," reflected changing attitudes toward technology and nature, and nearby venues were the sites of conferences and talks centered on ecological issues. A relatively small city, Spokane nevertheless attracted exhibits from nine foreign countries, including the Soviet Union, and more than sixty corporations. Expo '74 was a financial success, attracting more than 5.5 million visitors.

The Knoxville International Energy Exposition of 1982, with the theme "Energy Turns the World," was held in Tennessee. A total of twenty-one countries, thirty companies, and several states presented exhibits. A highlight of the fair, albeit unrelated to the theme, was an appearance by Erno Rubik, the inventor of the then-popular Rubik's cube puzzle, who appeared at the Hungary Pavilion.

Corporate sponsorship, a new innovation, defrayed the costs of the Knoxville fair. Under this arrangement, exhibiting companies could pay to have a product featured as an "official" drink/food/object of the fair. The practice helped the city break even financially. Like previous fairs, funding at Knoxville also came from a combination of corporate donations, private fundraising, and federal and state grants. Fair chairman Jake Butcher was president of United American Bank (UAB), which helped arrange the $25 million startup fund for the fair. In 1983, UAB declared bankruptcy, ruining plans for later development of the fair site and buildings and tarnishing the memory of the fair.

The Louisiana World Exposition, hosted by New Orleans in 1984, was the last great international fair of the twentieth century to be held in the United States. With twenty nations and less than two dozen corporations involved, the fair found itself competing for tourist dollars with the 1984 Summer Olympics, which was taking place in Los Angeles, California. New Orleans, situated on the Mississippi River, used "World of Rivers: Fresh Water as a Source of Life" as its theme. Rather than a towering architectural structure such as the Unisphere, a 2,600-foot-long mall known as Wonderwall was developed that contained shops, restaurants, and entertainment stages. The 7 million visitors to New Orleans fell short of projections, and the fair declared bankruptcy before it closed. The city was left with a new convention center and retail area, the Riverwalk, but cost overruns and lost business led Louisiana Governor Edwin Edwards to declare the fair a "disaster."

The question has been raised by some commentators: Has the day of the world's fair ended? Perhaps the public is no longer thrilled by the pavilions and inventions; such things can be seen on television or in neighborhood malls. Other countries produced fairs in the 1990s with some success, however, and a community foundation has been formed in Phoenix, Arizona, to develop plans for a world's fair there in 2008.

Vickey Kalambakal

See also: Theme Parks.

Bibliography

Chappell, Urso. "World's Fair History, Architecture, and Memorabilia." ExpoMuseum. http://expomuseum.com.

Rydell, Robert W., John E. Findling, and Kimberly D. Pelle. *Fair America: World's Fairs in the United States.* Washington, DC: Smithsonian Institution, 2000.

WOUNDED KNEE

A tiny village in the Black Hills of South Dakota, Wounded Knee became the site of a violent confrontation between law enforcement officials and activists from the radical American Indian Movement (AIM) in the winter and spring of 1973, as a dispute between factions within the native population escalated into protest against U.S. government Indian policy.

Led by members of AIM, residents of the Oglala Sioux Pine Ridge Reservation and representatives of seventy-five other tribes gathered on February 27, 1973, to reclaim Wounded Knee in the name of the Sioux Nation. The protestors took the hamlet by force, declaring it an independent nation, and they vowed to occupy the area until the U.S. government agreed to redress their list of grievances. The siege lasted seventy-one days, ending only after Bureau of Indian Affairs (BIA) officials agreed to negotiate with AIM and other tribal leaders.

The months leading up to the siege at Wounded Knee were marked by increasing tensions within Pine Ridge Reservation. There was a growing political division between members of the tribal government installed by the BIA and the more traditional members who wanted greater sovereignty from the federal government. Local Sioux groups accused Dick Wilson, president of the tribal council, of corruption, misappropriation of funds, and strong-arming political opponents.

Of even greater concern were Wilson's efforts to transfer valuable uranium-rich land to the U.S. Department of the Interior in exchange for government support of his campaign. When Oglala traditionalists resisted Wilson's attempt to seize their land, he created an enforcement group called the Guardians of Our Oglala Nation (GOONS). The GOONS were aided by a sixty-member SWAT team of federal marshals from Washington, D.C. By February 1973, violent confrontations between traditionalists and Wilson's GOONS were becoming an everyday occurrence at Pine Ridge.

Shortly after the arrival of the federal marshals in February, traditional Oglalas petitioned the members of AIM for assistance. AIM had been operating as an indigenous civil rights organization since 1968. Much like the Black Panthers, AIM sought to put an end to police brutality, high unemployment, and oppressive government policies toward Native Americans in the 1970s. Prior to the events at Wounded Knee, members of AIM had made a significant impact on the country's social awareness of the problems affecting native peoples with a series of symbolic demonstrations.

AIM activists were initially reluctant to come to Pine Ridge for fear of becoming involved in a local political dispute. After their arrival in South Dakota, however, it became apparent that the fight was not merely between two Sioux parties, but between the Sioux Nation and the federal government. Russell Means, AIM's leader, agreed with the traditional Oglalas' claim that the government was using Dick Wilson and the rest of his organization to terrorize and exploit the residents of Pine Ridge.

AIM and Oglala organizers devised a plan that would draw national attention to the atrocities being committed within the reservation. They intended to gather residents together in the hamlet at Wounded Knee and to hold a press conference detailing the government's corruption and misuse of local power. AIM chose Wounded Knee as the site for the protest because of its symbolic importance as the location of the last major massacre of Native Americans by U.S. troops in 1890.

Shortly after their arrival at Wounded Knee, however, the protestors were surrounded by Wilson's GOONS and agents of the BIA and the Federal Bureau of Investigation (FBI). The federal authorities demanded that the protestors surrender immediately or face an assault. AIM and the Oglalas decided to stand their ground.

Protestor Demands

The protestors demanded that the government investigate the misuse of tribal funds, violence on the part of the GOONS, and the BIA's and Department of Interior's handling of the Oglala Sioux tribe. They also called for the investigation of 371 treaties between the United States and various native nations that had been broken by the federal government.

The most important of these broken treaties was the 1868 Fort Laramie Treaty, granting the Black Hills to the Sioux Nation. The Black Hills carried a religious significance for the Sioux people, as well as a more tangible significance for the Oglalas. The federal government was strip-mining the land surrounding the Black Hills for deposits of uranium, and chemicals used in the mining were leaking into the reservation's water supply and causing a growing number of illnesses and birth defects among residents. According to the conditions set forth in the 1868 treaty, the Oglalas had the right to order the government to stop the mining of the land. Federal authorities refused to acknowledge the protestors' demands, and thus begun the seventy-one-day siege.

Federal authorities cut off all electricity and set up roadblocks surrounding the area to keep food and supplies from reaching the protestors. Despite the growing number of obstacles, additional supplies and supporters made their way into the area. For the next two months, the men and women inside Wounded Knee lived on minimal resources and engaged in daily bouts of heavy gunfire with surrounding authorities. Three blizzards and more than 5 million rounds of ammunition later, two AIM members were dead, twelve more were seriously wounded, and another thirteen had disappeared while carrying supplies across federal lines. On May 8, 1973, the protestors finally agreed to surrender, but only after the government had agreed to a meeting with tribal leaders concerning the 1868 Fort Laramie treaty.

Nearly 600 people were arrested at Wounded Knee, with another 600 arrested in the days following the siege. The years 1973 through 1976 are commonly referred to as "The Reign of Terror" among the Oglalas. During that time, sixty-four tribal members were victims of unsolved murders and hundreds more were harassed and beaten. Of the hundreds of Native Americans arrested following Wounded Knee, only fifteen were ever convicted of a crime.

Catherine Griffis

See also: Native Americans; Violence, Political.

Bibliography

Mattheissen, Peter. *In the Spirit of Crazy Horse.* New York: Penguin, 1992.

O'Neil, Floyd, June Lyman, and Susan McKay. *Wounded Knee 1973: A Personal Account.* Lincoln: University of Nebraska Press, 1991.

Smith, Paul Chaat. *Like a Hurricane: The Indian Movement from Alcatraz to Wounded Knee.* New York: New Press, 1996.

X ARTICLE

Short-hand for the seminal *Foreign Affairs* article, "Sources of Soviet Conduct," written by George F. Kennan in 1947 under the pseudonym "X," the "X article" introduced the term "containment" into the Cold War lexicon. It also outlined the broad parameters of the strategy that would drive U.S. foreign policy toward the Soviet Union in various incarnations for the next four decades.

The X article appeared in the middle of a critical year in the development of U.S. postwar foreign policy. Kennan's "Long Telegram" in February 1946 and the Clifford-Elsey memorandum the following September detailed the existence of both a fundamental conflict between the United States and the Soviet Union and a consensus among American policymakers on the need to restrain Soviet ambitions. By March 1947, U.S. policy toward the Soviet Union had hardened noticeably with the announcement of the Truman Doctrine; in June, the Marshall Plan was announced as the economic component of the evolving anticommunist policy.

Kennan never intended the X article to be a comprehensive statement of national strategy, and it was not a complete exposition of his ideas. Indeed, it had originally been written as a memorandum to Secretary of the Navy James Forrestal, who was head of the policy planning staff at the State Department. Yet when "X" was revealed to be Kennan by Arthur Krock, a reporter from *The New York Times*, the article gained the weight of an official policy pronouncement.

Kennan emphasized the ideological and psychological sources of Soviet motivations in the postwar international arena. He described Soviet ambitions as unlimited and argued that negotiations had no hope of resolving the irreconcilable differences that existed between the United States and the Soviet Union. He called for a policy of containment to protect the free institutions of the West, a policy that would be characterized by the "adroit and vigilant application of counter-force at a series of constantly shifting geo-graphical and political points, corresponding to the shifts and maneuvers of Soviet policy." Given that the Kremlin viewed the Soviet-American rivalry as "a duel of infinite duration," the ultimate goal of U.S. policy should be the "long-term, patient but firm and vigilant containment of Russian expansive tendencies" to thwart Soviet attempts to gain control of additional resources and to maintain a global balance of power favorable to the United States.

What was required, Kennan concluded, was a commitment to "promote tendencies which must eventually find their outlet in either the break-up or the gradual mellowing of Soviet power." He believed that, if properly applied, the containment policy he suggested would cause the Soviet state to disintegrate from within due to its inherent internal flaws. Kennan's policy formulation would undergo a transformation with the promulgation of NSC-68 (National Security Countil Report 68, a 1950 document arguing for a policy of containment vis-à-vis the Soviet Union) and the outbreak of the Korean War in 1950, which globalized the Cold War, and would find its ultimate expression in the Vietnam War.

The exact meaning of Kennan's containment policy continues to be debated by scholars: Did he intend to employ diplomatic, economic, and/or military means to achieve American aims? Whatever his intentions may have been, the X article provided the definition of and foundation for U.S. strategy during the Cold War.

Andrew L. Johns

See also: Containment; Kennan's Long Telegram; Soviet Union/ Russia, Relations with; Truman Doctrine.

Bibliography

Gaddis, John Lewis. *Strategies of Containment: A Critical Appraisal of Postwar American National Security Policy.* Rev. ed. New York: Oxford University Press, 2005.

Kennan, George F. *Memoirs, 1925–1950.* New York: Bantam, 1967.

X (George F. Kennan). "The Sources of Soviet Conduct." *Foreign Affairs* 25 (July 1947): 562–82.

Y

YIPPIES

Originally created as a prank by members of the disillusioned 1960s counterculture, the Youth International Party (YIP) became one of the primary targets of several government agencies. Formed by veteran political activists Jerry Rubin, Abbie Hoffman, Paul Krassner, Keith Lampe, and Stew Albert, YIP gained considerable notoriety through manipulation of national media outlets. Members of the group (known as Yippies) played an integral role in planning the demonstrations at the Democratic National Convention in Chicago in August 1968. It was at this point that the message of YIP seemed to change from one of peace and love to one of open revolution.

Formed in response to the perceived failure of electoral politics in America, YIP was designed to gain wide publicity and arouse revolutionary sentiment among the young people of the nation. The group created a fictitious leadership, as well as imaginary membership lists. It published flyers and used word of mouth to spread rumors concerning the rapid growth of the party and its extreme radical ideology. The campaign was so successful that *Newsweek* magazine published an article on the Yippies within a month of the group's conception. Some of the actual activities of the Yippies included mailing marijuana cigarettes to 3,000 randomly chosen addresses found in a phone book and creating chaos on the floor of the New York Stock Exchange by emptying bags filled with money from a balcony over the trading floor.

To add credibility to the party name, a headquarters was rented at 32 Union Square in Manhattan, where the door was always left open so that anyone would be able to man the phones as an official party spokesperson. This phase of the group's existence was characterized by the kind of playful and often humorous mischief that embodied many of the liberal aspects of the hippie counterculture. Members also regularly engaged in "guerrilla theater," skits performed at random in public designed to deceive witnesses into thinking they were real.

The Yippie movement took a significant turn beginning in March 1968. During a rally organized by the Yippies at New York's Grand Central Station, violence erupted between demonstrators and police. Some of the group's leaders, including Hoffman, were beaten into unconsciousness. Because of their wide press coverage, the Yippies became associated with violent protest. This was not seen as negative publicity by many of the party's members, however; they viewed media manipulation and the ability to shock the American public as their primary goal.

The Yippies were also instrumental in planning the "Festival of Life," a demonstration at the 1968 Democratic National Convention in Chicago. In organizing this demonstration, the Yippies collaborated with groups such as the Students for a Democratic Society and the Mobilization to End the War in Vietnam, both more politically oriented than the Yippies.

The event was fraught with problems from the beginning. The organizing groups debated nearly every detail, but each one ultimately made its own arrangements for the protest. The organizers could not get a permit to allow protestors to sleep in Lincoln Park, and the Chicago Police began arresting organizers days before the convention began. As usual, rumors concerning Yippie activities abounded. Local news broadcasts warned the population of Chicago of a threat to taint the public water supply with the hallucinogenic drug LSD. While the threat was only a rumor, it did serve to heighten the already tense atmosphere surrounding the convention.

The demonstrations themselves proved to be a nightmare for the city. Violence between police and demonstrators occurred every day, and eight organizers of the event, three of them Yippies, were arrested on conspiracy charges. The group gained notoriety as the "Chicago Seven," and their joint trial was marked by characteristically Yippie-type stunts: During court proceedings, the defendants sang songs, displayed the Viet Cong flag, and interrupted testimony.

While never taken seriously by many older activists, the Yippies embodied the radical psychedelic atmosphere of the 1960s. As the Vietnam War drew to a close and the counterculture generation grew older, the group gradually broke up and disappeared. Several activist groups have since tried to carry on the name, but none has managed to achieve the public notoriety of the original Yippies.

Benjamin Gworek

See also: Antiwar Movement, Vietnam Era; Counterculture; Education, Higher; New Left; Port Huron Statement; Students for a Democratic Society; Vietnam War; Weathermen.

Bibliography

Hoffman, Abbie. *Revolution for the Hell of It.* New York: Dial, 1968.

Stein, David Lewis. *Living the Revolution.* Indianapolis, IN: Bobbs-Merrill, 1969.

YOUNG AMERICANS FOR FREEDOM

Young Americans for Freedom (YAF) was the most successful conservative student organization of the 1960s. Drawing energy from the Cold War and the utopian idealism of the baby boom generation, YAF was the New Right's counter to Students for a Democratic Society (SDS). YAF's influence declined precipitously after 1964, but a resurgence in conservative politics during the 1980s revitalized the organization.

The organization began on September 9–11, 1960, when about 100 students from forty-four colleges and universities met at the Sharon, Connecticut, estate of William F. Buckley, Jr. The meeting galvanized conservatives from organizations such as Youth for Goldwater, Young Republican National Federation, and National Conservative Young Organization. "We were carrying the flag of conservatism at a time nobody really understood what that meant," one participant, Carol Dawson, later recalled. YAF members like Dawson wanted to be active in the Republican Party, while expressing their views independently of parents and teachers.

The document that resulted from these early meetings became known as the "Sharon Statement," a classic critique of American liberalism. Consisting of a preamble and twelve short articles, this statement of belief affirmed the principles of limited federal government, states' rights, a vigorous market economy, strong national defense, the primacy of the U.S. Constitution, and the "foremost" of all values, "God-given free will." In the shadow of the Cold War, the document denounced communism as the "greatest single threat to these liberties."

The YAF was busy on college campuses during the early 1960s. At its peak in 1964, YAF had 20,000 dues-paying members and another 35,000 occasional contributors. YAFers boycotted corporations that traded with Communist countries, sent reading material and medical supplies to servicemen overseas, recruited conservative college faculty, and countered the student Left with demonstrations for the Vietnam War and college Reserve Officers' Training Corps programs. Young conservatives everywhere were inspired by Buckley's magazine, *National Review.*

Besides campus activities, YAF was also involved in national electoral politics, most aggressively in 1964, when it backed Arizona Republican Senator Barry Goldwater's campaign for the presidency. Goldwater was said to represent "a nation and a world in which the individual is free." The message did not resonate with voters. Lyndon B. Johnson's overwhelming victory marked an affirmation of liberalism and the decline of the YAF. Johnson's introduction of ground troops in Vietnam in 1965 fractured YAF still further. The organization's libertarian ideology compelled it to oppose the draft, even while supporting the war.

In the 1980s, a number of early YAFers resurfaced as appointees in the administration of President Ronald Reagan. The resurrection of conservative politics, fueled by a coalition with the Christian right, aided YAF recruitment. A new generation of YAFers grew up admiring Reagan, who they believed returned patriotism to America and vanquished the dreaded beast, communism. These young people, who came of age in the 1990s, joined YAF in addressing a new set of conservative issues. Abortion, the federal minimum wage, and gun control were all vigorously attacked by YAFers in the early 2000s.

Jed Woodworth

See also: Conservatism; Election of 1964; Republican Party.

Bibliography

Andrew, John A., III. *The Other Side of the Sixties: Young Americans for Freedom and the Rise of Conservative Politics.* New Brunswick, NJ: Rutgers University Press, 1997.

Hatch, Rebecca E. *A Generation Divided: The New Left, the New Right, and the 1960s.* Berkeley: University of California Press, 1999.

Z

ZERO POPULATION GROWTH

Established in 1968 by ecologist Paul Ehrlich, Yale University biology professor Charles L. Remington, and Connecticut lawyer Richard Bowers, Zero Population Growth (ZPG) sought to heighten public awareness about the threat of overpopulation in the United States. It was the first politically active environmental group to focus specifically on the issue of population growth.

In his book *The Population Bomb* (1968), Ehrlich, a biology professor at Stanford University in California, maintained that overpopulation was the world's fundamental environmental problem, underlying famine, overcrowding, and pollution. Because Americans, with their high standard of living, consumed many times more resources per capita than people in poorer countries, Ehrlich argued that the United States was the most overpopulated nation on earth. Within a decade of its publication, *The Population Bomb* sold 3 million copies, making it the best-selling environmental book to date.

To build on the book's success, Ehrlich, Remington, and Bowers created Zero Population Growth in the fall of 1968. Within two years, the organization had 33,000 members in 380 chapters across the United States. To encourage smaller families, ZPG's straightforward message, found on bumper stickers, posters, and advertisements, was that couples should have only two children.

Originally a grassroots organization that sought to educate Americans that they had a population problem and to encourage family planning through birth control or sterilization, ZPG was soon advocating public policy. In 1970, it opened a lobbying office in Washington, D.C., to support such issues as contraceptive research and abortion rights.

Many Americans appeared receptive to ZPG's general message. Public opinion polls revealed that the majority agreed overpopulation either was a problem in the present or would soon become one. The fertility rate in the United States dropped from 3.4 children per woman in the early 1960s to 1.8 by 1975.

ZPG was also the target of sharp criticism. Barry Commoner, a prominent ecologist, questioned its central premise, noting that since World War II, pollution had increased far more than population in the United States. Thus, he contended, to focus on population growth was to miss more serious technological causes of the environmental crisis. Because population growth was lower among whites than blacks, some critics charged that ZPG's advocacy of family planning, especially sterilization, was racist. Ehrlich denied the accusation, countering that the lifestyles of white, middle-class Americans put greater strains on the environment.

By the late 1970s, white Americans were close to achieving zero population growth. The most significant factor in the nation's continued population growth was immigration, especially from Mexico and other Latin American countries. ZPG's call for immigration restrictions provoked intense opposition from Latinos.

After a decline in membership in the 1970s and 1980s, ZPG grew to 70,000 members in the 1990s. While still stressing the need to curb population growth, it also called increasing attention to poverty, political repression, and technology as environmental issues. In 2002, Zero Population Growth changed its name to Population Connection. The organization continues to maintain its headquarters in Washington, D.C.

Fred Nielsen

See also: Birth Control; Club of Rome Report.

Bibliography

Callahan, Daniel, ed. *The American Population Debate.* Garden City, NY: Doubleday, 1971.

Ehrlich, Paul. *The Population Bomb.* New York: Ballantine, 1968.

Gottlieb, Robert. *Forcing the Spring: The Transformation of the American Environmental Movement.* Washington, DC: Island, 1993.

Cultural Landmarks

Landmark items that fall into the categories of both print media (Literature and Journalism) and performance media (Film, Radio, Television, and Theater)—such as novels that are made into movies—are listed under the category for which they are best known. Where the work has had a strong cultural influence as both a book and a movie, the artifact generally appears in the Literature and Journalism section, with a "see also" under Film, Radio, Television, and Theater.

THE FORTIES AND FIFTIES

Literature and Journalism

Affluent Society, The (nonfiction, by John Kenneth Galbraith, 1958)

Political scientists regard *The Affluent Society* as the most influential work of the noted Harvard economist and government advisor John Kenneth Galbraith—and of its time. In it, Galbraith argues that American society in the mid-twentieth century was unique in world history in the number of people with disposable income, but he acknowledges that traditional assumptions and policies had impeded the equitable distribution of wealth. True affluence—the fair distribution of quality education, medical care, transportation, and access to public services—can be achieved through a variety of measures, Galbraith contends. *The Affluent Society* thus had a direct effect on the domestic policy initiatives of presidents John F. Kennedy and Lyndon B. Johnson.

Atlas Shrugged (novel, by Ayn Rand, 1957)

One of the best-known works of the procapitalist, proindividualist novelist Ayn Rand, *Atlas Shrugged* is perhaps the signature treatise outlining her philosophy of objectivism. Rand argues that selfishness is the key motivating factor behind all human behavior. Rather than seeing this is as potentially destructive and antisocial, she contends, in this novel depicting railroad tycoons, that selfishness is both constructive and good. The book suggests that America was built on the selfish pursuit of wealth and that government action to rein in that pursuit would be detrimental not only to individual achievement but to social harmony as well. From the time it was first published, *Atlas Shrugged* has remained popular with antigovernment conservatives.

Black Boy (novel, by Richard Wright, 1945; television documentary, 1995)

An influential work in both the annals of African American letters and the development of the American coming-of-age memoir, *Black Boy* is the semi-fictionalized account of a young African American boy growing up in Mississippi in the 1920s. While the book offers a searing indictment of Southern racism of the day, it is also a powerful family drama concerning an ailing mother and a father who leaves home. Eventually, the boy joins his aunt and moves to Chicago, where he encounters the more subtle racism existing in the North. At one point, he joins the Communist Party but becomes disillusioned by its rigid thinking. Still, he clings to his belief that American society must change, and he finds hope in that struggle. As the story of a boy growing into manhood, the book has become a perennial favorite among young readers, both black and white. A television documentary about Wright and this book was aired in 1995.

Blackboard Jungle, The (novel, by Evan Hunter, 1954; film, directed by Richard Brooks, 1955)

This novel follows the experiences of an idealistic English teacher who enters a New York City public school and finds the institution plagued by violence and rebelliousness. A best-seller, the book was turned into a film—directed by Richard Brooks and starring Glenn Ford, Anne Francis, Sidney Poitier, and Vic Morrow—the following year. Part of a genre of fictional school exposés—including *Up the Down Staircase* (play, 1965; film, 1967) and *To Sir with Love* (novel, 1959; film, 1967)—*The Blackboard Jungle* may seem melodramatic to modern readers and viewers. In the 1950s, however, it was considered a hard-hitting portrayal of juvenile delinquency, a growing public concern at that time, and was said to raise public consciousness about the problems of inner-city youth and schools.

Catcher in the Rye, The (novel, by J.D. Salinger, 1951)

One of the most popular young adult novels of all time, J.D. Salinger's classic coming-of-age story tells of two days in the life of Holden Caulfield, a recently expelled prep school student. Although he comes from a wealthy family and faces a life of material opportunity, the angst-ridden Holden feels alienated from a world that he sees as dominated by "phonies." Distraught at this bleak vision, Holden experiences a mental breakdown and ends up on a psychiatrist's couch. As an antihero who exposed rather than saved

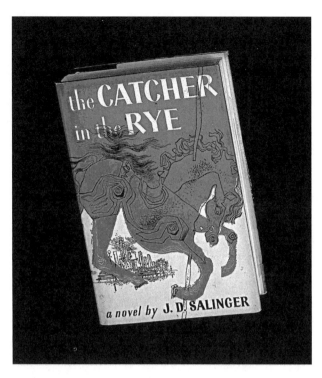

The narrator and protagonist of J. D. Salinger's *The Catcher in the Rye* (1951) challenges the mores and conventions of the time. *(Roberto Brosan/Time Life Pictures/Getty Images)*

society, Caulfield became a figure with whom generations of American teenagers came to identify.

Common Sense Book of Baby and Child Care, The (nonfiction, by Dr. Benjamin Spock, 1946)

One of the most revolutionary books of the postwar era, *Common Sense* was the first popular parenting book to present childhood as a unique stage in human development and to argue that children require special treatment. Before Spock's book, parenting guides depicted children as miniature adults who should be treated and disciplined as such. Cuddling, holding, and playing with the child too much, it had been contended, could arrest proper development. Earlier books also said that parents should defer to experts in how to raise their children. Spock's work turned all of this on its head. Accepting a child for who he or she is and indulging his or her need for play and affection, *Common Sense* maintains, leads to the healthy development of the child's psyche. Spock also urged parents to follow their own instincts on how to raise their children.

Millions of baby boom parents took Spock's advice. While the book has gone through multiple editions and sold in the tens of millions, it remains controversial to this day. Some have argued that Spock's "permissive" approach to child rearing in the 1950s led to the hedonism, casual sex, and drug abuse of the hippie generation of the 1960s and 1970s.

Dianetics: The Modern Science of Mental Health (nonfiction, by L. Ron Hubbard, 1950)

The book that launched the scientology movement and the Church of Scientology, *Dianetics* argues that there is something in the human brain called "the reactive mind"—full of fear and doubt—and that one must learn to control it in order to progress as a successful individual and member of society. Once one learns how to do this, scientologists contend, the powers within the brain are "unleashed" and can achieve their full potential.

While *Dianetics* continues to sell in the millions and is heavily promoted by the Church of Scientology, later practitioners have tended to deemphasize its influence, saying that the book took its ideas from many different religious traditions. One element of the book's continuing popularity has been that many Hollywood celebrities, including actors Tom Cruise and John Travolta, publicly discussed their devotion to its principles.

Fahrenheit 451 (novel, by Ray Bradbury, 1953; film, directed by François Truffaut, 1966)

This dark work of science fiction depicts a future in which it is illegal to possess and read books. Guy Montag, the protagonist, is a fireman charged with burning illegal books and the houses in which they are found. The title refers to the temperature at which books are said to combust spontaneously. Montag starts to question whether or not he should burn books after meeting Clarisse, a seventeen-year-old girl who has reservations about society's attitude toward critical thinking and knowledge. Confronted by his boss, whom he kills, Montag eventually goes into hiding with other book readers.

Like many science fiction books, *Farenheit 451* is an allegory, in this case about the dangers of censorship. Written during a period of anticommunist hysteria, when any work of literature with a hint of Marxism was considered anti-American, *Farenheit 451* has been understood by many readers as a portrait, albeit exaggerated, of 1950s America. A haunting film, directed by François Truffaut, came out in 1966 and was nominated for several international awards; a new version, being directed by Frank Darabont, was in production in 2006.

From Here to Eternity (novel, by James Jones, 1951; film, directed by Fred Zinnemann, 1953)

From Here to Eternity is set on a U.S. military base in Hawaii during the days leading up to the Japanese attack on Pearl Harbor in 1941. The main story line concerns a young soldier who reluctantly returns to a career in boxing after being harassed by his captain, who is eager to win an Army championship for the company. Because readers and audiences know that the action takes place before the outbreak of war, the story provides a kind of nostalgic look back at what was considered a more innocent time in American history, a time before the country took up the mantle of global leadership. The film starred Burt Lancaster and Deborah Kerr, whose lovemaking scene in the Hawaiian surf titillated 1950s audiences.

God and Man at Yale (nonfiction, by William F. Buckley, Jr., 1951)

Written by one of America's foremost conservatives, this book focuses on Buckley's experiences as an undergraduate at Yale University and his awakening to the process by which "traditional" American values of decency, duty, and respect for order were being slighted. The book had an enduring influence on young conservatives, especially during and after the liberal politics and legal reforms of the 1960s. Conservatives have liked the book's emphasis on unchanging values, as well as its argument that the removal of religion from schools and other public institutions was leading to the decline of Western civilization.

Hidden Persuaders, The (nonfiction, by Vance Packard, 1957)

While not the first book to examine the influence of advertisers and advertising on the American economy, society, and psyche, *The Hidden Persuaders* was the first to examine the subject in a manner accessible to a general readership. In the book, Packard discusses how advertisers create desires in consumers that they previously did not know they had and how advertising plays upon the fears and hopes of the general public. Written during the pro-business climate of the 1950s, when many experts claimed that advertising was a force for good, Packard's iconoclastic book argues that advertising has an insidious effect on the American people and their society.

How the Grinch Stole Christmas (children's storybook, by Dr. Seuss [Theodor Seuss Geisel], 1957; television film, directed by Chuck Jones and Ben Washam, 1966; film, directed by Ron Howard, 2000)

Perhaps the most popular Christmas book of the postwar era, *How the Grinch Stole Christmas* was an illustrated children's story by the best-selling author Dr. Seuss (born Theodor Seuss Geisel). The book relates the story of a town named Whoville, inhabited by decent, good-natured folks called the Whos. As the Whos prepare to celebrate Christmas, a local curmudgeon, the Grinch, steals all the presents. On one level a playful and fanciful children's story, *How the Grinch Stole Christmas* is also an allegory about individual greed versus the social good, a not-surprising theme for the lifelong Socialist writer. The book was later made into a children's television special in 1966, with Boris Karloff as the voice of the Grinch, and a Hollywood movie in 2000, with Jim Carrey in the title role.

Howl (poem, by Allen Ginsberg, 1956)

With his long poem "Howl" in 1956—a rant against the banality of postwar American culture—Allen Ginsberg established his reputation as a writer and unofficial spokesman for the Beat Generation, a movement of unconventional artists willing to challenge, in their work and lifestyles, the conformist society of the day. Ginsberg first read "Howl" to a live audience at the Six Gallery in San Francisco in October 1955. When it was published the following year, in a volume titled *Howl and Other Poems,* Ginsberg and his publisher, Lawrence Ferlinghetti (himself a Beat poet) of City Lights Books, were arrested on obscenity charges (of which they were later acquitted).

A social outcast in the 1950s, Ginsberg became one of the father figures of the counterculture movement of the 1960s. "Howl" became a kind of manifesto for hippies rebelling against conventional American culture.

Invisible Man (novel, by Ralph Ellison, 1952)

For many readers, both black and white, this work of African American alienation in white society retains its saliency more than fifty years after it was written. In it, Ellison describes the life of a young black man who grows up in the South, gets expelled from a black college for telling a trustee about racism at the institution, and moves to New York City, where he lives in the years following World War II. Throughout, the protagonist/narrator is continually taken advantage of because of his color, and he loses his identity. The title refers to the fact that everyone in the book sees the protagonist through his or her own racial blinders and that no one can see the real person behind the stereotypes they bring with them.

Kinsey Reports on Human Sexual Behavior (nonfiction, by Alfred Kinsey: *Sexual Behavior in the Human Male,* 1948, and *Sexual Behavior in the Human Female,* 1953)

The Kinsey Reports on Human Sexual Behavior were based on thousands of questionnaires distributed and analyzed by the Institute for Sex Research, now known as the Kinsey Institute, at Indiana University. These were the first large-scale studies of sex as a clinical subject, rather than as an issue of morality. Participants were questioned on a wide variety of sexual issues, and the results were tabulated in two books, one on men (1948) and one on women (1953).

The books demonstrated, among other things, that there was no link between premarital sex and divorce and that homosexuality was not deviant, both conclusions that challenged accepted beliefs of the time. The studies also found that many more people participated in extramarital sex, petting, homosexuality, oral and anal sex, and other "nontraditional" behaviors than previously had been believed. The results helped convince many in America that there was no normative sexual experience. Some sociologists cite the book as a key factor in the sexual revolution of the 1960s.

Little House on the Prairie (novels, by Laura Ingalls Wilder, 1932–1971; television series, 1974–1983)

This series of young-adult novels, later adapted into a popular television series, explores the theme of growing up on the American prairie in the late 1800s. The books tell of Wilder's early life in Wisconsin and the family's move to the Kansas plains, chronicling her own coming of age and married life. The series tries to present an honest account of nineteenth-century frontier life but leaves out much of the violence and poverty. In addition, the books portray Native Americans in a somewhat derogatory light. The television series, starring Melissa Gilbert (as Laura) and Michael

Landon (as her father), omitted much of the books' troubling anti-Native American commentary. Both the books and the TV series played on the desire of the American public for the family values of what was considered a simpler time.

Lolita (novel, by Vladimir Nabokov, 1955; film, directed by Stanley Kubrick, 1962; film, directed by Adrian Lyne, 1997)

One of the most controversial literary works of the postwar era, *Lolita* deals with the taboo subject of pederasty. The story revolves around a sophisticated European academic, Humbert Humbert, who takes a job at a small liberal arts college in the United States. There, he falls in love with a preteen girl named Lolita. To get close to the girl, he marries her mother, who, on discovering her new husband's secret desires, runs screaming into the street and is run over by a car and dies. Humbert then takes Lolita on a cross-country trip, which lasts until she gets tired of him and leaves.

After rejections from several U.S. publishers, author Vladimir Nabokov first published the book in France. Finally published in America in 1958, it became a best-seller and was turned into a critically acclaimed and popular movie directed by Stanley Kubrick four years later. In the 1962 film, the young Lolita was portrayed as a teenager so as not to offend audiences, but the 1997 remake by director Adrian Lyne featured a much younger Lolita.

Lonely Crowd, The (nonfiction, by David Riesman, Reuel Denney, and Nathan Glazer, 1950)

Initially criticized by sociologists but popular with the general reading public, *The Lonely Crowd* explores how large governmental and corporate organizations influence human behavior and the national character. According to the authors, people generally fit into one of three character types: "tradition-directed" (those who obey rules and fear change); "inner-directed" (self-confident and independent, but rigid); and "other directed" (willing to accommodate themselves to others and to social change). Of the three, the last type of person is deemed the most likely to succeed in modern American society. At a time of expanding bureaucracy, the book struck a chord with a public ambivalent about the conformism of postwar life.

Mad (magazine, 1952–present; television series, 1995–present)

Since its founding in 1952, *Mad* magazine has satirized American culture and society, offering timely parodies of hit films, TV shows, and advertisements. While the humor is broad and sophomoric, subtle social commentary about American values is embedded in the magazine's cartoons and comics. One early feature, "Spy vs. Spy," focused on two nearly identical characters who plotted violent mischief against one another; some recognized this as a not-so-subtle dig at the Cold War posturing of the United States and the Soviet Union.

The iconic image of the magazine is Alfred E. Neuman, a big-eared, freckle-faced boy who has appeared on virtually every cover. *Mad* has had a devoted following of both teenagers and adults. In 1995, the magazine spun off a modestly successful television variety show called *Mad TV,* which runs on the Comedy Central cable station.

Man in the Gray Flannel Suit, The (novel, by Sloan Wilson, 1955; film, directed by Nunnally Johnson, 1956)

The protagonist, Tom Rath, represents the typical World War II veteran who has returned from the war, gone to college, achieved a job in middle management, and is ready to get married. Tom, however, is not happy with his position, even though he has achieved what is supposed to be the American dream—he feels trapped and is haunted by nightmarish memories of his war years. A best-selling novel that captured the frustrations of white-collar veterans, *The Man in the Gray Flannel Suit* was turned into a movie starring Gregory Peck the year after it was published. While the novel was widely praised, the movie received mixed reviews and was only moderately successful at the box office.

Naked and the Dead, The (novel, by Norman Mailer, 1948; film, directed by Raoul Walsh, 1958)

During the early postwar period, World War II was a popular subject in fiction and movies, but few novels on the topic were more successful commercially and more influential for modern American literature than Norman Mailer's massive tome on the war in the Pacific, *The Naked and the Dead.* Brutally candid in its depiction of violence and war, the book chronicles a rescue mission by a platoon of U.S. soldiers across a jungled island contested by the Japanese. The novel depicts how war can debase the values of American soldiers who, in contrast to the Japanese, were often depicted in the media, in literature, and in fiction as noble warriors. One of the main themes of the book is how enlisted men and officers experienced the war in entirely different ways. A film version directed by Raoul Walsh appeared in 1958; much of the violence and coarseness of the book were left out.

Naked Lunch (novel, by William S. Burroughs, 1959; film, directed by David Cronenberg, 1991)

Burroughs's first successful novel, *Naked Lunch* established his reputation as one of the key figures in the Beat literary movement of the 1950s. Confronting American society in that decade of conformism, the Beats used both form and plot to challenge accepted values about literature and society. *Naked Lunch,* with its crude and fantastical language and its storyline about a heroin junkie and his hallucinogenic "trips," was the quintessential expression of the Beat perspective. Little noticed upon its publication in 1959, the book became popular in the later 1960s among younger Americans who were discovering illegal drugs. In 1991, Canadian horror film director David Cronenberg made a critically acclaimed movie based on the book.

National Enquirer, The (magazine, 1952–present)

Originally a New York-based, horse-racing paper, *The National Enquirer* was purchased in 1952 by the Italian publisher Generoso Pope, Jr., who quickly changed the format to feature bizarre incidents, grisly crimes, and celebrity news. The new content, combined with a new method of distribution—racks at grocery store and supermarket checkout counters—helped circulation soar past the 1 million mark by the end of the decade. In 1968, Pope overhauled the format once again, dropping the more grisly material for a focus on celebrities and ordinary people doing extraordinary things.

During most of its history, the tabloid has been treated as a joke by more mainstream publishers. With increased scrutiny on the sex lives of politicians in the late 1980s and 1990s, however, the *Enquirer* found itself quoted in such august papers as the *Washington Post* and *The New York Times.*

On the Road (novel, by Jack Kerouac, 1957)

Kerouac called the book a novel, but it is really more a memoir of the author's travels across the country in the company of his friend, a con artist and hustler named Neal Cassady. (Kerouac did change the names of the real-life characters; Cassady became Dean Moriarty, and Kerouac calls himself Sal Paradise.) The two drifters meet various characters along the way, engage in sex and crime, and slowly discover themselves in a meandering plot.

The book's free-flowing, stream-of-consciousness style influenced writers such as Richard Brautigan, LeRoi Jones (Amiri Baraka), and others coming out of the Beat literary movement of the 1950s, of which *On the Road* is perhaps the most famous prose work. It also has had a major impact on the culture at large, particularly in the decades following its publication, as young people took off on their own journeys of personal discovery across America. Although it was published in the 1950s, *On the Road* helped catalyze the hippie movement and turn it from a small group of social outcasts into a national social phenomenon.

Peanuts (cartoon strip, by Charles M. Schulz, 1950–2000)

Arguably the most famous and beloved of syndicated newspaper comic strips, "Peanuts," begun in 1950 by Charles M. Schulz, remains popular and widely distributed, despite the death of its creator in early 2000. (Reprints of the old strips continue to run in many newspapers.) The comic strip, collected in numerous books and the inspiration for several television specials, including the annually broadcast *A Charlie Brown Christmas* (1965; see page 1453), portrays a neighborhood of children familiar to generations of readers.

Although the characters are all young children, they represent distinct adult personality types and often speak in grown-up language and express sophisticated ideas and sentiments. The main protagonist is Charlie Brown, a much put-upon everyman. Other characters include the curmudgeonly Lucy, her younger brother, the philosophical Linus (with his trademark security blanket), and Charlie's eccentric dog Snoopy. The comic strip's enormous popularity has been said to be a product of its sly wit and the fact that its characters are fully rounded individuals, with all the strengths and foibles of ordinary people.

Peyton Place (novel, by Grace Metalious, 1956; film, directed by Mark Robson, 1957; television series, 1964–1969)

Based on both the 1956 best-selling novel by Grace Metalious and a 1957 hit movie starring Lana Turner, *Peyton Place* was the original prime-time soap opera.

Set in a New England town, the show followed the doings of two generations of the Harrington family. The television series sought to capitalize on the scandalous reputation that the novel and movie had gained for their explicit (for the time) depictions of sex and scandal, including plots revolving around extramarital affairs, illegitimate children, and premarital sex. ABC was rebuked for airing the show in prime time, but it was immensely popular. This show also is noteworthy for helping launch the careers of film stars Mia Farrow and Ryan O'Neal.

Both the movie and the series inspired movie and TV sequels titled *Return to Peyton Place,* with the movie coming out in 1961 and the TV series running from 1972 to 1974. Neither enjoyed the success of the original.

Playboy (magazine, 1953–present)

First published in December 1953, with a seminude Marilyn Monroe as the first of the magazine's trademark monthly centerfolds, *Playboy* was launched by publisher Hugh Hefner as a kind of guide to the bachelor's life. The magazine served as a foil to the family-conscious 1950s, when marriage and children were considered the only way to happiness and fulfillment. Instead, Hefner portrayed an exciting lifestyle for single men, complete with serial dating, apartments full of the latest consumer products, and tips on how to act in a sophisticated, man-of-the-world manner.

The monthly publication was best known for its photos of seminaked—and, by the 1970s, fully naked—young women. But *Playboy* was more than a single man's lifestyle guide; during its heyday from the 1950s through 1980s, it also offered some of the best short fiction published in America and included serious critiques of contemporary novels and movies. A popular feature of the magazine was, and remains, its lengthy in-depth interviews with major political and cultural figures. By the 1990s, however, *Playboy* appeared increasingly dated, and it had lost many of its readers—many of whom had picked up the magazine for the photos—to the Internet.

Power Elite, The (nonfiction, by C. Wright Mills, 1956)

Written by the leftist sociologist C. Wright Mills, *The Power Elite* challenged the 1950s Cold War American consensus that the United States was a democratic and egalitarian nation and the highest political achievement the world had yet seen. Although written by a scholar, the book had a wide crossover appeal with the general public and became a nonfiction best-seller.

Mills's basic thesis was that, like all countries, the United States had what he called a "power elite," who, while having to operate within a democratic system, actually controlled the destiny of the country. He divided the elite into three groups: those in the military, those in corporate America, and those in politics. In his famous farewell address, President Dwight D. Eisenhower picked up on Mills's ideas by warning of a "military-industrial complex" moving the nation toward a more aggressive posture overseas and taking control of the country's resources.

Power of Positive Thinking, The (nonfiction, by Norman Vincent Peale, 1952)

One of the best-selling books of the postwar period, *The Power of Positive Thinking* has sold more than 20 million copies in some forty-one languages. This upbeat self-help guide applies Christian principles to empower people in their daily lives. Sometimes called the "father of Christianized self-esteem," Peale advocates "positive thinking" as an antidote to doubt and fear, allowing people to unleash their spiritual, emotional, and intellectual potential. A pastor at the liberal Marble Collegiate Church in New York City from 1932 to 1984, Peale preached a message of self-empowerment and was extremely influential in the creation of the self-help genre of nonfiction. *The Power of Positive Thinking* fused two enormously powerful forces in twentieth-century American life: religion and psychology. Its basic message could be encapsulated as believing in oneself and trusting in God.

Profiles in Courage (nonfiction, by John F. Kennedy, 1956)

Profiles in Courage was a collection of vignettes of major—and some minor—figures in the history of American politics. In the book, John F. Kennedy included both Republicans and Democrats, as well as figures from other parties in early U.S. history. The theme running through the various portraits is of men (no women are included) who, despite the pressures of partisan politics, stood up for their principles, risking their political fortunes in doing so. The best-selling book, which won a Pulitzer Prize for biography in 1957, met with mixed reviews when it first came out. In subsequent years, some even questioned whether Kennedy wrote it himself. In any

event, the work added heft to the résumé of a young senator with aspirations to higher office.

Sports Illustrated (magazine, 1954–present)

Sports Illustrated, the first weekly magazine to focus on the subject of sports, was launched in 1954 by Time, Inc., founder Henry Luce, who foresaw sports as big business in America. It attracted few readers until the 1960s, when managing editor Andre Laguerre, writers Dan Jenkins and Frank Deford, and photographers Neil Leifer and Walter Iooss came on board. Their coverage of such sports giants as Muhammad Ali (who appeared on thirty-two covers) soon attracted a weekly circulation of 1 million readers. By the late 1980s, *Sports Illustrated* had nearly 3.5 million subscribers, and Luce's vision had come true: America was obsessed with sports.

A special winter issue featuring women in swimsuits appeared in 1964 and proved so popular with readers and advertisers that it became an annual tradition. This and other cross-marketing opportunities helped *Sports Illustrated* compete for an audience that was increasingly drawn to the multitude of sporting events shown on television. As Michael MacCambridge wrote in *The Franchise* (1997), a history of the magazine, *Sports Illustrated* served as a "counterbalance to the persistent hype of television." It made an art of in-depth sports reporting, he maintained, thereby elevating its prominence and popularity.

Status Seekers, The (nonfiction, by Vance Packard, 1959)

Differences between the classes were nearly nonexistent, sociologists argued, during the prosperity of the 1950s. Most people were comfortably "middle class," they said, and the American dream was being realized as never before. In 1959, the muckraking journalist Vance Packard disagreed in *The Status Seekers: An Exploration of Class Behavior in America and the Hidden Barriers That Affect You, Your Community, Your Future.* Status seekers, Packard wrote, are people "continually straining to surround themselves with visible evidence of the superior rank they are claiming."

Relying on hundreds of sociological and market research studies, Packard concluded that not only were there class differences in the United States, but the differences were hardening rather than withering away. This hardening, he maintained, was the result of the "merchandising of goods as status symbols by advertisers," businesses that made advancement difficult, and a move toward "bigness" by an increasingly bureaucratized society. Aimed at a popular audience rather than academics, *The Status Seekers* was a best-seller and put the phrase "status seeker" into the American vocabulary.

TV Guide (magazine, 1953–present)

A baby graced the cover of the first issue of *TV Guide,* dated April 3, 1953. This was not just any baby, but "Little Ricky" Ricardo, the real-life son of television's "first couple," Lucy (Lucille Ball) and Ricky Ricardo (Desi Arnaz). The United States was becoming a nation of TV watchers, as newly affluent families moved to the suburbs and purchased appliances and material goods as never before. That baby on the cover was symbolic of every baby born in the years after World War II. *TV Guide* gave their parents localized viewing guides, as well as television news and celebrity gossip.

The magazine was created by Walter H. Annenberg, who was inspired by a local Philadelphia magazine called *TV Digest.* Annenberg envisioned a national magazine, and the first *TV Guide* was published in ten editions. As television changed, so did *TV Guide,* with more than 100 regional editions, coverage of cable programming, and articles on television's social impact. By the end of the twentieth century, *TV Guide* was the most-read publication in the country. It had helped spread and legitimize the medium of television, while advancing the entertainment obsession of postwar America.

Ugly American, The (novel, by William J. Lederer and Eugene Burdick, 1958; film, directed by George Englund, 1963)

The Ugly American by William J. Lederer and Eugene Burdick is a series of short stories about the fictional Southeast Asian nation of Sarkhan. Ambassador Gilbert MacWhite (changed to Harrison MacWhite in the film) and other Americans in Sarkhan find themselves in the midst of a civil war, with a Soviet-financed Communist insurgency gaining strength. The book's thinly veiled jabs at U.S. foreign policy in Southeast Asia were not lost on contemporary readers, and *The Ugly American* became a best-seller. Even President Dwight D. Eisenhower looked to it for answers to U.S. foreign policy problems. A "slashing exposé of American arrogance, incompetence, and corruption in Southeast Asia," according to its publisher, W.W. Norton, *The Ugly American* coined a phrase that was used throughout the twentieth century to describe American blunders overseas. A film starring Marlon Brando was released in 1963, but it was the book version that continued to resonate in the twenty-first century, as the United States embarked on new ventures in the Middle East.

White Collar (nonfiction, by C. Wright Mills, 1951)

White Collar: The American Middle Classes was sociologist C. Wright Mills's seminal 1951 work on the new American middle class. In it, Mills theorizes that the middle class, growing by leaps and bounds in the prosperous 1950s, contained elements of the lower class and the upper class. Values learned in both social categories combined to create something new in American life. According to Mills, the "old" middle class of farmers and small merchants was gone, replaced by big business and its armies of clerical workers and managers. *The New York Times* called *White Collar* a negative view of the middle class, but said it had "grounds for hope through disillusion."

Mills consistently challenged conventional ideas of society, as evidenced in his earlier *The New Men of Power* (1948) and later *The Power Elite* (1956). In the latter, he posits that Americans might be gaining wealth but were losing control of the structures that governed their lives. His condemnation of the "power elite" and advocacy for labor and the middle class made Mills a role model for the counterculture and a prominent influence on the New Left.

Film, Radio, Television, and Theater

All About Eve (film, directed by Joseph L. Mankiewicz, 1950)

Nominated for a record-breaking fourteen Oscars (a total later equaled by *Titanic,* 1997) and winning six of them, *All About Eve* was a break from the typical film about Broadway and the entertainment industry. Whereas previous films on the subject inevitably portrayed sophisticated characters earnestly striving to achieve art, *Eve* was all about backstabbing and conniving to reach the top. The plot revolves around Eve Harrington (Anne Baxter), an up-and-coming Broadway actress who dethrones the reigning queen of Broadway, Margo Channing (Bette Davis), through ruthlessness and deceit. The arresting final scene shows Harrington, now the top actress in New York, encountering another pretty young actress, suggesting that the power struggle on Broadway never ends.

American Bandstand (television, 1952–1987; syndicated, 1987–1989)

One of the first television shows to focus on popular music, *American Bandstand* became an important vehicle for promoting the new sound of rock and roll in the 1950s. Hosted during its first four years by disk jockey Bob Horn (until his arrest on statutory rape charges), *American Bandstand* in 1956 was turned over to newscaster Dick Clark, who effectively maintained the show's squeaky clean, youthful image. The format of the show remained constant during its thirty-five-year run. Clark would invite recording artists to appear on the show, interview them, and play their latest hits to a studio full of dancing teenagers and young adults. Other segments included "rate a record," in which the teens on the show offered feedback on what they thought of a record. Clark used the show to create a music empire worth millions.

Amos 'n' Andy (radio, 1928–1960; television, 1951–1953)

A popular radio show that began in 1928, *Amos 'n' Andy* featured the comic goings-on in a black, urban neighborhood. The protagonists were Amos, a hard-working cab driver, Andy, a somewhat doltish layabout, and the Kingfish, a con man with a propensity for malapropisms. On radio, the show featured white actors doing the voices of blacks. Despite protests by the National Association for the Advancement of Colored People, CBS decided in 1951 to put the show on television—but with black actors. The show was popular with audiences on both sides of the color line; later African American comedians such as Redd Foxx and Bill Cosby said it served as artistic inspiration. Nevertheless, the show's stereotypes continued to offend, and CBS was forced to take it off the air within two years. (It remained in syndication until 1966.)

Asphalt Jungle, The (novel, by W.R. Burnett, 1949; film, directed by John Huston, 1950)

This classic film noir, based on the 1949 W.R. Burnett novel, depicts a burglary by a gang of petty hoodlums that goes awry. Each participant in the burglary has his own strengths but also his own fatal weaknesses, and the burglars are doomed to get caught. In its depiction of criminals as fully rounded characters with individual personalities, the film was greatly influential in the development of the crime film genre. Starring Sterling Hayden, Louis Calhern, and Sam Jaffe—the latter winning an Oscar for best actor in a supporting role—the film was directed by screen legend John Huston (*The Maltese Falcon,* 1941, and *The Treasure of the Sierra Madre,* 1948), and it helped confirm his status as one of America's premier filmmakers.

Bad Day at Black Rock (film, directed by John Sturges, 1955)

A powerful film about World War II and Japanese internment, *Bad Day at Black Rock* starred veteran actor Spencer Tracy in what many critics consider his finest role. Tracy plays a stranger, John J. Macreedy, who comes to the desert town of Black Rock to deliver a Congressional Medal of Honor. The townspeople, however, fear the revelation of crimes committed against local Japanese during the war and scheme to stop the medal from being delivered. Among the well-known actors who starred in the film were Lee Marvin, Robert Ryan, and Ernest Borgnine. *Bad Day* was nominated for three Academy Awards, and it claimed the best actor award for Spencer Tracy's performance at the Cannes film festival. The film is also cited as groundbreaking in its depiction of the intrigues of small-town life.

Ben-Hur (film, directed by William Wyler, 1959)

Hollywood's most successful movie set in biblical times, *Ben-Hur* won eleven Oscars, more than any film in history to date (later equaled by *Titanic,* 1997, and *Lord of the Rings: The Return of the King,* 2003). Based on the 1880 novel by Lew Wallace, everything about *Ben-Hur* was huge—the cast (including as many as 8,000 extras), the story, and the star, Charlton Heston. The plot tells the story of a rich young prince of Israel named Judah Ben-Hur, played by Heston, living under Roman occupation. A high-ranking army officer accuses Ben-Hur of plotting to kill him and exiles him to a life on galley ships. Ben-Hur escapes and seeks revenge. The film, enormously popular at the box office, is perhaps best remembered for its epic chariot race scene.

Best Years of Our Lives, The (film, directed by William Wyler, 1946)

The most authentic film about the experience of World War II veterans coming home, *The Best Years of Our Lives* is a bittersweet portrayal of a group of soldiers attempting to return to their small-town lives. Starring Fredric March, Harold Russell, and Dana Andrews, the film's basic message is that a wartime soldier really can't go home again, or, if he does, he and his home are no longer the same as when he left. One veteran returns as an amputee (played by World War II veteran and amputee Russell), and all have been irreversibly changed by their traumatic experiences in combat. At the same time, the townsfolk have been changed by the war. Much of the film focuses on uneasy relationships between the returning veterans and the people they once knew and loved. The film won seven Oscars, including best picture.

Big Sleep, The (film, directed by Howard Hawks, 1946; film, directed by Michael Winner, 1978)
Critically acclaimed and popular at the box office, *The Big Sleep,* nevertheless, features a plot that even people who saw the film multiple times had a hard time unraveling. Based on the 1939 novel by mystery writer Raymond Chandler, directed by Howard Hawks, and co-adapted for the screen by William Faulkner, the movie follows Los Angeles private eye Philip Marlowe (played by Humphrey Bogart), as he tries to get to the bottom of a wealthy family's mystery. With its complicated plot, *femme fatale* foil (played by Lauren Bacall), and hardboiled street language, *The Big Sleep* is considered a classic of the film noir genre. In 1978, the novel was remade as a film that is set in England but otherwise follows the original plot.

Bonanza (television, 1959–1973)
A highly popular series from the golden age of television Westerns, *Bonanza* depicted the frontier life of widower Ben Cartwright (played by Lorne Greene) and his three sons, Adam, Hoss, and Little Joe (Pernell Roberts, Dan Blocker, and Michael Landon, respectively) on and around the Ponderosa Ranch in the Sierra Nevada Mountains. The show's major innovation was that the characters were defending a home base, instead of wandering from place to place, as was more typical in earlier TV Westerns. Aside from *Gunsmoke, Bonanza* was the longest-running Western in television history.

Bridge on the River Kwai, The (film, directed by David Lean, 1957)
This big-budget Hollywood war drama, which won seven Academy Awards, including best picture, was based on a 1952 novel by the French author Pierre Boulle, rendered on screen by the British director David Lean, and starred Alec Guinness and William Holden. Set in the jungles of Southeast Asia during World War II, it tells the story of Allied prisoners forced to build a bridge over the eponymous river by their Japanese captors. The British commander, played by Guinness, is determined to build a proper bridge to show what his countrymen are made of, even though it helps the enemy cause. Just as the bridge is finished and the first Japanese train crosses it, a team of Allied commandoes blows it up. The film won critical acclaim for its depiction of cultures at odds with each other and the madness that war can produce in certain individuals.

Crucible, The (play, by Arthur Miller, 1953; film, directed by Nicholas Hytner, 1996)
A critical and popular success on Broadway, *The Crucible* was set in seventeenth-century Salem, Massachusetts, during the town's infamous witch trials. The play depicts the hysteria gripping the town and how essentially well-intentioned people can be led astray by manipulative leaders and their own fears to persecute people whose guilt is based on hearsay. In fact, *The Crucible* is a rather obvious allegory about the ongoing anticommunist hysteria that was gripping the United States in the early 1950s, when the play was written and first staged. In this work, Miller—whose *Death of a Salesman* (1949) had already established him as one of America's premier playwrights—expresses his outrage at the persecution of leftists by those whom liberals called "modern-day witch-hunters." A 1996 movie version was neither critically acclaimed nor highly successful at the box office.

Davy Crockett Show, The (television, 1954; film, *Davy Crockett, King of the Wild Frontier,* directed by Norman Foster, 1955).
Starring Fess Parker in both the TV and movie versions, this Walt Disney creation depicts the frontiersman Davy Crockett as a heroic figure who was able to conquer the wilderness, fight off Native Americans, and kill wild animals in his efforts to help settle the West. The film was first shot in three one-hour episodes for television, and its huge success led Disney to edit the episodes into one long motion picture for theatrical release.

Essentially recounting the stereotyped view of Western settlement as a noble white man's effort, the series and film are perhaps best remembered as a landmark in the history of marketing. Disney practically invented the art of what would later be called cross marketing, making millions of dollars on coonskin caps, lunchboxes, and other Crockett-related paraphernalia. Disney even incorporated the Crockett story into a ride at Disneyland, the Southern California amusement park that opened the year the film came out.

Death of a Salesman (play, by Arthur Miller, 1949; film, directed by László Benedek, 1951; television film, directed by Volker Schlöndorff, 1985)

Most critics recognize this hard-hitting drama as the finest by legendary playwright Arthur Miller; many regard it as among the finest works in twentieth-century American theater. *Death of a Salesman* portrays an unsuccessful traveling salesman named Willy Loman, who seeks to instill in his sons the values of the American dream. One son, Biff, finds it difficult to square the optimism his father teaches with the failure his father's life has become. The other son, Happy, wants no part of his father's dream. In the end, Loman is fired by his company and commits suicide.

The play was first staged in 1949, a time of transition for American society. Still recovering from the Great Depression and World War II, the country was about to launch itself into the consumer prosperity of the 1950s. *Salesman's* depiction of the dark underside of the American dream captured the imagination of critics and audiences. The play has twice been made into major films, once in 1951 for theatrical release and again in 1985 for television. It has been periodically revived on Broadway.

Donna Reed Show, The (television, 1958–1966)

One of the longest-running family sitcoms of the 1950s and 1960s, *The Donna Reed Show* followed the daily lives of the fictional Stone family, including husband Alex, wife Donna, and children Mary and Jeff. While intended to be typical and all-American, the Stones were, in fact, an idealized family: white, middle-class, and suburban, they experienced no money problems, never discussed politics, and almost never encountered anyone except other white, middle-class people. Embracing the classic nuclear family model of the 1950s and early 1960s, Donna stayed home, while Alex went off to work every day. Donna was the ideal wife, productive around the house but remaining true to the early postwar feminine ideal. Memorably, she was shown in the opening credits vacuuming the house in a stylish dress and pearls.

Dragnet (television, 1951–1959, 1967–1970, 1989–1990, 2003–2004; film, directed by Tom Mankiewicz, 1987)

With its trademark opening music—nine dour notes—*Dragnet* was one of the most popular police dramas in the history of American television. Set in Los Angeles in the 1950s and 1960s, the show chronicles the investigations of Detective Joe Friday, played with deadpan seriousness by show creator Jack Webb, and his partners, Officer Frank Smith in the 1950s (played by Ben Alexander) and Bill Gannon in the 1960s (played by Harry Morgan). What made the show unique was its effort at verisimilitude. The opening credits claimed that the cases being portrayed were pulled from real Los Angeles Police Department files—"the names have been changed to protect the innocent"—and each episode ended with the fate of the accused.

The show glorified the police, showing them as fair and businesslike, determined in their pursuit of criminals. The *Dragnet* series was revived in 1989–1990, starring two new young detectives. A tongue-in-cheek 1987 movie was based on the series, which was revived again, albeit briefly, as *L.A. Dragnet* in 2003–2004.

Ed Sullivan Show, The (television, 1948–1971)

The second-longest-running variety show in television history (after *Saturday Night Live*), *The Ed Sullivan Show* featured musical, comedy, and other acts in a one-hour format that aired on Sunday nights. Originally titled "Toast of the Town," it was renamed in 1955 to reflect the increasing popularity of its host, a stiff, but gracious, former journalist and vaudeville emcee. Sullivan was eclectic in his tastes and featured acts as diverse as ballet dancer Rudolf Nureyev and rock and roll singer Elvis Presley.

If an act was popular, Sullivan put it on the air, even if he occasionally toned down some of the performances. Presley, for example, was shown only from the waist up on his first appearance in 1956, so that television viewers could not see his scandalously swaying hips. Perhaps the best remembered act in the show's history was the 1964 U.S. debut of the Beatles.

Edge of Night, The (television, 1956–1984)

One of the most popular and longest running of television's daytime soap operas (it ran for 1,798 episodes), *The Edge of Night* was different from most in that it focused on mystery and detective work rather than romance. The main character was attorney Mike Karr (starring, successively, John Larkin, Lawrence Hugo, and Forrest Compton), who investigated and tried all cases that came to him. Like other soaps, however, *Edge of Night* featured a large ensemble cast and such common plot devices as illicit romance, divorce, murder, and amnesia. The name of the show came from its time slot at 4:30 P.M.

Father Knows Best (television, 1954–1960)

Among the most popular family situation comedies of the 1950s, *Father Knows Best* was adapted from a radio program of the same name. Set in a typical suburb, the show featured the comic doings of the Andersons, a wholesome family of five. Jim Anderson (played by veteran movie actor Robert Young) worked as an insurance agent and came home each night to his homemaker wife, Margaret (Jane Wyatt), and children, Betty, Bud, and Kathy (Elinor Donahue, Billy Gray, and Lauren Chapin, respectively). With its name and plot lines involving the father character sorting out the family's daily dilemmas, *Father Knows Best* highlighted the patriarchal ideal of 1950s America probably better than any other show on television.

Fibber McGee and Molly (radio, 1935–1959; television, 1959–1960)

Unlike many radio comedies that made the transition to television, *Fibber McGee and Molly* remained highly popular on the radio through the 1950s, even as its television incarnation was brief and not very successful. The show, which recounted the lives and misadventures of a Midwestern husband and wife, featured broad humor that played on the strong character traits of the stars: Fibber (played by Jim Jordan on radio and Bob Sweeney on television), a braggart who never finished anything he started, and Molly (played by Marian Driscoll Jordan on radio and Cathy Lewis on TV), a patient and level-headed woman. The show was rooted in small-town America, with each episode featuring visits by a cast of eccentric neighbors.

From Here to Eternity
SEE Literature and Journalism

Gentleman's Agreement (film, directed by Elia Kazan, 1947)

Gentlemen's Agreement was a popular, critically acclaimed movie about the insidious effects of anti-Semitism in America. Made shortly after World War II and the Holocaust, the movie focused on the subtle forms of prejudice infecting daily life in the United States in the early postwar years. Gregory Peck plays a journalist who pretends to be Jewish in order to write an exposé on anti-Semitism, discovering the depths of bigotry and hatred. Directed by Elia Kazan, who would go on to make such iconic American films as *A Streetcar Named Desire* (1951) and *On the Waterfront* (1954), *Gentlemen's Agreement* may strike modern audiences as melodramatic, but it won the Oscar for best picture in 1948.

George Burns and Gracie Allen Show, The (television, 1950–1958)

Among the first stage and radio comedians to make the transition to television, George Burns and Gracie Allen maintained the formula that had made them stars in the earlier media formats. The plots were usually simple; what made the show special were the two stars. Allen was the quintessential ditzy blonde who often outwitted Burns, if only by accident. But Burns was more than just Allen's straight man. Often stepping outside the scene to address the audience directly, Burns would offer his idiosyncratic views of the world. Each episode, in fact, began with him stepping through the proscenium of the theater set—trademark cigar in hand—to explain to the audience what they were about to see. The show was an early experiment in the possibilities of television comedy.

Gidget (film, directed by Paul Wendkos, 1959; television, 1965–1966)

One of the first, and easily the most popular, films of the surfing genre of the 1960s, *Gidget* virtually invented the teenage summer movie. Played by Sandra Dee, the eponymous heroine is a straight-A student at a California high school. Gidget seems uninterested in the opposite sex, until she meets a hip, but coolly indifferent, surfer named Moondoggie (played by James Darren), who rescues her from drowning one day at the beach. Gidget eventually falls in love with both Moondoggie and the surfing lifestyle. In the end, she gets the boy to go steady with her. Several sequels to the enormously popular film were made in the early 1960s, set in Rome and Hawaii. A short-lived TV series, starring Sally Field in the title role, aired in 1965–1966.

Gunsmoke (television, 1955–1975)

The longest-running dramatic series in television history, *Gunsmoke* played for twenty-one seasons. Over the course of its run, the Western classic went from a half-hour format in its first six seasons to an hour-long format and, after ten years in black and white, to color in its eleventh season. Two of the stars, James Arness (who played the lead character, Marshall Matt Dillon) and Milburn Stone (playing his friend, Doc Adams) stayed on for the entire run, while Amanda Blake (playing sexy saloon owner Kitty Russell) lasted nineteen seasons. The show portrays a Western town beset by violent outlaws, gunfights, and brawls, giving Arness much to do in each episode. While television Westerns are few and far between in the early 2000s, they dominated the airwaves in the 1950s and early 1960s. *Gunsmoke* was the standard against which all others were measured.

High Noon (film, directed by Fred Zinnemann, 1952)

This iconic film Western depicts a small-town lawman (played by Gary Cooper) nearing the end of his stint as town marshal. It recounts Marshal Will Kane's last day in office, which also is the day he is to be married to a beautiful young woman (played by Grace Kelly). On the verge of starting his new life, Kane faces an old enemy—a man he had once put in prison—who unexpectedly arrives in town. The marshal tries to rally the town's citizens against this evil presence, but everyone, including his future bride, urges him to leave town, rather than face the danger. Kane insists on staying and confronts his enemy alone in a shootout at high noon.

Many critics, at the time and since, have seen the movie as an allegory, with the townspeople standing in for an America that would not confront the evils of Joseph McCarthy and his anticommunist witch hunts. Cooper won an Oscar for best actor, and the film has been cited by many film societies and critics as the greatest Western ever made.

Honeymooners, The (television, 1955–1956)

Although it ran for only thirty-nine episodes, *The Honeymooners* remains one of the best-loved television shows of all time. (Several more episodes were made but never aired as part of the original series; found years later, they were released as "the lost episodes".) The weekly comedy starred Jackie Gleason as Ralph Kramden, a bus driver, with Audrey Meadows as Alice Kramden (Ralph's wife), Art Carney as Ed Norton (a sewer worker and neighbor), and Joyce Randolph as Trixie Norton (Ed's wife). Set almost exclusively in the Kramdens' small Brooklyn apartment, the show often revolved around Ralph's crazy money-making schemes,

which inevitably went sour, as the practical Alice predicted they would.

A rarity in television then and since, *The Honeymooners* featured working-class characters struggling with money and trying to grab their piece of the American dream. Popular at the time, the show has remained a favorite in syndicated reruns in the decades since. Several of its catch phrases—such as "To the moon, Alice!" and "One of these days, Alice, one of these days"—have entered popular speech.

Howdy Doody Show, The (television, 1947–1960)

Among the most popular children's programs in the early history of television, *The Howdy Doody Show* included a mix of real-life actors and marionettes in a fictional Western town called Doodyville. Originally called *The Puppet Playhouse,* the half-hour program was renamed in 1949 and aired on weekday afternoons. Produced in front of a live audience of children known as the Peanut Gallery, the shows featured the emcee Buffalo Bob Smith and a host of puppet characters, clowns, and crazy machines. With its famous opening lines—"Hey, kids! What time is it? . . . It's Howdy Doody Time!"—the show is remembered fondly by a generation of baby boomers. Its folksy tone and primitive set, along with competition from the rival *Mickey Mouse Club,* eventually led to a drop in viewership, the loss of sponsors, and cancellation in 1960.

I Love Lucy (television, 1951–1957)

Arguably the most popular situation comedy ever to appear on American television, *I Love Lucy* starred the veteran Broadway and movie actress Lucille Ball and her real-life husband, band leader and music producer Desi Arnaz, as a New York couple named Lucy and Ricky Ricardo. Other key players in the show were their neighbors and landlords, Fred and Ethel Mertz (William Frawley and Vivian Vance). Best remembered for its wacky situations and perfect comic timing, the show's episodes usually revolved around Lucy's crazy schemes at fame and fortune—and their disastrous outcomes.

The show was a landmark in other ways as well. When CBS insisted that Ball find an Anglo actor to play her husband, Lucy refused, breaking down a major barrier against the depiction of mixed ethnic couples on television. Later episodes featured Lucy's real-life pregnancy, another television first.

In 1957, the show went from a half-hour sitcom

format to a one-hour variety show called *The Lucy-Desi Comedy Hour.* In 1960, it returned to a half-hour sitcom called *Lucy in Connecticut.* After her divorce from Arnaz, Ball went solo on the *The Lucy Show,* a half-hour sitcom, from 1962 to 1968. *I Love Lucy* remains in syndication and is said to have been on the air every day, somewhere in the world, since it first appeared in 1951.

Inherit the Wind (play, by Jerome Lawrence and Robert E. Lee, 1955; film, directed by Stanley Kramer, 1960)

The stage and movie drama *Inherit the Wind* was loosely based on the 1925 Scopes "monkey" trial, in which a Tennessee high-school science teacher was convicted for breaking a state law against the teaching of evolution. At the time, the trial became a national sensation, when two great figures—former presidential candidate William Jennings Bryan and famed criminal defense lawyer Clarence Darrow—descended on the small town of Dayton to prosecute and defend, respectively, teacher John Scopes. By 1955, when the play became a hit on Broadway, many theatergoers saw it through the lens of modern events, as a polemic against the ideological intolerance of McCarthyism. In 1960, the play was turned into a critically acclaimed movie starring Fredric March (as Bryan) and Spencer Tracy (as Darrow).

Invasion of the Body Snatchers (film, directed by Donald Siegel, 1956; film, directed by Philip Kaufman, 1978)

One of the most haunting science fiction films in the annals of Hollywood, *Invasion of the Body Snatchers* is also recognized as one of the few movies whose original version (1956) and remake (1978) were equally lauded by critics and the film-going public. While the original was set in a small town in Northern California and the remake in San Francisco, both films tell the story of organisms from outer space that mysteriously duplicate and replace people, turning the human race into a conformist army of drones. Created shortly after the anticommunist hysteria of the early 1950s, the original has been seen as both an allegory for Communist and American anticommunist conformism. What the remake lost in social resonance, it made up for in fast-paced drama.

It's a Wonderful Life (film, directed by Frank Capra, 1946)

A commercial failure when it first came out, *It's a Wonderful Life* ranks with *Miracle on 34th Street* (1947) as one of the most enduringly popular Christmas movies ever made. The film opens with the attempted suicide of the protagonist, small-town bank president George Bailey (played by Jimmy Stewart), who is about to see his firm go bankrupt. Saved by his guardian angel, Bailey is permitted to see what would have happened to the town if he had never lived—it would have become a den of sin, greed, and violence. Still, a familiar theme resonates with viewers: the feeling of many people that their lives have not been worthwhile. In the end, the townspeople save the bank and the wealthiest and most evil man in town (played by stage veteran Lionel Barrymore) is thwarted in his efforts to take over the only institution he has yet to control. Over the years, *It's a Wonderful Life* has come to be aired on television regularly at Christmas time, gaining new fans each season.

Jack Paar Tonight Show, The (television, 1957–1962)

Almost single-handedly creating the format of the late night television talk show, *The Jack Paar Tonight Show,* with its eponymous host, featured a series of guests who would be interviewed by Paar about their careers, their personal lives, and general public issues. The original show was hosted by Steve Allen and focused largely on comedy sketches. Paar, while keeping the occasional sketch, turned it primarily into an interview show.

Possessing both a razor-sharp wit and a sentimental edge (he was known to cry on camera), Paar did not shy away from controversial issues or off-color jokes, which frequently got him in trouble with his bosses at NBC. He once temporarily quit the show—on camera—after the network edited out a joke about toilets. Tired of fighting the censors and keeping up with the grueling nightly schedule, Paar left the show and turned the hosting job over to Johnny Carson, who toned down the politics and played up the humor (see page 1439).

King and I, The (stage musical, by Richard Rodgers and Oscar Hammerstein II, 1951; film, directed by Walter Lang, 1956)

Both a hit Broadway musical and a popular movie, *The King and I* was based on a novel by British writer Margaret Landon about the true-life adventures of a British governess sent to the royal court of Siam to educate the king's children in English language and customs. The feisty Anna and the headstrong king frequently clash over questions of etiquette, the role of women, the rearing of children, and other matters. Behind the squabbling is an unfulfilled romantic tension between the two characters, a clash of cultures, and a political drama about the impact of the British Empire. Originally produced on Broadway in 1951, *The King and I* became the hit of the season and was turned into a movie five years later. Both starred Yul Brynner as the king; the play featured Gertrude Lawrence as Anna, and the film version starred Deborah Kerr.

Kukla, Fran, and Ollie (television, 1947–1957)

A popular children's show that enjoyed strong crossover appeal among adults, *Kukla, Fran, and Ollie* featured a series of puppets and starred Fran Allison as the host. Unlike other puppet shows, *Kukla, Fran, and Ollie* (Kukla and Ollie were the featured puppets) relied more on wit, urbane dialogue, and simple but profound storytelling, rather than slapstick comedy. Several television shows and specials from the 1960s through the 1980s continued to feature the puppets. *Kukla, Fran, and Ollie* is often seen as the inspiration for later children's television hits, such as *Sesame Street* and *The Electric Company*.

Lawrence Welk Show, The (television, 1955–1982)

One of the longest-running and most popular variety programs in television history, *The Lawrence Welk Show* featured the eponymous bandleader and his orchestra playing traditional music hits. The show also featured skits and dance routines. From the very beginning, the show was derided as corny and old-fashioned by television critics and younger viewers. Yet it remained so popular with older viewers that when ABC canceled it in 1971, Welk successfully lined up 200 independent stations to form an ad hoc network to air the show across the country. Over the years, Welk invited more and more outside performers to liven up the show, but its slow pace and oddly accented host—Welk came from an Alsatian immigrant family in North Dakota—never changed. This kept the show popular with an ever-aging audience.

Leave It to Beaver (television, 1957–1963)

Perhaps the most popular of the family-based sitcoms of the 1950s and early 1960s, *Leave It to Beaver* featured a "typical" middle-class suburban family, with a father who went off to an unidentified white-collar job and a mother who stayed home to care for the house and the family's two boys. Typical of such shows, the plots usually revolved around one of the children—usually Beaver (played by Jerry Mathers)—getting into mild trouble that had to be sorted out by the father when he came home from the office. As in other such sitcoms, much of the harsh reality of life and diversity of American society was left out. The family never had to deal with serious money or health issues, and the poor, blacks, and other minorities were conspicuous by their absence.

Life of Riley, The (television, 1949–1950)

This show, based on a story written by Groucho Marx, focused on a man named Riley, who worked in a manufacturing company. The show usually found him at home, however, where he wreaked havoc trying to solve minor problems. His favorite phrase entered the popular lexicon of the 1950s: "What a revoltin' development this is!" William Bendix played Chester Riley, and Marjorie Reynolds, his wife. Bendix, who had been the voice of Riley on radio, was one of that medium's few stars who proved able to maintain his character's popularity on television. The show's other characters included Jim Gillis, Riley's best friend (Tom D'Andrea); Honeybee Gillis, Jim's wife (Gloria Bondell); and Riley's two children (Wesley Morgan and Lugene Sanders).

Little House on the Prairie
SEE Literature and Journalism

Lone Ranger, The (radio, 1933–1955; television, 1949–1957

Originally a 1930s radio show based on a series of books by George Trendle, *The Lone Ranger* began airing on television in 1949. The first episode told the now-familiar story of how the Lone Ranger (played in different seasons by Clayton Moore and John Hart) got his nickname. Lured into an ambush by desperados, the Lone Ranger was the only one of six Texas Rangers to survive. Half dead, he was rescued by a laconic American Indian named Tonto. After avenging the deaths of the Rangers, the Lone Ranger, with the loyal Tonto at his side, traveled the West tracking down criminals.

Given the audience, the writers and producers kept the show's plots simple: there were bad guys and good guys, and the latter, after some close scrapes, inevitably prevailed. Although Tonto was played with an air of nobility by Native Canadian actor Jay Silverheels, the show maintained most of the stereotypes of the Old West—wild Indians, honest lawmen, good white townsfolk, and nary another ethnic minority in sight.

Many Loves of Dobie Gillis, The (television, 1959–1963)

Among the middle-class, family-based situation comedies of the 1950s and early 1960s, *The Many Loves of Dobie Gillis* stood out as an oddity. For one thing, its protagonist (played by Dwayne Hickman) was a late teen who was clean-cut but obsessed with girls and confused about what he should do with his life. Gillis's best friend was another oddball, the dopey beatnik Maynard G. Krebs (Bob Denver), and he was constantly being pursued by brainy but homely Zelda Gilroy (Sheila James). His main competitor for girls was wealthy Chatsworth Osborne, Jr. (Steve Franken).

This television show was unusual in that it dealt with class issues—after a fashion. Aspiring to riches, Gillis was constantly reminded of his lower-middle-class origins as the son of a small grocery store owner. Much to his chagrin, he was often forced to work in his father's store.

Meet the Press (television, 1947–present)

The original Sunday morning political talk show, *Meet the Press* presents national and occasionally foreign leaders, along with experts of various kinds, being interviewed about critical topics of the day. Originally thirty minutes in length—it was extended to an hour in 1992—*Meet the Press* features hard-hitting questions from the host reporter. *Meet the Press* has been hosted by nine high-profile TV journalists over the years; host Tim Russert took the reins in 1991. It remains the longest-running program on network television.

Mickey Mouse Club, The (television, 1955–1959; 1977–1978; 1989–1994)

Originally a vehicle for promoting the entertainment empire of Walt Disney, *The Mickey Mouse Club* went on to become the most popular children's program in the early history of television. Featuring a cast of young "Mouseketeers," along with skits and songs, the show is perhaps most notable for its pioneering marketing efforts. Millions of children were introduced to Disneyland and Disney movies via the daily after-school show, which offered viewers membership cards, Mickey Mouse hats, and other Disney paraphernalia. After continuing in syndicated reruns for

years, the show was resurrected in new versions that ran for two seasons starting in 1977, and from 1989 to 1994, but the new versions were never as successful as the original.

Milton Berle Show, The (television, 1948–1956, 1958–1959, 1966–1967)

Among the pioneers of early television, comedian Milton Berle and the show he hosted were a throwback to earlier times, featuring vaudeville-like gags, jokes, costume changes (including Berle dressed in drag), and corny skits. Despite, or perhaps because of, its transitional format, the show was enormously popular in its first incarnation in the late 1940s and early 1950s.

Known formally as the *Texaco Star Theater,* after its sponsor, the show made Milton Berle the number one television star of the early 1950s. Millions of Americans made sure they were home every Tuesday night to watch the show. Television historians say that Berle was more responsible for the explosion in television ownership than any other entertainer. He resurrected the show in the late 1950s and mid-1960s, but it had only limited success.

Texaco Star Theater made the comedian Milton Berle television's first major star. *(NBC Television/Getty Images)*

Mister Roberts (novel, by Thomas Heggen, 1946; play, by Thomas Heggen and Joshua Logan, 1948; film, directed by John Ford, 1955; television, 1965–1966)

A comedy set aboard a cargo ship in the Pacific theater during World War II, *Mister Roberts* originated as a best-selling novel by Thomas Heggen in 1946. Adapted for the stage, it enjoyed a successful run on Broadway, beginning in 1948. It was as a Hollywood film released in 1955, however, that *Mister Roberts* achieved its most enduring appeal. Henry Fonda stars as Lieutenant Doug Roberts, a not-so-young officer desperate to leave the supply ship and see real action in the war. Roberts, however, is continually thwarted by the ship's martinet captain, played by James Cagney, who refuses to sign his transfer. Comic relief is provided by a young Jack Lemmon, playing the lazy, but entrepreneurial, Ensign Pulver, who is willing to buy and sell anything if the price is right. World War II movies remained enormously popular from the 1940s through the mid-1960s, playing to veterans and those raised on stories about the war.

Music Man, The (stage musical, by Meredith Willson, 1957; film, directed by Morton DaCosta, 1962)

One of the most popular musicals in Broadway history, *The Music Man* tells the story of a con man, Harold Hill, who comes to the fictional small town of River City, Iowa, to make a few fast bucks off its good citizens. His plan is to get them to raise funds for a boys' marching band and then hightail it out of town with the money. Love, however, gets in the way. Failing to convince the wary Marian, a local librarian, that he is an honest man, Hill desperately tries to persuade her not to tell the townsfolk what he is up to. In the process, he falls in love and is, in fact, turned into an honest man. The show features a number of songs that have become American standards, including "Trouble in River City" and "Seventy-Six Trombones."

Night of the Hunter (film, directed by Charles Laughton, 1955)

A dark, idiosyncratic film noir, *Night of the Hunter,* based on a Depression-era novel, features veteran actor Robert Mitchum as an amoral, violent con man who comes to a small town posing as a member of the clergy. Mitchum is after two children whose hit man father has told them where he hid the money of the man he murdered and has warned them not to tell a soul. To achieve his ends, the smooth-talking Mitchum marries the children's mother (played by Shelley Winters). Unable to get the truth from the children, Mitchum turns increasingly abusive and violent. Largely overlooked by critics and the film-going public when it was released, *Night of the Hunter,* the only film ever directed by the legendary British actor Charles Laughton, has since been recognized as one of the finest American films in the noir tradition.

On the Waterfront (film, directed by Elia Kazan, 1954)

Featuring Marlon Brando in one of his best-known and most critically acclaimed roles, *On the Waterfront* tells the story of a former boxer named Terry Malloy (Brando) who had been forced by the mob to throw a fight that ended his career. Now a dockworker on the New York waterfront, Malloy is once again caught in gangster affairs, having witnessed the murder of a fellow worker by mob goons. Malloy is torn between his desire for justice, which means cooperating with a government investigation of mob activity on the docks, and his fear of becoming a "rat."

Set against the anticommunist investigations of the early 1950s, the film has been seen as a metaphor about people torn over whether they should give the names of Communist friends and colleagues to the House Committee on Un-American Activities (HUAC). In a real-life twist to the film, director Elia Kazan was ostracized by Hollywood for his willingness to cooperate with HUAC.

Ozzie and Harriet Show, The (television, 1952–1966)

Also known as *The Adventures of Ozzie and Harriet,* this highly successful family sitcom from the 1950s varied somewhat from the traditional form of the genre in that the family portrayed in the show, the Nelsons, was real. Despite this twist, the plots and characters were rather conventional. The working father, a bandleader (Ozzie Nelson), and the stay-at-home mom (Harriet Nelson) were parents of two boys (David and Ricky). Many of the episodes involve the parents sorting out the hi-jinks of their sons, particularly the younger brother, precocious Ricky. Because the show was aired for so many years and the characters were real, audiences watched David and Ricky grow up, attend school, marry, and begin their careers. Ricky, who looked a bit like Elvis Presley, followed in his father's footsteps and became a modestly successful rock and roll band leader.

Pillow Talk (film, directed by Michael Gordon, 1959)

A romantic comedy set in a New York City apartment building, *Pillow Talk* revolves around a telephone party line (two households sharing the same line). At one end is interior decorator Jan Morrow (played by Doris Day), at the other is songwriter Brad Allen (Rock Hudson). Morrow is infuriated by the fact that every time she picks up the phone, she hears Allen, an eligible bachelor, using the same pickup lines. Not having seen one another, each comes to despise the other—until Allen sees her at a nightclub. When he recognizes the voice, he goes back on the party line, posing as a rich Texan from out of town, and woos her. With its stilted flirting and absence of sex, the film may seem dated to modern viewers, but it represents the way Hollywood depicted the courting relationship among successful single people in the last years before the sexual revolution.

Playhouse 90 (television, 1956–1960)

Early television, as it was experimenting with ways to present drama and comedy to its audiences, often presented live theater over the airwaves—in part, because recording technology was still primitive. A latecomer to the genre, *Playhouse 90* is widely regarded as the finest example of American made-for-television theater. The show's producers recruited some of the finest writing, acting, and directing talent for its productions. Industry executives often pointed to the show to defend themselves against the charge that their medium was full of cheap, lowbrow entertainment— what one federal communications official would later call a "vast wasteland." Among the best-known plays staged for the show were *Requiem for a Heavyweight, The Time of Your Life,* and *Judgment at Nuremburg.*

Postman Always Rings Twice, The (novel, by James Cain, 1934; film, directed by Tay Garnett, 1946; film, directed by Bob Rafelson, 1981)

One of the classics of early postwar films noir, which depicted a dark world of petty criminals, hard-boiled detectives, and sexy but cynical women, *The Postman Always Rings Twice* was based on the 1934 first novel of mystery writer James Cain. It tells the story of a drifter Frank (played by John Garfield) who teams up with an unhappy, sexually unfulfilled housewife Cora

(Lana Turner) to kill her husband Nick, a mild-mannered gas station owner in Southern California. The drifter is eventually caught and tried for murder. Like many noir films, *Postman* is steeped in the existential philosophy of the early postwar years: Events are random, the world is dark and dangerous, and all one can do is seize the moment and live life fully. A 1981 remake, with Jack Nicholson playing the drifter and Jessica Lange as the housewife, was also popular with critics and the moviegoing public.

Price is Right, The (television, 1956–1963, 1963–1965, 1972–present)

The Price is Right, the longest-running game show in TV history, was unashamedly of, for, and about American consumerism. Contestants, selected at random from the studio audience, competed against each other for prizes by trying to guess the prices of ordinary household goods. The contestant who guessed closest won. In its original run during the 1950s and early 1960s, the show was hosted by Bill Cullen. Since 1972, it has been emceed by Bob Barker.

Queen for a Day (radio, 1945–1957; television, 1956–1964, 1969–1970)

This program started out as a radio show called *Queen for Today* in 1945, changed its name to *Queen for a Day* later that year, and moved to television in January 1956, where it remained until 1964; it was revived briefly in 1969–1970. The show also spawned a number of movies, including a 1951 film directed by Arthur Lubin. During its longest run, the show was hosted by Jack Bailey.

The mid-to-late 1950s were the golden age of TV game shows, with five of the top ten programs being of that genre. Episodes of *Queen for a Day* featured ordinary women who told the host why they wanted to be queen and what kinds of merchandise prizes they wanted. The audience then voted, indicating with its applause which contestant should win. A kind of popularity contest for regular women, the show was full of bathos, as contestants tried to outdo each other with their stories of need. At its height, the show commanded the highest advertising dollars on television to that time, an extraordinary $4,000 a minute.

Raisin in the Sun, A (play, by Lorraine Hansberry, 1959; film, directed by Daniel Petrie, 1961)

The first major drama by a black playwright to win a crossover audience of white theatergoers—and the first by a black woman to be produced on Broadway—Lorraine Hansberry's *Raisin in the Sun* opened to rave reviews in 1959. Taking its title from a poem by Langston Hughes about the frustrations of being black in America, the play is about inner-city black family members who receive a life insurance windfall after the death of the father. The family tries to move to a white suburb, but they encounter racism and prejudice along the way. Hansberry said that her own experience growing up in a middle-class black family in Chicago provided the inspiration for the drama. The 1961 film version starred Sidney Poitier.

Rawhide (television, 1959–1966)

Set on a cattle drive in the Old West, *Rawhide* was one of the most successful Western television series during the golden age of that genre. Led by trail boss Gil Favor (played by Eric Fleming), the cowboys on the show went through various adventures while trying to get their cattle to market. With its hostile American Indians, gun-slinging outlaws, and hearty pioneers, the show did little to dispel stereotypes of the Old West. It is known for having showcased the young actor Clint Eastwood in his first prominent role.

Rear Window (film, directed by Alfred Hitchcock, 1954; television film, directed by Jeff Bleckner, 1998)

One of the most popular and critically acclaimed films by director Alfred Hitchcock, the master of movie suspense, *Rear Window* stars Jimmy Stewart as an uncharacteristically edgy news photographer temporarily confined to his New York apartment by a broken leg; Grace Kelly plays his amorous girlfriend. Through the rear window of his apartment, Stewart observes the goings-on in a building across the way. Over the course of several days, he and Kelly come to the conclusion that a mysterious neighbor, played by Raymond Burr, has murdered his wife. The film was remade as a television movie in 1998, starring the paraplegic actor Christopher Reeve in Stewart's role.

Rebel Without a Cause (film, directed by Nicholas Ray, 1955)

Based on a sociological study from the 1940s, *Rebel Without a Cause* was the last film of teen idol James Dean, who died prematurely in a car accident shortly before the premier. The movie tells the story of a troubled teenager, played by Dean, whose family has

As the angst-ridden star of *Rebel Without a Cause* (1955), James Dean became a symbol and idol of his generation. *(John Kobal Foundation/Getty Images)*

recently moved to Los Angeles. Over the course of the movie, the boy attempts to find the love and human connectedness that his family cannot offer among the troubled youth of his high school. Like the contemporary films *Asphalt Jungle* (1950) and *The Wild One* (1953), *Rebel Without a Cause* was one of the finest examples of the 1950s subgenre films that attempted to explain the alienation of modern youth. A cult classic, *Rebel* also is famous for presenting screen legend Natalie Wood in her first adult role.

Salt of the Earth (film, directed by Herbert Biberman, 1954)

Salt of the Earth was a project in social criticism, not just in front of the camera, but also behind it. The film was released in 1954 by members of the Hollywood blacklist who were barred from work because of their alleged Communist ties. It is the story of a strike by the Union of Mine, Mill and Smelter Workers against a zinc mine in Bayard, New Mexico. Like the film's makers, the union was accused of Communist connections and expelled from the Congress of Industrial Organizations. Also like the film's makers, the members of the union were outsiders, mostly Mexican Americans playing themselves. Only two professional actors (Will Geer and Rosaura Revueltas) appeared in the movie. *Salt of the Earth* had only a limited release because of its controversial subject matter; the well-known critic Pauline Kael called it Communist propaganda. A relic of the Cold War, *Salt of the Earth* was selected by the Library of Congress as one of 100 films to preserve for posterity.

Searchers, The (film, directed by John Ford, 1956)

A classic John Ford Western starring John Wayne, *The Searchers* is the story of a man's five-year odyssey in search of his niece (Natalie Wood), who has been abducted by Comanche Indians. The story takes place in Texas in 1868 and addresses themes of racial prejudice, family ties, and obsession. The rugged landscape of the Southwest, as captured by cinematographer Winton C. Hoch, is a vivid symbol of the wildness and violence of the West, and Wayne is especially effective as an outsider bent on revenge. The film was not particularly successful when it was released, and it received no Academy Award nominations, but later audiences came to regard it as one of Ford's and Wayne's most important works—and one of Hollywood's greatest Westerns. *The Searchers* achieved mythical status when a new generation of filmmakers, including Martin Scorsese, Steven Spielberg, and George Lucas, touted it in the 1970s as a major influence on their work; its influence is evident in such later classics as *Taxi Driver* (1976) and *Star Wars* (1977).

See It Now (television, 1951–1958)

The first television news magazine, *See It Now* set standards for journalistic integrity and courage that all future programs of its kind have attempted to follow. The show evolved from a radio program called *Hear It Now,* which featured sound clips of historical events and narration by veteran broadcaster Edward R. Murrow. *See It Now* was filmed on location, did not rehearse interviews, and, in the series debut, featured the first live, coast-to-coast television transmission. Murrow broadcast from the studio, alternating with live reports from correspondents in the field.

See It Now covered the hottest topics of the day and did not flinch from the controversial. With a segment on how Cold War hysteria was affecting everyday people and a hard-hitting piece on Senator Joseph McCarthy himself, the show got into difficulties with network executives and sponsor Alcoa. In 1955, *See It Now* was replaced by a game show and relegated to a series of specials that aired until 1958, when CBS cancelled the program. Several *See It Now* alumni went on to create *60 Minutes,* its most direct and influential offspring.

Sergeant Bilko (television, 1955–1959)

Actually called *The Phil Silvers Show,* this popular television comedy became known as *Sergeant Bilko* after its memorable lead character. The show debuted in September 1955 and was set on a fictional Kansas army base called Fort Baxter, where Master Sergeant Ernie Bilko ran the motor pool. Smooth-talking and charismatic, Bilko would do anything to earn a buck or to make army life less taxing. His conscience was intact, however, and he always had the best interests of his men, blue-collar Americans, at heart. The show was created by Silvers, who played the title role, and Nat Hiken, the head writer, producer, and director. Within months of its debut, it surpassed the classic *Milton Berle Show* in the ratings and went on to win four Emmy Awards for its first season. The hilarious antics of Bilko and his crew appealed to a viewing public still not far from the military life of World War II. The show's influence was seen in later military situation comedies such as *McHale's Navy* and *MA3H.*

Seven Year Itch, The (film, directed by Billy Wilder, 1955)

Not generally regarded as director Billy Wilder's best farcical comedy (recognition most commonly accorded to the 1959 film *Some Like it Hot*), *The Seven Year Itch* did address a topic prohibited by the current film production code—adultery—and it helped open the way to Hollywood's treatment of more adult and occasionally controversial subjects. Tom Ewell plays Richard Sherman, whose wife and son are on vacation from Manhattan during a long, hot summer. In their absence, Sherman fantasizes about the busty blonde upstairs, known as the Girl (Marilyn Monroe). Much to his dismay, she wants to be friends, making his "seven-year itch" (the length of time he's been married) all the more irritating. Based on a Broadway play by George Axelrod, the film comedy of sex, marriage, and the girl next door features one of Monroe's best performances. Sherman was not the only married American male to fantasize about her.

77 Sunset Strip (television, 1958–1964)

Although it was introduced in the 1950s, *77 Sunset Strip* was the first of the hip detective television shows to become popular in the 1960s. The show followed Stu Bailey (Efrem Zimbalist, Jr.) and Jeff Spencer (Roger Smith) as they solved cases out of their private investigator (PI) office at 77 Sunset Strip in Los Angeles. At the front desk was a curvaceous French secretary named Suzanne. Next door was a swinging club called Dino's, where the PIs parked their fancy sports cars. First aired in October 1958, *77 Sunset Strip* was created by Roy Huggins, who also brought *Maverick, The Rockford Files,* and *The Fugitive* to the small screen. The cases solved by Bailey and Spencer were consistently simple and repetitive, often involving pretty women and murdered playboys.

After five seasons on the air, *77 Sunset Strip* was retooled in 1963 with new actors and a story line that included international espionage. The changes failed to revive the dying show, and it was canceled in February 1964. During its first five seasons, however, *77 Sunset Strip* was a huge hit, popularizing hipster slang and attitudes with 1960s audiences. The show influenced the many detective shows that followed in the 1960s.

Shane (film, directed by George Stevens, 1953)

The Western classic *Shane* is the second film in the self-declared trilogy of director/producer George Stevens (between *A Place in the Sun,* 1951, and *Giant,* 1956), dedicated to themes of love and honor. It is a simple story that takes place in a uniquely American setting—the Western frontier. Here, good battles evil, hard work is rewarded, and boys grow up with heroes. Alan Ladd's Shane is such a hero to young Joey Starrett, though Joey knows little about him. Shane's life before and after he arrives at the Starrett homestead is a mystery. A former gunslinger who abhors violence but is pushed to it by the West, he helps Starrett's father fight the corrupt cattle barons who threaten to take his land.

Filmed in scenic Jackson Hole, Wyoming (it received an Oscar for best cinematography, color), *Shane* was the most successful Western of the 1950s, and it is often cited as one of the best ever made. Joey's final cries of "Shane! Shane. Come back!" are some of the most haunting and familiar in film. He seems to be asking, "What happened to the true American heroes? Will they ever return?"

Singin' in the Rain (film, directed by Gene Kelly and Stanley Donen, 1952)

Often cited as the best movie musical ever made, *Singin' in the Rain* stars Gene Kelly, Donald O'Connor, and Debbie Reynolds in a tale of Hollywood at the beginning of the sound era. Kelly plays Don Lockwood, a suave, silent film star who becomes ridiculous when he makes his first talking picture. On a tight deadline, Lockwood decides to turn the movie into a musical and have his girlfriend anonymously dub the speaking parts to cover for his usual co-star, who has a grating voice. A movie about the history of Hollywood from vaudeville to silent pictures to the elaborate musicals of the 1940s, *Singin' in the Rain* is also a love story. Despite the fact that even songs like "Singin' in the Rain," "Good Mornin'," and "Make 'Em Laugh" and several rousing dance numbers did not earn the film an Oscar, *Singin' in the Rain* ranks number ten on the American Film Institute's list of the 100 Greatest Movies.

$64,000 Question, The (television, 1955–1958)

In a similar vein to the 1999 *Who Wants to be a Millionaire?, The $64,000 Question* was a summer replacement series that offered large cash prizes to contestants who could prove their smarts by answering general-knowledge questions. As such, it was the first of the big-money quiz shows. *The $64,000 Question* was based on a popular 1940s radio show called *Take It Or Leave It,* whose top prize was worth $64. Times had changed by 1955, as inflation and the ethic of upward mobility called for a spectacular jackpot. Contestants on *The $64,000 Question* answered questions in their area of expertise and then moved up to higher prize levels.

The atmosphere on the show was grave, with a security guard, "trust officer," and "question supervisor" presiding over the proceedings. Viewers came to favor certain contestants who appeared week after week, a phenomenon that actually led to the show's downfall. As congressional investigations later revealed, several quiz shows gave answers to the more popular contestants to ensure their continued appearance and better viewer ratings. At its height, *The $64,000 Question* attracted 47 million viewers and was a national phenomenon.

Some Like It Hot (film, directed by Billy Wilder, 1959)

According to rankings in 2000 by the American Film Institute, *Some Like It Hot* is the funniest motion picture ever made. Directed by Billy Wilder and starring Jack Lemmon, Tony Curtis, and Marilyn Monroe, it is the story of two 1920s musicians who run from the mob by joining an all-girl band. This requires them to dress and act like women, of course, which leads to uproarious antics as the band travels to gigs in Florida. The film's sexual innuendos, gender-bending story line, and spoofing of sexual stereotypes challenged the Hollywood production code, which was quickly losing influence. Audiences often missed the symbolism, however, as they were too busy laughing at Curtis and Lemmon in drag. *Some Like It Hot* was one of the top-grossing movies of 1959 and the highest-grossing film comedy to that time. It received six Academy Award nominations but lost out for best picture to *Ben Hur*.

South Pacific (novel by James Michener, 1947; stage musical by Richard Rodgers and Oscar Hammerstein II, 1949; film, directed by Joshua Logan, 1958)
James Michener's Pulitzer Prize-winning novel *Tales of the South Pacific* (1947), about love, prejudice, and war was made into a long-running Broadway play and a hit movie musical. The play, with songs by Richard Rodgers and Oscar Hammerstein and directed by Joshua Logan, premiered on Broadway in April 1949. Logan also directed the 1958 film version. The story of Nellie Forbush, a World War II nurse stationed in the South Pacific, where she falls in love with an older plantation owner, was more effective on stage than it is on screen, although the memorable songs were the brightest spots in both. "I'm Gonna Wash That Man Right Outa My Hair" and "Some Enchanted Evening" became instant classics. The Broadway version of *South Pacific* received Tony Awards for best musical and best score, among others.

Strangers on a Train (film, directed by Alfred Hitchcock, 1951)
Hitchcock's 1951 masterpiece *Strangers on a Train,* with a script by mystery writer Raymond Chandler, features all of the director's favorite motifs and techniques. It is the story of a murderous deal—you kill my father, I'll kill your wife—verbally agreed to by two strangers who meet on a train. As it turns out, tennis pro Guy Haines does not really agree to the deal, and he is shocked when Bruno Anthony carries out his end of the bargain by killing Guy's wife. Suspense then hinges on whether Guy will murder

Bruno's overbearing father and on how the effeminate Bruno will frame Guy for the murder of his wife. Some of Hitchcock's favorite motifs—dual identities and a conflicted hero—are played out against a backdrop of sports, politics, and true love. The director was at his best in this period, shooting most of his classics—among which *Strangers on a Train* must be included—before 1960.

Streetcar Named Desire, A (play by Tennessee Williams, 1947; film, directed by Elia Kazan, 1951)
Tennessee Williams's award-winning play *A Streetcar Named Desire* is widely regarded as one of the most powerful American dramas of the postwar era. The story is set in New Orleans, where Stella and Stanley Kowalski live in a squalid apartment with Stella's sister Blanche, who has come to visit. Blanche's effect is like a steam train barreling through the French Quarter. Savage in its language and realism, *Streetcar* shocked audiences when it opened on Broadway in 1947. Playing the lead role was a young Marlon Brando, who had been studying "method" acting at the Actors Studio in New York. Both on stage and in the 1951 film version, Brando did much to popularize the new technique (in which the actor sought to "inhabit" a character).

An allegory of the crumbling South and the way the world can beat a person down, the play won the Pulitzer Prize for drama in 1948. The film earned Academy Awards for best actress (Vivien Leigh), best supporting actor (Karl Malden), and best supporting actress (Kim Hunter). The play has been performed countless times since in professional and amateur theater, but never with the passion that Brando and his co-stars brought to Williams's rich dialogue.

Sunset Boulevard (film, directed by Billy Wilder, 1950)
Hollywood is a dangerous place, a place where washed-up stars descend into madness and young dreamers sell their souls for success, at least as portrayed by director Billy Wilder in the 1950 film classic *Sunset Boulevard.* Joe Gillis is such a dreamer, a bankrupt screenwriter who stumbles into the mansion of Norma Desmond, a silent film actress long past her prime. Joe, played by William Holden, agrees to help Desmond write her comeback script and becomes her lover. But when he tries to leave, she kills him, leaving him to narrate the film from the grave. "Nobody leaves a star," Desmond says.

Some critics called *Sunset Boulevard* a cruel film, in part, because Wilder hired actual silent film actors to star in it. Gloria Swanson played Desmond with all the drama and camp she once brought to the silent screen. In the role of Desmond's butler was Erich von Stroheim, another former silent film star. Wilder's black comedy has become a cult classic, known for such lines as "I'm ready for my close-up now, Mr. DeMille."

Sweet Smell of Success (film, directed by Alexander Mackendrick, 1957)

Like *Citizen Kane* (1941), *Sweet Smell of Success* is a fictionalized story about a controversial public figure. Burt Lancaster plays J. J. Hunsecker, a Manhattan gossip columnist who makes deals with publicity agents in order to get dirt for his column. The character of Hunsecker was said to be based on Walter Winchell, the nationally known gossip columnist and radio commentator. In the 1920s and 1930s, Winchell held power over celebrities and politicians from his accustomed seat at the exclusive Stork Club in New York.

A gossip peddler who advanced America's celebrity culture, Winchell strongly protested *Sweet Smell of Success* when it was released in 1957. The gritty film, with outstanding cinematography by James Wong Howe, took the celebrity-obsessed audience of the 1950s behind the scenes to a world few of them knew existed—a world in which slimy press agents like Sidney Falco (played by Tony Curtis) would do anything to get their clients in the papers, and gossip columnists could control the rise and fall of careers.

Today Show, The (television, 1952–present)

The first of the morning news programs to become a staple of network television, *The Today Show* debuted on January 14, 1952, with host Dave Garroway. Technical glitches were an inevitable part of the early live broadcasts, as Garroway read news reports and juggled segments from reporters around the world. Helping with the weather and entertainment news was the so-called "Today Girl," a different reporter every day. A succession of personalities hosted the show through the years, including John Chancellor, Hugh Downs, and Joe Garagiola. In 1963, Barbara Walters helped cover the Kennedy assassination, and she was the first Today Girl promoted to co-host in 1974.

Ratings slid after Walters's departure in 1976, but the new on-air team of Tom Brokaw and Jane Pauley brought *Today* back to prominence. It re-

mained on top among morning news shows in the 1990s with Katie Couric and Matt Lauer as hosts. In 1994, it moved into a new studio in Rockefeller Plaza looking out onto the streets of Manhattan and, much as it did in the 1950s, sought to include ordinary people in the broadcast. Couric left the show in 2006.

Tonight Show, The (television, 1954–present)

The Tonight Show has been entertaining late-night television viewers for more than fifty years. Its content has largely depended on the host, the first of whom was Steve Allen. With Allen as host from 1954 to 1957, the show was filled with musical numbers, improvisations, and audience participation. After Allen came Jack Paar, an interviewer more than a comedian. Paar interviewed a variety of guests on the air, from entertainers to politicians, and did not shy away from controversy.

By far the most famous and influential *Tonight Show* host was Johnny Carson, who took over for Paar in 1962 and led the show for thirty years. A comic who appealed to viewers from all regions of the country, Carson became a legendary figure in late-night TV entertainment. Upon his retirement in 1992, he was succeeded by Jay Leno, another comic specializing in witty monologues and man-on-the-street interviews. *The Tonight Show* has been challenged repeatedly as the late-night leader, most notably by David Letterman's *Late Show*, but it has managed to stay on or near the top of the ratings.

Touch of Evil (film directed by Orson Welles, 1958)

A classic film noir and perhaps the greatest B-movie ever made, *Touch of Evil* contains some of the stunning filmmaking techniques displayed by director Orson Welles in his 1941 classic, *Citizen Kane*. Yet unlike *Citizen Kane*, which Welles was permitted to make and release despite its controversial content, *Touch of Evil* was undermined by his studio, Universal International Pictures. Welles's version was reshot and cut without his permission, creating a confusing but shorter film that failed at the box office and with critics.

In 1998, a fifty-eight-page memo from Welles to the studio was discovered, detailing his original concepts for *Touch of Evil*. These changes were edited into a new version of the film released on DVD. *Touch of Evil* thus became more than a film about police corruption along the U.S.-Mexican border; it represents the difficulties auteur directors like Welles had in working within the commercial studio system. *Touch of Evil* was Welles's fifth and last film. Its desecration by the studio was the final straw for one of the most gifted directors in film history.

Treasure of the Sierra Madre, The (film, directed by John Huston, 1948)

The Treasure of the Sierra Madre is the definitive American film on greed and how the desire for wealth can corrupt men's souls. Directed by John Huston and released in 1948 (his first after the war), the film was both an adventure and a Western about a group of prospectors searching for gold in Mexico's Sierra Madre mountains. Performances by Humphrey Bogart and Walter Huston (the director's father) made *The Treasure of the Sierra Madre* a character-driven adventure film, one almost entirely lacking in violence. A box-office flop, the film received Academy Awards for best director and best writing, screenplay (John Huston), as well as best supporting actor (Walter Huston). John Huston was the first person to direct his father in an Oscar-winning performance; he would later direct his daughter to a win in *Prizzi's Honor* (1985).

12 Angry Men (television, 1954; film directed by Sidney Lumet, 1957)

The twelve angry men in the title are jurors charged with deciding the fate of a Puerto Rican teenager who is accused of killing his father with a knife. In real time and completely within the bounds of the jury room, *12 Angry Men* examines the judicial process, indicts the power it gives to individuals, and slowly works its way to the truth of the case, based on the reasonable doubt of one juror. The twelve men are all white and all middle class, and most begin the film believing in the guilt of the accused. Juror number eight, however, played by Henry Fonda, notes discrepancies in witness testimony and convinces his fellow jurors of the possibility of innocence.

12 Angry Men first appeared on television in 1954, and it was directed by Sidney Lumet for the larger screen. It was not a hit with audiences, but it did receive three Academy Award nominations, including best picture. While some of the film seems melodramatic to modern viewers, it nevertheless stands as a powerful testimony on the jury process and the way individual feelings, prejudices, and experiences can influence a juror's vote.

Twenty-One (television, 1956–1958)

A popular TV game show that aired at the height of that genre's craze from 1956 to 1958, *Twenty-One* became notorious after it was revealed that its star contestant, Columbia University professor Charles Van Doren, had been coaxed to cheat in order to increase viewer ratings. The disclosure convinced Congress to undertake an investigation of television game shows. On *Twenty-One,* two contestants in isolation booths answered trivia questions that ranged in point value from one to eleven. The first contestant to reach twenty-one points was the winner and received $500 for each point value. Van Doren was enormously popular with audiences and won $129,000 on the show, before a rival discovered that he had been given the answers beforehand. In the aftermath of the revelation, Van Doren was fired from his teaching position and called to testify before Congress. In 1994, Robert Redford directed a feature film about Van Doren and the *Twenty-One* scandal, called *Quiz Show* (1994).

Twilight Zone, The (television, 1959–1964, 1985–1989; film, directed by Joe Dante, John Landis, George Miller, and Steven Spielberg, 1983)

A sometimes creepy mix of science fiction, fantasy, and social commentary, *The Twilight Zone* was a series of half- and one-hour episodes that aired on CBS Television from 1959 to 1964. It was created by writer Rod Serling, who used the show as a forum for Cold War commentary on such issues as conformity, discrimination, alienation, and modern technology. *The Twilight Zone* was written by a variety of talented short-story writers (including Ray Bradbury), but Serling himself wrote ninety-two of the 156 broadcast episodes. He also introduced and closed each show, usually appearing on camera in a black suit.

The Twilight Zone was not a ratings hit in the 1960s, but it found an enduring audience in syndication, usually airing late at night or in marathons on holidays. Its themes, bizarre plot twists, and shocking resolutions attracted new viewers more than forty years after its original airing. A feature film was made in 1983, and a new television version aired from 1985 to 1989. But it was Serling's original episodes that still packed a punch, proving that television could be a showcase of ideas, even when masked in science fiction.

Vertigo (film, directed by Alfred Hitchcock, 1958)

An Alfred Hitchcock classic, *Vertigo* is a study in

obsession and lost love. Jimmy Stewart plays a vertigo-suffering detective who falls in love with a client and is devastated by her death. He meets a woman on the street who resembles her and attempts to remake her in the client's image, only to discover that they are one and the same. Artfully shot and edited, *Vertigo* was a difficult film for 1960s audiences, and it failed at the box office. In time, however, critics turned to it again and discovered one of Hitchcock's most notable achievements. Stewart's performance, miles outside his usual all-American persona, captured the obsessiveness of love to an unsettling degree. As in such other films as *Rear Window* (1954) and *Psycho* (1960), Hitchcock implicates viewers as opportunistic voyeurs who objectify women and are obsessed with watching life rather than participating.

View from the Bridge, A (play, by Arthur Miller, 1955; film, directed by Sidney Lumet, 1961)

A two-act play by acclaimed American dramatist Arthur Miller, *A View from the Bridge* was set in Brooklyn, New York, in 1955, and it explored life on the docks for Italian immigrants. The original screenplay, co-written with Elia Kazan, was titled *The Hook*. A chronicle of waterfront corruption, rather than a story of families living near the docks, the play was widely smeared as un-American and abandoned by Miller. Ultimately, it became Kazan's Oscar-winning film *On the Waterfront.*

Miller rewrote *The Hook* as *A View from the Bridge;* it appeared on Broadway in 1955 and flopped. Miller again retooled the play, lengthening it to two acts and filling out its dialogue and characters, especially that of Eddie Carbone, a longshoreman raising his niece Catherine. Carbone also has taken in two illegal Sicilian immigrants. When one of the immigrants falls in love with Catherine, Carbone's overprotectiveness and jealousy leads to tragedy. *A View from the Bridge* was staged in London in 1956, became a hit, and moved to Broadway. A film version directed by Sidney Lumet (titled *Vu Du Pont*) was released in 1961.

What's Opera, Doc? (cartoon, directed by Chuck Jones, 1957)

What's Opera, Doc? is animator Chuck Jones's seven-minute lampoon of Richard Wagner's eighteen-hour opera cycle, *The Ring of the Nibelung.* In it, Elmer Fudd is Siegfried, a mighty warrior on a rabbit hunt. To distract him, Bugs Bunny disguises himself as the lovely Viking Brunhilde. Fudd is smitten, and the

two make a duo in the ballet "Return My Love." When Brunhilde's headdress falls off, she is revealed as the "wascally wabbit." Fudd commands the heavens to "kill the wabbit," but is remorseful when Bugs dies. "Well, what did you expect in an opera, a happy ending?" Bugs asks in the closing scene. *What's Opera, Doc?* was chosen by the National Film Preservation Board of the Library of Congress as a "culturally, historically or aesthetically significant" film and added to the National Film Registry.

Wild One, The (film, directed by László Benedek, 1953)

Based on a real-life incident in which hoodlums spread destruction in the downtown of Hollister, California, *The Wild One* stars Marlon Brando as Johnny, the leader of the Black Rebels Motorcycle Club. Cruising the open road, the young rebels ride from town to town, stirring up trouble. They arrive in Wrightsville in "Middle America," and Johnny falls for the sheriff's daughter, a conservative girl who has never left the small town. To her, Johnny represents freedom and adventure.

The town erupts around the motorcycle club's arrival. Vigilantes attempt to expel the Black Rebels and members of a rival club called the Beetles; the townsfolks' violence turns out to be much stronger than that of the motorcyclists. Like other antisocial characters that followed (James Dean in *Rebel Without a Cause,* for example), Brando's Jimmy appealed to 1950s youth. Many older Americans, however, feared the film would lead to copycat revolts and even accused it of being Communist. *The Wild One* was the first film to dramatize the motorcycle culture, and it took years for motorcyclists to live down its reputation.

Wonderful World of Disney, The (television, 1954–present)

A pioneer in feature-film production, Walt Disney also was a vital figure in the early years of television. In 1954, *Disneyland* first aired on the ABC network; although it was little more than a theme park commercial masquerading as family entertainment, the show was a success and other Disney programs soon followed. The Disney studio had a cache of animated short films it could use on television to promote its longer feature films, and Walt Disney hosted the show himself from 1954 to 1966. This approach did much to further the Disney Company's image as *the* all-American source of family entertainment.

Renamed *The Wonderful World of Disney* in 1969, the regular Sunday night show introduced such popular movies as *Davy Crockett*. The program would go by several other names through the years (*Disney's Wonderful World, The Disney Sunday Movie,* and *The Magical World of Disney*) and appeared in various forms on all three broadcast networks—but the concept remained the same. *Wonderful World* returned to ABC in 1997, after the Disney Corporation acquired the network. It is the longest-running prime time show in television history.

You Bet Your Life (television, 1950–1961)

You Bet Your Life was a popular prime-time game show hosted by comedian Groucho Marx that aired on the NBC network from 1950 to 1961. It began as a radio quiz show in 1947 and moved to the small screen in 1950, the start of the television era. Contestants bet all or part of a purse given them at the start of the show, based on their ability to answer questions in a certain category. The questions were not difficult; the show's primary entertainment was Marx's verbal jabs at the contestants, who were chosen based on their ability to be his foils. A "secret word," revealed only to the viewing audience at the start of each show, was one of the program's running gags. The first contestant to say the word received $100, held in the mouth of a papier-mâché duck that dropped from the ceiling. In 1960, *You Bet Your Life* was renamed *The Groucho Show* in an effort to distance it from the quiz show scandals, but audiences turned away from the genre en masse, and Marx's show left the air in 1961.

Your Show of Shows (television, 1950–1954)

Your Show of Shows was among the most popular variety shows of television's golden age. Drawing from vaudeville, nightclub acts, and Broadway, *Your Show of Shows* was most popular with East Coast audiences, who saw it live. It was largely experimental, drawing on the most popular forms of American entertainment to create something new for the new medium of television. The stars of the show were Sid Caesar (with whom it became synonymous) and Imogene Coca, two talented comedians who spoofed everything from foreign films to gumball machines. The show also had a talented staff of writers behind the scenes that included Mel Brooks, Neil Simon, and Carl Reiner. Each ninety-minute program (originally part of a larger program called *Saturday Night Revue*) featured skits, large-scale production numbers, monologues, film parodies, and a bit part by a guest host. Singing, dancing, high-brow comedy, and sophisticated satire all came together in *Your Show of Shows,* which dominated Saturday night television from 1950 until 1954.

THE SIXTIES

Literature and Journalism

Autobiography of Malcolm X, The (nonfiction, by Malcolm X with the assistance of Alex Haley, 1965)

Co-written with author and journalist Alex Haley, *The Autobiography of Malcolm X* stands as the most important memoir of the African American experience in postwar urban America. In this book, the controversial black nationalist leader traces his life from childhood in Omaha, where he witnesses the death of his father by white racists (a fact questioned by some historians), to young adulthood in Boston and Harlem, New York, where he joins a criminal gang but is eventually caught and sent to prison. There, Malcolm Little (his original or, as he deemed it, his "slave" name) converts to the Muslim faith under the auspices of the Nation of Islam, a black nationalist organization.

Upon his release from prison, Malcolm—having replaced his surname with an "X," symbolizing the African heritage he says was stolen from him—becomes a speaker and organizer for the Black Muslims. He preaches the Black Muslim belief that white people are "devils" and that blacks must use "any means necessary," including violence, to defend themselves. In the final pages of the book, written shortly before his assassination in February 1965, Malcolm leaves the Nation of Islam after a pilgrimage to Mecca, where he sees Muslims of all colors worshipping together in peace.

Bell Jar, The (novel, by Sylvia Plath, 1963)

This semiautobiographical novel, first published under the pseudonym Victoria Lucas, recounts the summer experiences of a college student working as a magazine editor in New York. The central character suffers a mental breakdown—comparing her illness to a bell jar, airless and suffocating—similar to the author's own battle with insanity and thoughts of suicide. Plath was better known as a poet than as a memoirist or novelist, but *The Bell Jar* has remained a perennial best-seller since its publication in 1963. Like J.D. Salinger's *Catcher in the Rye* (1951), its coming-of-age narrative and ruminations on the shallowness of modern life have made it popular among young adult readers.

Plath took her own life at age thirty, shortly after the book was written but before it was published.

Black Like Me (nonfiction, by John Howard Griffin, 1961; film, directed by Carl Lerner, 1964)

In the tradition of journalists who have gone under cover to expose social problems, *Black Like Me* tells the story of author John Howard Griffin, a white man who undergoes pigmentation treatments to make him appear African American. Under this disguise, Griffin travels through the segregated South, experiencing the humiliation and legal restrictions that black Southerners faced every day. Despite the fact that he has a college degree, Griffin is repeatedly turned down for jobs and continually harassed. The book was both a best-seller and a literary sensation when it was published in 1961. *Black Like Me* was produced as a movie in 1964, starring James Whitmore.

Catch-22 (novel, by Joseph Heller, 1961; film, directed by Mike Nichols, 1970)

Arguably the greatest satirical novel about war in American letters, *Catch-22* tells the story of airmen serving on a U.S. base in Italy during World War II. The title refers to a fictional military regulation that states that the only way to get out of the service is to declare oneself insane—but that to do so means that one is, in fact, sane. There is, in short, no way out for protagonist John Yossarian.

The book highlights both the insanity and surrealism of war. One of its most memorable characters is Milo Minderbender, an entrepreneurial officer who cuts a deal with the Germans to have bombers attack their own base. The novel was popular when it first came out and became "required reading" in the antiwar movement later in the decade. It has enjoyed lasting acclaim on sheer literary merits, and the title has become a popular catch phrase for an unreasonable and problematic situation. A movie version starring Alan Arkin was released in 1970.

Conscience of a Conservative, The (nonfiction, by Barry Goldwater, 1960)

This brief book articulates the political philosophy of Barry Goldwater, a conservative Republican senator from Arizona who ran for president in 1964. The book's basic contention is that the United States is a profoundly conservative country that has been politically hijacked by liberals intent on expanding government programs and turning it into a socialist state. Ridiculed by a number of critics, the work won a strong following among far-right conservatives and became a kind of bible for the movement that helped Goldwater win the Republican nomination in 1964. Although Goldwater was ultimately swamped in the general election that November, the ideas in his book continued to resonate with conservatives; much of what he wrote was later adopted by a more successful conservative, Ronald Reagan. Many scholars consider *The Conscience of a Conservative* one of the most influential polemics in postwar America.

Death and Life of Great American Cities, The (nonfiction, by Jane Jacobs, 1961)

The Death and Life of Great American Cities was a book ahead of its time. In it, the self-educated urban planner Jane Jacobs denounces virtually everything that was considered gospel in the urban planning profession. In particular, she argues that urban renewal and slum clearance, while well intentioned, gut the living core of cities, replacing dense urban neighborhoods with alienating spaces and high-rises. Abhorring the impact of the automobile, she maintains that the automobile-based suburban lifestyle threatens to cut off social interaction, and highways cutting through downtown areas destroy city neighborhoods. All of this urban renewal, she concludes, destroys American cities. In its place, she advocates historical preservation and the construction of neighborhoods on a human scale. Widely read when it came out, the book presented ideas that have since become part of mainstream urban planning.

Double Helix, The (nonfiction, by James Watson, 1968)

Perhaps the single most important scientific development of the postwar era was the discovery of the molecular structure of DNA (deoxyribonucleic acid, the so-called "code of life") by biochemists James Watson, Francis Crick, and Maurice Wilkins in 1953. DNA is the genetic substance of living cells and viruses; its chemical structure carries the unique genetic traits of individual organisms. Watson's 1968 book, whose title refers to the three-dimensional shape of the DNA molecule, tells the story of the discovery of DNA and

explains its significance in layman's terms. The discovery is not cast as a story of science moving heroically and inexorably forward, but as an honest portrayal of the infighting among scientists and the author's own misgivings about the associate with whom he shared the Nobel Prize. Recent scholarship has shown that Watson was not entirely candid, failing to give credit to Rosalind Franklin, an associate of Maurice Wilkins, for her critical contribution.

Electric Kool-Aid Acid Test, The (nonfiction, by Tom Wolfe, 1968)

Journalist and author Tom Wolfe is widely regarded as a leading practitioner of, and spokesman for, the so-called New Journalism of the 1960s, and *The Electric Kool-Aid Acid Test* is regarded by many as his best book in this style. New Journalism was said to be characterized by several features: colorful and idiosyncratic language, unorthodox and even taboo subject matter, and the author's own narrative perspective on the story.

The Electric Kool-Aid Acid Test chronicles the story of novelist and counterculture hero Ken Kesey from his high school days, when he was voted the senior "most likely to succeed," to his leadership of an LSD-taking group of hippies known as the Merry Pranksters. Eventually, his followers abandon him, and the book ends on a bittersweet note about life and love in the counterculture movement.

Feminine Mystique, The (nonfiction, by Betty Friedan, 1963)

Perhaps the most influential book in the feminist movement of the postwar era, *The Feminine Mystique* offered a paradigm shift in the way many women saw themselves and their role in society. Author Betty Friedan was a highly educated graduate of Smith College in the 1950s; she began to feel frustrated that her skills and knowledge were going to waste in her role as housewife and mother—a role she claimed to have accepted because society and the media told her this was the highest aspiration a woman could achieve. Friedan then began to wonder if other women felt the same way. She surveyed her classmates and found that the frustration she felt was widespread.

Friedan tried to get her findings published as a magazine article, but editors told her that only mentally unbalanced women could be unhappy as housewives and mothers. Ultimately published as a book, Friedan's findings touched many women, helping to spark the women's movement of the 1960s and 1970s. She went on to help found the National Organization for Women, which became a major women's rights group in the late twentieth century.

Fire Next Time, The (nonfiction, by James Baldwin, 1963)

Published during the high tide of the civil rights movement, this powerful two-part essay is a biographical account of Baldwin's early years and a searing critique of racism in America. The solution to the race problem, he contends, is neither integration nor segregation, but acceptance. Baldwin argues that America must understand that it has always been a society of many races and that if blacks are not accepted by whites, the society will eventually become oppressive to whites as well. He also explores the role of religion in his own life, the hypocrisies he has found in it, and his encounter with Elijah Muhammad, the founder of the Black Muslim movement.

Forest People, The (nonfiction, by Colin Turnbull, 1961)

This book examines Turnbull's experiences living with the Bambuti Pygmies, an African tribe living in the forests of the Congo. In the tradition of anthropologist Margaret Mead, Turnbull lived among the Pygmies, observing and learning from them. The book struck a chord with American readers, living in their fast-paced, consumption-obsessed modern society. Turnbull portrayed a community that lived close to nature, found joy in simple things, and had few material possessions. It did not hurt the book's sales that it was written in an engaging, novelistic style. While some critics later pointed out that the book downplayed problems within Pygmy society, most readers accepted its basic contention that a simple, nonacquisitive people had somehow survived the onslaught of the civilized world.

I Know Why the Caged Bird Sings (nonfiction, by Maya Angelou, 1969)

A perennial on the reading lists of college literature classes, I Know Why the Caged Bird Sings is the first and most popular of a five-volume autobiography by the African American writer and poet Maya Angelou. The book recounts Angelou's childhood in a segregated town in Arkansas and her subsequent move to San Francisco. Among the life stories she recounts are growing up with her brother in her grandmother's household, a sexual assault at a young age, and her experiences with racism in a small Southern town.

I Lost It at the Movies (nonfiction, by Pauline Kael, 1965)

More than a guide to motion pictures and the modern film industry, Pauline Kael's I Lost It at the Movies is a personal account of the moviegoing experiences of perhaps the most noted film critic in the United States. In the book, Kael discusses some of her favorite movies and the changing character of the movie business. Known for her cutting wit and penchant for intellectually challenging and emotionally stirring films, Kael wrote about the movies for more than forty years, until her retirement in 1991. Her career included a long stint as the film critic for The New Yorker magazine.

I'm OK, You're OK: A Practical Guide to Transactional Analysis (nonfiction, by Thomas Harris, 1969)

Among the earliest and most influential books in the so-called self-help genre, I'm OK, You're OK has been through numerous editions in the years since it was first published in 1969. Along the way, it has won new generations of readers and sparked much controversy. The book's main thesis is that most people do not progress emotionally beyond childhood. Instead, they continually seek approval from others and get caught in a trap in which they perceive others as emotionally "OK" but see themselves as emotionally "not OK." Harries argues that such behavior leaves people emotionally "crippled" and offers a number of strategies for moving beyond that condition. Supporters of the book claim that millions have been helped on the road to emotional well-being. Critics have argued that it is a product of the permissive 1960s, in which all behavior, as long as it makes the individual happy, is acceptable.

In Cold Blood (nonfiction, by Truman Capote, 1965; film, directed by Richard Brooks, 1967)

One of the most harrowing accounts of violent crime in modern American nonfiction, In Cold Blood tells the story of two small-time criminals who commit a multiple murder of a Holcomb, Kansas, family in 1959. Author Truman Capote learned of the murders from a newspaper article and was intrigued by the contrast between the viciousness of the perpetrators and the wholesomeness of the victims. Readers shared Capote's fascination and made the book a best-seller.

Capote, controversial for his flamboyant personal style and provocative positions on public issues, differed from other New Journalists of the day, who often included themselves as characters in their own stories. Never doing this, Capote was able to maintain a greater distance from his subject matter. The movie version of *In Cold Blood* was released in 1967.

Machine in the Garden, The (nonfiction, by Leo Marx, 1964)

In this seminal book on the history of American technology, Leo Marx examines the ways in which technology has shaped the nation's culture and vice versa. The central thesis is that Europeans brought their attitudes and ideas with them to the new continent and, in doing so, sought to recreate nature in an image that matched their own perceptions of what an idealized landscape should look like. Carefully examining American literature of the nineteenth century, Marx argues that Americans used technology primarily to change their environment but, in the end, found that the technology they employed threatened the very environment they had created. Marx makes it clear that his book is not merely about the nineteenth century but has implications for the modern era as well.

Making of the President, 1960, The (nonfiction, by Theodore H. White, 1961)

One of the first book-length, journalistic treatments of a single political campaign, *The Making of the President, 1960* discusses the hard-fought and narrowly decided race for the presidency between Republican Vice President Richard M. Nixon and Democratic Senator John F. Kennedy. Republicans claimed the book was biased in Kennedy's favor, but White maintained that his more complete coverage of the Democrats' campaign was the result of their giving him more access. Predicting a Kennedy victory, White was at the Kennedy family compound at Hyannisport, Massachusetts, on election night, adding to the behind-the-scenes feel of the book.

Publishers were initially hesitant to publish the account, fearing that, with the campaign over, it would remain on bookstore shelves. But White's up-close reportage and engaging style captivated readers, making the book one of the best-selling political books of all time and single-handedly creating a subgenre of its own. White went on to publish books with the same title and approach on the 1964, 1968, and 1972 campaigns.

Mastering the Art of French Cooking (nonfiction, by Julia Child, Simone Beck, and Louisette Bertholle, 1961)

While cookbooks on foreign cuisine fill entire sections of bookstores today, few Americans felt comfortable following the difficult and unusual recipes associated with fine French cooking before Julia Child. More than any book, *Mastering the Art of French Cooking* introduced household chefs to French cuisine, walking them through the process in carefully explained steps, from buying the ingredients, to picking the right wine, to serving on the right plates. The best-selling cookbook established Child's reputation as America's first celebrity chef, an image cemented by her long-running television show.

Naked Ape, The (nonfiction, by Desmond Morris, 1967; film, directed by Donald Drive, 1973)

Subtitled "A Zoologist's Study of the Human Animal," *The Naked Ape* argues that the human race is not as different from the animal kingdom as people like to think. The book examines the age-old debate of nature versus nurture, or environment versus genetics, and comes down strongly on the side of nature and genetics. Morris argues that most of human prehistory occurred on the savannahs of Africa and that much of our physical and behavioral attributes were shaped there. In his studies of many human situations—from finding food and engaging in conflict to sexual contact and raising the young—Morris finds that humans display instincts that are distinctly primate. While none of this was new to biological scientists, Morris made the argument accessible to the general public, who, in turn, made the book a best-seller. A 1973 movie version proved unsuccessful.

National Lampoon, The (magazine, 1969–present)

The National Lampoon is a satirical magazine that was founded in 1969 by several veterans of the campus humor publication, *The Harvard Lampoon,* which itself dates back to 1876. Featuring humorous articles based on the latest news and cultural developments, the magazine became the most widely read publication on the nation's college campuses during the 1970s and 1980s. Other popular *Lampoon* productions include comedy recordings, a syndicated radio show called "The National Lampoon Radio Hour," and several films, including *Animal House* (1978).

One Flew Over the Cuckoo's Nest (novel, by Ken Kesey, 1962; film, directed by Milos Forman, 1975)

This best-selling, critically acclaimed novel by 1960s counterculture figure Ken Kesey tells the story of petty criminal Randle Patrick McMurphy, who avoids prison by getting a court to declare him insane. Sentenced to an Oregon mental hospital, McMurphy rallies the other patients in opposition to the dictatorial hospital administration, personified by a martinet nurse named Ratched. Kesey based many of the incidents and characters in the book on his real-life experiences working in a mental hospital. *Cuckoo's Nest* resonated with rebellious young readers of the 1960s and 1970s, who accepted the core tenet of the book that the hospital staff and wardens were no less insane than the patients—perhaps more so in their rigid application of rules. The 1975 film version, starring Jack Nicholson as McMurphy, won a total of five Academy Awards, including best picture.

One-Dimensional Man (nonfiction, by Herbert Marcuse, 1964)

An intellectual guru to many 1960s radicals, Herbert Marcuse was a student of the Frankfurt School of Philosophy in Germany during the early 1920s and early 1930s. An unorthodox Marxist thinker and a Jew, Marcuse was forced to flee his native land shortly after the Nazi takeover in 1933, becoming a professor at various universities in America. Arguably his most influential book, *One-Dimensional Man* became required reading among leftist critics of American capitalism during the 1960s. In it, Marcuse argues that elites have traditionally used technology to maintain control over the minds of the masses and that, by the 1960s, they had effectively reduced human freedom to narrow confines defined by the elites themselves. As the appeal of anticapitalist radicalism began to fade among American youth, so, too, did the popularity of Marcuse's work.

Other America, The (nonfiction, by Michael Harrington, 1962)

The most influential book on the subject of poverty to appear in the postwar era, Michael Harrington's *The Other America* was widely read by the general public and by policymakers in the presidential administrations of John F. Kennedy and Lyndon B. Johnson. Indeed, Johnson himself claimed the book was an inspiration for his War on Poverty program, a series of government initiatives that roughly halved the number of Americans living under the poverty line between 1965 and 1980. A short and highly readable work, *The Other America* examines the reasons for poverty, the experiences of people living in poverty, and possible solutions. The major impoverished groups are discussed: Harrington examines the lives of inner-city blacks, Native Americans on reservations, and white rural poor. Although he was himself a Socialist who harshly criticized capitalism as the cause of poverty, Harrington inspired liberal programs, which tried to use government to smooth the harder edges of capitalism.

Population Bomb, The (nonfiction, by Paul Ehrlich, 1968)

The Population Bomb did more to call attention to the dangers of exploding population growth than any work since that of Thomas Malthus in the late eighteenth century. Like Malthus, the biologist and educator Paul Ehrlich contends that the global population is quickly outpacing society's ability to feed, clothe, and house people, a condition that leads to famine, epidemics, conflict, and environmental degradation, and, eventually, will cause a collapse of civilization and a breakdown of the global order. But Ehrlich departs from Malthus on one crucial point: whereas the British economist had failed to take into account the effects of technological breakthroughs, Ehrlich cites advances in medicine and other advances that lower death rates as the very causes of overpopulation. Still, he fails to anticipate ongoing developments in agriculture—including new, high-yield crops—or to predict how growing wealth in the developing world would lead to higher rates of education and, ultimately, smaller families. Some scholars say the book's dire predictions have not been disproved, just put off further into the future.

Portnoy's Complaint (novel, by Philip Roth, 1969; film, directed by Ernest Lehman, 1972)

The most widely read example of the so-called Jewish renaissance in postwar American fiction, *Portnoy's Complaint* begins on a psychiatrist's couch as the eponymous protagonist explains the reasons for his neuroses and sexual hang-ups. Inevitably, this takes him back to his childhood in a guilt-ridden Jewish household in Newark, New Jersey, in the 1940s and 1950s. Both comedic and tragic, the book explores previously taboo subjects like premarital sex and masturbation. Such was the popularity of the book that the title became widely used by Americans to designate sexual neurosis. A film based on the book and starring Richard Benjamin was produced in 1972, but it met with mixed reviews and a lackluster reception at the box office.

Rabbit, Run (novel, by John Updike, 1960; film, directed by Jack Smight, 1970)

In telling the story of Harry "Rabbit" Angstrom, a former high school basketball star having a hard time adjusting to adulthood, John Updike contributed one of the postwar era's most critically acclaimed, best-selling novels of modern American angst. Married to an alcoholic and hating his job, Angstrom chooses to run away and eventually moves in with a prostitute. Much of the book is about the protagonist's inability to establish meaningful relationships with others or to find personal meaning in his own life. Yet Rabbit's likable character and the honest account of his struggle, as well as Updike's elegant prose style, struck a note with the reading public. Three sequels—*Rabbit Redux* (1971), *Rabbit Is Rich* (1981), and *Rabbit at Rest* (1990)—also met with popular success. The 1970 movie version of *Rabbit, Run* starred James Caan.

Rolling Stone (magazine, 1967–present)

A music and music industry magazine founded by entrepreneur Jann Wenner and critic Ralph Gleason in San Francisco, *Rolling Stone*—titled in homage to the rock band of a similar name—was the most successful of the many counterculture publications spawned during the hippie era. Later, however, it became far more mainstream in format, coverage, and presentation. Although Wenner once jokingly claimed that he founded the magazine in order to meet famous people, his agenda was more serious—to write about rock music, alternative lifestyles, and the counterculture in a way that avoided the condescension and sensationalism of the mainstream press. The magazine also fostered the unique style of personal journalism, the so-called New Journalism of writers such as Tom Wolfe, Norman Mailer, and Hunter S. Thompson who put themselves at the center of the stories they covered.

Silent Spring (nonfiction, by Rachel Carson, 1962)

So influential was Rachel Carson's *Silent Spring*—which began as a series of articles in *The New Yorker* magazine—that many people point to its publication in 1962 as the beginning of the modern environmental movement. The book brought to light the many negative effects of pesticides, especially DDT (dichloro diphenyl trichloroethane), which was far more pervasively used at the time than most Americans realized. "For the first time in history," Carson wrote, "every human being is now subjected to contact with dangerous chemicals, from the moment of conception until death."

Trained as a biologist, Carson was able to explain the impact of such chemicals on the environment in everyday language, which made the book a best-seller and ultimately led to sweeping changes in public policy. The book was the object of ridicule by the chemical industry, but a study by a federal commission upheld its findings. The result was a scaling back in pesticide use and a new awareness of the environment on the part of the American public.

Six Crises (nonfiction, by Richard M. Nixon, 1962)

One of ten books written by Richard M. Nixon, *Six Crises* details early events he considered important to his political career. The book begins in 1948, with Nixon's participation in the Alger Hiss case as a member of the U.S. House of Representatives. The hearings brought him to national prominence, and he ran for vice president on the Republican ticket with Dwight D. Eisenhower in 1952. The second crisis occurred during that campaign, when he was accused of taking bribes but saved his career by appearing on television with his family and dog Checkers. Eisenhower won the presidency, but suffered a heart attack in 1955, making Vice President Nixon acting president for several weeks, the third crisis. The fourth and fifth crises occurred in foreign countries—in Venezuela, when Nixon and his wife, Pat, were attacked by procommunist mobs, and in Russia, during the vice president's famous debate with Nikita Khrushchev. The sixth crisis was his failed 1960 campaign for the presidency against John F. Kennedy. Nixon's detached account of these events presents him as a rational, competent political figure, quite a different image from the one he would later project during the Watergate crisis.

Slaughterhouse Five (novel, by Kurt Vonnegut; 1969; film, directed by George Roy Hill, 1972)

A prisoner of war during World War II, when he witnessed the horrific bombing of Dresden, Germany, by Allied forces, novelist Kurt Vonnegut, provides a fictionalized account of his experience in *Slaughterhouse Five,* a novel released at the height of protest against the Vietnam War. The protagonist, Billy Pilgrim, tells the story in a circular, rather than a linear, structure, because he has become "unstuck in time," able to shift back and forth across various periods of his life. So the novel, too, moves between Pilgrim's wartime experiences, his optometry practice in Ilium, New York, and his visit to the planet Tralfamadore, where he is imprisoned as a human specimen and put on display. From the Tralfamordians, Pilgrim learns that all moments in the past, present, and future coexist. He is unafraid of death, even during the bombing that kills 130,000 Germans. The novel's satirical, psychedelic take on such issues as war and consumerism made it popular with 1960s audiences.

Structure of Scientific Revolutions, The (nonfiction, by Thomas Kuhn, 1962)

Thomas Kuhn had a distinguished career as a professor of philosophy and the history of science, but it was his *The Structure of Scientific Revolutions,* written while he was a doctoral student at Harvard, that made him known to the general public. Published in 1962, after appearing in the *International Encyclopedia of Unified Science,* the book put forth a new concept of science: a pursuit characterized by "a series of peaceful interludes punctuated by intellectually violent revolutions." For Kuhn, "normal science" is not a gradual accumulation of knowledge over time, but a tradition-shattering occurrence that changes worldviews. He coined the term "paradigm shift" to describe the process of one set of beliefs (a paradigm) being changed or replaced by another.

More than 1 million copies of *The Structure of Scientific Revolutions* were sold in sixteen languages, and it has influenced not only scientists, but also economists, historians, and sociologists. Upon Kuhn's death in 1996, *The New York Times* wrote that his "theory of scientific revolution became a profoundly influential landmark of 20th-century intellectual history."

To Kill a Mockingbird (novel, by Harper Lee, 1960; film, directed by Robert Mulligan, 1962)

To Kill a Mockingbird is one of the most-loved works of American fiction and film. Written by Harper Lee, it is the story of a Southern lawyer named Atticus Finch who defends an African American man falsely accused of rape. Lee tackles some of the biggest issues of the postwar era—race, class, and justice—through the eyes of Atticus's eight-year-old daughter, Scout. From the girl's perspective, the world is easily drawn in black and white; during the three years covered in the book, however, she comes to see that justice and kindness take many forms.

To Kill a Mockingbird is a modern classic that readers turn to again and again for its humor, heroism, and strong sense of place. It received the Pulitzer Prize and has sold over 30 million copies in more than forty languages. In 1962, a film version of *To Kill a Mockingbird* was released starring Gregory Peck as Atticus. It is the rare case of a film living up to the novel that preceded it. With the civil rights movement in full swing, its progressive message of tolerance was not lost on audiences or critics.

Understanding Media (nonfiction, by Marshall McLuhan, 1964)

Understanding Media, by Marshall McLuhan, was published in 1964, when the mass media were developing at a rapid pace but few had yet analyzed the implications of this development. In Part One of a somewhat rambling work, McLuhan coins the now-familiar phrase "the medium is the message." As he put it, "the 'message' of any medium or technology is the change of scale or pace or pattern that it introduces into human affairs." Here and throughout the book, McLuhan analyzes the various forms of mass media not just as news and entertainment devices, but as participants in society that have an influence on their audience. In subsequent chapters, McLuhan examines the nature and effect of the printed word, the typewriter, the telegraph, the telephone, the photograph, the phonograph, radio, movies, television, and automation. He was the first to use the phrase "global village," theorizing that electronic media could reunify the human race. The work gained poignancy and respect as the twentieth century wore on and the role of the mass media continued to expand.

Valley of the Dolls (novel, by Jacqueline Susann, 1966; film, directed by Mark Robson, 1967)

A sensationalist pulp novel, Jacqueline Susann's *Valley of the Dolls* was also a classic of feminist literature, even though it preceded the feminist movement itself. The story begins in affluent postwar America and follows twenty years in the lives of three starry-eyed women in their pursuit of glory in show business. Borrowing from her own experience of moving to New York for a Broadway career, Susann portrays characters who find success to varying degrees, only to discover that their lives are empty and meaningless. Living in the valley of the dolls

("dolls" are uppers, tranquilizers, and other pills), two characters meet tragic ends and another relies on her talent for a happy life. The 1967 film version of *Valley of the Dolls* became a cult classic. The original book and movie spawned a 1970 film sequel called *Beyond the Valley of the Dolls*.

Where the Wild Things Are (children's story-book, by Maurice Sendak, 1963)

Enormously popular with children and adults, *Where the Wild Things Are* has emerged as a modern classic of children's literature since its publication in 1963. Written and illustrated by Maurice Sendak, it is the story of Max, a mischievous boy who is sent to bed without dinner and travels in his imagination to where the wild things are. Max manages to tame the beasts and is made their king, but ultimately he misses home and wants "to be where someone loved him best of all." Max sails back to find his dinner, still hot, waiting in his room. Like so many other children who dream of running away, Max realizes that there's no place like home. *Where the Wild Things Are* was an unconventional children's book when it was published, but Sendak's marvelous illustrations earned it the Caldecott Medal in 1964.

Whole Earth Catalog (nonfiction, by Stewart Brand, 1968)

The *Whole Earth Catalog* was the bible of the counterculture of the 1960s and early 1970s, a one-stop shopping source for everything from books by Buckminster Fuller to Futuro houses. In retrospect, the catalog functioned much like the Internet would decades later. Stanford University professor Fred Turner has argued that the *Whole Earth Catalog* helped translate the ideals of the counterculture into resources for understanding the possibilities of digital networking. In 1968, however, hippie biologist Stewart Brand simply wanted a publication to guide the many people living communally, thinking environmentally, and eating healthfully. "We are as gods and might as well get used to it," the catalog opened.

Tools to help an individual conduct his own education, find his own inspiration, shape his own environment, and share his adventure were promoted in several editions of the *Whole Earth Catalog*. Items were listed in the catalog if they were useful as a tool, relevant to independent education, high-quality or low-cost, not already common knowledge, and easily available by mail. The *Whole Earth Catalog* was a network for alternative thinkers before such networks went online.

Film, Radio, Television, and Theater

Andy Griffith Show, The (television, 1960–1968)

Set in the small North Carolina town of Mayberry, *The Andy Griffith Show* chronicled the everyday lives of phlegmatic sheriff Andy Taylor (played by Andy Griffith), his inept deputy Barney Fife (Don Knotts), young son Opie (Ron Howard), and a host of slightly eccentric characters. Although set in a police station, the show rarely dealt with serious crime, focusing instead on small-town plot lines and wholesome Americana. Often, the jail cells contained but a single criminal, the town drunk Otis (Hal Smith). Indeed, the people and goings-on in Mayberry could not have been farther from the reality of a divided and tumultuous America in the 1960s—a distancing that may have explained the show's enormous popularity. A sequel called *Mayberry RFD* ran from 1968 to 1971.

Batman (television, 1966–1968; film, directed by Tim Burton, 1989)

In the original comic book, created in 1938, Batman represented the antithesis of the original superhero Superman. Whereas Superman stood for small-town, all-American values, Batman was a gritty urbanite. In the 1960s television show, however, Batman (played by Adam West) and his adventures were a camp parody of the superhero and his activities. The characters almost seemed to wink at the camera, and the villains—such as the Joker and the Riddler—while based on those in the comic books, were more comedic than threatening. The show also incorporated the pop art sensibility of the 1960s, with fight scenes punctuated by bursts of colorful action words ("pow!" "zap!") as in the paintings of Roy Lichtenstein. In 1989, Batman was produced as a Hollywood movie starring Michael Keaton. The film returned Batman to his comic book roots, making him a brooding character in a dark urban landscape. Several movie sequels have appeared since then.

Becket (play, by Jean Anouilh, 1961; film, directed by Peter Glenville, 1964)

Regarded as one of the best historical films ever made by Hollywood—and an unlikely hit—*Becket* told the story of the conflict between King Henry II of England

and St. Thomas Becket, the archbishop of Canterbury. When the previous archbishop dies in 1161, Henry decides to assert national sovereignty by appointing Becket, an old drinking friend, as the new archbishop rather than accept an overly pious priest from Rome. Becket, however, turns out to have his own ideas about how the church should be run and proves a worthy opponent to the king. The archbishop is assassinated in 1170, presumably under Henry's orders. Based on a 1961 play by Jean Anouilh, the movie pitted two of the most popular British stars of the day, Richard Burton and Peter O'Toole, as Becket and Henry, respectively, and it was nominated for twelve Oscars (winning only one—for best writing, screenplay).

Beverly Hillbillies, The (television, 1962–1971; film, directed by Penelope Spheeris, 1993)

The 1960s saw a series of hit television sitcoms based on small-town and rural life, including *The Andy Griffith Show, Green Acres,* and *Petticoat Junction.* Students of television history have argued that the popularity of such shows derived from the fact that they provided relief from the cultural and political unrest of the decade. Among the most watched of these shows was *The Beverly Hillbillies,* which provided a twist on the formula by relocating a poor Tennessee family to the elite confines of Beverly Hills, after oil is discovered on their land. The Clampett family—father Jedd, feisty Granny, sexy Elly May, and doltish cousin Jethro—were gently lampooned, but so were their snobby Beverly Hills neighbors. The television show spawned a movie version in 1993 that was panned by critics and the public.

Bewitched (television, 1964–1972; film, directed by Nora Ephron, 2005)

Bewitched starred the rising screen actress Elizabeth Montgomery as Samantha, both a wife and a witch and married to an advertising executive named Darrin Stephens (played by Dick York and later Dick Sargent). Most of the sitcom's episodes revolved around magic—perpetrated either by Samantha or her snide mother Endora (Agnes Moorehead)—gone awry. While Samantha has almost limitless powers, she happily chooses the role of a middle-class, stay-at-home housewife and, later, mother. It has been suggested that the popularity of the scenario—and a similar one in the roughly contemporary sitcom *I Dream of Jeannie*—was a reaction to the growing feminism of the 1960s. A film version came out in 2005 to lackluster reviews and box office.

Bonnie and Clyde (film, directed by Arthur Penn, 1967)

Bonnie and Clyde tells the story of the notorious Depression-era bank-robbing gang led by outlaws Bonnie Parker and Clyde Barrow. Although the action is set in the 1930s, the film is very much a product of the 1960s. In it, Bonnie and Clyde become counterculture heroes, engaging in free love as they hit the road, challenging authority, and discovering themselves and America in the process.

The film was also notable for its explicit use of violence. While gangster films had, by necessity, always been violent, director Arthur Penn slowed down the action and graphically showed the effects and aftermath of bullets entering human bodies. The groundbreaking film was both a critical and box office success and was nominated for ten Oscars, winning for best cinematography and best actress in a supporting role (Estelle Parsons) in a highly competitive year.

Brady Bunch, The (television, 1969–1974; film, directed by Betty Thomas, 1995; film, directed by Arlene Sanford, 1996)

A successful family sitcom when it first aired, *The Brady Bunch* grew in popularity in subsequent decades as a result of its campy sets and plots and growing nostalgia for the supposedly simpler times of the 1970s. In fact, the show was a breakthrough for its day, leaving behind the traditional nuclear family as depicted in the sitcoms of the 1950s and 1960s. In the show, two single parents (the father a widower, the mother either widowed or divorced) get married and move their six children in together. Problems between the two groups of children (three girls of varying ages on the mother's side and three boys of similar ages on the father's) are at the center of most episodes' plots. Despite the unorthodox makeup of the family, the show followed the traditional sitcom pattern in that the mother was a housewife who frequently turned to the father to resolve conflicts among the children. The show was turned into a variety show briefly in the late 1970s and two successful, albeit satirical, movies in 1995 (*The Brady Bunch Movie*) and 1996 (*A Very Brady Sequel*).

Bye Bye Birdie (stage musical by Charles Strouse and Lee Adams, 1960; film, directed by George Sidney, 1963)

The first major Broadway musical featuring the relatively new musical style of rock and roll, *Bye Bye*

The appearance of the Beatles on the *The Ed Sullivan Show* (see page 1427) on February 9, 1964, marked the beginning of the British Invasion—an influx of rock and roll performers and associated cultural influences. *(CBS Photo Archive/Getty Images)*

Birdie is loosely based on an episode from the life of Elvis Presley. It tells the story of a famous musician who travels to a small town to kiss his biggest fan and star in a farewell performance before he is drafted into the army, as Elvis was. The whole episode—dreamed up by an aspiring songwriter who wants Birdie to perform his song there—is to be filmed for a popular television variety show modeled on the real-life *Ed Sullivan Show.* Enormously successful on Broadway, the musical was turned into an equally popular film in 1963, starring Dick Van Dyke as the songwriter and Jesse Pearson as Birdie.

Candid Camera (television, 1960–1967)

Before there was reality television, there was *Candid Camera*—with the twist that contestants did not know they were being filmed. Each weekly show consisted of several episodes in which ordinary people were placed in unusual situations—often including actors who helped convince the contestants that the circumstances were real. The reactions of the contestants—from gag to revelation—were filmed by a hidden camera. Episodes were introduced by host Allen Lunt, the genial main host and producer of the show, or by his co-hosts, including the actor Arthur Godfrey and former Miss America Bess Myerson. While the contestants were often caught in embarrassing situations, the show treated them gently, never exposing them as angry or morally compromised. *Candid Camera,* which originated as a radio program called *Candid Microphone,* had several television incarnations from the 1950s through the early 2000s, but its most popular run lasted from 1960 to 1967.

Carol Burnett Show, The (television, 1967–1978)

Hosted by comedian Carol Burnett, the program consisted largely of comic skits in the vaudeville style of broad humor, usually including a guest star and featuring the show's cast of regulars—Harvey Korman, Tim Conway, Lyle Waggoner, and Vicki Lawrence. Many one-time skits were take-offs on popular movies and typically included slapstick and comic innuendo. There were also several long-running story lines, including one about a bitter and dysfunctional family with Lawrence playing the mean-spirited mother. In addition to the skits, *The Carol Burnett Show* included musical and dance routines.

CBS Evening News with Walter Cronkite (television, 1962–1981)

Media surveys conducted in the 1960s and 1970s declared the veteran journalist and *CBS Evening News* anchor Walter Cronkite to be the most trusted man in America. At a time of great social upheaval and deep distrust of the institutions of government and business, Cronkite represented both stability and integrity to his tens of millions of nightly viewers. Although his career stretched back to World War II, it was Cronkite's marathon coverage of the assassination and funeral of President John F. Kennedy in 1963 that established his towering reputation.

In the days before cable television and the Internet, network news programs were the primary source of current events information for most Americans, giving the anchors enormous influence. That influence was demonstrated during the 1968 Tet Offensive in Vietnam, when Cronkite spoke out against the war. President Lyndon B. Johnson remarked, "If I've lost Walter, I've lost Middle America." Cronkite resigned his anchor position in 1981 and was succeeded by Dan Rather.

Charlie Brown Christmas, A (television special, 1965)

Charles M. Schulz's Peanuts, featuring the put-upon "everyman" Charlie Brown and his friends, was the nation's most popular comic strip from the 1950s through the 1990s, syndicated in hundreds of newspapers. In 1965, many of the main Peanuts characters appeared in an animated Christmas special for television. The show tells the story of a Charlie Brown disillusioned by the commercial excesses of the season. Given the assignment of finding a Christmas tree for the school's pageant, Charlie shows up with a puny sapling, earning him the ridicule of the cast. The gang's resident philosopher, Linus, is the only one to stand up for Charlie Brown, lecturing all on the true meaning of Christmas. Whimsical and sentimental,

the show has become the most popular made-for-television Christmas special in history, airing every season. Its score, a series of simple jazz piano pieces by Vince Guaraldi, became a best-selling album.

Children's Hour, The (film, directed by William Wyler, 1961)

Based on the 1934 play by Lillian Hellman, who also adapted it for the screen, *The Children's Hour* was the first major Hollywood film to deal with the theme of homosexuality in a serious manner. Based on a true story, it tells of two female teachers accused of lesbianism by a disturbed and spiteful student. Starring Audrey Hepburn and Shirley MacLaine as the teachers, the film shows how their lives fall apart because of the accusation.

The 1961 film was director William Wyler's second attempt at the story. In the first production in 1936 (titled *These Three*), he had been forced to make several major compromises to get past Hollywood censors, including dropping the lesbian theme for an extramarital heterosexual affair. Easing social restrictions in the postwar era permitted him to film the original story as Hellman had written it. Although still controversial, the film was a critical success; a modest hit at the box office, it was nominated for five Oscars.

Cool Hand Luke (film, directed by Stuart Rosenberg, 1967)

With its iconic line "what we have here is a failure to communicate," *Cool Hand Luke* proved a favorite with the moviegoing public of the late 1960s. Paul Newman plays Luke, a petty criminal with charm and charisma to spare. Sentenced to a Southern chain gang, Luke refuses to accept the authority of the warden and the guards, earning the undying respect of his fellow inmates until being killed in an escape attempt. Although not explicitly political—indeed, it ignored the fact that most chain gangs were made up primarily of black prisoners—the film's theme of standing up to authority nevertheless struck a chord with young moviegoers of the period.

Days of Our Lives (television, 1965–present)

A relative latecomer to the soap opera scene, *Days of Our Lives* nevertheless has proved to be the most popular and enduring television program of that genre. As of 2006, it had been on the air for forty-two seasons. Soap operas got their name from their melodramatic story lines and typical sponsors—manufacturers of soap and other household products—that appealed to the afternoon audience of stay-at-home wives and mothers. Set in the fictional town of Salem, the show has featured a thicket of subplots with the standard soap opera themes of love, betrayal, and conspiracy. Over the years, the predominantly youthful cast has changed several times over.

Dick Cavett Show, The (television, 1969–1974, 1975, 1977–1982)

Regarded as the "thinking person's talk show" during its heyday in the late 1960s and early 1970s, *The Dick Cavett Show* did not differ from its competitors in format—a variety of guests would come on the set to chat with the host—as much as in the content of the discussions. Cavett refused to fawn over his guests and tried to steer conversations away from the standard fare of celebrity career developments. Instead, he attempted to elicit the candid opinions of his guests—many of them prominent, outspoken newsmakers—on the pressing issues of the day. Coming from a liberal perspective, Cavett could occasionally upset conservative guests. In one of his most famous broadcasts, segregationist Governor Lester Maddox actually stomped off the set midway through his appearance on the show. *The Dick Cavett Show* later ran in several incarnations on various cable networks.

Dick Van Dyke Show, The (television, 1961–1966)

Unusual for a time when most TV sitcoms were set in the home and featured a husband who worked in some undefined white-collar capacity, *The Dick Van Dyke Show* divided episodes between protagonist Rob Petrie's home life and his work as head writer on a popular television variety show. While plots included the standard situation fare of family dilemmas, most of the stories revolved around the office, where Petrie and his co-writers, Sally and Buddy (played by Rose Marie and Morey Amsterdam), struggled to write gags for their vain and demanding boss, the eponymous star of *The Alan Brady Show* (played by creator Carl Reiner). Somewhat more sophisticated in its humor than most situation comedies of the day, *The Dick Van Dyke Show* has remained popular in reruns on cable television.

Dr. Strangelove, or How I Learned to Stop Worrying and Love the Bomb (film, directed by Stanley Kubrick, 1964)

A savage parody of Cold War thinking, *Dr. Strangelove* begins with mad Air Force Colonel Jack Ripper (played by Sterling Hayden), who is convinced that Communists are poisoning his drinking water, launching a preemptive nuclear strike on the Soviet Union. The plot of the film follows several stories: a bomber crew set on delivering its payload, efforts by the Army to retake the Air Force base sealed off by Ripper, and attempts by the president and his military and political advisors to prevent the nuclear attack. No sacred political cow is left unslain by director Stanley Kubrick; the film ridicules the military, the Soviets, and the president. The cast includes a number of stellar Hollywood actors, but most scenes are stolen by Peter Sellers, who plays no less than three characters: Jack Ripper's sane but helpless British aide, the ineffectual President Merkin Muffley, and Dr. Strangelove, a former Nazi and now scientific advisor to the president, who makes a case for the benefits of nuclear Armageddon.

Easy Rider (film, directed by Dennis Hopper, 1969)

A low-budget production that has become one of the best-remembered films of the late 1960s, *Easy Rider* tells the story of two motorcycle riders (played by Peter Fonda and Dennis Hopper) who cruise across the country, headed to Mardi Gras in New Orleans. Along the way, they hook up with a disillusioned young lawyer played by newcomer Jack Nicholson. Both an on-the-road movie and a film of discovery, *Easy Rider* contrasts the idealism of the young hippie protagonists with the corruption, paranoia, bigotry, and violence of mainstream America. The movie ends with the two riders being gunned down on a back road by a shotgun-toting redneck in a pickup truck. The film, with its soundtrack featuring music by Jimi Hendrix, the band Steppenwolf, and other rock stars, became an instant counterculture classic.

Elvis: One Night with You (television special, 1968)

The greatest rock and roll star of the 1950s, Elvis Presley had lost much of his popularity by the late 1960s, a victim of his stint in the U.S. Army, a series of starring roles in hokey Grade B movies, and upstaging by a new generation of American and British rock stars. In this 1968 television special, however, Elvis made his return to superstardom. The program showcased old and new music, and Presley's performance made it clear to the huge television audience that he had not lost either his powerful singing voice or his onstage charisma. The show relaunched Elvis's career and made him one of the highest-paid, most popular performers on the Las Vegas stage until his premature death in 1977.

Fail Safe (film, directed by Sidney Lumet, 1964)
Released in the same year as *Dr. Strangelove,* but far more serious in tone, *Fail Safe* explored the possibility of Cold War dynamics leading to a nuclear attack. Inspired by the Cuban Missile Crisis of 1962, when the United States and the Soviet Union came within a hairsbreadth of nuclear war, *Fail Safe* took its name from the military term for the last point at which nuclear bombers could be called back from their mission. After a false alarm sends a squadron of bombers toward the Soviet Union, the president (played by Henry Fonda) and his advisers are unable to recall the lead airplane as its preflight orders were to ignore all callback messages. As it becomes inevitable that Moscow is to be bombed, the president is left with an agonizing choice—purposely bomb New York City as a compensating measure to placate the angry Soviets, or risk full-scale nuclear war. Adding to the drama is the fact that the president's wife and children are in New York. A critical success despite its chilling conclusion, *Fail Safe* was a hit with movie audiences.

Fiddler on the Roof (stage musical, by Jerry Bock, Joseph Stein, and Sheldon Harnick, 1964; film, directed by Norman Jewison, 1971)
Set in Russia before the Communist revolution of 1917, *Fiddler on the Roof* depicts the lives of Jews hanging on to tradition in the fast-changing world of urbanization and emigration to America. Based on the story *Tevye's Daughters* by Sholem Aleichem, it follows a humble dairyman, Tevye, as he confronts the fact that his eldest daughter refuses to marry the man he has chosen for her. Dealing with such themes as prejudice, violence, and family values, the musical features a number of songs that have since become standards, including "Matchmaker," "If I Were a Rich Man," and "Sunrise, Sunset." The lead role was played by Zero Mostel in the 1964 Broadway musical and by Topol in the 1971 movie. Both versions were hits.

Flintstones, The (television, 1960–1966; film, directed by Brian Levant, 1994)

Arguably, the most popular prime-time animated series until *The Simpsons* in the late 1980s, *The Flintsones* featured the goings-on of two prehistoric families: the Flintstones (husband Fred, wife Wilma, and baby girl Pebbles) and their neighbors, the Rubbles (husband Barney, wife Betty, and baby boy Bamm-Bamm). Set in the Stone Age town of Bedrock, the comedy had little of prehistoric reality about it. The characters and plot lines were much like those in sitcoms set in middle-class suburban America. Much of the humor was based on the incongruity of modern-day people living a contemporary existence with Stone Age technology. The animated set featured modern conveniences made out of stone and animals doing the work of machines. The series inspired a less than successful live-action movie in 1994.

Get Smart (television, 1965–1970)
A parody of popular 1960s-era spy shows such as *I Spy* and *The Man from U.N.C.L.E.,* as well as the popular James Bond movie series, *Get Smart* starred Don Adams as hapless secret agent Maxwell Smart working for a CIA-like organization known as Control. *Get Smart* turned the hero spy character on its head. Smart was anything but, forgetting important parts of his assignment, mistaking villains for good guys (and vice versa), and proving hopelessly incompetent with the high-tech gadgets provided to him. With a talent for misdirection and the help of his sexy colleague, Agent 99 (Barbara Feldon), Smart manages to accomplish his mission. Created by veteran comic actor, director, and producer Mel Brooks, *Get Smart* was hugely popular during its five-year run. A 1989 movie sequel and a follow-up TV series in 1995 were both unsuccessful, however.

Gilligan's Island (television, 1964–1967)
When cultural critics sought examples of the "dumbing down" of American television during the 1960s, they often pointed to *Gilligan's Island.* Indeed, the show, with its seven mismatched castaways on a desert island, had its share of goofy situations, inane dialogue, and slapstick humor. But the show's plots, usually revolving around efforts to get off the island, were a paean to community spirit; its characters provided a portrait of American society in miniature, including an aristocratic couple, an academic, an all-American girl, a movie actress, and two working-class stiffs, including the Skipper and his bumbling first mate Gilligan (played by Bob Denver). A modest hit during

its original run, *Gilligan's Island* became even more popular in rerun syndication. It also inspired several made-for-TV movies.

Goldfinger (film, directed by Guy Hamilton, 1964)

The third in the long-running series of James Bond films that continue to be produced, *Goldfinger* is regarded by many critics as the best. Invented by British novelist Ian Fleming, the character of James Bond is a secret agent of many skills, steely nerves, and a suaveness that wins him the attention of beautiful women. Equipped with the latest in gadgetry, Bond fells evil adversaries—some agents of Cold War enemies, others, greedy, self-absorbed villains. In *Goldfinger,* Bond (played by Sean Connery) is out to catch a criminal mastermind who intends to steal all the gold in Fort Knox and dispatch his enemies by painting them in gold. When this film first came out, Bond appealed to audiences—both male and female—who preferred to believe that a single action hero could still matter in a world of nuclear weapons and police bureaucracies.

Good, the Bad, and the Ugly, The (film, directed by Sergio Leone, 1966)

Ironically, some of the finest and best-remembered Western movies of the golden age of that genre were made by the Italian director Sergio Leone during the 1960s. His films, as well as others by lesser Italian directors, came to be called "spaghetti Westerns." The most popular and critically acclaimed of them was Leone's *The Good, the Bad, and the Ugly.* Starring Clint Eastwood, the film follows three characters in search of a treasure buried in a cemetery grave. Two of these men—played by Lee Van Cleef and Eli Wallach—would be happy to kill Eastwood's character, except for the fact that he is the only one who knows the exact grave where the treasure is located. *The Good, the Bad, and the Ugly* plays on the darker theme of such other contemporary Westerns as John Ford's *The Searchers* (1956), in which the hero is driven by the same greed as the villains (even if he is not as willing to kill innocent people to realize his goals). Leone's morally ambiguous Westerns played well with an American audience jaded by the violence and changing values of the 1960s.

Graduate, The (novel, by Charles Webb, 1963; film, directed by Mike Nichols, 1967)

With its haunting score by pop duo Simon and Garfunkel, the film *The Graduate,* based on the 1963 novel by Charles Webb, tells the story of a recent college graduate, Benjamin Braddock (played by screen newcomer Dustin Hoffman), who returns to his parents' upper-middle-class home in Southern California. His parents want him to pursue a business career and marry Elaine Robinson (Katharine Ross), the beautiful daughter of his father's business partner, but Benjamin is uncertain about what he wants to do with his life. Finally, he succumbs to the seductive wiles of Elaine's mother, Mrs. Robinson (Anne Bancroft).

Benjamin's ambivalence spoke to a generation of young people caught between the values of their parents' generation and the free-loving, anticonsumerist possibilities of the emerging counterculture. In the famous final sequence of the film, Benjamin seizes Elaine in the middle of her wedding ceremony to another man. The two board a bus to escape. In the final shot, the young couple is seen through the bus's rear window, appearing unsure that they have done the right thing or of what will come next.

Great White Hope, The (play, by Howard Sackler, 1967; film, directed by Martin Ritt, 1970)

The Great White Hope tells the story of Jack Johnson, the first African American to win the heavyweight boxing title. Johnson, whose career spanned the early years of the twentieth century, was a highly controversial figure, challenging convention by marrying a white woman. An engaging drama in its own right, the play also gained attention and box-office appeal from controversial events at the time of its release. In the months before its premier in Washington, D.C., the U.S. Supreme Court had overruled state laws banning interracial marriage, and several American cities had erupted in race rioting. A difficult drama to stage—it required more than 200 extras—*The Great White Hope* was produced as a big-budget film in 1970, starring James Earl Jones as Johnson and Jane Alexander as his wife. Both were nominated for acting Oscars.

Guess Who's Coming to Dinner (film, directed by Stanley Kramer, 1967)

Released during the height of the civil rights movement, just as ghetto rioting swept several major cities, *Guess Who's Coming to Dinner* was almost nostalgic in its depiction of racial issues, offering a tribute to tolerance and acceptance. The movie tells the story of a liberal San Francisco newspaper editor (played by Spencer Tracy) and his high-society wife

(Katharine Hepburn), whose live-away daughter (Katharine Houghton) brings her fiancé home to meet them. The fiancé (Sidney Poitier) is black. The girl's mother is more accepting than her father, who hides his prejudice behind the argument that a mixed-race couple is bound to have a harder time in life, given the prejudices of society at large. During the course of the evening, the fiancé's parents arrive as well, and they are no less disturbed by their child's choice of mate. Ultimately, Tracy comes around, giving a rousing speech about tolerance and love conquering all. Enormously successful at the box office, the film garnered ten Oscar nominations.

Hair (stage musical, by James Rado and Gerome Ragni, 1968; film, directed by Milos Forman, 1979)

The first major musical about the 1960s counterculture movement, *Hair* was a huge hit on Broadway. Celebrating the hippie lifestyle of drugs and free sex, the musical also offered a gentle antiwar message. The dialogue rambled, and the plot seemed to be about nothing at all, but audiences were drawn by the catchy, rock-inspired tunes (including "Aquarius," "Hair," and "Good Morning Sunshine") and the scandal of brief on-stage nudity. In 1979, celebrated movie director Milos Forman turned the musical into a popular, if merely nostalgic, Hollywood hit.

Hard Day's Night, A (film, directed by Richard Lester, 1964)

The first of several feature films starring the Beatles, *A Hard Day's Night* (the title of one of their hit songs) follows the enormously popular British rock group on a concert tour of southern England. With a barely comprehensible story line about responsibility to the band, the film had an ad-libbed feeling, as if the band members were engaging in antics and dialogue they invented as they went along. Yet, with its fast cuts and odd camera angles, the movie somehow captured the chaos of a rock and roll tour and the eccentric lifestyle of rock stars. The almost surrealistic moviemaking style of director Richard Lester would be widely imitated in future rock and roll videos. Most audiences went to see the movie for its stars, who performed some of their greatest early hits in it.

Hogan's Heroes (television, 1965–1971)

With perhaps the oddest premise of any sitcom in television history, *Hogan's Heroes* followed the comic doings of a band of Allied soldiers in a German prisoner-of-war camp during World War II. Also featured in the show were their buffoonish German captors. As odd as the premise was, typical plots challenged credulity beyond even sitcom norms. Most involved the fact that prisoners were an effective squad of saboteurs and spies living behind enemy lines in the guise of POWs. Still, the show, based loosely on the hit movie *Stalag 17* (1953), was immensely popular, perhaps because it served as a comic antidote to the many heavy-handed World War II movies of the day.

Hustler, The (film, directed by Robert Rossen, 1961)

Starring Paul Newman as a young pool player, "Fast" Eddie Felson, trying to break into the hustling game, *The Hustler* is a dark and gritty drama of an underworld culture that was widespread in America in its time but was unfamiliar to most of the movie-going public. Cocky and confident, Felson challenges the reigning champ, Minnesota Fats (played by Jackie Gleason) and loses. Broke and desperate, Felson joins up with a ruthless manager and realizes that to get to the top, he must sell his soul and, perhaps, lose the love and respect of his girlfriend. Popular at the box office, the movie also was nominated for nine Oscars. In a 1986 sequel by director Martin Scorsese, *The Color of Money,* Newman revived his role as Felson, now the older mentor to a new hustler, played by Tom Cruise.

I Spy (television, 1965–1968; film, directed by Betty Thomas, 2002)

A path-breaking dramatic television series that was the first to star a black actor (Bill Cosby) in a leading role, *I Spy* was also one of the first shows to play off the enormous popularity of the James Bond movie series. The show featured Cosby and Robert Culp as American agents going around the world to thwart the country's enemies while posing as a tennis coach and his star athlete. The show differed from the Bond series in that it featured complex plots and comic dialogue, rather than high-tech gadgets and beautiful women. The series was turned into a less than successful movie starring Eddie Murphy and Owen Wilson in 2002.

Jeopardy! (television, 1964–1975, 1978–1979, 1984–present)

The most popular knowledge-based game show in television history, *Jeopardy!* pits three contestants against each other. Each tries to form questions based on answers in a variety of topical categories, including science, history, and popular culture. Created by talk show host and television producer Merv Griffin, *Jeopardy!* was originally developed as an antidote to the game show scandals of the 1950s, in which popular contestants were secretly given the answers by producers. Griffin reasoned that if the contestants were given the answers and had to come up with the questions, it would appear more honest. Originally hosted by Art Fleming, the show ran from 1964 to 1975 and aired again in 1978–1979 with Fleming and John Harlan hosting. A subsequent series, featuring host Alex Trebek, premiered in 1984.

Jetsons, The (television, 1962–1969; film, directed by William Hanna and Joseph Barbera, 1990)
Another production from the successful animation house of Hanna-Barbera, producers of the prime-time animated hit *The Flintstones, The Jetsons* was similar to its prehistoric counterpart in that it featured a typical, middle-class American family in an incongruous setting. The difference was that *The Flintstones* took place in the Stone Age, while *The Jetsons* was set in a Space Age future of robots and flying cars. Like most family sitcoms of the day, *The Jetsons* featured a stay-at-home mother and a father who worked in an unspecified white-collar job. A full-length animated movie of the same name was released in 1990.

Laugh-In (television, 1968–1973)
This hit show, with Dave Rowan and Dick Martin as the hosts and an ensemble cast of future comic stars, was one of the first comedy sketch shows to air regularly on American television. It was also one of the first network programs to cash in on the popularity of the 1960s counterculture, with its bikini-clad dancers painted with flowers. The name of the program was a play on the 1960s cultural phenomenon known as the "love-in," or communal gathering. Full of puerile sexual jokes and innuendos, the show launched the careers of several television and movie celebrities—including Goldie Hawn, Lily Tomlin, and Flip Wilson. It also coined a number of popular catchphrases, such as "Sock it to me" (once uttered on the show by the very un-hip Republican presidential candidate Richard M. Nixon) and "Here come da' judge."

Lion in Winter, The (play, by James Goldman, 1966; film, directed by Anthony Harvey, 1968)

Like the medieval religious epic *Becket* (1964), *The Lion in Winter* was an unlikely candidate for box-office success when the film was released in 1968. But its superstar cast—including Katharine Hepburn as Eleanor of Aquitaine and Peter O'Toole as King Henry II—made this film about the royal succession crisis of twelfth-century England a hit. Based on a successful Broadway play, this story of royal intrigue, a scheming wife, and three competitive sons struck a chord with viewers caught up in the intrigues of one of America's most contested political seasons. The film also introduced future star Anthony Hopkins in his first major film role. Hepburn won an Oscar for best actress, and Goldman won the Oscar for best writing for a screenplay based on material from another medium.

Love, American Style (television, 1969–1974, 1985–1986)
A TV by-product of the sexual revolution of the 1960s, *Love American Style* was an hour-long comedy show (for most of its run) that consisted of several skits about romance and sex—even if the latter, given the censor's standards, was never portrayed explicitly. Still, the show explored themes of courtship and sexual pursuit in a bawdy style that had not been seen on network television before. Unlike most comedy skit shows, *Love, American Style* was shot in tightly scripted segments on realistic-looking sets. Many television celebrities acted in the sketches, including Flip Wilson and Soupy Sales. One of the episodes served as the pilot for the 1970s hit series *Happy Days.* The show was revived briefly and unsuccessfully in 1985–1986.

Man for All Seasons, A (play, by Robert Bolt, 1962; film, directed by Fred Zinnemann, 1966; film, directed by Charlton Heston, 1988)
Another in the string of surprising 1960s theater and film hits about events in the long-distant English past, *A Man for All Seasons* chronicles the events surrounding the sixteenth-century lives of Sir Thomas More and King Henry VIII. When Lord Chancellor More refuses to annul Henry's marriage to Catherine of Aragon so that he can marry Anne Boleyn, the king has More imprisoned in the Tower of London and pulls England out of the Catholic Church. More refuses to give in, declaring his love for the church stronger than his love for the crown, and two years later, he is executed. Opening on Broadway in 1962, the play was adapted for the screen in 1966, starring Paul Scofield and Robert Shaw as More and Henry, respectively;

Orson Welles played Cardinal Wolsey. *A Man for All Seasons* was produced as a television film in 1988 with Charlton Heston directing and playing More.

Manchurian Candidate, The (film, directed by John Frankenheimer, 1962; film, directed by Jonathan Demme, 2004)

A political thriller about conspiracy and paranoia, *The Manchurian Candidate* was only modestly successful with audiences and critics when it first was released in 1962, but it has grown in popularity and critical esteem in the decades since. The film tells the story of a squadron of American soldiers captured by the Chinese during the Korean War and brainwashed into being "sleeper" agents ready to be activated at any time by the enemy. Ultimately, one of them—the son of a prominent political family—is activated to commit a political assassination that will put his mother, herself an enemy agent, into a position to become the power behind the presidency. The film captures the paranoia of the McCarthy era—when anyone could be a Communist agent—but turns it on its head, as the most right wing, anticommunist politician of all is the one being manipulated by the mother agent. The assassination of President John F. Kennedy in 1963 led many to see the film as hauntingly prescient. Frank Sinatra stars as one of the brainwashed squadron who comes to realize what is happening to him and prevents the assassination. The film was remade as a big-screen release, starring Denzel Washington, in 2004.

Mary Poppins (film, directed by Robert Stevenson, 1964)

One of the most popular family-oriented movies of the postwar era, *Mary Poppins* starred the family movie personality and singer Julie Andrews as a British governess who arrives by flying umbrella at the household of a dour banker and helps teach the widower's two children how to have fun. A lighthearted affair from Walt Disney Productions, based on a 1934 children's book by P. L. Travers, the film features several tunes that became popular hits, including "Chim-Chim-Cheree," "A Spoonful of Sugar," and "Supercalifragilisticexpialidocious." Technically, the film set new standards for the interaction of live actors and animated sequences.

Medium Cool (film, directed by Haskell Wexler, 1969)

Medium Cool examines the 1968 Democratic National Convention and the larger political issues of the 1960s. A veteran newsman (played by Robert Forster) becomes hardened to the violence of the times as he reports on riots and demonstrations surrounding the war in Vietnam. He is shocked to discover that his network is allowing the Federal Bureau of Investigation (FBI) to examine tapes of his broadcasts to find and arrest suspects. Fired for arguing against this, he goes to the 1968 Democratic National Convention and becomes involved in the violent rioting there. More than a documentary about the convention, the film examines why American politics turned so violent in the 1960s.

Midnight Cowboy (film, directed by John Schlesinger, 1969)

One of the first X-rated films with a mainstream theatrical release, *Midnight Cowboy* tells the story of a dim young Texan, Joe Buck (played by Jon Voight), who goes to New York with plans to make his fortune as a gigolo to wealthy society women. Upon his arrival, he is hustled by con artist Ratso Rizzo (Dustin Hoffman), who agrees to manage Buck for $20 and then disappears. Buck hunts him down, ends up staying with Rizzo, and the two become friends. Ever hoping to strike it rich, the two friends are gradually broken by life in the city and finally seek an escape. Successful with audiences and critics, the film was a pioneer in the depiction of gritty street life, a theme that would become popular in the films of the 1970s. It won the Academy Award for best picture.

Miracle Worker, The (play, by William Gibson, 1957; film, directed by Arthur Penn, 1962)

Premiering on the *Playhouse 90* theatrical television show in 1957 and opening on Broadway in 1959, the play by William Gibson was adapted for the screen in 1962. It tells the true-life story of Helen Keller, a deaf, mute, and blind girl from Alabama. Made desperate by their increasingly stubborn and violent daughter (played on Broadway and in the movie by Patty Duke), Helen's parents send for a young teacher, Annie Sullivan (Anne Bancroft also starred in the Broadway play and film versions), to tutor their child. The story revolves around Sullivan's efforts—and her success—in teaching the girl to communicate and begin interacting with the world around her. Duke and Bancroft won Oscars for best actress in a supporting role and best actress, respectively.

Mission: Impossible (television, 1966–1973, 1988–1990; film, directed by Brian De Palma, 1996;

film, directed by John Woo, 2000; film, directed by J.J. Abrams, 2006)

One of several James Bond-inspired, spy-oriented television shows of the 1960s (also including *I Spy* and *Get Smart*), *Mission Impossible* differed in that it replaced a single superagent with an ensemble cast of undercover operatives and technicians. Each episode would begin with the Impossible Mission team leader (played by Peter Graves) receiving a taped message that laid out the task his superiors wanted him to complete. Most of the missions involved sophisticated ruses designed to lead the enemy to give away secret information. The show was reprised for a few seasons in the late 1980s and early 1990s, and it inspired three later *Mission Impossible* movies starring Tom Cruise.

Mister Ed (television, 1961–1966)

If the basis of most situation comedies in the 1950s was everyday middle-class family life, the rule for sitcoms in the 1960s seemed to be the more outlandish the premise, the more likely it was to be a hit. Perhaps no show was based on a more unlikely assumption than *Mister Ed,* an early 1960s comedy about a talking horse. And few shows were more popular. While each episode had its own situation to resolve, the main running gag of the series involved the fact that no one but Mister Ed's owner, Wilbur Post, could actually hear the horse talk—usually complaints about conditions in the stable or wisecracks about problems in Wilbur's life.

Mister Rogers' Neighborhood (television, 1968–2001)

One of the longest-running children's shows in American television history, *Mister Rogers' Neighborhood* featured Fred Rogers as host, with a variety of real-life and puppet characters. For any viewer over the age of four or five, the show seemed impossibly slow—but that was the point. The gentle pacing of the action and Rogers's soft-toned voice were geared to a very young audience, and his approach was popular with parents. A low-budget program with simple sets, the show attempted to explain important issues like hygiene, citizenship, cooperation, and violence to young children. The show originated on the Canadian Broadcasting System in 1963, before moving to the U.S. Public Broadcasting System (PBS) in February 1968. It remained on the air until 2001, always with the same host, until Rogers became too ill to continue.

Monkees, The (television, 1966–1968)

Following the enormous success of Director Richard Lester's movies about The Beatles—*A Hard Day's Night* (1964) and *Help!* (1965)—*The Monkees* was a late-1960s television show based on the same formula—four lovable rock and roll musicians, nonsensical dialogue, frantic pacing, and numerous breaks for musical numbers. The main difference, aside from that fact that three of the four group members were American—was that the Beatles were a genuine musical phenomenon and the Monkees were the creation of TV producers. Still, the show enjoyed popular success, and the group put out several Top Ten radio hits. The band and the show featured Davey Jones as lead singer, Peter Tork on rhythm guitar, Micky Dolenz on drums, and Mike Nesmith on bass guitar.

My Fair Lady (stage musical, by Frederick Loewe and Alan Jay Lerner, 1957; film, directed by George Cukor, 1964)

Based on George Bernard Shaw's play *Pygmalion* (1912), *My Fair Lady* opened on Broadway in 1957 to rave reviews and enthusiastic audience response. Even as it continued its hugely successful run in New York—more than 2,700 performances—it was produced as a big-budget Hollywood musical that premiered in 1964. The story concerns low-class flower peddler Eliza Doolittle (played by Julie Andrews on Broadway and Audrey Hepburn in the movie) who phonetics professor Henry Higgins (Rex Harrison in both the theatrical and movie versions) attempts to turn into a lady. Although Higgins initially feels little but contempt for the girl, he cannot resist the challenge. He eventually succeeds so well that she is able to pass in high society. Along the way, naturally, the teacher falls in love with his student. The show spawned such musical hits as "The Rain in Spain," "I Could Have Danced All Night," "Get Me to the Church on Time," "With a Little Bit of Luck," and others. The movie won eight Academy Awards, including one for best picture.

Night of the Living Dead (film, directed by George A. Romero, 1968; film, directed by Tom Savini, 1990)

According to many horror film aficionados, the original 1968 version of *Night of the Living Dead* is both the best zombie movie ever made and a model for almost all future films in that subgenre. Radiation from a falling satellite causes the newly dead to rise from their graves, seeking the brains of the living for sustenance. Several of the zombies' intended victims barricade themselves in a remote farmhouse, hoping to survive the night until the zombies return to their graves. Although produced on a low budget, the film achieves great suspense and has been a perennial favorite on late-night television. It has inspired several sequels, as well as a remake in 1990.

Nutty Professor, The (film, directed by Jerry Lewis, 1963; film, directed by Tom Shadyac, 1996)

Regarded by many critics as the best of Jerry Lewis's numerous comic films, *The Nutty Professor* tells the story of a shy and overweight science professor who seeks to become more sociable and better looking. To that end, he creates a secret potion that turns him into Buddy Love, a handsome, musically talented lady's man who is more smarmy than suave. But the potion wears off at odd moments, producing the film's more comic scenes. Although Lewis denies it, it has been suggested that the character of Love was based on Lewis's comic partner Dean Martin, from whom he had been professionally estranged. Successful in the United States, the film helped establish Lewis's reputation as one of the most beloved American film directors in France. A remake starring Eddie Murphy was released in 1996.

Odd Couple, The (play, by Neil Simon, 1966; film, directed by Gene Saks, 1968; television, 1970–1975)

One of the most favorite story lines in American postwar comedy, *The Odd Couple* began as a hit Broadway play in 1966, was made into a popular movie starring Walter Matthau and Jack Lemmon in 1968, and settled in as a long-running television show starring Jack Klugman and Tony Randall. Conceived by playwright Neil Simon, *The Odd Couple* in all its forms recounted the antics of Oscar Madison and Felix Unger, divorced roommates living in a Manhattan apartment. The comic premise is that Oscar is an inveterate slob and Felix a neat freak. Both the play and movie, however, were darker in tone than the TV show, highlighting Felix's near nervous breakdown after being thrown out of the house by his wife. The play went through several revivals on Broadway, and a sequel to the movie—again starring Matthau and Lemmon—enjoyed modest success in 1998.

Oh! Calcutta! (stage musical, multiple authors, 1969; film, directed by Jacques Levy, 1972)

Originally an off-Broadway musical, *Oh Calcutta!* enjoyed great success and a long run due to its provocative handling of sexual issues and its plentiful on-stage nudity. The seemingly nonsensical title—the story has nothing to with India—comes from a play on the French phrase *O Quelle Cutte!* ("What an ass!"). Featuring songs with sexual themes, the play offers ideas on free thinking, free expression, and alternative lifestyles. Largely dated now, the play is best remembered for having challenged taboos about sex and nudity and for the role of so many prominent figures who had a hand in its creation, including ex-Beatle John Lennon, playwright and cartoonist Jules Feiffer, playwright and actor Sam Shepard, and theater critic Kenneth Tynan. The play was turned into a modestly successful movie in 1972.

One Flew Over the Cuckoo's Nest
SEE Literature and Journalism

Planet of the Apes (film, directed by Franklin J. Schaffner, 1968; film, directed by Tim Burton, 2001)

One of the most popular science fiction films of all time, *Planet of the Apes* was based on the 1963 novel by French writer Pierre Boulle. The low-budget movie stars Charlton Heston as an astronaut, Commander Taylor, whose spacecraft has crash-landed on a strange planet where the apes are civilized and the humans live in preverbal barbarism. Taylor is captured by the apes, and his ability to speak and reason sets him apart from the other captive humans. It also challenges the apes' long-held stereotypes of ignorance and violence among humans. Gradually, however, some of the apes come to accept the idea that their prejudices about humans are wrong.

Both the book and film were written and produced at a time of changing attitudes about race, and many critics have come to see the film as an allegory of America's evolving racial relations. *Planet of the Apes* also has one of the great surprise endings in cinematic history. The movie inspired several sequels and a 2001 high-budget remake.

Producers, The (film, directed by Mel Brooks, 1968; stage musical, by Mel Brooks and others, 2001)

Written and directed by comedian Mel Brooks, *The Producers* tells the story of Max Bialystock, an aging

Broadway impresario, long past his glory days, and an insecure but clever accountant, Leo Bloom, who comes in to do his books. While going over Bialystock's collapsing finances, Bloom casually remarks that one could make more money with a flop than a hit by getting investors to put in more money than is needed and telling them, after the show has bombed, that all the money was lost. Following this scheme, the two produce an upbeat musical about Nazi Germany that they are sure is guaranteed to offend everyone.

Unfortunately for Bialystock and Bloom, the audience on opening night finds the musical unintentionally hilarious, ensuring a hit run for the play and a prison sentence on fraud charges for the producers. Considered a comic masterpiece, the film also showed that the horrors of Nazi Germany were far enough in the past in 1968 to inspire comic mockery. In a reversal of the usual pattern by which musicals are produced in movie form, the film version inspired an exceptionally successful Broadway musical in 2001.

Psycho (film, directed by Alfred Hitchcock, 1960; film, directed by Gus Van Sant, 1998)

Considered by many critics and filmgoers as the finest suspense movie ever made, *Psycho* tells the story of Norman Bates (played by Anthony Perkins), a strangely talkative recluse who runs a motel on a nearly abandoned highway in Arizona. The movie opens with a beautiful Phoenix secretary (Janet Leigh), who embezzles thousands of dollars from her boss and runs off, winding up late one night at Bates's motel. In the now iconic shower scene, Bates brutally murders her with a knife, then kills the private detective sent to look for her. As it turns out, Bates suffers from schizophrenia, periodically assuming his dead mother's overbearing personality. Filmmaker Alfred Hitchcock played on the 1950s-era fascination with the psychological profiling of criminals, then coming into its own among sociologists and criminology experts. A film remake in 1998 failed to approach the masterful suspense of the original.

Putney Swope (film, directed by Robert Downey, 1969)

A madcap, sometimes nearly incomprehensible film, *Putney Swope* imagines what would happen if a black man became the head of a top Madison Avenue advertising agency. Renaming the business Truth and Soul, Inc., and replacing the white executives with black soul brothers, the protagonist Putney Swope (played by Arnold Johnson) turns the agency and the ad world on its head. Swope also begins to act out the lifestyle of a white executive, hiring a white maid and treating her badly, as he believes wealthy whites do to black maids. A biting social satire, the film features a number of faux advertisements that portray the racism and commercialism seen by director Robert Downey as inherent to modern American capitalism.

Rosemary's Baby (novel, by Ira Levin, 1967; film, directed by Roman Polanski, 1968)

Based on the best-selling 1967 novel by Ira Levin, *Rosemary's Baby* was the first Hollywood film by Polish director Roman Polanski. A masterpiece of horror, it is about a beautiful, young housewife, Rosemary Woodhouse (played by Mia Farrow), who becomes the victim of a satanic cult that impregnates her with the antichrist. Although the group includes a neighbor couple (Sidney Blackmer and Ruth Gordon), her obstetrician (Ralph Bellamy), and even her husband (John Cassavetes), Rosemary becomes increasingly suspicious, as they try to isolate her from all outside contact. Numerous stars play cameo roles in the famous baby shower scene.

Sesame Street (television, 1969–present)

Can television help preschool children prepare for kindergarten? That was the underlying issue and enduring mission of *Sesame Street,* one of the longest-running and most highly regarded shows in the history of the medium. Created by the Children's Television Workshop in response to a perceived lack of high-quality educational shows for young children, *Sesame Street* first aired on the Public Broadcasting System (PBS) on November 10, 1969. The show featured puppets created by Jim Henson, adults and children of many races, and an urban neighborhood setting. Its goal was to teach simple skills such as learning numbers and the alphabet to children who might not have the benefit of preschool. The show was an immediate success, and it set new standards for children's television programming. Who knew that children's shows could be educational *and* fun? Children fell in love with such characters as Big Bird, Grover, Oscar the Grouch, Bert and Ernie, and Cookie Monster. *Sesame Street* was soon airing in more than 100 countries, making it the one street children all around the world know how to get to.

60 Minutes (television, 1968–present)

A television news magazine on the air since 1968, *60 Minutes* was rated in the Top Ten most watched shows for twenty-three consecutive seasons—a record unmatched by any other program. Produced by Don Hewitt, the program specializes in hard-hitting investigative journalism, covering domestic and foreign affairs, as well as arts and culture. Mike Wallace, heading the on-air team, became known as an aggressive interviewer, often putting his subjects on the spot.

In 1995, *60 Minutes* came under fire for suppressing a story revealing secrets about the tobacco industry. The dilemma of whether or not to air the segment was chronicled in the feature film *The Insider* (1999). More than thirty years after its debut, *60 Minutes* remained the most popular news magazine on television, emulated by such others as *Dateline NBC, 20/20,* and *48 Hours.* A weeknight edition, *60 Minutes II,* premiered in 1998.

Smothers Brothers Comedy Hour, The (television, 1967–1969)

Brothers Tommy and Dick Smothers had one of the most heavily censored shows on television in the 1960s. Their *Smothers Brothers Comedy Hour,* a variety show of stand-up comedy, musical acts, and skits, touched on such subjects as sex, the counterculture, drug use, the Vietnam War, and the presidency. The brothers looked conservative, but their irreverent style was a hit with young people, who switched away from *Bonanza* to catch the Smothers's sibling rivalry and satirical comedy after the show's debut in 1967. Whole segments were often cut by censors, which led to fights between the brothers and the CBS network. The show was finally canceled in 1969 after two and a half seasons. "Mom always liked you best" was the Smothers's popular catchphrase, but their popularity as a comedy duo long after *Comedy Hour* proved they had an audience beyond their mom.

Sound of Music, The (stage musical, by Richard Rogers and Oscar Hammerstein II, 1959; film, directed by Robert Wise, 1965)

A hit musical that first appeared on Broadway in 1959, *The Sound of Music* was released as a major motion picture in 1965. The true (though embellished) story of the von Trapp family, who left their home in Austria in 1938 after the invasion of the Nazis, it is both a drama about one European family in the years before World War II and a love story: Maria, a governess, falls in love with the family patriarch and endears herself to his seven children by teaching them to sing. Songs such as "My Favorite Things," "Do-Re-Mi," and "Climb Every Mountain" are some of Rodgers and Hammerstein's best. *The Sound of Music,* starring Mary Martin as Maria, won six Tony Awards on Broadway. The film version, starring Julie Andrews and Christopher Plummer, won the Academy Award for best picture.

Star Trek (television, 1966–1969, 1987–1994, 1993–1999; films, 1979–2002)

The original *Star Trek* series only aired on television for three seasons, but it spawned one of the most successful and enduring franchises in American popular culture. The story of the U.S.S. *Enterprise,* a twenty-third-century starship on a five-year mission to "boldly go where no man has gone before," has led to motion pictures, novels, comic books, spin-off television shows, and an international fan community whose members are known as Trekkies. *Star Trek* premiered on NBC in September 1966, starring William Shatner as Captain James T. Kirk and Leonard Nimoy as the half-Vulcan, half-human Mr. Spock. The sets were clumsy, the acting wooden, and the dialogue awkward, but viewers were drawn to the characters and the tales of friendship and exploration in outer space.

When NBC threatened to cancel the show after two seasons, fans staged a letter-writing campaign that held it off. *Star Trek* was finally canceled in 1969 after seventy-nine episodes, but it thrived in syndication. *Star Trek: The Motion Picture* was released in 1979 to satisfy fan cravings for new stories. Several spin-off television shows and movies followed from the 1980s into the 2000s. *Star Trek* is so ingrained in American popular culture that such phrases as "Beam me up, Scotty" have become commonplace.

Sunrise at Campobello (play, by Dore Schary, 1958; film, directed by Vincent J. Donehue, 1960)

Based on Dore Schary's Tony Award-winning play, *Sunrise at Campobello* was a 1960 film about the early career of Franklin D. Roosevelt and the effects of his struggle with polio. The title came from the Roosevelt family's summer home on the island of Campobello, New Brunswick, where Roosevelt contracted polio in August 1921. Public life in subsequent years required him to keep the degree of his disability largely hidden, and the film details the challenges he faced and his perseverance on a daily basis. Ralph

Bellamy portrays Roosevelt, with Greer Garson as his wife Eleanor. Making her first film appearance in five years, Garson received an Academy Award nomination for best actress, one of four received by the film.

Sunrise at Campobello was released during the 1960 presidential contest between John F. Kennedy and Richard M. Nixon. A Democrat, Schary seemed to have had an eye on the polls and voters who might be swayed by the appeal of a gallant young member of his own political party.

That Girl (television, 1966–1971)

That Girl was the first television series centered around a young, single, independent woman. It aired on the ABC network from 1966 to 1971, catering to the young female audience that had made *Gidget* and *The Patty Duke Show* hits. Marlo Thomas played Ann Marie, a meter maid from the town of Brewster, New York, who moves to Manhattan to become an actress. Cute and perky, Ann attracts many eligible bachelors but few acting jobs. Ann considers herself a feminist, but she is highly dependent on the men in her life, namely her boyfriend and her father.

Helen Gurley Brown and Jacqueline Susann had done much to popularize the single-girl lifestyle, but *That Girl* wasn't exactly grounded in reality. Ann wasn't a career woman, and her part-time jobs could not possibly have supported her "mod" clothes and apartment. Yet *That Girl* reached the airwaves at the height of the women's movement, and its main character was a role model to many. It also strongly influenced the women-oriented shows that followed, most notably *The Mary Tyler Moore Show.*

2001: A Space Odyssey (film, directed by Stanley Kubrick, 1968)

2001: A Space Odyssey is a cinematic poem about a journey into space and search for extraterrestrial intelligence. Filmed in nearly slow motion and with minimal dialogue by director Stanley Kubrick, it was released in 1968 at the height of the space race between the United States and Soviet Union. Still, critics

Stanley Kubrick's *2001: A Space Odyssey* (1968) was a cinematic milestone—if enigmatic to moviegoers of the day. *(Dmitri Kessel/Time Life Pictures/Getty Images)*

and audiences found it enigmatic and boring, and it had little impact at the box office. Subsequent re-release in theaters built a cult following of viewers who found their own meaning in the film's images.

By the actual year 2001, *A Space Odyssey* was widely regarded as one of the most innovative and imaginative science fiction films ever made. Its orchestral score and pioneering special effects were instantly recognizable, while the eerie voice of the computer "HAL" was commonly identified as the voice of the Computer Age itself. For its time, *2001: A Space Odyssey* was a unique achievement in film—beginning with the dawn of humanity and traveling to Jupiter and beyond with only forty minutes of dialogue. It received an Academy Award for best effects, special visual effects.

Virginian, The (television, 1962–1971)

The Virginian was a ninety-minute Western program that ran on the NBC network from 1962 to 1971. James Drury played the Virginian, a man with no other name, who worked as foreman of a Wyoming ranch in the 1890s. The show had a large cast of characters, but only a handful appeared in each episode. The stories were driven by these characters and probed such issues as tolerance, justice, and discrimination. Based on a novel by Owen Wister, *The Virginian* played on the theme of change, such as that faced by the frontier at the turn of the twentieth century. "It is a vanished world. No journeys, save those which memory can take, will bring you to it now," Wister wrote in 1902. *The Virginian* faced these changes by adhering to a moral code that was as timeless as the Wyoming prairie.

West Side Story (stage musical, by Leonard Bernstein and Stephen Sondheim, 1957; film, directed by Robert Wise and Jerome Robbins, 1961)

William Shakespeare never could have envisioned the many incarnations his story of Romeo and Juliet would take over the centuries, especially the jazzy musical adaptation called *West Side Story*. Here, Romeo is Tony, a Polish boy living on New York City's racially divided Upper West Side, and Juliet is Maria, a Puerto Rican. The feuding families of Shakespeare's play are represented by street gangs, the Jets and the Sharks.

First on Broadway and then on the big screen, the story of doomed young lovers was reenergized through modern dance, a Leonard Bernstein/Stephen

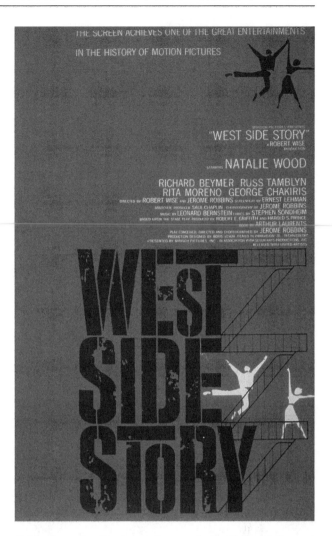

Aside from its timeless story and dazzling music and dance, *West Side Story* (1961) struck a chord with its focus on social issues. *(Hulton Archive/Getty Images)*

Sondheim score, and a 1950s setting that used gangs, violence, and urban strife to make it relevant to 1960s audiences. Considered the best movie musical of the 1960s, *West Side Story* received ten Academy Awards, including best picture. Choreographed on stage and screen by the legendary Jerome Robbins, the musical modernized an age-old story, proving Shakespeare's timeless appeal.

Who's Afraid of Virginia Woolf? (play, by Edward Albee, 1962; film, directed by Mike Nichols, 1966)

A grim domestic drama by Edward Albee, *Who's Afraid of Virginia Woolf?* was produced as a film starring the real-life married couple of Elizabeth Taylor and Richard Burton. A shocking black comedy, it had appeared on Broadway in 1962 and received the

Tony Award for best play. The 1966 film version kept the play's integrity and was filmed by first-time director Mike Nichols, much as if it were being performed on stage. Taylor and Burton played Martha and George, a couple living in a cruel and illusionary marriage. To help keep the peace, they invent an imaginary son, a secret between the two of them. On a night of drunken game playing with a younger couple, however, the secret son is revealed, laying open old wounds and clearing a path to a more truthful relationship. *Who's Afraid of Virginia Woolf* was called "perverse" and "dirty-minded" for its biting language, frank sexuality, and portrayal of a spiteful relationship, but it revolutionized American theater and film.

Wild Bunch, The (film, directed by Sam Peckinpah, 1969)

Peckinpah's elegiac Western masterpiece *The Wild Bunch* has influenced numerous films and filmmakers since its release in 1969. The story was based on Akira Kurosawa's film *The Seven Samurai* (1954), a Japanese classic whose Samurai warriors are easily transformed into Western outlaws in 1913 America. Faced with changing times and industrialization, the outlaws are on the run from bounty hunters committed to purging the West of its old-fashioned elements.

Unlike other Westerns of the time (*Butch Cassidy and the Sundance Kid* was released the same year), *The Wild Bunch* did not idealize the West or ignore its violence. Instead, it embraced the West's most violent aspects, book-ending the film with two elegantly filmed bloodbaths that nearly earned it an X rating. Like *Bonnie and Clyde* before it, *The Wild Bunch* used the past to comment on the violence raging in modern times: The wild bunch were symbolic of U.S. soldiers fighting in Vietnam. Directors Martin Scorsese, Quentin Tarantino, and John Woo later emulated *The Wild Bunch*'s graphic violence in their own films and repeatedly cited its influence.

THE SEVENTIES

Literature and Journalism

All the President's Men (nonfiction, by Bob Woodward and Carl Bernstein, 1974; film, directed by Alan J. Pakula, 1976)

Written by the two young *Washington Post* reporters who broke the story on the Watergate scandal, *All the President's Men* tells both the story of Watergate and the efforts by the two reporters to get the story out. The book chronicles their relentless digging for the facts, the machinations of the Nixon Administration to cover up the story, and the reporters' efforts to convince their editors of the reliability of those facts and the importance of the story. Published before Nixon's resignation in August 1974, the book covers most of the Watergate tale, from the initial break-in at the Democratic Party headquarters in June 1972 to the resignations of key administration officials in 1973. The book was made into a popular Hollywood film, starring Robert Redford as Woodward and Dustin Hoffman as Bernstein.

Being There (novel, by Jerzy Kosinski, 1971; film, directed by Hal Ashby, 1979)

Being There tells the story of Chance, a simple-minded gardener on a Washington, D.C., estate. Chance is cut off from society except through television, which provides his only connection to the outside world. When the owner of the estate dies, Chance is forced to leave. After being hit by a limousine, he is adopted by a wealthy old man and his sexually starved young wife, who tries to seduce him. Naive and full of wonder, Chance has a mind filled with the clichés of television and gardening aphorisms, but to a jaded media, which makes him a star, his utterances seem profound in their simplicity. Chance becomes both a political consultant to Washington power brokers and a sought-after television pundit. Although farcical in tone, the book offers a scathing commentary on the banality of mass media culture. The novel was turned into a popular film in 1979, with Peter Sellers as Chance.

Bury My Heart at Wounded Knee (nonfiction, by Dee Alexander Brown, 1970)

Unlike most traditional histories of the American West, this book recounts events from the perspective of Native Americans. It focuses on the thirty-year period from 1860, when the Navajos were forced off their land in parts of the Southwest, to 1890 and the Wounded Knee Massacre, in which hundreds of Sioux Indians in South Dakota were killed. While America's population more than doubled, from just over 31 million to nearly 63 million, the Native peoples were forced off their land and rounded up in

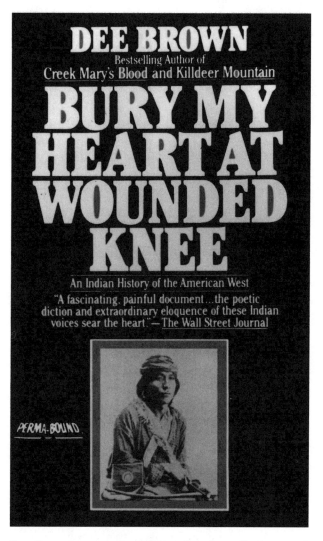

Dee Brown's account of Native American displacement and genocide in *Bury My Heart at Wounded Knee* (1970) overturned long-held "truths" about American history and how it is written. *(MPI/Getty Images)*

brutal fashion. The white perspective of Western history had prevailed for so long that the country was shocked by this chronicle of past racism and forgotten massacres. The book remained on best-seller lists for months; by 2005, it had sold more than 5 million copies.

Carrie (novel, by Stephen King, 1974; film, directed by Brian De Palma, 1976; television film, directed by David Carson, 2002)

Stephen King's first published novel, *Carrie,* launched his career as the modern master of the horror genre. In the novel, high school outcast Carrie White develops her telekinetic powers at the same time that she comes late to puberty. Attending the prom as the date of a boy who has asked her because his girlfriend, Sue, wants to make amends for cruel pranks, Carrie finds herself the butt of another humiliating joke in which she is doused in pig's blood after being mockingly crowned prom queen. Enraged, Carrie uses telekinesis to destroy the school and large portions of the town and to kill several people, including her abusive religious zealot of a mother. Her powers then overwhelm and kill her, ending the brief reign of terror.

The book, which gives a sympathetic portrait of Carrie and an inside look at the world of high school cruelty, spawned a movie starring Sissy Spacek. Though Carrie is dead at the end of the novel, the film, which concludes with Carrie's hand shooting up out of her grave, led to a sequel and a 2002 made-for-television version of the tale.

Deliverance (novel, by James Dickey, 1970; film, directed by John Boorman, 1972)

Set in the hills of Georgia, this novel was turned into a critically acclaimed 1972 movie starring Burt Reynolds, Jon Voigt, and Ned Beatty. It is the story of four urban Southerners, led by a macho amateur outdoorsman (Reynolds), who take a canoe trip down a river before it is turned into a lake by the construction of a dam. Deep in the wilderness, one of the men (Beatty) is captured by mountain men and raped. The leader of the group then kills one of the mountain men, and the rest escape. Although the flooding of the river covers up the body, the four rafters are haunted by the crime. Even as the story plays on the stereotypes of hillbillies, it reveals powerful truths about violence and the fragile veneer of modern civilization.

Doonesbury (comic strip, by Garry Trudeau, 1970–present)

Created by Garry Trudeau in the early 1970s, the widely syndicated *Doonesbury* comic strip has provided ongoing, often controversial, left wing political commentary and social satire since its inception. Trudeau began the strip as a student at Yale University, where he introduced such characters as B.D., Mike, and Zonker in the school newspaper. Trudeau won a Pulitzer Prize for *Doonesbury* in 1975, becoming the first cartoonist to earn this award. By 2005, the cartoon serial appeared in more than 1,400 newspapers, and compilations in dozens of books had sold more than 7 million copies. The strip also has inspired an animated TV film (1977) and a Broadway musical (1983).

Everything You Always Wanted To Know About Sex But Were Afraid To Ask (nonfiction, by David Reuben, 1972)

The two most important postwar books on human sexuality—*The Joy of Sex* and *Everything You Always Wanted To Know About Sex But Were Afraid To Ask* were published within months of each other in 1972. The invention of an oral contraception pill and the cultural iconoclasm of the 1960s coincided with the so-called sexual revolution, when taboos about premarital and extramarital sex, promiscuity, and even homosexuality began to fall away. Whether or not people were actually having more sex, they were certainly more open to talking about it. *Everything* offers an encyclopedic guide to all aspects of human sexuality in the form of frequently asked questions. Unlike *The Joy of Sex,* this book has no pictures—but it became a huge best-seller.

Executioner's Song, The (novel, by Norman Mailer, 1979; film, directed by Lawrence Schiller, 1982)

In January 1977, a year after the U.S. Supreme Court reinstated the death penalty, Gary Gilmore became the first person to be executed in the United States after a ten-year hiatus. On parole after a prison sentence for armed robbery, the Utah man killed a motel owner and a gas station attendant. What made his case unique was that Gilmore *requested* that he be put to death. In this novelistic treatment of the case, Mailer explores Gilmore's violent upbringing, his tempestuous romance with Nicole Baker, and the seemingly pointless murders in an attempt to understand what made Gilmore a killer and led to his request to die. A huge best-seller, the book was made into a hit television movie in 1982, with Tommy Lee Jones as Gilmore and Rosanna Arquette as Baker.

Fear and Loathing in Las Vegas (novel, by Hunter S. Thompson, 1971; film, directed by Terry Gilliam, 1998)

The book (and later movie) recount the journey of a journalist and his lawyer to Las Vegas purportedly to cover a sporting event, but really on a trip to find the American Dream. The piece was first published in 1971 in *Rolling Stone* magazine, and it came out in book form later that year. Consuming large amounts of drugs and alcohol on the journey, the two protagonists encounter a variety of bizarre characters, including hitchhikers, cops, and gamblers—but never the American Dream. The book was turned into a movie in 1998, starring Johnny Depp.

A landmark of the New Journalism, in which the reporter becomes central to the story, *Fear and Loathing* is a classic of the psychedelic fiction of the 1960s and 1970s. Thompson himself labeled the style "gonzo journalism" for the willingness of the reporter to explore the seamy underside of himself and his subject. Thompson later wrote *Fear and Loathing: On the Campaign Trail '72* (1973) and *Fear and Loathing in America: The Brutal Odyssey of an Outlaw Journalist, 1968–1976* (2000), a compilation of his earlier writings.

Fear of Flying (novel, by Erica Jong, 1973)

One of the most popular postwar novels with a feminist theme, *Fear of Flying* tells the story of a woman in search of herself. Unsure whether she is still in love with her husband, she has a passionate affair with another man. The book's explicit sex scenes and language scandalized many readers in the early 1970s. But the struggle of the protagonist to find happiness and exert power over her own life struck a chord with women readers, millions of whom were experiencing the same longings during the early years of the feminist movement.

Future Shock (nonfiction, by Alvin Toffler, 1970)

In this original and highly influential work, the "futurologist" Alvin Toffler discusses how modern technology had changed virtually every aspect of human society and how the trend was going to continue in the future. Toffler's main thesis is that the pace of change will accelerate so rapidly that individuals and society will undergo the kind of "shock" people expe-

rience by traumatic injury. In the same way, he contends, neither individuals nor society will always be able to cope with it. While many of the predictions offered by Toffler have come true—including the widespread use of computers and the breakdown of the traditional nuclear family—the book is best remembered for its pioneering exploration of the ways in which individuals and communities cope with rapid technological, cultural, and social change.

Gravity's Rainbow (novel, by Thomas Pynchon, 1973)

Written in the convoluted, psychedelic style for which Thomas Pynchon, the recluse of contemporary American letters, became famous, *Gravity's Rainbow*—the title describes the path of unguided missiles—takes place in London during World War II when the city was subjected to rocket attacks from Nazi Germany. At the center of the novel is Tyrone Slothrup, who appears to elicit the barrages every time he is sexually aroused, a result of having been subjected to medical experiments as a child. The somewhat nonsensical plot is, however, secondary to the language and mood of the novel, a kind of drug-induced rant. If perhaps difficult to follow, *Gravity's Rainbow* is regarded by many literary critics as a literary *tour de force* that invites readers to decipher the many allusions and clues hidden in the plot.

Great War and Modern Memory, The (nonfiction, by Paul Fussell, 1975)

A seminal work of twentieth-century history, *The Great War and Modern Memory* offers a reexamination of World War I. Unlike most other historical treatments of the subject, author Paul Fussell does not discuss the details of military or diplomatic history so much as people's memories of the war. His subjects include a number of literary figures, including Siegfried Sassoon, Robert Graves, David Jones, and Wilfred Owen. By this method, Fussell succeeds in demonstrating how the Great War was viewed by people at the time, how views of the war changed during the years in which it was fought, and how the war shaped events and society for the rest of the century.

Greening of America, The (nonfiction, Charles Reich, 1970)

Responding to the various social protest movements of the 1960s, in *The Greening of America* commentator

Charles Reich tells Americans that they need to undergo a fundamental shift in consciousness regarding their relationship with nature. In Reich's account, the United States began as an experiment in individualism, adapted to conformism in the age of industrialization and growing bureaucracy, and now needs to rebel against established ways of doing and thinking about things. The author was not blind to the faults of the 1960s protest era, however, arguing that the movement for change needed to mature beyond mere outrage to constructive action. Against conventional liberalism and conservatism, Reich argues for a third, radical force in American political and social life. A major best-seller, the book was highly influential among politically engaged Americans of the early 1970s.

Interview with the Vampire (novel, by Anne Rice, 1976; film, directed by Neil Jordan, 1994)

Set in late eighteenth-century New Orleans, *Interview with the Vampire* is the story of a young plantation owner, Louis, who has lost the will to live after the death of his wife. The vampire Lestat takes a liking to Louis and offers him immortality as a vampire. Louis accepts the offer, but he is disgusted by the vampire's need to kill humans and drink their blood. His concern for mortals angers Lestat and creates the tension that drives the plot. Much of the remainder of the book consists of Lestat's account of his own experiences as a vampire and his lessons on how to be one. *Interview with the Vampire* was the first in an enormously successful series of novels that author Anne Rice called "The Vampire Chronicles." A movie version of *Interview*, starring Tom Cruise as Lestat and Brad Pitt as Louis, was released in 1994.

Jonathan Livingston Seagull (novel, by Richard Bach, 1970)

In this simple but affecting allegory of individualism versus social conformity, Bach tells the story of the seagull who seeks to soar higher than all the others in his flock, thereby experiencing himself and his world in a new way. The other birds are dismissive of his goal and exile him from the flock. Both an inspirational tale and an exercise in pop philosophy attuned to the growing self-awareness movement of the late 1960s and early 1970s, the book was hugely popular, appearing on many of the nation's best-seller lists for nearly a year.

Joy of Sex, The (nonfiction, by Alex Comfort, 1972)

With a title borrowed from a perennially best-selling cookbook, *The Joy of Sex* was designed to offer a similar one-stop reference source for all things sexual. Full of pictures of couples in explicit sexual positions, the book set off a wave of controversy when it appeared in 1972. A product of the sexual revolution, the best-selling *The Joy of Sex* was intended by its author to help couples enjoy a healthier and happier sex life. While full of tips for heterosexuals, the book avoided homosexuality entirely and included only minimal information on more unconventional sexual practices, such as bondage. The book has been periodically updated and the latest edition includes more information on safe-sex practices, homosexuality, and "nontraditional" preferences.

Learning from Las Vegas (nonfiction, by Robert Venturi, 1972)

Although trained in the architectural tradition of modernism—form following function and a minimum of ornamental embellishment—Robert Venturi pioneered what later came to be called postmodernism. *Learning from Las Vegas*, which he co-wrote with his wife and graduate students, offers Venturi's thinking about what constituted architecture appropriate to the American landscape. Rather than trashing Las Vegas, as most elite architects did, Venturi argues that the gaudy desert city, with its huge signs and theme-based buildings, provides a new vernacular for American architecture. Las Vegas, he says, teaches several lessons, including the need for architects to be more whimsical and to consider the wants of ordinary people in their designs. The city's architecture, he points out, is hugely popular with visitors and residents alike. Architectural historians generally agree that *Learning from Las Vegas* is among the most influential postwar books on the subject.

Love Story (novel, by Erich Segal, 1970; film, directed by Arthur Hiller, 1970)

One of the best-selling novels of the postwar era, this short book tells the story of two young lovers from very different backgrounds. Oliver Barrett IV is a Harvard law student from a wealthy and well-regarded Boston family; Jennifer ("Jenny") Cavalleri is a working-class music student at Radcliffe. Oliver's father does not approve of the marriage and disowns his son, forcing the couple to live in poverty. Love conquers all, however, even if Jenny ultimately succumbs to a fatal disease. A sentimental tearjerker ("Love means never having to say you're sorry," went its most familiar line), the novel was made into an equally successful movie starring Ryan O'Neal as Oliver and Ali MacGraw as Jenny. The popularity of the book and movie, it has been suggested, reflected a desire among the American people to return to simple and traditional love stories amid the social unrest of the sexual revolution.

Monkey Wrench Gang, The (novel, by Edward Abbey, 1975)

This novel is the story of a Vietnam War veteran, George Washington Hayduke III, who returns to America and decides that modern development is threatening his beloved West. Hayduke joins forces with feminist Bonnie Abzug, guide Seldom Seen Smith, and Doc Sarvis to burn down billboards and sabotage mines, dams, highways, bridges, and other man-made blights on the environment. Instilled with humor and inspired by a desire to expose social hypocrisy, the members of the gang—which takes its name from the old adage about upsetting plans by "throwing a monkey wrench into the works"— nevertheless recognize that they cannot win in the end. The book became a cult classic, inspiring the formation of a number of radical environmental groups such as Earth First!

On Photography (nonfiction, by Susan Sontag, 1977)

In this seminal series of essays, literary critic and social commentator Susan Sontag trains her probing intellect on the subject of photography. Less a book about the technical aspects of the art, On Photography argues that photographers use their skills and artistry to penetrate the sheer abundance of images modern humans encounter in their lives to teach a new way of seeing. To be effective, photography must go beyond visual note taking and capture the artist's personal sensibility; the photographer must create not only a visual record but also a meaning behind that record.

Sontag also examines amateur photography, noting that picture taking on vacation allows the photographer to be productive while supposedly relaxing and pointing out that people from cultures with a strong work ethic such as Japan and Germany are inveterate holiday photographers. Sontag's book helped establish a theoretical basis for the postwar acceptance of photography as an art form.

Orientalism (nonfiction, by Edward Said, 1978)

A seminal book in several disciplines, especially literature and Middle East Studies, Orientalism examines how the West has interpreted the history and culture of non-Western societies, particularly Muslim, Arab, and Middle Eastern ones, to suit the needs of colonialism and neocolonialism. The book's title comes from the archaic name for the Western study of Middle Eastern and Asian cultures. Specifically, the author (born in Palestine but writing in the United States) argues that the West has traditionally viewed Arab and other non-Western societies as exotic, ahistorical, and "other"—different from European-based societies in ways that made them somehow inferior. The book, like the author, garnered its share of controversy, but it become a landmark in "deconstructivist" thought, whereby texts and other cultural artifacts are examined less for their intrinsic meaning than for how they are interpreted by the readers and viewers themselves.

People (magazine, 1974–present)

A milestone in the development of the postwar celebrity culture, People magazine was launched by Time Incorporated in 1974 (and was later published under the AOL Time Warner umbrella). Offering short, heavily illustrated articles on both celebrities and ordinary people doing extraordinary things, People was intended as a journalistically credible alternative to such mass-circulation celebrity tabloids as The National Enquirer. The new magazine was marketed in much the same way as the tabloids, relying on point-of-purchase sales at supermarket checkout aisles, but the introduction of People also went against conventional wisdom. At a time of shrinking magazine readership, when most new journals were aimed at specialty markets, People was the rare postwar general circulation magazine success.

Ragtime (novel, by E.L. Doctorow, 1975; film, directed by Milos Forman, 1981)

One of the most popular works by the acclaimed novelist E.L. Doctorow, Ragtime is set in early twentieth-century America, when ragtime was the popular music. Director Milos Forman's well-received film, like the novel, offers a number of intertwining storylines about characters from diverse race and class backgrounds. The main plot concerns a proud and stubborn black piano player named Coalhouse Walker, Jr. (played in the film by Howard E. Rollins, Jr.). Failing to win justice from authorities after his car is vandalized by a racist white fireman, Walker leads a team of angry black men, and one disaffected white, in taking over the New York library of financial tycoon J.P. Morgan. Walker threatens to destroy the library unless he receives an apology from the fireman. Like most of Doctorow's fiction, *Ragtime* offers a complex portrait of a specific era in the history of America.

Right Stuff, The (nonfiction, by Thomas Wolfe, 1979; film, directed by Philip Kaufman, 1983)

One of the pioneers of the New Journalism, in which the reporter becomes part of the story, Tom Wolfe examines the early history of the U.S. manned space program during the late 1950s and early 1960s, focusing on the seven astronauts selected to participate in Project Mercury. Selected from the various branches of the military, all seven were hotshot pilots, chosen for their flying skills, as well as their physical and mental fitness for space flight. The book reveals how the National Aeronautics and Space Administration (NASA) turned these men into American heroes, both for domestic political reasons (to ensure funding for NASA) and to combat the impression abroad that the United States lagged behind the Soviet Union in the space race. The book became a hit motion picture in 1983.

Scruples (novel, by Judith Krantz, 1978; television miniseries, 1980)

Krantz's first novel, *Scruples* initiated readers into what publishers began calling Planet Krantz, which she once described as being "about superficially wonderful things—clothes, settings, travel, houses." Krantz said she wrote *Scruples* after becoming bored at a bookstore and realizing that what women wanted to read about was drama, sex, and glamour in tantalizing, fast-moving stories. *Scruples* was about a Beverly Hills boutique and its employees, and, with it, Krantz reenergized the women's publishing genre. Other women writers immediately began emulating her style, further fueling the popular obsession with the lives of the rich and famous.

Krantz followed the success of *Scruples* with *Princess Daisy* (1980) and later published two *Scruples* sequels, *Scruples Two* (1992) and *Lovers* (1994)—all of which were best-sellers. How to explain her success with women's fiction? "I try to nourish my readers on a fantasy world that nobody really lives in, because glamour is an illusion," she once said. *Scruples* was turned into a television miniseries in 1980.

Snow Leopard, The (nonfiction, by Peter Matthiessen, 1978)

After his wife died of cancer, Matthiessen embarked on a five-week journey with zoologist George Schaller to the Himalayan region of Dolpo—"the last enclave of pure Tibetan culture on earth"—to study the Himalayan blue sheep and possibly catch a glimpse of the elusive Asian snow leopard. In his 1978 book, *The Snow Leopard*, Matthiessen describes their search and the grand Himalayan scenery they encountered. The book is a marvel of nature writing and the compelling account one man's mystical pursuit of something he cannot find. Nature, Buddhism, and the theme of pilgrimage come together in his account, which was well received by an American public newly interested in environmental renewal and Eastern thought. *The Snow Leopard* received the National Book Award for nonfiction in 1979.

Song of Solomon (novel, by Toni Morrison, 1977)

Morrison's *Song of Solomon* is the story of Macon Dead, Jr. (nicknamed "Milkman" because his mother nursed him somewhat longer than usual) and his attempt to forge a unique identity from his upwardly mobile Northern family and his Southern heritage. As a member of the richest African American family in a Midwestern town, he is torn between the life his father wants for him and the life of the lower class. He takes a journey of discovery to the South and finds a world he never knew existed.

Song of Solomon received the National Book Critics Circle Award in 1977 and was the first novel by an African American to be designated a Book-of-the-Month Club selection since Richard Wright's *Native Son* in 1940. *Song of Solomon*'s "description of the black world in life and legend" was specifically cited when Morrison received the Nobel Prize in Literature in 1993.

Sophie's Choice (novel, by William Styron, 1979; film, directed by Alan J. Pakula, 1982)

Sophie's Choice was the fifth novel by Pulitzer Prize-winning author William Styron. Like Styron as a young man, the book's narrator, Stingo, is a Southern writer transplanted to the North. Living in Brooklyn, New York, during the summer of 1947, where he hopes to write the Great American Novel, Stingo becomes friends with his upstairs neighbors, Sophie, a Holocaust survivor, and her boyfriend, Nathan. As the story unfolds, Sophie's and Nathan's pasts are gradually revealed—including Sophie's painful personal choice during the Holocaust, which she carries with her always. *Sophie's Choice* received the American Book Award for fiction in 1980, and it was made into a film in 1982. Meryl Streep's portrayal of Sophie earned her an Academy Award for best actress.

Ways of Seeing (nonfiction, by John Berger, 1972)
Ways of Seeing is John Berger's seminal 1972 work of art criticism, based on a BBC television program of the same name. The book is made up of seven essays, three pictorial and four textual. The latter address four topics: the mystification of art and history, the role of women in art and how they are viewed, European oil paintings from 1500 to 1900, and the role of publicity and advertising in art.

Written for a popular audience but also read by academics, *Ways of Seeing* was unique in its discussion of the commercialism of art. Berger opened readers' eyes not just to the importance of an artistic work, but also to the political and/or economic motives behind its commission, intended audience, and display placement. Berger's discussion of the objectification of women in art transcended art criticism and was relevant to discussions of such media as television and advertising.

Working (nonfiction, by Studs Terkel, 1974)
In the late 1960s and early 1970s, journalist Studs Terkel conducted in-depth interviews with ordinary Americans about their working lives. He compiled their stories in a book titled *Working: People Talk About What They Do All Day and How They Feel About What They Do*, which became a landmark of modern oral history. Terkel was famous for getting people to open up and discuss their lives honestly, which made *Working* both sociologically insightful and irresistible to readers. He talked to railroad workers, police officers, prostitutes, teachers, women executives, priests, and other professionals and blue-collar workers, many of them in his hometown of Chicago. *Working* gave its readers a window into the lives of other hard-working individuals, all dealing with common pressures, worries, happiness, and fear. A unique document of the lower and middle class in the 1970s, *Working* argued that most Americans "found a meaning to their work well over and beyond the reward of a paycheck."

World According to Garp, The (novel, by John Irving, 1978; film, directed by George Roy Hill, 1982)
The World According to Garp was first a novel by the best-selling author John Irving and then a 1982 Oscar-nominated film starring Robin Williams. The 1978 novel was the most well received to date by Irving, embraced by readers who appreciated his quirky style and event-filled narrative. The protagonist, T. S. Garp, is raised by a feminist single mother (played by Glenn Close in the film) who is a nurse at an all-boys school in New Hampshire. Garp excels at wrestling, grows up to become a semi-well-known author, has a family, loses a son, and is assassinated by a tongueless woman protesting women's lack of voice in the male-dominated world. One of *Garp*'s prominent themes is feminism, shown in three extremes by Garp's mother, the radical, tongueless Ellen James Society, and the transsexual Roberta Muldoon. *The World According to Garp* is a modern classic, and the book has sold more than 10 million copies in thirty languages.

Film, Radio, Television, and Theater

ABC After School Special (television, 1972–1988)
A popular television documentary series for young viewers, the *ABC After School Special* covered a range of historical and contemporary subjects, often of a controversial nature. Some shows went into greater depth than others, but each attempted to provide balanced and accurate coverage at a level understandable to teenage viewers. The producers did not shy away from sensitive historical topics, such as the rise of the Nazis in Germany, or those of immediate interest to teens, including pregnancy, AIDS, suicide, and drug abuse.

Alice Doesn't Live Here Anymore (film, directed by Martin Scorsese, 1974; television, 1976–1985)
A departure from the mean streets of New York for director Martin Scorsese, *Alice Doesn't Live Here Anymore* tells the story of a young widow (played by Ellen Burstyn) who flees her small-town life in New Mexico to make a career as a singer in California. Having

to support her eleven-year-old son, the heroine is forced to settle in Phoenix and take a job as a waitress until she can save enough money to complete the trip. There, she is courted by a warm-hearted customer (Kris Kristofferson). A gentle and humorous look at working-class life, the film features an eccentric ensemble cast, including a brassy fellow waitress (Diane Ladd), who often steals the scene. An extremely popular movie that was also hailed by critics, *Alice* won Burstyn an Oscar for best actress. The movie inspired a popular, long-running situation comedy, starring Linda Lavin as Alice.

All in the Family (television, 1971–1979)

Based on a British series called *Til Death Do Us Part*, *All in the Family* followed the lives of the Bunker household of Queens, New York. The family patriarch was Archie Bunker (Carroll O'Connor), a bigoted, misogynistic working-class husband and father. Edith (Jean Stapleton) was his sweet but ditzy wife.

While Archie clearly loved his daughter Gloria (Sally Struthers), he could not abide her liberal politics, flower-child sexuality, or radical graduate-student husband, Michael Stivic (Rob Reiner), whom Archie referred to as "Meathead." Created by the iconoclastic producer and writer Norman Lear, the show was a huge hit and groundbreaking in its political content, its willingness to confront racial and sexual stereotypes, and its depiction of the ordinary functions of life. Audiences in the early 1970s roared with laughter when they first heard a toilet flush on television.

Animal House (film, directed by John Landis, 1978)

Set in 1962 on the campus of Faber College, a fictional small liberal arts school, *Animal House* (aka *National Lampoon's Animal House*) tells the story of the members of Delta House, a raucous, rule-breaking fraternity. The fraternity brothers, from president down to pledge, are an eccentric bunch, none more than John "Bluto"

All in the Family, featuring Carroll O'Connor as the bigoted but lovable Archie Bunker, brought realism and social commentary to the TV sitcom. *(CBS Photo Archive/Getty Images)*

Blutarsky (John Belushi), the slightly psychotic but ultimately softhearted class clown. Because of their excessive partying and practical jokes, the fraternity is one prank away from losing their charter. When a few members finally cross the line, the sanctimonious members of a rival fraternity conspire with the mean-spirited college dean (John Vernon) to get Delta House expelled. Before they go, however, the boys of Delta House have the last laugh on their campus enemies in an all-out assault on the college's homecoming parade.

Annie (stage musical, by Peter Howard, Philip J. Lang, and Martin Charnin, 1977; film, directed by John Huston, 1982)

Based on the Depression-era comic strip *Little Orphan Annie*, the hit Broadway musical *Annie* tells the story of a young girl living in an orphanage presided over by a cruel matron. Annie is adopted by a wealthy munitions manufacturer, Oliver "Daddy" Warbucks. The sweet and precocious Annie wins the hearts of the entire Warbucks household, including the cold-hearted father, who posts a reward to find her biological parents. But the cruel orphanage matron gets accomplices to try to collect the reward by impersonating Annie's parents. The hit musical and modestly successful movie version represented one of the first major theatrical and Hollywood efforts to turn a comic strip into a live-action presentation.

Annie Hall (film, directed by Woody Allen, 1977)

Among the most popular of director and actor Woody Allen's many films, *Annie Hall* is a love story about two very different people. The eponymous heroine (played by Diane Keaton) is a happy-go-lucky, somewhat flaky woman from a small-town, white, Anglo-Saxon Protestant (WASP) family; her boyfriend, Alvy Singer (Woody Allen), is a neurotic comedy writer from a Brooklyn Jewish family. A touching love story with a bittersweet ending, *Annie Hall* is also a vehicle for Allen's biting comic commentary on relationships, American culture, and his beloved Manhattan. The movie was a hit with audiences and critics, picking up Oscars for best picture, best director, best original screenplay, and best actress.

Apocalypse Now (film, directed by Francis Ford Coppola, 1979, rereleased 2001)

Considered by film critics to be the finest movie made about the war in Vietnam, *Apocalypse Now* tells the story of Captain Willard (Martin Sheen), who is given the assignment of going upriver to "terminate with extreme prejudice" a renegade U.S. officer named Colonel Kurtz (Marlon Brando), who is rumored to have created an independent force of mountain tribesmen. As Willard travels upriver with the crew of a Navy gunboat, consisting largely of confused young draftees, he experiences many of the horrors and absurdities of the Vietnam War. Among the most memorable scenes are those of Lieutenant Colonel Bill Kilgore (Robert Duvall) who destroys a village while playing the music of Wagner over helicopter-borne loudspeakers. Eventually, Willard finds Kurtz and his army deep in the jungle. Kurtz has clearly gone mad, but his monologue on the theme of civilization versus barbarism offers a powerful indictment of the entire war.

Based on Joseph Conrad's novella *Heart of Darkness* (1902), *Apocalypse Now* was well received by audiences and critics in 1979, and it garnered eight Academy Award nominations. The film was rereleased in 2001 in a longer version entitled *Apocalypse Now Redux*, which included several scenes cut from the original. *Hearts of Darkness: A Filmmaker's Apocalpyse* was a 1991 documentary about the making of the film, including the many catastrophes that befell the crew.

Badlands (film, directed by Terrence Malik, 1973)

This film is loosely based on the real-life 1958 murder rampage of Charles Starkweather and Caril Ann Fugate on the Great Plains. The story begins in the town of Fort Dupree, South Dakota, where a young garbage collector (Martin Sheen) meets a sign painter's daughter (Sissy Spacek). The young man kills the woman's disapproving father, and the two head off toward the Badlands of western South Dakota, killing a total of ten people for no apparent reason. Simply told, with the exquisite cinematography for which director Terrence Malik is known, the film won high praise from critics, even if it did not enjoy widespread popularity beyond the art-house film circuit.

Blazing Saddles (film, directed by Mel Brooks, 1974)

A satirical comedy set in the Old West, *Blazing Saddles* established the reputation of director Mel Brooks as the king of Hollywood parodies in the 1970s and 1980s. Featuring Cleavon Little as a smooth-talking African American sheriff, the story follows the machinations of a wealthy crook (played by Harvey Korman) who tries to seize the land on which a railroad is to be built, and the efforts of the townspeople to

Francis Ford Coppola's *Apocalypse Now* (1979) was among the darkest, and most acclaimed, of a spate of films about the Vietnam War. *(Matthew Naythons/Getty Images Entertainment)*

thwart his plans. The movie is full of irreverent, ribald humor, including a signature scene in which bean-eating cowboys fart loudly around a campfire. In the final sequence, the movie dissolves into complete ridiculousness, as the characters punch through the cinematic fourth wall and find themselves on a studio back lot. Many critics lamented the juvenile gags, but audiences loved the film, making it one of the most popular movie parodies of all time.

Cabaret (stage musical, by John Kander and Fred Ebb, 1966; film, directed by Bob Fosse, 1972)

Based on the 1930s short stories of Christopher Isherwood, *Cabaret* tells of nightclub performers in Berlin shortly before and after the rise to power of Nazi leader Adolf Hitler. First turned into a dramatic production by John Van Druten in 1955—under the title *I Am a Camera*—Isherwood's book was then produced as a Tony Award-winning musical in 1966. Perhaps best remembered, however, is the 1972 movie, starring Liza Minnelli as Sally Bowles, a beau-

tiful cabaret singer living it up on other people's money, even as the society around her sinks into repression and militarism. The screenplay, written by Jay Allen, was a hit with filmgoers and critics alike, picking up eight Oscars, including best director for Fosse and best actress for Minnelli.

Charlie's Angels (television, 1976–1981; films, directed by John McNichol, 2000 and 2003)

A hugely popular TV series, *Charlie's Angels* featured three beautiful crime-solving women (initially, Farrah Fawcett, Jaclyn Smith, and Kate Jackson). Working for a detective agency headed by a mysterious man named Charlie (voice of John Forsythe) who gave them their instructions at the beginning of each episode, the three "angels" would go out to bring down the bad guys and protect the innocent. Often requiring them to go undercover, the cases were typically set in resort locales, giving the women the chance to show off their bodies in bikinis. This, say critics, was exactly the point: *Charlie's Angels* was the first to make female sensuality the focus of an entire series. The show inspired one of the most popular pin-ups in poster history (Fawcett in a one-piece bathing suit) and, much later, two Hollywood films (*Charlie's Angels: The Movie*, 2000) and (*Charlie's Angels: Full Throttle*, 2003).

Chinatown (film, directed by Roman Polanski, 1974)

Considered by many to be director Roman Polanski's finest work, *Chinatown* is an intricately plotted detective story involving Jake Gittes, a tough-talking 1940s-era Los Angeles private investigator played by Jack Nicholson. In the complex but tightly woven story line, Gittes is hired by Evelyn Mulwray (Faye Dunaway), the wife of the city water commissioner, whom she suspects of adultery. Mulwray is murdered, however, and Gittes finds himself caught up in a real-estate scandal involving Evelyn's father (John Huston) whom, Gittes eventually learns, had impregnated his own daughter. While the sexual aspects of the script are fictional, the real-estate scandal is based on a real-life plot (albeit much earlier in the century). Praised by critics and enormously successful at the box office, *Chinatown* was nominated for eleven Oscars. In 1990, Nicholson directed and starred in a modestly successful sequel titled *The Two Jakes*.

Chorus Line, A (stage musical, by Marvin Hamlisch and Edward Kleben, 1975; film, directed by Richard Attenborough, 1985)

By the time it closed in 1990, *A Chorus Line* had become the longest-running show in Broadway history with a total of 6,137 performances (later surpassed by *Cats*, *The Phantom of the Opera*, and *Les Miserables*). The show is set on a Broadway stage and tells the story of a group of dancers auditioning for the chorus line of a major musical. As the day progresses and the competition stiffens, more and more of the dancers are eliminated. In the end, only a dozen are left, all hungry for roles and eager to impress the director. Choreographed by Michael Bennett, with music by Marvin Hamlisch, the show also featured heartfelt monologues by individual dancers. The 1985 movie version starred Michael Douglas.

Clockwork Orange, A (film, directed by Stanley Kubrick, 1971)

Based on the 1962 novel by British writer Anthony Burgess, *A Clockwork Orange* depicts a dystopian future in which Soviet-style communism has melded with traditional capitalist culture to produce a society full of youthful predators and mind-controlling doctors. The story follows Alex (Malcolm McDowell), a young gang leader who engages in casual sex and violent crime. Eventually caught and convicted, Alex is offered a choice: Remain in prison or undergo an experimental aversion-therapy process. Utilizing violent imagery and the music of Beethoven, which Alex loves, the doctors are able to make Alex helpless in the face of violence. This leaves him woefully unprepared for life on the outside, and he is victimized by members of his former gang. Back in the hospital, Alex is seen as a victim of social engineering, and the process is reversed. Both the book and the movie captured the imagination of a reading and filmgoing public fearful of rising violent crime rates and both horrified and fascinated by the possibilities of psychological manipulation.

Dallas (television, 1978–1991)

The most popular prime-time soap opera in television history, *Dallas* chronicled the loves, intrigues, and adventures of the Ewing clan, a Texas family that made its fortune in oil. Although first aired in the late 1970s, the show is considered the quintessential media expression of the wealth- and power-obsessed 1980s. It featured an ensemble cast of characters, but the center of the ongoing drama was J.R. Ewing (Larry Hagman), a brilliant but amoral and manipulative executive. Most of the show's plots revolved around extramarital affairs, ruthless business dealings, and family backstabbing. The season-opening episode in 1980, which revealed who had shot J.R. at the end of the previous season, was the second-most watched regular series episode in TV history (after the final *MASH* episode in 1983), with 41 million U.S. households tuning in.

Deep Throat (film, directed by Gerard Damiano, 1972)

Such was the popularity of this 1972 pornographic film classic that when Watergate investigative reporters Bob Woodward and Carl Bernstein needed a cover name for their anonymous informant, they called him "Deep Throat." The movie, which featured Linda Lovelace (real name, Linda Boreman) as a woman adept at oral sex, *Deep Throat* was the first hardcore pornographic movie to gain widespread popularity—this in the age before videotape, when persons interested in such films had to see them in public. Shot on a shoestring budget, *Deep Throat* grossed more than $600 million by the early 2000s. Boreman later claimed that her husband used threats of violence to force her to perform in the film.

Dirty Harry (film, directed by Don Siegel, 1971)
Clint Eastwood's most memorable character, "Dirty" Harry Callahan is a San Francisco police detective who likes to take the law into his own hands, usually by threatening or shooting suspects with his .44 magnum sidearm. In *Dirty Harry*, Callahan seeks a psychopathic serial murderer, modeled after the notorious Zodiac Killer of the late 1960s and early 1970s. While hugely popular with audiences, particularly young males, the film alarmed liberals by its celebration of police violence and violations of civil liberties, all in the name of law enforcement. The film spawned no less than four sequels, all starring Eastwood as Callahan: *Magnum Force* (1973); *The Enforcer* (1976); *Sudden Impact* (1983); and *The Dead Pool* (1988).

Dog Day Afternoon (film, directed by Sidney Lumet, 1975)
Dog Day Afternoon was a kind of hybrid movie—a docudrama about a real bank robbery, a psychological portrait of the bank robbers themselves, and a comic adventure with a Murphy's Law theme: Everything that can go wrong will go wrong. Al Pacino plays Sonny Wortzik who, in 1972, tried to rob a bank on a hot summer's day in Brooklyn, New York. With his barely literate sidekick Sal (John Cazale), Wortzik finds himself trapped in the bank by 250 police, his only protection being the bank's staff and customers whom he has taken hostage. Much of the movie consists of the robbers' interaction with their hostages and a crowd of raucously sympathetic onlookers outside, as well as negotiations with police. In the course of the latter, as in the real-life drama, the audience learns that Wortzik has robbed the bank to pay for a sex change operation for his male lover. Finally, gaining a police escort out of the bank, Wortzik is killed by police at the airport. A critical and popular hit, *Dog Day Afternoon* garnered six Academy Award nominations, including best picture.

Don Kirshner's Rock Concert (television, 1973–1981)
Also known as *Rock Concert*, this show was on late night television and featured live rock and roll acts and music videos long before the birth of MTV. A variety of performers appeared on the show, including such rock titans as Rush, Black Sabbath, the Eagles, Van Halen, and KISS. Toward the end of its run, audiences declined, as the show failed to introduce new acts, choosing instead to feature well-established bands that were out of favor with younger viewers. *Rock Concert* did change with the times—bringing in disco, for example—but this tended to turn off many of its older fans. More cutting edge in its musical tastes and presentation than *American Bandstand*, the show introduced late-night viewers of all ages to some of the most important rock and roll music of the day.

Donahue (television, 1970–1996, 2002)
A pioneer of daytime talk shows that focused on issues as well as celebrities, *Donahue* (sometimes called *The Phil Donahue Show*) featured the eponymous host interviewing guests and soliciting questions and comments from the studio audience. Before *Donahue*, daytime television consisted largely of soap operas, game shows, and reruns. Based in Chicago, *Donahue* began as a more traditional talk show, focusing on the celebrity life. The host, however, known for his liberal social and political views, gradually began to reorient the program toward more controversial topics, including such once-forbidden hot-button issues as homosexuality. Extremely popular, the show served as a template for a raft of imitators, from the upbeat Oprah Winfrey to raunchy Jerry Springer. Donahue attempted to revive the show on NBC in 2002 but had little success.

Dukes of Hazzard, The (television, 1979– 1985; film, directed by Jay Chandrasekhar, 2005)
Playing off the late-1970s interest in all things Southern, a fad partially inspired by the growing conservatism of the era and rise to the presidency of Georgian peanut farmer Jimmy Carter, *The Dukes of Hazzard* followed the adventures of a couple of paroled "good ol' boy" cousins named Duke and their sexy female cousin Daisy. Despite their desire to be left alone, the Dukes have raised the ire of Hazzard County political bigwig Boss Hogg and his dimwitted flunky, Sheriff Rosco P. Coltraine.

Like its film inspiration, the 1977 hit *Smokey and the Bandit*, the series featured lots of chase scenes with the boys outrunning bad guys and the sheriff in their customized Dodge Charger, which they called the "General Lee" and bedecked with a large Confederate flag. A 2005 film version based on the series starred

Johnny Knoxville and Seann William Scott as the "thrillbilly" Dukes.

Elephant Man, The (play by Bernard Pomerance, 1979; film, directed by David Lynch, 1980)

Based on a 1971 book by anthropologist Ashley Montagu, *The Elephant Man* tells the true-life story of John Merrick (played by John Hurt in the film), who suffered from Proteus Syndrome, a disease that enlarges and horribly disfigures the face and parts of the body. Set in Victorian London, the play opens with Merrick being inhumanely displayed as a sideshow freak, until taken under the wing of a kindly doctor, Frederick Treves (Anthony Hopkins). While unable to treat the illness itself, Treves is able to help Merrick overcome his shame and isolation. Emerging as a gentleman of grace, charm, and cultural refinement, Merrick becomes a hit in London high society.

Enter the Dragon (film, directed by Robert Clouse, 1973)

One of the seminal action films of the postwar era, *Enter the Dragon* introduced both the Hong Kong martial arts movie and that genre's most popular star, Bruce Lee, to the American public. In this first American-produced film of the genre, Lee plays a martial arts expert recruited by authorities to penetrate the drug-smuggling ring of a Hong Kong crime boss who, as it turns out, was responsible for the suicide death of the protagonist's sister three years earlier. As with most martial arts films, however, the plot of *Enter the Dragon* is thin, little more than a vehicle to take the star from one fight to another. The fact that Lee died shortly after filming helped make it a cult classic. *Enter the Dragon* was not just an inspiration for martial arts films in America but almost single-handedly launched the martial arts fitness craze in the West as well.

Evita (stage musical, by Andrew Lloyd Webber and Tim Rice, 1979; film, directed by Alan Parker, 1996)

Another hit musical by the team of Andrew Lloyd Webber and Tim Rice, *Evita* recounts the story of Eva Perón, a nightclub singer who married Juan Perón, the powerful two-time president of Argentina. The play chronicles her life from an impoverished youth in rural Argentina to her career as a singer in Buenos Aires and ultimately the wife of the country's dictator. In that role, she enjoys a close connection to the poor and working class people of Argentina, whose adoration gives her enormous power. The musical was produced as a much-anticipated film starring Madonna as Evita (Eva), Jonathan Pryce as Juan Perón, and Antonio Banderas as the Argentine revolutionary, Ché Guevara. Both the musical and film take liberties with the true story of Eva Perón and the history of Argentina.

Exorcist, The (novel, by William Peter Blatty, 1971; film, directed by William Friedkin, 1973)

An immediate horror classic when it came out in 1973, *The Exorcist* was based on the best-selling 1971 novel of demonic possession by William Peter Blatty. It tells the story of twelve-year-old Regan MacNeil (Linda Blair), possessed by a spirit claiming to be Satan. After consulting several medical and psychiatric authorities, all of whom are unable to treat the girl successfully, the girl's mother (Ellen Burstyn) seeks out the help of a Catholic exorcist (Jason Miller), who is forced to confront his own questions of faith in the process. With its explicit sexual language and liberal use of bodily fluids and contortions, the movie shocked audiences—who made it a huge box office success. The film inspired four sequels, none of which enjoyed nearly the success of the original. A prequel, *Exorcist: The Beginning,* came out in 2004.

Five Easy Pieces (film, directed by Bob Rafelson, 1970)

Late 1960s radicalism produced a growing interest in class issues. One of Hollywood's most explicit and acclaimed explorations of that theme came in *Five Easy Pieces*, a film about a concert pianist named Robert Dupea (Jack Nicholson) who abandons his profession and upper-class background to pursue a working-class life as an oil rig roustabout. Learning that his father is dying, Dupea returns home with his waitress girlfriend and is forced to justify his choices in lifestyle and girlfriend to his family. A subtheme of the movie is the excesses of genius, as Dupea becomes increasingly erratic in his interactions with others. Popular with the public as well as critics, the film had a gritty, *cinema verité* quality, anticipating the new wave of street-oriented 1970s Hollywood filmmaking.

Flip Wilson Show, The (television, 1970–1974)

Among the many comedy variety programs that aired during the 1960s and 1970s, *The Flip Wilson Show* was unique in one key respect: It was the first and only one hosted by an African American. Wilson, who had gained television stardom as part of the ensemble 1960s comedy show, *Laugh-In*, was a versatile comic best known for his female alter ego, Geraldine, a sassy-talking lady from the wrong side of the tracks. Although its format was conventional, *The Flip Wilson Show* was yet another sign of white America's growing acceptance of blacks on network television.

French Connection, The (film, directed by William Friedkin, 1971)

In a run of movies about no-nonsense law enforcement officers, Hollywood capitalized on the social anxiety surrounding rising violent crime rates in the late 1960s and early 1970s. Among the earliest and best of such films was *The French Connection* in 1971. In it, two undercover New York detectives (played by Gene Hackman and Roy Scheider) try to foil an organized crime ring smuggling heroin from Paris to New York. Relying principally on the gritty streets of New York for its sets, the film has more the feel of a documentary than a standard police drama. *The French Connection* is especially famous for its pioneering car chase through crowded streets, with shots from inside the cars. The film was nominated for eight Oscars and won five, including best picture and best actor—the latter for Hackman in the role of detective "Popeye" Doyle.

Godfather, The (novel, by Mario Puzo, 1969; film, directed by Francis Ford Coppola, 1972)

When the young and relatively untried director Francis Ford Coppola was chosen to make this movie about the Mafia—the producers felt that for political reasons they needed an Italian American at the helm—he insisted that it be told as a family story. Before *The Godfather*, based on the best-selling 1969 novel of the same name by Mario Puzo, films about organized crime rarely depicted gangsters as human beings with families and friends. With several subplots concerning the members of a Mafia family and gang, the film focuses on the story of Don Vito Corleone (played by Marlon Brando), an old-style boss who refuses to get involved in the drug trade. Although the film invests members of organized crime with a sympathetic and moral human dimension, it does not shy away from the violence and amoral behavior in which they engage. Regarded by critics as one of the greatest American movies ever made, *The Godfather* won Academy Awards for best picture, best actor (Brando), and best screenplay based on material from another medium.

In 1974, Coppola co-produced and directed a sequel, *The Godfather, Part II*, which offered twin plots about the rise of Vito Corleone and his son, Michael. This picture also won the Oscar for best picture—the only sequel ever to be so honored. *The Godfather, Part III*, also directed by Coppola, came out in 1990; the response to it was tepid.

Gong Show, The (television, 1976–1980, 1989)

Produced by game show impresario Chuck Barris, who also starred as the emcee, *The Gong Show* was a parody of both the game show and the amateur talent show formats. Episodes featured a panel of celebrity judges who watched the sometimes painfully awful performances of off-key singers, clumsy jugglers, tin-eared musicians, and other amateur talents who often seemed pathetically unaware of their on-stage limitations. Eventually, when the performances became unbearable, one of the stars would pick up a mallet and strike a gong, ending the act. During all of this, the manic Barris would make faces and offer false encouragement. While more than twenty years separated *The Gong Show* from later amateur talent hits such as *American Idol*, it clearly was an inspiration. The show was briefly and unsuccessfully revived in the late 1980s.

Grease (stage musical, by Jim Jacobs and Warren Casey, 1972; film, directed by Randal Kleiser, 1978)

Another example of the 1970s fascination with all things fifties, *Grease* began as a hit Broadway musical (with more than 3,000 performances) and gained vast new audiences as a feature-length motion picture. In music, dance, and dialogue, *Grease* tells the story of a high school romance between Danny (Barry Bostwick in the musical and John Travolta in the movie), the head of a gang of greasers, and a new girl on campus, Sandy (Carole Demas in the musical, Olivia Newton John in the movie). To Danny's dismay, Sandy does not fit in with Danny's "cool" crowd. The plot of the movie, such as it is, revolves around Danny and Sandy overcoming various rivals for the other's attention, as well as a national dance competition that comes to the high school. A less than successful sequel called *Grease 2* was released in 1982.

Happy Days (television, 1974–1984)

Happy Days, a family-oriented TV sitcom, was the first show to capitalize on fifties nostalgia during the decade of the 1970s. A throwback to the time of stay-at-home moms, white-collar fathers, and children who got into regular, if harmless, trouble, *Happy Days* was inspired by the hit film *American Graffiti* (1973) but based on an episode from the comedy skit program *Love American Style*. Early episodes centered on the Cunningham family: father Howard (played by Tom Bosley), wife Marion (Marion Ross), teenage son Richie (Ron Howard), and preteen daughter Joanie (Erin Moran). Later shows focused more on the Fonz (Henry Winkler), a motorcycle-riding greaser character who mouthed a number of catch phrases imitated by millions. The show had several spin-offs, including two that became highly successful in their own right—*Laverne and Shirley* and *Mork and Mindy*.

Harlan County, U.S.A. (film, directed by Barbara Kopple, 1976)

One of the most influential documentary films of the postwar era, *Harlan County, U.S.A.* recounts the long and bitter strike by the United Mine Workers against the Eastover Mining Company of Harlan County, Kentucky in 1974. Viewers watch as the company tries to break the strike by hiring scabs and resorting to intimidation and violence. Kopple makes no pretense of presenting both sides objectively; the miners are portrayed in a far more sympathetic light than the owners. At the time of the film's release, this raised protests among critics, who also complained that the filmmaker rehashed old stereotypes of Appalachian poverty and ignorance. Still, the miners come across largely as heroes, standing up against powerful interests.

James at 15 (television movie and series, 1977–1978)

As the title indicates, this made-for-television movie and spin-off series focused on the experiences of a 15-year-old boy named James (Lance Kerwin in both the movie and series), whose family moves across the country. James misses his girlfriend Lacey (Melissa Sue Anderson in the movie; the character does not appear in the series) and runs away to be with her. While hitchhiking across the country, he meets a twentysomething woman who teaches him about love, sex, and other "life lessons." Both the movie and the weekly show attempted to deal realistically and honestly with serious adolescent issues like premarital sex and alcohol abuse. While the movie was hugely popular and rerun numerous times, the series was eventually canceled due to low ratings.

Jaws (novel, by Peter Benchley, 1974; film, directed by Steven Spielberg, 1975)

According to film-industry historians, no movie was more responsible for the advent of the summer block-buster than *Jaws*. Based on the 1974 best-seller by Peter Benchley, Spielberg's breakthrough film tells the story of a great white shark that attacks swimmers at a New England beach resort. After a woman is eaten alive, a shark expert named Matt Hooper (Richard Dreyfuss) is called in. Hooper warns the town that more attacks are certain, and he is able to convince the town's hydrophobic police chief Martin Brody (Roy Scheider) that the threat is real, but the mayor (Murray Hamilton) is afraid of scaring off tourists and allows the beaches to remain open. After more killings, Hooper and Brody hire grizzled, shark-obsessed, fisherman Quint (Robert Shaw) to join them in a deep-sea hunt for the killer shark. Ultimately, both the Ahab-like captain and the shark are killed. *Jaws* was a movie sensation during the summer of 1975, causing many people to think long and hard about venturing into the surf. It spawned three sequels, *Jaws 2* (1978), *Jaws 3-D* (1983), and *Jaws: The Revenge* (1987).

Jesus Christ Superstar (stage musical, by Andrew Lloyd Webber and Tim Rice, 1971; film, directed by Norman Jewison, 1973)

Among the cultural phenomena of the late 1960s was the so-called Jesus Movement, whose youthful members rediscovered their Christian faith and gave it a counterculture twist. *Jesus Christ Superstar* reflected this new view of Christianity. A rock and roll opera by the songwriting team of Andrew Lloyd Webber and Tim Rice, it tells the story of the last days of Christ in catchy tunes and elaborate dance numbers. Premiering on Broadway in 1971, the show enjoyed a run of 700 performances. In 1973, director Norman Jewison made a film version.

Julia (film, directed by Fred Zinnemann, 1977)

A powerful, critically acclaimed drama based on an incident from the autobiography of playwright Lillian Hellman (played by Jane Fonda), *Julia* tells the story of Hellman's efforts to smuggle money into Nazi Germany to help her lifelong friend, Julia (Vanessa Redgrave), finance an underground anti-Nazi movement. The story cuts back and forth between Julia in Germany and Hellman struggling with revisions to her latest play, while she is engaged in a tempestuous relationship with mystery writer Dashiell Hammett (Jason Robards). On the way to Russia for a writer's conference, Hellman stops in Germany to help Julia and, as a Jew on her way to Communist Russia, she gets in trouble with Nazi authorities. Hellman eventually gains her freedom but learns that Julia has been murdered. Surprisingly popular for such grim subject matter, the film was nominated for eleven Academy Awards.

Last Picture Show, The (film, directed by Peter Bogdanovich, 1971)

Using a small-town movie theater as a symbol for the decline of rural Texas life in the years immediately after World War II, *The Last Picture Show* is the story of two teenage boys—Duane Jackson (played by Jeff Bridges) and Sonny Crawford (Timothy Bottoms)—trying to decide whether they should leave the town for the opportunities of the city or stick with their money-losing inheritance of a pool hall and movie theater. Jackson is seeing a beautiful young girl (Cybill Shepherd), daughter of the richest man in town. Staying with her guarantees Jackson's financial security, but he is still unsure whether to seek his fortune elsewhere. Haunting and bittersweet, the movie was scripted by best-selling Western author Larry McMurtry from his own 1966 novel.

Last Tango in Paris (film, directed by Bernardo Bertolucci, 1972)

One of the first mainstream Hollywood movies to earn an "X" rating, *Last Tango in Paris* is the story of a mysterious American expatriate (played by Marlon Brando) and a beautiful young Parisian woman (Maria Schneider). The American, recovering from the suicide death of his wife, and the young woman, who is about to marry a documentary filmmaker, meet while apartment hunting and proceed to engage in a passionate (and explicitly depicted) love affair. Knowing that the relationship is not meant to last, the two decide not to tell each other their names. An exploration of sexual passion and its potentially profound effects on human behavior, the film was perhaps more controversial than popular among viewers.

Last Waltz, The (film, directed by Martin Scorsese, 1978)

Regarded by many critics as a film of the finest of all rock and roll concerts, *The Last Waltz* chronicles the last on-stage get-together of the legendary group The Band. A popular recording and concert group in its own right, as well as the backup for the legendary Bob Dylan, The Band specialized in country-influenced ballads and hard rock numbers. The concert featured tribute performances by some of rock's, country's, and the blues's greatest acts, including Dylan, Emmylou Harris, Muddy Waters, and Neil Young. The film intersperses footage of the concert with studio sessions and backstage interviews, but what makes it unique is its ability to capture not just the musical talents of the performers but their personalities and life stories as well.

Little Big Man (novel, by Thomas Berger, 1964; film, directed by Arthur Penn, 1970)

Based on a 1964 novel of the same name by best-selling author Thomas Berger, *Little Big Man* is the story of Jack Crabb (played by Dustin Hoffman), who claims to be the only white survivor of Custer's Last Stand. Using the plot device of an aged Crabb relating his lifetime of adventure, the film recounts his adoption by Native Americans, his marriage to a Native woman, and his life as a member of the tribe. Essentially a comedy, the film was still a breakthrough in Hollywood Westerns. It brought a disturbing new perspective on the Old West, with whites depicted as cruel and brutal, and American Indians portrayed as paragons of innocence and communal values.

Love Boat, The (television, 1977–1986)

Created by the prolific and highly successful television producer Aaron Spelling, this series followed the adventures of a cruise ship crew—in particular, the captain (played by Gavin MacLeod), doctor (Bernie Kopell), bartender (Ted Lange), cruise director (Lauren Tewes), and purser (Fred Grandy). The show was set on a real cruise ship and featured a new group of guest stars each week playing passengers of various sorts. Thus, the show could provide a popular mix of long-running plot lines, mostly about shipboard romances, and one-time stories about passengers, also focusing on romantic encounters. *The Love Boat* was extremely popular and ran for ten seasons. A remake, *The Love Boat: The Next Wave*, had a brief run in the late 1990s.

Mary Hartman, Mary Hartman (television, 1976–1978)

A decade of both cynicism and nostalgia, the 1970s witnessed a proliferation of film and television comedies that parodied the tried-and-true formulas of decades past. One of the most critically acclaimed was *Mary Hartman, Mary Hartman*. Starring comic actress Louise Lasser as the eponymous protagonist, the show resembled both a 1950s-style, family-based sitcom and an afternoon soap opera. But unlike those shows, *Mary Hartman*, set in the fictional small town of Fernwood,

Ohio, featured a series of eccentric characters and plots revolving around such offbeat subjects as religious cults and UFO sightings. Never a huge success—the show ran for only three seasons—it gained popularity in syndicated reruns and became a cult classic. It also produced a talk show parody called *Fernwood 2Nite*, starring *Mary Hartman* cast member Martin Mull.

Mary Tyler Moore Show, The (television, 1970–1977)

Playing off the women's liberation movement, *The Mary Tyler Moore Show*—starting with the title music's line, "you're gonna make it after all"—depicted women in a new television role: single and career oriented. The show followed the adventures of Mary Richards, a producer on a local television news show in Minneapolis. Episode plots generally revolved around issues at work and Mary's love life. While Mary was looking for the right guy, her pursuit of a meaningful relationship never took center stage—unlike that of her brassy neighbor Rhoda (played by Valerie Harper) who seemed obsessed with getting married. The show was also memorable for its ensemble cast, including a preening anchor (Ted Knight), hardboiled newsroom executive (Ed Asner), and sarcastic news writer (Gavin MacLeod).

MASH (novel, by Richard Hornberger, 1968; film, directed by Robert Altman, 1970; television, 1972–1983)

Despite its setting in the Korean War, *MASH*—in both its original film version and the television series it inspired—is a multilayered commentary on the Vietnam War era in which it was produced. An antiwar comedy, it portrays the experiences of the doctors, nurses, and staff of a Mobile Army Surgical Hospital (or MASH) unit in Korea. Based on the 1968 novel by Richard Hornberger (writing as Richard Hooker), *MASH* features an ensemble cast of eccentric characters, led by the irreverent surgeon Hawkeye Pierce (played by Elliott Gould in the film and Alan Alda on TV). In both versions, Pierce and fellow doctor Trapper John (Donald Sutherland in the movie, Wayne Rogers on TV) indulge in practical jokes and sexual escapades with nurses between long, grueling shifts trying to save the lives of wounded servicemen.

Mean Streets (film, directed by Martin Scorsese, 1973)

The first full-length feature by director Martin Scorsese to win both critical praise and popular audiences,

Mean Streets was a seminal film of the 1970s, introducing a gritty, *cinema verité* style to American filmmaking, as well as characters straight from the rough streets of New York's Little Italy. Starring Scorsese regulars Robert De Niro and Harvey Keitel in their first major roles, the film follows the story of a small-time organized crime debt collector, Charlie (Keitel), trying to break free from his gangster life. Charlie works for an uncle who disapproves of his plans to marry an epileptic young woman. Complicating Charlie's situation is his girlfriend's cousin Johnny Boy (De Niro), a psychotic whose failure to pay off his debts leads to a violent end.

Monday Night Football (television, 1970–present)

Until *Monday Night Football* (also known as *NFL Monday Night Football*) came around, television coverage of the sport was routine in scheduling (confined to Sunday afternoon) and staid in production, with commentary restricted to rote descriptions of action on the field. ABC producer Roone Arledge, for one, felt that professional football could succeed on prime-time television if it were livened up. The key, he believed, was an emphasis on personality. Players on the field would have to be portrayed as individuals with real-life stories.

Even more importantly, Arledge wanted a cast of characters in the reporting booth as well. Toward that end, he matched two telegenic former players, Don Meredith and Frank Gifford, with brash boxing reporter Howard Cosell. Sparks sometimes flew, but the team was charismatic. After a brief stumble, *Monday Night Football* appealed both to traditional football fans and a new audience of nonfans who were intrigued by the on-air antics of the three announcers. Although the announcing team has changed a number of times through the years, the show has remained a staple of ABC and the National Football League (NFL). In 2006, *Monday Night Football* moved to the cable network ESPN, owned by the Walt Disney Company, which also owns ABC.

Nashville (film, directed by Robert Altman, 1975)

A film about politics and music alike, *Nashville* helped confirm Altman's reputation as the finest ensemble cast director in Hollywood. The movie interweaves a series of subplots about various characters in the country music capital, including a female star on the verge of a nervous breakdown, a working-class couple with a troubled marriage and a disabled child, and a British Broadcasting Company (BBC) journalist full of her own importance. All of the stories are set against a political season in high gear, as a vaguely populist candidate—who is never seen—campaigns on the promise of ridding Congress of lawyers. Movie historians have praised the film for its effective depiction of a politically drifting, post-Vietnam, post-Watergate America. The film was nominated for five Oscars, including best picture, but it won just a single academy award for best music, original song ("I'm Easy," Keith Carradine).

Network (film, directed by Sydney Lumet, 1976)
Scripted by playwright Paddy Chayefsky, *Network* was one of the most powerful and popular films ever made on the subject of television journalism. Set in a fictional network newsroom, the acerbic comedy stars Peter Finch as aging anchorman Howard Beale, increasingly angry at the declining state of the country. Fired because of declining ratings, Beale explodes on the air, telling viewers to go to their windows and shout, "I'm mad as hell, and I'm not going to take it anymore." The response is electric, as millions follow Beale's advice. Cynical network executives realize they have a new star on their hands and develop a program featuring Beale in his mad Jeremiah persona. Released in the wake of the Vietnam War and Watergate scandals, *Network* sought to capture the angst of the times, even as it satirized a news department turning itself into another entertainment division of the network.

Poseidon Adventure, The (novel, by Paul Gallico, 1969; film, directed by Ronald Neame, 1972; film, directed by Wolfgang Petersen, 2006)
The first in a series of highly popular disaster films, *The Poseidon Adventure*, based on the best-selling 1969 novel by Paul Gallico, tells the story of cruise ship turned upside down in mid-ocean by a tsunami. The movie set the pattern for copycat films such as *Earthquake* (1974) and *The Towering Inferno* (1974), with an ensemble cast of major stars. Like other disaster movies, *The Poseidon Adventure* begins predisaster, establishing back stories for the major characters, so the audience will care whether they survive or not. The movie then portrays the disaster with realistic special effects and follows the characters as they struggle to make their way to the surface, some acting heroically along the way, others not so heroically. A remake came out in spring 2006 to generally poor reviews and a weak box office.

Prairie Home Companion, A (radio program, 1974–1987, 1989–present; film, directed by Robert Altman, 2006)
Featuring the dry Midwestern humor and mesmerizing baritone of host Garrison Keillor, *A Prairie Home Companion* is a weekly radio show that features musical guests, skits, commentary, talented special effects artists, and fictitious commercials. The featured story line, with new episodes each week, is set in the fictional town of Lake Wobegon, Minnesota, where, as Keillor says, "the women are strong, the men are good looking, and all of the children are above average." Originally taped in Minnesota, the show moved to New York in 1989 and back to Saint Paul in 1992, with Keillor and his crew also appearing before live audiences around the country. *A Prairie Home Companion* is one of the rare radio success stories of the television age and one of the most popular programs on National Public Radio. A film based on the program was released in 2006.

Pumping Iron (film, directed by George Butler and Robert Fiore, 1977)
Inspired by the novel *Stay Hungry* by Charles Gaines (produced as a dramatic movie of the same name in 1976), *Pumping Iron* is a documentary about a group of bodybuilders preparing for the Mr. Olympia and Mr. Universe competitions. Set in Gold's Gym in Brooklyn, New York, and elsewhere, the film depicts the workout routines, intensive dieting, and behind-the-scenes backbiting of the contestants. It also chronicles the lives of several bodybuilders, including the shy, deaf Lou Ferrigno (who later played the title role in *The Incredible Hulk* television series) and the witty but arrogant five-time champion Arnold Schwarzenegger, who manages to psychologically manipulate Ferrigno. The film was enormously influential in promoting bodybuilding as a participatory and a spectator sport and in launching the career of Schwarzenegger.

Rocky (film, directed by John G. Avildsen, 1976)
Ever uplifting, this 1976 boxing classic is the story of a small-time, big-hearted fighter from Philadelphia, Rocky Balboa (played by Sylvester Stallone, who also wrote the script), who works as an enforcer for a loan shark but gets a shot at the boxing big time. The heavyweight champion of the world, Apollo Creed (Carl Weathers), is scheduled to have a fight in Rocky's hometown, but his opponent backs out. Creed offers Rocky, a low-level amateur, a chance at the crown, believing he will be a pushover. But Rocky, inspired by his

feisty coach (Burgess Meredith), trains to within an inch of his life and ultimately boxes a surprised Creed to a draw. Hugely popular, *Rocky* became a film franchise unto itself with no fewer than four sequels. The original won an Academy Award for best picture.

Rocky Horror Picture Show, The (film, directed by Jim Sharman, 1975)

A cult classic that continues to play at midnight showings across the country—where audience members dress up as their favorite characters, shout lines at the screen, and throw things at various cues—*Rocky Horror Picture Show* is a musical spoof of the horror movie genre. It is the story of newlywed couple Janet (Susan Sarandon) and Brad (Barry Bostwick) who get lost in the rain and show up on the castle doorstep of transvestite Dr. Frank-N-Furter (Tim Curry) of the planet Transsexual in the galaxy Transylvania. Like Dr. Frankenstein, Frank-N-Furter has created a monster—Rocky Horror. Full of campy musical numbers, many featuring Frank-N-Furter, the film also features a cameo performance by rock musician Meat Loaf as the rebel Eddie.

Roots (novel, by Alex Haley, 1976; television miniseries, 1977)

One of the top-selling books in the history of African American letters, *Roots* also inspired the most watched miniseries in the history of television. The book and series gave a fictionalized account of the family history unearthed by journalist Alex Haley. In a *tour de force* of genealogical investigation, Haley was able to trace his ancestors back to the West African village where one of his ancestors, Kunte Kinte (played by LeVar Burton on television), was kidnapped by slave traders. The book and miniseries chronicle Kinte's offspring through several generations, from slavery to freedom.

In 1977, when ABC ran the twelve-hour miniseries based on the book, it took a risk by scheduling the programs over eight successive nights. The risk paid off. Not only was the series a critical and popular success, it also inspired a generation of Americans—of all backgrounds—to examine their own family trees.

Saturday Night Fever (film, directed by John Badham, 1977)

Saturday Night Fever and its soundtrack by the Bee Gees ushered in the disco era of the late 1970s and made John Travolta a star. Travolta plays Tony Manero, a cocky teenager in Brooklyn, New York, who works at a hardware store but excels at dancing. Going out dancing on Saturday nights as a respite from family, poverty, and worries about the future, Manero dreams of escaping Brooklyn for the bright lights of Manhattan. The film was a smash, and its soundtrack, featuring such hits as "Stayin' Alive" and "Night Fever," became a classic. Soon, people across the country were emulating the film's fashion and dancing. Though polyester suits and glittering disco balls would eventually seem dated, they came to symbolize the 1970s as a time of turmoil many teenagers longed to escape.

Saturday Night Live (television, 1975–present)

"Live from New York, it's Saturday Night!" Since its first airing on October 11, 1975, these words have opened one of television's most consistently funny and popular shows, *Saturday Night Live (SNL)*. Airing live on late-night screens, *SNL* features a ragtag ensemble of comedians performing satirical sketches with a celebrity host, interspersed with live musical performances by a guest band or artist. The show has been the launching ground for such comedic standouts as John Belushi, Dan Aykroyd, Bill Murray, Gilda Radner, Eddie Murphy, Chevy Chase, Steve Martin, and Adam Sandler. Although *SNL* has been routinely criticized for its behind-the-scenes treatment of minorities and women, young comics of both genders and all ethnicities aspire to an appearance. Since 1975, *SNL* has turned American news and culture upside down, putting a humorous spin on the week's events, ridiculing the U.S. government and politics, and introducing new catchphrases ("Well isn't that special") to the English language.

Scared Straight (film, directed by Arnold Shapiro, 1978)

In 1978, a group of seventeen troubled teenagers spent a day at Rahway State Prison in New Jersey. They had already committed such crimes as arson, armed robbery, and auto theft and were well on their way to a life behind bars. To scare them straight, the teens were invited to spend a day with real-life convicts as part of a crime prevention program. *Scared Straight*, narrated by actor Peter Falk, documents that day. In unflinching detail, the convicts tell the teens about life in maximum security; the group of cocky teenagers is reduced to quiet contemplation, some near tears. So as not to diminish the program's impact on viewers, the Federal

Communications Commission left its strong language uncensored. The film received the Academy Award for best documentary in 1979, the first to receive the award without a theatrical release.

Twenty years after *Scared Straight*, a new documentary followed up on the lives of the original teenagers. Amazingly, sixteen of the seventeen had stayed out of trouble, and many of the inmates were living productive lives out of prison.

Schoolhouse Rock (television, 1973–1985, 1995–1996)

The television cartoon show *Schoolhouse Rock* used catchy songs to teach kids three-minute lessons on government, math, grammar, history, and science. It was created by advertising executive David McCall, whose son knew every song on the radio but had trouble with multiplication. *Schoolhouse Rock* began airing on ABC in 1973 in breaks between Saturday morning cartoons, and its songs, such as "I'm Just a Bill," "The Great Melting Pot," "Zero, My Hero," "Conjunction Junction," and "Electricity," were soon being sung by children across the nation.

The show went off the air in 1985, but it became a cult classic for Generation X. In the 1990s, ABC began showing the old segments again on Saturday mornings and even produced a few new ones. The album *Schoolhouse Rock! Rocks* was released in 1996, featuring popular musical artists performing songs from the show. Like *Sesame Street*, *Schoolhouse Rock* was created by people who believed that television could both entertain and educate. For Generation Xers, it was a way they learned how a bill becomes a law, how to multiply, and where to put an adjective in a sentence.

Shaft (novel, by Ernest Tidyman, 1970; film, directed by Gordon Parks, 1971; film, directed by John Singleton, 2000)

"Who's the cat who won't cop out when there's danger all about?" John Shaft was the coolest, baddest private investigator of the 1970s. An African American who dressed sharp and took guff from no one, white or black, he helped usher in a series of so-called "blaxploitation" films during the 1970s. *Shaft* was released in 1971 to audiences that had never seen a black detective on film.

Based on a novel by Ernest Tidyman, the film starred Richard Roundtree in the title role. *Shaft* was groundbreaking for African American actors, as Roundtree played a kind of black crime-fighting su-

perhero, not a servant or sidekick. He was James Bond with sideburns and a leather coat—black power on the big screen. "Who is the man who would risk his neck for his brother man?" asked the Oscar-winning theme song by Isaac Hayes. A remake of the 1971 film starring Samuel L. Jackson and directed by John Singleton was released in 2000.

Soap (television, 1977–1981)

A combination satire and situation comedy created to spoof daytime soap operas, *Soap* ran on the ABC network from 1977 to 1981. The show generated controversy even before the pilot aired, as a news magazine had reported that in one episode a Catholic priest would be seduced inside a confessional. The article was wrong, but that did not prevent religious groups throughout the country from condemning the show and boycotting its sponsors. ABC struggled to find advertisers for the September 13, 1977, premiere.

The controversy died down over time, but some groups still protested the series for its frank treatment of such topics as adultery, homosexuality, racism, and mental illness. *Soap* featured the first openly homosexual character in prime time, Jodie Dallas, played by Billy Crystal. Clearly, television was changing—the Tate and Campbell families in *Soap* were portrayed as dysfunctional, and formerly taboo subjects were addressed in the open.

Sonny and Cher Comedy Hour, The (television, 1971–1974)

This prime-time show starred the popular recording and touring artists Sonny Bono and his wife Cher. The duo had a string of musical hits in the 1960s but had stopped recording by 1971, when a well-received appearance on *The Merv Griffin Show* convinced the head of CBS that they were perfect to replace the Smothers Brothers. CBS hoped Sonny and Cher would bring back young viewers who had left the network with the Smothers Brothers's cancellation. *The Sonny and Cher Comedy Hour* was like a Las Vegas lounge act with snappy banter between musical numbers. The show also featured a regular cast, including Sonny and Cher's toddler, and outlandish outfits designed by Bob Mackie. A virtual copy of the *Smothers Brothers Comedy Hour* but without the satirical teeth, it was a hit with audiences. The show stayed on the air until 1974, when Sonny filed for divorce from Cher, and the two refused to continue working together.

Soul Train (television, 1971–present)

Before there was MTV (Music Television) and BET (Black Entertainment Television), there was *American Bandstand* and *Soul Train*. The latter was a weekly dance show featuring African American artists, created and produced by Don Cornelius, a Chicago radio host. In the late 1960s, Cornelius pitched the idea of an African American dance show to Chicago television station WCIU. Cornelius funded the pilot, WCIU provided the studio, and on August 17, 1970, *Soul Train* went on the air five afternoons a week. The show was a hit in Chicago, and its producers expanded to national syndication in 1971. Soul, rhythm and blues, jazz, rap, and hip hop all have been showcased on *Soul Train*, which continues to air in syndication into the twenty-first century. In 1987, Cornelius launched the Soul Train Music Awards, which are broadcast annually.

Star Wars (film, directed by George Lucas, 1977)

With *Star Wars*, writer and director George Lucas drew from classical mythology and Hollywood Westerns to create one of the best-loved and most successful films of all time. Set "long ago in a galaxy far, far away," it is the story of Luke Skywalker, a young man on a coming-of-age mission. Aided by Han Solo, a Wookie, robots, and Ben Obi-Wan Kenobi, Skywalker uses the Force to end Darth Vader's tyranny over the galaxy. After a slew of gloomy science fiction films released in the 1970s, *Star Wars* was a breath of fresh air. Here were heroes and villains, rousing space battles and sword fights, the themes of faith and doubt, and an ending that left audiences cheering. The special effects in *Star Wars* were groundbreaking, but it was the story audiences loved most.

Released in 1977 and again in 1997, *Star Wars* made more than $460 million at the box office and launched a merchandising juggernaut. A number of filmmakers have attempted to emulate the success of the original Star Wars, most notably Lucas himself. The sequels *The Empire Strikes Back* and *Return of the Jedi* appeared in 1980 and 1983, respectively, and prequels were released in 1999, 2002, and 2005.

Taxi Driver (film, directed by Martin Scorsese, 1976)

Much of the central story of Martin Scorsese's *Taxi Driver* is a darker, urban retelling of the 1956 film *The Searchers*. In both films, an alienated war veteran searches for redemption by saving a young girl from a perceived evil. Travis Bickle (Robert De Niro), a men-

tally unstable loner, drives a taxi through New York City's worst neighborhoods at night. Trapped in a world of sex and violence, he dreams of washing "all this scum off the streets." Bickle arms himself for battle against those he sees as corrupting society, but his assassination attempt on a presidential candidate fails. (Some said that the 1981 assassination attempt on President Ronald Reagan by John Hinckley Jr., a mentally unbalanced man obsessed with Jody Foster, one of the stars of the film, was partly inspired by *Taxi Driver*.) Lusting for blood, Bickle befriends a twelve-year-old prostitute (Foster), and he is celebrated as a vigilante hero after killing her pimp. Released at a time of national pessimism after Vietnam and Watergate, *Taxi Driver* was a frightening commentary on modern urban life and a tale about the perils of alienation. *Taxi Driver* cemented De Niro's place as one of the finest American actors and Scorsese's as one of the best directors of the "new Hollywood."

Three's Company (television, 1977–1984)

Television's new obsession with sex was never more apparent than during the seven-year run of *Three's Company*. The show originally aired as a midseason replacement behind the hits *Happy Days* and *Laverne and Shirley,* but it soon surpassed both to become the most-watched comedy on television in 1979. It was a farce in which two unmarried women, Janet Wood and Chrissy Snow, lived with the bachelor Jack Tripper in a Santa Monica, California, apartment in order to save money. The landlord is uncomfortable with this swinging threesome cohabitating, so Jack pretends to be gay. Double entendres and suggestive dialogue made sex the show's primary topic, yet the roommates were never more than good friends.

Three's Company highlighted TV's so-called "jiggle era," in which sexually liberated women appeared in tight, skimpy clothing to the pleasure of male audiences. Critics assailed the show as mindless titillation, and feminists argued that it denigrated women. The actors and producers said it was all in good fun, perhaps with a few jabs at the conventional thinking of the time that men and women should not and could not live together platonically.

Towering Inferno, The (film, directed by John Guillermin and Irwin Allen, 1974)

Disaster movies spread like wildfire in 1970s Hollywood, and a leading example was *The Towering Inferno*, released in 1974. The film features an all-star cast that includes Paul Newman, Steve McQueen, Fred Astaire (who earned his first Oscar nomination for best actor in a supporting role), Faye Dunaway, Robert Wagner, Richard Chamberlain, and O. J. Simpson. Newman plays the architect of a San Francisco skyscraper that catches fire because of poor construction. Pyrotechnics and rescue sequences keep the action going during the nearly three-hour film. Unlike many other disaster movies, *The Towering Inferno* was a hit with viewers and critics, and it received an Academy Award nomination for best picture.

Unmarried Woman, An (film, directed by Paul Mazursky, 1978)

An Unmarried Woman was part of a wave of films in the 1970s that explored the ability of women to live without men. Directed by Paul Mazursky, who also wrote the script, this film was considered a touchstone of the women's movement, as it realistically portrayed the difficulty and excitement that women encounter when beginning a new, empowered life on their own. The title role is played by Jill Clayburgh, who brought a vulnerability to the part of an affluent New York wife whose husband leaves her for a woman he meets at Bloomingdale's. Navigating life on her own for the first time, she finds love on her own terms with a SoHo painter (Alan Bates). This last plot development was seen by some as a cop-out, but the film was nevertheless regarded as a hit of feminist filmmaking—and inspiring to many. The film received Academy Award nominations for best picture, best actress, and best screenplay.

Waltons, The (television, 1972–1981)

The first of several popular family dramas (including *Family*, *Eight Is Enough*, and *Little House on the Prairie*) that aired during the 1970s, *The Waltons*, about a large extended family who lived on Walton's Mountain in the Blue Ridge Mountains of Virginia in the 1930s, ran on the CBS network from 1972 to 1981. The stories were narrated by the oldest son, John-Boy, who aspired to be a writer.

The show was praised for capturing a specific time and place in American life, as well as for portraying poverty and community in a historical setting. In a way, however, it romanticized the Great Depression by sentimentalizing the strong family bonds forged by troubled times and a simpler way of life. In the midst of the troubled 1970s, *The Waltons* played on viewer nostalgia for simpler times and strong family values.

Way We Were, The (film, directed by Sydney Pollack, 1973)

Can liberals and conservatives fall in love? That's the question asked and answered in *The Way We Were*, a mid-twentieth-century saga directed by Sydney Pollack and starring Barbra Streisand and Robert Redford. Streisand plays Katie Morosky, a liberal activist and Young Communist leader who meets Hubbell Gardner, a conservative WASP writer, in the 1930s. They part, only to cross paths again in New York during World War II. Despite their differences, they fall in love, marry, move to California, and are caught up in the Hollywood blacklist, which drives them apart. Their politics are always at odds, and they divorce. *The Way We Were* was a favorite of fans of romantic movies for its doomed love story and strong leading characters. But the film is also a chronology of liberal causes in twentieth-century America, as Katie moves from procommunism to anti-nuclear war.

Woodstock (film, directed by Michael Wadleigh, 1970)

One of the most famous concert events in history, Woodstock was held on a 600-acre farm in upstate New York on August 15–17, 1969. The three days of music proved to be a gathering point for the counterculture, attended by 500,000 young people who lived in tents, played in the mud, and partook of illegal substances while listening to some of the greatest music of the day. Joan Baez, The Who, Jimi Hendrix, The Grateful Dead, and some thirty other performers entertained the delighted crowd, attendees at the greatest rock concert ever. If there was one high point of the counterculture movement, it was Woodstock, where the generation's music, casual sex, and drug use came together. Documentary director Michael Wadleigh captured the event on film, interspersing concert footage with attendee interviews.

THE EIGHTIES

Literature and Journalism

All I Really Need To Know I Learned in Kindergarten: Uncommon Thoughts on Common Things (nonfiction, by Robert Fulghum, 1988)

A book of simple aphorisms and helpful bits of advice, *All I Really Need To Know I Learned in Kindergarten* became a number one American best-seller upon publication. The central premise of the book is that the most important things for a happy and fulfilling life are both simple and learned at a young age. Fulghum playfully intersperses the big and small things we all can do, from sharing with others to flushing the toilet after each use. But whether big or small, the author uses these daily activities to reveal larger lessons. The book was one of a number of similar guides that came out in the late 1980s and early 1990s advocating a simpler life and a return to moral behavior in everyday life.

Bonfire of the Vanities, The (novel, by Tom Wolfe, 1987; film, directed by Brian De Palma, 1990)

While largely fictional, *The Bonfire of the Vanities* offers a lifelike portrait of New York City during the 1980s, with some of the characters based on real-life, public figures. The action begins when the mistress of financier Sherman McCoy, one of the self-styled Wall Street "masters of the universe," runs over an African American boy in the Bronx while driving with McCoy. The story is picked up by a sensation-mongering journalist and quickly becomes a *cause célèbre* of a radical black minister. The novel moves back and forth between satirical depictions of the city's racial and class politics and the gradual collapse of McCoy's life and sanity. The book was turned into a modestly successful, but critically panned, film starring Tom Hanks and Melanie Griffith.

Brief History of Time, A: From the Big Bang to Black Holes (nonfiction, by Stephen W. Hawking, 1988; film, directed by Errol Morris, 1991)

A surprising best-seller on physics and the nature of the universe, *A Brief History of Time* summarizes the theories of British physicist Stephen Hawking on black holes, the Big Bang, and other cosmological phenomena. Part of the fascination with this non-technical but difficult book concerns the life story of the author, who suffers from a degenerative nervous disorder, is confined to a wheelchair, and requires a voice synthesizer to speak. In 1991, documentary filmmaker Errol Morris adapted the book, with anecdotes of Hawking's life, into a film of the same name.

Bright Lights, Big City (novel, by Jay McInerney, 1984; film, directed by James Bridges, 1988)

Capturing the hip lifestyle of young Manhattanites during the go-go 1980s, Jay McInerney's *Bright Lights, Big City* tells the story of an unnamed narrator who goes to New York to work in the publishing business. Written in the second person, as if addressed personally to the reader, the book starts off with everything going well for the narrator—an interesting job, smart friends, and an exciting social life. After the death of his mother, however, the narrator turns to drugs, and the rest of the story chronicles his fall into substance abuse and despair. The book was produced as a moderately successful movie starring Michael J. Fox as the narrator.

Clear and Present Danger (novel, by Tom Clancy, 1989; film, directed by Phillip Noyce, 1994)

Arguably the most popular of Tom Clancy's many best-selling novels—sometimes referred to as "techno-military thrillers"—*Clear and Present Danger* puts CIA analyst Jack Ryan (played by Harrison Ford in the movie) in the midst of a power struggle among Colombian drug cartel leaders. As in many of Clancy's novels, however, everything is not as it seems. High-powered figures in the U.S. government are playing both sides against the middle; those who are supposed to be good guys are not, and those believed to be bad guys are often even more evil than first expected.

Over the years, Clancy has won a broad following among readers for his action-oriented plots and his attention to technical detail and accuracy. Several of his novels have been made into big-budget Hollywood pictures, including *The Hunt for Red October* (1990), *Patriot Games* (1992), and *Clear and Present Danger* (1994).

Closing of the American Mind, The: How Higher Education Has Failed Democracy and Impoverished the Souls of Today's Students (nonfiction, by Allan Bloom, 1987)

In this controversial work, Bloom, a professor of political philosophy at the University of Chicago, laments the decline of the humanities and the failure of the American educational establishment to teach students the classics of literature and philosophy. These failures have a detrimental effect on young Americans' understanding of themselves and their society, he argues, because the classics offer unique and unchanging truths about humanity and human society. Bloom also denounces the tendency in academia toward cultural relativism and multiculturalism. The book was lauded by conservatives as a warning about the decline of American culture and values and denounced by liberals as a reactionary defense of a culture dominated by "dead white men."

Color Purple, The (novel, by Alice Walker, 1982; film, directed by Steven Spielberg, 1985)

Among the best-selling works in the history of African American letters and postwar American fiction generally, *The Color Purple* tells the story of Celie, a young African American woman, growing up in the South in the early 1900s. A victim of sexual abuse, Celie is sold by her father into an unhappy marriage. Told in the form of a letter from Celie, the book chronicles the woman's struggle for her own kind of freedom. A Pulitzer Prize winner in 1983, *The Color Purple* was made into a major Hollywood movie by director Steven Spielberg, starring Whoopi Goldberg. Only modestly successful at the box office, the film—like the book—was criticized by many blacks for its harsh portrayal of African American men.

Confederacy of Dunces, The (novel, by John Kennedy Toole, 1980)

The Confederacy of Dunces was actually written in the 1960s, when the author was serving in the U.S. Army. Unsuccessful in his attempts to get it published, Toole put the manuscript in a drawer, where it remained until his mother discovered it after his suicide. With the help of novelist Walker Percy, she was able to find a publisher. The book tells of the slightly surrealistic adventures of Ignatius J. Reilly, an eccentric, overweight New Orleans man who can't hold a job and has serious problems relating to other people. Critics hailed the work as a masterpiece of comic fiction. The public agreed, making it a perennial best-seller.

Iacocca: An Autobiography (nonfiction, by Lee Iacocca with William Novak, 1984)

In 1978, the automotive engineer and Ford executive Lee Iacocca, known as the creator of the Mustang sports car in the 1960s, was fired from the company over differences with its chairman, Henry Ford II. Iacocca was quickly hired to run the nation's number three automaker Chrysler, where a run of bad management decisions and poorly designed cars had brought the company to the verge of bankruptcy. With the help of a federal bailout, in the form of a $1.5 billion loan guarantee, Iacocca ultimately succeeded in returning the company to profitability. In doing so, he became one of the most respected businessmen in America, during a time when that occupation was riding high in people's esteem; there was even talk of his running for president. The gruff but charming Iacocca helped stoke this popularity with his autobiography, the best-selling nonfiction book of 1984.

In Search of Excellence: Lesson's from America's Best-Run Companies (nonfiction, by Tom Peters and Robert H. Waterman, Jr., 1982)

No book did more to promote the importance of effective business management than *In Search of Excellence*, a book that contributed to the 1980s fascination with business executives and led to a series of best-selling management and executive biographies. Prior to *In Search of Excellence*, management techniques were usually confined to business schools and discussed among management scholars and students in academic, jargon-filled language. Authors Tom Peters and Robert Waterman changed that. Using examples from actual businesses and managers, the authors offer basic, almost commonsense, tips, like sticking close to one's expertise and always thinking of the customer's needs first.

In Search of Excellence rose to the top of *The New York Times* best-seller list in 1982, becoming one of the first in a cottage industry of management books written for the general reading public. This trend has continued with the success of such books as *One Minute Manager* (1982) and *Who Moved My Cheese?* (1998).

Jane Fonda's Workout Book (nonfiction, by Jane Fonda, 1981)

While running and other outdoor forms of exercise had gained in popularity during the 1970s, most of the literature on the subject of fitness, much of it aimed at men, called for a major commitment of time and energy. *Jane Fonda's Workout Book* helped change that, offering a simple aerobic exercise program geared toward working women and mothers who wanted to look better and feel more fit without having to sacrifice other aspects of their busy lives. Taking advantage of the rapidly growing presence of videocassette players in people's homes in the early 1980s, Fonda also introduced a best-selling videotape to accompany this enormously popular book. Physical fitness experts credit Fonda with almost single-handedly launching the aerobic exercise revolution in America.

Maus: A Survivor's Tale (cartoon fiction, by Art Spiegelman, 1986)

Long popular in Europe and Japan, graphic novels—incorporating a novel's complex plot and characterization with the artistry of comic books—enjoyed a small following in the United States. The release of *Maus: A Survivor's Tale* in 1986 helped changed that. This innovative work tells the story of a Jewish immigrant's son discovering the Holocaust experience of his parents. Using traditional comic book imagery, the Jewish victims in the tale are portrayed as mice and the Nazi villains as cats.

Maus elicited mixed reactions from critics and the public at large. Among the former were those who complained that the graphic novel genre, with its limited number of words, lacked the capacity to deal with complex issues, rounded character development, and complicated story lines. Some members of the Jewish community were offended at the exploration of such a sensitive subject in an art form usually associated—in the United States, at least—with light-hearted action adventure.

Mismeasure of Man, The (nonfiction, by Stephen Jay Gould, 1981)

Written by paleontologist Stephen Jay Gould, who had earned a reputation for introducing complex scientific topics to lay readers, *The Mismeasure of Man* examines human intelligence or, more specifically, how human intelligence has been measured and interpreted through history. Gould refers back to the turn of the twentieth century to tell the story of intelligence quotient (IQ) testing, how it was developed, how it was applied, and how its significance was over-

stated and misinterpreted. The author also provides an account of how countless individuals, particularly those from poor and minority backgrounds, suffered from the consequences of IQ testing. Politically on the left, Gould intended to use the book as a lesson to counter conservatives' emphasis on school testing, which, he said, discriminated against poor and disadvantaged students.

Neuromancer (novel, by William Gibson, 1984)

Achieving the unprecedented distinction of winning all of science fiction's three major awards—the Hugo, the Nebula, and the Philip K. Dick—*Neuromancer* is a science fiction novel set in an environmentally poisoned, class-divided, corporate-dominated future society. The people in this dystopia avoid an unpleasant reality by spending much of their time online in a computer-generated world. The novel, written a decade before the widespread use of the Internet, developed a strong cult following. Gibson is credited with inventing the subgenre of science fiction called "cyberpunk" (dealing with the possibilities of life inside cyberspace).

Official Preppie Handbook, The (nonfiction, by Lisa Birnbach, 1980)

Hugely popular, *The Official Preppie Handbook* satirized its subject even as it offered tongue-in-cheek tips to the reader on how to become one. A preppie is portrayed as someone who has attended an elite private college or preparatory high school, usually, but not always, a boarding school and popularly imagined as situated in a small New England town. More than that, the term signifies both a snob and a person from a socially prominent background.

Preppies were widely satirized in the media for their slang, conservative dress, and staid recreational activities. The book and the whole preppie fad were seen by many in the popular media as representing a transition from the hippie- and drug-influenced 1970s to the conservative, business-oriented 1980s.

Onion, The (magazine, 1988–present)

Founded as a photocopied handout featuring satirical news items about local personalities and events, *The Onion* ultimately became a mock newspaper satirizing politics, economics, and society. Begun by students at the University of Wisconsin, Madison, in 1988, it slowly began to gather a following of dedicated readers, even as it expanded its coverage to national and international issues. *The Onion* looked like the national newspaper *USA Today*, but all of the stories in the paper were fictional. The paper's best articles have been collected in several books, and a mock anthology of the most important news events of the twentieth century appeared in *Our Dumb Century* (1999). In 1996, *The Onion* went online, and its readership expanded exponentially.

Power of Myth, The (nonfiction, by Joseph Campbell, 1988; television miniseries, 1988)

This book was derived from the hugely popular PBS miniseries of the same name, which consisted of interviews by Bill Moyers with author and scholar Joseph Campbell. Among the myths discussed and analyzed by Campbell are creation stories, myths of heroes, myths of sacrifice, myths of eternity, and myths of love. Campbell discusses both the origin of these motifs and how they impact our everyday lives. The miniseries also contains an interview with George Lucas, creator of the *Star Wars* movie phenomenon, who utilized the theories in Campbell's book to create his popular science fiction series.

Trump: The Art of the Deal (nonfiction, by Donald Trump with Tony Schwartz, 1987)

Perhaps no figure personified the worship of wealth, consumption, and greed of the 1980s better than New York City real-estate tycoon Donald Trump. With his name prominently displayed on a host of skyscrapers and his personal life splashed across the social pages of newspapers in New York and across the country, he became a larger-than-life figure. *Trump: The Art of the Deal* is a boastful but charming biography that also examines New York City real estate—financing, development, and construction—in great detail. As the book's title indicates, Trump also offers tips on how to make money and get the best out of business negotiations. A number one best-seller, the book has been read by those fascinated with Trump, as well as those eager to learn his money-making secrets.

USA Today (newspaper, 1982–present)

Launched in 1982 as the first national, non-financial, daily newspaper in the country, *USA Today* utilized the latest satellite and computer technology to produce a newspaper that would be nearly identical in format and coverage in every major city in the United States—and available locally every Monday through Friday. Offering national news, sports, and weather coverage, *USA*

Today features bold graphics and brief stories to capture an audience of commuters and business travelers. Critics mocked the publication's breezy, feel-good style as "McNews" (the journalistic equivalent of McDonald's fast food), but the formula has been a success with readers. Within two years, the paper had a daily circulation in excess of one million; by early 2006, that number had increased to nearly 2.3 million.

White Noise (novel, by Don DeLillo, 1985)

"It's about fear, death, and technology. A comedy, of course," author Don DeLillo said of his National Book Award-winning novel *White Noise,* the story of a modern American family, in which the parents suffer an all-consuming fear of death. Jack Gladney teaches Hitler studies at a small college; his wife, Babette, takes pills that erase her fear of mortality. An "airborne toxic event," a black cloud of poisonous fumes, shakes the family out of its indifference and into the social problems that surround them, introducing them to a world of deceit and violence. The black cloud, paradoxically, becomes a symbol of the white noise that all Americans had become accustomed to in the second half of the twentieth century—television broadcasts, sirens, computers humming, horns honking.

Film, Radio, Television, and Theater

Airplane! (film, directed by Jim Abrahams and David Zucker, 1980)

A parody of a popular movie genre of the 1970s, *Airplane!* takes the plot of a conventional disaster film and uses it as a vehicle for a series of silly visual and verbal gags by Leslie Nielsen and others. Robert Hays plays Ted Striker, a pilot who has given up his profession after developing a fear of flying. When his flight attendant girlfriend (played by Julie Hagerty) leaves him, Striker follows her onto the plane she's working on. Once in the air, things go badly and the phobic pilot is required to land the plane. *Airplane!* was the first in a series of movie parodies by directors Abrams and Zucker, including *Airplane II: The Sequel* (1982).

Amadeus (play, by Peter Shaffer, 1980; film, directed by Milos Forman, 1984)

Told in flashback by Antonio Salieri, portrayed as a half-mad composer incarcerated in an insane asylum, the play and movie tell the fictional story of Salieri and

Wolfgang Amadeus Mozart, two musical rivals at the court of the Austro-Hungarian Empire in the late eighteenth century. The older Salieri is presented as a mediocre talent who takes the task of musical composition seriously. The much younger Mozart, by contrast, appears frivolous in his habits but is a true genius. Brilliant compositions seem to come to Mozart effortlessly, as if God has appointed him a vehicle for music of celestial beauty. The great irony is that Salieri is the person at court most able to appreciate Mozart's genius, even as he despises him personally. Ultimately, Salieri helps drive Mozart to an early grave.

The play and the film were highly praised by critics, won multiple awards, and were popular with audiences. But historians have pointed out that *Amadeus* took liberties with the real story: Mozart was not as eccentric and wild as portrayed, and Salieri was highly respected for his musical talents in his own time.

America's Most Wanted (television, 1988–present)

Hosted by John Walsh, whose own child had been murdered some years before, the show aims to assist in the capture of "America's most wanted" criminals. Each episode portrays several wanted criminals and reenacts their crimes in the hope that someone watching will have information about one of the criminals that might help lead to an arrest. For crimes that occurred far in the past, a computerized "age-lapsed" rendering of what the person might look like in later life is presented. As a result of the show, more than 3,000 criminals who had escaped capture for decades have been brought to justice. The show reflected both the rising victims' rights movement and tough-on-crime attitudes of the past two decades.

Back to the Future (film, directed by Robert Zemeckis, 1985)

A hugely successful film that spawned several popular sequels, *Back to the Future* stars Michael J. Fox as Marty McFly, a high school student from the small California town of Hill Valley who accidentally travels back in time to the 1950s to witness the meeting of his future mother and father. Unfortunately, as Marty learns, his father is a social misfit incapable of asking his mother on a date. If the two do not get together, Marty will never be born. Aided by the same mad scientist who invented the time machine in the first place (but, of course, when he was thirty years younger), Marty is able to bring his parents together

and go "back to the future." A 1989 sequel carries Marty into the future, and a third release in 1990 takes him back to the Old West.

Big Chill, The (film, directed by Lawrence Kasdan, 1983)

Perhaps the most successful of a string of early 1980s movies and television shows in which characters in their thirties contemplate where their lives have taken them thus far, *The Big Chill* features an all-star cast of characters who gather for the funeral of a mutual friend—the one who had seemed the most confident and the most likely to succeed. (The corpse is played by then-unknown Kevin Costner). Each of the characters has a unique personality and different life experiences. One (William Hurt) is an angry Vietnam veteran rendered impotent by an injury; another is a woman (Mary Kay Place) who fears that her biological time clock is ticking too fast for her to have a baby. They all share the same rueful longing for the idealism of their past. The movie features what became a hit soundtrack with songs from the 1960s and 1970s.

Blade Runner (film, directed by Ridley Scott, 1982)

While science fiction films of the 1950s and 1960s envision a bright future of space adventure and a world in which robots do the drudge work, the films of the 1970s portray a bleaker future. None more so than *Blade Runner*. Based on the 1968 novel *Do Androids Dream of Electric Sheep?* by science fiction writer Philip K. Dick, *Blade Runner* presents a dystopian future. Set in Los Angeles in the year 2017, when the city's population has climbed to over 100 million, *Blade Runner* tells of a detective (played by Harrison Ford) given the assignment of tracking down a killer android. The film's fascination, however, has less to do with the plot than the details and haunting imagery of the world in which it is set. Acid rain falls steadily over a city where the inhabitants speak in a strange patois of immigrant tongues.

Blue Velvet (film, directed by David Lynch, 1986)

When a man (played by Kyle MacLachlan) returns to his hometown, he discovers a severed human ear in a field. Dissatisfied with the police's lackadaisical investigation, he teams up with the police detective's daughter (Laura Dern) to find out who is responsible. Their investigations lead them to a beautiful and mysterious woman (Isabella Rossellini), who appears to be the mistress or sex slave of a man with perverse sexual tastes (Dennis Hopper).

While director David Lynch was already known for the cult film *Eraserhead* (1977) and the more conventional *Elephant Man* (1980), *Blue Velvet* established his reputation as the premier creator of contemporary filmic surrealism, a reputation he would use to persuade ABC to broadcast the bizarre but popular miniseries *Twin Peaks*. Both *Blue Velvet* and *Twin Peaks*, set in disconcertingly bright Technicolor towns in the Pacific Northwest, have developed strong cult followings over the years.

Blues Brothers, The (film, directed by John Landis, 1980)

A big-budget vehicle for two alumni of *Saturday Night Live's* original cast—co-writers John Belushi and Dan Aykroyd—*The Blues Brothers* tells the story of two white Chicago blues musicians, Jake and Elwood Blues. Based on a skit from *SNL*, the plot follows the brothers' attempts to remain one step ahead of the law—they're wanted as parking ticket scofflaws—while trying to save an orphanage by hosting a charity blues concert. The film's running gag is of white men trying to act like stereotypical blues musicians, right down to their old-fashioned suits and dark glasses Along the way, the Blues Brothers engage in song-and-dance routines, with cameo appearances by top names in rhythm and blues, including Ray Charles and Aretha Franklin. Some African Americans, angry that two white men received millions of dollars to make a movie about the blues, criticized the movie for its racial stereotyping. A sequel called *Blues Brothers 2000* was released in 1998, but without Belushi, who died of a drug overdose in 1982.

Brazil (film, directed by Terry Gilliam, 1985)

Borrowing from both George Orwell and Franz Kafka, *Brazil* tells the story of a bureaucrat in a dystopian future society named Sam Lowry (played by Jonathan Pryce) who dreams of escaping his dreary life to a fantastical place which, for some reason, he associates with the name "Brazil." Due to a snafu—a bug lands on a typewriter, causing his name to be substituted for that of a man wanted by the omnipresent and omniscient security forces—Lowry is arrested on charges of terrorism. He tries to point out the error, but the bureaucracy is incapable of admitting a mistake. Lowry is imprisoned and tortured, even as he imagines he escapes.

Directed by Terry Gilliam, one of the creators of the British comedy series *Monty Python*, the film was a scandal in Hollywood for its huge cost overruns and excessive length. Originally released in shorter form with a happy ending, it was a modest hit that won a cult audience with its elaborate sets and intricate plot.

Breakfast Club, The (film, directed by John Hughes, 1985)

During the 1980s, a group of young actors became known as the "brat pack," after the 1950s and 1960s rat pack of Frank Sinatra and company. Among the new generation of stars were Emilio Estevez, Anthony Michael Hall, Judd Nelson, Molly Ringwald, and Ally Sheedy. Like the earlier group, the brat pack actors both worked together and, more importantly, were seen together in public and at social functions, developing a kind of group celebrity identity.

Inside the studio, the brat pack made several films together, of which *The Breakfast Club* was the most popular. The plot is simple: Assigned to Saturday morning detention, a mismatched group of high school students—a jock, a society princess, a geek, an outcast, and a miscreant—are at first hostile to each other. But, over course of the movie, they learn to understand and even come to like one another.

Brighton Beach Memoirs (play, 1983, by Neil Simon; film, directed by Gene Saks, 1986)

Another of Neil Simon's successful Broadway plays that were turned into hit Hollywood movies, *Brighton Beach Memoirs* was the first film in Simon's fictionalized autobiographical trilogy (with *Biloxi Blues* and *Broadway Bound*, neither of which was as popular as the first). *Brighton Beach Memoirs* portrays the life of Eugene, a young Jewish boy, modeled after Simon himself, growing up in an extended family in Brooklyn, New York. The play follows Eugene through puberty and sexual awakening. Jonathan Silverman stars as Eugene in the 1986 film.

Cagney and Lacey (television, 1982–1988)

On one level, *Cagney and Lacey* was a typical police drama. Two detectives—one tough and the other sensitive—investigate crimes and track down villains. But this very popular series differed from previous cop shows in two important ways. Most obviously, the two detectives were women. Mary Beth Lacey (played by Tyne Daly) was a wife and mother of young children, and Chris Cagney (Sharon Gless) was a single woman.

While largely set on the job, the show sometimes included elements of the women's private lives. The show also was unusual in its willingness to tackle major social issues of the day, often concerning women and work.

Cats (stage musical, by Andrew Lloyd Webber, 1982)
After 7,485 performances, *Cats* closed on September 10, 2000, as the longest-running musical in Broadway history. Based on T.S. Eliot's *Old Possum's Book of Practical Cats*, the show features the music of Andrew Lloyd Webber, a junkyard set, actors in cat suits, and a choreography that sends the characters off the stage and into the aisles of the theater. The plot is basic, telling of an annual feline get-together where the cats decide which one deserves a better life in the following year. Its long run on Broadway made *Cats* a must-see attraction for visitors to New York.

Cheers (television, 1982–1993)
One of the most popular situation comedies in the history of television, *Cheers* offered an ensemble cast of characters and an atypical setting for a television show—a neighborhood bar in Boston. Many of the plot lines revolved around the romantic and sexual tension between bar owner and bartender Sam Malone (played by Ted Danson), a womanizing ex-baseball pitcher, and an intellectually pretentious waitress, Diane Chambers (Shelley Long). Rounding out the comedic cast were the bar's eccentric regulars: a phlegmatic drunk (George Wendt), a pompous mailman (John Ratzenberger), a goofy co-bartender (Woody Harrelson), and a pretentious psychologist, Frasier Crane (Kelsey Grammer), later the star of the popular spin-off show *Frasier*.

Children of a Lesser God (play, by Mark Medoff, 1980; film, directed by Randa Haines, 1986)
Children of a Lesser God tells the story of a teacher (played by William Hurt in the film) at a school for the deaf whose job it is to teach the students how to speak aloud. At the school, he meets a beautiful but moody student named Sarah (Marlee Matlin). Sarah refuses to learn how to speak, insisting on signing only, but behind her stubbornness is a fear of venturing out of the school into the larger world. At first, Sarah shuns the teacher, but gradually, they fall in love. Sentimental and emotional, the film was a huge hit with audiences and picked up five Academy Award nominations. Matlin won the Oscar for best actress.

Common Threads: Stories from the Quilt (film, directed by Rob Epstein and Jeffrey Friedman, 1989)
When this film about the AIDS memorial quilt came out, controversy over the disease was widespread. Many AIDS sufferers were shunned by a public still ignorant about the nature of the illness and willing to blame the victims for the lifestyle that supposedly caused them to become ill. The film includes footage of the making of the quilt and its display on the Washington Mall, as well as interviews with those suffering from AIDS and their families and friends. According to AIDS activists, *Common Threads* put a face on the disease, and it has helped those suffering from it win social acceptance. The film won an Oscar for best feature-length documentary.

Cosby Show, The (television, 1984–1992)
Created by veteran comedian and television personality Bill Cosby, *The Cosby Show* was the most widely viewed situation comedy of the 1980s. In many ways, the show was typical of the genre and the times. Both parents were working professionals: husband Cliff Huxtable (Cosby) was a doctor and wife Clair (Phylicia Rashad), a lawyer. Most episodes revolved around the family, with one or another of the kids getting into trouble and being set straight by their father. Unlike 1950s comedies, however, this father was often sarcastic with his kids. What really set this sitcom apart was the fact that the Huxtables were black and upper middle class. Unique for a program featuring nearly an all-African American cast, *The Cosby Show* was popular with both white and black audiences.

Crossfire (television, 1982–2005)
While debate shows or debate segments of news shows had been airing on television for decades, none was as successful in drawing audiences as CNN's *Crossfire*. The format was simple: two hosts—one conservative and one liberal—took on the hot-button topic of the day, usually by grilling guest politicians and experts. The liberal host went after the conservatives, while the conservative host confronted the liberals. Much of the show's popularity was owed to its high emotional content. Unlike earlier debate programs, *Crossfire* dispensed with the niceties; hosts cut off guests and each other in midsentence, and debates often descended into shouting matches. Over the years, the show featured a number of prominent

hosts, including Pat Buchanan, Michael Kinsley, James Carville, and Mary Matalin, among others.

Day After, The (film, directed by Nicholas Meyer, 1983)

Released as a television movie at the height of the 1980s Cold War tension between the United States and the Soviet Union, *The Day After* depicts what would happen to a typical small town (in this case, Lawrence, Kansas) in the wake of a full-scale nuclear war. The movie opens with scenes of bucolic small town life, even as news of war tensions escalate on television and radio broadcasts. About one-third way into the film, missiles are launched, and nearby Kansas City is obliterated, leaving the residents of Lawrence to cope with the aftermath, including long days in fallout shelters, radiation sickness, and violence among survivors.

The movie proved highly controversial. Conservatives criticized ABC, the network that produced it, for playing into the hands of the liberal antinuclear movement and for failing to make it clear in the movie that the Soviets were responsible for the fictional war.

Die Hard (film, directed by John McTiernan, 1988)

This enormously popular action adventure film stars Bruce Willis as New York cop John McClane. Visiting his estranged wife in Los Angeles, he arrives at her company Christmas party. McClane becomes an unwitting hero when a band of supposed European terrorists takes over the company's headquarters and holds its employees hostage. The terrorists plan to blow up the building to cover up their heist of the company vault; in the meantime, they string along the police who hope to rescue the hostages. McClane, hidden inside the building, realizes the criminals' ultimate plan and tries to warn authorities. The bad guys are eventually killed, and McClane rescues his wife. Sequels appeared in 1990 and 1995, with a fourth *Die Hard* movie expected to release in 2007.

Diner (film, directed by Barry Levinson, 1982)

The early 1980s saw a series of popular films about young adults waxing nostalgic over their youth, including *The Return of the Secaucus 7* (1980) and *The Big Chill* (1983). A coming-of-age movie set in Levinson's beloved home town of Baltimore, *Diner* tells the story of a group of former teenage friends, now young men, who get together for the impending wedding of one of their own. Set in the 1950s, the film, written by Levinson, is semi-autobiographical. As the story progresses, the young men come to realize that their teenage years

are behind them, and it is time to move on. Comic and bittersweet, *Diner* was a box-office smash that launched the careers of director Levinson and several stars, including Steve Guttenberg and Mickey Rourke.

Do the Right Thing (film, directed by Spike Lee, 1989)

The decade of the 1980s witnessed a stream of violent racial incidents on the streets of New York and other large American cities. In *Do the Right Thing*, African American director Spike Lee attempts to create a fictional incident that borrows from reality. The movie follows life in a black neighborhood in Brooklyn on the hottest day of the summer. The central plot concerns the growing tension between the son of an Italian pizza parlor owner (played by John Turturro) and the restaurant's black customers; Mookie (played by Lee) is a delivery boy. By the end of the day, these tensions have led to confrontation, as an angry crowd surrounds the restaurant. At the climactic moment, Mookie throws a trash can through the window, setting off a riot that destroys the pizza parlor.

With its ambiguous ending—Mookie is neither sad nor proud of what he has done—the film tries to convey the unresolved nature of racial issues in modern America. Many African Americans were upset that the critically acclaimed film was overlooked for a best picture Academy Award nomination, especially since a sweeter, more conventional film regarding race, *Driving Miss Daisy*, won that same year.

Dynasty (television, 1981–1989)

In the spirit of *Dallas*, the 1970s hit show *Dynasty* chronicled the loves, intrigues, and adventures of an oil-rich family, this time, based in Denver. While each character in the show had his or her own story, the main plot line concerned the efforts of the family patriarch (played by John Forsythe) to fight off the aggressive business maneuvers of his ex-wife (Joan Collins), also in the oil business. Like *Dallas*, *Dynasty* filled a seemingly insatiable appetite of television viewers in the 1980s for tales about the rich, famous, powerful, and nasty.

Entertainment Tonight (television, 1981–present)

Hosted by Mary Hart, John Tesh, and Leeza Gibbons, *Entertainment Tonight* was a television first, a news show entirely devoted to celebrities and the entertainment business. A television version of such tabloid newspapers and magazines as the *National En-*

quirer and *People, ET*, as the show was often called, featured gossip, brief interviews, film clips, and movie reviews by critic Leonard Maltin. The show covered all branches of the entertainment industry—film, television, music, and even sports—featuring anything and anyone who happened to be in the headlines that week.

E.T. The Extra-Terrestrial (film, directed by Steven Spielberg, 1982)

The most popular movie ever made about space aliens, *E.T.* ("extraterrestial") tells the story of a cuddly but highly evolved alien who finds itself stranded in a Southern California suburb after fellow aliens on its spaceship accidentally leave it behind. Trouble begins when the government learns about the presence of the alien and tries to capture it. E.T. has been adopted by a group of protective neighborhood children, who, eventually, help E.T. "phone home" to its spaceship and return to its own kind.

The often-humorous juxtaposition of an ordinary suburb and an event of world-shaping importance is part of the film's popularity, as is the cast of cute young actors and a lovable alien. Some critics also have seen a Christ-like allegory in E.T.'s "death" and "resurrection" at the film's end. *E.T.* was nominated for nine Oscars, including best picture.

Fame (film, directed by Alan Parker, 1980; television, 1982–1987)

Both a popular feature-length film and a spin-off television series, *Fame* was set in New York City's High School for the Performing Arts. The story line explores the grinding regimen of practice and intensely competitive atmosphere in this incubator of performing arts talent. The movie focuses on four students, two brash and confident and two shy and sensitive. Adding to the film and television series' success were the many rousing dance and musical numbers performed by the students.

Family Ties (television, 1982–1989)

One of the most successful family situation comedies of the 1980s, *Family Ties* offered typical plotlines and characters, although, in a bow to the times, both parents were working professionals—the father (played by Michael Gross), a local public television station manager, and the mother (Meredith Baxter), an architect. The twist in the show was their relationship with their three children. The parents are former hippies who have stayed loyal to their liberal politics, despite the conservatism of the times. While they had hoped their children would adopt their politics, things have turned out differently. The two daughters—Mallory and Jennifer (Justine Bateman and Tina Yothers) are apathetic politically, and the teenage son Alex (Michael J. Fox) is an archconservative. The show capitalized on the changing mood of the country, as the liberal 1970s gave way to the more conservative 1980s.

Fast Times at Ridgemont High (novel, by Cameron Crowe, 1981; film, directed by Amy Heckerling, 1982)

Based on a 1981 novel by rock journalist Cameron Crowe, *Fast Times at Ridgemont High* follows the goings-on of students and teachers at a Southern California high school. While the teachers try to inspire the students, most of the latter are simply interested in having a good time. The main plotline concerns a surfer, Jeff Spicoli (played by Sean Penn), who is about to fail history until convinced by his teacher, Mr. Hand (Ray Walston), that the subject actually matters to his life. The enduringly popular film helped launch the careers of several stars, including Penn, Judge Reinhold, and Forest Whitaker.

Fatal Attraction (film, directed by Adrian Lyne, 1987)

A controversial hit movie, *Fatal Attraction* tells the story of a successful, happily married New York lawyer, Dan Gallagher (played by Michael Douglas), who enjoys what he thinks is an innocent affair with a female colleague, Alex (Glenn Close), one weekend while his wife and children are out of town. The emotionally unstable woman thinks the weekend has meant more than it did to him, however, and she begins to obsess over Dan. Her stalking him and his family leads to a bloody and shocking conclusion.

Feminists complained that the film stereotyped single women as mentally unbalanced and portrayed Gallagher, who was also a willing a participant in the affair, as the injured party. The controversy, of course, only drove more people to see the film, which enjoyed one of the biggest box office returns of the decade for a dramatic, adult-themed film.

Fences (play, by August Wilson, 1987)

This Pulitzer Prize-winning drama by African American playwright August Wilson tells the story of a father and a son in the 1960s. The two have a troubled relationship, reflecting the generational miscommunication of the times. The play revolves around issues of prejudice and racism and how they infect all aspects of African American life, even within the family. The father, who had played in baseball's Negro Leagues, was a bit too old to make it in the white major leagues after they integrated in the late 1940s. The son wants to play football, but his father, still wary of professional sports, tries to stop him. The father also wants the son to take more responsibility for his life and not repeat his own mistakes. Among the topics dealt with in the play are infidelity, alcoholism and, of course, race.

Field of Dreams (film, directed by Phil Alden Robinson, 1989)

Based on the 1982 novel *Shoeless Joe* by W.P. Kinsella, *Field of Dreams* tells the story of an Iowa corn farmer (played by Kevin Costner) who hears voices in the cornfields telling him, "If you build it, they will come." As the son of a failed baseball player, the farmer interprets this to mean that he must build a baseball diamond. Once complete, the field draws the ghosts of Shoeless Joe Jackson and others thrown out of professional baseball following the infamous Black Sox scandal of 1919. Confused about what it all means, the farmer seeks out the advice of a retired sportswriter (James Earl Jones) in Chicago, who helps him discover the importance of memory, tradition, and following one's heart. Despite its mystical tone and abstruse plot, the film was extremely popular with movie audiences and was nominated for a best picture Oscar.

First Blood (film, directed by Ted Kotcheff, 1982)

In the era of Reagan conservatism during the early 1980s, many Americans began to reassess the meaning of the Vietnam War. Increasingly, some politicians and the media began to view America's defeat there as the result of domestic opponents who refused to let the soldiers fight to win. One manifestation of this sentiment was the series of *Rambo* films, featuring action star Sylvester Stallone in the lead role.

In *First Blood*, John Rambo is a traumatized Vietnam vet who wanders from town to town, seeking friends from his war years. In one town, he is arrested and tortured by a sadistic sheriff until he calls upon the fighting skills he honed in the military to escape. *First Blood* spawned two sequels (*Rambo: First Blood Part II* in 1985 and *Rambo III* in 1988), in which the title character goes to Vietnam and Afghanistan, respectively, to rescue captured U.S. soldiers. All three *Rambo* films were criticized by liberals for gratuitous violence and distorting the history of Vietnam.

Ghostbusters (film, directed by Ivan Reitman, 1984)

An enormously successful horror-comedy film starring two alumni of *Saturday Night Live*, Dan Aykroyd and Bill Murray, *Ghostbusters* tells the improbable story of a team of three spirit investigators (the third played by Harold Ramis) called in whenever there is trouble with ghosts and demons. Academics who have been fired after their grants have run out, the three set up a ghost-busting firm—only to be shut down by an overzealous government bureaucrat. But when an ancient Sumerian god is resurrected in the city, the team is called back into action. Silly and spirited, the movie featured a hit song of the same name and inspired a less than successful sequel in 1989.

Glory (film, directed by Edward Zwick, 1989)

This movie tells the true story of the all-black 54th Massachusetts Infantry, which served with distinction in the Civil War. The plot, derived from the letters of Colonel Robert Gould Shaw (played by Matthew Broderick), the white abolitionist commander who led the regiment, follows the militia from its creation to its baptism of fire at the battle of Fort Wagner, South Carolina. Denzel Washington and Morgan Freeman play two of the soldiers in the company. Besides showing the horrors of war, the movie also depicts the racism in both the Union and Confederate Armies. While parts of the film are fictionalized, it offers a realistic portrayal of the experiences of African American troops on and behind the battle lines. Washington won an Oscar for best supporting actor.

Heidi Chronicles, The (play, by Wendy Wasserstein, 1989; film, directed by Paul Bogart, 1995)

The best-known work of playwright Wendy Wasserstein, *The Heidi Chronicles* follows the life of a young woman of the baby boom generation trying to make her way in a society dominated by men. Many hailed the play as a feminist masterpiece, depicting a smart, strong, female character overcoming obstacles, while maintaining her humanity. Some critics thought the message was diluted by Wasserstein's penchant for the humor of television sitcoms and a pat ending; others said that Heidi, who speaks little in the company of her talkative male friends, was no feminist heroine at all. The play was made into a modestly successful movie starring Jamie Lee Curtis in 1995.

Hill Street Blues (television, 1981–1987)

The first television hit by innovative producer Steven Bochco, *Hill Street Blues* was a groundbreaking drama series about a police station in an unnamed American city. While police shows are almost as old as television itself, *Hill Street Blues* was the first to show officers as everyday human beings. There was plenty of crime-fighting action, to be sure, but many of the show's episodes focused on the private lives of the characters or the ordinary intrigues of the stationhouse—from love affairs to feuds. Never receiving very high ratings, the show nevertheless won a modest following of devoted fans who kept it on the air for seven seasons.

L.A. Law (television, 1986–1994)

A hugely successful television series by Steven Bochco, the creator of *Hill Street Blues*, *L.A. Law* featured a similar ensemble cast and episodes that interwove stories about the characters' professional and personal lives. As the title indicates, the show was set in a high-powered Los Angeles law firm. Episodes usually had a central plot line involving a major case one of the lawyers was trying, along with a number of subplots about minor and often comical cases or involving romantic relationships among the members of the firm. Like other popular shows of the 1980s, *L.A. Law* glamorized the rich and powerful, even as it tried to put forth a message that human relationships are more important than mere money and power. The show won fifteen Emmys in its nine-year run on NBC.

Larry King Live (television, 1985–present)

Call-in shows were long popular on radio, and talk shows were long popular on television, when journalist Larry King decided to combine the two for the upstart Cable News Network (CNN) in 1985. With his trademark suspenders and rambling style, King has interviewed many of the most high-profile personalities in America, from entertainment and politics alike. The only common denominator among the broad diversity of guests and topics has been timeliness—all were at the forefront of the news when they were interviewed. Critics of the show have said that King goes easy on his guests, asking them "soft" questions; admirers have countered that this has been his adept way of putting guests at ease so they reveal more about themselves.

Late Night/Late Show with David Letterman (television, 1982–1993, 1993–present)

At once a conventional late night talk show host and television innovator, David Letterman, a former local weatherman in Indiana, turned the genre upside down with his first show *Late Night*, which aired weeknights after the hugely popular *Tonight Show with Johnny Carson*. Letterman revolutionized the talk show format in major ways: He interviewed guests in a more confrontational manner than other hosts, lacing his questions and the show's opening monologue with ironic commentary, and he broke free of the studio format, going out in public to stage absurd pranks (even if the show's most popular features—Stupid Pet Tricks and the Top Ten List—were largely done in-studio). When Letterman was passed over in favor of Jay Leno as host of *The Tonight Show* upon Carson's retirement in 1992, he took his act to CBS. Fans of Letterman, however, have complained that the CBS show has less of an edge than its predecessor.

Les Misérables (stage musical, by Alain Boublil, Claude-Michel Schönberg, and Herbert Kretzmer, 1987; film, directed by Bille August, 1998)

Originating in Paris, moving to London, and opening on Broadway in 1987, *Les Misérables* billed itself as the world's most popular musical. *(James Keyser/Time Life Pictures/Getty Images)*

Based on Victor Hugo's 1862 novel of Napoleonic France, *Les Misérables* follows the travails of Jean Valjean, a victim of social injustice—he spends some twenty years in prison for stealing bread—whose virtue and goodness remain intact despite the meanness and corruption of the world. Exploring similar themes of freedom and justice, the rousing musical opened on Broadway in 1987 and promptly won eight Tony Awards. After nearly 6,700 performances, the show finally closed in 2003. A film version, featuring Liam Neeson as Valjean, was released in 1998.

Married with Children (television, 1987–1997)

At first glance, *Married with Children* was a typical family situation comedy—working father, stay-at-home mother, teenage daughter, and preteen son. But the tone of the show was very different from any previous family sitcom: It was, in a word, crude. Al, the father (played by Ed O'Neill), was a rude, misanthropic man who hated his wife and barely tolerated his children. The sex-starved wife Peg (Katey Segal) had equal contempt for her husband. The teenage daughter Kelly (Christina Applegate) was a loose sexpot who constantly teased her younger brother Bud (David Faustino). When the show first aired in 1987, critics charged the upstart Fox network with bringing television to a new low, but audiences loved the crudeness, understanding that much of it was tongue in cheek.

Miami Vice (television, 1984–1989)

A highly popular police drama, *Miami Vice* proved influential in several ways. By borrowing the fast cuts and pounding sound tracks of music videos, techniques since imitated in many police dramas, it added hipness and urgency to the episodes. It also helped change the image of Miami from a tired retirement village to a trendy, colorful hotspot. Perhaps most of all, it changed the sartorial style and shaving habits of millions of men, as the two stars—Don Johnson and Philip Michael Thomas—wore pastel colored suits, collarless shirts, and no socks, and let their facial hair grow to stubble length. Beyond that, the show featured standard plots of crime fighting, with an emphasis on drugs as befitting its day and locale.

Moonlighting (television, 1985–1989)

At once a romantic comedy and detective show, *Moonlighting* starred Bruce Willis as David Addison, Jr., a wisecracking private investigator, and Cybill Shepherd as Maddie Hayes, an ex-model and his new boss. While the plots were typical of private eye movies and shows—finding clues, following leads, nabbing bad guys—much of what made *Moonlighting* popular was the romantic and sexual tension between the two stars. The show was a further departure from standard fare in its willingness to penetrate the theatrical "fourth wall," with the actors occasionally stepping out of character to address the audience directly. *Moonlighting* went off the air not because of declining popularity but because of the burgeoning movie career of Willis, who left the show in 1989.

Moonstruck (film, directed by Norman Jewison, 1987)

A popular romantic comedy that won its star, the pop singer Cher, an Academy Award for best actress, *Moonstruck* tells the story of a widowed accountant, Loretta Castorini, living with her eccentric Italian American family in a Brooklyn brownstone. Several years have passed since her husband's accidental death, and Loretta is ready to get married again, this time to a kindly neighborhood baker, Johnny Cammareri (Danny Aiello). But along the way she meets his sexy but moody brother Ronny (Nicholas Cage) and has to choose between them. The quirky comedy was acclaimed by critics as well as by audiences.

Murphy Brown (television, 1988–1998)

Featuring film star Candice Bergen as the title character, *Murphy Brown* followed the doings of the cast and crew of a fictional television news magazine called FYI, of which Brown was co-anchor. Set in Washington, the show poked fun at real-life politics and politicians, usually with a liberal slant. Outside the newsroom, the show also included episodes about Brown's home life as a single working woman. During the 1992 season, Brown—realizing her biological clock was ticking—decided to have a baby without getting married. The story line captured national attention when Vice President Dan Quayle cited it as an example of how television was helping compromise America's "family values."

Nightline (television, 1980–present)

Hosted from the beginning by veteran television journalist Ted Koppel, *Nightline* hit the airwaves during the Iranian hostage crisis. Much of its coverage during the first year focused on that situation, but the late-night show won a solid audience with its in-depth coverage of a single topic in each installment. ABC decided to keep it on the air after the hostages were released in January 1981, and the show has continued to win praise for its commentaries by Koppel (and guest hosts), interviews with newsmakers, and short films providing background to whatever story is being covered that night. *Nightline* remained the only late-night news program on network television in the early 2000s. Koppel left the show in 2006.

Oprah Winfrey Show, The (television, 1986–present)

One of the most popular and influential daytime talk shows in the history of television, *The Oprah Winfrey Show* generally has taken the high ground, dealing with important topics in a sober fashion—especially compared to competitors such as *The Jerry Springer Show*. Most afternoon installments include a panel of guests discussing an important topic related to culture, health, education, and other areas of interest to women. The panels include both experts and ordinary people who have firsthand experience with the issue being discussed. Winfrey presides over the discussion and invites questions from the live studio audience. Promoting good books is one of Winfrey's passions, and the titles she introduces on the show often become best-sellers.

Ordinary People (novel, by Judith Guest, 1976; film, directed by Robert Redford, 1980)

Based on the best-selling novel by Judith Guest, the film tells the story of an upper-middle-class family who live in an exclusive lakeshore suburb of Chicago and the tragedy they endure. After the oldest son dies in a boating accident, the surviving members of the family grieve in their own ways and come into emotional conflict with each other. The tightly strung, overbearing mother (played by Mary Tyler Moore), who was very close to the dead boy, grows increasingly angry with the moody younger son (Timothy Hutton). The father (Donald Sutherland) is kindly, but he finds it difficult to keep mother and son from coming to verbal blows. Honest, brooding, and emotionally charged, *Ordinary People* struck a chord with audiences and won Oscars for best picture, best director, best adapted screenplay, and best supporting actor.

Pee-wee's Playhouse (television, 1986–1990)

A raucous children's show that aired on Saturday mornings, *Pee-wee's Playhouse* starred Pee-wee Herman (played by Paul Reubens) as a goofy and nerdy character with a subversive sense of humor. Dressed in a bow tie and speaking in an annoying (at least to adults) nasal voice, Herman led young viewers through a surrealistic studio set filled with a host of crazy imaginary friends. *Pee-wee's Playhouse* was essentially an update of traditional children's variety shows for the more ironic 1980s. It inspired several popular children's movies, including *Pee-wee's Big Adventure* (1985), *Back to the Beach* (1987), and *Big Top Pee-wee* (1988), before the star was arrested in Florida on morals charges in 1991.

Phantom of the Opera, The (stage musical, by Andrew Lloyd Webber and Charles Hart, 1988; film, directed by Joel Schumacher, 2004)

The second-longest-running musical in Broadway history, after *Cats*, *The Phantom of the Opera* was another hit by the acclaimed composer, director, and producer Andrew Lloyd Webber. Based on the 1911 novel of the same name by French author Gaston Leroux, which had been made into a number of films over the years, *Phantom* tells the story of a horribly disfigured man who hides behind a mask and lives in the bowels of a Paris opera house, where he falls in love with a beautiful singer and attempts to lure her down to his lair. Following its 1988 opening on Broadway, the show toured on every continent except Antarctica. The musical was turned into a film in 2004 starring Gerard Butler as the Phantom and Emmy Rossum as Christine, the singer.

Platoon (film, directed by Oliver Stone, 1986)

One of the most critically acclaimed and popular films about the war in Vietnam, *Platoon* recounts the experiences of a college student (played by Charlie Sheen) who volunteers for the infantry and is assigned to a platoon commanded by two sergeants—one good (Willem Dafoe) and one evil (Tom Berenger). Following members of the platoon as they patrol, fight, kill, and die in the jungles of Vietnam, the movie focuses on the massacre of civilian villagers precipitated by the evil sergeant. The brutality of war, and of the Vietnam conflict in particular, is portrayed in stark imagery and unflinching honesty. *Platoon* was the first in director Oliver Stone's film trilogy on the Vietnam War, followed by the successful *Born on the Fourth of July* (1989) and the less than successful *Heaven and Earth* (1993).

Raging Bull (film, directed by Martin Scorsese, 1980)

Based on the 1970 autobiography of former middleweight boxing champion Jake La Motta, *Raging Bull* goes beyond the standard sports biography picture, exploring the depths of his anger and violence in and out of the ring. Filmed in black and white, with veteran actor and Scorsese film regular Robert De Niro as La Motta, the film shocked audiences with its graphic depictions of his physical abuse of his wife and pugilistic fury against ring opponents. Boxing scenes are filmed in tight close-ups, showing the tremendous impact of La Motta's fists in slow motion. De Niro, who put on dozens of pounds to portray La Motta in his postfighting years, won an Academy Award for best actor.

Raiders of the Lost Ark (film, directed by Steven Spielberg, 1981)

In *Raiders of the Lost Ark*, director Steven Spielberg and writer George Lucas paid homage to the serial adventure films of the 1930s and 1940s—and, in doing so, scored a hit with modern audiences. The film is set in the 1940s and features a larger-than-life hero in Indiana Jones (played by Harrison Ford), a mild-mannered archaeology professor at home and a swashbuckling adventurer abroad, who uses his fists and trademark whip to get himself out of scrapes with villains. The plot focuses on the biblical Ark of the Covenant, sought by Nazis for the immense powers it is said to possess. To prevent the bad guys from getting the Ark, Jones travels to Egypt, where he runs into a sassy former girlfriend (Karen Allen). Together, they thwart the Germans and bring the Ark back to the United States. *Raiders of the Lost Ark* was one of the highest grossing pictures up to that time, and it spawned two successful sequels—*Indiana Jones and the Temple of Doom* (1984) and *Indiana Jones and the Last Crusade* (1989).

Rain Man (film, directed by Barry Levinson, 1988)

A traditional road movie with a twist, *Rain Man* tells the story of two brothers, Raymond (played by Dustin Hoffman) and Charlie (Tom Cruise). Raymond, institutionalized for autism, thrives on routine, has difficulty relating to other people, and displays astonishing powers of mathematical calculation. Charlie is a self-absorbed, smooth-talking hustler, whose wealthy father disowned him. When the father dies, he leaves his money to Raymond, and Charlie plots to take it away from him. Kidnapping Raymond from the hospital, Charlie takes him on a cross-country trip; along the way, he cashes in on his brother's calculation skills in a casino. During the course of the trip, however, Charlie comes to reassess his own character and undergoes a transformation. The performances of two of Hollywood's biggest stars made the film a hit. It also won Oscars for best picture, best director, and best actor (Hoffman).

Red Dawn (film, directed by John Milius, 1984)

Red Dawn tells the story of an imagined Soviet invasion of the United States, focusing on the effects of a Communist takeover in a small middle-American town. The story revolves around a group of high school students and refugees who go underground and turn themselves into a guerrilla force called the Wolverines. Together, they help turn the tide on the town's Communist occupiers. Released at the height of the 1980s Cold War, the movie draws on elements taken straight from the speeches of Ronald Reagan. The Soviets, for example, use Nicaragua as a base for launching their invasion of the United States. Once in charge, they establish concentration camps, known as reeducation centers, persecute religious organizations, and nationalize wealth and property.

River's Edge, The (film, directed by Tim Hunter, 1986)

A disturbing portrayal of high-school students in a small Northern California town and based on a real-life event, *The River's Edge* begins with a murder. A student named Samson has killed another student and shows his friends the body. Rather than condemn him or immediately turn him in, his friends have mixed reactions. Some want him to go to jail, others tell him to flee the state, and one ultimately informs the police. The low-budget film enjoyed a popular following for its real-life portrayal of teenagers caught on the horns of a moral dilemma, faced with the choice of standing together with their friend or obeying the law and social norms.

Roger and Me (film, directed by Michael Moore, 1989)

The film that helped establish Michael Moore as a preeminent documentary filmmaker and liberal gadfly, *Roger and Me* chronicles his pursuit of Roger Smith, the CEO of General Motors (GM) at a time when the huge automaker was closing its factories in Moore's hometown of Flint, Michigan, leaving behind an economically devastated landscape. Along the way, Moore encounters the victims of GM's policies, as well as various spokespersons for the corporation and others. The movie was the first to showcase Moore's talent for putting powerful people on camera and asking them uncomfortable questions. Its mix of humor, pathos, and social commentary made it a surprising hit with audiences across the country and around the world.

Roseanne (television, 1988–1997)

Based on a semiautobiographical character developed in standup routines by comedian Roseanne Barr, Roseanne (which starred Barr as Roseanne Conner) was unique for its time, portraying the comic trials and tribulations of a working-class family. The show had its share of typical sitcom one-liners, usually at the expense of husband Dan (John Goodman), but it also dealt with issues of importance to ordinary American families, including a number of episodes about the previously taboo on TV subject of making ends meet. Roseanne was also unusual for its less than happy endings and for the fact that the two stars were both overweight and less than glamorous.

Rush Limbaugh Show, The (radio, 1988–present)

Conservative talk show host Rush Limbaugh has become one of the most popular radio personalities in America since the late 1980s. His three-hour daily program, which retained its popularity through both Republican and Democratic administrations, has provided commentary from the host on late-breaking news and the activities of political and cultural personalities, calls from listeners—who affectionately call themselves "ditto heads," for their admittedly slavish acceptance of Limbaugh's views—and musical parodies, all with an unabashedly anti-Democrat and antiliberal bias. Limbaugh has capitalized on his enormous popularity with conservative listeners by publishing several books (including *The Way Things Ought to Be*, the number one nonfiction best-seller of 1992), a nationally distributed newsletter, and a short-lived television show in 1992. Critics of the radio program have charged that Limbaugh plays fast and loose with the facts—a charge that has left his legions of fans as unfazed as his 2003 admission of prescription drug abuse.

Seinfeld (television, 1989–1998)

A show that proclaimed to be about "nothing," *Seinfeld* has been selected by *TV Guide* magazine as the number one television program of all time. Starring the comedic ensemble of Jerry Seinfeld, Jason Alexander, Julia Louis-Dreyfus, and Michael Richards as shallow-minded, single friends living in New York City, *Seinfeld* took the most mundane aspects of life in the 1990s—dating, unemployment, eating out, going to the movies—and made them into the stuff of comedy. The show generated "water-cooler conversations" across the country, as people at work and in social situations discussed the exploits of Jerry, a stand-up comedian; George, a quintessential loser; Elaine, Jerry's neurotic ex-girlfriend; and Kramer, the wacky neighbor across the hall. *Seinfeld* aired on the NBC network for nine seasons. Its final episode in May 1998 was watched by 76 million viewers and ended with the four characters sentenced to prison for, essentially, being shallow. In syndication, the show has continued to be one of the most watched on television.

sex, lies and videotape (film, directed by Steven Soderbergh, 1989)

Independent film was not born in 1989 (many directors had long worked outside of the studio system), but it did achieve a new popularity and critical acclaim largely because of Steven Soderbergh's *sex, lies and videotape* of that year. The making of the film became legendary in Hollywood circles: The twenty-nine-year-old Soderbergh wrote the script in eight days and directed the film for just $1.8 million. A movie made for so little, whose sexiest moments occurred in conversation, could only be independent, but *sex, lies and videotape* found a large audience for its story of four people in sexual entanglements—a husband and wife who no longer have sex, the wife's sister (who is having an affair with the husband), and an impotent friend who videotapes women talking about their sexual fantasies. Purchased by a small studio called Miramax, *sex, lies and videotape* won the FIPRESCI Prize for best picture and the best actor award at the Cannes Film Festival. The film grossed more than $100 million, made Soderbergh one of Hollywood's most sought-after directors, and made Miramax the new home of small films.

Shining, The (novel, by Stephen King, 1977; film, directed by Stanley Kubrick, 1980; film, directed by Mick Garris, 1997)

Based on a best-selling horror novel by Stephen King, the 1980 film tells the story of a man and his family who agree to serve as caretakers of a deserted hotel high in the Colorado Rockies in the winter off-season. Jack Torrance, the father (played by Jack Nicholson), hopes to use the quiet months to write his novel. But the Overlook Hotel is full of murderous memories, and son Danny's psychic visions ("the shining") bring them rushing into the present, causing Jack to descend into madness. Kubrick's gothic horror and Nicholson's riveting performance terrified audiences and made the film a hit. King was reportedly unhappy with Kubrick's version, however; he worked with director Mick Garris on a 1997 film, released on television, that more closely followed his novel.

Simpsons, The (television, 1989–present)

The Simpsons is the longest-running sitcom of all time—and a cartoon. Not since *The Flintstones* in the 1960s has an animated program managed to hold its own in prime time. The program has become an American institution, satirizing popular culture and reflecting the foibles of a typical American family in each thirty-minute episode. *The Simpsons* first aired as a series of shorts on *The Tracey Ullman Show* and then in a December 1989 Christmas special. In January 1990, it became part of the Fox network's regular Sunday night lineup. Ironic and irreverent, the show chronicles the life of the Simpson family—Homer, the well-meaning but doltish and lazy father; Marge, the no-nonsense mother; Bart, the precocious son; Lisa, the brainy daughter; and toddler Maggie. The town of Springfield—an American "anytown"—with its cast of crazy residents, is the setting for their misadventures.

St. Elsewhere (television, 1982–1988)

American television in the 1980s excelled at drama, with such shows as *Hill Street Blues*, *Cagney and Lacey*, *thirtysomething*, and *St. Elsewhere*. The multiple storyline concept of *Hill Street Blues* shifted from a police station to a hospital in the acclaimed series *St. Elsewhere*, set in the fictional St. Eligius hospital in South Boston. It was a hospital of last resort, where patients turned when they were rejected by other facilities. Episodes followed the large cast, both in and out of the hospital, and addressed such emerging topics as homelessness, the spread of AIDS, and the rise of HMOs.

Beginning in October 1982, the show aired for six seasons, despite modest ratings, and the last episode aired in May 1988. It received thirteen Emmy Awards, primarily for acting and writing. It also launched the careers of several well-known film and television actors, including Tim Robbins, Denzel Washington, Ed Begly, Jr., David Morse, Howie Mandel, Mark Harmon, and Alfre Woodard.

Terminator, The (film, directed by James Cameron, 1984)

A sci-fi classic that made Arnold Schwarzenegger a star, *The Terminator* grossed nearly $40 million at the box office and made "I'll be back" a popular catchphrase. Schwarzenegger plays a cyborg—robotic components overlaid with human flesh—from the year 2029. He is sent to 1984 Los Angeles to kill Sarah Connor (played by Linda Hamilton), future mother of the man who will save the human race from the machines that will rule the world in the future. Also sent back in time to save her is Kyle Reese (Michael Biehn), a guerrilla fighter and father of her son.

The Terminator is a frightening look at the present and the future, worlds increasingly dependent on machines that feel "no pain, no pity, and no fear." Directed by James Cameron, the film is loaded with special effects and exciting action sequences that made it extremely popular with audiences. Sequels to *The Terminator* followed in 1991 and 2003. Schwarzenegger went on to star in some of the most popular action films of the 1980s and 1990s.

Thin Blue Line, The (film, directed by Errol Morris, 1988)

The Thin Blue Line was described by film critic Roger Ebert as a "documentary and drama, investigation and reverie, a meditation on the fact that Randall Adams was plucked from the center of his life and locked up forever for a crime that no reasonable person could seriously believe he committed." Directed by Errol Morris, the making of *The Thin Blue Line* resulted in Adams being released from a life sentence for the murder of a Dallas police officer in 1976.

Morris spent thirty months researching the case, putting the pieces together, interviewing witnesses and judges. He used dramatization, interviews, newspaper accounts, and diagrams for the film, resulting in a powerful condemnation of the Texas criminal justice system. In the film, Morris implies that the "thin blue line" of police officers charged with guarding the public safety also can threaten that safety in the name of justice. *The Thin Blue Line* is often shown in criminal justice classes and by those campaigning against the death penalty. The haunting score by Philip Glass and the intensity with which Morris pursued the truth makes *The Thin Blue Line* one of the most critically acclaimed documentaries ever made.

thirtysomething (television, 1987–1991)

The 1980s were filled with nostalgic attempts by baby boomers to reconcile their current middleclass existence with the more exciting lives they led in the 1960s. Protests, rock and roll, and psychedelic Volkswagen vans had been replaced by work, family, and station wagons. In theaters, *The Big Chill* (1983) captured the musings of the baby boomers, while on television, *thirtysomething* turned their lives into weekly drama. The program's look and soundtrack came to characterize the 1980s, a decade of looking back and looking forward.

Michael and Hope Steadman, Elliot and Nancy Weston, Gary Shepherd, Ellyn Warren—they were yuppies through and through, young urban professionals struggling to make the most of their marriages and careers. At times, *thirtysomething* bordered on sappy, but critics called it television drama at its best; "as close to the level of an art form as weekly television ever gets," *The New York Times* said. Created by Edward Zwick and Marshall Herskovitz, who went on to create other critically acclaimed dramas, *thirtysomething* aired on ABC from 1987 to 1991 and won an Emmy Award in 1988 for outstanding drama series.

This Is Spinal Tap (film, directed by Rob Reiner, 1984)

Since the Beatles raced around England in *A Hard Day's Night* (1964), viewers have enjoyed watching movies about rock and roll bands. Documentaries such as *Don't Look Back*, about Bob Dylan, *Gimme Shelter*, about the Rolling Stones, and *The Last Waltz*, about The Band, glamorized the rock lifestyle, while also satisfying curiosity about what went on behind the scenes of a rock tour. In 1984, director Rob Reiner parodied these films with a "mockumentary" about a fictional British heavy metal band called Spinal Tap on tour in the United States. Incompetent, accident-prone, and clueless, members of Spinal Tap believe they are the best band around. Starring Christopher Guest, Michael McKean, and Harry Shearer in largely improvised roles, *This Is Spinal Tap* was a cult hit that exposed the ridiculousness of the music business and skewered the most popular bands of the day.

Thorn Birds, The (novel, by Colleen McCullough, 1977; television, 1983)

Based on a 1977 best-selling novel by Colleen McCullough, *The Thorn Birds* was a popular miniseries that aired on ABC in 1983. It was the epic story of the Australian Cleary family, chronicling their lives over more than forty years. The central character, a priest played by Richard Chamberlain, was also the most controversial character, torn between the priesthood and his love for the family's only daughter, Meggie. This and other dramatic elements made *The Thorn Birds* extremely popular; it was watched by 110 million to 140 million viewers for part or all of its ten hours. The episode in which Father Ralph and Meggie consummated their relationship was the fourth-highest rated show in television history to that time. This was the height of television's miniseries craze that included *Roots* (1977), *Shogun* (1980), and *The Winds of War* (1983).

Times of Harvey Milk, The (film, directed by Rob Epstein, 1984)

Harvey Milk was the first openly gay person elected to public office in California. He served on the San Francisco Board of Supervisors from 1978 to 1979, when he and the mayor of San Francisco were shot and killed by another supervisor, Dan White, a former policeman. *The Times of Harvey Milk*, released in 1984, was a documentary chronicling Milk's rise in San Francisco politics and the turmoil that erupted after his murder. Directed by Rob Epstein, who had used the documentary format to tell other stories about American gays and lesbians, the film made Milk a hero to the gay community. Narrated by *Torch Song Trilogy* writer Harvey Fierstein, *The Times of Harvey Milk* received an Academy Award for best documentary, features, and the George Foster Peabody Award for excellence in broadcasting.

Tootsie (film, directed by Sydney Pollack, 1982)

Actor Dustin Hoffman had tears in his eyes when talking about *Tootsie* for an American Film Institute television special. To him, *Tootsie* was much more than a drag comedy in the tradition of *Some Like It Hot* (1959) and *Victor/Victoria* (1982). His time spent dressed as a woman for the role of an out-of-work actor who lands a job as an actress on a soap opera gave him insight, he claimed, into the life of women in 1980s America. *Tootsie*, directed by Sydney Pollack, explores some heavy themes for a comedy—acting, deception and disguise, love, and gender. Its intricate romance plot—a man posing as a woman in love with a woman and a man in love with a man posing as a woman—has all the twists of a Shakespeare play. The film is uproariously funny, but it is Hoffman's performance and obvious affection for his role as Dorothy Michaels that gives it added depth. *Tootsie* received ten Academy Award nominations, including best picture, but only Jessica Lange won an Oscar for her supporting role as Hoffman's love interest.

Top Gun (film, directed by Tony Scott, 1986)

Starring Tom Cruise as a brash young fighter pilot, *Top Gun* is a Cold War movie set to a rock soundtrack that was a huge hit with audiences in 1986. It glamorizes military life on an aircraft carrier, where "the need for speed" fuels staged air battles, overly aggressive volleyball matches, and off-base hijinks. The final air clash with Soviet fighter jets results in an American victory and new respect for Cruise's Maverick, a rule breaker despised by the military brass. In spirit and theme, *Top Gun* epitomized the nationalism and military bravado of Americans in the Cold War 1980s.

Torch Song Trilogy (stage musical, by Harvey Fierstein, 1982; film, directed by Paul Bogart, 1988)

The play *Torch Song Trilogy* opened on Broadway on June 10, 1982, one of the first mainstream theatrical productions to feature homosexual themes. It originally appeared off-Broadway as three plays—*The International Stud*, *Fugue in a Nursery*, and *Widows and Children First*—that were combined into *Torch Song Trilogy*. Written by and starring Harvey Fierstein as a drag queen looking for love and acceptance, *Torch Song Trilogy* received the Tony Award for best play in 1983; Fierstein also received a Tony for best actor. In 1988, the play was made into a feature film, also starring Fierstein in the role of Arnold Beckoff. Matthew Broderick plays the role of Arnold's lover. On stage and screen, *Torch Song Trilogy* was a funny and touching look at gay life in the 1970s, before the AIDS catastrophe, when coming out and finding love were the biggest issues facing gay men.

True West (play, by Sam Shepard, 1980)

The play *True West* premiered in San Francisco in 1980 and then moved to New York City's Cherry Lane Theatre in 1982. The play portrays the dynamic between two brothers as they housesit for their mother. One brother is a Hollywood screenwriter, and the other a drifter and thief. During the course of the play, they alternately switch roles, as the thieving brother writes a screenplay and the scriptwriter commits petty larceny. Considered the most important work by influential playwright Sam Shepard, the play explores the duality within every person's character, as well as the superficiality of life in Southern California. In a 2000 Broadway revival, actors Philip Seymour Hoffman and John C. Reilly alternated the roles of the two brothers on different nights, adding a new dimension to the work's exploration of the dual nature of the human personality.

Urban Cowboy (film, directed by James Bridges, 1980)

Hot on the heels of his disco movie hit *Saturday Night Fever*, John Travolta played the title character in this film set in Houston, Texas. Bud, Travolta's character, an oil worker, spends many of his nights at a honky tonk bar, trying to prove his manhood by riding a mechanical bull. At the same time, the film follows his troubled relationship with his girlfriend Sissy, played by Debra Winger. The film's exploration of gender identity in the macho world of the Southwestern oil industry won it praise from critics. Its popularity with the movie-going public helped spread the reach of country music and line-dancing to more urban audiences and made mechanical bull-riding a fad in the early 1980s.

Victor/Victoria (film, directed by Blake Edwards, 1982; stage musical, by Blake Edwards, 1995)

Victor/Victoria, starring Julie Andrews in the title role, was popular on both stage and screen. As Victoria, a struggling singer who poses as a gay man in drag to find work in a stage show, Andrews brought dignity to a role that could have sunk into campy stereotype. Blake Edwards, her real-life husband, directed the film, which co-starred James Garner as a macho club owner who falls for Victor/Victoria. With humor and catchy songs by Henry Mancini, *Victor/Victoria* toyed with themes of gender perception, show business disguises, and sexual identity just as the country was beginning to look at homosexuality in a new light. The film, one of the last great musical comedies, was so popular that Edwards converted it into a Broadway show in 1995. It was an even bigger hit on stage, where it ran for 734 performances until July 1997.

Director Oliver Stone (right) poses with actor Charlie Sheen on the set of *Wall Street* (1987), a morality tale of the go-go 1980s. *(Mario Ruiz/Time Life Pictures/Getty Images)*

Wall Street (film, directed by Oliver Stone, 1987)

A scathing indictment of Wall Street in the go-go years of the 1980s, the movie tells the story of a young stockbroker named Bud Fox (Charley Sheen) who spends his free time trying to find a business deal that might link him to an extremely successful but ruthless broker, Gordon Gekko (Michael Douglas). Fox finally succeeds in working with Gekko—whose motto, "greed is good," became a popular catchphrase of the day—and starts to enjoy the money, power, and women that come with successful dealing on Wall Street. Eventually, however, Fox comes to learn that Gekko earns his fortune on the backs of ordinary workers. When one of the deals involves a company in which his father works, Fox turns on Gekko.

Wheel of Fortune (television, 1983–present)

In *Wheel of Fortune*, a top-rated television game show that has aired in syndication since 1983, contestants spin a wheel for dollar values and guess letters to fill in the blanks of a word or phrase (as in the old-fashioned word game "Hangman"). The first person to complete the word or phrase wins. Created by game show legend Merv Griffin, *Wheel of Fortune* debuted as a daytime game show in January 1975. In 1981, Pat Sajak, a fomer TV weatherman in Los Angeles, joined the show as its host. Turning the letters since 1982 has been Vanna White, a former model who became a household name and a key factor in the show's success. (White was recognized in *The Guinness Book of World Records* as "Television's Most Frequent Clapper.") The show's phrase, "I'd like to buy a vowel," became part of everyday usage. In 2003, *Wheel of Fortune* celebrated its 4,000th episode and was the number one syndicated series on television.

Witness (film, directed by Peter Weir, 1985)

Witness is a critically acclaimed film about a Philadelphia police detective hiding out with an Amish family in Pennsylvania's Amish country. Lukas Haas plays a wide-eyed Amish boy who witnesses a murder in a city train station. When the boy implicates a police officer in the crime and high-ranking corruption is revealed, Detective John Book (Harrison Ford) protects the boy and himself by moving to Lancaster, Pennsylvania, and passing as Amish. He finds the Amish alien yet appealing in their loyalty to family and community, and he falls for the widowed Rachel Lapp (Kelly McGillis). Directed by Peter Weir, *Witness* was nominated for best picture.

Wonder Years, The (television, 1988–1993)

In its six-year run on the ABC network, *The Wonder Years* appealed to baby boomers' sense of nostalgia for their 1960s childhoods. Narrated by Daniel Stern, the show starred Fred Savage as Kevin Arnold, the youngest child in a suburban family trying to cope with the sweeping changes of the 1960s. The gruff father, homemaker mother, hippie sister, and bullying older brother were used to define a unique era of American life. At the same time, Kevin's teenage problems were universal. *The Wonder Years* appealed to parents, who remembered the 1960s, and children, who recognized themselves in Kevin and his friends. It was about a time of innocence, when twentysomethings were protesting the war and discrimination and thirteen-year-olds were protesting curfews. *The Wonder Years* was succeeded by other dramas, such as *American Dreams*, that also romanticized the 1960s and catered to a baby boomer audience.

THE NINETIES TO THE PRESENT

Literature and Journalism

American Psycho (novel, by Bret Easton Ellis, 1991; film, directed by Mary Harron, 2000)

When asked by a young woman he is dating what business he's in, the successful stockbroker and protagonist Patrick Bateman of *American Psycho* tells her he's in "murders and executions," a play on "mergers and acquisitions." She thinks he is joking, but he is not. It is never entirely clear why Bateman (played by Christian Bale in the film) murders—hatred, jealously, the thrill of the kill—but murder he does: more than twenty colleagues, romantic partners, friends, and strangers by novel's end. He kills anyone who stands in his way, as well as those who just cross his path. Told in brutal detail by controversial author Bret Easton Ellis, the killings become metaphors for the ruthless behavior of Wall Street financiers, a popular theme in 1980s and 1990s fiction and film.

Backlash: The Undeclared War Against American Women (nonfiction, by Susan Faludi, 1991)

This book contends that the 1980s saw a backlash, promoted by conservatives and some in the media, against the gains that the feminist movement had made in the 1960s and 1970s. Faludi holds that women who seek to succeed in business are not man haters, antisocial, or husband-starved. She contests two arguments popular in the 1980s: Women who put their career first have trouble finding mates, and such women suffer from an "infertility epidemic." A popular and critically acclaimed book, *Backlash* put the feminist movement and the backlash against it into historical perspective for lay readers.

Bell Curve, The: Intelligence and Class Structure in Modern Society (nonfiction, by Richard J. Herrnstein and Charles Murray, 1994)

A controversial best-selling book by conservative social theorists Richard J. Herrnstein and Charles Murray, *The Bell Curve* offers two contentious main ideas. First, it argues that not all people are created equal as far as intelligence is concerned and that intelligence among a given population can be traced on a "bell curve" (a few at the top, most in the middle, and a few at the bottom). Second, it argues that success in a given society has less to do with environment, poverty or wealth, and education than inherent intelligence. While the authors explicitly disclaim any connection between race and class on the one hand and intelligence on the other, their general conclusions implicitly do so. The book touched off a storm of debate and continues to be cited by those arguing one side or another of the nature versus nurture debate.

Bible Code, The (nonfiction, by Michael Drosnin, 1997)

A huge best-seller when it came out, *The Bible Code* is journalist Michael Drosnin's explanation of the efforts by an Israeli mathematician to unlock a secret numerical code embedded in the Bible. Once deciphered, the mathematician contended, the code reveals a litany of historical events down through the 1995 assassination of Israeli Prime Minister Yitzhak Rabin. A self-professed skeptic, Drosnin claims that the mathematician, using the code predicted Rabin's assassination a year before it occurred. Widely and hotly debated, the book sent millions of people to their Bibles in an effort to see what the code revealed.

Bridges of Madison County, The (novel, by Robert James Waller, 1992; film, directed by Clint Eastwood, 1995)

Even its legions of fans admitted that *The Bridges of Madison County* was unabashedly sentimental, but the book sold in the millions and became one of the most popular romance novels of all times. The story is a simple one. Photographer Robert Kincaid (played by Clint Eastwood in the film) is a *National Geographic* photographer on assignment to capture images of the historic covered bridges of Madison County, Iowa. Stopping to ask for directions, he meets Francesca Johnson (Meryl Streep), a farm wife whose inattentive husband is off at the state fair with the couple's children. The love affair between the middle-aged Kincaid and Johnson is brief, but the latter remembers it all her life. The movie version earned Streep an Oscar nomination for best actress.

Chicken Soup for the Soul (nonfiction, by Jack Canfield and Mark Victor Hansen, 1993)

An enormously successful book, *Chicken Soup for the Soul* has spawned a seemingly unending series of books addressed to specific audiences from pet lovers to prisoners. The books consist of brief inspirational stories, involving self-help and human compassion, many of them submitted by readers of previous editions. The accounts were chosen and edited by Jack Canfield and Mark Victor Hansen, both of whom have worked as public speakers and have given seminars on the theme of self-esteem. The series has a Christian tone, but the books generally avoid sectarianism and preachiness, emphasizing common sense and good-natured advice about building a contented and moral life.

Corrections, The (novel, by Jonathan Franzen, 2001)

The late 1990s and early 2000s saw a renewed interest in both memoirs and novels based on seemingly normal but actually dysfunctional families. Perhaps the most popular of the genre, *The Corrections* examines one such family in the post-Cold War world. International political events form the backdrop of this portrait of a family in disarray: The father is slipping into senility, one son is struggling with a new career, another is struggling with marriage, and the daughter is trying to launch her own restaurant. The mother, striving to maintain the fiction of a happy family life, merely wishes all of them to return home for one final good Christmas together.

Da Vinci Code, The (novel, by Dan Brown, 2003; film, directed by Ron Howard, 2006)

More than a best-seller, author Dan Brown's *The Da Vinci Code* is an international cultural phenomenon, selling more than 30 million copies in some forty languages. Aside from Brown's page-turning writing style, the book's appeal has been its controversial premise. American religious scholar Robert Langdon (played by Tom Hanks in the movie) is brought in by French police to investigate the murder of a curator at the Louvre Museum in Paris. Assisted by a French cryptologist (played by Audrey Tautou), Langdon uncovers a huge conspiracy perpetrated by a cabal within the Catholic Church, a 2,000-year-old cover-up of the fact that Jesus had a wife and a child whose descendants live on to the present day. The criticism that the novel sparked from Rome and Christian leaders intensified after the release of a movie version of the book in 2006.

Firm, The (novel, by John Grisham, 1991; film, directed by Sydney Pollack, 1993)

Beginning in the 1980s, Mississippi lawyer and author John Grisham has made a fortune writing a series of hugely popular lawyer-oriented novels set in the South. In this, one of his most popular, a promising young law school graduate named Mitch McDeere (played by Tom Cruise in the film) is approached by a mob-controlled law firm and offered money and gifts to hire on with them. McDeere accepts. But after two associates at the firm are murdered and the Federal Bureau of Investigation (FBI) gets involved, McDeere is faced with a choice of cooperating with the FBI or staying loyal to the firm. All Grisham's novels are noted for their taut pacing, starkly cast moral dilemmas, and richness of legal detail.

Generation X: Tales for an Accelerated Culture (nonfiction, by Douglas Coupland, 1992)

Whether Douglas Coupland, a Canadian-born journalist, invented the term "generation X" or not (the etymology is disputed), his book of that title made it popular shorthand for a generation of Americans born in the immediate wake of the baby boom. (Coupland calculated that those born roughly between the early 1960s and the late 1970s were the tenth—Roman numeral X—generation since the beginning of the American republic in 1776.) Employing a mix of words, graphics, and ephemera along the margins of the main text, Coupland portrays a series of twentysomething people living in California trying to envision a future for themselves better than their unemployed and directionless present. Unlike their baby boom predecessors, the Generation Xers are less interested in politics than in getting by financially or escaping the problems of the 1990s by fleeing to Mexico.

Greatest Generation, The (nonfiction, by Tom Brokaw, 1998)

In *The Greatest Generation*, NBC news anchor and author Tom Brokaw chronicles the lives of fifty veterans and civilians who lived through the Great Depression and World War II—a group he calls the "greatest generation" for having helped the nation survive the two most traumatic events of the twentieth century. The compelling stories—of individuals on the military fronts in Europe and the Pacific, as well as those on the home front—are presented in the form of oral history. The theme throughout is how great events affect ordinary people and how ordinary people affect great events. The book was enormously popular with aging veterans, their children, and even their grandchildren. Social commentators have explained its popularity as a product of nostalgia on the part of the older generation and gratitude on the part of the younger.

How We Die: Reflections on Life's Final Chapter (nonfiction, by Sherwin B. Nuland, 1994)

Author Sherwin Nuland, a practicing physician, uses his own experiences with the dying and the deaths of friends, relatives, and patients to examine how our society deals with these events. Most dying today, he notes, is done privately in hospitals or hospices, rather than in the more comforting environment of the home, surrounded by friends and family, as in times past. This, he says, makes the modern experience of death more mysterious and terrifying than in times past. A central topic of the book is the controversy over assisted suicide for the terminally ill who face severe pain—a practice that Nuland supports, with reservations.

Men Are from Mars, Women Are from Venus: A Practical Guide for Improving Communication and Getting What You Want in Your Relationships (nonfiction, by John Gray, 1992)

In this groundbreaking, best-selling book, John Gray argues that gender differences do exist and are immutable. They are so great, in fact, that one can say, metaphorically, men are from Mars (the planet associated with violence and war) and women are from Venus (the planet associated with romance and love). Key to these differences are the ways in which men and women perceive things—from relationships to language to money. Gray, a trained psychotherapist, says that accommodating these differences enables men and women to better live, love, and work together. Critics have questioned his credentials and have argued that some of his conclusions are simplistic, but the book has become so popular that its metaphor is commonplace in everyday conversation about gender difference.

Midnight in the Garden of Good and Evil (novel, by John Berendt, 1994; film, directed by Clint Eastwood, 1997)

Based on a true story of love and murder in the seaside Georgia city of Savannah, *Midnight in the Garden of Good and Evil* was a hit with readers in 1994. Offering a panorama of real-life characters, the story is told from the perspective of John Kelso (played by John Cusack in the film), a magazine reporter sent to do a feature article on a lavish annual Christmas party hosted by high-living, semi-closeted gay art collector Jim Williams (Kevin Spacey). At the party, Kelso is fascinated by Williams's young and violent lover Billy (Jude Law). After Billy ends up dead, Kelso covers the subsequent murder trial. In the tradition of southern gothic novels, *Midnight* updates the genre with a 1990s gay love affair.

Rules, The (nonfiction, by Ellen Fein and Sherri Schneider, 1996)

Following such other best-sellers as *How to Marry the Man of Your Choice*, this popular work examines the perennially popular topic of dating and relationships. Subtitled "Time-Tested Secrets for Capturing the Heart of Mr. Right," the book argues for a return to the pre-1960s approach to dating. Essentially, it advises women to play hard to get and let the man take the lead in relationships. According to the famous Rule 5, "Don't call him and rarely return his calls." The book spawned two sequels, *Rules II: More Rules to Live and Love By* and *The Rules for Online Dating: Capturing the Heart of Mr. Right in Cyberspace*. Feminists have argued that such rules are both unrealistic and demeaning to women, a throwback to the patriarchal days before women's liberation.

From the imagination of British fantasy writer J.K. Rowling, the adventures of wizard-in-training Harry Potter were a U.S. publishing and motion picture phenomenon in the 1990s and early 2000s. *(Justin Sullivan/Getty Images News)*

Slaves in the Family (nonfiction, by Edward Ball, 1998)

Edward Ball was living in New York City writing for the *Village Voice* when he was invited to a Ball family reunion in Charleston, South Carolina, in 1993. Gazing at the area where the wealthy family's plantations once stood, he wondered why no one ever discussed the hundreds of slaves the family had owned in the years before the Civil War.

Slaves in the Family describes Ball's efforts to learn about the slaves, how they affected his family history, and how they affected his own life. The journey is at once enlightening, depressing, and humorous, taking him all the way to Sierra Leone, Africa, where the slaves originated in the seventeenth century. Like Alex Haley's *Roots*, but from the point of view of white owners, *Slaves in the Family* is an attempt to come to terms with the "peculiar institution" of slavery and its long-term effects on American society.

Film, Radio, Television, and Theater

Ally McBeal (television, 1997–2002)

On the surface, just another show about big-city lawyers and their cases, *Ally McBeal* diverged from the typical lawyer show with its emphasis on the love life of the protagonist (played by Calista Flockhart), a sexy, flirty, mini-dress-wearing attorney. The backstory was her longtime infatuation with law partner Billy Thomas (Gil Bellows). The two had grown up together and vowed to marry, until Thomas married another woman. The show followed the tangled relationships of McBeal, Thomas, and their friends, with frequent breaks for scenes based on McBeal's fantasies. Genre busting and popular, the show aired for six seasons, usually near the top of the ratings.

American Idol (television, 2002–present)

American Idol follows in a long tradition of amateur talent shows going back to *Ted Mack's Original Amateur Hour* of the 1950s and *The Gong Show* of the 1970s, but none of its predecessor enjoyed the popularity or had the cultural impact of *American Idol*. Along with a much larger studio and television audience, the show is different from its predecessors in that it includes background stories about the contestants' lives, allowing

Actor Justin Kirk attends the 2003 film premier of *Angels in America*, Tony Kushner's 1993 Pulitzer Prize–winning drama about AIDS and gay life. *(Arnaldo Magnani/Getty Images Entertainment)*

audiences to identify and empathize with them. Hundreds of amateur singers and musicians audition before celebrity judges, and ten finalists compete for the prize, a recording contract with a major label. Along with the winners, the real stars of the show are the celebrity judges—singer Paula Abdul and music producers Randy Jackson and Simon Cowell. The latter, in particular, with his British-inflected, no-holds-barred criticism of the contestants, has become a star in his own right.

Angels in America: Millennium Approaches; Angels in America: Perestroika (play, by Tony Kushner, 1993–1994; television film, directed by Mike Nichols, 2003)

Angels in America, a two-part, seven-hour epic drama, is an allegory of AIDS, a society in decay, and salvation. The play opened on Broadway in 1993 and won that year's Pulitzer Prize for Drama and Tony Award for Best Play. It is an epic in the true sense of the word, including numerous characters and multiple plot lines in a story that moves across great stretches of time and space. While the subject of gay life in America and AIDS lies at the core, subplots address the collapse of communism, the 1953 execution of Julius and Ethel Rosenberg for selling atomic bomb secrets to Moscow, Mormonism, and immigrants adjusting to life in the United States. For all its complexity, *Angels* is about people experiencing fears and overcoming them, and about the transformation that triumph brings. HBO produced and aired a made-for-television movie in 2003.

Bachelor, The/Bachelorette, The (television, 2002–present)

During the early 2000s, a proliferation of so-called reality shows established the dominant trend in American television. (Some critics prefer the term "unscripted television," pointing out that many of the shows have little to do with reality.) They essentially came in three types: talent shows such as *American Idol*, adventure shows such as *Survivor*, and romance shows. Of the last group, arguably the most popular has been *The Bachelor* (or *The Bachelorette* when the central contestant is a woman). Over eight to ten episodes, the bachelor or bachelorette in question meets a few dozen suitors who try to woo him or her. Ultimately, the bachelor or bachelorette picks one and asks for her or his hand in marriage. The show mixes salacious, arranged overnight dates, and hints of sexual encounters, with the traditional, formal marriage proposal. In a 2003 show, the wedding of the first bachelorette was made into a TV special and featured on the cover of a number of celebrity magazines.

Barney and Friends (television, 1992–present)

During the 1990s, a number of shows aimed at very young viewers—under the age of five—began appearing on television. Among the most popular was *Barney and Friends*, featuring a large, live-action, purple dinosaur of the same name. Aimed at pre-school audiences, Barney and his friends—including dinosaurs Baby Bop and B.J. and a host of children—engage in all kinds of simple adventures. Filled with dialogue and songs, *Barney and Friends* has become one of the most-watched television shows for the under-five set. It also has spawned a feature-length movie, *Barney's Great Adventure* (1998), and a merchandising bonanza.

Beauty and the Beast (film, directed by Gary Trousdale and Kirk Wise, 1991; stage musical, 1994–present)

The Walt Disney Company has built an empire by remaking fairy tales and fables into modern animated film. Among the most successful of these is the classic story of the "Beauty and the Beast," in which, a mean-spirited prince is turned into a beast by a witch. The only way he can return to being a man is to find someone to love him as a beast. Gradually, a local beauty falls in love with the beast/prince, even as she turns him into a more compassionate person. Like most Disney adaptations, *Beauty and the Beast* softens the violence and brutality of the original tale, perhaps offending purists but winning huge audiences.

Buffy the Vampire Slayer (television, 1997–2001, 2001–2003)

Enormously popular with teenage and young adult audiences, this show took the teen horror movie formula and translated it into a weekly one-hour television drama. The story follows Buffy Summers (played by Sarah Michelle Gellar), a high school student in the ordinary small town of Sunnydale—ordinary except for the fact that it lies atop a "hellmouth," where demons from the underworld emerge into the real world. Episodes generally revolve around Buffy's talent at slaying demons. Even hardened television critics expressed a soft spot for the show, which continues in reruns, with its consciously campy dialogue and gender-bending use of a sexy, preppy, teenage girl as the scourge of the underworld.

Civil War, The (television film, 1990)

Perhaps the most widely watched documentary film in the history of television, *The Civil War* ran for more than eleven hours on successive nights. The expanded time frame allowed filmmaker and historian Ken Burns to explore every aspect of the war, from the battles and generals to life on the home front. Utilizing a vast array of primary sources, both written and visual, the film had an elegiac quality. Personal journal accounts and letters were read by some of Hollywood's biggest stars, as the camera panned across old photographs and modern-day film clips of historical sites. Adding to the richness of the presentation was a haunting folk music score.

While many historians lauded Burns for his prodigious research, elegant filmmaking style, and the mere fact of bringing the event to a television audience in such detail, others complained that he did not probe deeply enough into racial and economic issues surrounding the war. The techniques used in this film proved influential on future historicl documentaries. Burns went on to make popular, multiepisode historical documentaries on baseball, jazz, and other distinctively American subjects.

Dances with Wolves (novel, by Michael Blake, 1988; film, directed by Kevin Costner, 1990)

Telling the story of Civil War officer John Dunbar (played by Kevin Costner), whose wild behavior on the battlefield leads to his exile to an outpost on the Great Plains, the enormously popular and ciritically acclaimed *Dances with Wolves* almost single-handedly revived the Western as a box office draw in the 1990s. On one level, the film, based on a 1988 novel by Michael Blake (he also wrote the screenplay), is typical of the genre, featuring conflict between whites and American Indians set against a majestic Western backdrop. But this is no typical Western. Aside from Dunbar, who develops friendly relations with the local Lakota Sioux—and a love affair with a white women adopted and raised by the tribe—the whites in the film are depicted as venal, brutal, and ignorant, while the Native Americans come across as dignified, generous, and wise. Nominated for twelve Academy Awards, it picked up seven wins, including best picture and best director (also Costner).

Ellen (television, 1994–1998)

On one level, *Ellen* was a conventional situation comedy about a single woman named Ellen Morgan (played by Ellen DeGeneres) who flees Los Angeles for her small hometown, after losing her high-powered job at a doomed Internet company. Back home, she copes with her family and interacts with various eccentric characters in typical sitcom episodes with lots of one-liners. But the show made headlines in 1997 when the title character came out of the closet as a lesbian, even as the star did in real life. Liberals hailed the show as a pathbreaking step in network television's willingness to treat gays as normal human beings; some conservatives said the show promoted an unacceptable gay lifestyle. DeGeneres's outspoken humor helped her land an afternoon talk show in 2003.

ER (television, 1994–present)

Set in an emergency room at a Chicago hospital, *ER* follows the professional and private lives of the doctors, nurses, and administrators who work there. While hardly the first medical drama to hit the small screen, this series has been a pioneer in several ways. Like the contemporaneous cop shows *Homicide* and *NYPD Blue*, *ER* features an ensemble cast, fast music-video-type editing, and plots that revolve around workplace romances and problems in characters' home lives, updating the old hospital dramas such as *Dr. Kildare* and *General Hospital*. During much of its run, the show—created by best-selling author Michael Crichton—has been among the most watched on television.

Fahrenheit 9/11 (film, directed by Michael Moore, 2004)

The highest-grossing documentary in the history of American film, *Fahrenheit 9/11* is director and political agitator Michael Moore's scathing examination of American foreign policy under President George W. Bush. The movie begins with a look at the disputed 2000 election and continues through the war in Iraq. *Fahrenheit 9/11* diverges from the director's earlier films—such as *Roger and Me* (1989)—in that it includes fewer of Moore's trademark in-your-face interviews designed to embarrass the rich and powerful. Instead, Moore uses little- or never-seen footage of familiar events to provide a view of recent American history from a leftist perspective. The controversial film generated much talk in the media, particularly regarding its potential influence on the 2004 presidential election.

Fargo (film, directed by Joel Coen, 1996)

The filmmaking team of the Coen brothers—producer Ethan and director Joel—had already established a reputation for distinctive and unusual films, but their release of *Fargo* in 1996 marked a creative and critical breakthrough. Set near the title city, the movie follows the story of ruthless but bumbling big city criminals hired by a financially strapped car salesman, Jerry Lundegaard (played by William Macy), to kidnap his wife and split the ransom they will get from his father-in-law. The crime goes horribly wrong, and innocent people die before a pregnant small-town police chief (Frances McDormand) can track down the criminals. The portrayal of good-natured innocents in the upper Midwest rings true and stands in sharp contrast to the murderous criminals. *Fargo* was nominated for seven Academy Awards, including best picture; it won for best actress (McDormand) and best original screenplay (the Coen brothers).

Forrest Gump (film, directed by Robert Zemeckis, 1994)

A cultural phenomenon as much as hit Hollywood film, *Forrest Gump* starred Tom Hanks as the title character, a mentally challenged man who somehow manages to be at the center of key events of the 1950s and 1960s—from Martin Luther King, Jr.'s "I Have a Dream" speech to the jungles of Vietnam. Offering simple aphorisms, a romantic but ultimately frustrated love affair, and a quick tour of postwar American history, *Forrest Gump* has been quoted and interpreted endlessly. Among the familiar lines are, "Life is like a box of chocolates; you never know what you are going to get."

Above all, perhaps, the film was technically innovative at the time of its release; it used sophisticated computer editing to place Gump in the presence of major historical figures at key moments in America's past. *Forrest Gump* won six Academy Awards, including best picture, best director, and best actor.

Friends (television, 1994–2004)

This hugely popular situation comedy followed the doings of six Manhattan-based friends, three men and three women. All in their twenties when the show began, the main characters struggled to find love, careers, and friendship in a hip urban setting. Much like the earlier *Seinfeld*, on which it was loosely based, the show generally did not feature conventional sitcom plots in which a single comic dilemma was resolved by the end of the episode. Instead, to borrow the *Seinfeld* expression, the show was often "about nothing." Episode plots frequently meandered along without a clear ending but left plenty of room for comic misunderstandings and one-liners along the way. The show made headlines of its own when the ensemble cast demanded an unprecedented $1 million each per episode. The cast members' desire to explore other career opportunities contributed to *Friends* going off the air in 2004.

GoodFellas (film, directed by Martin Scorsese, 1990)

A cinematic exploration of the organized crime subculture in America, *GoodFellas* is based on an autobiography by a former Irish American gangster, Henry Hill. (The title comes from the nickname Hill and his fellow gangsters gave themselves). Unlike *The Godfather*, which presents life among Mafia bosses and their families, *GoodFellas* is about low-level mobsters trying to work their way up through truck hijackings, drug dealing, and various forms of extortion. Over the course of the film, the narrator and protagonist, Hill (played by Ray Liotta), becomes ever more addicted to the cocaine he is dealing; as he descends into addiction, the film takes on a disturbing paranoid quality. Despite its graphic violence, *GoodFellas* was very popular. It was nominated for six Academy Awards, including best picture.

Home Alone (film, directed by Chris Columbus, 1990)

One of the most popular Christmas movies of any era, *Home Alone* tells the story of an eight-year-old boy named Kevin (played by Macaulay Culkin) who is accidentally left at home in an upper-middle-class suburb of Chicago when the rest of his family takes a holiday vacation in France. At first upset and frightened, Kevin learns to enjoy his solitude and freedom, until a couple of bumbling burglars (Joe Pesci and Daniel Stern) eye what they think is an empty house. Rather than run away or hide from them, Kevin goes on the offensive, unleashing a series of booby traps that leave the burglars looking rather stupid. Full of good-natured humor and slapstick comedy, the film spawned three sequels and made Culkin an instant child star.

Homicide: Life on the Street (television, 1993–1999)

Typical of the gritty police shows of the 1980s and 1990s, with their fast, music-video style of editing and pounding scores, *Homicide: Life on the* Street, set in a Baltimore police station, was also willing to depict cops in a less than favorable light—unheard of in cop shows of previous decades. In addition, and like other recent police dramas, the show's episodes included several subplots, mixing stories from the professional and personal lives of the main characters.

Howard Stern Show, The (radio, 1994–present, syndicated; television, 1998–2001)

Radio host Howard Stern called himself the "king of all media" and, for much of the late 1990s and early 2000s, he boasted millions of listeners. The host of a hit radio program and popular television show, Stern turned best-selling author with his 1993 autobiography *Private Parts*. Critics called Stern a "shock jock," who gained his audience through crude sexual reference, and criticized his show—which featured salacious commentary and interviews—for playing to the lowest common denominator of American society. To his many fans, Stern was simply hilarious and his open discussion of sex a reflection of what everybody thinks about anyway. In 2004, a number of radio stations hosting Stern's show were penalized for obscenity by the Federal Communications Commission (FCC), and several took him off the air. In 2006, Stern began a new stage in his career, broadcasting his show on the subscription-based Sirius satellite radio network, beyond the FCC's reach.

In Living Color (television, 1990–1994)

A hip, urban variety show, *In Living Color* was often called a black *Saturday Night Live* for its mix of comedy sketches, musical and dance numbers, and largely African American cast. A number of the sketches were based on stock characters, including one of the most memorable, a dyspeptic birthday party entertainer named "Homey D. Clown." The host and star of the show was Keenan Ivory Wayans; comedians David Alan Greer, Jim Carrey, and Jamie Foxx, as well as several of Wayans's brothers, also were featured. Jennifer Lopez made her network debut as one of the show's dancing "fly girls."

Jerry Springer Show, The (television, 1991–present, syndicated)

The Jerry Springer Show is a daytime talk show that features a panel of usually noncelebrity guests confronting major problems in their personal lives. The host, a former Cincinnati mayor and news anchor, moderates and takes questions for the guests from the studio audience. The show has a notorious reputation as "gutter" television (or worse). The topics covered are typically sexual in one way or another, involving illicit love affairs, incest, spousal abuse, and the like. Guests are often pitted against one another—a perpetrator of abuse versus his or her victim, for example—resulting in shouting matches and even physical assaults.

JFK (film, directed by Oliver Stone, 1991)

Hailed by its fans as a brilliant piece of filmmaking and a much-needed exposé of the cover-up of the Kennedy assassination, Stone's *JFK* has also been widely denounced as historically inaccurate and an indulgence in the worst kind of conspiracy thinking. Based largely on the 1988 book *On the Trail of the Assassins* by Jim Garrison, a former New Orleans prosecutor who pursued his own investigation of the 1963 killing in Dallas, *JFK*

comes to no conclusions about who was ultimately responsible. Yet, it makes a case for a cabal within the U.S. intelligence services, angry at Kennedy for failing to support Cuban exiles seeking to overthrow Fidel Castro and worried that the president was not willing to commit enough military resources to sustaining the anticommunist regime in South Vietnam.

Larry Sanders Show, The (television, 1992–1998)

The subscription cable television station HBO began making a reputation for itself in the 1990s as the producer of edgy, unconventional television series. Most of the shows took familiar formats and gave them new twists. Among the first was *The Larry Sanders Show*, a series about the making of a television talk show of the same name. Featuring the eponymous host (played by comedian Garry Shandling), it offered an inside look at the venality of television industry people, most notably the insecure and vain Sanders. To add verisimilitude, the show cut back and forth between behind-the-scenes action and the fictional talk show, presented as if it were real. Dry-humored and cynical, *The Larry Sanders Show* developed a devoted following.

Matrix, The (film, directed by Andy Wachowski and Larry Wachowski, 1999)

A cultural and commercial phenomenon, as well as a technological breakthrough, the Internet in 1999 provoked endless fascination in the American mainstream as a new way of meeting others, doing business, and consuming. *The Matrix*, the first of three films about a future in which human beings are unknowingly plugged into an advanced Internet known as the Matrix, likewise fascinated filmgoers. This decidedly negative vision of the Internet contrasted, however, with society's predominantly utopian vision of the medium's potential in its early years.

The Matrix depicts a decidedly dystopian future, in which humans are allowed to live out their lives in a computer-constructed reality, while computers feed off the energy expended by their bodies. A small underground of human rebels is determined to overthrow the rule of the computers. Especially eye-catching are the film's special effects, highlighted by its slow-motion fight scenes.

NYPD Blue (television, 1993–2005)

Arguably the most popular police drama in television history, *NYPD Blue* is set in a downtown Manhattan detective squad headquarters. Each episode revolves around murders being solved by the detectives on duty. At the same time, the show explores the personal lives of the main characters. While many came and went over the years, one of them—gruff detective Andy Sipowicz (played by Dennis Franz), who struggled through the early seasons with an alcohol problem—remained throughout. The show helped pioneer the use of music video imagery and fast-cut editing in network dramatic series. Featuring sex scenes and partial nudity, it also sparked controversy for pushing television's censorship boundaries.

Passion of the Christ, The (film, directed by Mel Gibson, 2004)

Films recounting the life of Jesus Christ are nothing new in Hollywood, dating back to the silent era. But popular Hollywood actor and award-winning director Mel Gibson's recounting of the last twelve hours of Jesus Christ's life is something different—in its production, its handling of the topic, and its reception at the box office. Gibson raised the money for the film himself, viewing the Hollywood studio system as unwilling to finance the kind of religious film he sought to make. For authenticity, all of the characters in the film speak Latin, Hebrew, and Aramatic, the native tongue in the Holy Land at the time of Christ. The film is also extremely graphic in depicting the violence that, according to various interpretations of the New Testament, was perpetrated against Jesus in his last hours on Earth. Some biblical scholars have claimed the film is riddled with error, and liberal theologians have decried Gibson's emphasis on Jesus's pain and suffering. But audiences, particularly evangelical ones—many attended the film on the advice of their pastors—flocked to movie theaters, earning the film worldwide revenues of over $600 million. It was nominated for three Academy Awards.

Philadelphia (film, directed by Jonathan Demme, 1993)

One of the few big-budget Hollywood movies to address the subjects of homosexuality and AIDS—and the most successful at the box office—Philadelphia tells the story of a gay lawyer, Andrew Beckett (played by Tom Hanks), who works at a high-powered law firm in the title city. When Beckett contracts AIDS, he tries to hide the symptoms from his coworkers and bosses; when that becomes impossible, he is fired. The only lawyer Beckett can find to represent him in a civil suit against the firm is homophobic ambulance chaser Joe Miller (Denzel Washington). Gradually, the two establish a friendship, and Miller helps Beckett win his case. The film was a Hollywood breakthrough in exploring the social issues surrounding AIDS, and it won Hanks an Oscar for best actor.

Pulp Fiction (film, directed by Quentin Tarantino, 1994)

Quentin Tarantino, a former video store worker who made a name for himself as a director with the 1992 heist film Reservoir Dogs, followed that up two years later with the highly popular, critically acclaimed Pulp Fiction. The movie consists of a series of plots about petty criminals and others—mostly strangers—violently attacking and being attacked by each other. Even more than in Reservoir Dogs, Tarantino pays homage to crime movies past and foreign (especially Hong Kong films) in Pulp Fiction, which cuts narrative time into pieces and begins and ends in the middle of the story. Like all Tarantino films, Pulp Fiction is extremely violent, though its many fans argue that its violence is so comic as to seem slightly unreal and therefore less disturbing. Pulp Fiction was nominated for seven Academy Awards, including best picture.

Queer as Folk (television, 2000–present)

Based on a British show of the same name, Queer as Folk was the first American television series to feature gay men as the central characters. The weekly cable program focuses on the lives of five gay men living in Pittsburgh, following their romantic relationships, sexual encounters, professional lives, and health problems. A subplot follows the lives of their lesbian friends. Besides its gay themes, the show is also different from most dramatic series in that it often deals with political issues such as AIDS funding and gay marriage.

Real World, The (television, 1992–present)

Arguably the first modern reality program, The Real World is a series of multi-episode shows in which a group of young adults, picked by the producers, live in a large residence together and are filmed over a period of time. Shot in various cities in the United States and Europe, the show monitors the recreational, romantic, and professional lives of the participants, usually seven in number. Perhaps the most interesting aspect of the show is the stories—some loving and some hateful—that develop between these former strangers, selected for their diverse personality types, living in close quarters.

Rent (stage musical, by Jonathan Larson, 1996; film, directed by Chris Columbus, 2005)

Rent takes Puccini's nineteenth-century opera *La Boheme* and sets it in present-day America. Instead of Puccini's Paris, the musical is set in New York; instead of tuberculosis haunting the characters, it is the scourge of AIDS. Emphasizing the tragic message of the story and giving the musical much publicity, the composer, Jonathan Larson, died of the disease on the very night of its New York premiere. Hip, urban, and upbeat, despite its plot of disease and suffering, *Rent* offers a blend of musical styles from rock to disco to gospel. The musical won a Pulitzer Prize and four Tony Awards. The film version was released in 2005 to mixed reviews and a lackluster box office.

Saving Private Ryan (film, directed by Steven Spielberg, 1998)

Starring Tom Hanks and directed by Steven Spielberg, *Saving Private Ryan* features one of the most gut-wrenching opening sequences in the history of film, depicting the Allied landing at Normandy on June 6, 1944. Thousands of soldiers are slaughtered as they attempt to make their way onto the shores of France. After surviving D-Day, the job of Hanks's character is to find Private James Ryan. Ryan's three brothers have been killed in the war, and the government wants to send him home to save his mother further grief. The search for Ryan is an arduous journey that ends in a heroic standoff.

Saving Private Ryan was nominated for an Academy Award for best picture but lost to the independent film *Shakespeare in Love* in a year that marked the triumph of independent film. Spielberg, however, did win the Oscar for best director, his second after *Schindler's List* (1993). The success of *Saving Private Ryan*, along with Tom Brokaw's book *The Greatest Generation* (1998) and Stephen Ambrose's *Band of Brothers* (1992), reflected a continuing fascination with the World War II generation.

Schindler's List (film, directed by Steven Spielberg, 1993)

For director Steven Spielberg, *Schindler's List* was a break from his usual mass-appeal projects, such as *Jaws*, *E.T.*, and the *Indiana Jones* trilogy. Told in gritty black and white, the film portrays the real-life story of Oskar Schindler, a German businessman who used his factory to shelter Jews during the Holocaust. Based on the 1982 book by Thomas Keneally, the film is shocking in its intensity, depicting the experiences of Jews in Nazi Germany and concentration camps during World War II. Filmed testimony by real people saved by Schindler appears at the end of the three-hour film. *Schindler's List* collected seven Academy Awards, including best picture and best director. After completing *Schindler's List*, Spielberg established the Shoah Foundation, a nonprofit organization that collects eyewitness testimonies of Holocaust survivors and witnesses.

Sex and the City (television, 1998–2004)

Premiering on the HBO cable network in June 1998, *Sex and the City* shocked and thrilled audiences with its blatant sexual theme, strong language, and edgy fashions. Its stories of dating and friendship among four successful single women—Carrie Bradshaw (Sarah Jessica Parker), Miranda Hobbes (Cynthia Nixon), Samantha Jones (Kim Cattrall), and Charlotte York (Kristin Davis)—were based on Candace Bushnell's best-selling book *Sex and the City* (1996). The women slept with new men every week and talked openly about their experiences at the city's hottest restaurants, bars, and cafés. And they spent an unprecedented amount of money on clothes, handbags, and shoes. With single "never-marrieds" constituting more than 40 percent of the U.S. population, according to the 2000 census, *Sex and the City* became a hit with many young female viewers. Even if they could not afford the lifestyle of the show's characters, said critics, they could relate to the romantic dilemmas.

Shawshank Redemption, The (film, directed by Frank Darabont, 1994)

Written and directed by Frank Darabont, the film is an adaptation of a Stephen King novella, *Rita Hayworth and the Shawshank Redemption* (1982). The setting is Maine's Shawshank State Prison, where banker Andy Dufresne (played by Tim Robbins) is sent in 1947 on a false conviction of killing his wife. Soon thereafter, he begins chipping his way out with a small rock hammer obtained from "Red" Redding (Morgan Freeman), who becomes his closest friend in prison. A poster of Rita Hayworth, followed by other starlets over time, covers the hole in Dufresne's cell through which he escapes in 1966. In the meantime, he keeps the prison's books and helps the corrupt

Perennially acclaimed—and criticized by Italian American groups for its stereotypes—HBO's *The Sopranos* features James Gandolfini (center) as mob boss and family man Tony Soprano. *(Anthony Neste/Time Life Pictures/Getty Images)*

warden skim money. Unbeknown to the warden, Dufresne funnels more than $300,000 into bank accounts across the state. After his escape, he retrieves the money and travels to Mexico, where Red joins him upon parole the following year. Television replay helped make this tale of friendship and salvation one of the most popular films of the 1990s.

Silence of the Lambs (novel, by Thomas Harris, 1988; film, directed by Jonathan Demme, 1991)

Starring Anthony Hopkins and Jodie Foster, *Silence of the Lambs* won the Academy Award for best picture. Based on a best-selling novel of the same name by Thomas Harris, this psychological thriller is about a novice FBI agent, Clarice Starling (Foster) tracking a serial killer. To help in the search, she solicits the insights of Hannibal "The Cannibal" Lecter (Hopkins), an incarcerated psychiatrist-turned-psychopath who kills and then eats his victims. Lecter helps Starling see inside the criminal mind, but he also burrows into her own past and motivations. Tension builds as

Starling closes in on the killer. Lecter's escape from prison at the conclusion set up a sequel, *Hannibal* (2001), starring Julianne Moore as Starling.

Sopranos, The (television, 1999–present)

A weekly series that has turned the media's view of the mob family on its head, *The Sopranos* features a local organized crime boss, Tony Soprano (played by James Gandolfini) as a suburban family man with a wife, kids, and a nagging mother who tries to have him killed. Set in Northern New Jersey, the plot switches back and forth between Soprano's efforts to run a fractious syndicate of hit men and extortionists and his daily interactions in a dysfunctional family. The pressure puts Soprano into therapy, where he tries to grapple with the emotional weight of being a mobster and a father. Like other popular Mafia dramas, such as *The Godfather* trilogy and *GoodFellas*, *The Sopranos* set off an uproar in the Italian American community for its portrayal of that ethnic group as a collection of thugs. Despite such protests, the show has enjoyed enormous success, helping cement HBO's reputation for innovative, theater-quality drama.

Survivor (television, 2000–present)

Survivor was one of the first of many so-called "reality shows" that began appearing on American television in the late 1990s and early 2000s. The concept was simple: Film sixteen people living on an island for thirty-nine days, allow them to vote the least popular and least capable members off the island, and give the "sole survivor" $1 million at the end. The first episode aired in May 2000 and was watched by 15 million people. Viewers were appalled at the participants' Machiavellian maneuvers, backstabbing, and physical deterioration, but they watched enthralled week after week. *Survivor* single-handedly pulled the CBS network out of the ratings doldrums—especially the first season's final episode, when 51 million people watched an openly gay contestant claim the $1 million prize. Subsequent episodes have been filmed in Australia, Africa, South America, Thailand, Palau, and Panama. Although its ratings fell after the first two seasons as reality shows became more common, *Survivor* consistently ranked in the top five shows each week.

Thelma & Louise (film, directed by Ridley Scott, 1991)

Thelma and Louise stars Susan Sarandon and Geena Davis as two friends—both tired of their jobs and the men in their lives—who decide to take a road trip. Misadventure soon occurs, as Louise shoots a man who is attempting to rape Thelma, and they find themselves on the run from the law. After further escapades and an extended pursuit, the two women are finally tracked down by police, yet they resist capture to the end. Feminists cheered *Thelma and Louise* as a declaration of women's freedom. Others have objected to the two renegades taking the law into their own hands and the negative stereotyping of the male characters.

Titanic (film, directed by James Cameron, 1997)

Costing more then $250 million to produce, *Titanic* could have been the biggest box-office disaster in movie history. Instead, it tied or broke nearly every record, from its worldwide box office gross revenues of more than $1 billion to its eleven Academy Awards (tied with *Ben-Hur*, 1959, and *The Lord of the Rings: The Return of the King*, 2003, for the most ever), including best picture. At once a disaster film and a love story—about a wealthy girl in first class (played by Kate Winslet) and a poor boy in steerage (Leonardo DiCaprio)—*Titanic* personalized the story of the greatest shipping disaster of the twentieth century. What most viewers remember about the film, however, is its epic scale. To do justice to the size of the ship and the scope of the disaster, Cameron had a full-scale model of the vessel built at a specially designed studio on the coast of Baja California.

Toy Story (film, directed by John Lasseter, 1995)

Utilizing the latest developments in computer animation, *Toy Story* was a creatively and commercially successful film released by the Walt Disney Company and Pixar Animation Studios. Departing from their hand-drawn animation techniques—*Snow White and the Seven Dwarfs* (1937) was the first-ever animated feature—they delved into computer animation. This was a lengthy and painstaking process (it took nine years to create *Toy Story*), but the result was an incredibly lifelike and vivid animated film. The story of a cowboy named Woody who must make room for the new toy Buzz Lightyear, the movie is a funny and sweet story of friendship. With characters voiced by Tom Hanks, Tim Allen, and other notable actors, *Toy Story* was a hit with children and adults alike.

Toy Story grossed $192 million at the U.S. box office and received a special achievement award as the first feature-length computer-animated film at the Academy Awards. A sequel, *Toy Story 2*, was released in 1999. *Toy Story* started a revolution in animated film; in 2003, Disney dramatically downsized its traditional animation division in favor of computer animation.

Twin Peaks (television, 1990–1991)

"Who killed Laura Palmer?" This was the key question in an eerie and surrealistic television series that aired on ABC in 1990 and 1991—and millions asked it in water-cooler conversations for months. Directed by the iconoclastic David Lynch (known for the feature-length films *Eraserhead*, *The Elephant Man*, and *Blue Velvet*), *Twin Peaks* offered viewers an unusual combination of art house film—with its emphasis on symbolism and convoluted plot—and traditional television miniseries.

The show was originally produced as an eight-episode miniseries, but the mystery surrounding Palmer's death and its investigation by a mysterious FBI agent was stretched to a complete season and renewed for a second one. The supernatural storyline (involving more than a hundred characters) struggled to keep viewers' attention after the initial episodes, as Palmer's case remained unsolved. Questions were answered early in the second season, but critical acclaim had dwindled, and ABC cancelled the series after a total of thirty episodes. *Twin Peaks* apparently triggered a taste for the eccentric, however, and it was followed by such quirky fare as *Northern Exposure*, *Picket Fences*, and *The X-Files*.

Unforgiven (film, directed by Clint Eastwood, 1992)

Clint Eastwood's *Unforgiven* earned the Academy Award for best picture of 1992, becoming only the third Western ever to do so, after *Cimarron* (1931) and *Dances with Wolves* (1990). In *Unforgiven*, an aging gunfighter, William Munny (Eastwood), embarks on a bounty hunt for men who have disfigured a prostitute. The film ends in a bloody showdown of moral vengeance for Munny's murdered African American friend (Morgan Freeman).

On one level, *Unforgiven* was a traditional Western, as screenwriter David Webb Peoples incorporated into its script themes of violence, revenge, justice, and honor. At the same time, it subverts the genre with a revisionist view of Western morality. Munny is both hero and antihero, taking on the original task for money rather than any principles of justice.

War Room, The (film, directed by D.A. Pennebaker and Chris Hegedus, 1993)

In 1992, documentary filmmaker D.A. Pennebaker and his wife Chris Hegedus were granted an inside look at Arkansas governor Bill Clinton's campaign for the presidency. The result was *The War Room*, released in 1993. By then, everyone knew how the film would end—with Clinton's victory over President George Bush—but few knew what had happened behind the scenes along the way. The filmmakers focused their cameras not on Clinton but on his campaign staff, primarily strategist James Carville and media director George Stephanopoulos. This was a new type of campaign, run by young politicos and driven by media image making. Watching *The War Room*, viewers marveled at the machinery of a modern political campaign, which had rarely been caught uncensored on camera.

Who Wants to Be a Millionaire (television, 1999–2002, syndicated)

The television game show *Who Wants to Be a Millionaire* set off a short-lived, prime-time game show craze in 1999 and 2000. It had been many years since a new game show had had any success in the prime-time hours. On *Who Wants to Be a Millionaire* contestants sat in a "hot seat," answered multiple-choice questions from host Regis Philbin, and worked their way up to different prize levels, with a top prize of $1 million. If stumped, contestants had three "lifelines": they could phone a friend, poll the audience, or have the possible answers reduced from four to two. ABC was floundering in prime time before the debut of *Who Wants to Be a Millionaire*, but it soon surged to the top of the ratings on the strength of the show's 29 million viewers. The network began airing *Who Wants to Be a Millionaire* several nights a week, and oversaturation finally led to its cancellation in June 2002. The show has continued to air in syndication, and foreign versions have been popular around the world.

X-Files, The (television, 1993–2002)

Historians have long noted the American fascination with conspiracy theories, and the 1990s marked a revival of the trend. Evidence included the popularity of Oliver Stone's film *JFK* (1991), which challenged the official explanation of the Kennedy assassination, and the rise of Roswell, New Mexico, believed by many to be the site of a government UFO cover-up in the 1940s, as a popular tourist destination. Likewise, in 1993, *The X-Files*, which devoted an hour each week to alien conspiracies, began airing on the Fox network.

David Duchovny played Fox Mulder, an openminded FBI agent assigned to investigate the paranormal. Gillian Anderson played his partner, Dana Scully, a skeptic. A potential romance between the two provided an undercurrent of sexual tension in many episodes. After eight seasons, however, Duchovny left the program. The show carried on without him for one season before its cancellation in 2002.

Glossary

Glossary

A

Acid rain. Rain or snow containing high levels of sulfur dioxide and nitrogen oxide that have entered the atmosphere through emissions. It can be highly toxic and damaging to the environment.

Act of Chapultepec. Passed as an outcome of the Inter-American Conference held in Mexico City over February and March 1945, this act of March 3, 1945 established the first multilateral collective security system in the Western Hemisphere by calling for a combined response in case of an attack on any signatory state. It signaled a new period of inter-American cooperation in the postwar era.

Agricultural Research and Marketing Act (RMA). This 1946 act established a five-year research and marketing program for U.S. agriculture, and it increased federal funding in this area.

Air Quality Act of 1967. Passed during the administration of Lyndon B. Johnson, this act introduced comprehensive air pollution control at the federal level for the first time. It set ambient air quality standards based on a set of criteria as defined by the federal government, and it provided a basis for the Clean Air Act of 1970.

Amerasian Homecoming Act. An act written in 1987 and implemented in 1989 that allowed for Amerasians (mostly the children of American servicemen) born in Vietnam between January 1, 1962, and January 1, 1976, to emigrate to the United States with their immediate family members.

American Bar Association (ABA). Founded in 1878 in Saratoga Springs, New York, the ABA is the national representative of the legal profession of the United States. It aims to ensure the promotion of justice, professional standards, and respect for the law.

American Civil Liberties Union (ACLU). An organization founded in 1920, the ACLU has been active ever since in campaigning for individual rights, against the death penalty, and to protect the rights of minorities.

American Farm Bureau Federation. This organization was established in 1919 to represent the interests and concerns of agricultural producers at all levels. In the postwar era, the federation not only lobbied the federal government on behalf of agricultural producers, but it also was involved in activities ranging from citizenship programs (1950s) to food safety education campaigns (1990s).

American Federation of Labor (AFL). An organization of labor unions formed in 1886 by Samuel Gompers, which began as a federation of craft unions but eventually turned to industrial organizing as well. It merged with the Congress of Industrial Organizations to form the AFL-CIO in 1955.

American Institute of Public Opinion (AIPO). Established in 1935 by Dr. George Gallup to measure public opinion on social, political, and economic issues—primarily through the collation and analysis of data gained from national surveys—and to report such findings.

American Legion. This veterans' organization was founded by soldiers of the American Expeditionary Force at the end of World War I in 1919. It has represented the interests of military veterans and has played an important role in shaping postwar America through its emphasis on patriotism and service.

Amerika. A term used primarily by subversive and protest movements to indicate what they consider the "fascist" nature of the American government and state and the "evil" of the United States. The word first emerged during the Vietnam period, and it also has been used in rhetoric and protest against the Gulf and Iraq wars.

Amnesty International. Founded in 1961 in the United Kingdom, with its first U.S. branch established in 1962, Amnesty International is an international organization that seeks to protect human rights under the guidelines of the Universal Declaration of Human Rights. In the United States, for example, Amnesty International has campaigned against the death penalty.

Anti-Defamation League (ADL). Established in 1913, this league fights anti-Semitism and discrimination against the Jewish people and other victimized groups. In the years following World War II, the ADL's initiatives included opposing McCarthyism, initiating programs for Holocaust education, and supporting Jews in the Soviet Union.

Antiterrorism and Effective Death Penalty Act (1996). This act was passed on April 24, 1996, "to deter terrorism, provide justice for victims, [and] provide for an effective death penalty." The act imposes a limit on appeals in capital punishment cases; makes terrorism a crime punishable by death; aids in investigation, capture, and trial of terrorists; disallows fundraising that supports terrorist organizations; and is intended to prevent terrorists from entering the United States.

Anzus Treaty. A treaty promulgated in 1951 between the United States, Australia, and New Zealand that pledged the three nations to ensure each other's security.

Arab League. Formed on March 22, 1945, the Arab League aims to coordinate communications, health-related issues, and economic, cultural, and social affairs among member organizations. It also forbids the use of force between member states.

Atomic Energy Commission. A federal agency established in 1946 to control and direct all research into atomic energy and its applications.

B

Barbie. A doll produced by the Mattel Corporation, this representation of the "perfect woman" has sold in the millions, along with a variety of accessories. Barbie has become a cultural phenomenon and has been criticized as presenting an impossible and prejudicial ideal of women in terms of shape and color.

Barrio. A Spanish-speaking area in an American town or city. Barrios have provided an important locus for the development of Hispanic identity, community, and activism.

Beatniks or Beats. A subculture of the 1950s with a literate, philosophical focus. Its members rejected material possessions and established social mores, and they often embraced anarchistic views.

Beehive. A popular hairdo of the 1960s, also known as the B-52, the beehive was a teased and sprayed big-hair style that went from fad to kitsch symbol.

Beltway. An interstate highway encircling Washington, D.C. Also a term used to describe the issues and concerns of the federal government, the contractors who work for it, the lobbyists who pressure it, and the media that is focused on all of them (as in the phrase "inside the Beltway").

Berlin Blockade. From June 1948 to May 1949, the Soviet Union blocked railroad and street access to West Berlin by the Western occupying powers. In response, the British, French, and Americans airlifted food and provisions to Berliners. The incident marked one of the first steps in the Cold War.

Blaxploitation. A genre of films produced in the late 1960s and early 1970s for an African American audience, featuring strong African American characters and often set in an urban environment. Blaxploitation films included *Shaft* (1971), directed by Gordon Parks.

Blog. Short for "weblog," a blog is a journal, diary, or newsletter on the World Wide Web, frequently added to and updated, and aimed at a general audience. Blogs are an increasingly important means of public communication, and these Web pages can focus on any and all topics of interest.

Boat people. This term came to describe refugees from Communist rule after the Vietnam War who fled their country in small boats. Many eventually resettled in other countries, including the United States. The term is now occasionally used for any refugees who attempt to reach another country by small boat (for instance, from Cuba to America).

Braceros. Mexican workers who entered the United States under a program to make up agricultural labor shortages between 1942 and 1964.

Break dancing. A type of urban dancing that forms an important element of hip hop culture. Usually performed to rap music, break dancing is done solo and involves rapid acrobatic movements with different parts of the body touching the ground. Break dancing emerged in the 1970s, but it became a popular part of mainstream culture in the 1980s.

Bureau of African Affairs (BAA). Part of the U.S. Department of State, the bureau was established in 1958 and focuses on the United States's relationship with sub-Saharan Africa.

Bureau of Indian Affairs (BIA). Founded in 1824, the BIA is responsible for managing and administering 55.7 million acres held in trust by the United States for various Native American tribes and Natives of Alaska. Its work includes leasing assets on these lands, protecting water and land rights, developing and maintaining infrastructure, and providing education services to the native peoples. The BIA's role in managing American Indian affairs has been controversial.

Bureau of Public Roads. This agency, established in 1949, supervised the federal-state highway construction program, administered the highway beautification program, constructed defense highways and roads in national parks and forests, and conducted research into transportation and highway design. It was absorbed into the Federal Highway Administration in 1970.

C

Cable television. A form of television requiring payment and offering viewers a wider range of programming choices than free broadcast stations. It was first started as "community antenna television" in 1948, and rapidly spread; pay television over the cable system was introduced in 1972.

Cape Canaveral. The home of the Kennedy Space Center, located on the east coast of Florida, which is used for manned and unmanned launches of space missions.

CB radio. A form of radio (CB stands for "citizen's band") whereby individuals can broadcast messages to each other over a short distance on one of 40 channels. CB communication was widespread in the 1970s among truckers and other drivers. It became less popular with the advent of cellular phones but remains in use.

CFCs. Abbreviation for chloroflourocarbons, a category of chemical compounds that were first developed in the early 1930s and used in industrial, commercial, and household applications, such as refrigerators and aerosols. CFCs were subsequently discovered to be one of the factors responsible for ozone depletion.

Christian Identity Movement. A movement that takes in conservative Christian churches and religious organizations and right wing political groups. Popularized by Wesley Swift in the mid-1940s, the movement has been associated with anti-Semitism and political extremism.

Christmas bombing. An intensive U.S. bombing campaign against North Vietnam undertaken on December 18–30, 1972, despite peace negotiations taking place at the time. This bombing, initiated by the Nixon Administration, was widely condemned.

Clean Air Act of 1963. An early piece of legislation aimed at improving air quality in the United States, this act aimed to reduce air pollution by setting emissions standards for stationary sources of pollution, such as power plants and steel mills.

CNN. Acronym for Cable News Network, founded by Ted Turner and first broadcast in 1980. CNN is a continuous-news channel, and the network also runs its own news coverage programs.

COINTELPRO (Counter Intelligence Program). Begun in 1956 and discontinued in 1971, this program run by the Federal Bureau of Investigation targeted alleged radical and politically dissident groups and individuals. Much of this domestic intelligence activity was covert, and some of it was seen as violating the constitutional guarantees of freedom of speech and of association.

Commission on Civil Rights. Established in 1957, this commission has aimed to examine and resolve issues relating to race, ethnicity, religion, and sexual orientation.

Communist Control Act. Legislation passed in 1954 that invoked "national security" as a reason to deprive members and supporters of the Communist Party of their civil liberties.

Congress of Industrial Organizations (CIO). A federation of trade unions established in 1935 to represent manufacturing interests initially not represented by the American Federation of Labor (AFL). The CIO merged with the AFL in 1955.

Congress of Racial Equality (CORE). A coalition founded in 1942 and dedicated to nonviolent protest against racial discrimination. CORE was a major force behind the civil rights movement of the 1960s.

Consumer Union. An independent, nonprofit organization that aims to provide consumers with information and advice about products and services. Established in

1936, the organization derives its income from its monthly publication, *Consumer Reports.*

Contract with America. A legislative program initiated by Congressman Newt Gingrich (Republican of Georgia) in 1994 that promoted a conservative program for the Republican Party and supported such policies as welfare reform, getting tough on crime, and a balanced budget. It helped Republicans regain control of Congress for the first time in forty years.

Council of Energy Resource Tribes. An intertribal corporation that seeks to manage and develop the resources of member tribes. The organization allows for tribes to participate in the management of their resources and to develop relationships with industry.

Crack. An addictive, crystalline form of cocaine made by treating cocaine hydrochloride with a base of baking soda, resulting in "rocks" that are smoked in pipes to achieve a euphoric high. Crack cocaine is considered a drug made and used by the poor, primarily in inner cities, in contrast with the powdered form, which is associated with the middle and upper classes.

Creationism. The belief that the Earth was created by God as described in the Bible. Creationists actively oppose the theory of evolution. Variations among creationist beliefs range from the conviction that the Earth was created literally as described in the book of Genesis (in six days) to the neo-creationist theory of "intelligent design," which argues that the universe must be the product of some intelligent designer/greater power. Controversies over the teaching of creationism and evolution in U.S. public schools continue.

Cuban American National Foundation. A nonprofit organization established in 1981 by Jorge Mas Canosa, dedicated to overthrowing the Cuban government of Fidel Castro. The foundation has lobbied the U.S. government to gain bipartisan opposition to Castro's government. In recent years, however, it has been linked to questionable activities involving acts of terrorism perpetrated in Cuba.

Culture wars. A movement in American politics and culture over the closing decades of the twentieth century that saw the polarization of Americans (especially academics and intellectuals) over the way American culture, politics, and society should operate. The two camps might be seen as progressive (left wing) and traditional (right wing). Certain issues, such as gay rights, abortion, versions of national history, religious beliefs, and affirmative action, have all been hotly debated as part of the culture wars.

D

DDT. The abbreviation for dichloro diphenyl trichloroethane, an insecticide discovered in 1939 and used extensively in American agriculture. Subsequently found to be highly toxic and damaging to the environment over a long period, it was banned in the United States in 1972.

Department of Agriculture. Founded in 1862, the Department of Agriculture plays an important role in contemporary America. It provides food stamps and school lunch programs, guardianship of national forests and rangelands, conservation activities, rural infrastructure work, food safety regulation, and open markets for U.S. agricultural products.

Department of Homeland Security. This government department has three primary aims: to prevent terrorist attacks within the United States, to reduce America's vulnerability to terrorism, and to minimize damage from potential attacks and natural disasters. The department was established in the wake of the terrorist attacks of September 11, 2001, but it did not come into existence officially until January 24, 2003.

Department of Veterans Affairs. This department succeeded the Veterans Administration in 1989. It oversees the provision of benefits to veterans and their families, including education, medical care, and pensions.

Detroit riots. Among the most violent in the nation's history, these riots were instigated in July 1967 by a police raid on a party at an after-hours drinking club in a depressed black neighborhood in central Detroit. About 10,000 people, both blacks and whites, took part in the rioting, which was fueled by racial tensions, police abuse, economic disparity, and high unemployment rates, among other factors. Forty-three people were killed and 467 injured in the five-day riots.

Development Loan Fund (DLF). This fund was created in 1957 after the passing of the Mutual Security Act. It functioned as the lending arm of the International Cooperation Administration, established in 1954 to administer foreign aid for economic, political, and social development purposes.

Disc jockey. A disc jockey, or DJ, selects pre-recorded music for an intended audience, typically on the radio or at a dance. The DJ was very much a product of the postwar period, as a "teen culture" emerged, and rock and pop music became big business. Famous DJs of the postwar period include Alan Freed and Wolfman Jack.

Disneyland. This amusement park designed by animator and filmmaker Walt Disney opened in Anaheim, California, in 1955. It encompasses a variety of themed areas, including Main Street USA, Frontierland, and Tomorrowland. It has been a huge attraction ever since its opening.

Disneyworld. Walt Disney's sequel to Disneyland, this more modern amusement park opened in Orlando, Florida, in 1971. Among other differences from its West Coast counterpart, the Florida park includes the EPCOT Center, designed to present a futuristic and utopian vision for American society. Disneyworld also has been a huge attraction.

Displaced Persons Act. Passed in 1948, this act allowed some 200,000 displaced persons (DPs) to enter the United States. Many of these DPs were Jewish refugees, although the initial act contained anti-Semitic elements. The act was modified in 1950.

Dixiecrats. Southern conservatives who left the Democratic Party in 1948 over the issue of desegregation. They formed a States' Rights Party, which ran Strom Thurmond as a candidate in the 1948 election, and continued to oppose federal efforts to end discrimination and desegregation in the South.

DMZ. Short for "demilitarized zone," referring to a buffer zone between two enemies. Both the Korean War and the Vietnam War featured a demilitarized zone, and the term DMZ entered the general vocabulary.

E

eBay. Founded in 1995, eBay is an Internet marketplace for buying, selling, and trading an enormous variety and a vast number of items. Open to everyone, it has expanded into an international phenomenon, and it is arguably the most popular Web site on the Internet, with over 100 million registered members.

Eco-feminism. A strain of feminism that argues that patriarchal philosophies harm not only women but also all living things. Eco-feminists resist patriarchy as part of a broader effort to prevent the destruction of the natural environment.

F

Farmers Home Administration (FmHA). This government lending institution was established in 1946 to help provide struggling farmers with credit. The FmHA generally offered financing in rural areas for such things as housing, community facilities, and business ventures. It was closed down in 1994.

Federal Aviation Administration (FAA). Previously the Federal Aviation Agency (established 1958), the FAA became part of the Department of Transportation in 1967. It is responsible for the safety of civilian aviation, overseeing airspace and air traffic management, issuing and enforcing regulations and standards regarding aviation, and engaging in research, engineering, and development.

Federal Bureau of Investigation (FBI). This federal agency was established in 1908 by Attorney General Charles Bonaparte to investigate crimes and activities that crossed state jurisdictions. The FBI has been an important influence in the postwar period, for example, in its attempts to control radical activities in the 1960s and 1970s.

Federal Election Campaign Act of 1971. This act was passed to increase disclosure of the sources of contributions for federal campaigns. It was amended in 1974 to limit campaign contributions.

Federal Energy Regulatory Commission (FERC). This commission is responsible for regulating and overseeing energy industries for economic, safety, and environmental purposes. Its activities include regulating the transmission of oil by pipeline in interstate commerce, as well as monitoring and investigating energy markets.

Federal Highway Act of 1956. This act passed during the Eisenhower Administration established the nation's interstate highway system by providing for the construction and financing of 41,000 miles of new highways over a ten-year period.

Federal Trade Commission (FTC). Founded in 1914 to prevent unfair methods of competition in commerce, the FTC is an independent agency that reports to Congress and is responsible for overseeing and preventing anticompetitive practices.

Fiancees Act. This act, passed in 1946 in the aftermath of World War II, allowed foreign-born fiancé(e)s of U.S. service people to enter the United States.

Fish-in. A form of protest undertaken by a number of Native American tribes, mostly in the Pacific Northwest in the 1960s and 1970s, to protest their being harassed for fishing on non-reservation lands, even if the lands were tribal. In Washington State, American Indian tribes gained more open fishing rights.

Flower children. A term describing hippies who advocated universal peace and love and often embraced alternate lifestyles, including communal living. The name was derived from the flowers they wore in their hair and randomly gave to people on the street.

Flower Power. Slogan of the hippie movement, especially during the 1960s, invoking the spirit of peace and love.

Foreign Assistance Act. Passed on September 4, 1961, this act authorized the creation of the U.S. Agency for International Development (USAID), which focused on long-range economic assistance to developing nations.

Free Speech Movement. A student and activist movement formed to overturn restrictions on political speech at the Berkeley campus of the University of California in 1964.

Freedom Summer. A campaign held over the summer of 1964, when many civil rights activists went to the Deep South to sign up African Americans for the voting rolls. The campaign included the organization of the Mississippi Freedom Party and the establishment of Freedom Schools to address the racial inequalities in Southern schools.

Friends of the Earth. Founded in 1979 in San Francisco, this international organization campaigns on environmental issues, including protesting dam building projects, fighting against international whaling, and advocating the regulation of strip mining and oil tankers.

G

Gallup Polls. Public opinion surveys that have been influential in American history since George Gallup popularized them in 1935.

Gated community. A residential area, usually segregated by having walls surrounding it and by restricting access for security, and often status, purposes. These communities are generally sold as havens from the problems of urban life.

General Motors (GM). Founded in 1908 in Michigan, General Motors is a U.S.-based automobile manufacturing company. GM has produced many iconic American cars, including the Buick, Cadillac, and Pontiac, and it has been a major employer of American workers.

Generation X. This generation follows the baby boomers and includes people born roughly between 1961 and 1981. The stereotype of Generation Xers is that they are slackers and cynics, but the qualities that actually define Generation X continue to be debated.

G.I. Joe. A popular doll designed to represent the perfect soldier. Launched in 1963, it has proven to be one of the steadiest selling toys. It also is popular with collectors.

Glam rock. Also known as "glitter rock," glam rock was a popular music style of the 1970s. Predominantly a British phenomenon, it made gains in the United States through artists such as Alice Cooper and the popularity of the 1975 movie *The Rocky Horror Picture Show.*

Global warming. A theory that the temperature of the Earth and its oceans is increasing, largely as a result of human activity that produces carbon dioxide and other greenhouse gases. Although most scientists agree that the temperature increase has human causes, scientists, politicians, and the public continue to debate the future effects of global warming on the climate and the environment, and what action should be taken.

Grassy knoll. A term used by conspiracy theorists who argue that President John F. Kennedy was killed not by Lee Harvey Oswald shooting from the Texas Book Repository but rather by shots fired from a "grassy knoll" near the motorcade. It has become a more generic term to refer to hidden plots and conspiracies.

Green revolution. The development and application of new scientific methods to increase crop yields, particularly in famine-prone areas of the developing world.

H

Habitat for Humanity. Founded in 1976, this international organization works to build housing for those in need. More than 175,000 houses have been built through its program, which has been notably supported by former president Jimmy Carter.

Highway Trust Fund. Created through the Highway Revenue Act of 1956, this fund provides a secure source of financing for the national system of highways. Money comes from highway-use taxes.

(House) Interstate and Foreign Commerce Committee. Established in 1892 as the U.S. House of Representatives' Committee on Commerce and reorganized in 1946, this committee's duties included overseeing the regulating of interstate and foreign commerce, interstate and foreign transportation, and interstate and foreign communications. It also oversaw the weather bureau and public health and quarantine, among many other duties. The committee was in existence until 1968.

Human Rights Watch. The largest human rights organization based in the United States, it researches and publicizes human rights abuses in all regions of the world. It began as Helsinki Watch in 1978 to monitor compliance with the Helsinki Accords. In the 1980s, Americas Watch was created because of human rights abuses in Central America. Other Watch communities sprang up, and, in 1988, they all were merged into Human Rights Watch.

I

ICBM. The acronym for intercontinental ballistic missile, ICBMs are launched from a stationary or mobile platform and are designed for long-range delivery (5,000 miles or more) of single or multiple nuclear warheads.

Immigration Act of 1990. This act increased the number of immigrants allowed into the United States each year. It also created an immigration lottery, which assigned a number of visas randomly (not based on the country of origin) in an attempt to make the immigration system more equitable.

Immigration and Naturalization Service (INS). This agency was responsible for issues involving immigration, including permanent residence, illegal immigration, and asylum. It existed until 2003, when it was replaced by the U.S. Citizenship and Immigration Service within the Department of Homeland Security.

Indian Claims Commission (ICC). Established in 1946 for the purpose of settling Native American tribal land claims and treaty land disputes. Before the commission closed in 1979, 370 petitions representing 852 claims had been made by more than 200 tribes and groups.

Indian Educational Assistance and Self-Determination Act of 1975. This act was watershed self-determination legislation. It reduced the power of the Bureau of Indian Affairs to control Native American tribal finances by permitting the tribes to contract for tribal services.

Institute for Creation Research. Founded in 1970, this organization is devoted to the research, publication, and teaching of "creation science," essentially the creationist interpretation of scientific data relating to the origins of the Earth.

Inter-American Development Bank. This institution was established in 1959 to support economic and social development in Latin America and the Caribbean. It has helped to develop social, economic, health, and educational institutions, has supported regional integration initiatives, and has invested in private enterprises. This bank provided a model for other regional development banks.

International Atomic Energy Agency (IAEA). Created in 1957 to respond to the development of nuclear energy, this agency is dedicated to the missions of nuclear verification and security, safety, and technology transfer. It promotes international treaties and cooperative behavior to govern the development and use of nuclear energy.

International Brotherhood of Teamsters (IBT). Established in 1903, the IBT claims 1.4 million members and bills itself as "the world's most powerful labor union." It has evolved into an umbrella organization for hundreds of local unions that represent a wide range of skills and professions. It allegedly has had strong ties to organized crime.

International Monetary Fund (IMF). Established in 1945 and headquartered in Washington, D.C., the IMF's mission is to help promote the health of the world economy. As of mid 2006, this international organization has 184 member countries and lists as some of its goals the promotion of international monetary cooperation, the fostering of economic growth and high levels of employment, and providing temporary financial assistance to countries to help ease balance-of-payments adjustments.

IUD (Intrauterine Device). A contraceptive that consists of a small plastic and copper device inserted into the uterus, it is an effective, long-term form of contraception. Some of these devices have caused health problems in women.

J

Jim Crow laws. Laws that were in existence from the late 1800s until the 1960s in the American South that enforced a system of racial segregation. They were named after a minstrel character of the late nineteenth century. These laws were overturned during the civil rights era of the 1960s.

K

Kerner Commission. A special commission appointed by President Lyndon B. Johnson to investigate race riots in U.S. cities in the late 1960s. The commission pointed to deep-rooted problems of inequality and racism in urban areas.

Knights of Columbus. Established in 1881 in Connecticut and incorporated in 1882, this fraternal society is dedicated to upholding Christopher Columbus's ideal of defending Christianity in the New World. The Knights work to support the Catholic Church and provide education programs and civic aid.

Ku Klux Klan (KKK). Founded in the immediate aftermath of the American Civil War, the Ku Klux Klan has been a significant white supremacist organization in the United States. Its main activity in the postwar era was to violently oppose the civil rights movement of the 1960s. Versions of the KKK continue to flourish, many advocating Christian identity and racial integrity.

L

League for Industrial Democracy. Founded in 1905 by Socialists, including Jack London and Upton Sinclair, the league addressed numerous social problems, especially those concerned with labor. In the postwar era, the League allied itself with anticommunist forces and devoted itself to overthrowing communism. More recently, it has focused mostly on democracy-building programs in underdeveloped nations and has been largely dominated by conservatives.

League of Women Shoppers. This group was founded in 1935 by women who wanted to use their power as consumers to achieve justice for workers. It had close relations with both progressive and labor organizations in the pre–World War II period and subsequently supported the war effort. Its influence lessened after the war.

League of Women Voters. Established in 1920, the league is a grassroots organization dedicated to improving the system of government and influencing public policy. It is a nonpartisan organization that focuses on issues of general relevance, not just those of concern to women. Men have been allowed to join the league since 1974.

Levittown (1947–1950). Mass-produced housing built after World War II, originally in Hicksville, Long Island, New York. The houses could be produced and constructed quickly and cheaply, supporting the idea that all Americans could be homeowners. The Levittown phenomenon promoted the development of suburbia.

M

Mariel boatlift. In 1980, a large number of refugees escaped Fidel Castro's Cuba and headed for the United States in small boats, in a wave of arrivals that overwhelmed the U.S. Coast Guard. Many lives were in jeopardy, and a number of refugees died on the way, but many of them made it safely to the United States.

Military-industrial complex. This term, coined by President Dwight D. Eisenhower in his farewell address in 1961, refers to the postwar growth of the armed forces and the arms industry, and the political and commercial interests attached to them. It has a negative connotation, suggesting that government might be unduly influenced or controlled by industrial and military power.

Mississippi Freedom Democratic Party (MFDP). A party formed in 1964 to support civil rights and oppose the white-dominated Democratic Party of that Deep South state. The MFDP sent delegates to the 1964 Democratic Convention.

Model minority. A stereotypical term often used to describe Asian Americans, suggesting that among all the minority ethnic groups in the United States, Asian Americans are mostly likely to be law-abiding, hard-working citizens who contribute to rather than detract from the community.

Montana Freemen. A Christian Patriot group based in Montana, the Freemen embraced the notion of individual sovereignty and denied the authority of the federal government, seeking to establish their own institutions separate from the rest of the country. In 1996, the Freemen were involved in a standoff with U.S. federal marshals for eighty-one days; the conflict ended peacefully, and some Freemen were subsequently imprisoned. A number of such groups exist in the United States.

Moral Majority. A political movement attached to the rise of evangelical religion and the politically conservative right wing since the 1970s. It lobbies government on the basis of a religiously influenced political agenda.

MTV. Abbreviation for Music Television, a cable network channel launched in 1981 with music videos as its primary programming. MTV influenced the music industry's use of visual impressions to sell music and also helped to promote the spread of cable television. Its programming has since changed to include a broader range of shows aimed at young viewers.

Mutual Security Agency (MSA). The MSA was established in 1951 to provide military, economic, and technical assistance to friendly nations in the interest of international peace and security. It existed only until

1953, when its responsibilities were transferred to the Foreign Operations Administration.

N

Nation of Islam. Founded in the 1930s by Wallace Fard Muhammad, this religious and political organization seeks to improve the conditions of African Americans economically, socially, and spiritually. It grew rapidly in the postwar years, converting many African Americans to Islam. Parts of the organization have advocated a paramilitary approach to race relations, which has led to division in the membership. It was reorganized in 1978 under the leadership of Louis Farrakhan and has focused on political campaigning and protests such as the Million Man March.

National Academy of Sciences (NAS). Founded in 1863, the NAS advises the government on scientific and technological issues as they relate to the public good. Its membership consists of about 2,000 distinguished scholars.

National Aeronautics and Space Administration (NASA). An agency created in 1958 to coordinate the U.S. space flight program and aerospace research for military and civilian purposes. NASA has conducted numerous human explorations in space, including the Apollo missions to the moon (the first men landing on the moon were Neil Armstrong and Edwin "Buzz" Aldrin in 1969), Skylab, and the space shuttle, as well as robotic missions to other planets in the solar system.

National Association of Evangelicals (NAE). Established in April 1942, the NAE works to facilitate Christian unity and cooperative ministry among evangelical denominations, congregations, educational institutions, and service agencies. Its initial aim was to revive evangelical Christianity in the United States. Since World War II, evangelical Christianity has played an expanding role in American culture, society, and politics.

National Association of Manufacturers (NAM). Founded in Ohio in 1895, this association has promoted the interests of manufacturers in the United States— for example, by developing trade links with overseas countries. In the years following World War II, it has played an important role in shaping industrial relations policies, pushing for trade missions to a variety of countries, including the Soviet Union and Middle Eastern nations, and lobbying government over such issues as the exchange rate and interest rates.

National Governors Association. A bipartisan organization that represents the governors of the states of the United States. It is influential in creating public policy and represents the interests of the governors to the federal government.

National Indian Youth Council (NIYC). Founded in Gallup, New Mexico, in 1961, the NIYC has become an important national representative of the interests of American Indians. It began as a civil rights organization and also has been involved in environmental issues affecting the communities and land of native peoples. The NIYC is controlled and operated by Native Americans, and it continues to promote policies that ensure the survival of their communities.

National Missile Defense (NMD). This program aims to develop and maintain the option to deploy a cost-effective, operationally effective system compliant with the Anti-Ballistic Missile Treaty to protect the United States against limited ballistic missile threats, especially from rogue nations.

National Organization for Women (NOW). Founded in 1966, NOW is dedicated to achieving equal rights for women. It played an important role in the feminist movement of the 1960s and 1970s, fighting discrimination against women in the workplace, campaigning to secure birth control and reproductive rights for women, and promoting justice and equality in society.

National Peace Action Coalition. Established in June 1970, this major anti–Vietnam War organization held numerous antiwar demonstrations across the nation.

National Rifle Association (NRA). The origins of the NRA are in the American Rifle Association, founded in New York in 1871. The NRA aims to protect the right of citizens to own firearms, which they argue is guaranteed by the Second Amendment of the Constitution. The association funds and supports political candidates sympathetic to their aims. It also promotes gun safety and education programs.

National Security Act of 1947. This act reorganized the military, security, and foreign policy instruments that the president relies on to establish and carry out U.S. foreign policy, including the National Security Council and the Central Intelligence Agency.

National Security Council (NSC). Created by the National Security Act of 1947, the NSC is the president's principal arm for coordinating national security and foreign policy among federal agencies.

Nationalist Socialist White People's Party. This organization was formerly known as the American Nazi Party (its name was changed in 1967). It promotes national socialism as a political alternative and advocates Holocaust revisionism. It is an anti-Semitic, politically extreme organization.

9/11. The commonly used name for the events of September 11, 2001. On that date, four American passenger planes were hijacked by al-Qaeda terrorists, who flew two of them into the Twin Towers of the World Trade Center in New York City and one into the Pentagon in Washington, D.C. The fourth plane crashed in a field near Shanksville, Pennsylvania, after passengers disabled the rogue pilots. The attack killed 2,749 people, including a number of New York fire fighters and police officers when the Twin Towers collapsed. The event marked the beginning of what President George W. Bush has called the War on Terrorism.

North American Free Trade Agreement (NAFTA). In January 1994, this agreement established a free trade zone between the United States, Mexico, and Canada. It opened opportunities for future economic growth among these nations and has served as a model of trade liberalization.

O

Office of Price Administration. The federal government established this agency, which existed from 1942 to 1947, to prevent wartime inflation and to administer price controls.

Office of Strategic Services (OSS). This intelligence agency was established during World War II to gather strategic information and analyze it for the Joint Chiefs of Staff. It was a precursor to the Central Intelligence Agency.

OPEC (Organization of the Petroleum Producing Countries). Organized by oil-producing nations in 1960, OPEC aims to coordinate and unify petroleum policies among its member countries in order to secure fair prices for producer nations and an efficient, regular supply to consumer nations. It currently has eleven member nations.

Operation Wetback (1954). Put into place in 1954, Operation Wetback was an attempt by the U.S. Immigration and Naturalization Service to crack down on illegal immigration, particularly from Mexico. The operation targeted Mexican American communities and led to large-scale deportations, but it tended toward racial stereotyping and harassing Mexican Americans.

Orderly Departure Program. This program instituted in 1979 was designed to permit the entry of Vietnamese refugees into the United States in the wake of the Vietnam War.

Organization of Eastern Caribbean States. A major regional institution formed in 1981 to promote unity and development of its member nations.

Oslo Accords (1993). A peace agreement between Israel and the Palestine Liberation Organization, brokered by Norway and signed in Washington, D.C., by Yitzhak Rabin and Yasir Arafat. The hopes for peace that these accords outlined had not yet been realized by mid 2006.

Overseas Private Investment Corporation. This agency was established in 1971 to help U.S. businesses invest overseas, foster economic development in new and emerging markets, and support U.S. foreign policy. It supports projects intended to encourage political stability, free market reforms, and the values of the United States.

P

Pac-Man. A popular computer and arcade game of the 1980s, Pac-Man featured a yellow sphere with a mouth that ate dots and ghosts that attempted to catch it.

People for the Ethical Treatment of Animals (PETA). An international nonprofit organization founded in 1980, PETA is dedicated to establishing and defending the rights of all animals. Its work involves education, consumer boycotts, publicity campaigns, and lobbying government.

Planned Parenthood. With its origins in Margaret Sanger's American Birth Control League incorporated in 1922, Planned Parenthood (known by that name since 1942) has advocated and supported birth control and reproductive health support and education. It advocates the right of reproductive self-determination for all people and takes a pro-choice stance on the issue of abortion.

Playboy Clubs. These clubs for men were established in the 1960s and featured scantily clad waitresses in bunny costumes. The clubs were based on the popular *Playboy* magazine, edited by Hugh Hefner, and promoted a bachelor lifestyle.

Profumo case. British secretary of state for war John Profumo became embroiled in a scandal around his affair with call girl Christine Keeler, who also was involved with an attaché from the Soviet embassy. Profumo's involvement was seen as a potential breach of international security during the Cold War, and he was forced to resign. This case contributed to the fall of the Conservative government the following year.

Pulitzer Prize. An annual prize awarded by Columbia University to recognize special achievements in journalism, letters, drama, and music.

R

Reality television. This form of television programming focuses on "real life" situations. In one show, for example, a group of people are left on a remote island to fend for themselves and to vote one another off until only one person remains (*Survivor*). Other situations have involved dating (*The Bachelor, The Bachelorette*), and daily police activity (*Cops*). These shows are extremely polular and have achieved very high ratings.

Red Power. In the 1970s, this movement of Native American activism began with protestors occupying the island of Alcatraz off the California coast. Involving ethnic pride and a resurgence of American Indian identity, this movement has had a strong urban base.

Refugee Relief Act (1953). This act allowed for the admission into the United States of 214,000 refugees from Eastern Europe over three years. At least 186,000 had to be from Communist countries.

Roe v. Wade (1971). This decision by the U.S. Supreme Court determined that laws against abortion violated a woman's constitutional right to privacy. The decision overturned state laws that banned or restricted abortion. The decision was, and has been, very controversial, as many Americans continue to campaign either against abortion or for pro-choice.

Rubik's Cube. A puzzle composed of a cube made up of smaller, turning cubes, each with its six faces bearing different colors. The goal is to line up the smaller cubes so that each side of the larger cube is uniform in color. The cube proved to be phenomenally popular in the early years of the 1980s.

S

Securities and Exchange Commission (SEC). This government agency was established in 1934 to regulate the securities industry in order to protect investors, maintain fair markets, and facilitate capital formation.

"Shock and awe." A method of warfare predicated on the principle of destroying an adversary's will to fight through impressive displays of power. It is part of the theory of rapid dominance conceived by Harlan Ullman and James Wade, whereby large-scale missile strikes are used to psychologically dominate the enemy. This method was applied to U.S. military policy in the 2003 invasion of Iraq.

Shock jock. Derived from the term disc jockey (DJ), this describes a radio host who attempts to attract listeners by being offensive, usually using obscene humor or taking deliberately provocative stands on popular issues.

Sierra Club. An environmental organization founded in 1892 that works to protect wilderness areas, practice and promote responsible use of resources, provide education about use of the environment, and improve the quality of the natural and human environment.

Soccer mom. This term came into popular discourse in the 1990s and typically refers to an upper-middle-class, suburban, white mother who drives an SUV or minivan to take her children to their soccer games and other after-school activities. Soccer moms were credited with providing important support to Bill Clinton during his presidential campaigns, but they later came to be seen as swing voters sought by both parties.

Sputnik. The launch of this early Soviet satellite in 1957 spurred fears that the United States was falling behind the Russians in developing rocketry and exploring outer space.

Starr Report. The 1998 report by independent counsel Kenneth Starr on the investigation of a number of alleged scandals surrounding President Bill Clinton. The Starr report addressed Clinton's involvement with White House intern Monica Lewinsky and his alleged perjury and abuse of authority. The report called for Clinton's impeachment, though he was not convicted of any of the charges, and so remained in office. The Starr Report was notorious for its details on the Clinton-Lewinsky liaison; some saw it as a witch-hunt against Clinton.

T

Teach for America. A program established by Wendy Kopp, based on her senior thesis at Princeton University in 1989, to address the problems of inadequate education in low-income areas in the United States. It engages recent college graduates to commit two years to teaching in urban and rural public schools.

Televangelist. A church minister who preaches via the medium of television. The rise of televangelism occurred during the 1970s and 1980s. Famous televangelists included Jim Bakker, Jimmy Swaggart, Jerry Falwell, and Pat Robertson. Bakker and Swaggart became embroiled in sexual scandals, but television programming remains a popular means of promoting evangelical Christianity.

Theosophy. A set of beliefs promoted by the Theosophical Society, founded in 1875 by Helena Blavatsky. Theosophists believe that humans are capable of intuitive insight into the nature of God; they use yoga and meditation to gain wisdom and insight. Theosophy has a continuing following in the United States.

Third World. This term came into usage in the 1960s to distinguish countries that were neither part of the capitalist West nor of the Communist East. They are the poorer nations of the world, and many are in debt to the richer countries. Less frequently used in the post–Cold War era, the term is often seen as pejorative.

Title VII. A part of the Civil Rights Act of 1964 that prevents discrimination in employment on the basis of race, color, gender, age, creed, religion, disability, veteran status, or national origin.

U

U-2. A high-altitude U.S. military plane used to spy on enemy installations before the satellite era.

Unabomber. Before his identity was discovered, this was the name applied to Theodore Kaczynski, a mathematician convicted of killing three people and injuring twenty-nine through a number of mail bombs. He saw himself as fighting against the evils of technological progress. The name was derived from the Federal Bureau of Investigation's code name for him, "Unabom," a combination of "university" and "airline bomber."

United Auto Workers (UAW). Under its full title—United Automobile, Aerospace and Agricultural Implement Workers of America—this organization, founded in 1935, is one of the largest unions in the United States. It represents the interests of a diverse range of workers with the goal of securing economic and social justice for all members of the community.

United Farm Workers (UFW). Formed in the early 1960s from labor unions organized by César Chávez, Dolores Huerta, and others, the UFW strives to improve the conditions of farmworkers, especially in California, many of whom are Hispanic. The UFW took on many of the issues affecting Hispanic civil rights in the 1970s and beyond.

United States Information Agency (USIA). An agency that existed from 1953 to 1999 and was responsible for "public diplomacy"—the spreading of information about the United States and its values to other countries. It focused on cultural and education exchange.

USA PATRIOT Act. The title of this act is an acronym for Uniting and Strengthening America by Providing Appropriate Tools Required to Intercept and Obstruct Terrorism. Passed as a response to the terrorist attacks of September 11, 2001, the act expanded the authority of the U.S. government and law enforcement in investigating alleged or suspected terrorist activity. Rights activists have criticized the act for its possible infringements on civil liberties.

V

Viagra. A medication for men suffering from erectile dysfunction, Viagra has taken on some currency in popular culture through its supposed effects in fueling older men's sex lives.

W

Weapons of Mass Destruction (WMD). These may include nuclear, chemical, and biological weapons that produce a catastrophically damaging effect. The term became particularly popular in the lead-up to the attack on Iraq, when the United States alleged that Saddam Hussein's Iraqi regime secretly possessed such weapons.

Weather Underground Organization. A radical offshoot of Students for a Democratic Society, this organization was formed in the late 1960s as the Weathermen. It turned to violence in its campaign against the government and authority in general.

Welfare Reform Act (1996). The actual name of this act is the Personal Responsibility and Work Opportunity Reconciliation Act of 1996. It was passed to overhaul the American welfare system by moving more people from welfare into employment,

White flight. A term used to describe the movement of white upper- and middle-class people to areas less likely to have nonwhite elements in the population, often from urban to suburban areas. It has been a significant issue since the end of World War II and has shaped much of the demographic landscape of postwar America.

White trash. An epithet for poor white people who are stereotyped as having bad manners, low moral standards, and little education. The term is essentially class-based, although it does have some geographical currency, referring to those who live in particular areas of the United States, wear a certain style of clothing, and have lowbrow cultural preferences.

Wilderness Society. This organization was established in 1935 to protect and promote the conservation of America's wilderness areas. Based on scientific principles, the society has worked on such projects as protecting the Arctic Wildlife Refuge from oil and gas drilling and preventing logging and road building in undeveloped national forests.

World Trade Organization (WTO). Established in 1995, this international organization deals with the rules of trade between nations. Its functions include administering WTO trade agreements, handling trade disputes, and providing a forum for international trade negotiations.

Y

Young People's Socialist League (YPSL). The YPSL, which emerged in 1907, has been the official youth affiliate of the Socialist Party in America since 1913. The league was active in the years following World War II, including organizing a nuclear test ban march in 1962. It focuses on education, direct action such as protests, and supporting candidates for public office.

Bibliography

Bibliography

Arts and Culture

Abrahamson, David. *Magazine-Made America: The Cultural Transformation of the Postwar Periodical.* Cresskill, NJ: Hampton, 1996.

Amott, Teresa L., and Julie A. Matthaei. *Race, Gender, and Work: A Multicultural Economic History of Women in the United States.* Boston: South End, 1991.

Anderson, Terry H. *The Movement and the Sixties.* New York: Oxford University Press, 1995.

Anderson, Will. *Where Have You Gone, Starlight Cafe?: America's Golden Era Roadside Restaurants.* Portland, ME: Anderson and Sons, 1998.

Arnaz, Desi. *A Book.* Cutchogue, NY: Buccaneer, 1977.

Bailey, Beth L. *From Front Porch to Back Seat: Courtship in Twentieth-Century America.* Baltimore: Johns Hopkins University Press, 1988.

Baritz, Loren. *Backfire: A History of How American Culture Led Us into Vietnam and Made Us Fight the Way We Did.* New York: William Morrow, 1985.

Barkin, Steve M. *American Television News: The Media Marketplace and the Public Interest.* Armonk, NY: M.E. Sharpe, 2003.

Barnouw, Erik. *Tube of Plenty: The Evolution of American Television.* New York: Oxford University Press, 1975

Baughman, James L. *The Republic of Mass Culture: Journalism, Filmmaking, and Broadcasting in America Since 1941.* Baltimore: Johns Hopkins University Press, 1992.

Bellah, Robert N., Richard Madsen, William M. Sullivan, Ann Swidler, and Steven M. Tipton. *Habits of the Heart: Individualism and Commitment in American Life.* Berkeley: University of California Press, 1985.

Belz, Carl. *The Story of Rock.* New York: Oxford University Press, 1972.

Berman, Paul. *A Tale of Two Utopias: The Political Journey of the Generation of 1968.* New York: W.W. Norton, 1996.

Bongco, Mila. *Reading Comics: Language, Culture, and the Concept of the Superhero in Comic Books.* New York: Garland, 2000.

Boorstin, Daniel J. *Democracy and Its Discontents: Reflections on Everyday America.* New York: Random House, 1974.

Boyer, Paul S. *By the Bomb's Early Light: American Thought and Culture at the Dawn of the Atomic Age.* New York: Pantheon, 1985.

———. *When Time Shall Be No More: Prophecy Belief in Modern American Culture.* Cambridge, MA: Harvard University Press, 1992.

Braden, William. *The Age of Aquarius: Technology and the Cultural Revolution.* Chicago: Quadrangle, 1970.

Brady, Kathleen. *Lucille: The Life of Lucille Ball.* New York: Hyperion, 1994.

Bravin, Jess. *Squeaky: The Life and Times of Lynette Alice Fromme.* New York: St. Martin's, 1997.

Brochu, Jim. *Lucy in the Afternoon: An Intimate Memoir of Lucille Ball.* New York: William Morrow, 1990.

Bugliosi, Vincent. *Outrage: The Five Reasons Why O.J. Simpson Got Away with Murder.* New York: W.W. Norton, 1996.

Bugliosi, Vincent, and Curt Gentry. *Helter Skelter: The True Story of the Manson Murders.* New York: W.W. Norton, 1974.

Burt, Larry W. *Tribalism in Crisis: Federal Indian Policy, 1953–1961.* Albuquerque: University of New Mexico Press, 1982.

Buzzanco, Robert. *Masters of War: Military Dissent and Politics in the Vietnam Era.* Cambridge, UK: Cambridge University Press, 1997.

Chalmers, David Mark. *And the Crooked Places Made Straight: The Struggle for Social Change in the 1960s.* Baltimore: Johns Hopkins University Press, 1996.

Clark, Marcia, and Teresa Carpenter. *Without a Doubt.* New York: Viking, 1997.

Collins, Jim, ed. *High-Pop: Making Culture into Popular Entertainment.* Malden, MA: Blackwell, 2002.

Conrad, Barnaby. *Snoopy's Guide to the Writing Life.* Cincinnati, OH: Writer's Digest, 2002.

Cook, Bruce. *The Beat Generation.* Westport, CT: Greenwood, 1983.

Coontz, Stephanie. *The Way We Never Were: American Families and the Nostalgia Trap.* New York: Basic Books, 1992.

Cooper, David Edward. *The Manson Murders: A Philosophical Inquiry.* Cambridge, MA: Schenkman, 1974.

Corber, Robert J. *In the Name of National Security: Hitchcock, Homophobia, and the Political Construction of Gender in Postwar America.* Durham, NC: Duke University Press, 1993.

Courtwright, David T. *Violent Land: Single Men and Social Disorder from the Frontier to the Inner City.* Cambridge, MA: Harvard University Press, 1996.

Cruikshank, Margaret. *The Gay and Lesbian Liberation Movement.* New York: Routledge, 1992.

Darden, Christopher A., and Jess Walter. *In Contempt.* New York: ReganBooks, 1996.

DeBenedetti, Charles. *An American Ordeal: The Antiwar*

Movement of the Vietnam Era. Syracuse, NY: Syracuse University Press, 1990.

Denisoff, R. Serge. *Great Day Coming: Folk Music and the American Left.* Urbana: University of Illinois Press, 1971.

Dickstein, Morris. *Gates of Eden: American Culture in the Sixties.* New York: Basic Books, 1977.

Easterlin, Richard A. *Birth and Fortune: The Impact of Numbers on Personal Welfare.* New York: Basic Books, 1980.

Ehrenhalt, Alan. *The Lost City: Discovering the Forgotten Virtues of Community in the Chicago of the 1950s.* New York: Basic Books, 1995.

Elliott, Michael. *The Day Before Yesterday: Reconsidering America's Past, Rediscovering the Present.* New York: Simon and Schuster, 1996.

Endleman, Robert. *Jonestown and the Manson Family: Race, Sexuality, and Collective Madness.* New York: Psyche, 1993.

Escott, Colin. *Roadkill on the Three-Chord Highway: Art and Trash in American Popular Music.* New York: Routledge, 2002.

Faith, Karlene. *The Long Prison Journey of Leslie Van Houten: Life Beyond the Cult.* Boston: Northeastern University Press, 2001.

Farber, David R. *Chicago '68.* Chicago: University of Chicago Press, 1988.

———, ed. *The Sixties: From Memory to History.* Chapel Hill: University of North Carolina Press, 1994.

Farley, Reynolds. *The New American Reality: Who We Are, How We Got Here, Where We Are Going.* New York: Russell Sage Foundation, 1996.

Fidelman, Geoffrey Mark. *The Lucy Book: A Complete Guide to Her Five Decades on Television.* Los Angeles: Renaissance, 1999.

Fiske, John. *Media Matters: Everyday Culture and Political Change.* Minneapolis: University of Minnesota Press, 1996.

Fox, Richard Wightman. *Reinhold Niebuhr: A Biography.* New York: Pantheon, 1985.

Frankel, Max. *The Times of My Life and My Life with the Times.* New York: Random House, 1999.

Fraser, Steven, and Joshua B. Freeman, eds. *Audacious Democracy: Labor, Intellectuals, and the Social Reconstruction of America.* Boston: Houghton Mifflin, 1997.

Friedberg, Anne. *Window Shopping: Cinema and the Postmodern.* Berkeley: University of California Press, 1993.

Gabler, Neal. *Winchell: Gossip, Power, and the Culture of Celebrity.* New York: Alfred A. Knopf, 1994.

Galbraith, John Kenneth. *The Affluent Society.* Boston: Houghton Mifflin, 1984.

Gans, Herbert J. *The Levittowners: Ways of Life and Politics in a New Suburban Community.* New York: Pantheon, 1967.

Gates, Henry Louis, Jr. *Loose Canons: Notes on the Culture Wars.* New York: Oxford University Press, 1992.

Gathorne-Hardy, Jonathan. *Sex the Measure of All Things: A Life of Alfred C. Kinsey.* Bloomington: Indiana University Press, 2000.

George, Edward, and Dary Matera. *Taming the Beast: Charles Manson's Life Behind Bars.* New York: St. Martin's, 1998.

Gilbert, James Burkhart. *A Cycle of Outrage: America's Reaction to the Juvenile Delinquent in the 1950s.* New York: Oxford University Press, 1986.

Gillett, Charlie. *The Sound of the City: The Rise of Rock and Roll.* New York: Da Capo, 1996.

Gitlin, Todd. *Media Unlimited: How the Torrent of Images and Sounds Overwhelms Our Lives.* New York: Metropolitan, 2002.

———. *The Twilight of Common Dreams: Why America Is Wracked by Culture Wars.* New York: Metropolitan, 1995.

———. *The Whole World Is Watching: Mass Media in the Making & Unmaking of the New Left.* Berkeley: University of California Press, 1980.

Glazer, Nathan, ed. *Clamor at the Gates: The New American Immigration.* San Francisco: ICS, 1985.

Goldstein, Richard. *Reporting the Counterculture.* Boston: Unwin Hyman, 1989.

Goodman, Paul. *Growing Up Absurd: Problems of Youth in the Organized System.* New York: Random House, 1960.

Goodwin, Andrew. *Dancing in the Distraction Factory: Music Television and Popular Culture.* Minneapolis: University of Minnesota Press, 1992.

Graebner, William. *Coming of Age in Buffalo: Youth and Authority in the Postwar Era.* Philadelphia: Temple University Press, 1990.

Grunwald, Henry A. *One Man's America: A Journalist's Search for the Heart of His Country.* New York: Doubleday, 1997.

Guilbaut, Serge. *How New York Stole the Idea of Modern Art: Abstract Expressionism, Freedom, and the Cold War.* Chicago: University of Chicago Press, 1985.

Haddow, Robert H. *Pavilions of Plenty: Exhibiting American Culture Abroad in the 1950s.* Washington, DC: Smithsonian Institution Press, 1997.

Haining, Peter. *The Classic Era of the American Pulp Magazine.* Chicago: Chicago Review, 2001.

Harrington, Michael. *The Other America: Poverty in the United States.* Baltimore: Penguin, 1966.

———. *The Politics at God's Funeral: The Spiritual Crisis of Western Civilization.* New York: Holt, Rinehart and Winston, 1983.

Harris, Warren G. *Lucy & Desi: The Legendary Love Story of Television's Most Famous Couple.* New York: Simon and Schuster, 1991.

Heineman, Kenneth J. *Campus Wars: The Peace Movement at American State Universities in the Vietnam Era.* New York: New York University Press, 1993.

Hendershot, Cynthia. *Anti-Communism and Popular Culture in Mid-Century America.* Jefferson, NC: McFarland, 2003.

Henriksen, Margot A. *Dr. Strangelove's America: Society and Culture in the Atomic Age.* Berkeley: University of California Press, 1997.

Herrnstein, Richard J., and Charles Murray. *The Bell Curve: Intelligence and Class Structure in American Life.* New York: Simon and Schuster, 1996.

Himelhoch, Jerome, and Sylvia Fleis Fava. *Sexual Behavior in American Society; An Appraisal of the First Two Kinsey Reports.* New York: W.W. Norton, 1955.

Hing, Bill Ong. *To Be an American: Cultural Pluralism and the Rhetoric of Assimilation.* New York: New York University Press, 1997.

Hixson, Walter L. *Parting the Curtain: Propaganda, Culture, and the Cold War, 1945–1961.* New York: St. Martin's, 1998

Hohenberg, John. *The Professional Journalist: A Guide to the Practices and Principles of the News Media.* New York: Holt, Rinehart and Winston, 1978.

———. *The Pulitzer Prizes: A History of the Awards in Books, Drama, Music, and Journalism, Based on the Private Files over Six Decades.* New York: Columbia University Press, 1974.

Hollinger, David A. *Postethnic America: Beyond Multiculturalism.* New York: Basic Books, 1995.

Horn, Maurice. *Women in the Comics.* 3 vols. Philadelphia: Chelsea House, 2001.

Hughes, Robert. *Culture of Complaint: The Fraying of America.* New York: Warner, 1993.

Hunter, James Davison. *Culture Wars: The Struggle to Define America.* New York: Basic Books, 1991.

Inge, M. Thomas. *Charles M. Schulz: Conversations.* Jackson: University Press of Mississippi, 2000.

Isserman, Maurice. *If I Had a Hammer—: The Death of the Old Left and the Birth of the New Left.* New York: Basic Books, 1987.

Jackson, Kenneth T. *Crabgrass Frontier: The Suburbanization of the United States.* New York: Oxford University Press, 1985.

Jamieson, Kathleen Hall, and Karlyn Kohrs Campbell. *The Interplay of Influence: News, Advertising, Politics, and the Mass Media.* Belmont, CA: Wadsworth, 1997.

Jeffords, Susan. *The Remasculinization of America: Gender and the Vietnam War.* Bloomington: Indiana University Press, 1989.

Jencks, Christopher. *The Homeless.* Cambridge, MA: Harvard University Press, 1994.

———. *Rethinking Social Policy: Race, Poverty, and the Underclass.* Cambridge, MA: Harvard University Press, 1992.

Johnson, Rheta Grimsley. *Good Grief: The Story of Charles M. Schulz.* New York: Pharos, 1989.

Jones, Jacqueline. *American Work: Four Centuries of Black and White Labor.* New York: W.W. Norton, 1998.

———. *The Dispossessed: America's Underclasses from the Civil War to the Present.* New York: Basic Books, 1992.

Jones, James H. *Alfred C. Kinsey: A Public/Private Life.* New York: W.W. Norton, 1997.

Kaplan, Judy, and Linn Shapiro, eds. *Red Diapers: Growing Up in the Communist Left.* Urbana: University of Illinois Press, 1998.

Katz, Michael B. *The Undeserving Poor: From the War on Poverty to the War on Welfare.* New York: Pantheon, 1990.

Kellner, Douglas. *Media Culture: Cultural Studies, Identity, and Politics Between the Modern and the Postmodern.* London: Routledge, 1995.

Kimball, Roger. *The Long March: How the Cultural Revolution of the 1960s Changed America.* San Francisco: Encounter, 2000.

Kinder, Marsha. *Playing with Power in Movies, Television, and Video Games: From Muppet Babies to Teenage Mutant Ninja Turtles.* Berkeley: University of California Press, 1991.

Kirchberg, Connie. *Elvis Presley, Richard Nixon, and the American Dream.* Jefferson, NC: McFarland, 1999.

Kling, Rob, Spencer Olin, and Mark Poster, eds. *Postsuburban California: The Transformation of Orange County Since World War II.* Berkeley: University of California Press, 1995.

Knight, Peter. *Conspiracy Culture: From the Kennedy Assassination to The X-files.* New York: Routledge, 2000.

Kovach, Bill, and Tom Rosenstiel. *The Elements of Journalism: What Newspeople Should Know and the Public Should Expect.* New York: Crown, 2001.

Kozol, Jonathan. *Savage Inequalities: Children in America's Schools.* New York: HarperPerennial, 1992.

Lasch, Christopher. *The Culture of Narcissism: American Life in an Age of Diminishing Expectations.* New York: Warner, 1979.

Lauter, Paul. *From Walden Pond to Jurassic Park: Activism, Culture, & American Studies.* Durham, NC: Duke University Press, 2001.

Lee, Henry C., and Jerry Labriola. *Famous Crimes Revisited: From Sacco-Vanzetti to O.J. Simpson.* Southington, CT: Strong, 2001.

Lee, Martin A., and Bruce Shlain. *Acid Dreams: The CIA, LSD, and the Sixties Rebellion.* New York: Grove, 1985.

Levy, David W. *The Debate over Vietnam.* Baltimore: Johns Hopkins University Press, 1995.

Lhamon, W.T. *Deliberate Speed: The Origins of a Cultural Style in the American 1950s.* Washington, DC: Smithsonian Institution Press, 1990.

Lipsitz, George. *Class and Culture in Cold War America: A Rainbow at Midnight.* New York: Praeger, 1981.

Lyons, Paul. *New Left, New Right, and the Legacy of the Sixties.* Philadelphia: Temple University Press, 1996.

Magnussen, Anne, and Hans-Christian Christiansen.

Comics & Culture: Analytical and Theoretical Approaches to Comics. Copenhagen, Denmark: Museum Tusculanum, 2000.

Manson, Charles, and Nuel Emmons. *Manson in His Own Words.* New York: Grove, 1986.

Marc, David. *Bonfire of the Humanities: Television, Subliteracy, and Long-Term Memory Loss.* Syracuse, NY: Syracuse University Press, 1995.

———. *Comic Visions: Television Comedy and American Culture.* Boston: Unwin Hyman, 1989.

———. *Demographic Vistas: Television in American Culture.* Philadelphia: University of Pennsylvania Press, 1996.

Marling, Karal Ann. *As Seen on TV: The Visual Culture of Everyday Life in the 1950s.* Cambridge, MA: Harvard University Press, 1994.

Martin, Andrew. *Receptions of War: Vietnam in American Culture.* Norman: University of Oklahoma Press, 1993.

Matusow, Barbara. *The Evening Stars: The Making of the Network News Anchors.* Boston: Houghton Mifflin, 1983.

May, Elaine Tyler. *Homeward Bound: American Families in the Cold War Era.* New York: Basic Books, 1988.

McAlister, Melani. *Epic Encounters: Culture, Media, and U.S. Interests in the Middle East, 1945–2000.* Berkeley: University of California Press, 2001.

McCloud, Scott. *Reinventing Comics: How Imagination and Technology Are Revolutionizing an Art Form.* New York: Perennial, 2001.

McWhirter, David P., Stephanie A. Sanders, and June Machover Reinisch. *Homosexuality/Heterosexuality: Concepts of Sexual Orientation.* New York: Oxford University Press, 1990.

McWilliams, John C. *The 1960s Cultural Revolution.* Westport, CT: Greenwood, 2000.

Melley, Timothy. *Empire of Conspiracy: The Culture of Paranoia in Postwar America.* Ithaca, NY: Cornell University Press, 2000.

Miller, Timothy. *The Hippies and American Values.* Knoxville: University of Tennessee Press, 1991.

Mills, C. Wright. *The Power Elite.* New York: Oxford University Press, 1956.

Moore, Joan W., and John Hagedorn. *Female Gangs: A Focus on Research.* Washington, DC: U.S. Dept. of Justice, Office of Justice Programs, Office of Juvenile Justice and Delinquency Prevention, 2001.

Nadel, Alan. *Containment Culture: American Narrative, Postmodernism, and the Atomic Age.* Durham, NC: Duke University Press, 1995.

Neville, John F. *The Press, the Rosenbergs, and the Cold War.* Westport, CT: Praeger, 1995.

Numbers, Ronald L. *The Creationists.* New York: Alfred A. Knopf, 1992.

Oakes, Guy. *The Imaginary War: Civil Defense and American Cold War Culture.* New York: Oxford University Press, 1994

Oakley, J. Ronald. *God's Country: America in the Fifties.* New York: Dembner, 1986.

O'Connor, John E. *American History, American Television: Interpreting the Video Past.* New York: Ungar, 1983.

Ovnick, Merry. *Los Angeles, The End of the Rainbow.* Los Angeles: Balcony, 1994.

Page One: One Hundred Years of Headlines as Presented in the New York Times. New York: Galahad, 2000.

Perkinson, Henry J. *Getting Better: Television and Moral Progress.* New Brunswick, NJ: Transaction, 1991.

Polan, Dana B. *Power and Paranoia: History, Narrative, and the American Cinema, 1940–1950.* New York: Columbia University Press, 1986.

Pomeroy, Wardell Baxter. *Dr. Kinsey and the Institute for Sex Research.* New York: Harper and Row, 1972.

Portes, Alejandro, and Alex Stepick. *City on the Edge: The Transformation of Miami.* Berkeley: University of California Press, 1993.

Raskin, Jonah. *For the Hell of It: The Life and Times of Abbie Hoffman.* Berkeley: University of California Press, 1996.

Reed, David. *The Popular Magazine in Britain and the United States, 1880–1960.* Toronto: University of Toronto Press, 1997.

Robinson, Paul A. *The Modernization of Sex: Havelock Ellis, Alfred Kinsey, William Masters, and Virginia Johnson.* New York: Harper and Row, 1976.

Rood, Karen L., ed. *American Culture After World War II.* Detroit: Gale Research, 1994.

Rorabaugh, W. J. *Berkeley at War, the 1960s.* New York: Oxford University Press, 1989.

Rose, Dan. *Patterns of American Culture: Ethnography & Estrangement.* Philadelphia: University of Pennsylvania Press, 1989.

Rose, Mark H. *Interstate: Express Highway Politics, 1941–1956.* Lawrence, KS: Regents, 1979.

Ross, Andrew. *No Respect: Intellectuals & Popular Culture.* New York: Routledge, 1989.

Roszak, Theodore. *The Making of a Counter Culture: Reflections on the Technocratic Society and Its Youthful Opposition.* Garden City, NY: Doubleday, 1969.

Rowe, John Carlos, and Richard Berg. *The Vietnam War and American Culture.* New York: Columbia University Press, 1991.

Rupp, Leila J., and Verta Taylor. *Survival in the Doldrums: The American Women's Rights Movement, 1945 to the 1960s.* New York: Oxford University Press, 1987.

Sabin, Roger. *Comics, Comix & Graphic Novels: A History of Graphic Novels.* London: Phaidon, 2001.

Salamone, Frank A. *Popular Culture in the Fifties.* Lanham, MD: University Press of America, 2001.

Sale, Kirkpatrick. *The Green Revolution: The American Environmental Movement, 1962–1992.* New York: Hill and Wang, 1993.

————. *SDS*. New York: Random House, 1973.

Samuelson, Robert J. *The Good Life and Its Discontents: The American Dream in the Age of Entitlement, 1945–1995*. New York: Times Books, 1995.

Sanders, Coyne Steven, and Thomas W. Gilbert. *Desilu: The Story of Lucille Ball and Desi Arnaz*. New York: William Morrow, 1993.

Sayre, Nora. *Previous Convictions: A Journey Through the 1950s*. New Brunswick, NJ: Rutgers University Press, 1995.

Schlesinger, Arthur Meier. *The Disuniting of America*. New York: W.W. Norton, 1992.

Schuetz, Janice E., and Lin S. Lilley. *The O.J. Simpson Trials: Rhetoric, Media, and the Law*. Carbondale: Southern Illinois University Press, 1999.

Schulz, Charles M., and David Larkin. *Peanuts: A Golden Celebration: The Art and the Story of the World's Best-Loved Comic Strip*. New York: HarperCollins, 1999.

Scott, Allen J., and Edward W. Soja, eds. *The City: Los Angeles and Urban Theory at the End of the Twentieth Century*. Berkeley: University of California Press, 1996.

Shabecoff, Philip. *A Fierce Green Fire: The American Environmental Movement*. New York: Hill and Wang, 1993.

Students for a Democratic Society. *The Port Huron Statement*. New York: No publisher, 1964.

Sugrue, Thomas J. *The Origins of the Urban Crisis: Race and Inequality in Postwar Detroit*. Princeton, NJ: Princeton University Press, 1996.

Tatalovich, Raymond. *Nativism Reborn?: The Official English Language Movement and the American States*. Lexington: University Press of Kentucky, 1995.

Teaford, Jon C. *The Rough Road to Renaissance: Urban Revitalization in America, 1940–1985*. Baltimore: Johns Hopkins University Press, 1990.

Tebbel, John William, and Mary Ellen Zuckerman. *The Magazine in America, 1741–1990*. New York: Oxford University Press, 1991.

Terkel, Studs. *The Great Divide: Second Thoughts on the American Dream*. New York: Pantheon, 1988.

Terry, Maury. *The Ultimate Evil: An Investigation into a Dangerous Satanic Cult*. New York: Bantam, 1989.

Thompson, Hunter S. *Fear and Loathing in America: The Brutal Odyssey of an Outlaw Journalist, 1968–1976*. Edited by Douglas Brinkley. New York: Simon and Schuster, 2000.

————. *Fear and Loathing in Las Vegas: A Savage Journey to the Heart of the American Dream*. New York: Vintage Books, 1989.

————. *Hell's Angels: A Strange and Terrible Saga*. New York: Ballantine, 1996.

Tichi, Cecelia. *Electronic Hearth: Creating an American Television Culture*. New York: Oxford University Press, 1991.

Tifft, Susan E., and Alex S. Jones. *The Trust: The Private and Powerful Family Behind the New York Times*. Boston: Little, Brown, 1999.

Toch, Thomas. *In the Name of Excellence: The Struggle to Reform the Nation's Schools, Why It's Failing, and What Should Be Done*. New York: Oxford University Press, 1991.

Trencher, Susan R. *Mirrored Images: American Anthropology and American Culture, 1960–1980*. Westport, CT: Bergin and Garvey, 2000.

Turow, Joseph. *Breaking Up America: Advertisers and the New Media World*. Chicago: University of Chicago Press, 1997.

Twerski, Abraham J., and Charles M. Schulz. *When Do the Good Things Start?* New York: Topper, 1988.

Varnum, Robin, and Christina Gibbons. *The Language of Comics: Word and Image*. Jackson: University Press of Mississippi, 2002.

Waldinger, Roger, ed. *Strangers at the Gates: New Immigrants in Urban America*. Berkeley: University of California Press, 2001.

Walker, Brian. *The Comics: Since 1945*. New York: Harry N. Abrams, 2002.

Ward, Ed, Geoffrey Stokes, and Ken Tucker. *Rock of Ages: The Rolling Stone History of Rock & Roll*. New York: Rolling Stone, 1986.

Wells, Tom. *The War Within: America's Battle over Vietnam*. New York: Henry Holt, 1996.

West, Cornel. *Prophetic Fragments: Illuminations of the Crisis in American Religion and Culture*. Grand Rapids, MI: W.B. Eerdmans, 1993.

West, Philip, and Chi-mun So. *Remembering the "Forgotten War": The Korean War Through Literature and Art*. Armonk, NY: M.E. Sharpe, 2001.

Whitfield, Stephen J. *The Culture of the Cold War*. Baltimore: Johns Hopkins University Press, 1991.

Whyte, William Hollingsworth. *The Organization Man*. Garden City, NY: Doubleday, 1957.

Wolfe, Tom. *From Bauhaus to Our House*. New York: Farrar, Straus and Giroux, 1981.

Worster, Donald. *Rivers of Empire: Water, Aridity, and the Growth of the American West*. New York: Pantheon, 1985.

Wright, Lawrence. *In the New World: Growing Up with America, 1960–1984*. New York: Alfred A. Knopf, 1988.

Wyatt, David. *Out of the Sixties: Storytelling and the Vietnam Generation*. Cambridge, UK: Cambridge University Press, 1993.

Zelizer, Barbie. *Covering the Body: The Kennedy Assassination, the Media, and the Shaping of Collective Memory*. Chicago: University of Chicago Press, 1992.

Zucker, Norman L., and Naomi Flink Zucker. *Desperate Crossings: Seeking Refuge in America*. Armonk, NY: M.E. Sharpe, 1996.

Business, Economics, and Labor

Ackerman, Bruce, and Anne Alstott. *The Stakeholder Society.* New Haven: Yale University Press, 1999.

Aldrich, Nelson W. *Old Money: The Mythology of America's Upper Class.* New York: Alfred A. Knopf, 1988.

Allen, Michael Patrick. *The Founding Fortunes: A New Anatomy of the Corporate-Rich Families in America.* New York: Truman Talley, 1987.

Auletta, Ken. *The Underclass.* Woodstock, NY: Overlook, 1999.

Bane, Mary Jo, and David T. Ellwood. *Welfare Realities: From Rhetoric to Reform.* Cambridge, MA: Harvard University Press, 1994.

Barnard, John. *Walter Reuther and the Rise of the Auto Workers.* Boston: Little, Brown, 1983.

Barnett, Rosalind C., and Caryl Rivers. *She Works/He Works: How Two-Income Families Are Happier, Healthier, and Better-off.* San Francisco: HarperSanFrancisco, 1996.

Berkowitz, Edward D. *America's Welfare State: From Roosevelt to Reagan.* Baltimore: Johns Hopkins University Press, 1991.

Bernstein, Irving. *Guns or Butter: The Presidency of Lyndon Johnson.* New York: Oxford University Press, 1996.

Bernstein, Michael A., and David E. Adler, eds. *Understanding American Economic Decline.* Cambridge, UK: Cambridge University Press, 1994.

Bluestone, Barry, and Bennett Harrison. *The Deindustrialization of America: Plant Closings, Community Abandonment, and the Dismantling of Basic Industry.* New York: Basic Books, 1982.

———. *Growing Prosperity: The Battle for Growth with Equity in the Twenty-First Century.* Boston: Houghton Mifflin, 2000.

Boyle, Kevin. *The UAW and the Heyday of American Liberalism, 1945–1968.* Ithaca, NY: Cornell University Press, 1995.

Calleo, David P. *The Imperious Economy.* Cambridge, MA: Harvard University Press, 1982.

Campagna, Anthony S. *The Economy in the Reagan Years: The Economic Consequences of the Reagan Administrations.* Westport, CT: Greenwood, 1994.

———. *U.S. National Economic Policy, 1917–1985.* New York: Praeger, 1987.

Chicago Tribune Staff. *The American Millstone: An Examination of the Nation's Permanent Underclass.* Chicago: Contemporary Books, 1986.

Commoner, Barry. *The Politics of Energy.* New York: Alfred A. Knopf, 1979.

Dandaneau, Steven P. *A Town Abandoned: Flint, Michigan, Confronts Deindustrialization.* Albany: State University of New York Press, 1996.

Davies, Gareth. *From Opportunity to Entitlement: The Transformation and Decline of Great Society Liberalism.* Lawrence: University Press of Kansas, 1996.

Davis, Mike. *City of Quartz: Excavating the Future in Los Angeles.* London: Verso, 1990.

De Graaf, John, David Wann, and Thomas H. Naylor. *Affluenza: The All Consuming Epidemic.* San Francisco: Berrett-Koehler, 2001.

Dietrich, William S. *In the Shadow of the Rising Sun: The Political Roots of American Economic Decline.* University Park: Pennsylvania State University Press, 1991.

Duncan, Greg J., with Richard D. Coe. *Years of Poverty, Years of Plenty: The Changing Economic Fortunes of American Workers and Families.* Ann Arbor: Survey Research Center, Institute for Social Research, University of Michigan, 1984.

Edsall, Thomas Byrne. *The New Politics of Inequality.* New York: W.W. Norton, 1984.

Ehrenreich, Barbara. *Nickel and Dimed: On (Not) Getting By in America.* New York: Metropolitan, 2001.

———. *The Worst Years of Our Lives: Irreverent Notes From a Decade of Greed.* New York: Pantheon, 1990.

Fraser, Steven, and Joshua B. Freeman, eds. *Audacious Democracy: Labor, Intellectuals, and the Social Reconstruction of America.* Boston: Houghton Mifflin, 1997.

Galinsky, Ellen. *Ask the Children: What America's Children Really Think About Working Parents.* New York: William Morrow, 1999.

Gilder, George F. *Wealth and Poverty.* New York: Basic Books, 1981.

Gillette, Michael L. *Launching the War on Poverty: An Oral History.* New York: Twayne, 1996.

Goldfield, Michael. *The Decline of Organized Labor in the United States.* Chicago: University of Chicago Press, 1987.

Graham, Otis L. *Losing Time: The Industrial Policy Debate.* Cambridge, MA: Harvard University Press, 1992.

Hargrove, Erwin C. *Prisoners of Myth: The Leadership of the Tennessee Valley Authority, 1933–1990.* Princeton, NJ: Princeton University Press, 1994.

Harrington, Michael. *The New American Poverty.* New York: Holt, Rinehart and Winston, 1984.

———. *The Other America: Poverty in the United States.* Baltimore: Penguin, 1966.

Heath, Jim F. *John F. Kennedy and the Business Community.* Chicago: University of Chicago Press, 1969.

Hochschild, Arlie Russell. *The Time Bind: When Work Becomes Home and Home Becomes Work.* New York: Metropolitan, 1997.

Hochschild, Arlie Russell, and Anne Machung. *The Second Shift: Working Parents and the Revolution at Home.* New York: Viking, 1989.

Hodgson, Geoffrey M. *Economics and Utopia: Why the Learning Economy Is Not the End of History.* London: Routledge, 1999.

Hodgson, Geoffrey M., and Ernesto Screpanti, eds. *Rethinking Economics: Markets, Technology, and Economic Evolution.* Brookfield, VT: E. Elgar, 1991.

Hogan, Michael J. *The Marshall Plan: America, Britain, and the Reconstruction of Western Europe, 1947–1952.* Cambridge, UK: Cambridge University Press, 1987.

Isserman, Maurice. *The Other American: The Life of Michael Harrington.* New York: PublicAffairs, 2000.

Jackson, Jesse, Sr., and Jesse Jackson, Jr. *It's About the Money!: The Fourth Movement of the Freedom Symphony: How to Build Wealth, Get Access to Capital, and Achieve Your Financial Dreams.* New York: Times Business, 1999.

Jencks, Christopher. *Rethinking Social Policy: Race, Poverty, and the Underclass.* Cambridge, MA: Harvard University Press, 1992.

Jones, Jacqueline. *The Dispossessed: America's Underclasses from the Civil War to the Present.* New York: Basic Books, 1992.

Kimball, Gayle. *50–50 Parenting: Sharing Family Rewards and Responsibilities.* Lexington, MA: Lexington, 1988.

King, Ronald Frederick. *Money, Time & Politics: Investment Tax Subsidies & American Democracy.* New Haven: Yale University Press, 1993.

Kirsch, M.M. *How to Get Off the Fast Track—and Live a Life Money Can't Buy.* Los Angeles: Lowell House, 1991.

Kirstein, George G. *The Rich: Are They Different?* Boston: Houghton Mifflin, 1968.

Krugman, Paul R. *Peddling Prosperity: Economic Sense and Nonsense in the Age of Diminished Expectations.* New York: W.W. Norton, 1994.

Kunz, Diane B. *The Economic Diplomacy of the Suez Crisis.* Chapel Hill: University of North Carolina Press, 1991.

LaFeber, Walter. *Michael Jordan and the New Global Capitalism.* New York: W.W. Norton, 1999.

Lapham, Lewis H. *Money and Class in America: Notes and Observations on a Civil Religion.* New York: Weidenfeld and Nicolson, 1988.

Levering, Robert. *A Great Place to Work: What Makes Some Employers So Good, and Most So Bad.* New York: Random House, 1988.

Levy, Frank. *Dollars and Dreams: The Changing American Income Distribution.* New York: Russell Sage Foundation for the National Committee for Research on the 1980 Census, 1987.

Lichtenstein, Nelson. *The Most Dangerous Man in Detroit: Walter Reuther and the Fate of American Labor.* New York: Basic Books, 1995.

Magaziner, Ira C., and Robert B. Reich. *Minding America's Business: The Decline and Rise of the American Economy.* New York: Harcourt Brace Jovanovich, 1982.

Matusow, Allen J. *Nixon's Economy: Booms, Busts, Dollars, and Votes.* Lawrence: University Press of Kansas, 1998.

McWilliams, John-Roger, and Peter McWilliams. *Wealth 101: Getting What You Want—Enjoying What You've Got.* Los Angeles: Prelude, 1992.

Melosi, Martin V. *Coping with Abundance: Energy and Environment in Industrial America.* New York: Alfred A. Knopf, 1985.

Meyerowitz, Joanne J. *Not June Cleaver: Women and Gender in Postwar America, 1945–1960.* Philadelphia: Temple University Press, 1994.

Milkman, Ruth. *Farewell to the Factory: Auto Workers in the Late Twentieth Century.* Berkeley: University of California Press, 1997.

Miller, Roger LeRoy, and Raburn M. Williams. *The New Economics of Richard Nixon: Freezes, Floats, and Fiscal Policy.* New York: Harper's Magazine, 1972.

Mills, C. Wright. *White Collar: The American Middle Classes.* New York: Oxford University Press, 1956.

Mohl, Raymond A., ed. *Searching for the Sunbelt: Historical Perspectives on a Region.* Knoxville: University of Tennessee Press, 1990.

Murray, Charles A. *Losing Ground: American Social Policy, 1950–1980.* New York: Basic Books, 1984.

Nau, Henry R. *The Myth of America's Decline: Leading the World Economy into the 1990s.* New York: Oxford University Press, 1990.

———. *Trade and Security: U.S. Policies at Cross-Purposes.* Washington, DC: American Enterprise Institute, 1995.

Nocera, Joseph. *A Piece of the Action: How the Middle Class Joined the Money Class.* New York: Simon and Schuster, 1994.

O'Connor, Alice. *Poverty Knowledge: Social Science, Social Policy, and the Poor in Twentieth-Century U.S. History.* Princeton, NJ: Princeton University Press, 2001.

Oliver, Melvin L., and Thomas M. Shapiro. *Black Wealth/White Wealth: A New Perspective on Racial Inequality.* New York: Routledge, 1995.

Packard, Vance Oakley. *The Ultra Rich: How Much Is Too Much?* Boston: Little, Brown, 1989.

Patterson, James T. *America's Struggle Against Poverty in the Twentieth Century.* Cambridge, MA: Harvard University Press, 2000.

Phillips, Kevin P. *Arrogant Capital: Washington, Wall Street, and the Frustration of American Politics.* Boston: Little, Brown, 1994.

———. *Wealth and Democracy: A Political History of the American Rich.* New York: Broadway, 2002.

Potter, David Morris. *People of Plenty: Economic Abundance and the American Character.* Chicago: University of Chicago Press, 1954.

Reich, Robert B. *The Work of Nations: Preparing Ourselves for 21st-Century Capitalism.* New York: Alfred A. Knopf, 1991.

Reuther, Victor G. *The Brothers Reuther and the Story of the UAW: A Memoir.* Boston: Houghton Mifflin, 1976.

Rose, Mark H. *Interstate: Express Highway Politics, 1941–1956.* Lawrence, KS: Regents, 1979.

Schachter, Oscar. *Sharing the World's Resources.* New York: Columbia University Press, 1977.

Schapsmeier, Edward L., and Frederick H. Schapsmeier. *Ezra Taft Benson and the Politics of Agriculture: The Eisenhower Years, 1953–1961.* Danville, IL: Interstate, 1975.

Schmidt, Jeff. *Disciplined Minds: A Critical Look at Salaried Professionals and the Soul-Battering System That Shapes Their Lives.* Lanham, MD: Rowman and Littlefield, 2000.

Schor, Juliet. *The Overspent American: Upscaling, Downshifting, and the New Consumer.* New York: Basic Books, 1998.

———. *The Overworked American: The Unexpected Decline of Leisure.* New York: Basic Books, 1991.

Schulman, Bruce J. *From Cotton Belt to Sunbelt: Federal Policy, Economic Development, and the Transformation of the South, 1938–1980.* New York: Oxford University Press, 1991.

Shetty, Y. Krishna, and Vernon M. Buehler. *Productivity and Quality Through People: Practices of Well-Managed Companies.* Westport, CT: Quorum, 1985.

Stolper, Michael, with Everett Mattlin. *Wealth: An Owner's Manual: A Sensible, Steady, Sure Course to Becoming and Staying Rich.* New York: HarperBusiness, 1992.

Tynes, Sheryl R. *Turning Points in Social Security: From "Cruel Hoax" to "Sacred Entitlement."* Stanford, CA: Stanford University Press, 1996.

Wheat, Leonard F., and William H. Crown. *State Per-Capita Income Change Since 1950: Sharecropping's Collapse and Other Causes of Convergence.* Westport, CT: Greenwood, 1995.

Williamson, Jeffrey G. *American Inequality: A Macroeconomic History.* New York: Academic Press, 1980.

Wilson, William J. *When Work Disappears: The World of the New Urban Poor.* New York: Alfred A. Knopf, 1996.

Woodward, Bob. *Maestro: Greenspan's Fed and the American Boom.* New York: Simon and Schuster, 2000.

Yergin, Daniel, ed. *The Dependence Dilemma: Gasoline Consumption and America's Security.* Cambridge, MA: Center for International Affairs, Harvard University, 1980.

———. *The Prize: The Epic Quest for Oil, Money, and Power.* New York: Simon and Schuster, 1991.

Yergin, Daniel, and Joseph Stanislaw. *The Commanding Heights: The Battle Between Government and the Marketplace That Is Remaking the Modern World.* New York: Simon and Schuster, 1998.

Zundel, Alan F. *Declarations of Dependency: The Civic Republican Tradition in U.S. Poverty Policy.* Albany: State University of New York Press, 2000.

Family, Community, and Society

Abt, Samuel, and James D. Startt. *Lance Armstrong's Comeback from Cancer: A Scrapbook of the Tour de France Winner's Dramatic Career.* San Francisco: Poole, 2000.

Ackerman, David M. *Prayer and Religion in the Public Schools.* New York: Novinka, 2001.

Aikman, J. Kurt, and Robert F. Lang. *Olympic Security: Inside the Fence at the Olympic Village, 1996 Summer Olympic Games, Atlanta, Georgia.* Atlanta: Georgia Tech Research Security, 1997.

André, Rae. *Homemakers, the Forgotten Workers.* Chicago: University of Chicago Press, 1981.

Andrisani, John. *Think Like Tiger: An Analysis of Tiger Woods' Mental Game.* New York: G. P. Putnam's Sons, 2002.

Antoun, Richard T., and Mary Elaine Hegland, eds. *Religious Resurgence: Contemporary Cases in Islam, Christianity, and Judaism.* Syracuse, NY: Syracuse University Press, 1987.

Aronson, Virginia, and Elaine K. Andrews. *Venus Williams.* Philadelphia: Chelsea House, 1999.

Asirvatham, Sandy. *Venus Williams.* Philadelphia: Chelsea House, 2002.

Baird, Robert M., and Stuart E. Rosenbaum. *Same-Sex Marriage: The Moral and Legal Debate.* Amherst, NY: Prometheus, 1997.

Barkley, Charles, and Rick Reilly. *Sir Charles: The Wit and Wisdom of Charles Barkley.* New York: Warner, 1994.

Barrett, Norman S. *The Centennial Olympic Games.* New York: Carlton, 1996.

Bellah, Robert N., Richard Madsen, Steven M. Tipton, William M. Sullivan, and Ann Swidler. *The Good Society.* New York: Vintage Books, 1992.

———. *Habits of the Heart: Individualism and Commitment in American Life.* Berkeley: University of California Press, 1985.

Berger, Brigitte. *The Family in the Modern Age: More than a Lifestyle Choice.* New Brunswick, NJ: Transaction, 2002.

Berger, Brigitte, and Peter L. Berger. *The War over the Family: Capturing the Middle Ground.* Garden City, NY: Anchor/Doubleday, 1983.

Berger, Gilda. *Violence and Sports.* New York: F. Watts, 1990.

Berger, Phil. *Blood Season: Mike Tyson and the World of Boxing.* 2nd ed. New York: Four Walls Eight Windows, 1996.

Berk, Sarah Fenstermaker. *The Gender Factory: The Apportionment of Work in American Households.* New York: Plenum, 1985.

Bill, James A., and John Alden Williams. *Roman Catholics & Shi'i Muslims: Prayer, Passion & Politics.* Chapel Hill: University of North Carolina Press, 2002.

Bingham, Howard L., and Max Wallace. *Muhammad Ali's Greatest Fight: Cassius Clay vs. the United States of America.* New York: M. Evans, 2000.

Blanchard, Dallas A. *The Anti-Abortion Movement and the Rise of the Religious Right: From Polite to Fiery Protest.* New York: Twayne, 1994.

Blau, Francine D. *The Economics of Women, Men, and Work.* Englewood Cliffs, NJ: Prentice-Hall, 1992.

Boyer, Paul S. *Purity in Print: Book Censorship in America from the Gilded Age to the Computer Age.* Madison: University of Wisconsin Press, 2002.

Brenner, Richard J. *Shaquille O'Neal & Larry Johnson.* Syosset, NY: East End, 1993.

Brown, Bruce W. *Images of Family Life in Magazine Advertising, 1920–1978.* New York: Praeger, 1981.

Burby, Liza N. *Sheryl Swoopes, All-Star Basketball Player.* New York: Rosen, 1997.

Callahan, Tom. *In Search of Tiger Woods: A Journey Through Golf with Tiger Woods.* New York: Crown, 2003.

Cameron, Steve. *Brett Favre: Huck Finn Grows Up.* Indianapolis, IN: Masters, 1996.

Carter, Stephen L. *The Culture of Disbelief: How American Law and Politics Trivialize Religious Devotion.* New York: Basic Books, 1993.

Christopher, Matt. *On the Field With—Mia Hamm.* Boston: Little, Brown, 1988.

Coyle, Maureen, Rita Sullivan, and Jeanne Tang. *Official WNBA Guide and Register.* St. Louis: WNBA Enterprises, 2002.

Curry, Hayden. *A Legal Guide for Lesbian and Gay Couples.* Berkeley, CA: Nolo, 1998.

Daly, Wendy. *Tara and Michelle: The Road to Gold.* New York: Random House, 1997.

Detwiler, Fritz. *Standing on the Premises of God*: The Christian Right's Fight to Redefine America's Public Schools. New York: New York University Press, 1999.

Dyson, Michael Eric. *Open Mike: Reflections on Philosophy, Race, Sex, Culture and Religion.* New York: Basic Civitas, 2003.

Elias, Robert, ed. *Baseball and the American Dream: Race, Class, Gender, and the National Pastime.* Armonk, NY: M.E. Sharpe, 2001.

Eskridge, William N. *Equality Practice: Civil Unions and the Future of Gay Rights.* New York: Routledge, 2002.

Findlay, James F. *Church People in the Struggle: The National Council of Churches and the Black Freedom Movement, 1950–1970.* New York: Oxford University Press, 1993.

Follis, Anne Bowen. *I'm Not a Women's Libber, but—and Other Confessions of a Christian Feminist.* Nashville, TN: Abingdon, 1981.

Fraser, James W. *Between Church and State: Religion and Public Education in a Multicultural America.* New York: St. Martin's, 1999.

Freeman, Jo. *Social Movements of the Sixties and Seventies.* New York: Longman, 1983.

Gaines, Ann. *Sammy Sosa.* Philadelphia: Chelsea House, 2000.

Garrison, J. Gregory, and Randy Roberts. *Heavy Justice: The State of Indiana v. Michael G. Tyson.* Reading, MA: Addison-Wesley, 1994.

Gilbert, James Burkhart. *A Cycle of Outrage: America's Reaction to the Juvenile Delinquent in the 1950s.* New York: Oxford University Press, 1986.

Gottlieb, Sherry Gershon. *Hell No, We Won't Go!: Resisting the Draft During the Vietnam War.* New York: Viking, 1991.

Grabowski, John F. *The Los Angeles Lakers.* San Diego, CA: Lucent, 2002.

Griffin, David Ray. *God and Religion in the Postmodern World: Essays in Postmodern Theology.* Albany: State University of New York Press, 1989.

Gutelle, Andrew. *Tiger Woods.* New York: Grosset and Dunlap, 2002.

Gutman, Bill. *Cal Ripken, Jr.: Baseball's Iron Man.* Brookfield, CT: Millbrook, 1998.

———. *Shooting Stars: The Women of Pro Basketball.* New York: Random House, 1998.

———. *Venus & Serena: The Grand Slam Williams Sisters.* New York: Scholastic, 2001.

Gutman, Dan. *Gymnastics.* New York: Viking, 1996.

Halberstam, David. *Playing for Keeps: Michael Jordan and the World He Made.* New York: Random House, 1999.

Harriss, John, ed. *The Family: A Social History of the Twentieth Century.* Oxford, UK: Oxford University Press, 1991.

Hauser, Thomas. *Muhammad Ali: His Life and Times.* New York: Simon and Schuster, 1991.

Heller, Peter. *Bad Intentions: The Mike Tyson Story.* New York: Da Capo, 1995.

Herberg, Will. *Protestant, Catholic, Jew: An Essay in American Religious Sociology.* Garden City, NY: Anchor, 1960.

Herman, Didi, and Carl Stychin. *Legal Inversions: Lesbians, Gay Men, and the Politics of Law.* Philadelphia: Temple University Press, 1995.

Hoffer, Richard. *A Savage Business: The Comeback and Comedown of Mike Tyson.* New York: Simon and Schuster, 1998.

Howard, Gregory Allen, Stephen J. Rivele and Diana Landau. *Ali: The Movie and the Man.* New York: Newmarket, 2001.

Hunt, Thomas C., and James C. Carper. *Religion and Schooling in Contemporary America: Confronting Our Cultural Pluralism.* New York: Garland, 1997.

Hunter, Bruce. *Shaq Impaq.* Chicago: Bonus Books, 1993.

Jackson, Kenneth T. *Crabgrass Frontier: The Suburbanization of the United States.* New York: Oxford University Press, 1985.

Jackson, Phil, and Charles Rosen. *More Than a Game.* New York: Seven Stories, 2001.

Johnson, Mary Anne, and James Olsen. *Exiles from the American Dream: First-Person Accounts of Our Disenchanted Youth.* New York: Walker, 1975.

Jones, Chris. *Falling Hard: A Rookie's Year in Boxing.* New York: Arcade, 2002.

Jones, Landon Y. *Great Expectations: America and the Baby Boom Generation.* New York: Coward, McCann and Geoghegan, 1980.

Karolyi, Bela, and Nancy Ann Richardson. *Feel No Fear: The Power, Passion, and Politics of a Life in Gymnastics.* New York: Hyperion, 1994.

Kaye, Elizabeth. *Ain't No Tomorrow: Kobe, Shaq, and the Making of a Lakers Dynasty.* Chicago: Contemporary Books, 2002.

King, Billie Jean, and Kim Chapin. *Billie Jean.* New York: Harper and Row, 1974.

Klatell, David A., and Norman Marcus. *Sports for Sale: Television, Money, and the Fans.* New York: Oxford University Press, 1988.

Kusch, Frank. *All American Boys: Draft Dodgers in Canada from the Vietnam War.* Westport, CT: Praeger, 2001.

Kwan, Michelle, and Laura James. *Michelle Kwan, Heart of a Champion: An Autobiography.* New York: Scholastic, 1997.

Kwitny, Jonathan. *Man of the Century: The Life and Times of Pope John Paul II.* New York: Henry Holt, 1997.

LaFeber, Walter. *Michael Jordan and the New Global Capitalism.* New York: W.W. Norton, 1999.

Lash, Jonathan, Katherine Gillman, and David Sheridan. *A Season of Spoils: The Reagan Administration's Attack on the Environment.* New York: Pantheon, 1984.

Lienesch, Michael. *Redeeming America: Piety and Politics in the New Christian Right.* Chapel Hill: University of North Carolina Press, 1993.

Lipinski, Tara, Simon Bruty, and Mark Zeigler. *Totally Tara: An Olympic Journey.* New York: Universe, 1998.

Lischer, Richard. *The Preacher King: Martin Luther King, Jr. and the Word that Moved America.* New York: Oxford University Press, 1995.

Longman, Jere. *The Girls of Summer: The U.S. Women's Soccer Team and How It Changed the World.* New York: HarperCollins, 2000.

Lovitt, Chip. *Skating for the Gold: Michelle Kwan & Tara Lipinski.* New York: Pocket Books, 1997.

Lukas, J. Anthony. *Common Ground: A Turbulent Decade in the Lives of Three American Families.* New York: Alfred A. Knopf, 1985.

Lyon, David. *Jesus in Disneyland: Religion in Postmodern Times.* Malden, MA: Polity, 2000.

Macnow, Glen. *Sports Great Tiger Woods.* Berkeley Heights, NJ: Enslow, 2001.

Marsden, George. *Evangelicalism and Modern America.* Grand Rapids, MI: W.B. Eerdmans, 1984.

Martin, William C. *A Prophet with Honor: The Billy Graham Story.* New York: William Morrow, 1991.

McKenna, George, and Stanley Feingold. *Taking Sides: Clashing Views on Controversial Political Issues.* Guilford, CT: Dushkin, 1997.

McNeil, William. *Ruth, Maris, McGwire and Sosa: Baseball's Single Season Home Run Champions.* Jefferson, NC: McFarland, 1999.

Merin, Yuval. *Equality for Same-Sex Couples: The Legal Recognition of Gay Partnerships in Europe and the United States.* Chicago: University of Chicago Press, 2002.

Miller, Marla. *All-American Girls: The U.S. Women's National Soccer Team.* New York: Pocket Books, 1999.

Moceanu, Dominique, and Steve Woodward. *Dominique Moceanu, an American Champion: An Autobiography.* New York: Bantam, 1996.

Mooney, Martin J. *Brett Favre.* Philadelphia: Chelsea House, 1997.

Mottram, D.R. *Drugs in Sports.* London: E.&F.N. Spon, 1996.

Navratilova, Martina, and Mary Carillo Bowden. *Tennis My Way.* New York: Scribner's, 1983.

Noden, Merrell. *Home Run Heroes: Mark McGwire, Sammy Sosa, and a Season for the Ages.* New York: Simon and Schuster, 1998.

Olasky, Marvin N. *Abortion Rites: A Social History of Abortion in America.* Wheaton, IL: Crossways, 1992.

Owen, David. *The Chosen One: Tiger Woods and the Dilemma of Greatness.* New York: Simon and Schuster, 2001.

Paisner, Daniel. *The Ball: Mark McGwire's 70th Home Run Ball and the Marketing of the American Dream.* New York: Viking, 1999.

Peale, Norman Vincent. *The Positive Principle Today: How to Renew and Sustain the Power of Positive Thinking.* Englewood Cliffs, NJ: Prentice-Hall, 1976.

Piparo, C.A., and Cheryl Nathan. *Brett Favre: Quarterback Dreams.* Ridgewood, NJ: Infinity Plus One, 1998.

Ponti, James. *WNBA: Stars of Women's Basketball.* New York: Pocket Books, 1999.

Quayle, Dan, and Diane Medved. *The American Family: Discovering the Values That Make Us Strong.* New York: HarperCollins, 1996.

Quiner, Krista. *Dominique Moceanu: A Gymnastics Sensation: A Biography.* East Hanover, NJ: Bradford, 1997.

Rappoport, Ken. *Sheryl Swoopes, Star Forward.* Berkeley Heights, NJ: Enslow, 2002.

Reilly, Rick. *The Life of Reilly: The Best of Sports Illustrated's Rick Reilly.* New York: Total Sports Illustrated, 2000.

———. *Missing Links.* New York: Doubleday, 1996.

———. *Slo-Mo!: My Untrue Story.* New York: Doubleday, 1999.

Remnick, David. *King of the World: Muhammad Ali and the Rise of an American Hero.* New York: Random House, 1998.

Retton, Mary Lou, Bela Karolyi, and John Powers. *Mary Lou: Creating an Olympic Champion.* New York: McGraw-Hill, 1986.

Riesman, David, in collaboration with Reuel Denney and Nathan Glazer. *The Lonely Crowd: A Study of the Changing American Character.* New Haven: Yale University Press, 1950.

Ripken, Cal, and Mike Bryan. *The Only Way I Know.* New York: Viking, 1997.

Roberts, Michael. *Fans! How We Go Crazy over Sports.* Washington, DC: New Republic, 1976.

Rosaforte, Tim, Byron Nelson, and Gary Player. *Raising the Bar: The Championship Years of Tiger Woods.* New York: St. Martin's, 2002.

Rutledge, Rachel. *Mia Hamm: Striking Superstar.* Brookfield, CT: Millbrook, 2000.

Ryan, Joan. *Little Girls in Pretty Boxes: The Making and Breaking of Elite Gymnasts and Figure Skaters.* New York: Doubleday, 1995.

Sampson, Curt. *Chasing Tiger.* New York: Atria, 2002.

Shiner, David, and David Quentin Voigt. *Baseball's Greatest Players: The Saga Continues.* Bridgewater, NJ: SuperiorBooks.com, 2001.

Silk, Mark. *Spiritual Politics: Religion and America Since World War II.* New York: Simon and Schuster, 1988.

Skolnick, Arlene S. *Embattled Paradise: The American Family in an Age of Uncertainty.* New York: Basic Books, 1991.

Smelser, Marshall. *The Life That Ruth Built: A Biography.* Lincoln: University of Nebraska Press, 1993.

Sperber, Murray A. *Beer and Circus: How Big-Time College Sports Is Crippling Undergraduate Education.* New York: Henry Holt, 2000.

Spigel, Lynn. *Make Room for TV: Television and the Family Ideal in Postwar America.* Chicago: University of Chicago Press, 1992.

Stewart, Mark. *Sweet Victory: Lance Armstrong's Incredible Journey, the Amazing Story of the Greatest Comeback in Sports.* Brookfield, CT: Millbrook, 2000.

Stewart, Mark, and Mike Kennedy. *Home Run Heroes: Mark McGwire & Sammy Sosa.* Brookfield, CT: Millbrook, 1999.

Stewart, Omer Call. *Peyote Religion: A History.* Norman: University of Oklahoma Press, 1987.

Strasser, Mark Philip. *On Same-Sex Marriage, Civil Unions, and the Rule of Law: Constitutional Interpretation at the Crossroads.* Westport, CT: Praeger, 2002.

Tabor, James D. *Why Waco?: Cults and the Battle for Religious Freedom in America.* Berkeley: University of California Press, 1995.

Watson, Mary Ann. *The Expanding Vista: American Television in the Kennedy Years.* New York: Oxford University Press, 1990.

Wells, David R. *Consumerism and the Movement of Housewives into Wage Work: The Interaction of Patriarchy, Class, and Capitalism in Twentieth Century America.* Brookfield, VT: Ashgate, 1998.

Whannel, Garry. *Media Sport Stars: Masculinities and Moralities.* London: Routledge, 2002.

Whiteside, Kelly. *WNBA: A Celebration: Commemorating the Birth of a League.* New York: HarperHorizon, 1998.

Whitfield, Stephen. *American Space, Jewish Time: Essays in Modern Culture and Politics.* Armonk, NY: M.E. Sharpe, 1996.

Will, George F. *Men at Work: The Craft of Baseball.* New York: Macmillan, 1990.

Foreign Policy and Military Affairs

Acheson, Dean. *Present at the Creation: My Years in the State Department.* New York: W.W. Norton, 1987.

Allison, Graham T. *Essence of Decision: Explaining the Cuban Missile Crisis.* Boston: Little, Brown, 1971.

Alteras, Isaac. *Eisenhower and Israel: U.S.-Israeli Relations, 1953–1960.* Gainesville: University Press of Florida, 1993.

Anderson, David L. *Trapped by Success: The Eisenhower Administration and Vietnam, 1953–1961.* New York: Columbia University Press, 1991.

Appy, Christian G. *Working-Class War: American Combat Soldiers and Vietnam.* Chapel Hill: University of North Carolina Press, 1993.

Baritz, Loren. *Backfire: A History of How American Culture Led Us into Vietnam and Made Us Fight the Way We Did.* New York: William Morrow, 1985.

Berman, Larry. *No Peace, No Honor: Nixon, Kissinger, and Betrayal in Vietnam.* New York: Free Press, 2001.

———. *Planning a Tragedy: The Americanization of the War in Vietnam.* New York: W.W. Norton, 1982.

Berman, William C. *William Fulbright and the Vietnam War: The Dissent of a Political Realist.* Kent, OH: Kent State University Press, 1988.

Beschloss, Michael R. *The Crisis Years: Kennedy and Khrushchev, 1960–1963.* New York: Edward Burlingame, 1991.

———. *MAYDAY: Eisenhower, Khrushchev, and the U-2 Affair.* New York: Harper and Row, 1986.

Beschloss, Michael R., and Strobe Talbott. *At the Highest Levels: The Inside Story of the End of the Cold War.* Boston: Little, Brown, 1993.

Bill, James A. *The Eagle and the Lion: The Tragedy of American-Iranian Relations.* New Haven: Yale University Press, 1988.

———. *George Ball: Behind the Scenes in U.S. Foreign Policy.* New Haven: Yale University Press, 1997.

Blair, Clay. *The Forgotten War: America in Korea, 1950–1953.* New York: Times Books, 1987.

Blight, James G. *Cuba on the Brink: Castro, The Missile Crisis, and the Soviet Collapse.* Lanham, MD: Rowman and Littlefield, 2002.

Blum, Robert M. *Drawing the Line: The Origin of the American Containment Policy in East Asia.* New York: W.W. Norton, 1982.

Blumenthal, Sidney. *Pledging Allegiance: The Last Campaign of the Cold War.* New York: HarperCollins, 1990.

Bonner, Raymond. *Waltzing with a Dictator: The Marcoses and the Making of American Policy.* New York: Times Books, 1987.

———. *Weakness and Deceit: U.S. Policy and El Salvador.* New York: Times Books, 1984.

Bowers, William T., William M. Hammond, and George L. MacGarrigle. *Black Soldier, White Army: The 24th Infantry Regiment in Korea.* Washington, DC: Center of Military History, U.S. Army, 1996.

Brands, H.W. *The Devil We Knew: Americans and the Cold War.* New York: Oxford University Press, 1993.

———. *The Wages of Globalism: Lyndon Johnson and the Limits of American Power.* New York: Oxford University Press, 1995.

Brinkley, Douglas. *Dean Acheson: The Cold War Years, 1953–71.* New Haven: Yale University Press, 1992.

Broad, William J. *Teller's War: The Top-Secret Story Behind the Star Wars Deception.* New York: Simon and Schuster, 1993.

Broadwater, Jeff. *Eisenhower & the Anti-Communist Crusade.* Chapel Hill: University of North Carolina Press, 1992.

Brzezinski, Zbigniew K. *Power and Principle: Memoirs of the National Security Advisor, 1977–1981.* New York: Farrar, Straus and Giroux, 1983.

Buzzanco, Robert. *Masters of War: Military Dissent and Politics in the Vietnam Era.* Cambridge, UK: Cambridge University Press, 1997.

Cable, Larry E. *Conflict of Myths: The Development of American Counterinsurgency Doctrine and the Vietnam War.* New York: New York University Press, 1986.

Carroll, John M., and George C. Herring. *Modern American Diplomacy.* Wilmington, DE: Scholarly Resources, 1986.

Chomsky, Noam. *Rethinking Camelot: JFK, the Vietnam War, and U.S. Political Culture.* Boston: South End, 1993.

Clodfelter, Mark. *The Limits of Air Power: The American Bombing of North Vietnam.* New York: Free Press, 1989.

Cockburn, Andrew, and Leslie Cockburn. *Dangerous Liaison: The Inside Story of the U.S.-Israeli Covert Relationship.* New York: HarperCollins, 1991

Cockburn, Leslie. *Out of Control: The Story of the Reagan Administration's Secret War in Nicaragua, the Illegal Arms Pipeline, and the Contra Drug Connection.* New York: Atlantic Monthly, 1987.

Cohen, Warren I. *America's Response to China: A History of Sino-American Relations.* New York: Columbia University Press, 1990.

———, ed. *The Cambridge History of American Foreign Relations.* Cambridge, UK: Cambridge University Press, 1993.

———. *Dean Rusk.* Totowa, NJ: Cooper Square, 1980.

Cohen, William S. *Men of Zeal: A Candid Inside Story of the Iran-Contra Hearings.* New York: Penguin, 1989.

Coker, Christopher. *The United States and South Africa, 1968–1985: Constructive Engagement and Its Critics.* Durham, NC: Duke University Press, 1986.

Coleman, Kenneth M., and George C. Herring. *Understanding the Central American Crisis: Sources of Conflict, U.S. Policy, and Options for Peace.* Wilmington, DE: SR, 1991.

Cook, Blanche Wiesen. *The Declassified Eisenhower: A Divided Legacy.* Garden City, NY: Doubleday, 1981.

Cullather, Nick. *Secret History: The CIA's Classified Account of Its Operations in Guatemala, 1952–1954.* Stanford, CA: Stanford University Press, 1999.

Cumings, Bruce, ed. *Child of Conflict: The Korean-American Relationship, 1943–1953.* Seattle: University of Washington Press, 1983.

———. *The Origins of the Korean War: Liberation and the Emergence of Separate Regimes, 1945–1947.* Princeton, NJ: Princeton University Press, 1981.

Dalfiume, Richard M. *Desegregation of the U.S. Armed Forces; Fighting on Two Fronts, 1939–1953.* Columbia: University of Missouri Press, 1969.

DiLeo, David L. *George Ball, Vietnam, and the Rethinking of Containment.* Chapel Hill: University of North Carolina Press, 1991.

Divine, Robert A. *Eisenhower and the Cold War.* New York: Oxford University Press, 1981.

Dumbrell, John. *American Foreign Policy: Carter to Clinton.* New York: St. Martin's, 1997.

———. *A Special Relationship: Anglo-American Relations in the Cold War and After.* Houndmills, Hampshire, UK: Macmillan; New York: St. Martin's, 2001.

Firestone, Bernard J., and Robert C. Vogt, eds. *Lyndon Baines Johnson and the Uses of Power.* New York: Greenwood, 1988.

FitzGerald, Frances. *Fire in the Lake: The Vietnamese and the Americans in Vietnam.* New York: Vintage Books, 1989.

Freedman, Lawrence. *The Gulf Conflict, 1990–1991: Diplomacy and War in the New World Order.* Princeton, NJ: Princeton University Press, 1993.

———. *Kennedy's Wars: Berlin, Cuba, Laos, and Vietnam.* New York: Oxford University Press, 2000.

Friedman, Thomas L. *From Beirut to Jerusalem.* New York: Anchor, 1995.

Fulbright, J. William, with Seth P. Tillman. *The Price of Empire.* New York: Pantheon, 1989.

Fursenko, A.V., and Timothy Naftali. *"One Hell of a Gamble": Khrushchev, Castro, and Kennedy, 1958–1964.* New York: W.W. Norton, 1997.

Gaddis, John Lewis. *Strategies of Containment: A Critical Appraisal of Postwar American National Security Policy.* New York: Oxford University Press, 1982.

———. *The United States and the End of the Cold War: Implications, Reconsiderations, Provocations.* New York: Oxford University Press, 1992.

————. *We Now Know: Rethinking Cold War History.* Oxford, UK: Clarendon, 1997.

Gardner, Lloyd C. *Approaching Vietnam: From World War II Through Dienbienphu, 1941–1954.* New York: W.W. Norton, 1988.

————. *Architects of Illusion: Men and Ideas in American Foreign Policy, 1941–1949.* Chicago: Quadrangle, 1970.

Garrison, Jean A. *Games Advisors Play: Foreign Policy in the Nixon and Carter Administrations.* College Station: Texas A&M University Press, 1999.

Garthoff, Raymond L. *Detente and Confrontation: American-Soviet Relations from Nixon to Reagan.* Washington, DC: Brookings Institution, 1994.

Geelhoed, E. Bruce, and Anthony O. Edmonds. *Eisenhower, Macmillan, and Allied Unity, 1957–1961.* New York: Palgrave Macmillan, 2003.

Gelb, Leslie H., with Richard K. Betts. *The Irony of Vietnam: The System Worked.* Washington, DC: Brookings Institution, 1979.

Green, David. *The Containment of Latin America: A History of the Myths and Realities of the Good Neighbor Policy.* Chicago: Quadrangle, 1971.

Gutman, Roy. *Banana Diplomacy: The Making of American Policy in Nicaragua, 1981–1987.* New York: Simon and Schuster, 1988.

Haddow, Robert H. *Pavilions of Plenty: Exhibiting American Culture Abroad in the 1950s.* Washington, DC: Smithsonian Institution Press, 1997.

Haig, Alexander Meigs. *Caveat: Realism, Reagan, and Foreign Policy.* New York: Macmillan, 1984.

Halberstam, David. *The Best and the Brightest.* New York: Penguin, 1983.

————. *The Making of a Quagmire: America and Vietnam During the Kennedy Era.* New York: Alfred A. Knopf, 1988.

————. *War in a Time of Peace: Bush, Clinton, and the Generals.* New York: Scribner's, 2001.

Halliday, John, and Bruce Cumings. *Korea: The Unknown War.* London: Viking, 1988.

Hallion, Richard. *The Naval Air War in Korea.* Baltimore: Nautical and Aviation Publishing Company of America, 1986.

————. *Storm over Iraq: Air Power and the Gulf War.* Washington, DC: Smithsonian Institution Press, 1992.

Hayslip, Le Ly. *When Heaven and Earth Changed Places: A Vietnamese Woman's Journey from War to Peace.* New York: Plume, 1990.

Head, William, and Earl H. Tilford, Jr., eds. *The Eagle in the Desert: Looking Back on U.S. Involvement in the Persian Gulf War.* Westport, CT: Praeger, 1996.

Herken, Gregg. *The Winning Weapon: The Atomic Bomb in the Cold War, 1945–1950.* New York: Alfred A. Knopf, 1980.

Herring, George C. *America's Longest War: The United States and Vietnam, 1950–1975.* New York: McGraw-Hill, 1996.

————. *LBJ and Vietnam: A Different Kind of War.* Austin: University of Texas Press, 1994.

Hersh, Seymour M. *The Samson Option: Israel's Nuclear Arsenal and American Foreign Policy.* New York: Random House, 1991.

Hess, Gary R. *Presidential Decisions for War: Korea, Vietnam, and the Persian Gulf.* Baltimore: Johns Hopkins University Press, 2001.

————. *The United States' Emergence as a Southeast Asian Power, 1940–1950.* New York: Columbia University Press, 1987.

Heyck, Denis Lynn Daly, ed. *Life Stories of the Nicaraguan Revolution.* New York: Routledge, 1990.

Higgins, Trumbull. *The Perfect Failure: Kennedy, Eisenhower, and the C.I.A. at the Bay of Pigs.* New York: W.W. Norton, 1987.

Hiro, Dilip. *Desert Shield to Desert Storm: The Second Gulf War.* New York: Routledge, 1992.

Hirsh, Michael. *At War with Ourselves: Why America Is Squandering Its Chance to Build a Better World.* New York: Oxford University Press, 2003.

Hixson, Walter L. *Parting the Curtain: Propaganda, Culture, and the Cold War, 1945–1961.* New York: St. Martin's, 1998

Hogan, Michael J., ed. *The End of the Cold War: Its Meaning and Implications.* Cambridge, UK: Cambridge University Press, 1992

————. *Hiroshima in History and Memory.* Cambridge, UK: Cambridge University Press, 1996.

————. *The Marshall Plan: America, Britain, and the Reconstruction of Western Europe, 1947–1952.* Cambridge, UK: Cambridge University Press, 1987.

Hohenberg, John. *Israel at 50: A Journalist's Perspective.* Syracuse, NY: Syracuse University Press, 1998.

Hoopes, Townsend. *The Devil and John Foster Dulles.* Boston: Little, Brown, 1973.

Hunt, Michael H. *Lyndon Johnson's War: America's Cold War Crusade in Vietnam, 1945–1968.* New York: Hill and Wang, 1996.

Immerman, Richard H. *The CIA in Guatemala: The Foreign Policy of Intervention.* Austin: University of Texas Press, 1982

Iriye, Akira. *The Cold War in Asia: A Historical Introduction.* Englewood Cliffs, NJ: Prentice-Hall, 1974.

Isaacson, Walter, and Evan Thomas. *The Wise Men: Six Friends and the World They Made: Acheson, Bohlen, Harriman, Kennan, Lovett, McCloy.* New York: Simon and Schuster, 1986.

Jackson, Henry F. *From the Congo to Soweto: U.S. Foreign Policy Toward Africa Since 1960.* New York: William Morrow, 1982.

Jentleson, Bruce W., ed. *Opportunities Missed, Opportunities*

Seized: Preventive Diplomacy in the Post-Cold War World. Lanham, MD: Rowman and Littlefield, 2000.

————. *With Friends Like These: Reagan, Bush, and Saddam, 1982–1990.* New York: W.W. Norton, 1994.

Johnson, Haynes Bonner, et al. *The Bay of Pigs: The Leaders' Story of Brigade 2506.* New York: W.W. Norton, 1964.

Johnson, Loch K. *America's Secret Power: The CIA in a Democratic Society.* New York: Oxford University Press, 1989.

Kahin, George McTurnan. *Intervention: How America Became Involved in Vietnam.* New York: Alfred A. Knopf, 1986.

Kaiser, David E. *American Tragedy: Kennedy, Johnson, and the Origins of the Vietnam War.* Cambridge, MA: Harvard University Press, 2000.

Kaplan, Fred M. *The Wizards of Armageddon.* New York: Simon and Schuster, 1983.

Kaplan, Lawrence S. *The United States and NATO: The Formative Years.* Lexington: University Press of Kentucky, 1984.

Kaplan, Robert D. *Balkan Ghosts: A Journey Through History.* New York: St. Martin's, 1993.

Karnow, Stanley. *Vietnam: A History.* New York: Viking, 1983.

————. *Vietnam, the War Nobody Won.* New York: Foreign Policy Association, 1983.

Kaufman, Burton Ira. *The Korean War: Challenges in Crisis, Credibility, and Command.* Philadelphia: Temple University Press, 1986.

————. *Trade and Aid: Eisenhower's Foreign Economic Policy, 1953–1961.* Baltimore: Johns Hopkins University Press, 1982.

Kellner, Douglas. *From 9/11 to Terror War: The Dangers of the Bush Legacy.* Lanham, MD: Rowman and Littlefield, 2003.

————. *The Persian Gulf TV War.* Boulder, CO: Westview, 1992.

Kennan, George Frost. *Memoirs.* New York: Pantheon, 1983.

————. *The Nuclear Delusion: Soviet-American Relations in the Atomic Age.* New York: Pantheon, 1983.

Kennedy, Paul M. *The Rise and Fall of the Great Powers: Economic Change and Military Conflict from 1500 to 2000.* New York: Vintage Books, 1989.

Kerry, J. Robert. *The United States and Southeast Asia: A Policy Agenda for a New Administration: Report of an Independent Task Force Sponsored by the Council on Foreign Relations.* New York: Council on Foreign Relations, 2001.

Kingseed, Cole C. *Eisenhower and the Suez Crisis of 1956.* Baton Rouge: Louisiana State University Press, 1995.

Kolko, Gabriel. *Anatomy of a War: Vietnam, the United States, and the Modern Historical Experience.* New York: Pantheon, 1985.

Krenn, Michael L. *The Chains of Interdependence: U.S. Policy Toward Central America, 1945–1954.* Armonk, NY: M.E. Sharpe, 1996.

Krepinevich, Andrew F. *The Army and Vietnam.* Baltimore: Johns Hopkins University Press, 1986.

Kuniholm, Bruce Robellet. *The Origins of the Cold War in the Near East: Great Power Conflict and Diplomacy in Iran, Turkey, and Greece.* Princeton, NJ: Princeton University Press, 1980.

————. *The Persian Gulf and United States Policy: A Guide to Issues and References.* Claremont, CA: Regina, 1984.

Kunz, Diane B. *The Economic Diplomacy of the Suez Crisis.* Chapel Hill: University of North Carolina Press, 1991.

Kwitny, Jonathan. *Endless Enemies: The Making of an Unfriendly World.* New York: Penguin, 1986.

LaFeber, Walter. *America, Russia, and the Cold War, 1945–1992.* New York: McGraw-Hill, 1993.

————. *Inevitable Revolutions: The United States in Central America.* New York: W.W. Norton, 1993.

————. *The Panama Canal: The Crisis in Historical Perspective.* New York: Oxford University Press, 1989.

Ledeen, Michael Arthur, and William Lewis. *Debacle, the American Failure in Iran.* New York: Alfred A. Knopf, 1981

Lee, Steven Hugh. *Outposts of Empire: Korea, Vietnam, and the Origins of the Cold War in Asia, 1949–1954.* Montreal: McGill-Queen's University Press, 1996.

Leffler, Melvyn P. *A Preponderance of Power: National Security, the Truman Administration, and the Cold War.* Stanford, CA: Stanford University Press, 1992.

Leslie, Stuart W. *The Cold War and American Science: The Military-Industrial-Academic Complex at MIT and Stanford.* New York: Columbia University Press, 1993.

Lesser, Ian O. *The United States and Southern Europe After the Cold War.* Santa Monica, CA: Rand, 1990.

Levy, David W. *The Debate over Vietnam.* Baltimore: Johns Hopkins University Press, 1995.

Litwak, Robert. *Détente and the Nixon Doctrine: American Foreign Policy and the Pursuit of Stability, 1969–1976.* Cambridge, UK: Cambridge University Press, 1984.

————. *Rogue States and U.S. Foreign Policy: Containment After the Cold War.* Washington, DC: Woodrow Wilson Center, 2000.

Litwak, Robert S., and Samuel F. Wells, Jr., eds. *Superpower Competition and Security in the Third World.* Cambridge, MA: Ballinger, 1987.

Lowenthal, Abraham F. *Partners in Conflict, the United States and Latin America.* Baltimore: Johns Hopkins University Press, 1987.

Lytle, Mark H. *The Origins of the Iranian-American Alliance, 1941–1953.* New York: Holmes and Meier, 1987.

Maga, Timothy P. *John F. Kennedy and New Frontier Diplomacy, 1961–1963.* Malabar, FL: Krieger, 1994.

Mahoney, Richard D. *JFK: Ordeal in Africa.* New York: Oxford University Press, 1983.

Mann, Robert. *A Grand Delusion: America's Descent into Vietnam.* New York: Basic Books, 2001.

Marks, Frederick W. *Power and Peace: The Diplomacy of John Foster Dulles.* Westport, CT: Praeger, 1993.

Marshall, Kathryn. *In the Combat Zone: An Oral History of American Women in Vietnam, 1966–1975.* Boston: Little, Brown, 1987.

May, Elaine Tyler. *Homeward Bound: American Families in the Cold War Era.* New York: Basic Books, 1988.

May, Ernest R., and Philip D. Zelikow, eds. *The Kennedy Tapes: Inside the White House During the Cuban Missile Crisis.* Cambridge, MA: Harvard University Press, 1997.

McDougall, Walter A. *The Heavens and the Earth: A Political History of the Space Age.* New York: Basic Books, 1985.

Melanson, Richard A., and David Mayers, eds. *Reevaluating Eisenhower: American Foreign Policy in the 1950s.* Urbana: University of Illinois Press, 1987.

Miller, James Edward. *The United States and Italy, 1940–1950: The Politics and Diplomacy of Stabilization.* Chapel Hill: University of North Carolina Press, 1986.

Moise, Edwin E. *Tonkin Gulf and the Escalation of the Vietnam War.* Chapel Hill: University of North Carolina Press, 1996.

Moore, Harold G., and Joseph L. Galloway. *We Were Soldiers Once—and Young: Ia Drang, the Battle That Changed the War in Vietnam.* New York: Random House, 1992.

Morley, Morris H. *Unfinished Business: America and Cuba After the Cold War, 1989–2001.* Cambridge, UK: Cambridge University Press, 2002.

————. *Washington, Somoza, and the Sandinistas: State and Regime in U.S. Policy Toward Nicaragua, 1969–1981.* Cambridge, UK: Cambridge University Press, 1994.

Mueller, John E. *Policy and Opinion in the Gulf War.* Chicago: University of Chicago Press, 1994.

Nau, Henry R. *Domestic Trade Politics and the Uruguay Round.* New York: Columbia University Press, 1989.

————. *Technology Transfer and U.S. Foreign Policy.* New York: Praeger, 1976.

Nixon, Richard M. *No More Vietnams.* New York: Arbor House, 1985.

Noer, Thomas J. *Cold War and Black Liberation: The United States and White Rule in Africa, 1948–1968.* Columbia: University of Missouri Press, 1985.

Palmer, Bruce. *The 25-Year War: America's Military Role in Vietnam.* Lexington: University Press of Kentucky, 1984.

Pastor, Robert A. *Condemned to Repetition: The United States and Nicaragua.* Princeton, NJ: Princeton University Press, 1988.

————. *Whirlpool: U.S. Foreign Policy Toward Latin America and the Caribbean.* Princeton, NJ: Princeton University Press, 1992.

Paterson, Thomas G. *Contesting Castro: The United States and the Triumph of the Cuban Revolution.* New York: Oxford University Press, 1994.

————, ed. *Kennedy's Quest for Victory: American Foreign Policy, 1961–1963.* New York: Oxford University Press, 1989.

————. *Meeting the Communist Threat: Truman to Reagan.* New York: Oxford University Press, 1988.

————. *On Every Front: The Making and Unmaking of the Cold War.* New York: W.W. Norton, 1992.

Patti, Archimedes L.A. *Why Viet Nam?: Prelude to America's Albatross.* Berkeley: University of California Press, 1980.

Pemberton, William E. *Harry S. Truman: Fair Dealer and Cold Warrior.* Boston: Twayne, 1989.

The Pentagon Papers: As Published by The New York Times, Based on the Investigative Reporting by Neil Sheehan, written by Neil Sheehan {and others}. Articles and documents edited by Gerald Gold, Allan M. Siegel, and Samuel Abt. New York and Toronto: Bantam, 1971.

Petras, James F., and Morris Morley. *The United States and Chile: Imperialism and the Overthrow of the Allende Government.* New York: Monthly Review, 1975.

Pickett, William B. *Eisenhower Decides to Run: Presidential Politics and Cold War Strategy.* Chicago: Ivan R. Dee, 2000.

Pipes, Richard. *Communism: A History.* New York: Modern Library, 2001.

————. *U.S.–Soviet Relations in the Era of Détente: A Tragedy of Errors.* Boulder, CO: Westview, 1981.

Pisani, Sallie. *The CIA and the Marshall Plan.* Lawrence: University Press of Kansas, 1991.

Plummer, Brenda Gayle. *Rising Wind: Black Americans and U.S. Foreign Affairs, 1935–1960.* Chapel Hill: University of North Carolina Press, 1996.

Potter, Lawrence G., and Gary G. Sick, eds. *Security in the Persian Gulf: Origins, Obstacles, and the Search for Consensus.* New York: Palgrave, 2002

Prados, John. *Presidents' Secret Wars: CIA and Pentagon Covert Operations from World War II Through the Persian Gulf.* Chicago: Ivan R. Dee, 1996.

Pruessen, Ronald W. *John Foster Dulles: The Road to Power.* New York: Free Press, 1982.

Quandt, William B. *Camp David: Peacemaking and Politics.* Washington, DC: Brookings Institution, 1986.

Rhodes, Richard. *Dark Sun: The Making of the Hydrogen Bomb.* New York: Simon and Schuster, 1996.

Rice, Gerard T. *The Bold Experiment: JFK's Peace Corps.* Notre Dame, IN: University of Notre Dame Press, 1985.

Rotter, Andrew Jon. *The Path to Vietnam: Origins of the American Commitment to Southeast Asia.* Ithaca, NY: Cornell University Press, 1987.

Rubenberg, Cheryl. *Israel and the American National Inter-*

est: A Critical Examination. Urbana: University of Illinois Press, 1986.

Santoli, Al, ed. *Everything We Had: An Oral History of the Vietnam War by Thirty-Three American Soldiers Who Fought it.* New York: Ballantine, 1982.

Saunders, Bonnie F. *The United States and Arab Nationalism: The Syrian Case, 1953–1960.* Westport, CT: Praeger, 1996.

Schaller, Michael. *The American Occupation of Japan: The Origins of the Cold War in Asia.* New York: Oxford University Press, 1985.

———. *The United States and China in the Twentieth Century.* New York: Oxford University Press, 1990.

Schell, Jonathan. *The Fate of the Earth.* New York: Alfred A. Knopf, 1982.

———. *The Gift of Time: The Case for Abolishing Nuclear Weapons Now.* New York: Henry Holt, 1998.

Schoenbaum, David. *The United States and the State of Israel.* New York: Oxford University Press, 1993.

Schubert, Frank N., and Theresa L. Kraus, eds. *The Whirlwind War: The United States Army in Operations Desert Shield and Desert Storm.* Washington, DC: Center of Military History, U.S. Army, 1995.

Schulzinger, Robert D. *Henry Kissinger: Doctor of Diplomacy.* New York: Columbia University Press, 1989.

———. *A Time for War: The United States and Vietnam, 1941–1975.* New York: Oxford University Press, 1997.

Shawcross, William. *Deliver Us from Evil: Peacekeepers, Warlords and a World of Endless Conflict.* New York: Simon and Schuster, 2000.

———. *The Shah's Last Ride: The Fate of an Ally.* New York: Simon and Schuster, 1988.

———. *Sideshow: Kissinger, Nixon, and the Destruction of Cambodia.* New York: Simon and Schuster, 1979.

Sheehan, Neil. *A Bright Shining Lie: John Paul Vann and America in Vietnam.* New York: Random House, 1988.

Sick, Gary. *All Fall Down: America's Tragic Encounter with Iran.* New York: Random House, 1985.

Sick, Gary, and Lawrence G. Potter, eds. *The Persian Gulf at the Millennium: Essays in Politics, Economy, Security, and Religion.* New York: St. Martin's, 1997.

Skidmore, David. *Reversing Course: Carter's Foreign Policy, Domestic Politics, and the Failure of Reform.* Nashville, TN: Vanderbilt University Press, 1996.

Slotkin, Richard. *Gunfighter Nation: The Myth of the Frontier in Twentieth-Century America.* New York: Atheneum, 1992.

Smith, Gaddis. *Dean Acheson.* New York: Cooper Square, 1972.

———. *The Last Years of the Monroe Doctrine, 1945–1993.* New York: Hill and Wang, 1994.

———. *Morality, Reason, and Power: American Diplomacy in the Carter Years.* New York: Hill and Wang, 1986.

Smith, R.B. *An International History of the Vietnam War.* New York: St. Martin's, 1983.

Soderbergh, Peter A. *Women Marines in the Korean War Era.* Westport, CT: Praeger, 1994.

Spanier, John W. *The Truman-MacArthur Controversy and the Korean War.* New York: W.W. Norton, 1965.

Spector, Ronald H. *After Tet: The Bloodiest Year in Vietnam.* New York: Free Press, 1993.

Stueck, William Whitney. *The Korean War: An International History.* Princeton, NJ: Princeton University Press, 1997.

———. *Rethinking the Korean War: A New Diplomatic and Strategic History.* Princeton, NJ: Princeton University Press, 2002.

———. *The Road to Confrontation: American Policy Toward China and Korea, 1947–1950.* Chapel Hill: University of North Carolina Press, 1981.

Summers, Harry G. *On Strategy: A Critical Analysis of the Vietnam War.* Novato, CA: Presidio, 1982.

Sutter, Robert G. *The China Quandary: Domestic Determinants of U.S. China Policy, 1972–1982.* Boulder, CO: Westview, 1983.

———. *Chinese Policy Priorities and Their Implications for the United States.* Lanham, MD: Rowman and Littlefield, 2000.

Takaki, Ronald T. *Hiroshima: Why America Dropped the Atomic Bomb.* Boston: Little, Brown, 1995.

Talbott, Strobe. *Deadly Gambits: The Reagan Administration and the Stalemate in Nuclear Arms Control.* New York: Alfred A. Knopf, 1984.

———. *The Russia Hand: A Memoir of Presidential Diplomacy.* New York: Random House, 2002.

———. *The Russians and Reagan.* New York: Vintage Books, 1984.

Talbott, Strobe, and Nayan Chanda, eds. *The Age of Terror: America and the World After September 11.* New York: Basic Books, 2001.

Terry, Wallace, ed. *Bloods: An Oral History of the Vietnam War by Black Veterans.* New York: Ballantine, 1992.

Theoharis, Athan G. *The Yalta Myths: An Issue in U.S. Politics, 1945–1955.* Columbia: University of Missouri Press, 1970.

Thomas, Evan. *The Very Best Men: Four Who Dared: The Early Years of the CIA.* New York: Simon and Schuster, 1995.

Tillman, Seth P. *The United States in the Middle East, Interests and Obstacles.* Bloomington: Indiana University Press, 1982.

Tucker, Nancy Bernkopf. *Patterns in the Dust: Chinese-American Relations and the Recognition Controversy, 1949–1950.* New York: Columbia University Press, 1983.

———. *Taiwan, Hong Kong, and the United States, 1945–1992: Uncertain Friendships.* New York: Maxwell Macmillan International, 1994.

Turley, William S. *The Second Indochina War: A Short Political and Military History, 1954–1975.* Boulder, CO: Westview, 1986.

Ulam, Adam Bruno. *The Rivals: America and Russia Since World War II.* New York, Viking, 1971.

Ungar, Sanford J. *Africa: The People and Politics of an Emerging Continent.* New York: Simon and Schuster, 1985.

Vance, Cyrus R. *Hard Choices: Critical Years in America's Foreign Policy.* New York: Simon and Schuster, 1983.

Walker, Martin. *The Cold War: A History.* New York: Henry Holt, 1994.

Walker, Thomas W., ed. *Reagan Versus the Sandinistas: The Undeclared War on Nicaragua.* Boulder, CO: Westview, 1987.

Warner, Roger. *Back Fire: The CIA's Secret War in Laos and Its Link to the War in Vietnam.* New York: Simon and Schuster, 1995.

Welch, Richard E. *Response to Revolution: The United States and the Cuban Revolution, 1959–1961.* Chapel Hill: University of North Carolina Press, 1985.

Westheider, James E. *Fighting on Two Fronts: African Americans and the Vietnam War.* New York: New York University Press, 1997.

White, Mark J., ed. *The Kennedys and Cuba: The Declassified Documentary History.* Chicago: Ivan R. Dee, 1999.

———. *Missiles in Cuba: Kennedy, Khrushchev, Castro, and the 1962 Crisis.* Chicago: Ivan R. Dee, 1997.

Whitfield, Stephen J. *The Culture of the Cold War.* Baltimore: Johns Hopkins University Press, 1991.

Wilson, Jim. *The Sons of Bardstown: 25 Years of Vietnam in an American Town.* New York: Crown, 1994.

Wirls, Daniel. *Buildup: The Politics of Defense in the Reagan Era.* Ithaca, NY: Cornell University Press, 1992.

Wirtz, James J. *The Tet Offensive: Intelligence Failure in War.* Ithaca, NY: Cornell University Press, 1991.

Wittner, Lawrence S. *Cold War America; from Hiroshima to Watergate.* New York, Praeger, 1974.

Wood, Bryce. *The Dismantling of the Good Neighbor Policy.* Austin: University of Texas Press, 1985.

Woodward, Bob. *Veil: The Secret Wars of the CIA, 1981–1987.* New York: Simon and Schuster, 1987.

Yergin, Daniel. *Shattered Peace: The Origins of the Cold War.* New York: Penguin, 1990.

Young, Marilyn Blatt. *The Vietnam Wars: 1945–1990.* New York: HarperCollins, 1991.

Politics and Government

Alderman, Ellen, and Caroline Kennedy. *In Our Defense: The Bill of Rights in Action.* New York: William Morrow, 1991.

Allen, Charles F. *The Comeback Kid: The Life and Career of Bill Clinton.* New York: Carol, 1992.

American Civil Liberties Union. *Censorship in a Box: Why Blocking Software Is Wrong for Public Libraries.* Wye Mills, MD: ACLU, 1998.

American Municipal Association. *Loyalty Oaths for Municipal Employees: Report of an Inquiry to State Leagues and Associations of Municipalities.* Chicago: No publisher, 1954.

Andrew, John A. *Lyndon Johnson and the Great Society.* Chicago: Ivan R. Dee, 1998.

———. *The Other Side of the Sixties: Young Americans for Freedom and the Rise of Conservative Politics.* New Brunswick, NJ: Rutgers University Press, 1997.

Armor, David J. *Forced Justice: School Desegregation and the Law.* New York: Oxford University Press, 1995.

Bagley, Constance E., and Christy A. Haubegger. *Cutting Edge Cases in the Legal Environment of Business.* Minneapolis/St. Paul: West, 1993.

Baird, Robert M., and Stuart E. Rosenbaum. *The Ethics of Abortion: Pro-Life vs. Pro-Choice.* Buffalo, NY: Prometheus, 1993.

———. *Hatred, Bigotry, and Prejudice: Definitions, Causes & Solutions.* Amherst, NY: Prometheus, 1999.

Balkin, J.M., and Bruce A. Ackerman. *What Brown v. Board of Education Should Have Said: The Nation's Top Legal Experts Rewrite America's Landmark Civil Rights Decision.* New York: New York University Press, 2001.

Ball, Howard. *The Bakke Case: Race, Education, and Affirmative Action.* Lawrence: University Press of Kansas, 2000.

———. *Hugo L. Black: Cold Steel Warrior.* New York: Oxford University Press, 1996.

Ball, Howard, and Phillip J. Cooper. *Of Power and Right: Hugo Black, William O. Douglas, and America's Constitutional Revolution.* New York: Oxford University Press, 1992.

Banks, Christopher P., and John Clifford Green. *Superintending Democracy: The Courts and the Political Process.* Akron, OH: University of Akron Press, 2001.

Banner, Stuart. *The Death Penalty: An American History.* Cambridge, MA: Harvard University Press, 2002.

Bartley, Numan V. *The Rise of Massive Resistance: Race and Politics in the South During the 1950s.* Baton Rouge: Louisiana State University Press, 1999.

Bayer, Linda N. *Ruth Bader Ginsburg.* Philadelphia: Chelsea House, 2000.

Beals, Melba. *Warriors Don't Cry: A Searing Memoir of the Battle to Integrate Little Rock's Central High.* New York: Pocket Books, 1994.

Belknap, Michal R. *Cold War Political Justice: The Smith Act, the Communist Party, and American Civil Liberties.* Westport, CT: Greenwood, 1977.

Belli, Marvin M., and Maurice C. Carroll. *Dallas Justice: The Real Story of Jack Ruby and His Trial.* New York: McKay, 1964.

Berman, William C. *America's Right Turn: From Nixon to Clinton.* Baltimore: Johns Hopkins University Press, 1998.

———. *From the Center to the Edge: The Politics and Policies of the Clinton Presidency.* Lanham, MD: Rowman and Littlefield, 2001.

———. *William Fulbright and the Vietnam War: The Dissent of a Political Realist.* Kent, OH: Kent State University Press, 1988.

Bernstein, Carl, and Bob Woodward. *All the President's Men.* New York: Simon and Schuster, 1994.

Bernstein, Irving. *Guns or Butter: The Presidency of Lyndon Johnson.* New York: Oxford University Press, 1996.

Berry, Mary Frances. *Stability, Security, and Continuity: Mr. Justice Burton and Decision-Making in the Supreme Court, 1945–1958.* Westport, CT: Greenwood, 1978.

Beschloss, Michael R., ed. *Taking Charge: The Johnson White House Tapes, 1963–1964.* New York: Simon and Schuster, 1997

Bezanson, Randall P. *Speech Stories: How Free Can Speech Be?* New York: New York University Press, 1998.

Black, Earl. *The Rise of Southern Republicans.* Cambridge, MA: Belknap Press of Harvard University Press, 2002.

Blumenthal, Sidney. *Our Long National Daydream: A Political Pageant of the Reagan Era.* New York: Harper and Row, 1988.

———. *Pledging Allegiance: The Last Campaign of the Cold War.* New York: HarperCollins, 1990.

Blumenthal, Sidney, and Thomas Byrne Edsall, eds. *The Reagan Legacy.* New York: Pantheon, 1988.

Bollinger, Lee C., and Geoffrey R. Stone. *Eternally Vigilant: Free Speech in the Modern Era.* Chicago: University of Chicago Press, 2002.

Bork, Robert H. *The Tempting of America: The Political Seduction of the Law.* New York: Free Press, 1990.

Bosco, Antoinette. *Choosing Mercy: A Mother of Murder Victims Pleads to End the Death Penalty.* Maryknoll, NY: Orbis, 2001.

Bosmajian, Haig A. *The Freedom Not to Speak.* New York: New York University Press, 1999.

Boxly, George T. *The Twelve: A Lawyer Looks at the Case.* New York: New Century, 1949.

Boyer, Paul S., ed. *Reagan as President: Contemporary Views of the Man, His Politics, and His Policies.* Chicago: Ivan R. Dee, 1990.

Brauer, Carl M. *John F. Kennedy and the Second Reconstruction.* New York: Columbia University Press, 1977.

Breines, Wini. *Community and Organization in the New Left, 1962–1968: The Great Refusal.* New York: Praeger, 1982.

Brendon, Piers. *Ike, His Life and Times.* New York: Harper and Row, 1986.

Brennan, Mary C. *Turning Right in the Sixties: The Conservative Capture of the GOP.* Chapel Hill: University of North Carolina Press, 1995.

Brennan, William J. *The Conscience of the Court: Selected Opinions of Justice William J. Brennan, Jr. on Freedom and Equality.* Edited by Stephen L. Sepinuck and Mary Pat

Treuthart. Carbondale: Southern Illinois University Press, 1999.

Brisbin, Richard A. *Justice Antonin Scalia and the Conservative Revival.* Baltimore: Johns Hopkins University Press, 1997.

Broadwater, Jeff. *Eisenhower & the Anti-Communist Crusade.* Chapel Hill: University of North Carolina Press, 1992.

Broder, David S., and Bob Woodward. *The Man Who Would Be President: Dan Quayle.* New York: Simon and Schuster, 1992.

Bronner, Ethan. *Battle for Justice: How the Bork Nomination Shook America.* New York: W.W. Norton, 1989.

Brown, Joe B., and Diane Holloway, eds. *Dallas and the Jack Ruby Trial: Memoir of Judge Joe B. Brown.* San Jose, CA: Authors Choice, 2001.

Bryson, Joseph E. *Legality of Loyalty Oath and Non-Oath Requirements for Public School Teachers.* Boone, NC: 1963.

Bugliosi, Vincent. *The Betrayal of America: How the Supreme Court Undermined the Constitution and Chose Our President.* New York: Thunder's Mouth, 2001.

———. *No Island of Sanity: Paula Jones v. Bill Clinton: The Supreme Court on Trial.* New York: Ballantine, 1998.

Burner, David. *The Torch Is Passed: The Kennedy Brothers & American Liberalism.* New York: Atheneum, 1984.

Burnett, Betty. *The Trial of Julius and Ethel Rosenberg: A Primary Source Account.* New York: Rosen, 2003.

Burt, Larry W. *Tribalism in Crisis: Federal Indian Policy, 1953–1961.* Albuquerque: University of New Mexico Press, 1982.

Buzzanco, Robert. *Masters of War: Military Dissent and Politics in the Vietnam Era.* Cambridge, UK: Cambridge University Press, 1997.

Califano, Joseph A. *The Triumph & Tragedy of Lyndon Johnson: The White House Years.* College Station: Texas A&M University Press, 2000.

Campaign Finance Study Group. *An Analysis of the Impact of the Federal Election Campaign Act, 1972–1978, from the Institute of Politics, John F. Kennedy School of Government, Harvard University.* Washington, DC: U.S. Government Printing Office, 1979.

Cannon, James M. *Time and Chance: Gerald Ford's Appointment with History.* New York: HarperCollins, 1994.

Cannon, Lou. *Official Negligence: How Rodney King and the Riots Changed Los Angeles and the LAPD.* New York: Times Books, 1997.

———. *President Reagan: The Role of a Lifetime.* New York: Simon and Schuster, 1991.

Carmichael, Virginia. *Framing History: The Rosenberg Story and the Cold War.* Minneapolis: University of Minnesota Press, 1993.

Caro, Robert A. *The Years of Lyndon Johnson.* New York: Alfred A. Knopf, 1982.

Carter, Dan T. *The Politics of Rage: George Wallace, the Ori-*

gins of the New Conservatism, and the Transformation of American Politics. New York: Simon and Schuster, 1995.

Carter, Jimmy. *Keeping Faith: Memoirs of a President.* Toronto: Bantam, 1982.

———. *To Assure Pride and Confidence in the Electoral Process.* Washington, DC: Brookings Institution, 2002.

Carter, Rosalynn. *First Lady from Plains.* Boston: Houghton Mifflin, 1984.

Carter, Stephen L. *God's Name in Vain: The Wrongs and Rights of Religion in Politics.* New York: Basic Books, 2000.

Carville, James. *. . . and the Horse He Rode in on: The People v. Kenneth Starr.* New York: Simon and Schuster, 1998.

———. *Stickin': The Case for Loyalty.* New York: Simon and Schuster, 2000.

Carville, James, and Paul Begala. *Buck Up, Suck Up—and Come Back When You Foul Up: 12 Winning Secrets from the War Room.* New York: Simon and Schuster, 2002.

Causey, Max, and John Mark Dempsey. *The Jack Ruby Trial Revisited: The Diary of Jury Foreman Max Causey.* Denton: University of North Texas Press, 2000.

Caute, David. *The Great Fear: The Anti-Communist Purge Under Truman and Eisenhower.* New York: Simon and Schuster, 1978.

———. *The Year of the Barricades: A Journey Through 1968.* New York: Harper and Row, 1988.

Chomsky, Noam. *Rethinking Camelot: JFK, the Vietnam War, and U.S. Political Culture.* Boston: South End, 1993.

Clifford, Clark M., with Richard Holbrooke. *Counsel to the President: A Memoir.* New York: Random House, 1991.

Clowse, Barbara Barksdale. *Brainpower for the Cold War: The Sputnik Crisis and National Defense Education Act of 1958.* Westport, CT: Greenwood, 1981.

Conkin, Paul Keith. *Big Daddy from the Pedernales: Lyndon Baines Johnson.* Boston: Twayne, 1986.

Cortner, Richard C. *Civil Rights and Public Accommodations: The Heart of Atlanta Motel and McClung Cases.* Lawrence: University Press of Kansas, 2001.

Counts, I. Wilmer, Will D. Campbell, Ernest Dumas, and Robert S. McCord. *A Life Is More Than a Moment: The Desegregation of Little Rock's Central High.* Bloomington: Indiana University Press, 1999.

Craig, Barbara Hinkson, and David M. O'Brien. *Abortion and American Politics.* Chatham, NJ: Chatham House, 1993.

Cray, Ed. *Chief Justice: A Biography of Earl Warren.* New York: Simon and Schuster, 1997.

Critchlow, Donald T., ed. *The Politics of Abortion and Birth Control in Historical Perspective.* University Park: Pennsylvania State University Press, 1996.

Crowley, Monica. *Nixon in Winter: The Final Revelations.* London: I.B. Tauris, 1998.

Curry, George E., and Cornel West. *The Affirmative Action Debate.* Reading, MA: Addison-Wesley, 1996.

Dallek, Matthew. *The Right Moment: Ronald Reagan's First Victory and the Decisive Turning Point in American Politics.* New York: Free Press, 2000.

Dallek, Robert. *Flawed Giant: Lyndon Johnson and His Times, 1961–1973.* New York: Oxford University Press, 1998.

———. *Lone Star Rising: Lyndon Johnson and His Times, 1908–1960.* New York: Oxford University Press, 1991.

———. *Ronald Reagan: The Politics of Symbolism, with a New Preface.* Cambridge, MA: Harvard University Press, 1999.

Danforth, John C. *Resurrection: The Confirmation of Clarence Thomas.* New York: Viking, 1994.

Davies, Gareth. *From Opportunity to Entitlement: The Transformation and Decline of Great Society Liberalism.* Lawrence: University Press of Kansas, 1996.

Davis, Sue Justice. *Rehnquist and the Constitution.* Princeton, NJ: Princeton University Press, 1989.

Dean, John W. *Blind Ambition: The White House Years.* New York: Simon and Schuster, 1976.

Deaver, Michael K. *A Different Drummer: My Thirty Years with Ronald Reagan.* New York: HarperCollins, 2001.

DeBenedetti, Charles. *An American Ordeal: The Antiwar Movement of the Vietnam Era.* Syracuse, NY: Syracuse University Press, 1990.

Deitz, Robert. *Willful Injustice: A Post-O.J. Look at Rodney King, American Justice, and Trial by Race.* Washington, DC: Regnery, 1996.

Dellinger, David T., and Bobby Seale. *Chicago Conspiracy Contempt Briefs.* New York: Distributed by the Center for Constitutional Rights, 1970.

Dennis, Eugene. *Letters from Prison.* New York: International, 1956.

Denton, Robert E., Jr. *The Primetime Presidency of Ronald Reagan: The Era of the Television Presidency.* New York: Praeger, 1988.

Dershowitz, Alan M. *Sexual McCarthyism: Clinton, Starr, and the Emerging Constitutional Crisis.* New York: Basic Books, 1998.

Diamond, Sara. *Roads to Dominion: Right-Wing Movements and Political Power in the United States.* New York: Guilford, 1995.

Dick, Bernard F. *Radical Innocence: A Critical Study of the Hollywood Ten.* Lexington: University Press of Kentucky, 1988.

DiLeo, David L. *George Ball, Vietnam, and the Rethinking of Containment.* Chapel Hill: University of North Carolina Press, 1991.

Dionne, E.J. *Why Americans Hate Politics.* New York: Simon and Schuster, 1992.

Divine, Robert A. *Blowing on the Wind: The Nuclear Test Ban Debate, 1954–1960.* New York: Oxford University Press, 1978.

Dixon, Robert Galloway. *The Right of Privacy; a Symposium*

on the Implications of Griswold v. Connecticut, 381 U.S. 497 (1965). New York: Da Capo, 1971.

Dole, Robert J. *Project on the Independent Counsel Statute: Report and Recommendations.* Washington, DC: American Enterprise Institute, 1999.

Douglas, Davison M. *School Busing: Constitutional and Political Developments.* New York: Garland, 1994.

Douglas, William O. *The Court Years, 1939–1975: The Autobiography of William O. Douglas.* New York: Random House, 1980.

Draper, Theodore. *A Very Thin Line: The Iran-Contra Affairs.* New York: Hill and Wang, 1991.

Draper, Timothy Dean, David Paul Nord, and Timothy J. Gilfoyle. *Revisiting 1968.* Chicago: Chicago Historical Society, 2002.

Drew, Elizabeth. *On the Edge: The Clinton Presidency.* New York: Simon and Schuster, 1994.

Dudley, William. *The Bill of Rights: Opposing Viewpoints.* San Diego, CA: Greenhaven, 1994.

———. *Watergate.* San Diego, CA: Greenhaven, 2002.

Duffy, Michael, and Dan Goodgame. *Marching in Place: The Status Quo Presidency of George Bush.* New York: Simon and Schuster, 1992.

Dugger, Ronnie. *The Politician: The Life and Times of Lyndon Johnson: The Drive for Power, from the Frontier to Master of the Senate.* New York: W.W. Norton, 1982.

Dunar, Andrew J. *The Truman Scandals and the Politics of Morality.* Columbia: University of Missouri Press, 1984.

Eastland, Terry. *Freedom of Expression in the Supreme Court: The Defining Cases.* Lanham, MD: Rowman and Littlefield, 2000.

———. *Religious Liberty in the Supreme Court: The Cases That Define the Debate Over Church and State.* Washington, DC: Ethics and Public Policy Center, 1993.

Echeverria, John D., and Raymond Booth Eby. *Let the People Judge: Wise Use and the Private Property Rights Movement.* Washington, DC: Island, 1995.

Edelman, Peter B. *Searching for America's Heart: RFK and the Renewal of Hope.* Boston: Houghton Mifflin, 2001.

Ehrlichman, John. *Witness to Power: The Nixon Years.* New York: Pocket Books, 1982.

Eisler, Kim Isaac. *A Justice for All: William J. Brennan, Jr., and the Decisions That Transformed America.* New York: Simon and Schuster, 1993.

Ellis, Charley. *If We Remain Silent . . .* Los Angeles: United Defense Committee Against "Loyalty" Checks, 1950.

Ellsberg, Daniel. *Secrets: A Memoir of Vietnam and the Pentagon Papers.* New York: Viking, 2002.

Emerson, Gloria. *Winners & Losers: Battles, Retreats, Gains, Losses, and Ruins from the Vietnam War.* New York: W.W. Norton, 1992.

Epstein, Jason. *The Great Conspiracy Trial; an Essay on Law,* *Liberty, and the Constitution.* New York: Random House, 1970.

Farber, David R. *Chicago '68.* Chicago: University of Chicago Press, 1988.

Farish, Leah. *Lemon v. Kurtzman: The Religion and Public Funds Case.* Berkeley Heights, NJ: Enslow, 2000.

Feiffer, Jules. *Pictures at a Prosecution; Drawings & Text from the Chicago Conspiracy Trial.* New York: Grove, 1971.

Feinberg, Joel, and Hyman Gross. *Justice: Selected Readings.* Encino, CA: Dickenson, 1977.

Ferrell, Robert H. *Harry S. Truman: A Life.* Columbia: University of Missouri Press, 1994.

———. *Harry S. Truman and the Modern American Presidency.* Boston: Little, Brown, 1983.

Fink, Gary M., and Hugh Davis Graham, eds. *The Carter Presidency: Policy Choices in the Post-New Deal Era.* Lawrence: University Press of Kansas, 1998.

Fischer, Beth A. *The Reagan Reversal: Foreign Policy and the End of the Cold War.* Columbia: University of Missouri Press, 1997.

FitzGerald, Frances. *Way Out There in the Blue: Reagan, Star Wars, and the End of the Cold War.* New York: Simon and Schuster, 2000.

Fixico, Donald Lee. *Termination and Relocation: Federal Indian Policy, 1945–1960.* Albuquerque: University of New Mexico Press, 1986.

Ford, Gerald R. *A Time to Heal: The Autobiography of Gerald R. Ford.* New York: Harper and Row, 1979.

Frank, John Paul. *Inside Justice Hugo L. Black: The Letters.* Austin: Jamail Center for Legal Research, the University of Texas at Austin, 2000.

Franklin, John Hope, and August Meier. *Black Leaders of the Twentieth Century.* Urbana: University of Illinois Press, 1982.

Fraser, Steve, and Gary Gerstle, eds. *The Rise and Fall of the New Deal Order, 1930–1980.* Princeton, NJ: Princeton University Press, 1989.

Freedman, Lawrence, ed. *Superterrorism: Policy Responses.* Malden, MA: Blackwell, 2002.

Fried, Albert. *McCarthyism: The Great American Red Scare: A Documentary History.* New York: Oxford University Press, 1997.

Fried, Richard M. *Nightmare in Red: The McCarthy Era in Perspective.* New York: Oxford University Press, 1990.

Galub, Arthur L. *The Burger Court, 1968–1984.* Danbury, CT: Grolier Educational, 1995.

Garber, Marjorie B., and Rebecca L. Walkowitz. *Secret Agents: The Rosenberg Case, McCarthyism, and Fifties America.* New York: Routledge, 1995.

Garcia, Alfredo. *The Fifth Amendment: A Comprehensive Approach.* Westport, CT: Greenwood, 2002.

Garment, Leonard. *In Search of Deep Throat: The Greatest Political Mystery of Our Time.* New York: Basic Books, 2000.

Garrow, David J. *Liberty and Sexuality: The Right to Privacy and the Making of Roe v. Wade.* New York: Macmillan, 1994.

Gerber, Scott Douglas. *First Principles: The Jurisprudence of Clarence Thomas.* New York: New York University Press, 1999.

Germond, Jack W., and Jules Witcover. *Blue Smoke and Mirrors: How Reagan Won and Why Carter Lost the Election of 1980.* New York: Viking, 1981.

———. *Mad as Hell: Revolt at the Ballot Box, 1992.* New York: Warner, 1993.

Gibbs, Jewelle Taylor. *Race and Justice: Rodney King and O.J. Simpson in a House Divided.* San Francisco: Jossey-Bass, 1996.

Gibson, James William. *Warrior Dreams: Paramilitary Culture in Post-Vietnam America.* New York: Hill and Wang, 1994.

Giglio, James N. *The Presidency of John F. Kennedy.* Lawrence: University Press of Kansas, 1991.

Gitenstein, Mark. *Matters of Principle: An Insider's Account of America's Rejection of Robert Bork's Nomination to the Supreme Court.* New York: Simon and Schuster, 1992.

Goldberg, Robert Alan. *Barry Goldwater.* New Haven: Yale University Press, 1995.

Goldfarb, Ronald L. *Perfect Villains, Imperfect Heroes: Robert F. Kennedy's War Against Organized Crime.* New York: Random House, 1995.

Goldfield, David R. *Black, White, and Southern: Race Relations and Southern Culture, 1940 to the Present.* Baton Rouge: Louisiana State University Press, 1991.

Goldman, Eric Frederick. *The Crucial Decade—and After: America, 1945–1960.* New York: Vintage Books, 1960.

Goldman, Roger L., William J. Brennan, and David Gallen. *Justice William J. Brennan, Jr.: Freedom First.* New York: Carroll and Graf, 1994.

Goodwin, Doris Kearns. *Lyndon Johnson and the American Dream.* New York: Harper and Row, 1976.

Gordon-Reed, Annette. *Race on Trial: Law and Justice in American History.* New York: Oxford University Press, 2002.

Gormley, Ken. *Archibald Cox: Conscience of a Nation.* Reading, MA: Addison-Wesley, 1997.

Green, David. *The Language of Politics in America: Shaping Political Consciousness from McKinley to Reagan.* Ithaca, NY: Cornell University Press, 1992.

Greenberg, Gerald S. *Historical Encyclopedia of U.S. Independent Counsel Investigations.* Westport, CT: Greenwood, 2000.

Greene, John Robert. *The Crusade: The Presidential Election of 1952.* Lanham, MD: University Press of America, 1985.

———. *The Limits of Power: The Nixon and Ford Administrations.* Bloomington: Indiana University Press, 1992.

———. *The Presidency of George Bush.* Lawrence: University Press of Kansas, 2000.

———. *The Presidency of Gerald R. Ford.* Lawrence: University Press of Kansas, 1995.

Greenhalgh, William W. *The Fourth Amendment Handbook: A Chronological Survey of Supreme Court Decisions.* Chicago: Criminal Justice Section, American Bar Association, 1995.

Greenstein, Fred I. *The Hidden-Hand Presidency: Eisenhower as Leader.* New York: Basic Books, 1982.

Gugin, Linda C., and James E. St. Clair. *Sherman Minton: New Deal Senator, Cold War Justice.* Indianapolis: Indiana Historical Society, 1997.

Gutiérrez, David. *Walls and Mirrors: Mexican Americans, Mexican Immigrants, and the Politics of Ethnicity.* Berkeley: University of California Press, 1995.

Hacker, Jacob S. *The Divided Welfare State: The Battle over Public and Private Social Benefits in the United States.* Cambridge, UK: Cambridge University Press, 2002.

Haldeman, H.R. *The Haldeman Diaries: Inside the Nixon White House.* New York: G.P. Putnam's, 1994.

Hall, John Wesley. *Search and Seizure.* 3rd ed. Charlottesville, VA: LEXIS Law, 2000.

Hamby, Alonzo L. *Man of the People: A Life of Harry S. Truman.* New York: Oxford University Press, 1995.

Hamilton, Nigel. *JFK, Reckless Youth.* New York: Random House, 1992.

Hargrove, Erwin C. *Jimmy Carter as President: Leadership and the Politics of the Public Good.* Baton Rouge: Louisiana State University Press, 1988.

Harrington, Michael. *The Other America: Poverty in the United States.* Baltimore: Penguin, 1966.

Harrison, Maureen, and Steve Gilbert. *Abortion Decisions of the United States Supreme Court: The 1990's.* Beverly Hills, CA: Excellent Books, 1993.

———. *Landmark Decisions of the United States Supreme Court IV.* La Jolla, CA: Excellent Books, 1994.

———. *Obscenity and Pornography Decisions of the United States Supreme Court.* Carlsbad, CA: Excellent Books, 2000.

Hartmann, Susan M. *Truman and the 80th Congress.* Columbia: University of Missouri Press, 1971.

Heale, M.J. *McCarthy's Americans: Red Scare Politics in State and Nation, 1935–1965.* Athens: University of Georgia Press, 1998.

Heath, Jim F. *John F. Kennedy and the Business Community.* Chicago: University of Chicago Press, 1969.

Heins, Marjorie. *Not in Front of the Children: "Indecency," Censorship and the Innocence of Youth.* New York: Hill and Wang, 2001.

Herda, D.J. *New York Times v. United States: National Security and Censorship.* Hillside, NJ: Enslow, 1994.

Herman, Arthur. *Joseph McCarthy: Reexamining the Life and Legacy of America's Most Hated Senator.* New York: Free Press, 2000.

Herman, Didi. *The Antigay Agenda: Orthodox Vision and the*

Christian Right. Chicago: University of Chicago Press, 1998.

Hersh, Seymour M. *The Dark Side of Camelot.* Boston: Little, Brown, 1997.

———. *The Price of Power: Kissinger in the Nixon White House.* New York: Summit, 1983.

Heumann, Milton, Thomas W. Church, and David P. Redlawsk. *Hate Speech on Campus: Cases, Case Studies, and Commentary.* Boston: Northeastern University Press, 1997.

Higgins, Trumbull. *The Perfect Failure: Kennedy, Eisenhower, and the C.I.A. at the Bay of Pigs.* New York: W.W. Norton, 1987.

Himmelstein, Jerome L. *To the Right: The Transformation of American Conservatism.* Berkeley: University of California Press, 1990.

Hine, Thomas. *Populuxe.* New York: Alfred A. Knopf, 1986.

Hockett, Jeffrey D. *New Deal Justice: The Constitutional Jurisprudence of Hugo L. Black, Felix Frankfurter, and Robert H. Jackson.* Lanham, MD: Rowman and Littlefield, 1996.

Hoeveler, J. David. *Watch on the Right: Conservative Intellectuals in the Reagan Era.* Madison: University of Wisconsin Press, 1991.

Hoff, Joan. *Nixon Reconsidered.* New York: Basic Books, 1994.

Hogan, Michael J. *A Cross of Iron: Harry S. Truman and the Origins of the National Security State, 1945–1954.* Cambridge, UK: Cambridge University Press, 2000.

Hohenberg, John. *The Bill Clinton Story: Winning the Presidency.* Syracuse, NY: Syracuse University Press, 1994.

———. *Reelecting Bill Clinton: Why America Chose a "New" Democrat.* Syracuse, NY: Syracuse University Press, 1997.

Hopkins, W. Wat. *Actual Malice: Twenty-Five Years After Times v. Sullivan.* New York: Praeger, 1989.

———. *Mr. Justice Brennan and Freedom of Expression.* New York: Praeger, 1991.

Horwitz, Morton J. *The Warren Court and the Pursuit of Justice: A Critical Issue.* New York: Hill and Wang, 1998.

Hutchinson, Dennis J. *The Man Who Once Was Whizzer White: A Portrait of Justice Byron R. White.* New York: Free Press, 1998.

Hyman, Harold Melvin. *To Try Men's Souls: Loyalty Tests in American History.* Berkeley: University of California Press, 1960.

Irons, Peter H. *Brennan vs. Rehnquist: The Battle for the Constitution.* New York: Alfred A. Knopf, 1994.

Irons, Peter H., and Stephanie Guitton. *May It Please the Court: The Most Significant Oral Arguments Made Before the Supreme Court Since 1955.* New York: New Press, 1993.

Isaacson, Walter. *Kissinger: A Biography.* New York: Simon and Schuster, 1992.

Isserman, Maurice. *America Divided: The Civil War of the 1960s.* New York: Oxford University Press, 2000.

———. *If I Had a Hammer—: The Death of the Old Left and the Birth of the New Left.* New York: Basic Books, 1987.

Italia, Bob, and Paul J. Deegan. *John Paul Stevens.* Edina, MN: Abdo and Daughters, 1992.

Jackson, Jesse L., Sr., Jesse L. Jackson, Jr., and Bruce Shapiro. *Legal Lynching: The Death Penalty and America's Future.* New York: New Press, 2001.

Jamieson, Kathleen Hall. *Packaging the Presidency: A History and Criticism of Presidential Campaign Advertising.* New York: Oxford University Press, 1996.

Jamieson, Kathleen Hall, and Paul Waldman. *The Press Effect: Politicians, Journalists, and the Stories That Shape the Political World.* Oxford, UK: Oxford University Press, 2003.

Jaworski, Leon. *The Right and the Power: The Prosecution of Watergate.* New York: Reader's Digest, 1976.

Jeffries, John Calvin. *Justice Lewis F. Powell, Jr.* New York: Charles Scribner's Sons, 1994.

Jelen, Ted G., ed. *Ross for Boss: The Perot Phenomenon and Beyond.* Albany: State University of New York Press, 2001.

Jezer, Marty. *Abbie Hoffman, American Rebel.* New Brunswick, NJ: Rutgers University Press, 1992.

Johnson, Charles A., and Danette Brickman. *Independent Counsel: The Law and the Investigations.* Washington, DC: Congressional Quarterly, 2001.

Johnson, Haynes Bonner. *The Best of Times: America in the Clinton Years.* New York: Harcourt, 2001.

———. *Sleepwalking Through History: America in the Reagan Years.* New York: W.W. Norton, 1991.

———. *The System: The American Way of Politics at the Breaking Point.* Boston: Little, Brown, 1996.

Kantor, Seth. *Who Was Jack Ruby?* New York: Everest House, 1978.

Kaufman, Burton Ira. *The Korean Conflict.* Westport, CT: Greenwood, 1999.

———. *The Presidency of James Earl Carter, Jr.* Lawrence: University Press of Kansas, 1993.

Kellner, Douglas. *Grand Theft 2000: Media Spectacle and a Stolen Election.* Lanham, MD: Rowman and Littlefield, 2001.

———. *Television and the Crisis of Democracy.* Boulder, CO: Westview, 1990.

Khalifah, H. Khalif, ed. *Rodney King and the L.A. Rebellion: A 1992 Black Rebellion in the United States.* Hampton, VA: U.B.&U.S. Communications Systems, 1992.

Kissinger, Henry. *White House Years.* Boston: Little, Brown, 1979.

———. *Years of Renewal.* New York: Simon and Schuster, 1999.

Kluger, Richard. *Simple Justice: The History of "Brown v.*

Board of Education" and Black America's Struggle for Equality. New York: Vintage Books, 1975.

Knight, Douglas M. *Street of Dreams: The Nature and Legacy of the 1960s.* Durham, NC: Duke University Press, 1989.

Krenn, Michael L. *Black Diplomacy: African Americans and the State Department, 1945–1969.* Armonk, NY: M.E. Sharpe, 1999.

Kurtz, Michael L. *Crime of the Century: The Kennedy Assassination from a Historian's Perspective.* Knoxville: University of Tennessee Press, 1993.

Kutler, Stanley I., ed. *Abuse of Power: The New Nixon Tapes.* New York: Free Press, 1997.

———. *The American Inquisition: Justice and Injustice in the Cold War.* New York: Hill and Wang, 1982.

———. *The Wars of Watergate: The Last Crisis of Richard Nixon.* New York: Alfred A. Knopf, 1990.

LaFave, Wayne R. *Search and Seizure: A Treatise on the Fourth Amendment.* 3rd ed. St. Paul, MN: West, 1996.

Lamphere, Robert J., and Tom Shachtman. *The FBI-KGB War: A Special Agent's Story.* New York: Random House, 1986.

LaRue, L.H. *Political Discourse: A Case Study of the Watergate Affair.* Athens: University of Georgia Press, 1988.

Lasby, Clarence G. *Eisenhower's Heart Attack: How Ike Beat Heart Disease and Held on to the Presidency.* Lawrence: University Press of Kansas, 1997.

Lassiter, Matthew D., and Andrew B. Lewis. *The Moderates' Dilemma: Massive Resistance to School Desegregation in Virginia.* Charlottesville: University Press of Virginia, 1998.

Leidholdt, Alexander. *Standing Before the Shouting Mob: Lenoir Chambers and Virginia's Massive Resistance to Public-School Integration.* Tuscaloosa: University of Alabama Press, 1997.

Leo, Richard A., and George C. Thomas. *The Miranda Debate: Law, Justice, and Policing.* Boston: Northeastern University Press, 1998.

Levy, Leonard Williams. *Origins of the Bill of Rights.* New Haven: Yale University Press, 1999.

———. *Origins of the Fifth Amendment; the Right Against Self-Incrimination.* New York: Oxford University Press, 1968.

Lewis, Anthony. *Gideon's Trumpet.* New York: Random House, 1964.

———. *Make No Law: The Sullivan Case and the First Amendment.* New York: Vintage Books, 1992.

Lienesch, Michael. *New Order of the Ages: Time, the Constitution, and the Making of Modern American Political Thought.* Princeton, NJ: Princeton University Press, 1988.

———. *Redeeming America: Piety and Politics in the New Christian Right.* Chapel Hill: University of North Carolina Press, 1993.

Linder, Marc. *"Moments Are the Elements of Profit": Overtime and the Deregulation of Working Hours Under the Fair Labor Standards Act.* Iowa City, IA: Fănpìhuà, 2000.

Lipschultz, Jeremy Harris. *Free Expression in the Age of the Internet: Social and Legal Boundaries.* Boulder, CO: Westview, 2000.

Loevy, Robert D., ed. *The Civil Rights Act of 1964: The Passage of the Law That Ended Racial Segregation.* Albany: State University of New York Press, 1997.

Lowi, Theodore J. *The End of the Republican Era.* Norman: University of Oklahoma Press, 1995.

Lowi, Theodore J., and Joseph Romance. *A Republic of Parties?: Debating the Two-Party System.* Lanham, MD: Rowman and Littlefield, 1998.

Lukas, J. Anthony. *Nightmare: The Underside of the Nixon Years.* Athens: Ohio University Press, 1999.

Luna, Christopher. *Campaign Finance Reform.* New York: H.W. Wilson, 2001.

MacCoun, Robert J., and Peter Reuter. *Drug War Heresies: Learning from Other Vices, Times, and Places.* Cambridge, UK: Cambridge University Press, 2001.

Mackey, Thomas C. *Pornography on Trial: A Handbook with Cases, Laws, and Documents.* Santa Barbara, CA: ABC-CLIO, 2002.

MacPherson, Myra. *Long Time Passing: Vietnam and the Haunted Generation.* Garden City, NY: Doubleday, 1984.

Mailer, Norman. *The Armies of the Night: History as a Novel, the Novel as History.* New York: Plume, 1994.

Maltz, Earl M. *The Chief Justiceship of Warren Burger, 1969–1986.* Columbia: University of South Carolina Press, 2000.

Maraniss, David. *First in His Class: A Biography of Bill Clinton.* New York: Simon and Schuster, 1995.

Matusow, Allen J. *Farm Policies and Politics in the Truman Years.* Cambridge, MA: Harvard University Press, 1967.

Mauro, Tony. *Illustrated Great Decisions of the Supreme Court.* Washington, DC: Congressional Quarterly, 2000.

McAdam, Doug. *Political Process and the Development of Black Insurgency, 1930–1970.* Chicago: University of Chicago Press, 1999.

McCormack, Wayne. *The Bakke Decision: Implications for Higher Education Admissions: A Report.* Washington, DC: American Council on Education, Association of American Law Schools, 1978.

McCoy, Donald R. *The Presidency of Harry S. Truman.* Lawrence: University Press of Kansas, 1984.

McCullough, David G. *Truman.* New York: Simon and Schuster, 1992.

McQuaid, Kim. *The Anxious Years: America in the Vietnam-Watergate Era.* New York: Basic Books, 1989.

Meador, Daniel John. *Preludes to Gideon; Notes on Appellate Advocacy, Habeas Corpus, and Constitutional Litigation.* Charlottesville, VA: Michie, 1967.

Meeropol, Robert, and Michael Meeropol. *We Are Your Sons: The Legacy of Ethel and Julius Rosenberg.* Boston: Houghton Mifflin, 1975.

Mello, Michael. *Against the Death Penalty: The Relentless Dissents of Justices Brennan and Marshall.* Boston: Northeastern University Press, 1996.

Mersky, Roy M., J. Myron Jacobstein, and Robert H. Bork. *The Supreme Court of the United States: Hearings and Reports on Successful and Unsuccessful Nominations of Supreme Court Justices by the Senate Judiciary Committee, 1916–1987.* Buffalo, NY: W.S. Hein, 1990.

Mervin, David. *Ronald Reagan and the American Presidency.* New York: Longman, 1990.

Milbrath, Lester W. *Environmentalists, Vanguard for a New Society.* Albany: State University of New York Press, 1984.

Miller, Jim. *"Democracy Is in the Streets": From Port Huron to the Siege of Chicago.* New York: Simon and Schuster, 1988.

Miller, Merle. *Plain Speaking: An Oral Biography of Harry S. Truman.* New York: Berkley, 1974.

Miller, Richard Lawrence. *Truman: The Rise to Power.* New York: McGraw-Hill, 1986.

Moran, Rachel F. *Interracial Intimacy: The Regulation of Race & Romance.* Chicago: University of Chicago Press, 2001.

Morris, Kenneth Earl. *Jimmy Carter: American Moralist.* Athens: University of Georgia Press, 1996.

Morris, Roger. *Richard Milhous Nixon: The Rise of an American Politician.* New York: Henry Holt, 1990.

Moss, Norman. *Klaus Fuchs: The Man Who Stole the Atom Bomb.* New York: St. Martin's, 1987.

Moyers, Bill D. *The Secret Government: The Constitution in Crisis, with Excerpts from "An Essay on Watergate."* Cabin John, MD: Seven Locks, 1988.

Murphy, Bruce Allen. *Wild Bill: The Legend and Life of William O. Douglas.* New York: Random House, 2002.

Murphy, Paul L. *The Constitution in Crisis Times, 1918–1969.* New York: Harper and Row, 1972.

Nash, George H. *The Conservative Intellectual Movement in America, Since 1945.* New York: Basic Books, 1976.

Nash, Roderick. *The Rights of Nature: A History of Environmental Ethics.* Madison: University of Wisconsin Press, 1989.

Navasky, Victor S. *Kennedy Justice.* New York: Atheneum, 1971.

———. *Naming Names.* New York: Viking, 1980.

Nelson, Deborah. *Pursuing Privacy in Cold War America.* New York: Columbia University Press, 2002.

Nelson, Patricia M. *Affirmative Action Revisited.* Huntington, NY: Nova Science, 2001.

Neville, John F. *The Press, the Rosenbergs, and the Cold War.* Westport, CT: Praeger, 1995.

Newman, John. *Oswald and the CIA.* New York: Carroll and Graf, 1995.

Newman, Robert P. *Owen Lattimore and the "Loss" of China.* Berkeley: University of California Press, 1992.

Nixon, Richard M. *In the Arena: A Memoir of Victory, Defeat, and Renewal.* New York: Simon and Schuster, 1990.

———. *RN: The Memoirs of Richard Nixon, with a New Introduction.* New York: Simon and Schuster, 1990.

Noble, Charles. *Welfare as We Knew It: A Political History of the American Welfare State.* New York: Oxford University Press, 1997.

Noonan, John Thomas, and Edward McGlynn Gaffney. *Religious Freedom: History, Cases, and Other Materials on the Interaction of Religion and Government.* New York: Foundation, 2001.

North, Oliver, and William Novak. *Under Fire: An American Story.* New York: HarperCollins, 1991.

Olmsted, Kathryn. *Challenging the Secret Government: The Post-Watergate Investigations of the CIA and FBI.* Chapel Hill: University of North Carolina Press, 1996.

O'Neill, William L. *A Better World: The Great Schism: Stalinism and the American Intellectuals.* New York: Simon and Schuster, 1982.

O'Reilly, Kenneth. *Racial Matters: The FBI's Secret File on Black America, 1960–1972.* New York: Free Press, 1991.

Oshinsky, David M. *A Conspiracy So Immense: The World of Joe McCarthy.* New York: Free Press; London: Collier Macmillan, 1983.

Pach, Chester J. *The Presidency of Dwight D. Eisenhower.* Lawrence: University Press of Kansas, 1991.

Palmer, Jan. *The Vinson Court Era: The Supreme Court's Conference Votes: Data and Analysis.* New York: AMS, 1990.

Parker, Richard A. *Free Speech on Trial: Communication Perspectives on Landmark Supreme Court Decisions.* Tuscaloosa: University of Alabama Press, 2003.

Parmet, Herbert S. *Eisenhower and the American Crusades.* New York: Macmillan, 1972.

———. *George Bush: The Life of a Lone Star Yankee.* New York: Scribner's, 1997.

———. *JFK, the Presidency of John F. Kennedy.* New York: Dial, 1983.

———. *Richard Nixon and His America.* Boston: Little, Brown, 1990.

Parmet, Herbert S., and Marie B. Hecht. *Never Again: A President Runs for a Third Term.* New York: Macmillan, 1968.

Pastor, Robert A. *Congress and the Politics of U.S. Foreign Economic Policy, 1929–1976.* Berkeley: University of California Press, 1980.

Patterson, James T. *Brown v. Board of Education: A Civil Rights Milestone and Its Troubled Legacy.* Oxford, UK: Oxford University Press, 2001.

Pells, Richard H. *The Liberal Mind in a Conservative Age: American Intellectuals in the 1940s and 1950s.* New York: Harper and Row, 1985.

Pemberton, William E. *Exit with Honor: The Life and Presidency of Ronald Reagan.* Armonk, NY: M.E. Sharpe, 1997.

Petras, James F., and Morris Morley. *Empire or Republic?: American Global Power and Domestic Decay.* New York: Routledge, 1995.

Phelps, Timothy M., and Helen Winternitz. *Capitol Games: Clarence Thomas, Anita Hill, and the Story of a Supreme Court Nomination.* New York: Hyperion, 1991.

Phillips, Kevin P. *Boiling Point: Republicans, Democrats, and the Decline of Middle-Class Prosperity.* New York: Random House, 1993.

———. *The Politics of Rich and Poor: Wealth and the American Electorate in the Reagan Aftermath.* New York: Random House, 1990.

———. *Wealth and Democracy: A Political History of the American Rich.* New York: Broadway, 2002.

Pickett, William B. *Eisenhower Decides to Run: Presidential Politics and Cold War Strategy.* Chicago: Ivan R. Dee, 2000.

Poen, Monte M. *Harry S. Truman Versus the Medical Lobby: The Genesis of Medicare.* Columbia: University of Missouri Press, 1979.

Posner, Gerald L. *Case Closed: Lee Harvey Oswald and the Assassination of JFK.* New York: Random House, 1993.

Posner, Richard A. *An Affair of State: The Investigation, Impeachment, and Trial of President Clinton.* Cambridge, MA: Harvard University Press, 1999.

Powe, L. A. Scot. *The Warren Court and American Politics.* Cambridge, MA: Harvard University Press, 2000.

Quayle, Dan. *Standing Firm: A Vice-Presidential Memoir.* New York: HarperCollins, 1994.

Radcliff, William Franklin. *Sherman Minton: Indiana's Supreme Court Justice.* Indianapolis: Guild Press of Indiana, 1996.

Radosh, Ronald, and Joyce Milton. *The Rosenberg File with a New Introduction Containing Revelations from National Security Agency and Soviet Sources.* 2nd ed. New Haven, CT: Yale University Press, 1997.

Raskin, Jamin B. *We the Students: Supreme Court Decisions For and About Students.* Washington, DC: Congressional Quarterly, 2000.

Raza, M. Ali, A. Janell Anderson, and Harry Glynn Custred. *The Ups and Downs of Affirmative Action Preferences.* Westport, CT: Praeger, 1999.

Reeves, Richard. *President Kennedy: Profile of Power.* New York: Simon and Schuster, 1993.

Reeves, Thomas C. *The Life and Times of Joe McCarthy: A Biography.* New York: Stein and Day, 1982.

———. *A Question of Character: A Life of John F. Kennedy.* New York: Free Press, 1991.

Regan, Donald T. *For the Record: From Wall Street to Washington.* New York: St. Martin's, 1989.

Reich, Robert B. *Locked in the Cabinet.* New York: Alfred A. Knopf, 1997.

Reichley, James. *Conservatives in an Age of Change: The Nixon and Ford Administrations.* Washington, DC: Brookings Institution, 1981.

Reinhard, David W. *The Republican Right Since 1945.* Lexington: University Press of Kentucky, 1983.

Reisner, Marc. *Cadillac Desert: The American West and Its Disappearing Water.* New York: Penguin, 1993.

Riddle, John M. *Eve's Herbs: A History of Contraception and Abortion in the West.* Cambridge, MA: Harvard University Press, 1997.

Roberts, Sam. *The Brother: The Untold Story of Atomic Spy David Greenglass and How He Sent His Sister, Ethel Rosenberg, to the Electric Chair.* New York: Random House, 2001.

Rose, Mark H. *Interstate: Express Highway Politics, 1939–1989.* Knoxville: University of Tennessee Press, 1990.

Rosenberg, Julius, Ethel Rosenberg, and Michael Meeropol. *The Rosenberg Letters: A Complete Edition of the Prison Correspondence of Julius and Ethel Rosenberg.* New York: Garland, 1994.

Rosenkranz, E. Joshua, and Bernard Schwartz. *Reason and Passion: Justice Brennan's Enduring Influence.* New York: W.W. Norton, 1997.

Rosenstiel, Tom. *Strange Bedfellows: How Television and the Presidential Candidates Changed American Politics, 1992.* New York: Hyperion, 1993.

Rosteck, Thomas. *See It Now Confronts McCarthyism: Television Documentary and the Politics of Representation.* Tuscaloosa: University of Alabama Press, 1994.

Rovere, Richard Halworth. *Senator Joe McCarthy.* New York: Meridian, 1960.

Rowan, Roy. *The Four Days of Mayaguez.* New York: W.W. Norton, 1975.

Roy, Beth. *Bitters in the Honey: Tales of Hope and Disappointment Across Divides of Race and Time.* Fayetteville: University of Arkansas Press, 1999.

Ruby and Oswald Affair, a Microfilm Documentary. Fresno, CA: AMCO Microfilming Historical Archive Department, 1964.

Rudenstine, David. *The Day the Presses Stopped: A History of the Pentagon Papers Case.* Berkeley: University of California Press, 1996.

Sarat, Austin. *Race, Law, and Culture: Reflections on Brown v. Board of Education.* New York: Oxford University Press, 1997.

———. *When the State Kills: Capital Punishment and the American Condition.* Princeton, NJ: Princeton University Press, 2001.

Schaller, Michael. *Reckoning with Reagan: America and Its President in the 1980s.* New York: Oxford University Press, 1992.

Schapsmeier, Edward L., and Frederick H. Schapsmeier. *Prophet in Politics: Henry A. Wallace and the War Years, 1940–1965.* Ames: Iowa State University Press, 1971.

Schlesinger, Arthur Meier, Jr. *A Thousand Days: John F. Kennedy in the White House.* Boston: Houghton Mifflin, 1965.

Schmidt, Susan, and Michael Weisskopf. *Truth at Any Cost: Ken Starr and the Unmaking of Bill Clinton.* New York: HarperCollins, 2000.

Schrag, Peter. *Test of Loyalty: Daniel Ellsberg and the Rituals of Secret Government.* New York: Simon and Schuster, 1974.

Schrecker, Ellen. *Many Are the Crimes: McCarthyism in America.* Boston: Little, Brown, 1998.

———. *No Ivory Tower: McCarthyism and the Universities.* New York: Oxford University Press, 1986.

Schudson, Michael. *Watergate in American Memory: How We Remember, Forget, and Reconstruct the Past.* New York: Basic Books, 1993.

Schultz, David A., and Christopher E. Smith. *The Jurisprudential Vision of Justice Antonin Scalia.* Lanham, MD: Rowman and Littlefield, 1996.

Schultz, John. *The Chicago Conspiracy Trial.* New York: Da Capo, 1993.

Schwartz, Bernard. *The Ascent of Pragmatism: The Burger Court in Action.* Reading, MA: Addison-Wesley, 1990.

———. *Swann's Way: The School Busing Case and the Supreme Court.* New York: Oxford University Press, 1986.

———. *The Warren Court: A Retrospective.* New York: Oxford University Press, 1996.

Scott, Peter Dale. *Deep Politics and the Death of JFK.* Berkeley: University of California Press, 1993.

Segers, Mary C., and Ted G. Jelen. *A Wall of Separation?: Debating the Public Role of Religion.* Lanham, MD: Rowman and Littlefield, 1998.

Shilts, Randy. *And the Band Played On: Politics, People, and the AIDS Epidemic.* New York: St. Martin's, 1987.

Shoup, Laurence H. *The Carter Presidency, and Beyond: Power and Politics in the 1980s.* Palo Alto, CA: Ramparts, 1980.

Sick, Gary. *October Surprise: America's Hostages in Iran and the Election of Ronald Reagan.* New York: Times Books, 1991.

Sickels, Robert J. *John Paul Stevens and the Constitution: A Search for Balance.* University Park: Pennsylvania State University Press, 1988.

Simon, James F. *The Antagonists: Hugo Black, Felix Frankfurter and Civil Liberties in Modern America.* New York: Simon and Schuster, 1989.

Simon, Paul. *P.S.: The Autobiography of Paul Simon.* Chicago: Bonus Books, 1999.

Sloane, Arthur A. *Hoffa.* Cambridge, MA: MIT Press, 1992.

Small, Melvin. *Antiwarriors: The Vietnam War and the Battle for America's Hearts and Minds.* Wilmington, DE: Scholarly Resources, 2002.

———. *The Presidency of Richard Nixon.* Lawrence: University Press of Kansas, 1999.

Smith, Paul Chaat. *Like a Hurricane: The Indian Movement from Alcatraz to Wounded Knee.* New York: New Press, 1996.

Smolla, Rodney A. *The First Amendment: Freedom of Expression, Regulation of Mass Media, Freedom of Religion.* Durham, NC: Carolina Academic Press, 1999.

Sorensen, Theodore C. *Kennedy.* New York: Harper and Row, 1965.

Spann, Girardeau A. *The Law of Affirmative Action: Twenty-Five Years of Supreme Court Decisions on Race and Remedies.* New York: New York University Press, 2000.

Spear, Joseph C. *Presidents and the Press: The Nixon Legacy.* Cambridge, MA: MIT Press, 1986.

St. Clair, James E., and Linda C. Gugin. *Chief Justice Fred M. Vinson of Kentucky: A Political Biography.* Lexington: University Press of Kentucky, 2002.

Starr, Kenneth. *First Among Equals: The Supreme Court in American Life.* New York: Warner, 2002.

Stephen, John A. *Officer's Search and Seizure Handbook.* New York: Lexis, 2000.

Stern, Mark. *Calculating Visions: Kennedy, Johnson, and Civil Rights.* New Brunswick, NJ: Rutgers University Press, 1992.

Stock, Catherine McNicol. *Rural Radicals: From Bacon's Rebellion to the Oklahoma City Bombing.* New York: Penguin, 1997.

Stockman, David Alan. *The Triumph of Politics: Why the Reagan Revolution Failed.* New York: Harper and Row, 1986.

Strauch, A. Bruce. *Publishing and the Law: Current Legal Issues.* New York: Haworth Information, 2001.

Sullivan, John J. *A Guide to the Laws of Search and Seizure for New York State Law Enforcement Officers.* Rev. ed. Flushing, NY: Looseleaf Law, 1996.

Sullivan, Kathleen M., and Gerald Gunther. *First Amendment Law.* New York: Foundation, 1999.

Swerdlow, Amy. *Women Strike for Peace: Traditional Motherhood and Radical Politics in the 1960s.* Chicago: University of Chicago Press, 1993.

Tabor, James D., and Eugene V. Gallagher. *Why Waco?: Cults and the Battle for Religious Freedom in America.* Berkeley: University of California Press, 1995.

Tanenhaus, Sam. *Whittaker Chambers: A Biography.* New York: Random House, 1997.

Theoharis, Athan G. *Seeds of Repression: Harry S. Truman and the Origins of McCarthyism.* Chicago: Quadrangle, 1971.

———. *Spying on Americans: Political Surveillance from Hoover to the Huston Plan.* Philadelphia: Temple University Press, 1978

Thomas, Evan. *Robert Kennedy: His Life.* New York: Simon and Schuster, 2000.

Toobin, Jeffrey. *A Vast Conspiracy: The Real Story of the Sex Scandal That Nearly Brought Down a President.* New York: Random House, 2000

Tucker, D.F.B. *The Rehnquist Court and Civil Rights.* Aldershot, UK: Dartmouth, 1995.

Tushnet, Mark V. *Making Civil Rights Law: Thurgood Marshall and the Supreme Court, 1936–1961.* New York: Oxford University Press, 1994.

———. *Making Constitutional Law: Thurgood Marshall and the Supreme Court, 1961–1991.* New York: Oxford University Press, 1997.

Ungar, Sanford J. *The Papers & the Papers: An Account of the Legal and Political Battle over the Pentagon Papers.* New York: Columbia University Press, 1989.

Urofsky, Melvin I. *A Conflict of Rights: The Supreme Court and Affirmative Action.* New York: Charles Scribner's Sons, 1991.

———. *Division and Discord: The Supreme Court Under Stone and Vinson, 1941–1953.* Columbia: University of South Carolina Press, 1997.

———. *Felix Frankfurter: Judicial Restraint and Individual Liberties.* Boston: Twayne, 1991.

———. *The Warren Court: Justices, Rulings, and Legacy.* Santa Barbara, CA: ABC-CLIO, 2001.

Utter, Glenn H., and Ruth Ann Strickland. *Campaign and Election Reform: A Reference Handbook.* Santa Barbara, CA: ABC-CLIO, 1997.

Van Sickel, Robert W. *Not a Particularly Different Voice: The Jurisprudence of Sandra Day O'Connor.* New York: P. Lang, 1998.

Van Tassel, Emily Field, and Paul Finkelman. *Impeachable Offenses: A Documentary History from 1787 to the Present.* Washington, DC: Congressional Quarterly, 1999.

VanBurkleo, Sandra F., Kermit Hall, and Robert J. Kaczorowski. *Constitutionalism and American Culture: Writing the New Constitutional History.* Lawrence: University Press of Kansas, 2002.

Vaughn, Stephen. *Ronald Reagan in Hollywood: Movies and Politics.* Cambridge, UK: Cambridge University Press, 1994.

Walker, Martin. *The President We Deserve: Bill Clinton, His Rise, Falls, and Comebacks.* New York: Crown, 1996.

Walker, Samuel. *Hate Speech: The History of an American Controversy.* Lincoln: University of Nebraska Press, 1994.

Warren, Earl. *The Memoirs of Earl Warren.* Garden City, NY: Doubleday, 1977.

Wasby, Stephen L. *"He Shall Not Pass This Way Again": The Legacy of Justice William O. Douglas.* Pittsburgh, PA: University of Pittsburgh Press for the William O. Douglas Institute, 1990.

Watkins, John T. *The Watkins Decision of the United States Supreme Court, June 17, 1957: An Historic Rebuke to the Committee on Un-American Activities of the House of Representatives.* New York: Emergency Civil Liberties Committee, 1957.

Wattenberg, Martin P. *The Decline of American Political Parties, 1952–1980.* Cambridge, MA: Harvard University Press, 1984.

Weinstein, Allen. *Perjury: The Hiss-Chambers Case.* New York: Random House, 1997.

Welch, Susan, and John Gruhl. *Affirmative Action and Minority Enrollments in Medical and Law Schools.* Ann Arbor: University of Michigan Press, 1998.

Wells, Tom. *Wild Man: The Life and Times of Daniel Ellsberg.* New York: Palgrave, 2001.

Wetterer, Charles M. *The Fourth Amendment: Search and Seizure.* Springfield, NJ: Enslow, 1998.

White, John Kenneth, and Philip John Davies, eds. *Political Parties and the Collapse of the Old Orders.* Albany: State University of New York Press, 1998.

White, Mark J., ed. *Kennedy: The New Frontier Revisited.* New York: New York University Press, 1998.

———. *The Kennedys and Cuba: The Declassified Documentary History.* Rev. ed. Chicago: Ivan R. Dee, 2001.

White, Theodore Harold. *The Making of the President, 1960.* New York: Atheneum, 1961.

———. *The Making of the President, 1968.* New York: Atheneum, 1969.

White, Welsh S. *Miranda's Waning Protections: Police Interrogation Practices after Dickerson.* Ann Arbor: University of Michigan Press, 2001.

Wice, Paul B. *Miranda v. Arizona: "You Have the Right to Remain Silent."* New York: Franklin Watts, 1996.

Wicker, Tom. *JFK and LBJ: The Influence of Personality upon Politics.* Baltimore: Penguin, 1970.

———. *One of Us: Richard Nixon and the American Dream.* New York: Random House, 1991.

Williams, Juan. *Thurgood Marshall: American Revolutionary.* New York: Times Books, 1998.

Williams, Robert Chadwell. *Klaus Fuchs, Atom Spy.* Cambridge, MA: Harvard University Press, 1987.

Wills, Garry. *The Kennedy Imprisonment: A Meditation on Power.* Boston: Little, Brown, 1982.

———. *Nixon Agonistes: The Crisis of the Self-Made Man.* Atlanta, GA: Cherokee, 1990.

———. *Reagan's America.* New York: Penguin, 2000.

Wilson, Bradford P. *Enforcing the Fourth Amendment: A Jurisprudential History.* New York: Garland, 1986.

Wilson, Paul E. *A Time to Lose: Representing Kansas in Brown v. Board of Education.* Lawrence: University Press of Kansas, 1995.

Winters, Paul A. *The Death Penalty: Opposing Viewpoints.* 3rd ed. San Diego, CA: Greenhaven, 1997.

Wirls, Daniel. *Buildup: The Politics of Defense in the Reagan Era.* Ithaca, NY: Cornell University Press, 1992.

Witt, Elder. *A Different Justice: Reagan and the Supreme Court.* Washington, DC: Congressional Quarterly, 1986.

Wittner, Lawrence S. *Rebels Against War: The American Peace Movement, 1933–1983.* Philadelphia: Temple University Press, 1984.

Wolters, Raymond. *Right Turn: William Bradford Reynolds, the Reagan Administration, and Black Civil Rights.* New Brunswick, NJ: Transaction, 1996.

Woods, Randall Bennett. *Vietnam and the American Political Tradition: The Politics of Dissent.* Cambridge, UK: Cambridge University Press, 2003.

Woods, Randall Bennett, and Howard Jones. *Dawning of the Cold War: The United States' Quest for Order.* Athens: University of Georgia Press, 1991.

Woodward, Bob. *The Agenda: Inside the Clinton White House.* New York: Simon and Schuster, 1994.

Woodward, Bob, and Scott Armstrong. *The Brethren: Inside the Supreme Court.* New York: Simon and Schuster, 1979.

Yarbrough, Tinsley E. *The Burger Court: Justices, Rulings, and Legacy.* Santa Barbara, CA: ABC-CLIO, 2000.

———. *John Marshall Harlan: Great Dissenter of the Warren Court.* New York: Oxford University Press, 1992.

———. *The Rehnquist Court and the Constitution.* Oxford, UK: Oxford University Press, 2000.

Yarnell, Allen. *Democrats and Progressives: The 1948 Presidential Election as a Test of Postwar Liberalism.* Berkeley: University of California Press, 1974.

Yergin, Daniel, and Joseph Stanislaw. *The Commanding Heights: The Battle Between Government and the Marketplace That Is Remaking the Modern World.* New York: Simon and Schuster, 1998.

Zaroulis, N.L., and Gerald Sullivan. *Who Spoke Up?: American Protest Against the War in Vietnam, 1963–1975.* Garden City, NY: Doubleday, 1984.

Zelezny, John D. *Communications Law: Liberties, Restraints, and the Modern Media.* 3rd ed. Belmont, CA: Wadsworth/Thomson Learning, 2001.

Zelizer, Barbie. *Covering the Body: The Kennedy Assassination, the Media, and the Shaping of Collective Memory.* Chicago: University of Chicago Press, 1992.

Race, Ethnicity, and Gender

Acuña, Rodolfo. *Occupied America: A History of Chicanos.* New York: Longman, 2000.

Adam, Barry D. *The Rise of a Gay and Lesbian Movement.* New York: Twayne, 1995.

Adam, Barry D., Jan Willem Duyvendak, and André Krouwel, eds. *The Global Emergence of Gay and Lesbian Politics: National Imprints of a Worldwide Movement.* Philadelphia: Temple University Press, 1999.

Alderman, Ellen, and Caroline Kennedy. *In Our Defense: The Bill of Rights in Action.* New York: William Morrow, 1991.

Armor, David J. *Forced Justice: School Desegregation and the Law.* New York: Oxford University Press, 1995.

Baird, Robert M., and M. Katherine Baird. *Homosexuality: Debating the Issues.* Amherst, NY: Prometheus, 1995.

Barrera, Mario. *Race and Class in the Southwest: A Theory of Racial Inequality.* Notre Dame, IN: University of Notre Dame Press, 1979.

Bartley, Numan V. *The Rise of Massive Resistance; Race and Politics in the South During the 1950's.* Baton Rouge: Louisiana State University Press, 1969.

Bass, Jack. *Unlikely Heroes: The Dramatic Story of the Southern Judges of the Fifth Circuit Who Translated the Supreme Court's Brown Decision into a Revolution for Equality.* New York: Simon and Schuster, 1981.

Belknap, Michal R. *Federal Law and Southern Order: Racial Violence and Constitutional Conflict in the Post-Brown South.* Athens: University of Georgia Press, 1987.

Bell, Derrick A. *And We Are Not Saved: The Elusive Quest for Racial Justice.* New York: Basic Books, 1987.

Berman, William C. *The Politics of Civil Rights in the Truman Administration.* Columbus: Ohio State University Press, 1970.

Berry, Mary Frances. *The Politics of Parenthood: Child Care, Women's Rights, and the Myth of the Good Mother.* New York: Viking, 1993.

———. *Why ERA Failed: Politics, Women's Rights, and the Amending Process of the Constitution.* Bloomington: Indiana University Press, 1988.

Bloom, Jack M. *Class, Race, and the Civil Rights Movement.* Bloomington: Indiana University Press, 1987.

Bowers, William T., William M. Hammond, and George L. MacGarrigle. *Black Soldier, White Army: The 24th Infantry Regiment in Korea.* Washington, DC: Center of Military History, U.S. Army, 1996.

Branch, Taylor. *Parting the Waters: America in the King Years, 1954–1963.* New York: Simon and Schuster, 1988.

———. *Pillar of Fire: America in the King Years, 1963–65.* New York: Simon and Schuster, 1998.

Brauer, Carl M. *John F. Kennedy and the Second Reconstruction.* New York: Columbia University Press, 1977.

Breines, Wini. *Young, White, and Miserable: Growing Up Female in the Fifties.* Boston: Beacon, 1992.

Bright, Susan, ed. *Feminist Family Values Forum: Mililani Trask, Gloria Steinem, Angela Davis, María Jiménez.* Austin, TX: Plain View, 1996.

Brodie, Laura Fairchild. *Breaking Out: VMI and the Coming of Women.* New York: Pantheon, 2000.

Bugliosi, Vincent. *Outrage: The Five Reasons Why O.J. Simpson Got Away with Murder.* New York: W.W. Norton, 1996.

Burner, Eric. *And Gently He Shall Lead Them: Robert Parris Moses and Civil Rights in Mississippi.* New York: New York University Press, 1994.

Burns, Stewart. *Daybreak of Freedom: The Montgomery Bus Boycott.* Chapel Hill: University of North Carolina Press, 1997.

Burt, Larry W. *Tribalism in Crisis: Federal Indian Policy, 1953–1961.* Albuquerque: University of New Mexico Press, 1982.

Byerly, Victoria Morris. *Hard Times Cotton Mill Girls: Personal Histories of Womanhood and Poverty in the South.* Ithaca: New York State School of Industrial and Labor Relations, Cornell University, 1986.

Camarillo, Albert, ed. *Latinos in the United States: A Historical Bibliography.* Santa Barbara, CA: ABC-CLIO, 1986.

Carmichael, Stokely. *Black Power: The Politics of Liberation in America.* New York: Random House, 1967.

Carson, Clayborne. *In Struggle: SNCC and the Black Awakening of the 1960s.* Cambridge, MA: Harvard University Press, 1981.

Carter, Dan T. *From George Wallace to Newt Gingrich: Race in the Conservative Counterrevolution, 1963–1994.* Baton Rouge: Louisiana State University Press, 1996.

———. *The Politics of Rage: George Wallace, the Origins of the New Conservatism, and the Transformation of American Politics.* Baton Rouge: Louisiana State University Press, 1996.

Chafe, William Henry. *Civilities and Civil Rights: Greensboro, North Carolina, and the Black Struggle for Equality.* New York: Oxford University Press, 1980.

Chalmers, David Mark. *Backfire: How the Ku Klux Klan Helped the Civil Rights Movement.* Lanham, MD: Rowman and Littlefield, 2003.

Cleaver, Eldridge. *Eldridge Cleaver: Post-Prison Writings and Speeches.* New York: Random House, 1969.

———. *Soul on Ice.* New York: Delta Trade, 1999.

Cose, Ellis. *Color-Blind: Seeing Beyond Race in a Race-Obsessed World.* New York: HarperCollins, 1997.

———. *The Rage of a Privileged Class.* New York: HarperCollins, 1993.

Cronin, Mary M. *An Analysis of a Wartime Agenda: The Korean War Reporting of Marguerite Higgins.* No publisher, 1990.

Cushman, Clare, and Talbot D'Alemberte. *Supreme Court Decisions and Women's Rights: Milestones to Equality.* Washington, DC: Congressional Quarterly, 2001.

Dalfiume, Richard M. *Desegregation of the U.S. Armed Forces; Fighting on Two Fronts, 1939–1953.* Columbia: University of Missouri Press, 1969.

Daniels, Roger, Sandra C. Taylor, and Harry H.L. Kitano, eds. *Japanese Americans, from Relocation to Redress.* Salt Lake City: University of Utah Press, 1986.

Davis, Angela Yvonne. *Women, Race & Class.* New York: Vintage Books, 1983.

DeCaro, Louis A. *On the Side of My People: A Religious Life of Malcolm X.* New York: New York University Press, 1996.

Dees, Morris, and James Corcoran. *Gathering Storm: America's Militia Threat.* New York: HarperCollins, 1996.

Dees, Morris, and Steve Fiffer. *Hate on Trial: The Case Against America's Most Dangerous Neo-Nazi.* New York: Villard, 1993.

Deloria, Vine. *Behind the Trail of Broken Treaties: An Indian Declaration of Independence.* New York: Delacorte, 1974.

D'Emilio, John. *Sexual Politics, Sexual Communities: The Making of a Homosexual Minority in the United States, 1940–1970.* Chicago: University of Chicago Press, 1983.

D'Emilio, John, and Estelle B. Freedman. *Intimate Matters: A History of Sexuality in America.* Chicago: University of Chicago Press, 1997.

D'Emilio, John, William B. Turner, and Urvashi Vaid. *Creating Change: Sexuality, Public Policy, and Civil Rights.* New York: St. Martin's, 2000.

Dittmer, John. *Local People: The Struggle for Civil Rights in Mississippi.* Urbana: University of Illinois Press, 1994.

Douglas, Susan J. *Where the Girls Are: Growing Up Female with the Mass Media.* New York: Times Books, 1995.

Drucker, Dan. *Abortion Decisions of the Supreme Court, 1973 Through 1989: A Comprehensive Review with Historical Commentary.* Jefferson, NC: McFarland, 1990.

Duberman, Martin B. *Stonewall.* New York: E.P. Dutton, 1993.

Dudziak, Mary L. *Cold War Civil Rights: Race and the Image of American Democracy.* Princeton, NJ: Princeton University Press, 2000.

Duram, James C. *A Moderate Among Extremists: Dwight D. Eisenhower and the School Desegregation Crisis.* Chicago: Nelson-Hall, 1981.

Dworkin, Andrea. *Heartbreak: The Political Memoir of a Feminist Militant.* New York: Basic Books, 2002.

———. *Right-Wing Women.* New York: Perigee, 1983.

Dyson, Michael Eric. *Between God and Gangsta Rap: Bearing Witness to Black Culture.* New York: Oxford University Press, 1996.

———. *Making Malcolm: The Myth and Meaning of Malcolm X.* New York: Oxford University Press, 1995.

Echols, Alice. *Daring to Be Bad: Radical Feminism in America, 1967–1975.* Minneapolis: University of Minnesota Press, 1989.

Edsall, Thomas Byrne, and Mary D. Edsall. *Chain Reaction.* New York: W.W. Norton, 1991.

Egerton, John. *Speak Now Against the Day: The Generation Before the Civil Rights Movement in the South.* Chapel Hill: University of North Carolina Press, 1995.

Ehrenreich, Barbara. *The Hearts of Men: American Dreams and the Flight from Commitment.* Garden City, NY: Anchor Press/Doubleday, 1983.

Ehrenreich, Barbara, and Arlie Russell Hochschild, eds. *Global Woman: Nannies, Maids, and Sex Workers in the New Economy.* New York: Metropolitan, 2003.

Epstein, Steven. *Impure Science: AIDS, Activism, and the Politics of Knowledge.* Berkeley: University of California Press, 1996.

Faludi, Susan. *Backlash: The Undeclared War Against American Women.* New York: Crown, 1991.

———. *Stiffed: The Betrayal of the American Man.* New York: HarperPerennial, 2000.

Farley, Reynolds, and Walter Allen. *The Color Line and the Quality of Life in America.* New York: Russell Sage Foundation, 1987.

Ferguson, Russell, et al., eds. *Out There: Marginalization and Contemporary Cultures.* Cambridge, MA: MIT Press, 1990.

Findlay, James F. *Church People in the Struggle: The National Council of Churches and the Black Freedom Movement, 1950–1970.* New York: Oxford University Press, 1993.

Fixico, Donald Lee. *Termination and Relocation: Federal Indian Policy, 1945–1960.* Albuquerque: University of New Mexico Press, 1986.

Formisano, Ronald P. *Boston Against Busing: Race, Class, and Ethnicity in the 1960s and 1970s.* Chapel Hill: University of North Carolina Press, 1991.

Francke, Linda Bird. *Ground Zero: The Gender Wars in the Military.* New York: Simon and Schuster, 1997.

Franklin, John Hope, and August Meier. *Black Leaders of the Twentieth Century.* Urbana: University of Illinois Press, 1982.

Freeman, Jo. *The Politics of Women's Liberation: A Case Study of an Emerging Social Movement and Its Relation to the Policy Process.* New York: Longman/David McKay, 1975.

———. *A Room at a Time: How Women Entered Party Politics.* Lanham, MD: Rowman and Littlefield, 2000.

Friedan, Betty. *The Feminine Mystique.* With a new introduction and epilogue by the author. New York: Dell, 1984.

Fuchs, Lawrence H. *The American Kaleidoscope: Race, Ethnicity, and the Civic Culture.* Hanover, NH: Wesleyan University Press, 1990.

García, Mario T. *Mexican Americans: Leadership, Ideology & Identity, 1930–1960.* New Haven: Yale University Press, 1989.

Garrow, David J. *Bearing the Cross: Martin Luther King, Jr., and the Southern Christian Leadership Conference, 1955–1968.* New York: William Morrow, 1986.

———. *The FBI and Martin Luther King, Jr.* New York: Penguin, 1983.

———. *Liberty and Sexuality: The Right to Privacy and the Making of Roe v. Wade.* New York: Macmillan, 1994.

Gates, Henry Louis. *Colored People: A Memoir.* New York: Vintage Books, 1995.

Gates, Henry Louis, and Cornel West. *The African-American Century: How Black Americans Have Shaped Our Country.* New York: Free Press, 2000.

Gibbs, Jewelle Taylor. *Race and Justice: Rodney King and O.J. Simpson in a House Divided.* San Francisco: Jossey-Bass, 1996.

Gilligan, Carol. *The Birth of Pleasure.* New York: Alfred A. Knopf, 2002.

———. *In a Different Voice: Psychological Theory and Women's Development.* Cambridge, MA: Harvard University Press, 1993.

Gilliom, John. *Surveillance, Privacy, and the Law: Employee Drug Testing and the Politics of Social Control.* Ann Arbor: University of Michigan Press, 1994.

Glasgow, Douglas G. *The Black Underclass: Poverty, Unemployment, and Entrapment of Ghetto Youth.* San Francisco: Jossey-Bass, 1980.

Gold, Susan Dudley. *Roberts v. U.S. Jaycees (1984): Women's Rights.* New York: Twenty-First Century Books, 1995.

Goldfield, Michael. *The Color of Politics: Race and the Mainsprings of American Politics.* New York: New Press, 1997.

Goldstein, Leslie Friedman. *Contemporary Cases in Women's Rights.* Madison: University of Wisconsin Press, 1994.

Graham, Hugh Davis. *Civil Rights and the Presidency: Race and Gender in American Politics, 1960–1972.* New York: Oxford University Press, 1992.

Griswold del Castillo, Richard, and Richard A. Garcia. *César Chávez: A Triumph of Spirit.* Norman: University of Oklahoma Press, 1995.

Guitton, Stephanie, and Peter H. Irons. *May It Please the Court: Arguments on Abortion.* New York: New Press, 1995.

Gutiérrez, David. *Walls and Mirrors: Mexican Americans, Mexican Immigrants, and the Politics of Ethnicity.* Berkeley: University of California Press, 1995.

Hacker, Andrew. *Two Nations: Black and White, Separate, Hostile, Unequal.* New York: Scribner, 1992.

Halberstam, David. *The Children.* New York: Random House, 1998.

Hampton, Henry, Steve Fayer, and Sarah Flynn. *Voices of Freedom: An Oral History of the Civil Rights Movement From the 1950s Through the 1980s.* New York: Bantam, 1990.

Harding, Vincent. *There Is a River: The Black Struggle for Freedom in America.* New York: Vintage Books, 1983.

Harding, Vincent, Robin D.G. Kelley, and Earl Lewis. *We Changed the World: African Americans, 1945–1970.* New York: Oxford University Press, 1997.

Harrison, Maureen, and Steve Gilbert. *Abortion Decisions of the United States Supreme Court: The 1980's.* Beverly Hills, CA: Excellent Books, 1993.

Hartmann, Susan M. *From Margin to Mainstream: American Women and Politics Since 1960.* New York: Alfred A. Knopf, 1989.

———. *The Home Front and Beyond: American Women in the 1940s.* Boston: Twayne, 1982.

Hill, Anita, and Emma Coleman Jordan. *Race, Gender, and Power in America: The Legacy of the Hill-Thomas Hearings.* New York: Oxford University Press, 1995.

Hochschild, Jennifer L. *Facing Up to the American Dream: Race, Class, and the Soul of the Nation.* Princeton, NJ: Princeton University Press, 1995.

Hoff, Joan. *Law, Gender, and Injustice: A Legal History of U.S. Women.* New York: New York University Press, 1991.

Hollinger, David A. *Postethnic America: Beyond Multiculturalism.* New York: Basic Books, 1995.

Hondagneu-Sotelo, Pierrette. *Gendered Transitions: Mexican Experiences of Immigration.* Berkeley: University of California Press, 1994.

Hooks, Bell. *Black Looks: Race and Representation.* Boston: South End, 1992.

Horowitz, Daniel. *Betty Friedan and the Making of The Feminine Mystique: The American Left, the Cold War, and Modern Feminism.* Amherst: University of Massachusetts Press, 1998.

Hull, Gloria T., Patricia Bell Scott, and Barbara Smith, eds. *All the Women Are White, All the Blacks Are Men, but Some of Us Are Brave: Black Women's Studies.* Old Westbury, NY: Feminist, 1982.

Irons, Peter H., and Stephanie Guitton. *May It Please the Court: The Most Significant Oral Arguments Made Before the Supreme Court Since 1955.* New York: New Press, 1984.

Italia, Bob, and Paul J. Deegan. *Anthony Kennedy.* Edina, MN: Abdo and Daughters, 1992.

Iverson, Peter. *The Navajo Nation.* Westport, CT: Greenwood, 1981.

Jackson, James E. *At the Funeral of Medgar Evers in Jackson, Mississippi: A Tribute in Tears and a Thrust for Freedom.* New York: Publisher's New Press, 1963.

Jamieson, Kathleen Hall. *Beyond the Double Bind: Women and Leadership.* New York: Oxford University Press, 1995.

Jeffords, Susan. *The Remasculinization of America: Gender and the Vietnam War.* Bloomington: Indiana University Press, 1989.

Jencks, Christopher. *Rethinking Social Policy: Race, Poverty, and the Underclass.* Cambridge, MA: Harvard University Press, 1992.

Jones, Brenn. *Learning About Equal Rights from the Life of Ruth Bader Ginsburg.* New York: Rosen, 2002.

Jussim, Daniel. *Drug Tests and Polygraphs: Essential Tools or Violations of Privacy?* New York: Messner, 1987.

Kaplan, Elaine Bell. *Not Our Kind of Girl: Unraveling the Myths of Black Teenage Motherhood.* Berkeley: University of California Press, 1997.

Kennedy, Susan Estabrook. *If All We Did Was to Weep at Home: A History of White Working-Class Women in America.* Bloomington: Indiana University Press, 1979.

Kerber, Linda K., Alice Kessler-Harris, and Kathryn Kish Sklar, eds. *U.S. History as Women's History: New Feminist Essays.* Chapel Hill: University of North Carolina Press, 1995.

Kessler-Harris, Alice. *In Pursuit of Equity: Women, Men, and the Quest for Economic Citizenship in 20th-century America.* Oxford, UK: Oxford University Press, 2001.

———. *Out to Work: The History of Wage-Earning Women in the United States.* New York: Oxford University Press, 1982.

Klein, Alan M. *Baseball on the Border: A Tale of Two Laredos.* Princeton, NJ: Princeton University Press, 1997.

Kluger, Richard. *Simple Justice: The History of Brown v. Board of Education and Black America's Struggle for Equality.* New York: Vintage Books, 1975.

Lemann, Nicholas. *The Promised Land: The Great Black Migration and How It Changed America.* New York: Vintage Books, 1992.

Levy, Anne, and Michele Antoinette Paludi. *Workplace Sexual Harassment.* 2nd ed. Upper Saddle River, NJ: Prentice Hall, 2002.

Levy, Peter B. *Documentary History of the Modern Civil Rights Movement.* New York: Greenwood, 1992.

Lischer, Richard. *The Preacher King: Martin Luther King, Jr. and the Word That Moved America.* New York: Oxford University Press, 1995.

Luker, Kristin. *Abortion and the Politics of Motherhood.* Berkeley: University of California Press, 1984.

MacKinnon, Catharine A. *Feminism Unmodified: Discourses on Life and Law.* Cambridge, MA: Harvard University Press, 1987.

———. *Sex Equality.* New York: Foundation, 2001.

MacKinnon, Catharine A., and Andrea Dworkin, eds. *In Harm's Way: The Pornography Civil Rights Hearings.* Cambridge, MA: Harvard University Press, 1997.

Manegold, Catherine S. *In Glory's Shadow: Shannon Faulkner, the Citadel, and a Changing America.* New York: Alfred A. Knopf, 2000.

Mansbridge, Jane J. *Why We Lost the ERA.* Chicago: University of Chicago Press, 1986.

Martínez, Oscar J. *Border People: Life and Society in the U.S.-Mexico Borderlands.* Tucson: University of Arizona Press, 1994.

Massengill, Reed. *Portrait of a Racist: The Man Who Killed Medgar Evers?* New York: St. Martin's, 1994.

Mathews, Donald G., and Jane Sherron De Hart. *Sex, Gender, and the Politics of ERA: A State and the Nation.* New York: Oxford University Press, 1992.

May, Antoinette. *Witness to War: A Biography of Marguerite Higgins.* New York: Beaufort, 1983.

McAdam, Doug. *Freedom Summer.* New York: Oxford University Press, 1988.

———. *Political Process and the Development of Black Insurgency, 1930–1970.* Chicago: University of Chicago Press, 1999.

McCoy, Donald R. *Quest and Response: Minority Rights and the Truman Administration.* Lawrence: University Press of Kansas, 1973.

McMillian, Willie. *Women in the Military: Sexual Harassment.* Carlisle Barracks, PA: U.S. Army War College, 1993.

McNickle, D'Arcy. *Native American Tribalism: Indian Survivals and Renewals.* New York: Published for the Institute of Race Relations by Oxford University Press, 1973.

Meier, August. *A White Scholar and the Black Community, 1945–1965: Essays and Reflections.* Amherst: University of Massachusetts Press, 1992.

Meier, August, and Elliott Rudwick. *CORE: A Study in the Civil Rights Movement, 1942–1968.* New York: Oxford University Press, 1973.

Meier, August, Elliott Rudwick, and John Bracey, Jr., eds. *Black Protest in the Sixties.* 2nd ed. New York: M. Wiener, 1991.

Meier, Matt S., and Feliciano Rivera. *The Chicanos: A History of Mexican Americans.* New York: Hill and Wang, 1972.

Meyerowitz, Joanne, ed. *Not June Cleaver: Women and Gender in Postwar America, 1945–1960.* Philadelphia: Temple University Press, 1994.

Millett, Kate. *Sexual Politics.* New York: Avon, 1971.

Min, Pyong Gap. *Caught in the Middle: Korean Merchants in America's Multiethnic Cities.* Berkeley: University of California Press, 1996.

Mintz, Steven, and Susan Kellogg. *Domestic Revolutions: A Social History of American Family Life.* New York: Free Press, 1988.

Moore, Joan W. *Hispanics in the United States.* Englewood Cliffs, NJ: Prentice-Hall, 1985.

Moore, Joan W., et al. *Homeboys: Gangs, Drugs, and Prison in the Barrios of Los Angeles.* Philadelphia: Temple University Press, 1978.

Morris, Willie. *The Ghosts of Medgar Evers: A Tale of Race, Murder, Mississippi, and Hollywood.* New York: Random House, 1998.

Morrison, Toni. *Race-ing Justice, En-gendering power: Essays on Anita Hill, Clarence Thomas, and the Construction of Social Reality.* New York: Pantheon, 1992.

Muldoon, Maureen. *The Abortion Debate in the United States and Canada: A Source Book.* New York: Garland, 1991.

Nichols, Roger L. *Indians in the United States and Canada: A Comparative History.* Lincoln: University of Nebraska Press, 1998.

Nossiter, Adam. *Of Long Memory: Mississippi and the Murder of Medgar Evers.* Reading, MA: Addison-Wesley, 1994.

Oates, Stephen B. *Let the Trumpet Sound: The Life of Martin Luther King, Jr.* New York: Harper and Row, 1982.

Okihiro, Gary Y. *Common Ground: Reimagining American History.* Princeton, NJ: Princeton University Press, 2001.

Olson, James Stuart, and Raymond Wilson. *Native Americans in the Twentieth Century.* Urbana: University of Illinois Press, 1984.

O'Neill, Timothy J. *Bakke and the Politics of Equality: Friends and Foes in the Public School of Litigation.* Middletown, CT: Wesleyan University Press, 1984.

O'Reilly, Kenneth. *Racial Matters: The FBI's Secret File on Black America, 1960–1972.* New York: Free Press, 1991.

Payne, Charles M. *I've Got the Light of Freedom: The Organizing Tradition and the Mississippi Freedom Struggle.* Berkeley: University of California Press, 1995.

Pearson, Hugh. *The Shadow of the Panther: Huey Newton and the Price of Black Power in America.* Reading, MA: Addison-Wesley, 1994.

Perry, Bruce. *Malcolm: The Life of a Man Who Changed Black America.* Barrytown, NY: Station Hill, 1991.

Plummer, Brenda Gayle. *Rising Wind: Black Americans and U.S. Foreign Affairs, 1935–1960.* Chapel Hill: University of North Carolina Press, 1996.

Reagan, Leslie J. *When Abortion Was a Crime: Women, Medicine, and Law in the United States, 1867–1973.* Berkeley: University of California Press, 1997.

Reed, Adolph L. *The Jesse Jackson Phenomenon: The Crisis of Purpose in Afro-American Politics.* New Haven: Yale University Press, 1986.

Roberts, Sam. *Who We Are: A Portrait of America Based on the Latest U.S. Census.* New York: Times Books, 1994.

Robinson, Jo Ann Gibson, and David J. Garrow. *The Montgomery Bus Boycott and the Women Who Started It: The Memoir of Jo Ann Gibson Robinson.* Knoxville: University of Tennessee Press, 1987.

Rodgers-Rose, La Frances. *The Black Woman.* Beverly Hills, CA: Sage, 1980.

Rodríguez, Clara E., and Virginia Sánchez Korrol, eds. *Historical Perspectives on Puerto Rican Survival in the U.S.* Princeton, NJ: Markus Wiener, 1996.

Rose, Douglas D. *The Emergence of David Duke and the Politics of Race.* Chapel Hill: University of North Carolina Press, 1992.

Rosenberg, Rosalind. *Divided Lives: American Women in the Twentieth Century.* New York: Hill and Wang, 1992.

Salzman, Jack, and Cornel West, eds. *Struggles in the Promised Land: Toward a History of Black-Jewish Relations in the United States.* New York: Oxford University Press, 1997.

Sánchez Korrol, Virginia. *From Colonia to Community: The History of Puerto Ricans in New York City, 1917–1948.* Westport, CT: Greenwood, 1983.

Sarat, Austin. *Race, Law, and Culture: Reflections on Brown v. Board of Education.* New York: Oxford University Press, 1997.

Sayer, John William. *Ghost Dancing the Law: The Wounded Knee Trials.* Cambridge, MA: Harvard University Press, 1997.

Schultz, David A., and Christopher E. Smith. *The Jurisprudential Vision of Justice Antonin Scalia.* Lanham, MD: Rowman and Littlefield, 1996.

Sebba, Anne. *Battling for News: The Rise of the Woman Reporter.* London: Hodder and Stoughton, 1994.

Sitkoff, Harvard. *The Struggle for Black Equality, 1954–1992.* New York: Hill and Wang, 1993.

Skerry, Peter. *Counting on the Census?: Race, Group Identity, and the Evasion of Politics.* Washington, DC: Brookings Institution, 2000.

———. *Mexican Americans: The Ambivalent Minority.* New York: Free Press, 1993.

Smith, Robert Charles. *Racism in the Post-Civil Rights Era: Now You See It, Now You Don't.* Albany: State University of New York Press, 1995.

Staggenborg, Suzanne. *The Pro-Choice Movement: Organization and Activism in the Abortion Conflict.* New York: Oxford University Press, 1991.

Stallard, Karin, Barbara Ehrenreich, and Holly Sklar. *Poverty in the American Dream: Women & Children First.* New York: Institute for New Communications, 1983.

Stanton, Bill. *Klanwatch: Bringing the Ku Klux Klan to Justice.* New York: Weidenfeld, 1991.

Steinem, Gloria. *Outrageous Acts and Everyday Rebellions.* New York: Holt, Rinehart and Winston, 1983.

Stern, Mark. *Calculating Visions: Kennedy, Johnson, and Civil Rights.* New Brunswick, NJ: Rutgers University Press, 1992.

Stoper, Emily. *The Student Nonviolent Coordinating Committee: The Growth of Radicalism in a Civil Rights Organization.* Brooklyn, NY: Carlson, 1989.

Strasser, Susan. *Never Done: A History of American Housework.* New York: Pantheon, 1982.

Strickland, Rennard. *Tonto's Revenge: Reflections on American Indian Culture and Policy.* Albuquerque: University of New Mexico Press, 1997.

Strum, Philippa. *Women in the Barracks: The VMI Case and Equal Rights.* Lawrence: University Press of Kansas, 2002.

Stychin, Carl, and Didi Herman, eds. *Law and Sexuality: The Global Arena.* Minneapolis: University of Minnesota Press, 2001.

Sugrue, Thomas J. *The Origins of the Urban Crisis: Race and Inequality in Postwar Detroit.* Princeton, NJ: Princeton University Press, 1996.

Takaki, Ronald. *A Different Mirror: A History of Multicultural America.* Boston: Little, Brown, 1993.

———. *From Different Shores: Perspectives on Race and Ethnicity in America.* New York: Oxford University Press, 1987.

———. *Strangers from a Different Shore: A History of Asian Americans.* Boston: Little, Brown, 1989.

Taylor, Jill McLean, Carol Gilligan, and Amy M. Sullivan. *Between Voice and Silence: Women and Girls, Race and Relationship.* Cambridge, MA: Harvard University Press, 1995.

Taylor, Ronald B. *Chavez and the Farm Workers.* Boston: Beacon, 1975.

Thernstrom, Stephan, and Abigail Thernstrom. *America in Black and White: One Nation, Indivisible.* New York: Simon and Schuster, 1997.

Trejo, Arnulfo D., ed. *The Chicanos: As We See Ourselves.* Tucson: University of Arizona Press, 1979.

Tsai, Shih-shan Henry. *The Chinese Experience in America.* Bloomington: Indiana University Press, 1986.

Turner, Patricia A. *I Heard It Through the Grapevine: Rumor in African-American Culture.* Berkeley: University of California Press, 1993.

Tushnet, Mark V. *Making Civil Rights Law: Thurgood Marshall and the Supreme Court, 1936–1961.* New York: Oxford University Press, 1994.

Tygiel, Jules. *Baseball's Great Experiment: Jackie Robinson and His Legacy.* New York: Oxford University Press, 1993.

Vollers, Maryanne. *Ghosts of Mississippi: The Murder of Medgar Evers, the Trials of Byron de la Beckwith, and the Haunting of the New South.* Boston: Little, Brown, 1995.

Wagenheim, Kal. *Puerto Rico: A Profile.* New York: Praeger, 1975.

Wagenheim, Kal, and Olga Jiménez de Wagenheim, eds. *The Puerto Ricans: A Documentary History.* Princeton, NJ: Markus Wiener, 1994.

Waldinger, Roger David. *Still the Promised City?: African-Americans and New Immigrants in Postindustrial New York.* Cambridge, MA: Harvard University Press, 1996.

Warren, Carol A. B. *Madwives: Schizophrenic Women in the 1950s.* New Brunswick, NJ: Rutgers University Press, 1987.

West, Cornel. *Restoring Hope: Conversations on the Future of Black America: A Project of the Obsidian Society.* Boston: Beacon, 1997.

Westheider, James E. *Fighting on Two Fronts: African Americans and the Vietnam War.* New York: New York University Press, 1997.

Whitfield, Stephen J. *A Death in the Delta: The Story of Emmett Till.* Baltimore: Johns Hopkins University Press, 1991.

Williams, Juan. *Eyes on the Prize: America's Civil Rights Years, 1954–1965.* New York: Viking, 1987.

Wofford, Harris. *Of Kennedys and Kings: Making Sense of the Sixties.* New York: Farrar, Straus and Giroux, 1980.

Wolfenstein, E. Victor. *The Victims of Democracy: Malcolm X and the Black Revolution.* Berkeley: University of California Press, 1981.

Wolff, Miles. *Lunch at the Five and Ten, the Greensboro Sit-ins: A Contemporary History.* New York: Stein and Day, 1970.

Woodward, C. Vann. *The Strange Career of Jim Crow.* New York: Oxford University Press, 1974.

X, Malcolm, with the assistance of Alex Haley. *The Autobiography of Malcolm X.* New York: Ballantine, 1992.

Science, Medicine, and Technology

Abbate, Janet. *Inventing the Internet.* Cambridge, MA: MIT Press, 1999.

Aiken, Tonia D. *Legal and Ethical Issues in Health Occupations.* Philadelphia: W.B. Saunders, 2002.

Balogh, Brian. *Chain Reaction: Expert Debate and Public Participation in American Commercial Nuclear Power, 1945–1975.* Cambridge, UK, and New York: Cambridge University Press, 1991.

Battin, M. Pabst, Rosamond Rhodes, and Anita Silvers. *Physician Assisted Suicide: Expanding the Debate.* New York: Routledge, 1998.

Bhat, Vasanthakumar N. *Medical Malpractice: A Comprehensive Analysis.* Westport, CT: Auburn House, 2001.

Brown, Fred. *Progress in Polio Eradication: Vaccine Strategies for the End Game: Institut Pasteur, Paris, June 28–30 2000.* New York: Basel, 2001.

Carson, Rachel. *Silent Spring.* Boston: Houghton Mifflin, 1994.

Carter, Richard. *Breakthrough: The Saga of Jonas Salk.* New York: Trident, 1966.

Casper, Barry M. *Powerline: The First Battle of America's Energy War.* Amherst: University of Massachusetts Press, 1981.

Colten, Craig E., and Peter N. Skinner. *The Road to Love Canal: Managing Industrial Waste Before EPA.* Austin: University of Texas Press, 1996.

Cortada, James W. *The Computer in the United States: from Laboratory to Market, 1930 to 1960.* Armonk, NY: M.E. Sharpe, 1993.

Cowdrey, Albert E. *This Land, This South: An Environmental History.* Lexington: University Press of Kentucky, 1996.

Cravens, Hamilton, Alan I. Marcus, and David M. Katzman, eds. *Technical Knowledge in American Culture: Science, Technology, and Medicine Since the Early 1800s.* Tuscaloosa: University of Alabama Press, 1996.

Demy, Timothy J., and Gary Stewart. *Suicide: A Christian Response: Crucial Considerations for Choosing Life.* Grand Rapids, MI: Kregel, 1998.

Divine, Robert A. *Blowing on the Wind: The Nuclear Test Ban Debate, 1954–1960.* New York: Oxford University Press, 1978.

———. *The Sputnik Challenge.* New York: Oxford University Press, 1993.

Dunlap, Thomas R. *DDT: Scientists, Citizens, and Public Policy.* Princeton, NJ: Princeton University Press, 1981.

Fee, Elizabeth, and Daniel M. Fox. *AIDS: The Making of a Chronic Disease.* Berkeley: University of California Press, 1992.

Fowler, Robert Booth. *The Greening of Protestant Thought.* Chapel Hill: University of North Carolina Press, 1995.

Franklin, H. Bruce. *War Stars: The Superweapon and the American Imagination.* New York: Oxford University Press, 1988.

Goldstein, Marc, and Michael Feldberg. *The Vasectomy Book: A Complete Guide to Decision Making.* Los Angeles: J.P. Tarcher, 1982.

Gould, Stephen Jay. *Ever Since Darwin: Reflections in Natural History.* New York: W.W. Norton, 1977.

Graham, Hugh Davis. *The Rise of American Research Universities: Elites and Challengers in the Postwar Era.* Baltimore: Johns Hopkins University Press, 1997.

Haught, John F. *God After Darwin: A Theology of Evolution.* Boulder, CO: Westview, 2000.

Herken, Gregg. *Brotherhood of the Bomb: The Tangled Lives and Loyalties of Robert Oppenheimer, Ernest Lawrence, and Edward Teller.* New York: Henry Holt, 2002.

———. *The Winning Weapon: The Atomic Bomb in the Cold War, 1945–1950.* New York: Alfred A, Knopf, 1980.

Hollinger, David A. *Science, Jews, and Secular Culture: Studies in Mid-Twentieth-Century American Intellectual History.* Princeton, NJ: Princeton University Press, 1996.

Horn, Carl, Donald H. Caldwell, and D. Christopher Osborn. *Law for Physicians: An Overview of Medical Legal Issues.* Chicago: American Medical Association, 2000.

Jasper, Margaret C. *The Law of Medical Malpractice.* Dobbs Ferry, NY: Oceana, 2001.

Jenkins, Dominick. *The Final Frontier: America, Science, and Terror.* London: Verso, 2002.

Jones, James H. *Bad Blood: The Tuskegee Syphilis Experiment.* New York: Free Press, 1982.

Kehoe, Terence. *Cleaning Up the Great Lakes: From Cooperation to Confrontation.* DeKalb: Northern Illinois University Press, 1997.

Kevorkian, Jack. *Prescription—Medicide: The Goodness of Planned Death.* Buffalo, NY: Prometheus, 1991.

Kwitny, Jonathan. *Acceptable Risks.* New York: Poseidon, 1992.

Larson, Edward J. *Summer for the Gods: The Scopes Trial and America's Continuing Debate over Science and Religion.* New York: Basic Books, 1997.

———. *Trial and Error: The American Controversy over Creation and Evolution.* Oxford, UK: Oxford University Press, 2003.

Lasby, Clarence G. *Eisenhower's Heart Attack: How Ike Beat Heart Disease and Held on to the Presidency.* Lawrence: University Press of Kansas, 1997.

Leslie, Stuart W. *The Cold War and American Science: The Military-Industrial-Academic Complex at MIT and Stanford.* New York: Columbia University Press, 1993.

Levy, Steven. *Crypto: How the Code Rebels Beat the Government, Saving Privacy in the Digital Age.* New York: Viking, 2001.

———. *Insanely Great: The Life and Times of Macintosh, the Computer That Changed Everything.* New York: Viking, 1994.

Loving, Carol. *My Son, My Sorrow: The Tragic Tale of Dr. Kevorkian's Youngest Patient.* Far Hills, NJ: New Horizon, 1998.

Mann, Alfred K. *For Better or for Worse: The Marriage of Science and Government in the United States.* New York: Columbia University Press, 2000.

Martin, Daniel. *Three Mile Island: Prologue or Epilogue?* Cambridge, MA: Ballinger, 1980.

Miller, Kenneth R. *Finding Darwin's God: A Scientist's Search for Common Ground Between God and Evolution.* New York: Cliff Street, 1999.

Morreim, E. Haavi. *Holding Health Care Accountable: Law and the New Medical Marketplace.* New York: Oxford University Press, 2001.

Numbers, Ronald L. *The Creationists.* New York: Alfred A. Knopf, 1992.

Numbers, Ronald L., and Charles E. Rosenberg, eds. *The Scientific Enterprise in America: Readings from Isis.* Chicago: University of Chicago Press, 1996.

Rhodes, Richard. *Dark Sun: The Making of the Hydrogen Bomb.* New York: Simon and Schuster, 1996.

Rostow, Victoria P., and Roger J. Bulger. *Medical Professional Liability and the Delivery of Obstetrical Care.* Washington, DC: National Academy Press, 1989.

Shilts, Randy. *And the Band Played on: Politics, People, and the AIDS Epidemic.* New York: St. Martin's, 1987.

Uhlmann, Michael M. *Last Rights?: Assisted Suicide and Euthanasia Debated.* Washington, DC: Ethics and Public Policy Center, 1998.

Vaughan, Diane. *The Challenger Launch Decision: Risky Technology, Culture, and Deviance at NASA.* Chicago: University of Chicago Press, 1996.

Wang, Jessica. *American Science in an Age of Anxiety: Scientists, Anticommunism, and the Cold War.* Chapel Hill: University of North Carolina Press, 1999.

Waymack, Mark H., and George Taler. *Medical Ethics and the Elderly: A Case Book.* Chicago: Pluribus, 1988.

Westwick, Peter J. *The National Labs: Science in an American System, 1947–1974.* Cambridge, MA: Harvard University Press, 2003.

Survey Histories and General Interest

Dubofsky, Melvyn, and Athan Theoharis. *Imperial Democracy: The United States Since 1945.* Englewood Cliffs, NJ: Prentice-Hall, 1983.

Hodgson, Godfrey. *America in Our Time.* New York: Vintage Books, 1978.

Jezer, Marty. *The Dark Ages: Life in the United States, 1945–1960.* Boston: South End, 1982.

Leuchtenburg, William E., ed. *The Unfinished Century: America Since 1900.* Boston: Little, Brown, 1973.

Marcus, Robert D., and David Burner, eds. *America Since 1945.* New York: St. Martin's, 1972.

Reeves, Thomas C. *Twentieth-Century America: A Brief History.* New York: Oxford University Press, 2000.

Terkel, Studs. *Coming of Age: The Story of Our Century by Those Who've Lived It.* New York: New Press, 1995.

Surveys on Specific Decades

The 1940s

Diggins, John P. *The Proud Decades: America in War and in Peace, 1941–1960.* New York: W.W. Norton, 1989.

Patterson, James T. *Grand Expectations: The United States, 1945–1974.* New York: Oxford University Press, 1996.

The 1950s

Carter, Paul Allen. *Another Part of the Fifties.* New York: Columbia University Press, 1983.

Halberstam, David. *The Fifties.* New York: Villard, 1993.

Oakley, J. Ronald. *God's Country: America in the Fifties.* New York: Dembner, 1986.

O'Neill, William L. *American High: The Years of Confidence, 1945–1960.* New York: Free Press, 1986.

The 1960s

Blum, John Morton. *Years of Discord: American Politics and Society, 1961–1974.* New York: W.W. Norton, 1991.

Farber, David R. *The Age of Great Dreams: America in the 1960s.* New York: Hill and Wang, 1994.

Gitlin, Todd. *The Sixties: Years of Hope, Days of Rage.* Toronto: Bantam, 1987.

Goodwin, Richard N. *Remembering America: A Voice from the Sixties.* New York: Perennial Library, 1989.

Heath, Jim F. *Decade of Disillusionment: The Kennedy-Johnson Years.* Bloomington: Indiana University Press, 1975.

Matusow, Allen J. *The Unraveling of America: A History of Liberalism in the 1960s.* New York: Harper and Row, 1986.

Morgan, Edward P. *The 60s Experience: Hard Lessons About Modern America.* Philadelphia: Temple University Press, 1991.

O'Neill, William L. *Coming Apart: An Informal History of America in the 1960s.* Chicago: Quadrangle, 1971.

Wright, Lawrence. *In the New World: Growing Up with America, 1960–1984.* New York: Alfred A. Knopf, 1988.

The 1970s

Bailey, Beth L., and Dave Farber, eds. *America in the Seventies.* Lawrence: University Press of Kansas, 2004.

Schulman, Bruce J. *The Seventies: The Great Shift in American Culture, Society, and Politics.* New York: Free Press, 2001.

The 1980s

Johnson, Haynes. *Sleepwalking Through History: America in the Reagan Years.* New York: W.W. Norton, 2003.

Philips, Kevin. *The Politics of Rich and Poor: Wealth and the American Electorate in the Reagan Aftermath.* New York: Random House, 1987

Wills, Garry. *Reagan's America.* New York: Penguin, 2000.

The 1990s

Farley, Reynolds, ed. *State of the Union: America in the 1990s.* New York: Russell Sage Foundation, 1995.

Johnson, Haynes Bonner. *Divided We Fall: Gambling with History in the Nineties.* New York: W.W. Norton, 1995.

Indexes

General Index

W

Wachowski, Andy, 4:1516
Wachowski, Larry, 4:1516
Waco, Texas, 3:957–58; 4:1241,
   1337–38, *1338*
   See also Texas
Wade, Henry, 3:1077–78
Wade, Virgil, 1:145–46
Wadleigh, Michael, 4:1488
Waggoner, Lyle, 4:1452–53
Wagner, George, 3:1177
Wagner, Richard, 4:1441
Wagner, Robert, 4:1487–88
Wagner Act (1935), 3:1197; 4:1224
Wahlberg, Mark, 1:136, 137–38
Waking, The (Roethke), 3:984
Wal-Mart, 1:297; 3:1114, 1116,
   1117–18, 1122; 4:1399–1400
Walcott, Joe, 1:168; 3:1176–77
Walken, Christopher, 1:347
Walker, Alice, 4:1490
Walker, T-Bone, 3:1056
Walker, Walton, 2:764, 766–67
Walker, William, 1:199
Wall Street, 4:1507, *1507*
Wall Street. *See* Stock market
Wall Street Journal, 1:4; 3:934, 935,
   1039–40, 1188, 1199
Wallace, George C.
   civil rights movement, 1:146, 232;
      3:811–12, 1104, 1183; 4:1381
   political elections
      1964, 2:427
      1968, 1:45–46, 157–58, 287, 350,
         378; 2:454; 3:1052, 1157,
         1190; 4:1262
      1972, 1:46, 157–58; 2:455, 456;
         4:1326–27
      1976, 2:457
Wallace, Henry A.
   political election of 1946, 2:443
   political election of 1948, 1:52, 53, 55,
      377, 397; 2:444–45, 524, 559;
      3:1004–6; 4:1262
Wallace, Lew, 4:1425
Wallace, Mike, 4:1463
Wallace, Violetta, 3:1037
Wallach, Eli, 4:1456
Waller, James, 2:662
Waller, Robert James, 4:1509
Wallis, Jim, 1:224; 2:511, 513
Walsh, John, 4:1493
Walsh, Lawrence E., 2:709
Walsh, Raoul, 4:1421
Walsh-Healey Public Contracts Act, 3:951
Walston, Ray, 4:1497
Walt Disney Corporation, 3:830–31;
   4:1426–27, 1432, 1441–42, 1459,
   1483, 1513, 1520

Walter, Francis E., 3:821–22
Walters, Barbara, 4:1439
Walton, Sam, 3:1116
Waltons, The, 4:1488
Wanger, Walter, 2:555
Wanniski, Jude, 3:1039–40, 1216
War Brides Act (1945), 1:90; 2:681
War on Drugs, 1:229, 404, 407, 410;
   3:968
   See also Drug abuse; Drug culture; Drug
      trafficking
War on Poverty. *See* Johnson, Lyndon B.
War on Terrorism
   civil liberties, 1:226, 229–30
   East Asia, 2:761
   immigration, 2:687, 717
   military defense spending, 1:375–76
   Muslims, 2:717, 718–19
   national security policy, 3:900, 903–4
   Southeast Asia, 3:1152
   United Nations (UN), 4:1308–9
   See also Terrorism, domestic; Terrorism,
      foreign; Weapons of mass
      destruction (WMD)
War Powers Act (1973), 1:279;
   4:1345–46
War Resisters League, 1:59–60
War Room, The, 4:1521
Ward, Anita, 1:394
Ward, Mary Jane, 3:840, 1012
Wardell, Dave, 3:1006–7
Wards Cove Packing Co. v. Antonio (1989),
   1:16
Ware, Chris, 1:258
Warhol, Andy, 1:80, 80–81, 301, 406–7;
   2:555–56
Warner, Jack, 1:51; 2:663
Warner Brothers (WB), 2:547, 551, 554,
   557, 663; 4:1230, 1232–36
Warren, Earl
   administrative term, 1:160, 230, 292,
      322, 322–24, 326; 2:444, 749;
      4:1326, 1346–48, *1347*
   court cases, 1:173–74, 349–50; 2:578,
      625, 807; 3:867, 891
Warren, Robert Penn, 2:549
Warren Commission (1963), 2:749;
   4:1346–48, *1347*
Warsaw Pact (1955), 1:41, 42, 43; 2:414,
   701; 3:864, 919, 943, 1160
Washam, Ben, 4:1419
Washington, Booker T., 3:890
Washington, D.C.
   abortion, 1:5–6
   anti-nuclear power movement, 1:58
   arts funding, 1:83–84, 85, 86
   civil rights movement
      disabled population, 1:392; 2:428
      education, 2:426–28, 431, 435
      Freedom Riders, 1:237, 244; 2:428

Washington, D.C.
   civil rights movement *(continued)*
      gay and lesbian population, 1:237
      March on Washington (1963),
         1:233, 241, 242–43, 281;
         3:811–13, *812*
      Million Man March (1995), 1:151;
         2:717; 3:866, 866–67
      Poor People's Campaign (1968),
         1:244; 3:987–89, 1155, 1158;
         4:1368
   Congress, 1:274–81
   constitutional amendments, 1:293–95
   gambling, 2:584
   Kennedy Center, 1:*362*
   sports, 1:122
   think tanks, 1:286
   urbanization, 2:691, 694
   Vietnam War protest movement, 1:60,
      61–62, 66, 67
   See also Terrorism, domestic; Watergate
      (1972); *specific court case*
Washington, Denzel, 4:1459, 1498,
   1504, 1517
Washington, Dinah, 3:1057
Washington, George, 1:39, 144; 3:942
Washington, Harold, 1:378
Washington Post, 1:110, 143, 303–4, 329;
   2:411, 480; 3:827, 935, 975, 1094;
   4:1294, *1294*, 1295, 1354, 1421,
   1467
Washington Star, 3:933
Washington State
   abortion, 1:5
   consumerism, 1:299
   drug rehabilitation programs, 1:410
   education, 1:177; 2:439, 440
   environmentalism, 4:1391, 1392, 1393
   public activism, 2:610, *610*, 611, 612
   sexual crime, 1:342
   sports, 1:122, 251; 2:565
   welfare system, 2:532
   World's Fair, 4:1404, 1405
   *See also specific court case or political
      representative*
Washington Times, 3:877
Washington v. Glucksberg (1997), 3:1060
Wasserstein, Wendy, 4:1258, 1498
Water pollution, 2:492, 493, *493*,
   494–95, 498, 499; 4:1348–51,
   1349
   See also Environmentalism; *specific
      legislation*
Water Pollution Control Act (1948/
   1972), 2:494, 500; 4:1348, 1349–51
Water Resources Development Act
   (1986), 4:1350
Watergate (1972), 1:183, 261, 328, 329,
   456–57; 2:534; 4:1351–55, *1354*
   incident development, 4:1351–54

Biographical Index

Geographical Index